Lord Strathcona

A BIOGRAPHY OF DONALD ALEXANDER SMITH

•

DONNA McDONALD

Dundurn Press
Toronto • Oxford

Editor: Rae Fleming
Design: Sebastian Vasile
Printer: Transcontinental

National Library of Canada Cataloguing in Publication Data

McDonald, Donna, 1942-
Lord Strathcona : a biography of Donald Alexander Smith / Donna McDonald.

Includes bibliographical references and index.
ISBN 1-55002-266-0 (bound).—ISBN 1-55002-397-7 (pbk.)

1. Strathcona and Mount Royal, Donald Alexander Smith, Baron, 1820-1914.
2. Capitalists and financiers--Canada--Biography. 3. Hudson's Bay Company--Biography.
4. Canadian Pacific Railway Company--Biography. 5. Canada--History--1841-. I. Title.

FC506.S9M28 1996 971.05'092 C96-990074-0 F1033.S9M28 1996

We acknowledge the support of the **Canada Council for the Arts** and the **Ontario Arts Council** for our publishing program. We also acknowledge the financial support of the **Government of Canada** through the **Book Publishing Industry Development Program** and **The Association for the Export of Canadian Books**, and the **Government of Ontario** through the **Ontario Book Publishers Tax Credit** program.

Care has been taken to trace the ownership of copyright material used in this book. The author and the publisher welcome any information enabling them to rectify any references or credit in subsequent editions.

J. Kirk Howard, President

Printed and bound in Canada.
Printed on recycled paper.
www.dundurn.com

Dundurn Press
8 Market Street
Suite 200
Toronto, Ontario, Canada
M5E 1M6

Dundurn Press
73 Lime Walk
Headington, Oxford,
England
OX3 7AD

Dundurn Press
2250 Military Road
Tonawanda NY
U.S.A. 14150

Lord Strathcona

A BIOGRAPHY OF DONALD ALEXANDER SMITH

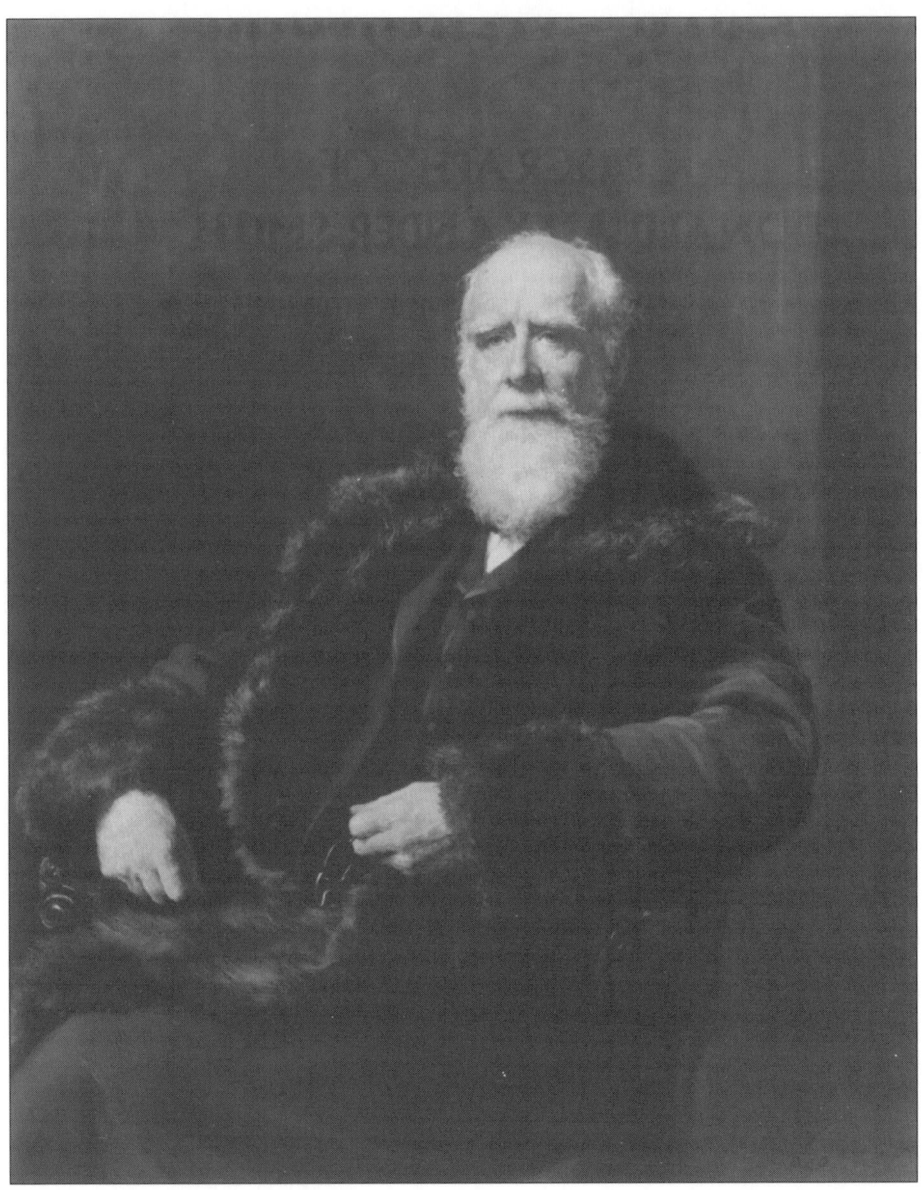

Walter William Ouless, R.A., Sir Donald Smith, 1890

TABLE OF CONTENTS

For my mother and father

FOREWORD

The nineteenth century in Europe and North America saw more changes than any of its predecessors and, it may be argued, more than the twentieth century which has been remarkable less for the number of changes than for the speed with which they have happened.

Donald Smith was a nineteenth century man and his life mirrors the developments of his era. He saw the change from stage coach to railway transport, from sail driven transatlantic crossings to steam powered liners; horses and shoe leather gave way to the automobile. The typewriter, the telephone and the telegram became important tools for the businessman in his lifetime, bringing with them a commercial etiquette which is only now, a hundred years later, being replaced by a new code of manners dictated by the computer, the answering machine and the fax.

But Donald Smith's life does more than reflect his century. It closely mirrors Canada's passage to nationhood. He spent a quarter of a century in the inhospitable territory of uninhabited Quebec and Labrador, emerging from this cold cocoon in time for Confederation, and in time to play a significant and sometimes decisive role in the progress from colonial dependency to full nationhood. He was a principal figure in the peaceful resolution of the first Riel uprising, a major player in the handing over of Hudson's Bay territories to the Canadian government, a powerful force in the creation of the Canadian Pacific Railway and a seminal influence in the establishment of both the Royal Canadian Mounted Police and Canada's independent military. He also made a major contribution to the establishment of both medical science and women's education in Canada. On the international scene, he was involved in the first steps towards the creation of the British Commonwealth, in the development of a world wide cable network and in the British navy's transition from steam to the internal combustion engine and the consequent creation of British Petroleum.

It could be assumed that a subject with such a pedigree would have fathered numerous biographies. In fact, he has elicited numerous attempts and to my predecessors, both successful and otherwise, I owe many thanks. The task, as they all knew, is not an easy one. Beckles Willson published the first study in 1902 without the cooperation of Lord Strathcona, his family and friends (though he knew many of them, including "the old Lord") and it is flawed as a result. Indeed, it and the two subsequent biographies are flawed in the way such books usually are when the author knows his subject. W.T.R. Preston had a venomous streak and reserved much of his spite for Lord Strathcona, giving his malice free rein in his 1914 biography which also contains numerous factual errors. Beckles Willson's two volume account, published in 1915 and sometimes inaccurately described as the authorized version, is a huge improvement on his earlier study but Sir William Van Horne and John Sterling, Lord Strathcona's American lawyer, exercised editorial control which they doubtless felt entitled to do since they were also providing financial support. Willson did, however, have access to some of the early correspondence and he did know the principal players. As a result, his book provides an invaluable reference, even if it is one with which to disagree on the basis of new information or a different perspective. It is doubly important since much of the material which he was able to read has since been destroyed.

It has been argued, especially by Lord Strathcona's family (though not by the present generation of descendants) that he did not want a biography. This cannot be true. His granddaughter, Frances Kitson, and her husband helped to remove pile upon pile of correspondence, all neatly tied with blue ribbon, from the attic of Lord Strathcona's last house in London. Not only were there letters, there were Hudson's Bay Company journals, accounts, maps and plans, books and reports. These spanned a lifetime, from his earliest letters to his mother to his last communications with his solicitors. These documents travelled from the King's Posts on the north shore of the St. Lawrence River to Labrador, to Montreal and to London. In both cities they were moved more than once. Following Lord Strathcona's death, papers were shipped from Montreal to London, including copies of all letters written up to 1892, a series of daily journals covering most years from 1869 to 1891 and ten boxes of personal and business letters and other papers. Donald Smith did not keep what others may regard as ephemera because he wanted to be encumbered by paper. He kept the evidence of his activities initially because he hoped to play an important part on the world's stage and latterly because he knew he had done so. In short, he knew his life merited a biography, knew his papers reflected many important aspects of nineteenth century history, and valued them accordingly. Unfortunately, some of his heirs did not do so.

The present Lord Strathcona has been exceedingly courteous and cooperative as have been many other members of the family, particularly his sister, Diana Faber, and her husband, and his brother, Barnaby Howard, and to all of them I am very grateful. Others before them, however, have not recognized the value of the documents in their possession and much has been destroyed. The early correspondence, which Beckles Willson saw, seems to have been among the material which was burned, together with documents such as bills which would have provided wonderful clues to a personality which was coincidentally both proud and modest. This intentional conflagration and an accidental one at the Board of Trade Building in Montreal in 1901 have done much to impede the biographer and it is hardly surprising that my predecessors have fallen by the wayside. The late W.L. Morton's manuscript and research notes in the Provincial Archives of Manitoba reveal how barren the territory is and how desperately one must grasp for clues. I am grateful to Mrs. Morton for encouraging me to read this material and to pursue my own research. The archives staff in Winnipeg were consistently helpful and friendly.

Another major source of information on Lord Strathcona can be found in the dusty trunks of his Scottish solicitors, Skene Edwards and Garson. Not only have they retained the meticulous Scottish solicitors' accounts of most of their dealings with his lordship, they have also kept many of his other papers, including Hudson's Bay Company documents, papers on his Canadian investments and details of his financial dealings in the latter years of his life. The richness of the information on the Persian Oil Company, however, is matched by the poverty of personal correspondence. I am nonetheless grateful to Messrs Skene Edwards and Garson for permission to consult this material and to the Scottish Record Office for providing it and the facilities in which to read it.

The National Archives of Canada has a hodgepodge of material in its Strathcona files but, more importantly, it houses as originals or on microfilm most of the major collections with relevant material. All the Canadian prime ministers from Macdonald to Borden and all the senior politicians from Confederation to the first world war had dealings with Lord Strathcona, whether in his capacity as Government Commissioner, Hudson's Bay Company executive, CPR director, Canadian High Commissioner or patron of the arts and of many Canadian educational and charitable institutions. The National Archives is one of the easiest national depositories in the world in which to work and the unfailing courtesy and helpfulness of the staff, coupled with the understanding that researchers do not live nine to five lives, has made it a pleasure to work there. Both Bruce Wilson and Bill Russell, during their periods on the Archives staff in London, went out of their way to assist me, as did Timothy Dubé in Ottawa.

The Hudson's Bay Company Archives, of course, provide a wealth of material on Lord Strathcona and microfilm copies have meant that I have been able to fight with Donald Smith's appalling handwriting at the Public Record Office in London as well as at the company's archival headquarters in Winnipeg. To Meryl Foster and the staff at the Public Record Office and to Judith Hudson Beattie and the staff at the HBC Archives, I am especially grateful. Both women have been outstandingly helpful. During my research, the Hudson's Bay Company gave its collection of papers and artifacts to the provincial archives and museum in Manitoba, a gesture which will ensure that a rich source of information about many aspects of Canadian life will be secured for generations to come.

Thanks also are due to W. Thomas White, curator at the James J. Hill Library in Saint Paul where Hill's papers have been preserved for the benefit of scholars and historians. I am grateful to Dr. White for his unfailing courtesy and helpfulness and to the library's grants programme for an award to enable me to tease out the threads of Donald Smith's involvement with the Saint Paul, Minneapolis and Manitoba Railway.

Bequests from my aunt, Elizabeth Griffith, and from John and Lotte Hecht have been used to support the research for this book. Though they did not leave money to me for that specific purpose, their unanticipated generosity helped bring this volume closer to completion.

The Hardisty family papers which have been given to the Glenbow Museum and Archives in Calgary have helped me to piece together Lady Strathcona's own background and to discover much about her life with Donald Smith in Labrador. Staff at the Glenbow were generous with their time and advice and their kindness is much appreciated.

Cleophas Belvin kindly lent me a copy of his thesis on Lord Strathcona's early career and Nora Hague at the McCord Museum went out of her way to be helpful when I was researching photographs for this volume.

The reader will see that in addition to the major depositories mentioned above, I have consulted a plethora of material in public and private hands. To each library, archive or private individual, I am deeply grateful.

Quotations from the Hill Papers are reproduced with permission as are quotations from the Hudson's Bay Company Archives. The Master, Fellows and Scholars of St. John's College, Cambridge, have given permission to quote from documents concerning Lord Strathcona's connection with the college, and the trustees of the Bowood manuscripts have given permission to quote from the correspondence of Lord Lansdowne.

As a school child in Canada, I was familiar with the nation's most famous photograph showing an old man (with nearly a third of his life ahead of him) driving the last spike of the Canadian Pacific Railway at Craigellachie. Indeed, I was at copy-cat ceremonies when the Pacific Great Eastern finally reached Prince George. But I could not have told you the name of the man at that pivotal point in Canadian history and find that most of my compatriots cannot either. I hope this book will go some way towards changing that.

I first encountered Lord Strathcona (schools, streets and parks apart) when I was working for the government of New Brunswick, looking for anything connected with that province's history as it prepared to celebrate its bicentennial. I came across some of the Skene Edwards and Garson papers, then on loan to the Scottish Record Office, and immediately wanted to know more about the man who had amassed such a collection. The question lay at the back of my mind until Kirk Howard, publisher of Dundurn Press, began throwing possible subjects for a biography at me one night in Toronto. One by one I rejected the women who went to Canada from England and painted. Having written about Juliana Horatia Ewing with great pleasure, I wanted to tackle other fields. Finally, in exasperation, I pointed out that I could write about men too.

"Lord Strathcona."

"Right. I'll do it!"

A publisher must have certain qualifications: a good business head, good spelling, grammar and vocabulary, an appreciation of the language, a wide ranging interest in all manner of subjects, patience and a willingness to take his/her authors out to dinner. In all these areas, Kirk is eminently qualified. As the recipient of more dinners than spelling corrections, I am most appreciative. I am also grateful to him for choosing Rae Fleming as my editor. Knowing that the manuscript was to be dealt with by an historian who was familiar with nineteenth century Canada and railway construction has been a great comfort.

Special thanks are due to Dominic d'Angelo who, besides helping with the transmission of proofs, gave up his time to read the manuscript, thereby saving me from many mistakes.

My husband, Robert McDonald, has patiently listened to endless hypotheses about Lord Strathcona's in-laws, financial dealings, art interests and political inclinations and has made invaluable suggestions for improvements to the book. His tolerance of Lord Strathcona as the other man in my life has been matched by his ability and apparent willingness to prepare breakfast/lunch/dinner while I researched and wrote. I am the more grateful to him when I recall that he has his own books to write.

The list of people to whom I owe thanks is very long. Neither they nor those mentioned above are responsible for any errors; these are entirely of my own doing. I would, however, like to express my sincere gratitude to Elsie Angus, Richard Aston at the Wellcome Institute for the History of Medicine, Nancy Brock, Robert Burke, S.J., Maureen Covell, Louis Cyr, S.J., Martin Dalby, Sister Dougan at Glencoe Hospital, William Fong, Alex Fraser, Catherine Graham, Saul and Liliane Grey, Peter Horton at the Royal College of Music, Janet Hulton at the Moravian Union, Jonathan King, Robert Kitson, Eric Lawson, Nicholas McConnell, Frank McDonald, Judy McGrath at *Them Days*, Tony Mew, Ann Moran, Norman Napier, Christine Reynolds at Westminster Abbey, Colin and Ann Scarfe, Mike and Cindy Shea, Greg Smith, Patricia Stewart-Bam, Cathy and Ernie Stigant, Malcolm Underwood, archivist at St. John's College, Cambridge, Simon Waegemaekers, Graham Wilson at the Moray Department of Leisure and Libraries, Joan Yeats and Susan Young.

Generally speaking, I have retained the spelling and punctuation used by my sources but where a full stop has, for example, been omitted in haste, I have supplied it. I have tried not to impede the flow of the text with scholarly brackets. On the other hand, where spelling errors and eccentric punctuation help to give the flavour of the writer, I have retained them. Abbreviations, especially those such as Alex^{ndr} I have generally rendered in full.

Donna McDonald
London, August 1996

On doit des égards aux vivants; on ne doit aux morts que la verité.

Voltaire

CHAPTER ONE

THE EARLY YEARS 1820–1838

How far is't called to Forres?
Macbeth, I, iii

The town of Forres lies on the northeast coast of the Scottish mainland. At first established because it was near a fording point on the turbulent Findhorn River, Forres grew in importance when a road was constructed to follow the coast from Inverness, through Forres and Elgin, before turning southeast to Aberdeen. The town itself straddles a stream, the Burn of Mosset, which runs parallel to the Findhorn, both of them debouching into Findhorn Bay on the southern shores of the Moray Firth. Here the Gulf Stream, which modifies the northern temperatures of the British Isles, ends its long journey, giving Forres a more temperate climate than east coast Scottish cities further south. Writers in 1842 and again a hundred years later noted the love of gardening to be found among the people of Forres, who discovered in the remnants of the Gulf Stream some compensation for their poor soil.[1]

The town's main claim to fame, however, is that the kings of Scotia had their castles there. According to Shakespeare, Macbeth and Banquo were on their way to Duncan I's court when they encountered three of the witches for which Forres was then notorious. The play says Duncan was murdered at Macbeth's castle in nearby Inverness but many historians would argue that he was slain at home in Forres like other Scotian kings before him.

The ruins of Duncan's fortress lie at the top of Castle Hill while the Burn of Mosset curls around the base before making its way to the sea. In a thatched stone house between the foot of the hill and the burn, Donald Alexander Smith was born on August 6, 1820. He was the fourth child of Alexander Smith and Barbara Stuart, and their second son. A healthy baby with fair red hair and blue-grey eyes, he was christened in the parish kirk, dedicated to St. Laurence, on October 4.

Both Barbara Stuart and Alexander Smith belonged to Clan Grant whose members were concentrated in the Spey Valley which runs parallel to the Moray Firth and has long been famous as one of the prime centres of Scotch whisky distillation. The Smiths had been married in Grantown-on-Spey in 1813, three years after their betrothal. Barbara had grown up on a farm on the edge of the Abernethy Forest on the southern side of the Spey Valley and recalled her childhood as an idyllically happy time. While her family was not wealthy, they were hard working, decent men and women who had farmed that spot for generations and the familial bond was strong and loving. Though Alexander Smith came from a respectable, steady family, living further downriver in the parish of Knockando, he himself preferred the cheerful companionship of the tavern to the effort of making a living. He had already tried his hand at soldiering and farming before settling in Grantown as a saddler in the year he and Barbara became engaged.

Their first child was born in Grantown and named Margaret after her mother's youngest sister who had been drowned when a ship capsized en route to Orkney. In 1815, when Barbara was 31 and her husband was 35, she gave birth to her second child, John Stuart, named after her favourite brother. This baby was born in Cromdale, near Grantown, where Barbara probably took herself and Margaret in order to be with her family during her confinement. The Smiths' third child, Jane, was almost certainly born in Grantown, probably about 1817. Three years after Donald came James M'Grigor and he was followed by Marianne, the Smiths' last child.

Grantown was one of the first planned towns to be created in Scotland. Laid out by Sir James Grant in 1776, it was meant to attract investment and wealth to the region but the town languished till the Victorians discovered the health-giving properties of bracing highland air. A handsome but not prosperous town was no place for a tradesman like Alexander Smith and in 1818 the family moved to Forres, a busier centre, rivalling Elgin in those days. As a stopover for the stage and a collection point for the mail coaches, Forres, with its surrounding agricultural land, should have offered greater opportunities to a resourceful saddler, but Alexander's neighbours recalled a volatile temper and a continuing preference for a drink and good company. His workshop was next door to the premises of Mr. Downie, a wine merchant, and within a stone's throw of several other drinking establishments, the proximity of which were doubtless temptation enough.[2]

It was Barbara who was the stronger of the two and she held the family together, stressing to her children the value of education and learning, emphasizing the importance of courtesy and politeness and consideration for others at all times, teaching them the principles and practice of the Scots Presbyterian faith, and imbuing them with the history and traditions of their Scottish ancestry.

"She set great store by courtesy and good manners and our bonnets were always off in her presence," Donald recalled of his mother in later years. She taught her boys and girls to memorize the psalms which, paraphrased and made to rhyme, were for so long a feature of Scottish Protestant life. They tested the memory and powers of elocution and reinforced the message of the church. A boy who learned the metrical paraphrases at his mother's knee remembered them for life.[3]

Donald Alexander, named after his maternal grandfather and his father, was three, when his younger brother was born. The new baby was a sickly child who needed much of his mother's attention, so keeping an eye on the toddler often fell to Margaret. She was an intelligent girl, but a girl nonetheless, and the attitude to female education current in the early nineteenth century, coupled with the fact that the Smith family had no money for private tutors or governesses, meant her scholarly ambitions were thwarted. Donald, with his keen mind and eagerness to learn, became a favourite and a strong and lasting tie developed between them. It was probably reinforced in 1825 when Marianne was born and again in 1826 when James M'Grigor died and the children were thrown on their own resources in the face of their mother's worry and grief.

Margaret would have had her hands full with a lively child. The Mosset was close enough to the front door to be a constant danger and the house was adjacent to Castle Bridge which crossed the burn. The steep stone steps leading from the embankment to the High Street would have been a perpetual temptation to an enquiring mind too young to appreciate the dangers of tumbling off them or the risks of the fast moving carriages should he succeed in reaching the top undetected.

Before long, however, Donald was heading up the steps with his brother John to walk along the High Street, past the market cross and the tollbooth with its weather vane in the shape of a golden cock, to the Anderson Institution. James Anderson, a native of Forres, had moved to Glasgow to make his fortune, investing some of his money in Cowlairs, now a residential area in the northern part of the city. On his death, Anderson bequeathed Cowlairs land to his native town with instructions to build a school with the profits from the land and employ a teacher, so that boys from Forres and the neighbouring parishes of Rafford and Kinloss, whose parents could not afford to send them away to private schools, could be "instructed in reading, writing, arithmetic, and such branches of education as the Provost, Magistrates and Town Council should deem proper." The neo-Grecian building, with a spire and a public clock, opened in 1824.[4]

The Anderson Institution was an elementary school and parents who wanted more than the rudiments of learning for their boys were then obliged to send them to the Forres Academy, a fee paying school with so high a reputation that, at one point, boys from all over Scotland were being sent there for their education. Like so many private schools of the time, the staff were primarily, though not exclusively, clergymen who favoured languages and classics over the sciences.

Keeping a boy in school was an expensive business for a father because a teenaged son needed to be fed and clothed but, while at school, could make no financial contribution to his own upkeep or that of his family. The expense, coupled with the lost income, often forced men to withdraw their sons, but, as Donald was to observe several decades later, "many a parent in Forres at that time was determined to give, and did give far beyond really what under other circumstances or for any other purpose they would have been justified in giving, that they might have a school in which a sound education would be given to their children." This was true in the case of Donald's father "who out of small means gave much more for the purposes of education year by year than really perhaps he ought to have done."[5]

Donald was one of the school's top scholars, though he recalled his great disappointment one year, when he was first in his class and anticipated receiving the prize which was to be awarded for this achievement, only to have it snatched away from him when he was promoted to another class. He and his classmates seem to have been well trained at the Forres Academy, but, after they graduated, they laughed at one of their teachers, the Rev. John Longmuir, and his incessant repetition of the stories told him by his father who had met Dr. Johnson and James Boswell in August 1775 when the travellers spent the night in Forres en route to the Western Isles. The fact that the lexicographer found nothing to remark about the town, let alone about those he met there, cannot have swelled the schoolteacher's pride any more than the fact that Boswell commented only on the inn and the fact that it was kept by a wine cooper from London.

This same teacher fancied himself as a Shakespeare scholar and quite naturally focused the boys' attention on *Macbeth*. "He was very severe on southern ignorance in pronouncing 'Dunsinane' with the accent on the last syllable," Donald remembered, and insisted the boys learn the accepted Scottish alternative to the famous passage in Act V, rendering it "Till Birnam forest to Dunsinane come."[6]

The reverend gentleman's passions stayed fixed in the boys' minds, though not always in the way he might have wished. One year, he took Donald and his school fellows to Nelson's Tower which admirers of the admiral had erected in 1806 to commemorate him and his victory at Trafalgar. Situated on Cluny Hill, next to Castle Hill, it offers a superb view of Forres and the cultivated plains between the town and Findhorn Bay —a sight which so impressed one of the school's lesser intellects that he excitedly declared he could see where Dr. Johnson had poisoned Banquo.

Forres was rich with distractions for boys let out of school. Games of hide and seek on Castle Hill, where the stone arches of Duncan's castle still remained, occupied the long summer evenings. The stables and byres built into the ruined castle walls attracted lads who were not running errands, and fishing for trout in the shallow burn was a pleasure available to those without chores. The little ones chased each other around the clothes drying on the green by the Mosset while older boys headed upstream to the mills. Beyond the brewery making table beer, they came to a distiller, and mills for flour, meal and barley. Here they would beg peas from the miller and the streets and hills of Forres would resound with laughter as they chased each other, and unsuspecting adults, with their pea shooters.[7]

In winter, a small loch at the base of the hill sometimes froze and the children would pull off their boots and go sliding. It was not a sight to gladden a mother's heart and any lad appearing at the hearth with huge holes in his stockings was unlikely to risk maternal disapproval twice.[8]

On Victoria Road, as the High Street becomes beyond the school, Donald and his friends would have examined the witch's stones. According to local legend, each of three witches was placed in a barrel into which spikes had been driven, and rolled down Cluny Hill; the stones mark the places where two of the barrels came to rest and where the witches, if any life remained, were executed. In fact, the stone nearest the school is now thought to have been a Pictish altar to the sun god, though an imaginative schoolboy might have provided any number of histories for it.

Even greater stories could be told around Sueno's Stone, including the fables then accepted by the scholars of Forres. The slim obelisk, standing twenty-three feet high, is covered with elaborate carvings depicting a battle on one side and, on the other, a Celtic cross. Its name derives from Sweyne of Denmark who defeated Malcolm II in 1008 but archaeologists today do not accept that the stone has anything to do with him. The discovery of skeletons on the site in 1813 indicates a battle which the stone probably commemorates but the most detailed and realistic accounts of it appear to exist, now as in 1830, in the minds of local schoolboys.

A dovecote stood next to Sueno's Stone and boys amused themselves by throwing stones at the birds. The chances of young Donald ever having hit one are remote. His aim, as an adult, was terrible and only marginally better than his skill with a ball or a stone in his youth.[9]

As the boys of Forres matured, the tollbooth and market cross became increasingly attractive. The market was held there, where the High Street spread out to accommodate the sellers of fish from the Moray Firth and vendors of agricultural produce from the nearby fields. This was also the site of the town pump where "the lads used to pump the water for their sweethearts."[10]

On a Saturday in July, the square came alive with the annual feeing market. Here farm labourers and housemaids indentured their services for the coming year or years. As in towns throughout Scotland, this business transaction was coupled with a fair. Candies, gingerbread and other edible treats were on sale in Forres and so were fresh fish, shoes and jewellery. Here were the luckenbooths, the locked booths from which the more valuable trinkets were dispensed. When romance had progressed from water pumping to betrothal, a young man would purchase for his intended a luckenbooth pin in the shape of a pair of interlocked hearts. Generally of the simplest design, they were and are worn by the wives and sweethearts of Scottish men as a highly esteemed love token.

The fair had its rougher side as well, attracting itinerant strong men, singers of lewd ballads and others of doubtful repute. The farmers generally left about four o'clock and the local servant girls appeared about six. The beer and whisky flowed and some of the men became increasingly drunk. It was then that the recruiting sergeants from the 72nd, 92nd or 93rd Highlanders or the Rifle Brigade successfully offered the king's shilling to young men who would wake the next morning to find themselves "gone for a sodger." Barbara Smith's boys were too canny for that trick and her husband was too old, but they doubtless knew the stories of unwilling "volunteers."[11]

Besides this summer diversion, the Smith family amused itself with occasional holidays to Abernethy, to visit Barbara's family, and perhaps called on Mr. Cumming, a kinsman who lived at Logie on the banks of the Findhorn River. Here the water drops off the high moors and tumbles through narrow gorges, edged by beautiful woodlands. Randolph's Leap, a particularly attractive spot, marks the point where one of young Donald's distant relatives, Alistair Cumming, had leapt across the gorge to evade capture by Thomas Randolph, newly created Earl of Moray.

As a Grant, Donald would also have learned about two rocks, each called Craigellachie and each used as a site for warning beacons when the Grants were under threat. One, where Strathspey spreads out into the alluvial plain, marks the northeastern end of Grant territory while the other, thirty-seven miles upriver at Aviemore, is the rock of alarm and gathering point for the Grants in time of danger. "Stand fast, Craigellachie!" is the Clan Grant rallying cry. The need for these precautions had long passed by the time Donald was born, but parents still taught their children the salient points in the clan's history and customs. Familiarity with the landscape and the stories attached to it linked the men and women in the valley and provided a touchstone for Grants in whatever corner of the world they found themselves.

Alexander Smith's family lived in the parish of Knockando near the eastern Craigellachie. A visit, *en famille*, by stage coach would have been prohibitively expensive but, as a saddler, Smith might well have had access to horses and carts from time to time and family exchanges may well have taken place. There is, however, no reason to think that Donald met his father's sister, Elspet, or her family, until many years later.

Other family holidays, however, saw Donald with his brother and sisters on the sandy beaches of Findhorn Bay, eyeing the small fishing boats and the boat builders' yards. Their parents looked askance at the Findhorn custom which compelled the women to carry their menfolk on their backs from the shore to their boats and thought how much better things were handled a mile away at Forres. At Findhorn, the children could watch the coasters offloading coal, slates and lime and taking on board the oak timbers and potatoes which the district exported to the south, and they could ponder the mysterious stories of Findhorn's past, for two previous villages have been covered over by the shifting sands and shingles of the estuary.

Whatever the pleasures of other summers, it was that of 1829 which Donald and everyone else in Forres, Findhorn and Strathspey remembered for the rest of their lives. May, June and July were exceptionally hot and the aurora borealis was particularly prominent in July. Strangely, changes in barometric pressure did not presage changes in the weather, though occasional short, sharp cloudbursts brought about very localized flooding, attributed by some to heavenly retribution for the recent vote in parliament in favour of Catholic emancipation.

As July turned to August, storms developed in the north and strong winds pushed water-laden clouds up the Moray Firth, stacking them against the Grampian Mountains. On August 3, the clouds burst and torrents of rain lashed down, loosening rocky debris in all the gullies and culverts and hurling it down to the river valleys. Ten inches of rain fell in forty-eight hours. It roared through the Spey Valley, taking bridges and houses with it. At Randolph's Leap, the Findhorn rose fifty feet to the top of the gorge. The Findhorn and the Burn of Mosset, normally about two miles apart, converged at Castle Bridge next to the Smith home in Forres. When Donald awoke on August 4, if indeed he had managed to sleep, he found the bridge had been split longitudinally and across the remaining half, families from outlying regions struggled to the safety of the Forres hills.

Sir Thomas Dick Lauder was travelling in the region at the time and wrote a best-seller about the great flood which

> spread over the rich and variously cropped fields, and over hedges, gardens, orchards and plantations. In this "world of water," the mansions of proprietors, the farm-houses and offices, the trees, and especially the hedge-rows, giving its peculiarly English appearance to the environs of Forres, — the ricks of hay, and here and there a few patches of corn standing on situations more elevated than the rest, presented a truly wonderful scene. Terror was painted on the countenances of some, and amazement in those of everyone.[12]

On the morning of the fourth, with the rain still thundering down, the fishermen of Findhorn launched their boats inland to rescue the families stranded on hillocks, rooftops or in the upper rooms of their homes. The *Nancy* tried to run up the channel of the Mosset but the current was so strong that she was driven onto the bank and was forced to journey cross-country. Lauder noted that he "saw a man catch a fine salmon in one of the fields a-starboard."[13]

In forty-eight hours, the floods totally destroyed over sixty houses, twenty-two bridges, twenty other buildings and a thousand acres of farmland. Over six hundred families were made homeless and six people died. Three of these were at Forres, among them one of Donald's schoolmates. Whether on his own initiative or at his mother's prompting, he called on the boy's parents to commiserate with them in their loss. On leaving, he asked them to "accept a slight token in memory of his friend. He handed them over all of his pocket-money, amounting to a shilling and some odd coppers."[14]

The incident is generally seen as a foretaste of later generosity, but it is more important for revealing a child who was keen to do the right thing, to behave in the correct manner and to follow the established rules of social intercourse. The drowning of Donald's school chum came only three years after the death of his little brother, James M'Grigor, and it is easy to imagine that on that occasion a friend or relative offered Barbara Smith financial support. With five children to feed and a husband whose earnings did not always make their way to the family purse, she would doubtless have been grateful for help in meeting the costs of a funeral. Her son, a few days short of his ninth birthday when the flood swept through Morayshire and killed his friend, emulated the form without understanding the context.

The shy often conceal themselves behind a facade of formality and Donald learned to use this mask to disguise his insecurity. The ritual of good manners was encouraged by his mother whose real intention was that her children should sincerely practise the courtesy and consideration which properly underlie conventional social forms. For her, one judged a man's worth by his concern for others; it was that which made him a true gentleman. Many years later, when Donald tried to impress her with tales of the rich and titled ladies he had met, she responded quietly, "Tell me, were they *gentlewomen*?"[15]

In the towns and villages of early nineteenth century Morayshire, with their interlinking families of Grants, Stuarts, Cummings and Smiths, each child learned which branch of his clan he and his parents belonged to and how his family related to others in the branch and to other branches of the clan. Kinship crossed barriers of class and wealth and wise parents knew how to use this network to benefit their offspring.

Barbara and Alexander Smith had put what resources they could into the education of their first son, John Stuart. When he left school in Forres, he enrolled at Marischal College, Aberdeen and progressed from there to the University of Edinburgh where he completed his medical studies in 1839. The Smiths then sought help from Barbara's kinsman, Sir James M'Grigor, after whom the youngest Smith boy had been named. A Grant of Lethendry (in the parish of Cromdale) on his mother's side, as was his wife, M'Grigor was the head of Wellington's medical services during the Peninsular War and in 1815, the year John was born, he was appointed director general of the Army Medical Department, a post he held until 1851. In November 1839, he secured for the newly qualified Dr. Smith a posting as Assistant Surgeon with the 55th Regiment of Foot (the Westmoreland Regiment).

Smith's army medical career took him to India, China and Australasia, and, in that respect, he was a typical product of Strathspey and the settlements on the coastal plain. People were the region's greatest export, especially after the landowners enclosed the hilly pastures and forced the crofters to move to the towns where they had not the wherewithal to feed themselves. The surplus labour in the towns and the economic depression of the late 1820s and early 1830s exacerbated already difficult conditions and drove many from the region. Thousands emigrated to Canada and the United States. In 1833, Alexander Kerr, who had left Forres for work at the naval dockyards in Chatham, explained to James Alves, a Forres carpenter who had gone to Upper Canada the year before, "Times are very much chinged at home since you left there for there are nothing to be done now for tredsmen nor labrors and they cannot be well off."[16]

Grants were merchants in London, Manchester and Montreal. They served in the army throughout the world and they had been leading figures in the North West Company which, prior to 1821, traded furs in competition with the Hudson's Bay Company in North America. When the mail coaches drew up at the inn on the High Street of Forres, the shouts and laughter and sweating horses signalled news of family and friends from all quarters of the globe. For Donald Smith, they reinforced the conviction that he, too, would make his career far from his native land.

The North West Company and the Hudson's Bay Company were enterprises of which young Donald would have heard a great deal as he grew up. Charles Grant and his son, also Charles, merchants who backed the North West Company, were relatives as were the Nor'Westers, Robert and Cuthbert Grant. Cuthbert's son, also Cuthbert, was sent for his education to Scotland where, his father and uncle having died, he was cared for by Donald's Stuart relatives.[17]

But two North West men were especially important to Donald, for Barbara Smith's brothers, Robert and John, had joined the company. Robert had been stationed in New Caledonia and drowned when a canoe capsized in the Columbia River. He saved the lives of two of his companions who could not swim and was struggling to shore with the third on his back when his strength gave out. John was Barbara's favourite brother and the one after whom her first son had been named. He had joined the North West Company in 1799 and had explored the Fraser River with Simon Fraser and Jules Quesnel in 1808. It was Stuart who named the river after the leader of the expedition. Two years earlier, the men had established Fort St. James on the southern tip of the beautiful lake which bears John Stuart's name. A watercolour of the lake hung in the Smith household at Forres, a reminder not only of family overseas but also of adventures which a young man might encounter there.[18]

John Stuart was admired throughout the Northwest, both by the Nor'Westers with whom he had worked and by the officers of the Hudson's Bay Company with which the North West Company amalgamated in 1821. Hudson's Bay Governor George Simpson, in his account of his journey to the Columbia in 1828, described Stuart as

> the Father or founder of New Caledonia; where for 20 years of his Life, he was doomed to all the misery and privation, which that inhospitable region could bring forth, and who with a degree of exertion, of which few men were capable, overcame difficulties, to which the business of no other part of the country was exposed; bringing its returns to near about their present standing, and leaving the District as a Monument of his unwearied industry and extraordinary perseverance, which will long reflect the highest credit on his name and character, as an Indian Trader.[19]

Stuart equally enjoyed a reputation as a highly literate man who took pleasure in discussing his reading with his correspondents.

In 1835, he was granted his first furlough since 1819 and at the end of October arrived in London. Soon after, he reached Forres for a long awaited reunion with his sister and a first meeting with his nephew and nieces. His uncle's charm, his erudition and his stories of the Pacific Northwest convinced Donald Smith that his future lay in Canada. Stuart, who knew the hardships of long cold winters, poor food and loneliness, advised against rash decisions and suggested his nephew might have an aptitude for the law. He was planning to visit fur trade cronies in Scotland and England, to see his brother Peter, who was Fort Major at Belfast, and to spend a year touring on the Continent. If, when he returned, Donald was still keen on Canada, he would do what he could to smooth the way.

Donald and his parents accepted this proposal and, after he completed his schooling in 1836, the young man was set to work in the office of Robert Watson, the town clerk, where his achievements as a Latin scholar meant that his copying of legal texts tended to be accurate and, as his handwriting had not yet deteriorated, legible. It was, however, a job of unmitigated boredom and he dreamed of escape. If he did not join the Hudson's Bay Company, he might take up farming in Upper Canada or find employment with one of the companies which had purchased large tracts of land at favourable prices and now sold small sections to immigrants. The British American Land Company had an agent in northern Scotland and regular newspaper advertisements heralded the advantages of land in the Eastern Townships of Lower Canada while the Canada Company, founded by the novelist John Galt, promoted the benefits of the two million acres it owned between Lake Huron and Lake Erie in Upper Canada.

In 1837, however, neither Upper nor Lower Canada were as attractive as they had been a year before. Rebellions in support of more representative government had broken out in both provinces and the Morayshire papers carried front page stories of fighting. News of friends and relatives was eagerly looked for, the more so in Forres because William Alves, who had emigrated from there with his family in 1832, was one of the insurgents.

A country in turmoil is not one to attract immigrants and in 1838, the papers were reporting that the floods of newcomers, who had been pouring into the Canadas since the end of the last century, had substantially abated. Though political instability seemed to rule out the Canadian option, Donald was still determined to put the town clerk's office behind him, and the Smiths began to consider other options. Through his paternal grandmother, Donald was related to the family of Grants who had established cotton weaving and printing mills in Manchester. Britain's cotton mills were thriving on new technology which processed the cheap, raw cotton imported from India and the Grants, who provided the model for the Cheeryble Brothers in Dickens' *Nicholas Nickelby*, were quick to respond to Mrs. Smith's enquiring letter with the offer of a clerkship. The proposal exchanged the law for commerce but the quill and the bottle of ink were much the same. Donald was reluctant to accept. Sir James M'Grigor was applied to again and, probably through his brother-in-law, Colonel Alexander Grant, a senior figure in the Madras Army, he arranged employment with the East India Company. Though another clerk's post, it at least offered travel and the possibility of adventure and Donald was tempted. It was not, however, what he really wanted. Canada was still in his mind.

Early in 1838, John Stuart decided that he would not, after all, be returning to Canada but would retire from the Hudson's Bay Company. Fur traders who had long been away from the pressures and pleasures of civilised life knew that they might have difficulties settling into towns and cities and many took a year or two off at the end of their working lives in order to discover if they could adjust. Some moved to small Canadian towns such as Cobourg or Brockville where fur traders clustered and neither moccasins nor half-breed children occasioned comment. Others settled in Britain, especially Scotland where most of them had been born, and John Stuart was soon to find himself occupying a house with a large garden in Forres, there being, as his sister wrote to him "no prescription better to be recommended than that of breathing his native air again."[20]

From the Continent, Stuart sent his sister a letter to say that he would be returning to London in a few weeks and if Donald was still determined to go to Canada, he would do what he could to help. By March, the *Inverness Courier* was reporting that there now seemed to be no evidence of armed rebellion in the Canadas and Donald needed no further encouragement.

A trunk was packed: clothes, bedding, a Bible and, from his mother, a plaid. His friends Kenneth and Stewart, assuming their surnames would never be forgotten, procured a powder horn to which they affixed a silver plaque reading, "Presented to Donald Smith Aged 18 on being put into clerkship with The Hudson Bay Company from his friends Stewart and Kenneth Forres Morayshire 1838." He was, in fact, four months short of his eighteenth birthday and had certainly not decided to join the Hudson's Bay Company about which his uncle had many misgivings. It may be that they sent the powder horn to him later in the year when he had entered the company, but it seems more likely that they jumped the gun. Another leave-taking present was a silver watch, made by James Ross of Forres, and engraved "Donald Smith Forres" on the inside of the dustcover. Almost certainly it was his father's farewell token.

On Saturday, April 14, the day before Easter, Donald Smith set out on foot for Aberdeen, his trunk being sent on ahead. It seems a curious day for a young man from a God-fearing household to start such a journey and no clues now exist to suggest a reason, though he did want to be in London as soon as possible in order to take the earliest available passage for Canada. It was important to arrive there in the summer when the roads were passable, so that he could reach whatever place he settled on for his final destination. Travel in the autumn, when the roads were a sea of mud, was difficult and in the late fall, when they were frozen but not covered with snow, it was virtually impossible.

Having found his trunk and obtained a passage on a coastal vessel, Donald would undoubtedly have made time to visit Marischal College, then still housed in the old Greyfriars monastic buildings, where his brother had studied for his B.A. The fabulous seventeenth century Mercat Cross, topped by a unicorn, was also a short distance from the docks and demanded attention. But Donald devoted little time to sightseeing and was soon bound for London where he arrived early on the morning of April 29.

Thinking it imprudent to call on his uncle before ten o'clock, Donald made his way to the coach office in Ludgate Hill where he delivered a parcel to be called for by Mrs. Grant, yet another member of the far-flung clan. From the coach office, he headed north to Clerkenwell where his uncle was staying and discovered him about to set off for a business meeting. Together they took a stage to Hanover Square, just south of Oxford Street, and Donald amused himself as a tourist before returning to Clerkenwell to dine with his uncle and a friend.

"London," he observed in his first letter to his mother, "is a very gay place at this season of the year," and on the following morning he set out to see more of it,

> walking all the way from the Mansion House where the Lord Mayor resides, to Hyde Park, where the aristocracy are to be seen riding and driving. You have heard of Rotten Row; it is a fine place. Here the trees and flowers are a good month in advance of ours in Scotland or at least in Forres. Had I been in the Park an hour later or earlier, I should have been rewarded by the spectacle of Her Majesty. The Queen and the Duchess of Kent, her mother, drive every day, I am told; so I shall hope to enjoy the privilege.[21]

Victoria was to be crowned at the end of June and Donald was not alone in wanting a glimpse of this plain young lady who was undertaking such great responsibility so early in life. The fact that they were virtually coevals, Victoria having been born fifteen months before this particular Scottish subject, added to his curiosity.

John Stuart took his nephew to the Palace of Westminster where they heard a debate in the House of Commons and unsuccessfully tried to gain admission to the House of Lords. The Houses of Parliament had been destroyed by fire in 1834 and the Commons was sitting in the old Court of Requests, which had previously been occupied by the House of Lords, while the peers were temporarily accommodated in what had been the Painted Chamber before the fire. The MPs were surrounded by ruins and by the building works that marked the beginning of Charles Barry's long struggle to provide a new home for the national government.

While Donald enjoyed his visits to the various attractions of the capital, he did not allow himself to lose sight of his main reason for being there. First, he had to learn more about the Hudson's Bay Company from conversations with his uncle and by visiting the company's headquarters in Fenchurch Street. By the time he wrote his mother on April 30, Donald had already been exposed to some of John Stuart's doubts about a career with the company.

> Openings in the Indian Country are much more difficult and less profitable than formerly. The prospects of a great decrease in the price of beaver is everywhere spoken of. My uncle assured me that if he had to begin his career afresh, he would have nothing to do with the Honourable Company or with the Indian country, but would settle in Upper Canada, where land is cheap and quite large towns are springing up in all parts.[22]

On the first of May, Donald went to see William Smith, soon to be assistant secretary of the Hudson's Bay Company. These senior executives of the organisation wielded considerable power but were kept closely in check by the directors. Stuart's advice was that the young man should present himself, indicate his interest in working for the company but not accept a clerkship if Smith offered it. This was because George Simpson, who was normally based in Lower Canada, exercised supreme power over Hudson's Bay Company activities in North America and an appointment for which he was responsible was much more likely to attract his attention and support than one which was thrust upon him by someone else. This tactic also gave Donald a chance to assess the other opportunities for employment in Canada before committing himself to the Hudson's Bay.

In the spring of 1838, Simpson was in England where he had been called for preparatory discussions prior to travelling to St. Petersburg for negotiations with the Russians about supplying their fur trading posts on the Pacific coast. He seems not to have been in London when Donald Smith was there, but shortly after Easter, John Stuart had taken steps to win over Simpson who, on April 20, wrote James Keith in Canada with reference to a vacant post which they had discussed earlier. "You will hear of a very promising, well educated, young man named Donald Smith from Mr. James McKenzie [the company's agent at Quebec]; if he be willing to accept the appointment you will be pleased to let him have it; on the contrary you may give it to any other of whom you may think favorably."[23]

Five days later, Stuart procured for his nephew a letter which simultaneously introduced the young Scot and advised Keith to appoint Donald Smith to the vacant clerkship "sending him forthwith to winter quarters." It also noted that "his passage money and all expenses connected with his voyage and journey ... have been defrayed by his friends." "Friends" meant John Stuart.[24]

The business with the Hudson's Bay Company settled, Donald turned his attention to learning as much as he could about the country to which he was now committed. Years later, he recalled, "As I was going out to Canada, I made it my business to inform myself as thoroughly as I could of the political situation there. I read every newspaper and pamphlet I could come at, and afterwards went to the *Morning Herald* office and looked up the Canadian articles and debates in Parliament of Canadian affairs."[25]

The visit to London also introduced him to William Stuart, John Stuart's cousin and the guardian of his son, Donald. Donald Smith knew about his namesake, who was at school in England, and hoped to meet him in London, but however interesting it may have been to encounter a Canadian of very nearly his own age, Donald Smith was to be better served by his encounter with his uncle's cousin. Banking in Britain was relatively primitive in those days and, in the remote farms or trading posts where Donald might expect to find himself, it was non-existent. Men therefore needed an honest and respectable friend who could accept and disburse cash when called on to do so. For many years, William had acted in this capacity for his cousin and he now undertook to do so for Donald, assuming, of course, that the young man would one day have sufficient earnings to repay his uncle and then to contribute to his family's upkeep in Scotland. At that point, he had not even made a decision about his future career, as he explained to his mother.

> It is still doubtful whether I shall enter the service of the Hudson's Bay Company in any capacity. At present my own view favours Upper Canada.... My uncle strongly advises me, on arrival at Montreal, to push on westward. Canada is at present in a most troubled state and trade is in consequence suffering. Lord Durham sailed for Quebec in the *Hastings* a fortnight ago with royal powers to effect a settlement of the troubles and administer punishment to the rebels.[26]

By perusing the newspapers and perhaps by personal interview as well, Donald and his uncle discovered the *Royal William*, a 340 ton brig built in Prince Edward Island in 1831 and subsequently sold in England where she was registered in Scarborough on the Yorkshire coast. A timber vessel, like so many British North American-built ships of the period, she had been carrying lumber between Quebec and Dublin and was now in London seeking cargo for her return to Canada. On May 9, Donald wrote his mother that he expected to sail late that night or the following morning, "according to tide and cargo." Captain Agar seems to have been unduly optimistic about obtaining cargo and delayed the ship's departure for a week, but in the end, she sailed in ballast. Shortly after midnight on May 16, as the tide pulled out of the great Thames estuary, the *Royal William* slipped from her moorings and headed out to sea. She worked her way through the English Channel, skirted the south coast of Ireland and headed out to the rough open waters of the Atlantic. If Donald Smith looked back, it was to a land he was not to see again for twenty-eight years. In spirit, however, he was looking ahead.[27]

CHAPTER TWO

THE LITTLE EMPEROR AND THE KING'S POSTS 1838–1847

O happy is the man who hears
instruction's warning voice
Eleventh Paraphrase[1]

The *Royal William* carried two passengers in addition to Donald Smith. One was Mr. Ross who had owned land in Upper Canada and had sold it to go into the lumber business in what is now Quebec. He and the courteous young Scot, who was poring over the prospectus of the Canada Company and perusing guides for emigrants, soon fell into conversation. Ross held forth on the conditions of the timber business from which a profit could then be made, even if a ship returned to Canada in ballast. Despite being seasick throughout much of the long journey, Donald considered carefully all that he heard and read: it was his introduction to the economics of transport, and he remembered it.

The voyage was beset by fogs and icebergs and the *Royal William* did not enter the Gulf of St. Lawrence till the middle of June. By that time, the young highlander had also made a good impression on Captain Agar who took him ashore with him when they stopped at Fraserville on the south bank of the St. Lawrence River. The reason for calling there was undoubtedly to pick up a pilot to guide them through the narrow channels of the river but Malcolm Fraser, the local seigneur, declared that Donald was making a propitious start to his Canadian life by taking his first steps on the soil of a highland Fraser. It was certainly an initiation into the changes the new world could bring about in its settlers. Now called Rivière du Loup, Fraserville was originally named after a captain who had served under General Wolfe in the taking of Canada from the French, but his grandson, Malcolm Fraser, spoke scarcely a word of English and only enough Gaelic to toast the new arrival. This branch of the Frasers spoke French.

On the morning of Friday, June 18, the *Royal William* nosed into the harbour at Quebec. The lower town bustled with all the activity of Canada's principal civilian port. Sailors, freight agents, stevedores, boarding house keepers and ships' chandlers thronged the narrow, wooden-planked streets while high above them towered the ramparts of the great citadel. Sunlight glinted from the steep tin roofs of the city and everywhere there was the bustle of people committed to doing a year's shipping business in eight ice-free months. Added excitement was provided by the presence of *HMS Vestal* and her rather tense crew who were waiting to take charge of eight Lower Canada rebels about to be deported to Bermuda.

One of Donald's first calls in Quebec was on James McKenzie. An old fur trader who had worked for the North West Company along the north shore of the St. Lawrence, where he had a reputation for selling watered rum and Indian women, McKenzie had been both the Nor'Westers' agent and an independent trader before becoming the Hudson's Bay Company agent in 1827. He procured supplies for the company's posts in the St. Lawrence and Labrador districts, forwarded the shipments from these posts to London, and distributed supplies from England. The previous Saturday, when he had sent a shipment to Montreal, he had forgotten to enclose a parcel of bills and some papers, so Donald was welcomed as much as a courier as for his own sake. McKenzie added to Donald's letters of introduction by providing another to James Keith who was in charge in Montreal. In it, he alerted Keith, who had also served with the North West Company, to the fact that the young man was not merely recommended by George Simpson; he was the nephew of their old colleague John Stuart, and therefore someone in whom they too might take an interest.[2]

In Quebec, Mr. Ross continued to keep an eye on his new friend and arranged a meeting with William Price who was rapidly becoming one of Canada's foremost timber merchants. A conservative businessman with extensive lumber interests throughout the eastern part of Lower Canada, he was ill at ease in cities and both he and his equally dour son preferred spending their time at their mills in the bush. Ross obviously thought that Donald would make a good addition to Price's staff and the shipboard conversation about the timber trade had roused the young man's interest, but no prospect of employment emerged from the meeting.

Ross also took Donald to dinner at the newly opened Victoria Hotel where the city's businessmen, merchants and lumbermen congregated. Here, the conversation was all of the new Governor General, Lord Durham, who had landed at Quebec two weeks earlier and whose investigations into the 1837 Rebellion were proceeding with great dispatch. Durham had placed a firm hand on the reins of government, had granted some amnesties, authorised some executions and sanctioned some deportations. His decisive action was lauded by the diners who felt he was creating conditions in which they could profitably do business again. London, being unaware of the views of the colonial businessmen, condemned its envoy for exceeding his authority — but it was Durham's report which was to establish the framework for uniting Upper and Lower Canada under one government and for encouraging the Anglophones and the Francophones of British North America to work together to their mutual advantage.

Late in the day, Donald bade farewell to his new acquaintances and boarded a steamer for Montreal. It made slow progress, dodging the small sailing ships anchored in the roads outside the port. Along both sides of the river, vessels took on cargoes of timber while pilot boats and tugs guided the larger ships through the narrow channels of the St. Lawrence.

Early on June 20, the steamer docked at Montreal. Founded on an island in the middle of the St. Lawrence River, the city was fast establishing itself as the heart of Canada's commercial network. While Quebec was a seat of government and catered for the large seafaring ships which could not navigate the shoals and narrows above it, Montreal was already identified as Canada's financial and distributive centre. The city's docks and wharfage were negligible compared to Quebec's, but vessels with a shallow draft carried goods and passengers between the two cities, and from Montreal small boats, barges and freight canoes had access to the inland waterways which allowed communication with Upper Canada, the interiors of both provinces and the hinterland beyond.

Donald considered the letters of introduction in his pocket and set out to see the man who was easily the most powerful. This was Edward Ellice, a merchant who had supplied the North West Company, who owned estates in Canada and Scotland and who prided himself on being an influential figure who could effect compromises and bring about resolutions to conflicts from which he stood to gain only further prestige. He was nicknamed "Bear", "rather for his oiliness than for any trace of ferocity ever seen in him," Thomas Carlyle observed, but the allusion to his connection with the fur trade was equally apt. His son, also Edward, was following in his footsteps and was at that time in Canada as Lord Durham's secretary. Ellice senior was absent but Donald left his uncle's letter and in due course was rewarded with a dinner invitation and the opportunity to meet some of Canada's most important public figures.[3]

His immediate needs were, however, more pressing, and from Bear Ellice's sumptuous Montreal home, he trudged to Lachine, on the western outskirts of the city. The village, with its solid, squat, grey stone buildings, housed the Hudson's Bay Company's Canadian headquarters but, since it was Sunday, Donald went to see Lewis Grant, son of one of the Forres Grants, to whom he also had a letter of introduction from John Stuart. Grant had no suggestions for employment. On Monday morning, Donald called at the HBC offices to deliver the mail from Quebec but he avoided committing himself to employment until he had met Alexander Stewart, to whom his uncle had also written.

Sandy Stewart was another Nor'Wester whose kindness and patience endeared him as much to the Indians with whom he had traded as to his North West and Hudson's Bay Company colleagues. Ill health had forced him to retire from the fur trade and he had established himself and his mixed-blood family in Boucherville on the south shore of the St. Lawrence opposite Montreal. He kept in touch with his old friends and was glad to hear from John Stuart.

> You will probably see my nephew and will not like him the worse for being the son of my sister. He is, I believe, a fine lad, acknowledged by all to be of an excellent character. He goes *à l'aventure*; and if it is possible that through your friends you could procure any situation for him better than that of entering the service of the Hudson's Bay Company, I know that for my sake you will do it.[4]

Stewart welcomed Donald into his home and offered guidance on the course he should pursue. The Canada Company was unlikely to give him a situation:

immigration had been greatly reduced by the rebellion and was unlikely to pick up for at least another year. As for buying land from the company, assuming he could afford it, those plots which were easy to clear had already been taken and it would require back-breaking work to remove the trees on those which were now available. Furthermore, Donald had no experience of farming or animal husbandry and, alone on a remote homestead, he would have no one to turn to for guidance or support.

As for the Hudson's Bay Company option, there were three main points to consider. First, it would be a long time before he could expect substantial financial recompense for the effort he would be required to make on the company's behalf. Second, it had already been made clear that if he did join, he would be assigned either to one of the posts along the north shore of the St. Lawrence River or to Ungava in the far north of Labrador. The company's power base, however, was in the area north and west of the Great Lakes. It was where all the great fur traders had served and where both George Simpson and James Keith, now controlling the operation from Lachine, had gained their experience. Men were very rarely posted from one department to another and if Donald started in the Gulf of St. Lawrence, he should expect to go no further than Labrador.

Set against these discouraging points was the fact that the Hudson's Bay Company had a place earmarked for him. The company found work for the sons of its employees wherever possible and Donald would be treated kindly as John Stuart's nephew. The company rewarded diligence and hard work and Donald had many of the qualities which it valued. He was intelligent and better educated than many men employed by the company, and he was possessed of that rather old fashioned, formal courtesy which was the hallmark of Hudson's Bay Company officers. In any case, his first contract would be for five years and he could then leave with honour if he wished to do so.

There was really no choice: he took himself back across the river to Montreal and out to Lachine for an appointment with James Keith. By the end of it, Donald was an apprentice clerk in the Hudson's Bay Company. As decreed from London by George Simpson, he signed the usual contract, giving him £20 in the first year, £25 in the second, £30 in the third, £40 in the fourth and £50 in the final year. Board and lodging were provided by the company.[5]

In joining the Hudson's Bay Company, Donald Smith was entering an organisation which was quite unlike any other; it had its own transportation system, its own banking system and its own currency; it had its own rules and customs, its own social and professional hierarchy, its own vocabulary and a financial year which took precedence over the calendar year in most communications.

The company had been established in 1670 when Charles II granted a charter to his cousin, Prince Rupert, Count Palatine of the Rhine, and his seventeen associates. The charter created a joint stock company called "the Governor and Company of Adventurers of England tradeing into Hudsons Bay" and, as with the memorandum and articles of association of any company established in England today, the charter set out who the first members were to be, how many of them were to be directors and how they were to be chosen. It outlined the way in which the company was to be run. The charter also provided the shareholders with a land grant but, as the territory was unmapped, neither the king nor the first members of the company comprehended that, with a few strokes of the pen, hundreds of thousands of acres had passed into the company's control. The charter granted "the sole Trade and Commerce" of all the land draining into Hudson Straits "that are not already actually possessed by or granted to any of our Subjectes or possessed by the Subjectes of any other Christian Prince or State." It included fishing and mineral rights as well.[6]

In short, the company acquired almost all of present day Alberta and Saskatchewan, all of Manitoba, much of the North West Territories, and a large portion of northern Ontario and northern Quebec. Moreover, the charter granted it to the company forever. As Donald Smith was to remark nearly sixty years after he first signed his contract, "The earth-hunger of Christian monarchs in those days was not limited by exact geographical considerations, nor was much regard shown to the claims of other nations." Prince Rupert was appointed the first Governor and the charter determined that "the said Land bee from henceforth reckoned and reputed as one of our Plantacions or Colonyes in America called *Ruperts Land*."[7]

Rupert's Land was not, however, a colony in the way that Nova Scotia or Canada or Massachusetts were. Rupert's Land was administered as a business by businessmen. The company made the rules and regulations which governed the lives of its employees, and settlers were neither desired nor taken into account. Reference to the monarch or to parliament in London was neither required nor sought.

The preamble to the charter did make reference to efforts to find the North West Passage but this was an embellishment designed to praise the shareholders who had already financed one journey to the Arctic seas. As the king, Prince Rupert and his colleagues all knew, the company was established as a trading operation, sending European goods into the north in exchange for furs. Metal was largely unknown to the Indians at that time and the company swapped firearms and ammunition, cooking utensils and the ubiquitous Venetian glass beads for furs. Especially sought after were beaver pelts because European gentlemen, whether civilian, clergy or military, all wanted to wear hats of beaver felt. Not only were they fashionable, they were waterproof, a not unimportant consideration in a northern European winter.

Pierre-Esprit Radisson and Médard Chouart, Sieur de Groseilliers, had demonstrated that the fastest route from northern Europe to the fur lands of the new world was via Hudson Bay and, further, that it was possible to get in and out in one season without being trapped by the ice. The company was established to take advantage of that fact. Over the years, it developed a system whereby pelts were sent by canoe or York boat to York Factory on the west coast of Hudson Bay, and later to other posts in Hudson or James Bay, as soon as the ice melted on the rivers and the season of navigation opened. The ships arrived from London carrying the trade goods, provisions for the traders and new staff. The outfit, that is the goods and provisions which had been indented for the previous year, was transferred from the ships to the inland boats and canoes and the return, that is the pelts, was passed from the boats to the ships. It was a system which required careful timing, preparedness and being alert to seasonal changes which could be used to advantage or could trap a canoe or a ship for the winter.

By the time Donald Smith became an employee in 1838, the Hudson's Bay Company had added two considerable stretches of territory to the North American holdings granted by King Charles. Through a series of leases, it acquired Labrador, concentrating in particular on the area around Hamilton Inlet. It also acquired the King's Posts, so called because they were first the property of the French monarch. These were dotted along the north shore of the St. Lawrence River and included Tadoussac, Isle Jeremie, Bersimis, Godbout and Sept Iles, and two inland posts at Chicoutimi and Lake St. John. As well, the company occupied, without clear title, the Seigneury of Mingan in a sheltered bay at the mouth of the Mingan River. The company thus had a sweep of coastal stations from Rigolet at the entrance to Hamilton Inlet to Tadoussac, half way up the St. Lawrence.

The second, larger, acquisition gave the company all of British Columbia, including Vancouver Island, and the northern part of Washington State. This had been worked primarily by the North West Company, a partnership of fur traders who had been based in Montreal and who had developed a transportation network through the Great Lakes and the river systems of the interior. Simon Fraser, John Stuart and his fur trading friends, and Alexander Mackenzie, the first man to travel overland to the Pacific from Canada, which then meant southern Ontario and Quebec, were all North West Company men. A bitter rivalry, leading occasionally to bloodshed, developed between the Hudson's Bay men and the Nor'Westers who were encroaching on their monopoly. By the early part of the nineteenth century, the Montreal men were under increasing financial pressure. It took two years to turn a profit on a beaver pelt using the southern route because canoes taking goods in through the St. Lawrence could not reach the remote fur lands and return with the skins in one season, especially if the Nor'Westers had to hunt for their food en route. Each time the Hudson's Bay Company diverted Indians to its own posts to trade, it also secured the food which would otherwise have been sold to the competition. The struggle to maintain their long supply line virtually bankrupted the Nor'Westers and in 1821 they sought an accommodation with the Hudson's Bay Company. It was negotiated by Bear Ellice.

By the Deed Poll of 1821, which confirmed the amalgamation of the two bodies, the Hudson's Bay Company acquired undisputed command of the river system to enhance its main supply route through the bay, and an enlarged and more secure monopoly. Not long before Donald arrived in 1838, a licence to trade west of its chartered territories gave official sanction to the occupation of the North West Company's forts between the Rocky Mountains and the Pacific Ocean. George Simpson's journey to St. Petersburg was destined to settle arrangements with the Russian trading posts which still remained along the Pacific coast and effectively gave the company control over them as well.

By the Deed Poll of 1821, the English company also acquired a new relationship with its employees because it adopted two significant features of the Nor'Westers' management. The first was an annual council of senior staff at which they discussed the administration of the business and made suggestions for its improvement. The second meant that the senior men became partners, not employees, and were paid from dividends. In the North West Company, the men who wintered at the fur posts rather than in Montreal were known as wintering partners and the term was adopted when the companies amalgamated. Men such as labourers, apprentices and clerks, were on salary, as were the resident governor and one or two other senior managers in Canada, and all the staff in London.

Among the many Hudson's Bay Company features to be retained was the division of the territory into two departments. An imaginary line, drawn from a point midway between York Factory and the mouth of the Severn River through what is now Winnipeg to the American boundary, separated the Northern and Southern Departments. New Caledonia, meaning the territory between the Rocky Mountains and the Pacific Ocean, with the Sandwich Islands as an added bonus, made a third department when the licence to trade there was officially granted. In due course, the Montreal Department was created by uniting the King's Posts, Labrador and a sweep of land carved out of the Southern Department above the Great Lakes.

With the unification of the two companies, opposing trading forts were amalgamated, staff was pruned and business was streamlined. The man appointed to oversee this in the Northern Department was George Simpson who controlled every minute detail of the lives of Hudson's Bay Company employees from Lake Superior to the mountains. He was an indefatigable traveller throughout his territory, intimidating most of the company's officers, whatever their seniority.

When Donald Smith signed his contract as an apprentice clerk, Simpson was still in Europe. When he returned to Canada the following spring, he was Governor-in-Chief for all of North America, a title which merely confirmed that Simpson was entitled to do as he had already been doing, namely managing the Southern Department, and the King's Posts and Labrador, in addition to the Northern Department. Dubbed the Little Emperor in reference to his size and his power, he was arrogant, inconsiderate, and peremptory but, under his aegis, the Hudson's Bay Company was to become an efficient business organisation, constantly honing its methods, improving its supply routes, and developing new products for the European market. As John Stuart warned his nephew, Simpson was a man who would have to be treated with the greatest of care.

> You are dependent on the good-will and caprice of one man, who is a little too much addicted to prejudices for speedy advancement; but this is probably true in many other spheres of commercial endeavour. I wish it were in my power to assist you in his good graces; but as you know I am quitting the service and against his wish, which is by no means a present recommendation to his favour. There is, I may say, no man who is more appreciative of downright hard work coupled with intelligence, or one more intolerant of *puppyism*, by which I mean carelessness and presumption. Depend upon it, the Governor soon finds means of driving that sort of youth out of the service. In fact, I think he will stand idleness sooner than the least trace of presumption. It is his *foible* to exact not only strict obedience but deference to the point of humility. As long as you pay him in that coin you will quickly get on his sunny side and find yourself in a few years a trader at a congenial post, with promotion in sight.[8]

It was wise to warn the HBC novice that mention of Stuart's name would not necessarily help in his dealings with the governor. Though George Simpson had at one time been a great admirer of John Stuart, the two had fallen out when Simpson abandoned his country wife, Margaret Taylor, and her children and, with no warning, married his young English cousin, Frances Simpson. While Simpson was in England on business and the unsuspected courtship in 1829, Stuart had been left in charge of Margaret, sister of his own country wife Mary, and had faithfully reported on her health and welfare and on the birth of Simpson's second child by her. Stuart was as shocked as Margaret, Mary and many of the fur traders were when Simpson callously turned his back on her. "The commodity," as he referred to Margaret, was superfluous as far as he was concerned, and Stuart was instructed to marry her off to someone else. He had abandoned other "bits of brown," as he contemptuously called the Indian and half-breed women for whom he saw no purpose beyond sexual gratification, but it was generally supposed that the relationship with Margaret was more substantial.

Matters were made worse in the winter of 1830 when Stuart was also instructed by Simpson to resettle the country wife of John George McTavish and the seven children she had borne him. Stuart wrote scathingly to McTavish, who had emulated his mentor and taken a young Scottish bride in the winter of 1829, and it was clear to Simpson that the condemnation applied equally to him. Simpson retaliated, speaking slightingly to the Governor and Committee of the fur trader whom he had once admired and praised. Stuart was probably flattering himself in thinking that Simpson did not want him to retire, but in recommending to his nephew "deference to the point of humility", he knew whereof he spoke.[9]

For the moment, however, George Simpson was in London preparing to go to St. Petersburg and Donald had only to contend with the meticulous and formal James Keith.

The weeks from July till early October were the Hudson's Bay Company's busiest time. The English ships delivered provisions and trade goods in the Bay and at Quebec where they had to be checked and prepared for onward shipment. Furs, buffalo robes and other commodities poured into York Factory and the warehouses at Lachine where they had to be counted, assessed for quality and packed for England. Bills of lading had to be drawn up and checked, indents for the following year had to be approved or modified, and accounts had to be made ready for London. There were never enough hands for the work. Donald was immediately set to counting muskrat skins. The stiff, rough hides ripped into the delicate flesh of the young clerk, tearing it to shreds, and the pain in his hands was worsened by the laughter of his more experienced colleagues who finally explained that he should be wearing sturdy gloves for such a job.[10]

For an apprentice clerk determined to make his mark, there was much to see and learn at Lachine. For a start the name, generally spelled La Chine in those days, meant precisely what it appeared to mean. In the seventeenth century, René-Robert Cavalier, Sieur de La Salle had been granted the land by the Sulpician Fathers. An explorer, La Salle expected that it was only a matter of time before he located the passage through the waterways to the west which would lead him to China. His neighbours thought otherwise and renamed the land on the edge of the St. Lawrence to save him the journey.

The village of Lachine developed just above the Lachine Rapids, where the river, rushing eastwards, drops seven feet in a little over a mile, effectively halting traffic in both directions. The fur depot there was constructed by the North West

Company which also built canoe sheds and warehouses to store provisions and trade goods for the west bound journey. Across the river was Kahnawake, home of the Mohawks who manned the North West Company's canoes and, later, the Hudson's Bay Company's brigades and Simpson's private canoes. Following the 1821 amalgamation, the storage facilities were taken over by the HBC and in 1833 Simpson moved the company's entire administrative operation there from Fort Garry (Winnipeg) in the Northern Department. The office, which was also Simpson's home, was a large, almost elegant, pillared building which had once served as an inn. It stood on the edge of the Lachine Canal which the government had built between 1821 and 1825 to enable vessels to bypass the torrent. A footbridge across the canal took the unmarried clerks from the fur sheds to their lodgings at Mr. Norton's.

At the commencement of the season of navigation, huge, gaily decorated birch bark canoes gathered in the canal to load provisions for those inland posts which were more easily equipped from Montreal; at the end of the season, they clustered by the warehouses, offloading their produce. The canoes were famous for their size and for the speed and dexterity with which their crews managed them. When Lord Durham arrived in Montreal in July 1838, he dropped a word to his secretary, Edward Ellice, that he would like to have a look at a "trading canoe." He was to embark at Lachine on Wednesday, July 18 and head up the St. Lawrence to the Ellice estate at Beauharnois to spend the night before proceeding to Upper Canada. Ellice explained to James Keith that the company should "show a mark of esteem" to the Governor General and suggested a flotilla of canoes, "manned with Indians," to escort him to Beauharnois. No doubt this procession would also enhance the Ellice reputation there. And thus it was that Donald Smith, who knew better, made his first *faux pas* in the eyes of the Hudson's Bay Company. The clerks rushed from their work for a glimpse of the queen's *locum tenens* and in the excitement Donald forgot to remove his cap as a mark of respect. He was, quite properly, rebuked by Mr. Keith.[11]

But Donald was not to spend long under James Keith's eagle eye. On July 7, William Connolly had written from Tadoussac in the Gulf of St. Lawrence, requesting "that Mr. D.A. Smith be sent down as soon as you may find it convenient." A month later, the request was urgent: he needed an assistant as soon as possible. The ink was scarcely dry on Donald's contract when Connolly wrote his first letter. He had been promised help and the HBC grapevine, which worked with remarkable efficiency in even the most adverse circumstances, had revealed that John Stuart's nephew was going to be sent to him. When he wrote his uncle on July 29, Donald was quite unaware that he was about to pack his bags again, but six weeks after he had landed in Quebec, he was back on James McKenzie's doorstep and, on August 14, he sailed in the schooner *Otter* down the river to Tadoussac. This seems to have been a temporary posting, designed to help Connolly prepare the accounts and perhaps to provide cover so that Connolly could make a quick tour of the other posts for which he was also responsible. In November, Connolly took the accounts to Montreal and it seems that Donald accompanied him. He was certainly there at the beginning of November, writing excitedly to his mother about a new outbreak of violence and the declaration of martial law.[12]

> At another place called Beauharnois a body of four hundred attacked a house where our Mr. Ellice and many other ladies and gentlemen were. They were summoned to surrender, which they did after half an hour's fighting. Mrs. Ellice, Mrs. Balfour, and other ladies who had taken refuge in the cellar were shamefully treated, and Mr. Ellice and his host, Mr. Brown, were carried off prisoners to Napierville. In Montreal there is great excitement and there are guards before the Montreal Bank and the principal buildings. The Company's storehouses are also guarded, and the clerks and labourers enrolled as constables. You may remember my writing of Mr. Lewis Grant, son of Mr. Grant, of Forres, who has a business establishment at Lachine. He was on a visit to Mr. McDonald of Chateauguay, formerly one of the Company's men. Mr. McDonald's store, I hear, had been pillaged and both he and Mr. Grant taken prisoners and carried off.
>
> Montreal is a scene of great martial enthusiasm and the people put every reliance in the troops who have been and are daily being despatched to the scene of the outbreak. Yesterday, the 71st Regiment, part of the 93rd, and the Grenadier Guards departed by steamer, and some of us went down to see them off, their bands playing Highland airs. It is said General Colborne and General McDonell will leave in person to-day and this time it is certain the rebels will be shown no mercy. If it is not crushed soon, the civil and loyal population will enlist *en masse* and you may expect to hear of my going as a soldier. I write this in haste to catch the last packet this season.[13]

In fact the excitement soon died down and order was restored.

Connolly's business in Montreal, his native city, probably included persuading James Keith to allow him to keep the new apprentice clerk and when he returned to the King's Posts he would have had Donald in tow. Donald's account for Outfit 1838 (June 1, 1838-May 31, 1839) shows that he spent nearly eighty-five percent of his salary that year. A small amount would be explained by postage but the majority of his expenditure would have been on the acquisition of appropriate clothes for the work he was now doing. He outfitted himself with homespun trousers, flannel shirts, a toque, moccasins, a leather jacket and anything else he may have needed to ward off the cold. The value of goods, whether acquired on his behalf in Montreal, Quebec or London, or provided by the trading post, was then debited against his London account with the company to which his salary was credited. An annual statement was provided which enabled employees to check that payments had been made and that both income and expenditure were properly recorded. Men at the trading posts had little use for cash and scarcely ever saw it except in rare cases where they were purchasing furs rather than trading for them.[14]

Tadoussac, where Donald spent his first Canadian winter, derives from *totoushac*, an Algonkian word meaning *nipples* and referring to the rounded hills of rock which guard the narrow entrance to the Saguenay River where the post was situated. Here Jacques Cartier traded for furs in 1535 and here the French established Canada's oldest fur trading post in 1600. In 1658, the King of France granted a lease conferring exclusive hunting, fishing, and trading rights on the north shore from Isle-aux-Coudres at the mouth of Baie St. Paul to Sept Iles over 300 miles further east. This Domaine du Roi, the King's Posts, extended north to the headwaters of the rivers which drained that section of the coast. In 1661, the Compagnie des Cents-Associés was granted a monopoly on the Seigneurie de Mingan. Those boundaries were never clearly defined, but were understood to extend from the King's Posts to Goynish River. When France ceded New France to Britain in 1763, this string of fur trading posts was included and Britain promptly leased the lot to the highest bidder. In 1802, this was the North West Company whose twenty year lease expired the year after the amalgamation with the Hudson's Bay Company. Concern about keeping down costs meant that the company allowed bits of leases to be purchased, creating a complex legal tangle which it was still trying to sort out in the last quarter of the century. In 1832, it managed to reunite all but Mingan and the posts were put under the management of William Connolly. In 1835, the Mingan lease, covering the mainland trading post and an archipelago of twenty-nine small islands, was purchased and added to his responsibilities.

This collection of leases gave the company exclusive rights over all fishing and trading activities at Mingan; at the King's Posts, it had the sole right to the seal fishery and to trade with the Indians but was otherwise placed on an equal footing with the rest of the public except that, before 1842, the public was not allowed to settle. Business was highly competitive and the company's staff had to be constantly on the alert for traders offering more attractive deals on furs or setting their nets in the more desirable salmon rivers. North of Tadoussac, Donald's lumbering acquaintance, William Price, had his operations and there were perpetual arguments about encroachment and the damming of salmon streams.

Donald found that Tadoussac was no more than a scattering of little houses tucked against the mountains at the mouth of the river. One served as a cookhouse while another was used to store furs and trade goods. William Connolly, who had recently married a wealthy young Montreal lady, had his own quarters, while Donald and the other unmarried men had rooms in a nearby building and were expected to mess together. In many posts, the company's office was in this building as well. Though at the western end of the department, Tadoussac was the administrative centre to which the other King's Posts and Mingan reported. The company had its own schooners, such as the *Otter*, which travelled between these places in the season of navigation, gathering the returns and taking them to Quebec for forwarding to England in the company's ship.

In the late autumn and early winter, Indians arrived at the posts and "took debt." They were given guns, ammunition, flour, blankets and other provisions, the value of which determined the number of made beaver (dressed beaver skins) required to pay for them. (In the Northwest, the unit of currency was the robe, or dressed buffalo hide.) More valuable furs such as fox and less esteemed ones such as rabbit were priced in relation to the made beaver. Thus, it took many rabbit skins to equal one made beaver, but a good fox was worth several made beaver. In the summer and fall, the Indians were expected to return with furs at least equal to the value of the goods with which they had been issued. If they brought more, additional goods could be taken; rarely, if ever, did they maintain a credit in case the next season's hunting failed. The difficulty at Tadoussac and the other posts along the north shore was that free traders often enticed the Indians to part with their furs, with the result that the company, having bankrolled the winter hunt, got nothing in return. This, coupled with the presence of a number of mixed-blood hunters who were happier dealing in cash, induced the company to reduce the amount of bartering it did and in September 1845 Simpson issued instructions that it was to be abandoned altogether. Henceforward, furs were to be purchased and goods and provisions were to be sold for ready money. In fact, bartering continued alongside cash transactions and in 1864 the company was still instructing its men in the posts below Quebec to abandon the credit system.

Donald's apprenticeship as a clerk was not confined to learning the financial idiosyncrasies of the Hudson's Bay Company. He had to learn to judge the value of furs in cash terms, in relation to the trade goods available and in relation to each other. Their worth fluctuated according to the prices fetched at auction in Montreal or London and the traders most admired were the ones who could get the best furs for the lowest cost and who were also sensitive to the variations in the fur market. News of the prices obtained for furs was treated confidentially, partly to egg on the young clerks to better deals but primarily to keep the information out of the hands of competitors. If prices were on the upswing, you could afford to pay a little more and thus encourage the hunters to bring in more and better furs. If your competitor paid more for furs than he should have when the market was declining, you stood a better chance of driving him out of business.

An apprentice clerk in Donald Smith's day could also expect to spend long hours copying documents. Copies needed to be kept of outgoing correspondence and duplicate records of income and expenditure had to be maintained. The accounts for Mingan and Sept Iles, for instance, would be made up at those posts and a fair copy sent to Tadoussac. There all the figures for the district would have to be correlated to show how the area was doing as a whole, to indicate whether individual posts were improving or declining, and to reveal any weak spots.

Winter at Tadoussac was not a pleasant experience. It was colder than Donald had ever known, and, as always on the St. Lawrence, the fog and mists shrouded the mountain tops and filled the long, deep Saguenay valley. As winter turned to spring, attention once again turned to accounts. By the end of May, a complete inventory of the post's supplies had to be completed so that the men, and more importantly, George Simpson, knew exactly what was being carried forward to the next financial year. For Simpson, careful management meant knowing that half a bag of sugar or a pound of nails were available and he was quite capable of telling one post to pass on its surplus to another where goods were in short supply. This, of course, required credits and debits to be entered in the accounts to keep the books straight. In the last analysis, the viability of each post was determined, not merely by the amount of furs or salmon or seal oil it returned, but by the value of these items in relation to what it cost to maintain the post. Profit and loss was assessed post by post and district by district as well as for the company overall, and the King's Posts were always on the verge of being shut down. They survived as long as they did because they served as a buffer to keep intruders from the wealthier interior regions.

As the months passed at Tadoussac, Donald began to learn about the land he was living in and the men and women who populated it. When communication with the outside world resumed, he wrote to his family, explaining that the Indians with whom he was dealing were Montagnais.

> All the country to the north-east of here is the Montagnais country as far as Swanipie where you meet the Nascopies and after that the Esquimaux. I have tried to ascertain how many Montagnais or Mountaineers there are. Some say 5000, which is probably a high figure.
>
> I was astonished to see the Montagnais in the woods teaching their children to read according to the principles they had imbibed from the missionaries. Time hangs heavily on their hands and they turn in the family circle for entertainment to the alphabet.

"Canada," he told them, was a Montagnais word meaning "coming and going from some place" while "Quebec" meant "land here." These derivations he had learned from Père Leblanc. "He has often heard an Indian call out 'Quebec' when he wanted the canoe to put ashore. I tried it myself on my guide to-day, and he understood at once. I made him repeat it, and to me it sounded more like 'Ke-buc' or 'boc'. But it is an altogether different derivation from that accepted by the historians of this country." The accepted derivations, then as now, are that Canada derives from the Iroquois *kanata*, meaning a village or community, while Quebec is an Algonkian word meaning "the river narrows here."[15]

Donald's interest in the language and customs of the Montagnais was not married to an awareness that the native peoples did not always share his European values. In time his understanding would grow and bring with it greater empathy but, for the present, he found "the Indians hereabouts careless about everything." As he wrote to his sister Margaret,

> I think you would have to travel the whole world over to find a greater contrast to the Scotch than these same Indians. If civilization consists in frugality and foresight, then the Montagnais are far worse than dogs, who at least have sense enough to bury a bone against an evil day. In some of their lodges even before winter has properly begun, their rations have come to an end. Everything about the place has been swallowed that can be swallowed and starvation stares them in the face. They stalk in the tracks of a solitary caribou and in the excitement forget their own hunger, but this does not make their families forget theirs. The caribou eludes them. They wander farther afield and at length bring down a bear. They cut him up and return to find their families dying or dead, which is what happened last month near Manwan Lake.[16]

For Margaret and her parents, tales such as this must have made Donald seem very far away indeed. Their news to him, when the first mail arrived in 1839, was about the details of their lives in Forres and the progress of John's medical career. In fact, thanks to John Stuart, he had received a loan from George Simpson to tide him over till Sir James M'Grigor secured him his position in the Army Medical Department.

In the meantime, Governor Simpson had reappeared at Lachine and wasted no time in taking himself to the Saguenay. Simpson was an inveterate traveller who annually inspected as many of the company's posts as he could manage. He pushed his oarsmen to paddle as fast as possible and thought nothing of starting at three or four in the morning in order to cover the route in the time he had allotted. Once at a post, he noted every detail, quizzing staff on their work and making suggestions for improvements. Though stubborn, he was not malicious unless crossed, and he was always prepared to advance the career of a young man who met his exacting standards. John Stuart's nephew made a good first impression.

In November, however, Tadoussac and Montreal were at loggerheads over the seal oil which had been shipped from Tadoussac in April and from Godbout in June. James McKenzie had reported to Montreal that it was substandard but Connolly understood that it had found a buyer in Quebec almost as soon as it was received. "How comes it then," he fumed at the end of November, "that no notice was taken of the alleged impurities until five or six months after it was disposed of?" This was a serious allegation. The oil was used for lighting, and the parlours of Montreal and Quebec would be dirtied if spluttering lamps belched forth smoky black grease. Connolly, however, was sure that McKenzie was misinformed and, as testimony to the Tadoussac oil, appended a certificate from Mr. D.A. Smith.

> Having been present at the measuring and filling up of the casks with the oil made at Tadoussac in April last, I affirm that previously to its being poured into the coolers it was thoroughly strained and that in filling up the casks from out of the coolers, the dross remaining at the bottom was always taken out and thrown into a vessel apart, and further that the casks containing the oil were made expressly for that purpose, and were perfectly tight.[17]

This was a useful lesson. With care, and marshalling all the available facts, one could fight the Montreal mandarins.

The year 1840 unrolled much as its predecessor had done, except that the longed for mail from home brought sad news. In January, Donald's favourite sister, Margaret, had succumbed to small pox which had raged through Scotland that winter, and, to increase his distress, he had dreamt of her death at the moment when it in fact occurred. Pangs of homesickness wrenched at Donald's heart as he realized just how cut off he was from those he loved best. His sister had been buried in the graveyard of the St. Laurence kirk six months before he discovered her fate and it would be at least another two before his letter of commiseration reached Forres. He could do little to comfort his mother and there was nothing she could do to comfort him.[18]

After the flurry of sending off the returns, the winter months were once again occupied with travelling to negotiate for furs, in hopes of outwitting the free traders who were always on the lookout for ways of encroaching on the company's territory. The long evenings at the post gave opportunity to read, and books and old newspapers were diligently perused and shared among the officers and clerks. Tadoussac, being closer to Quebec and the civilised world and in more frequent communication with it, was richer in reading material than most of the company's far flung posts, but, throughout the fur empire, a handful of self-taught scholars provided themselves with an education which, though generally out of date when it came to current affairs, would not otherwise be scorned by Europe's intelligentsia. John Stuart had been one such and his nephew was following in his footsteps.

In June, at the beginning of Outfit 1841, William Connolly retired and was replaced by Murdoch McPherson. In sending him to the King's Posts from the MacKenzie River District in the far north west, Simpson, now Sir George, was doing McPherson a favour for it brought him closer to Nova Scotia where his wife's father, an old fur trader, had retired, and it gave him a better opportunity to see to the education of his sons. McPherson, another Nor'Wester who had known John Stuart, took a kindly interest in the young clerk and talked to him about life on the other side of the continent and about the people who worked there.

And always, there were the accounts. Most apprentice contracts assume a two way bargain. The young man is to serve diligently for a pittance but in return is educated in his chosen craft or profession. The Hudson's Bay Company contracts, however, made no mention of training and the company imposed no obligation on its senior staff to provide it. It was a matter of chance whether an apprentice clerk received a formal induction into the management of a trading post and the keeping of accounts according to the company's somewhat esoteric regulations. A young man who found himself with a good senior officer would observe methods and techniques which he might emulate. With luck, he would be taught both how and why to do his paper work in a certain way. More often, however, he was expected to learn by copying and even that was difficult if, as sometimes happened, the chief kept the accounts close to his chest and never showed them to his juniors. Donald Smith did see the accounts of the King's Posts and worked on them, but he received no training whatsoever. Nor is there any reason to believe that McPherson was capable of training him. For all he was genial, well educated and sympathetic, he was not versed in the competitive ways of the St. Lawrence River posts and financial management had never been his strong suit. In 1832, Governor Simpson had noted that he was "equal to the management of any Trading Post but not sufficiently conversant with Accounts or general business to be useful at a Depot." By October 1843, Simpson was complaining of a "want of system and energy in the whole business below Quebec" and "a laxity of discipline," and he ordered McPherson to return to the MacKenzie River District as soon as a replacement for him could be found.[19]

Though he had received no training, Donald was still considered sufficiently responsible to be posted as clerk in charge at Chicoutimi, about seventy miles up the Saguenay River from Tadoussac. In the summer of 1841, however, he was brought back to Tadoussac to take charge while McPherson conducted a tour of inspection. When the older man returned, he found his clerk both depressed and unwell. No record of his illness now exists but it was almost certainly a severe cold which had turned to bronchitis or pleurisy, the curse of his winter months. The depression was caused by the after effects of the news of Margaret's death and the new information that in May his youngest sister, Marianne, had been attacked by "a species of hectic fever of no ordinary kind," as her uncle called it. Though she was fighting it vigorously, the question was not whether she would die but when. Moreover his brother had scarcely set foot in India on his first army posting before he too was ill with "a severe attack of fever and inflammation in the liver that had nearly brought him to the grave."[20]

In October, McPherson sent Donald to Quebec with the remainder of that year's returns. His journey was described as "private business," which was not something in which apprentice clerks were normally allowed to indulge, but the visit was meant to give him a chance to seek medical help and to send his unhappy mother a sympathetic letter before the river froze and severed all but the most urgent communications. He almost certainly stayed with James McKenzie and made himself useful in his office, for, at the end of May 1842, he was again in Quebec specifically to help McKenzie as the ships arrived with the outfits from London. McPherson was equally keen to have him in Tadoussac so he could help with the accounts for Outfit 1841 and in July wrote to McKenzie to send him back. The winter of 1842-1843 proved an exceptionally mild one, with temperatures only once dropping below -14°F, but this made no difference to Donald's winter routine and he was off work sick for two weeks.

By the spring of 1843, John Stuart was sufficiently worried about his nephew's health and the circumstances in which he was working to redouble his efforts to seek an improvement. In January of the previous year, he had suggested to James Keith that he give Donald a year's experience in the Montreal office, saying it would "make a man of him" and at the end of April he had written asking Keith to allow Donald to go to Quebec or Lachine for medical assistance if necessary. In April 1843, with Donald's apprenticeship coming to an end he broached the subject again and doubtless raised it with George Simpson whom he saw in London that month. He wanted the young man to have at least a summer and preferably a year in Keith's office. The intention was that he should acquire an overview of the business and be close to medical advice should he need it. Stuart, who had not consulted Donald and did not know his wishes, added that he "could not ask either you or Governor Simpson to use your influence in procuring him another situation, nor do I know that he wishes it, but I believe that he is neither contented nor happy where he now is and I would not have him sent under present circumstances out of the Montreal Department on any consideration whatsoever."[21]

Simpson was not having his business dictated to him by retired officers such as John Stuart, whose nephew was promptly posted to Lake St. John. Here, for the first time, Donald demonstrated some of the independent thinking of which he was capable and which he could turn to the advantage of the company. The lake was a short distance above Chicoutimi where the post had been usurped by a free trader after the company had abandoned it. By the simple expedient of associating himself with the Catholic missionary who now performed his annual service at the lake, Donald was able to persuade the Indians to bring their furs to the new HBC outpost in future.

He was back in Tadoussac in the autumn and was meant to take charge at Isle Jeremie, further up the St. Lawrence, where his new responsibilities would be commensurate with his new contract as a clerk, at a salary of £100 a year. But the move was forestalled by a report from Mingan where George Ross was said to be seriously ill. It was influenza, though reports of paralysis suggest the virus might have masked a stroke, and when Ross reached Quebec on November 18, James McKenzie observed that he was "not settled in his mind." The seigneury was far too important to leave unattended by an officer and Donald was immediately despatched to provide at least temporary cover. At Sept Iles, he was incorrectly told that the stories of Ross' ill health were a false alarm, so he turned back. On November 14, he was officially posted to Mingan; gales at Godbout detained him on November 21 but fair weather followed and the schooner delivered him to his new assignment by the end of the month.[22]

Mingan lies at the entrance to the St. Lawrence River. Like a tongue in the river's gaping mouth, Anticosti Island divides the approach, with Honguedo Passage along the southern side and Jacques Cartier Passage along the other. Close to the north shore, the Mingan Islands rise out of the water while just below the surface their reefs require the cautious sailor to thread his way with care through the narrow channel leading to Mingan's little harbour. Mingan means *sea-wolf* in Algonkian and the imagination easily conceives a malevolent creature which drives vessels onto the treacherous reefs while hidden by the fog and mists that envelop the river mouth for much of the year. Scores of ships have foundered since explorers first discovered that the Gulf of St. Lawrence was not a bay but the entrance to a great river leading into the interior of the North American continent.

In fact, a *sea-wolf* is a seal and the creatures frolic in the waters around the Mingan Islands. Though buffeted by stormy winds at all seasons of the year, the islands sheltered the trading post which was prettily situated on the mainland above a beach that stretches "for six leagues level enough for a coach and six to drive on," as James McKenzie remarked in a report on the area which he prepared for the North West Company in 1808. The Mingan and the Romaine Rivers, one at either end of the beach, offered the Hudson's Bay Company a plentiful salmon harvest and at the same time were the conduits for the Montagnais and Naskapi people coming to trade. In winter, the water between the islands and the mainland froze, allowing easy communication by sleigh or foot to the islands and to Esquimo Point beyond the Romaine River. In front of the trading post stood a cannon which had been brought from Egg Island where, in August 1711, the British fleet, on its way to capture Quebec, had smashed on the rocks.

Mingan's boundaries stretched at least as far east as Musquarro and Donald had charge of the outposts there and at Natashquan (which the company usually referred to as Natasquen). It was the largest territory for which he had yet been responsible and the post at Mingan was, itself, one of the biggest he had encountered. (In the winter of 1861-1862, James Anderson, one of his successors, housed and fed one hundred and five survivors from the ship wrecked *North Britain.*)[23]

Mingan was significant both as a fur trading centre and for its production of cured salmon and seal oil but it was at least as important as a barbican for the Labrador trade to the north and the King's Posts to the west. The company's exclusive rights at the seigneury meant that it could halt interlopers at Mingan and consequently deter them from proceeding further inland or further up the St. Lawrence where the law did not so clearly favour the HBC. But constant vigilance was required to defend those rights and drive off the intruders from Newfoundland, Nova Scotia, New Brunswick and across the river at Gaspé.

Whether Donald Smith, at the age of twenty-three, had the maturity or experience to manage the men under his command and the work at hand is open to doubt. Certainly Murdoch McPherson felt he did not and aired his views to George Simpson. The governor, who knew the reputation better than he knew the young clerk, disagreed. "From the favorable report I have had of that gentleman, who has now been 5 years in the service, I should hope he will be found quite competent for the charge; if not so now at his present age & after the experience he has had, we can have little to hope for from his future services in the management of an establishment." He reiterated his views to George Barnston who had replaced McPherson at Tadoussac, saying that he had a very high opinion "both as regards zeal and efficiency."[24]

Still, it was a lonely life for a young man, most of whose staff were a good deal older than he was. His natural intelligence and curiosity did not lead to easy companionship with the scarcely literate fishermen and the labourers who processed the seal oil, built and repaired the small boats, and performed a multitude of other tasks around the posts. He did, however, find friendship amongst the Oblate Fathers whose mission included the King's Posts and Mingan. He could not share their creed, but appreciated their education in general and their knowledge of the region in particular. "You must not be surprised," he wrote to his staunchly Presbyterian family from Mingan, "to hear that I am very friendly with the Catholic missionaries of this country whenever and wherever I find them. The Company's policy has always been well disposed towards these brave men: and I am so on personal grounds. The priest at L'Anse St. Jean is a kindly young man, who has suffered many hardships and is ready to suffer more without complaint. I owe a good deal of my proficiency in French and many hours of companionship to him."[25]

At Mingan, Donald began to refine his understanding of the relationship between Canada's native people and the game on which they depended, and to see how the presence of European traders affected that relationship. Cycles of profusion and scarcity are a natural occurrence when the game population is not interfered with. Predators significantly reduce one species and that species' usual victims flourish as a consequence. The Montagnais, like other tribes, were fat or starving depending on which creatures were thriving. Migration in pursuit of game discouraged the Indians' development of sophisticated food storage techniques and the provision of flour by white traders reinforced the belief that tomorrow would take care of itself. It was a concept that was completely alien to the white man and anathema to careful Scots like Donald Smith. The Montagnais "live from hand to mouth and never can tell of what their dinner to-morrow will consist until they trap or shoot it. It may be bear or partridge or caribou or beaver or salmon. The flesh satisfies their hunger and the skins — a secondary consideration — they sell to the trader."[26]

The winter of 1843-1844 was a difficult one for the Montagnais and prompted a formal petition to the governor general. Donald thought that it emanated from, "or rather has been imposed upon, but a small number of Indians, belonging principally to the Post of Jeremie." Nevertheless, he and others along the north shore were required to contribute to a response to the petition. For a start, he said, there had not been an "annual bounty" during his time at the King's Posts and Mingan and the company's officers had never been asked, as alleged in the petition, to distribute presents on behalf of the government, though in their capacity as Hudson's Bay Company employees, they had assisted widows and orphans. He agreed that Montagnais did die during the winter but claimed that their relatives said it was from disease rather than hunger. Those who were ill and reached Mingan were fed and clothed and maintained at the post until their relatives had hunted enough food to support them.

More interesting are allegations which reveal the gulf in understanding between the HBC and the Indians, and perhaps also between the company and the missionary or free trader who, it is implied, inspired the complaint. The petition claimed the cost of goods along the river was high and the price obtained for furs was low. Donald pointed out that the company's posts operated with a fixed tariff and this, being set by Montreal and London, gave little freedom to manoeuvre. It was true, he agreed, that the company drove off certain people but in the company's eyes, these were those bent on robbery, not on helping native people in trouble. It was also true that Indians from the south shore had been coming to the opposite side but the seigneury had declined to give most of them advances in order to reserve the benefit of the hunt to its own Indians. The company perceived that it had a relationship with the native people in a loosely defined geographical area and referred to them as "our" Indians whose duty it was to hunt, bringing furs and occasionally other provisions to the trading post. Conversely, they expected that the Indians thought of a particular centre as "theirs" and that they perceived the duty of the traders to be to provision the hunters. In reality, of course, the concept was one sided and disintegrated when the native people, for their own reasons, chose to hunt and trade in other areas. The challenge to the trader was to induce fidelity without excessive dependence and experience of trading bred knowledge and sympathy which made this easier to achieve. It also meant that many traders were quick to spring to the defence or support of "their" Indians when occasion demanded. While not expounding on these wider issues, Donald gave a spirited defence against the allegations in the petition and, when it landed on George Simpson's desk towards the end of March 1845, it encouraged his plan to visit the King's Posts and Mingan later in the year.[27]

Simpson had other reasons for wanting to take a closer look at Mingan and the young man who had charge there. Shipping had been excessively delayed at Mingan in the summer of 1844 and it appeared that this had happened because the accounts were not ready. It was Donald's responsibility to gather and check the accounts from the various outposts within the seigneury and correlate these with the Mingan figures, sending an integrated financial statement to Tadoussac where the accounts would be checked and incorporated into a statement for the King's Posts and Mingan. This document was forwarded to Montreal where the figures would again be checked before being compiled into a report for London where accountants repeated the process yet again, adding into the mix the cost of the London operation and UK earnings. The further away from Montreal one was, the earlier the accounting operation had to be commenced. It was Donald's first year in Mingan and it seems that no one reminded him of the need to get things done sooner and he did not think of it himself. In a letter to George Barnston on August 17, he noted that the *Otter* had arrived on August 9 and departed the following day. He could not complete the general accounts until she returned with papers from other posts. On August 24, he excused himself by saying that no one had told him the accounts were wanted earlier and he had therefore asked for the documents at the usual time. Usual for Tadoussac, perhaps, but not for Mingan.

The *Otter* was kept busy scurrying between the various posts throughout the summer, but in October, found herself at Mingan unable to budge because the documents were not ready. She was thus prevented from making any of the late autumn journeys which were carefully judged to take advantage of every available hour of ice-free water. Barnston was livid and wasted no time in expressing his views forcefully. Duncan Finlayson, who had replaced James Keith at Montreal, was equally annoyed and proposed sending off another blast but Barnston dissuaded him. "With regard to the stay of the Schooner at Mingan I believe you will think enough has been said, and Mr. Smith's management being otherwise unexceptionable, it is probable his reply will render it unnecessary to make further comment." The reply, he assumed, would be a generous serving of humble pie of the sort which John Stuart had advocated in dealing with George Simpson. In this he erred, for though a tone of humility permeated the response, Donald had never learned to deal with criticism and his letter justified his actions.[28]

In her earlier voyages, the *Otter* had not been detained at Mingan except by adverse wind, Donald noted, and it was not his fault if its last journey between Musquarro and Mingan had not been expeditious.

> On her arrival from off her last trip to Musquaro, her sails were anything but fit to sustain a heavy gale; she was destitute of stove pipes, these having been left at Tadoussac or Quebec, and expected down by the schooner Tadoussac; and even after the arrival of our Blksmith, by the latter vessel, we had the utmost difficulty in furnishing a sufficiency of stove pipes for her.

Furthermore, he said, he did not know until he received Barnston's letter on October 11 whether the *Otter* was to be laid up for the winter at Mingan or Tadoussac. The wind was fair while they were loading the vessel, but then turned stormy.

> Again on Thursday the 17th the wind was from the South East, with most tempestuous weather, for a very short time, succeeded by a Gale from the west, which, & Capn Hovington admitted it to be so, must inevitably have driven both vessels back, & would in all probability have torn the Otter's sails to shreds; and not from that date, till the day on which they did start, had we one breath of favorable wind. I am also satisfied Capn Hovington will admit, that both he and his son strongly recommended that the Otter, from the bad state of her sails, should sail in company with the Tadoussac.

In addition, he said, he had been ill, primarily from having had little sleep because he had been obliged to keep watch to prevent interlopers from trading in the harbour. "On whom could I depend for such a duty, was it on the only winterer then at the post, the idiot Boutin; or on the summermen, men who, often themselves of indifferent character, would readily aid their pilfering countrymen." He then dropped his bombshell, saying that he might be inferior to some but, if he was accused of "want of application," he offered his resignation.[29]

Barnston seized the first opportunity to try to defuse the situation. On March 18, 1845, he wrote thanking Donald for his "full and free" communication, a euphemism which acknowledged that the young man had let off steam and not worried about the expenditure of ink. He would not have reverted to the subject of the schooner again, said Barnston, but for the last paragraph suggesting that the general management of the Mingan business was objected to "which is very far from being the case."

> On the matter of your giving up your charge, I must say, that I am just as unwilling to part with an able assistant and respected young officer, as I am to approve of the keeping of our schooners for so long a time as they were at Mingan last fall. Such detention you must now be aware, cannot fail to cause much anxiety, and be attended with much serious Embarrassment to the District's Business. Talking to Captain Hovington on the subject, he informs me he repeatedly besought you to let him have the papers that he might go, and certainly our vessels should always be ready for sea within three days after receiving their cargo.

He continued in a moderate tone, explaining the ramifications of such delays and the difficulties caused to everyone else as a consequence. He also made it perfectly clear that he knew the *Otter* had been delayed because the accounts were not ready and the wind was a poor excuse. Other vessels had sailed from Mingan while Hovington idled. Barnston's approach was well suited to the circumstances. In describing Donald Smith as "able" and "respected," he gave the first indication that the company had any regard for him at all and, in explaining that dealing with the schooners promptly was a matter of consideration for others, he immediately evoked a sympathetic response, for this was no more than a variant on Barbara Smith's lessons on courtesy and gentlemanly behaviour.[30]

The reasons for describing Donald as "able" had begun to appear as soon as letters started to arrive from Mingan in the summer of 1844. Intermingled with the correspondence, in which it becomes increasingly clear that the accounts are going to be late, are comments on the business at his new post which show that he had a well developed capacity to pull back from quotidian events and see the broader picture. As a result, he was able to perceive that an adjustment in the transport arrangements or a different way of provisioning a post would improve the efficiency, not just of a post, but of a whole district. With more experience, he would have foreseen the ramifications of delaying the *Otter*, though whether that would have improved his handling of the accounts is open to doubt.

In his letter of August 17, he addressed the issue of short term contracts. "The mode of engaging servants for short periods is much to be condemned, as it not only causes great inconvenience and additional expense, but likewise hinders the men from forming that attachment for the service, which under longer engagement they generally contract." He also explained that it was not a sound economy to reduce the flour supply because the Indians, with insufficient flour, would hunt deer rather than fur bearing animals. Simpson saw the logic and increased the provision of flour but he denied a request for a horse, saying that oxen were better suited to the post. In this he was mistaken since the horse was required as a means of transport as well as a beast of burden at Mingan.[31]

Before he responded to Barnston's rebuke over the detention of the *Otter*, Donald surveyed the competition at Mingan. He had learned Latin at the Forres Academy where the boys were required to commit long passages to memory. Sections of Livy's *History* came unbidden to Donald's mind throughout his life and this work or some other Latin text was evidently in his thoughts as he composed this portion of his letter with its Latin grammatical structure.

> Mingan district may be said to be environed by Evils. On the one hand is the Kings Posts Domain; and on the other are the settlements on the Labradore: these are avowed enemies; that, a doubtful friend, for tho' opposition 'twixt the posts of Seven Islands & Mingan ceased on the transfer to the H.B. Co. of the K. Posts, it was soon revived, at least on the part of the former post, under the cloak of expediency, and has since continued more or less to this moment.[32]

At Esquimaux Bay, the company's territory in Labrador, he claimed about a dozen Mingan families had been trading for several years. It was the responsibility of each post, he thought, to confine its trade to its own Indians, an argument which acknowledges that seasonal migrations of hunters followed a pattern which was generally consistent from year to year unless the animals' movements or, more likely, the temptations of a new trading post intervened. Mingan's other "evil" was "scores of the very dross of society" which prowled along the shore in the summer, "seeking what they can catch, without regard to the means by which it may be obtained." To counter this, he proposed a coast guard, a suggestion which kept cropping up at the King's Posts and Mingan and which George Simpson approved, though nothing further was ever done.[33]

When Simpson was in London in the winter of 1844-1845, he spoke to Lloyd's, which controlled the British marine insurance market, and proposed that Hudson's Bay Company officers at the King's Posts and Mingan be appointed Lloyd's agents. There were known to be wreckers working the St. Lawrence coast and if the company's men could not prevent ships being lured onto the rocks, they could at least make efforts to protect the wrecks for the benefit of their owners. This was not an altruistic plan but another means of encouraging his officers to patrol their territory and discourage competition. Had Lloyd's paid promptly for services rendered, the scheme might have worked to everyone's advantage but it did not and, within a year of becoming an agent, George Barnston had resigned and advised Donald to do likewise.[34]

For his part, Donald was finding that he had adventures enough without shipwrecks. In the spring of 1845, William Baker called at Mingan to say that he would be going to Natashquan to fish for cod but had no intention of interfering with the company's business. In fact, as soon as he arrived, he set about trading for furs; he put salmon nets in the river and refused to remove them when called upon to do so. The man in charge at Natashquan, reported Donald, was intimidated by his bluster. In August, Baker returned to the coast with three other schooners from Gaspé, this time heading for the St. Jean River which runs parallel to the Mingan about eighteen miles further west. Here the intruders, about thirty in all, took up a position across the river from the salmon shed which the company had erected the preceding winter. With five men from one of the company's boats, Donald immediately rode over and ordered the intruders out. They refused, insisting on their right to remain and reinforcing their intentions by making it clear that they were armed.

> They still insisted on their right to remain, nay further even to trade, on which, having previously seen that each of our party loaded his gun with ball, I again ordered them to quit, and informed them, in the event of their still refusing to go we should set about cutting their cables, and should they offer resistance we would then fire on them, but that only as a dernier resort, or in the event of their firing the first shot.[35]

Finally, they agreed to go but the wind was against them so they requested permission to wait for the tide the following morning. Donald agreed, but returned to order them out again when he found they were still in the river thirty-six hours later.

Baker was not to be deterred by a young man reading the order book at him and in October returned with six men, this time to Kegashka which is next door to Musquarro and thirty miles inside the seigneury's supposed boundaries. They laid up the schooner for the winter and built a house, while a Canadian (by which the company's officers and servants always meant a French Canadian) named Robitaille and two Inuit women constructed a hut a little further west. Donald got wind of this from a party of Indians about the middle of November and immediately set out to evict the interloper again. As Baker had gambled, travel from Mingan was almost impossible. The roads, such as they were, were a quagmire and the river was full of lethal, floating ice. It was the tenth of December before he reached the encampment.

"To have ejected him at that advanced season," he wrote to Finlayson, obviously pleased with how he had handled the situation, "was of course out of the question, his schooner being fast in the ice & the Bays all frozen over." Donald explained that Baker could be prosecuted for violating the company's rights, "cautioned him against having any dealings whatsoever with the natives & warned him that if he did not leave the domaine at the earliest possible period in the ensuring spring he could look for little leniency at our hands."[36]

The warning was repeated three days later and Baker solemnly gave his promise which, moreover, he kept, doubtless helped by the fact that he was under surveillance throughout the winter. What galled both Baker and Donald Smith, though for opposite reasons, was that before Donald learned of Baker's presence at Kegashka, two men from Musquarro, Edouard Thibeault and I.F. Capaille, having been sent from Musquarro to another post for provisions, saw Baker's house and went ashore to investigate. Their inquiries took two weeks after which they proceeded on their errand. When Donald reached Musquarro after his first visit to Baker, he found that Bryson, who was in charge at Musquarro, "had as much idea of Mr. Baker's proceedings as of what was passing on the moon." Thibeault and Capaille had plausibly explained that their delay had been occasioned by a difficult voyage. "Not a word was said of the sumptuous manner in which they had fared: the many glasses of Jamaica they had swallowed were not spoken of: in fact neither Baker's nor Robitaille's name was once mentioned. Suspecting that they had been bribed to silence I made strict inquiry and Thibeault at length admitted such had been the case."[37]

Thereafter, Baker kept his distance for the better part of a year, instead pursuing his demand to trade in the seigneury through a petition to the governor general. In truth, both Donald and Baker were bluffing because neither knew the boundaries of the seigneury and both insisted they were within their rights.

In the summer of 1845, when Governor Simpson visited the King's Posts and Mingan, Donald had some reason to be satisfied with himself and his work. He had driven Baker out of the St. Jean River; the returns looked promising and in fact amounted to twenty times more fish than the post had produced the previous year; he had managed to send his mother £30 in 1842, £28 in 1843, £33 at the beginning of 1845 and was to send another £30 in October; and he had saved enough to get himself a new set of summer clothes.

By the autumn, however, the complexion of things had changed. The potato crop was a comparative failure, so feeding the men would be difficult in the winter which gave every sign of coming early: on August 22, it was so cold the leaves froze to the ground. The winds were playing havoc with shipping arrangements and, on the eleventh of October, the *Otter* was stuck in Mingan harbour, unable to get out because the breeze was so light while Captain Dunn was lingering in the river in the *Marten*, unable to get in for the same reason. The *Otter* finally got out on the twenty-first and was five miles from Sept Iles when she was driven back by gales from the west, though the *Marten,* being a larger, sturdier vessel, was not defeated by the storm.

Much worse, however, was the arrival of a scathing letter from Sir George Simpson. He was aware, he said, of Donald's desire to do his work well, and would therefore not remind him of the importance of having everything ready so that "no delay be occasioned to any of the vessels in awaiting either cargo or papers." But he had been appalled by the state of the accounts he had found at Mingan.

> Your countinghouse department appeared to me in a very slovenly condition, so much so, that I could make very little of any document that came under my notice. Your scheme of outfits were really curiously perplexing, & such as I trust I may never see again, while letters, invoices and accounts were to be found tossing about as waste papers in almost every room of the house. I am aware that, during the pressure of summer business, you have not much time to devote to the neat arrangement of papers, but your winters are very long with little or no out door work to occupy your attention; and if you were but to give a

> few hours a week to the arrangement of your papers your bureau would be in a very different state to that in which I found it.

The letter continued by giving instructions about what was to be included in inventories and notes that, had they been done properly in the past, "there would have been no occasion for ordering new scales, while those which I found in the store seem to have been overlooked for years."[38]

On October 15, while the *Otter* and the *Marten* were jockeying to get out of and into the harbour, Donald replied to Simpson, thanking him for acknowledging that he did, indeed, want to conduct the business in a proper manner and regretting that he had merited such an extreme degree of censure. "I do readily admit that on your arrival the office, nay indeed, the interior of the house in general, was not in apple pie order, nor so neatly arranged as I could have desired, but should hope that the appearance of the trading stores and other outdoor matters met your approval." By way of excuse, he pointed out that the house had been undergoing repairs prior to Simpson's arrival and that the man responsible for the indoor work had had a stroke. He accepted that there were papers lying about, but claimed they were his private papers and not "public documents." None of his excuses addressed the fact that the accounts were a shambles and that even if every scrap of paper had been in its proper place, Simpson was still unable to make sense of the figures.[39]

Simpson was something of a martinet but the severity of his rebuke also reflects his disappointment at finding that his hopes for the young clerk might have been misplaced. Donald's letters showed him to be far more intelligent than the majority of those who worked for the HBC, but the efficient organisation the governor had created assumed that all the company's officers would pay meticulous attention to detail, and if Donald was to play a part in the HBC's future, he would need to use his time more efficiently and be more fastidious about financial matters. Donald, however, was more interested in the broad sweep of ideas than he was in bookkeeping minutiae, though his superb memory for figures meant that ledgers sometimes seemed superfluous to him. The dishevelled state of his paper work reflected his lack of interest in the written accounts as much as it demonstrated the fact that he was still having to discover for himself how the books were to be kept.[40]

Through the long winter months, Donald brooded on Simpson's letter. He tidied up the house, planned the next season's work more carefully, and resolved that when it came time to turn in the next year's accounts, they would not give rise to complaint; but occasionally he wondered if he should not leave the service and find some other employment where he could give greater satisfaction. The fact that the fur returns were going to be poor did nothing to cheer him up and matters were not helped by the isolation he continued to feel within the post itself. Even if his French had improved to the point where he could comfortably converse with the Canadian labourers, there was little of substance about which they might want to talk. In addition there was, for him, the problem of the women. At least one of his staff was a married man with a family and in the autumn his wife was in a "delicate state" which would "soon require the attentions of 2 Indian women who remain at the post." He knew nothing about such matters except that they made him feel ill at ease and he tried to deal with his discomfort by suggesting that trading posts were unsuitable for married men.[41]

His spirits lifted as spring came on in 1846. Simpson had summoned George Barnston to Lachine in February and one of the consequences of their discussions was that Bryson was removed from Musquarro at the end of the summer and replaced by the lively and intelligent Robert Hamilton. When Baker returned to Kegashka yet again in the autumn of 1846, Hamilton refused to be intimidated and forced Baker out of the seigneury.

The summer was a dry one and the water was low in the rivers, making transport exceedingly difficult, though the salmon catch was so high that the *Marten* could not carry it all. On the ninth of August, calamity struck at Mingan when the wooden house, like tinder after the rainless summer, caught fire. Donald and most of the men who shared it with him had retired for the night when the alarm was raised.

> To such an extent had the fire spread ere being discovered and so rapid its progress that all our efforts to extinguish it proved unavailing. With the exception of the building the property lost to the Company is of but trifling value consisting of the household furniture which was old and of very common quality and you will be glad to know that the more important papers indeed almost all of them and the whole of the cash except perhaps ten or fifteen dollars have been saved. My personal property has been wholly lost, as I had to make my escape in my shirt without either coat hat or shoes. Our stoves and stovepipes have been rendered perfectly useless and I have to beg as I am given to understand that none of the Company's vessels will again visit us this season, that you would be good enough to send down by return of Mr. Hoffman's schooner, which is to make another trip to Labrador, a stove — a double one of 2½ or 3 feet would answer best — with 11 lengths and 2 elbows of stovepipe.[42]

Nearly a month had elapsed after the fire before he was able to find a passing schooner, en route for Quebec, which took this report to James McKenzie with a request that he pass on the news to Tadoussac and Lachine. The kitchen, which was attached to the house, survived "in a half consumed state" and accommodated the men until a new house could be built. The extent of Donald's personal loss can be judged by the ledgers which show that he was obliged to spend £30 on new clothes, a substantial sum in view of the fact that his new summer jacket and trousers the previous year had cost a little over £6. He did, however, manage to salvage the plaid his mother had given him when he left Forres. What the report fails to mention is that Donald was very badly singed about the face and eyes, the damage to his sight being worse than he at first realized.[43]

The letter is also far from reliable in its information about the accounts and other papers which had been saved. Donald gave priority to providing accommodation for his men and completing the season's business, but when he finally came to deal with the paper work, he discovered he had virtually nothing on which to base his report. In September and October, he had to ask the outposts to repeat their figures and was obliged to ask the men around the posts what they had received so he could calculate what their debts might be. The inventory which gave him the figure to carry forward into the accounts for Outfit 1846 could not be repeated because the flour, the tea and most of the other items left over from the previous year were now mixed with the outfit which had been received via the ships from London and Quebec. However good his memory was, he could not produce the sort of detail which Simpson would require and there was no time to think about the indent for Outfit 1847. In November, he promised to send the accounts to Tadoussac with two servants who were retiring from Musquarro, but they arrived empty handed.[44]

As with the delayed schooner in the summer of 1844, the ramifications of the missing Mingan accounts were felt along the line: in December, George Simpson was writing tetchily to George Barnston at Tadoussac to say, "We have no advices from Mingan & the accounts of this department, which it is customary to send to England by the December mail, are necessarily kept back, awaiting the Mingan accounts." Hogmanay or no, Simpson was at his desk on January 1, 1847, writing again to Barnston. "I cannot understand Mr. Smith's want of attention to the transmission of his accounts in proper shape: he is very active but appears to me to be wanting in method." Three weeks later he sent off another blast. Even if the retiring servants had drowned "that wld not be a satisfactory explanation, as the accts ought to have been ready to be forwarded when the last of his returns were sent up." At that point, he had had more than enough and instructed that Robert Miles, for whom Simpson had the highest regard as an accountant, was to be sent from Chicoutimi to Mingan to deal with the accounts, inventories and indents.[45]

On March 19, as Miles prepared to return to Tadoussac with the still incomplete accounts, Donald responded to George Barnston's letter which Miles had brought down with him. Barnston had conveyed the brunt of Simpson's complaints, embellishing them where he thought it would be useful. Donald's lengthy reply was not the model of humility his uncle had recommended. On the matter of the accounts, he hid the fact that his eyes were still so painful that paper work was all but impossible and concentrated instead on explaining why he had not sent up the accounts as he had said he would.

> Had I the most remote idea that anything approaching [the inconvenience] should have been experienced on that head, I should have sent them up in the autumn as I first intended, but, after making them up in a sort of way I found them so very incomplete that I decided on retaining them till spring with the intention of sending them out by the first vessel, which, under the peculiar circumstances of the case I imagined would answer equally well. It was my intention to have proceeded within a short time to Musquarrow, and after communicating with the persons at the different stations, I should have been enabled to make out the document in a more satisfactory manner. The Requisition is, however, now sent up by Mr. Miles, and the servants' accounts shall follow it within a few days, that is, so soon as I shall have communicated with the posts below this.[46]

The word "active" was a high compliment in the Hudson's Bay Company vocabulary, especially when it came from George Simpson, and in the past, Donald's "activeness" had compensated for the fact that he neither understood nor particularly cared about the accounts. But in the winter of 1846-1847, he was not active. He could have gone to Musquarro during the winter, as he had managed to do under very difficult conditions when he got wind of Baker's encampment, but he remained at Mingan. In part, his behaviour can be explained by the fact that his eyes were seriously hurt by the fire and his capacity to work was severely curtailed as a result. The physical damage was compounded by psychological stress, for the failure to recover his sight raised the spectre of his mother's progressive blindness which had begun before he left Scotland and was becoming increasingly apparent with every letter from home. He was still smarting from Simpson's attack on his "countinghouse department" when the fire wiped out all his diligent efforts to show that he could prepare the accounts properly and submit them on time. There seemed little reason to be active when so much conspired against him: the inertia of his depression was tinged with fear and he had neither friend nor family to support him in his black mood or to goad him into action.

Insult was quite literally added to injury when Miles arrived and Donald found himself unjustly accused of carelessness. The Quebec cooper, Morrison, had been the subject of complaint by every post which was obliged to use his casks and Simpson stubbornly refused to believe his officers' criticism of the quality of his work. Morrison's latest line of self-defence had been to claim that at Godbout, Sept Iles and Mingan the casks were kept in the open air and rolled over rough ground to the ships. This was not the case at Mingan where they were stored under cover and carefully rolled along wooden planking to the waiting vessels. "The casks received from Morrison are generally not only badly made up, but composed of wood of a very inferior quality, requiring the greatest attention on the part of our coopers in filling up worm holes rents etc which if left in the state received from him would indeed occasion great loss of oil or any other liquid which might be put into the casks." When he was in Quebec helping McKenzie in 1842, Morrison as much as admitted that he sold shoddy goods and lied about their quality.[47]

If the company preferred to believe men like Morrison rather than men like himself, Donald thought, why should he want to devote his life to such a business? Consequently, when Barnston's letter concluded with a suggestion that Sir George Simpson was threatening to recommend that "certain persons" be allowed to retire, Donald retorted that it gave him "no uneasiness." He was confident that he had acted in the best interests of his employers and to the best of his abilities and judgement. "I shall on retiring be free from self-reproach, and shall, I hope, with the blessing of God be enabled to push my way in some other line of life."[48]

When Miles returned to Tadoussac, he reported that the missing accounts indicated a much more serious malaise. Barnston was a highly educated Scot with so fine a sense of honour that he had fought one duel and been second in another. He was, as Simpson had observed many years earlier, sometimes of a "gloomy desponding turn of mind," to the point where Simpson feared that he might commit suicide. In such a mood, he had written a highly intemperate letter to the Governor and Committee and had been so insulting in a letter to Simpson that it surprised everyone he was not turned out of the service forthwith. In 1839, perhaps because of his promotion to the King's Posts, his despair lifted but he was still sufficiently familiar with its manifestations to recognize the symptoms in Donald Smith. He was therefore quick to take up Simpson's suggestion that a change should be made at Mingan and promptly sent Miles from Chicoutimi to relieve Donald. "If the latter Gentleman be in the state of health represented, the sooner he comes up the better, and I am in hopes that, upon his voyage and change of residence, his spirits will improve, and he will be expeditious in the Copying and Closing of our district Books."[49]

Barnston was quite right to demonstrate the concern for Donald's well being and to understand that showing consideration for his physical and mental health was the first step to guide him towards recuperation. But he was wrong if he thought matters would not deteriorate. That summer's mail from Scotland reported that John Stuart had died at his home in Forres on January 14. His body had been taken for burial to Abernethy Parish Church, near Leanchoil farm where he and Donald's mother had spent such a happy childhood. But far worse than the loss of this kind uncle who had done so much to further the education and careers of his nieces and nephews was the unhappy news that Donald's father had died on the third of March. After the deaths of Margaret and Marianne, his parents, together with Jane, now his only surviving sister, had left the scene of their sorrow and moved to Alexander Smith's old home of Archiestown. Now, it was clearly Donald's duty to be there as well to support his mother and settle his father's estate, but before he could arrange his departure, he received word that his brother had been able to get compassionate leave from the army and, with Donald's power of attorney, was able to sort out the family affairs.[50]

Deprived of any opportunity to mourn or to externalize his grief by helping his family, Donald was forced to keep his sorrow bottled within himself. To this was added genuine worry, for while he grieved for his father, his much greater concern was for his mother and Jane. Who in Archiestown would help them? It was a man's responsibility to care for the women in his family — not merely to provide for them but to manage their financial affairs, to deal with the civic authorities when necessary, to ensure they had homes and were secure. John Stuart, whose benevolent hand had supported the Smiths on so many occasions, could succour them no more, while the nephew who bore his name could be stationed in whatever corner of the earth it pleased the army to send him. And Donald, at the mouth of the Saguenay River, in some windswept cabin on the St. Lawrence shore, or in frozen isolation at any of the fur trading posts to which he might be assigned, could do nothing for those who were dearest to him. He could neither comfort nor be comforted.

From the depths of his despondency, Donald made a decision. He would resign the service at the expiration of his contract and return to Britain. The Grants in Manchester wanted him to work in their woollen business and he stood at least as much chance of advancement with them as he did with the Hudson's Bay Company. Having made that decision, he slowly began to climb his way out of his black hole of despair.[51]

There was still, however, the question of his eyes and still the fear that the damage might be permanent. "Upon arrival here his eyes were like Balls of Fire!" Barnston reported to Finlayson in Montreal. He was, Barnston confided in July "rather delicate" and as soon as he could be spared, he would be allowed to visit Quebec, "unless he do not pick up health & Spirits in the Interim. I shall say to him, if he be visiting Montreal, that you will be happy to see him at Lachine." Finlayson agreed, but Donald postponed the trip in hopes of completing the accounts. This, however, was an exceedingly slow process. He could not work by candlelight and his days were generally spent in the saleshop, much like a rural general store, where cash was now paid for the commodities supplied and for the furs purchased. The psychological benefits were considerable, for Donald's innate courtesy met a favourable response from customers and helped to buoy up his spirits. At Tadoussac he formed a brief acquaintance with Murdoch McPherson's son, Joseph, whose lack of application had proved a source of concern to both his father and his grandfather, and he also met a hot headed teenager named James Grant who, with experience, was thought to have a promising career before him. But it was George Barnston's consideration which, more than anything else, helped Donald pull his life together.[52]

Nevertheless, by November, it was clear that his eyes had not made the improvement he had hoped for and he arranged to take the accounts on the *Otter* to Quebec where he would seek medical advice, carrying on to Montreal if necessary. In writing George Simpson at the beginning of November, Barnston mentioned that Donald was considering resigning but said he trusted the young man would be sent back to Tadoussac for the winter because his services were required.[53]

Governor Simpson, however, had other plans entirely. In the summer of 1847, William Nourse, in charge in Esquimaux Bay, had written that his arm had been severely injured in an accident; he was unable to do the work of the district and sought permission to obtain medical advice in Canada. Simpson had his eye on Donald Smith for a Labrador assignment and was not to be deterred by news that the young man intended to resign. "Want of method" was Donald's weakness and method could be learned; other young clerks might be as eager to do well but few of them were as energetic as Donald was when he was well and none of them had his capacity to see beyond quotidian duties to the broader picture.

In response to Barnston's letter, Simpson penned one announcing that "if Mr. Smith comes up to Quebec for medical advice, he will not return to the Kings Posts but be re-employed in another part of the country, shld he continue in the service. In that or in any other case, you had better put the accounts and shop under the charge of Mr. Miles, as [from] the specimens we have had of Mr. Smith's counting house qualifications, it is evident he is quite unfit for that department." Joseph McPherson had been sent on to Labrador in the summer and, by Simpson's latest letter, Barnston was informed that his department was considered overstaffed and he should be prepared to forward others to Esquimaux Bay as well.[54]

At the beginning of December, Barnston told Donald what was in store for him, noting that the journey to Esquimaux Bay would be in winter and by foot. To Simpson he wrote that he really could spare no more clerks because that would only leave him with the apprentice, James Grant, who was too young to take charge of a post. Of Donald, he wrote with affectionate concern.

> Mr. Smith tho' having arrived here in bad health has been most serviceable in bringing up the accounts, which he would have completed at a much earlier period, had it not been for his weak eyes, and the constant attendance necessary on the shop Business. I should regret his leaving the service, for in many quarters he would be found a valuable acquisition.... Mr. Smith possesses the best of principles and is clever and well informed. He has suffered much distress from the misfortune at Mingan, and the late Death of his Father.[55]

On December 13, Donald finally reached Quebec, "drenched in the rain which has been the case with him ever since he left Tadoussac five days ago." At Quebec, he was detained because the Green Line stage could not run, there being no snow. Finally, on the eighteenth, he was able to set out for Montreal.[56]

Once in the city, Donald saw a doctor who assured him that the injury to his eyes would heal in time and that he need fear no relationship between his own problems and those his mother suffered. Rest would provide the best cure.

As for George Simpson, for a callous and inconsiderate man, he displayed unexpected sympathy for those who suffered depression. He had himself tasted it when the first child of his marriage died at the age of seven months in 1832 but, even before that, he had been more than tolerant of George Barnston's behaviour. In Donald, he saw a man whom he was determined to keep in the service, despite his ineptitude in the accounts department. He was convinced that Donald was the right man for Esquimaux Bay where both energy and tact were needed to deal with commercial competitors and he intended, if all went well, that he would take charge of the district in a few years time. Donald tended to think for himself which meant that sometimes he did not hesitate to break the rules by, for example, ordering the new stove for Mingan directly from Quebec rather than passing on a request through a superior officer. In this case, Simpson recognized full well that he was entirely justified in doing what he had done under the circumstances and could find no fault with him for it.

The governor used a judicious amount of flattery and cajolery. He pulled aside the curtain enough to give Donald a sense of what the future might hold for him if stayed with the company. The more the two men talked, the more it became apparent that Donald's earnest desire to do the best he could was coupled with an analytical mind which sought solutions to all the problems he encountered. Guided and supported by Simpson, he could bring great improvements to Labrador. Simpson encouraged Donald to think of him as a confidant and to write him freely on any aspect of the business which he thought worthy of attention. But first Donald would have to withdraw his intention of resigning. He did so, assuming that he had before him a few weeks to follow his doctor's advice and rest his eyes. A few days later, on January 19, 1848, Donald Smith was instructed to set out for Labrador. Immediately.[57]

CHAPTER THREE

ESQUIMAUX BAY 1847-1852

God made the earth in six days and on the seventh he threw stones at Labrador.
Labrador folk saying

Many years later, a friend, on hearing how Sir George Simpson had sent Donald Smith to Labrador with but a few hour's notice, declared that he would have told Simpson to go to hell and to take the Hudson's Bay Company with him.

"Well," responded Donald Smith, by then Lord Strathcona, "I too felt like that for a moment. Then I said to myself, 'If Governor Simpson can bring himself to give such an order as that, I can bring myself to carry it out.' And I went."[1]

George Simpson controlled his staff by a mixture of callousness, an extensive knowledge of precisely what was happening at each of the fur trading posts in his widespread empire and a tight-lipped secrecy which meant that he did not reveal his plans until they were fully formulated and ready to be implemented. The Labrador changes had been developing in his mind for the better part of a year.

In May 1847, when Simpson wrote George Barnston at Tadoussac, he noted that Barnabas Verral, who had resigned when he left Esquimaux Bay, was expected to re-enter the service, in which case he would replace Donald Smith at Mingan, but he said nothing of Donald's future beyond the fact that he was being pulled back to Tadoussac. In November, he revealed that if Donald left Tadoussac for medical treatment, he would then be sent to another post. On the eleventh of December, Simpson unveiled the entire scheme in a letter to the Governor and Committee, though even London was not advised of the names of those involved. James Grant, the apprentice from Tadoussac, would be sent to Esquimaux Bay, together with Donald Smith, and the experienced Verral would be sent to the St. Lawrence in exchange. When a letter from Richard Hardisty, in charge at the Southern Department post of Matawagamingue, arrived in the autumn of 1847 with a request for permission to visit Montreal the following summer, it presented itself as an option for replacing William Nourse if his condition had not improved. Despite having determined all these moves on the HBC chessboard and hinted at some of them, it was only on January 18 that Simpson wrote Barnston to reveal the changes which would affect Tadoussac, but the letter would only be delivered when Donald arrived, en route to his new post. Donald's own letter of instructions was not written until the following day — though he was probably given verbal orders on the eighteenth. He was told that a carter would take him, together with three boatmen from Kahnawake, to "a stage about 10 miles below Quebec" and from here he was to arrange a conveyance to take the party to Black River from which point they would travel by snowshoe to Esquimaux Bay. He would have to acquire the snowshoes in Quebec.[2]

Simpson's conversations had generated in Donald an enthusiasm and energy which had been lacking for months. They rekindled his ambition and his pride and sparked a determination to prove his mettle to the governor. Simpson was often not altogether truthful with his senior officers, so the letter which Donald carried to William Nourse stated, "From Mr. Smith's habits of business and experience, he is qualified for any charge in the District; and Grant, who is a very promising young man, might be usefully employed as an assistant with yourself, whereby he would acquire a knowledge of accounts, and experience to qualify him, next year if necessary, for the charge of a post." Nothing was said of Donald's health or his "countinghouse business" and no reference was made to the concern that Grant might not be strong enough for what Simpson described as a "forced march." The men were under tremendous pressure to be in Esquimaux Bay by March because Simpson believed that if they were not, it would be impossible to provision some of the interior posts. At this point, he was not convinced that Nourse's injury was as serious as he claimed and hoped that extra help would suffice.[3]

Donald's suggestion in later years that he was ready to leave "in a couple of hours" after receiving his orders helps to embellish Simpson's reputation for issuing peremptory commands. In fact, he set out in the early hours of January 20 after writing a letter to his mother telling her that he was about to start for Labrador, where he expected to arrive in the middle of April, and another to Simpson confirming that he wished him to purchase for him from London a silver watch at the agreed cost of £10.[4]

The men reached Quebec at eleven o'clock on the morning of January 24 and about an hour later set out for Black River in two carioles which James McKenzie had procured for them. On the way to McKenzie's house, they bought snowshoes in the street and equipped themselves for the next part of their journey. They spent the night of the twenty-fourth in a hotel about twenty-four miles beyond Quebec and, averaging about forty-five miles a day, managed to reach Port au Persil late on the night of January 26. Here they dismissed the carioles and, with a cart for their luggage, began to walk towards Tadoussac. There was scarcely six inches of snow on the ground and travel was slow.[5]

The morning of January 28 found them on the west side of the Saguenay which had not frozen but was full of floating ice that had been driven in by strong gales from the east. Finally, at the end of the month, they were able to cross and avail themselves of the two days "to recruit" which Simpson had allowed. Early on the morning of February 3, Donald and the three Mohawks (almost always referred to by the HBC as Iroquois since they are one of the Five Nations which make up this tribe) were back on the trail, now accompanied by James Grant and a guide named Tshiask who was to take them to Isle Jeremie and, if no replacement could be found for him there, on to Godbout.[6]

At Jeremie, where they arrived on February 9, they paused to have their snowshoes repaired and to gather fresh provisions. Their journey from Tadoussac had taken much longer than anticipated because the bays were not frozen over and they were constantly delayed by snow storms. The men from Kahnawake were proving troublesome as well. "The Iroquois, I regret to say, do not appear to be good carriers, complaining much of from eighteen to twenty pounds weight in which are included their own clothes." Alexander Comeau, one of the company's officers who had business further along the coast, joined them at Isle Jeremie, but again they were delayed. "Joseph Sougueinas, one of the Iroquois, who has been complaining ever since our departure, and by lagging behind has not a little retarded us" was finally left behind at Trinity Bay because his constitution was "quite gone.... Another of the Iroquois, Louis, is but an indifferent walker not having been accustomed to use the snowshoe for many years back." Grant, whose strength had been doubted, had so far managed to keep pace and, when they left Trinity on February 18, they were expecting "to get on much better than we have hitherto done, as we have procured a good guide, an advantage till now denied us, as no Indian capable of acting as such was to be procured at either Tadoussac or Isle Jeremie." Tshiask, it would seem, was not what Barnston had promised.[7]

After a brief stop at Sept Iles, Donald, James Grant, two of the Mohawks and a guide set out on February 25 for Mingan. Eight days later, on March 3, they trudged into Donald's old post where he sent off yet another note to George Simpson. "After a toilsome march across a mountainous track of country, we yesterday arrived at this place. This portion of the coast is seldom attempted on foot, parties tripping generally waiting, till the ice having cleared off along shore, more difficult parts may be passed either by canoe or flat. Had we done so we might not have got here for ten days to come, and, advanced as the season now is, I should have been loath to lose a single day for the sake of saving a little personal fatigue."

The situation with James Grant, however, was now rather different. "I regret to say that the fatigue of the voyage from Tadoussac will incapacitate Mr. James Grant for proceeding beyond this establishment. For some days he has been complaining of pain in the back and general weakness, and assures me his strength is not equal to the task of continuing the march. Under these circumstances I should not feel myself justified in insisting on his going forward." Simpson had authorized this course of action, just as he had said Robert Hamilton from Musquarro was to replace Donald should his health prove unequal to the journey.[8]

More worrying was the fact that they had not managed to procure a guide to take them overland to Hamilton Inlet. Rather, they had found an Indian who was well acquainted with the route, but he was on crutches. Donald made notes on the track to be followed and hoped they might suffice. At Mingan, he added a young Orkney boatman named Alex Hunter to his party and hired Alexis Bellefleur to help carry supplies.

After Mingan, the weather was "boisterous in the extreme," except on the twelfth of March, and the men were glad to reach Musquarro on the fifteenth. The rain was "pouring down in torrents" and, while Donald said he did not mind it, the Iroquois were going from bad to worse. He was concerned that their health would deteriorate further when they added to their packs the provisions necessary for the overland journey. At Musquarro, Donald encountered a group of Indians who had come in to trade and they reported that there had been less snow that winter than any in their memory. Travel had been close to impossible, as Donald and his group could confirm from their own experience. Stories of a scarcity of game in the interior did not bode well for the next stage of their journey either. On the other hand, the Indians said that, although they did not know the route to Esquimaux Bay, they knew someone who did and would return with him on March 18. This they failed to do.

Donald was determined not to be defeated by the task Simpson had allocated him and went in search of the dilatory Indians. The pounding rain obliterated their tracks and it was not until the twenty-sixth of March that he finally located their camp. Here, he discovered that the guide had met with an accident during the winter and was now a helpless cripple. A guide was essential for the next stage of the journey, partly because Donald needed directions and partly because it was inadvisable to attempt to traverse uncharted territory without the help of an Indian or someone who, like the Indians, knew how to survive in the bush: how to interpret the signs which indicated the presence of wild animals which might feed the travellers and how to read the messages left by other native people to mark the tracks and portages. The men from Kahnawake were from a different landscape and a different cultural tradition and could not be relied on for this vital work.

Donald thought the journey might be made with a compass and someone with survival skills, but the Indians refused to accompany him under such circumstances and Alexis Bellefleur, a half-breed who was acquainted with the Indian way of life, declared that he would rather give up all his wages than attempt the crossing without a guide. Robert Hamilton, in charge at Musquarro, supported Bellefleur in this, as did many others who assured Donald that he would be courting certain destruction to enter the woods without a guide. Hamilton and Donald made a journey fifty miles to the east of Musquarro in hopes of finding a guide there, but that too proved fruitless. Finally, Donald had to admit that his intention of walking overland was doomed and he settled down to make himself useful around the post and watch the rain and sleet pummel the surrounding fields. When the ice broke on the inland waterways and the Indians appeared from the interior, he would procure a guide and push on by canoe.[9]

The delay was not without its benefits. It enabled all the travellers to recoup their strength, including James Grant who proceeded from Mingan to join them. Alex Hunter was "attacked by feaver of a typhoid character which brought him very low" but there was time enough for him to recover before they set out again. At Musquarro, Donald passed a good many hours with Robert Hamilton who proved to be the friend and companion he had lacked since joining the company. Their days in the rain at the trading post cemented an enduring friendship. It was also while at Musquarro that he met Father Durocher who ministered to the Indians of the King's Posts and Mingan and, in observing his activities and talking to him, Donald realized that the alliance between the company and the church which had worked when he was briefly at Lake St. John could equally well be turned to advantage at Esquimaux Bay. Durocher wanted to visit that district and indicated that he intended to seek permission from George Simpson. In this he was supported by Donald, who, in a letter written that summer, nonetheless felt obliged to make sure the governor did not think he also shared the priest's religious views.

> Whether or not his ministrations may be beneficial in a spiritual sense, is not for me to judge, but he has certainly succeeded in attaching to the posts on the Seigniory many Indians who formerly traded the whole of their hunts with the settlers on the Labradore, and I think it would tend to benefit the interests of the Company were he to visit Esquimaux Bay. I would however beg of you to understand, that this recommendation I take the liberty

> of making, solely as being likely to improve the trade by keeping the Indians attached to their posts, & deterring them from resorting to the Establishments on the Gulf shore, which they will assuredly do, if denied the opportunity of seeing a priest on their own grounds, and without regarding it in a religious view.[10]

The argument made sense and had been seen to work but it found no sympathy with George Simpson who feared that the Catholics might take unfair advantage of any assistance they were offered; he also hesitated to risk alienating the Church of England with which the company had good relations in the Northern Department. Henceforth, the request and its denial would regularly punctuate the correspondence between Esquimaux Bay and Montreal.

If the winter of 1847-1848 was unusually mild and free of snow, the spring compensated by coming abnormally late. It was not until the end of May that the party was able to begin the final lap. By the tenth of June, they were at Coquatshen at the mouth of the St. Augustine River and a few days later they began paddling upstream. There were forty portages, most of them poorly marked. One took them across to the Kenamu River system which finally brought them to Hamilton Inlet and the post at North West River on the evening of June 27. "The journey across land occupied a fortnight, the shortest time in which it has yet been made, and had our guide been better acquainted with the route it might have been accomplished within twelve days," Donald reported to Sir George with just a hint of pride. It also poured rain almost every day, which further slowed them down, though he made no mention of the weather to Simpson.[11]

At some point towards the end of their journey, they fell in with Donald Henderson, one of the junior clerks in the district, and Joseph McPherson, whose father had been in charge of Tadoussac for part of the time that Donald was there. They too were en route to North West River, the headquarters for the Esquimaux Bay District. Nourse had left for Rigolet, on the coast, the day before Donald and James Grant finally made their appearance, and on the first of July, in company with Joseph McPherson, they set out to meet him. Grant stayed behind at Rigolet while Donald and McPherson returned to North West River in the district's schooner, the *Willie*, in order to prepare the outfits for the inland posts. It was hot work, with the temperature up to 85°F on the twenty-third of July and 94° in the shade on the afternoon of August 5. Flies and mosquitoes swarmed everywhere.

Before the summer was out, the two men also had a little adventure which Donald was amused to report to his mother.

> We heard piercing yells, and hastening towards the spot found a rather pretty Esquimaux girl who had sprained her ankle. Her attempt to walk had only made it worse; it had swollen to about twice its normal size. There was nothing to do but to carry her nearly a mile into the Esquimaux camp. You would hardly believe that this was a very repugnant task; as a matter of fact, none in my experience was ever more so. The odour of these people when they are sufficiently animated is not very pleasant: the effluvia of this young lady was really overpowering, and we were glad when our job was over, and we deposited her with her parents. Even

> then we were considerably delayed, first by explanation, which at first they refused to believe, and afterwards by their gratitude. There was a good deal of merriment when we returned to the house, for the others had somehow got *wind* of the affair.[12]

Donald's aroma, after a hot day packing outfits for the interior, is unlikely to have been of the most delicate, but both he and his brother were fastidious about their personal hygiene. Of sixty officers in the Afghanistan campaign of 1878, only Dr. Smith and his commanding officer continued to shave and they were the only ones with white collars. Donald had opted for a beard but the cleanliness of his linen occasioned comment.

Poor Mrs. Smith would have been delighted to receive Donald's letter, not because she particularly wanted to know of her son's gallantry but because it proved that he had survived the journey to Esquimaux Bay. She had not yet grasped how infrequently the district could communicate with the outside world and in June had compelled Jane to write the company's London office seeking news. The reply, informing the women that there had been no information and that none was expected for a month or two, offered little consolation.[13]

Donald Smith had received his new watch at Rigolet and immediately after his return to North West River, he found an opportunity to write Simpson a private note to thank him and to report on Nourse's health. "The whole of his right arm, and indeed the whole of the right side is very much affected with paralysis, the fingers being greatly contracted. He is also subject to almost daily fits of cramp, which cause the most excruciating pains, his body being occasionally all but doubled up." Donald thought he should see a doctor as soon as possible. In fact, the decision to allow Nourse to leave had probably already been made, for Richard Hardisty and his family set out from Lachine on the evening of July 26.[14]

For the Hudson's Bay Company, the work of Esquimaux Bay focused on Hamilton Inlet, the long channel which pushes inland in the southern third of Labrador. The mouth is choked with little islands; from the south, a spit of land curls north and west with Mount Gnat sitting like a solitary pustule on its tip. A long, narrow peninsula runs parallel to the north shore of the inlet, nearly touching the southern protrusion, while the space between them is jammed by Henrietta Island. The tide rips through the narrows, rising six feet on a normal day, and all but the smallest boats were obliged to wait for the tide to carry them in and out of the inlet. The ferocity of the currents at this point led some people to call the area Cross Waters Bay and even in the most severe winters, the water never froze except among the rocks on the shore. On the north side of the windy peninsula, the aptly named Double Mer forms a cul de sac to delude the unwary eastbound navigator while at its tip, Rigolet supervised the company's transatlantic and coastal shipping, receiving and forwarding supplies and collecting the district's returns. Few vessels, whatever their size, could slip through the narrows unobserved by the staff at Rigolet.

Beyond the narrows, the inlet widens to such an extent that it is sometimes referred to as Lake Melville. The mountains along the northern shore are rather monotonous but the Mealy Mountains along the south are a stunning geological oddity. About two miles from the inlet, they march along in parallel with it, "not conical, not pyramidal, not serrated, but a succession of colossal thumbs, or haycocks of gigantic dimensions, which Titans have half toppled over in sport, and all trending southerly. They are wholly barren of vegetation."[15]

At its western end, Hamilton Inlet forks, with the southern branch fed by Hamilton (now Churchill) River and the northern by Grand Lake and North West River. A French post, established in 1758 on the east shore of the northern fork, near the mouth of North West River, was called Esquimaux Bay and the name became synonymous with the whole region. The HBC post was on the same shore, about a mile and a half from the mouth of the river, and sat between the sandy bank and the gently sloping hills beyond. About twenty red painted, one storey buildings, including stores, shops, the men's houses and the senior officer's residence, with its red HBC flag flapping in the breeze, were spread out along the strand. Nearby was a circle of Naskapi lodge frames which the natives would cover with skins when they came to trade.[16]

North West River was a comparatively secure post, its greatest threat coming from the company's own operation at the King's Posts and Mingan, as Donald had already had occasion to notice from the opposite perspective. The company's principal inland post was Fort Nascopie (as Naskapi was always written by the company), while the other important post on the seaboard was Kibokok, as the company usually spelled it, just south of the fifty-fifth parallel on Kaipokok Bay. Fort Chimo, at the southern tip of Ungava Bay, had been the responsibility of the Southern Department but had been abandoned some years earlier. On the northern shores of Labrador, the Moravian missionaries maintained posts at Hopedale, Hebron and Nain, primarily in pursuit of their religious work, but they used trade as a means of inducing the Inuit and the Naskapi to visit and were thus a thorn in the flesh of the HBC which perceived the Germans to be a particular threat to the operation at Kibokok.[17]

All along the southern half of the Labrador coast were families who hunted, trapped and fished, and sold their surplus produce either to the company or to independent traders who were generally based in Newfoundland, though Hunt and Henley, who had a post at Sandwich Bay near the mouth of Hamilton Inlet, were based in London. Most of these fishing families, many of mixed-blood, were "livyers" because they "lived here" all year round. More frequently, they were referred to as planters. They had fixed summer and winter camps and travelled between them. The general boundaries of each family's territory were understood and respected though, as game became increasingly scarce, the trappers and hunters found themselves having to travel progressively further inland in pursuit of it. The trading posts got along with each other quite well on the whole, partly because they were licensed to work in certain areas and tended not to poach and partly because the HBC had hitherto concentrated on fur rather than fish. One look at the accounts of Esquimaux Bay, however, was sufficient to prove that the fisheries needed to be developed to ensure the district's economic viability.

In the middle of August, Donald left North West River for Rigolet where he was to be in charge. There were fourteen buildings at his new post, including houses for the officers and servants, a bakery, warehouses for furs and other goods, and a shop for the sale of food, clothing, fishing tackle, traps and other necessities of life on the Labrador. There was a building for the cooper, another for making seal oil, one for salting fish and another for packing goods for shipment. Some were frame buildings constructed from wooden planks, while others were made of logs. In front of the house was a turnip patch from which the dogs were kept by old fishing nets stretched between poles. If one ignored the mosquitoes, Rigolet was beautiful in the August light, as Charles Hallock noted when he visited in 1860.

> Four six-pound cannons and one eighteen-pounder, ranged before the principal store and pointed down the bay, give the post a rather war-like aspect; but these have never been used except on Queen's birthdays, or to greet the arrival of officers of the Company, or in manifestation of peace and good-will on other special occasions. There are nets hung on pickets to dry; and nets for salmon sweep out into the cove in semi-circles, like mammoth necklaces of beads. Here and there a sly old seal is seen prowling near, to rob the nets of their prize — doubly vigilant, inasmuch as he has one eye constantly on the fish, and the other on the man who sits with a gun watching for *him*.

Alders, willows and spruce grew about the post, tinting the landscape with the pale yellows and mature greens of early autumn.

> From the summit of the neighbouring hills is an extended view of the broad bay below, with its many islands and the expanse of inland water above the Narrows; Mount Nat [sic] standing alone in his grandeur; the distant ocean drawn like a silver ribbon upon the horizon; and more impressive and sublimer than all, the long chain of Mealy Mountains looming up in soft, slaty clouds against the massive blue, thirty miles away — cloud-capped, and brilliant with the gleaming snow that crests their summits.[18]

On the twenty-third of August, the guns of Rigolet announced the arrival of the *Marten*, the company ship which brought the last of the supplies and collected the remaining returns; it brought the final mail of the season and took away to Montreal the last of the correspondence from Esquimaux Bay. In 1848, it took William Nourse to Canada and brought Richard Hardisty to replace him. With Hardisty came his wife, Margaret, and four of their children.

The Hardistys were typical of Hudson's Bay Company families of the period in that their lives were totally immersed in the activities of the company and the children accepted as completely normal the pattern of life which the company's requirements imposed. Their education, careers and marriages were all shaped by the limitations and opportunities of fur trading life as, indeed, had been their mother's life and, to a very large extent, their father's as well.

Richard Hardisty had been born in London in 1790, the son of William and Mary Hardisty. Two brothers and a sister had been born before him and one brother followed. The family lived in the parish of St. Martin-in-the-Fields, an area packed with tenement blocks where many parents struggled to find enough room and enough money to raise and educate their children. William Hardisty is listed in the street directories of the period as a lighterman at Hungerford Market which suggests that he managed several small boats, since a man with only one is unlikely to have been able to afford an entry or to have thought it worth his while. Hungerford Market could offer a good living to a man who was prepared to work hard and Richard may have found employment there for a time as well, for an early Hudson's Bay Company character report notes that "besides being possessed of some Experience & Practise as a Tradesman he is also competent in Writing and accounts, assiduous and indefatigable[,] Qualifications not often found united in One Person in this part of the World."[19]

His "Experience & Practise as a Tradesman" came to a halt about 1811 when he joined the army Commissariat. Late in 1813, he was in Belgium and in June 1815 he was at Waterloo, supplying the troops when Wellington defeated Napoleon. Peace meant a scaled down army and by the end of 1816 Richard was back in Britain, vainly searching for a job in a market crowded with recently demobilized soldiers. One of his friends from the Commissariat had managed to find himself work and, early in 1817, decided to do something for Richard, though the job he had in mind was not one he would have taken himself because the pay was poor and the living conditions were abominable. At parties, he had met William Smith, then the assistant secretary at the Hudson's Bay Company headquarters in London, and, armed with a supporting letter from a mutual friend, he called on Smith to see if there were openings for Richard Hardisty. He discovered that two apprentice clerks were to be sent from England that spring and an application would be entertained.

That evening, Richard had a visitor.

> After being in his company some time, I said "Hardisty, do you know any one who would willingly enter the Hudson's Bay Company's Service as a Clerk *with a small salary, and plenty of the worst difficulties and discomfitures*" he replied most emphatically "I do." Who said I? "Why myself" was his reply. I told him then many of the objections I had but he overruled them all, finding that to be the case, I gave him my card and told him to call with it on Mr. Smith the following morning but whether he signed the contract that morning, or the one after, I forget, however in a very few days after he received instructions to embark.[20]

The *Eddystone* sailed from Gravesend on May 17, 1817 and deposited Richard Hardisty at Moose Factory on the shores of Hudson Bay three months later. He was assigned to the Southern Department and gradually rose in seniority, taking responsibility for larger and more complex trading operations. Early in his career with the company, probably in the autumn of 1818, he took the sixteen year old Margaret Sutherland as his wife. Richard was a quiet but committed Anglican and the wedding ceremony was almost certainly conducted by the senior Hudson's Bay Company officer, who had authority to do so in the absence of clergy.

Margaret Sutherland was the younger daughter of John Sutherland, a Scot, generally said to be from Caithness, though on one occasion he is described as an Orkneyman. He entered the company's service in 1778 and was soon earning a bonus for residing in the hinterland. Together with Donald Mackay, he paddled further and further away from the bay, ranging ever southwards and west in search of pelts. "Has been uncommonly assiduous in pushing inland," his superiors noted in 1787, adding that "he is under no contract being too far off to send him one." He knew his worth to the company and, when his contract was up for renewal, he invariably negotiated a higher salary than the one offered.[21]

By 1794, Sutherland was on the Assiniboine River. He was driven by the spirit of exploration which sends men into uncharted territory but he was also compelled to move inland by the fierce competition between the Hudson's Bay Company, the North West Company and the free traders who had crossed the ill defined American boundary. In earlier years, the company had been content to establish posts around the bay and wait for the Indians to come to trade. By Sutherland's time, they were obliged to take the trade goods to the hunters, as their competitors did.

Like many such men, who needed the support of women who could make moccasins, repair canoes and snowshoes, and skin animals, Sutherland had a native born companion. Her English name was Jeanny and her intelligence and abilities provoked admiring comments from the traders and explorers who clustered along the Assiniboine at the turn of the century. She was noted for making pemmican and curing skins and her social skills were equally appreciated. Archibald McLeod, a North West Company trader, confided to his diary on November 26, 1800 that he had "had the *Honor* of playing *Cribbage* with Jeanny." A month later, Daniel Harmon, a Nor'Wester who became a close friend of Donald Smith's uncle, John Stuart, noted in his journal,

> Yesterday, I went to see the fort of the Hudson's Bay Company, which is situated about nine miles down this river [the Upper Assiniboine] and is in the charge of a Mr. Sutherland. He has a woman of this country, for a wife, who, I was pleased to find, could speak the English language, tolerably well. I understand, also, that she can read and write it, which she learned to do at Hudson's Bay, where the Company have a school. She speaks, likewise, the Cree and Sauteux [Chippewa] tongues. She appears to possess natural good sense, and is far from being deficient, in acquired knowledge.[22]

The relationship between Jeanny and Sutherland seems to have been based on genuine affection, despite the fact that Sutherland was an alcoholic. Sober, he showed concern for his family and their well-being, and was admired by his colleagues for his diligence, his skills as a hunter and his understanding of the forests and rivers in which he worked. Drunk, he was scorned by the Nor'Westers, who called him Mr. Sugar Royall in reference to his weakness for rum, and he was the object of great concern to his Hudson's Bay colleagues. In October 1809, three of them, under his command at Osnaburgh House, complained to John Hodgson, chief at Albany, that "he drinks 'till he is not able to walk nor set, and there he lies on the Floor, which it is pitifull to see, and if it was not for his Wife he would set the place on Fire, never blows out his Candle, lies in Bed, and drinks 'till he loses his Senses entirely." Hodgson responded more in sorrow than in anger, for he had warned Sutherland of what would happen if his drinking continued. He was relieved of his command and in September 1810 went home on leave. In 1811, he was allowed to return to Albany but a year later the post journal records that he was drunk and setting a bad example for younger officers and men "and altho' he has been warned by the Superintendent & myself that his behaviour cannot be tolerated, & his dismissal from the service will be the consequence of his persisting in it, he appears incorrigible and I am concerned to add there are no hopes of his reformation." A year later, he was dismissed and in May 1814, when he requested permission to join his family at Albany, the Governor and Committee, meeting in London, denied his application.[23]

John Sutherland had two daughters and, though it cannot be said with certainty that their mother was Jeanny, there seems every reason to believe she was, as she was living with him when Sutherland's girls were born. The elder, Charlotte, was born about 1799, and first married a man named McPherson by whom she had a son, John, about 1817. The boy was adopted by her second husband, Thomas Corcoran, an Irish Catholic of increasingly proselytizing bent. By him Charlotte had four children, Margaret, Jane Isabella, Richard Edwards and a boy who died about 1843.

John Sutherland's younger daughter, Margaret, born about 1802, had six sons and four daughters by her husband, Richard Hardisty. Three of the girls and the youngest boy, Thomas, who was born in 1842, travelled with them to Esquimaux Bay. The oldest boy, William Lucas, was born in 1822, Joseph Wordsworth arrived in 1828, Richard Charles in 1831, George in 1835 and Henry in 1836. All five boys were sent to the Red River Academy which had been established at Fort Garry for the sons and daughters of Hudson's Bay Company officers. When Donald Smith first met the Hardistys, William was working for the company and Joseph had just joined, as Richard was to do when he graduated. Sir George Simpson refused to have the remaining three boys, however, on the grounds that he could not give that much patronage to one family, but after his death these three also joined the service.

The oldest of the girls, Hannah, was the Hardistys' first child. Born in 1820, she married Walter Faries, a junior Hudson's Bay Company officer at Matawagamingue and the son of Hugh Faries, a company interpreter; she was well on her way to producing a large family when her parents arrived at Rigolet. Mary Fletcher, the third daughter, was born in 1833. When she was twelve, her father was keen to have her educated at Red River with her brothers, but "could not think of sending her so great a distance without any other female." He compromised both his wishes for his daughter and his principles by sending her to the Convent of the Sacred Heart, run by the Sisters of Charity on the northern outskirts of Montreal. Here her cousin Margaret was a nun and could offer some companionship in an alien world.[24]

Her father worried about the influence of a Catholic environment "and I should hope that those I have entrusted her to are too honourable to use any unfair means to convert her," he told George Simpson. To be sure, he had asked for permission to visit her in the summer of 1848. When the family arrived, they found her seriously ill and removed her from the convent to nurse her themselves at Lachine. Not long after, Simpson activated the next stage of his scheme for Labrador by announcing that Hardisty was to be sent to Esquimaux Bay, with the result that Mary accompanied her parents. She later lamented that neither she nor Hannah had been educated, though both girls, like their youngest sister Charlotte, who was four when the family moved to Esquimaux Bay, got a thorough grounding in basic skills from their father. Their mother had herself learned to write but gave it up in the face of her husband's superior ability. In 1865, Richard lamented that she had not written anyone for forty-four years. "She could then write well and I would not be ashamed to shew her letters to anyone. I am vexed now that she gave up writing as people may think she never learnt to write." When she was widowed, Margaret Hardisty once again took up correspondence and the surviving letters confirm her husband's comments on her ability.[25]

While he was unable to provide much by way of formal instruction for Hannah and Mary, Richard Hardisty took great care over the education of his second daughter, Isabella Sophia, who was obviously very intelligent. She was born on May 4, 1825 in the Rupert River District south east of James Bay. A year later, on July 5, she was baptized at Rupert's House by her father's chief, Joseph Beioley, who, together with his mixed-blood wife, Isabella, stood sponsor for her. The little girl soon demonstrated a spunky independence, married to a good deal of common sense, and her father decided it would be safe to allow her to travel to school in England without the close supervision of her relatives or reliable mature women. In September 1838, he entrusted her to the care of Robert Royal, master of the Hudson's Bay Company's *Prince of Wales*, and she sailed with him from Moose Factory to London.[26]

There she studied, first with Mrs. Pooly and then with Mrs. Knaggs, ladies who doubtless believed that appropriate manners and dress would stand a young woman in better stead than an excess of science or philosophy. The damp and foggy London winters interfered with her academic progress and caused her father to fret. "I now regret much she was not sent to Red River instead of to England, as judging from her state of health while in this country I am fully impressed with the belief that she would there have enjoyed uninterrupted good Health, and that consequently she would have made much greater progress in her Studies than her State of Health in England has enabled her to do."[27]

Bell, as she was then known, viewed her English experience quite differently. "I enjoyed myself very much all the time I was in England," she wrote to her brother Richard, "and have many kind friends there, who were all very sorry to part with me, I certainly think London a wonderful place."[28]

Her schooling did nothing to dampen her spirits: she was due to go back to Rupert's Land in the summer of 1843 but the usual problem of accompanying females occurred, so the trip was postponed till 1845 when it was thought the daughter of another company officer would be returning. If that was not the case, Joseph Beioley, who had recently retired, was asked to send his goddaughter back under the captain's care. This he did, but in 1844. Arriving at Moose on August 27, she found, of course, that there was no one to meet her. A month later, she greeted her startled parents at Matawagamingue "having come up from Moose accompanied by only Indians," her surprised father reported, adding that he would have sent her Mama to meet her had he known. Margaret, then seven months pregnant with Charlotte, was probably glad he did not.[29]

There was not much to occupy a lively, intelligent, unmarried young woman like Bella at a place like Matawagamingue. She helped her mother with the two youngest, Thomas and Charlotte, kept up an energetic correspondence with her brothers insofar as her isolation allowed, and generally made herself useful. By one of the late canoes in 1845, she was sent to spend the winter with her aunt, Charlotte Corcoran, at Albany on the western shores of James Bay. Here she stood a better chance of meeting a suitable young man. At the end of January 1846, however, the post burned to the ground and Bella, with her cousin Jane, moved to Moose Factory for the rest of the winter. In the spring, she returned to her parents. Bella felt no obligation to marry and was quite happy to take life as she found it. As far as she was concerned, her first visit to Montreal and all the excitement of the move to Esquimaux Bay kept her more than sufficiently occupied in 1848.

Most of the Hardisty children were fortunate in inheriting their mother's large, dark eyes and high cheek bones, and less fortunate in also having her thin lips. If Bella were unwell or upset for any length of time, her face became thin and drawn and this, with her thick, dark hair pulled tightly back, tended to make her appear more severe than she actually was. Her visage was saved by a strong jaw, inherited from her father, while her brothers, Richard and Joseph, and her sister Mary had high cheek bones and long, narrow jaws which gave them an air of being hollow cheeked. Joseph, especially in old age, could look quite cadaverous. William and Tom were on the stocky side, like their father, but the rest of the family were slim.[30]

Having arranged the final shipments for the season, the HBC staff at Esquimaux Bay settled down to their winter work. While Donald took charge at Rigolet, the Hardistys moved into the house at North West River where James Grant was also assigned, in accordance with Governor Simpson's wishes. Joseph McPherson seems to have wintered there as well, though he travelled about the district a good deal. William Cameron was at Kibokok. Donald Henderson retired from the service and his place at Fort Nascopie was taken by Henry Connolly, the son of William Connolly who had been Donald's first senior officer at Tadoussac. The winter proved a difficult one for the Naskapi, who did not get sufficient ammunition from Henderson in the spring and were unable to kill enough deer to sustain themselves. Believing that Henderson was still at Fort Nascopie, they thought they would be wasting their time if they returned. In September 1849, when Hardisty reported to London and Lachine, he thought that ninety-seven people had died, though the death toll was later revealed to be fifty-four because a feeble old man had been able to snare some migrating deer. A year later, Governor Simpson wrote that he had quizzed Henderson who refused to be blamed, pointing out that he had supplied the usual amount of ammunition and neither he nor the Indians could have been aware that the deer would not migrate, as usual, through the "barren grounds."[31]

At Rigolet, Donald occupied himself with getting to know the families who lived and worked in his area. Most had Inuit blood and were the children or grandchildren of women who had married Hudson's Bay Company labourers, who were generally from Orkney. Donald, who was always moderate in matters of food and drink, was by turns astonished and appalled by the Inuit capacity to eat and drink plentifully when opportunity arose, storing in human fat the energy which would be needed when fish and game were scarce. "Unless you have actually been a witness of their table performances," he wrote to his mother, "you would not believe what an Esquimaux family can consume at a single sitting. They will eat such a breakfast as a hearty white man will put away, and this merely as a relish. I have also seen one man drink eleven cups of coffee, each with several spoonfuls of sugar as an accompaniment to a meal of bread, pancakes, bear's meat, half-raw fish, and other delicacies."[32]

Apart from a quick run to North West River in March 1849, Donald had little but work to occupy his mind. At some point, probably after his return from North West River, he fell, dislocating his ankle and breaking his arm. He was still limping and moving his arm with difficulty when the summer's shipping business was upon him and Rigolet was inundated with incoming supplies and produce. More distressing was his discovery that the salmon from the outposts was in very poor condition, and, since none of the men at Rigolet knew anything about salmon beyond telling whether or not they had been cleaned, Donald was obliged to do much of the work himself. The *Marten* had then to be loaded and prepared for its final departure, while, simultaneously, he was playing host to Mrs. Hardisty and her children who had accompanied their father to Rigolet, where he was supervising the shipping and dealing with last minute accounts and correspondence.[33]

Immediately before the departure of the *Marten*, Richard Hardisty completed his report to George Simpson, speaking well of both Donald and James Grant.

> Mr. James Grant passed the Winter along with me at NW River, I had consequently every opportunity of making myself acquainted with his Character. I am glad to say that I find him to be a very active, intelligent young man, and always ready and willing to do his utmost for the interest of the Company. Mr. Donald A. Smith has had the charge of Rigolet during the last year, and continues to hold the same charge as I am quite confident that a more active, indefatigable, and interested person for the Company could not be found. He is just the person fitted for the Post where there is much Trade carried on with the Esquimaux, and Freemen.[34]

Despite his injury and the distractions of the shipping season, Donald was "active" enough to complete his accounts and do all that was required of him by the company, but in doing so, he pushed his own interests aside: he wrote neither George Simpson nor his mother. A year later, he claimed to Simpson that the exertion of loading the ship had led to an inflammation and fear of tetanus and that, for a brief while, his life "hung on a very slender thread," an exaggeration which the governor recognized as an excuse rather than an explanation.[35]

Simpson may have been disappointed at not hearing from Donald, even if he was pleased with the evidence that his protégé was finally measuring up to what was expected of him. Donald's mother, however, had no information at all. Not surprisingly, at the beginning of January, a fretful Barbara Smith dictated a letter for Jane to send to Governor Simpson. "As I have not heard from my son for a much longer time than usual I am most anxious about him he being when I heard last in a far distant & far out of the world place at Esquimaux Bay." Simpson's reply was prompt and a model of courtesy in which he prevaricated by suggesting that Donald's letters had miscarried. He assured Mrs. Smith that her son was well and told her that she would have two opportunities to send mail to Esquimaux Bay, once when the company ship left England in May and once when the *Marten* sailed from Quebec in August. Simpson had taken a special interest in the young man at Esquimaux Bay and the tenor of his reply was in keeping with that interest. On the other hand, the Smiths were proving a little troublesome to the company and it was wise not to provoke them further.[36]

The problem arose from the fact that John Stuart's will, drawn up in 1832, left money to Mary Taylor, his country wife and the mother of his one surviving son. She had followed Stuart to England in the autumn of 1837 but, when he refused to marry her, she returned to Canada. Following Stuart's death, his family discovered a draft of a new will which excluded Mary and left money instead to Mrs. Smith and the descendants of their deceased sister, Grace Cameron. Barbara Smith and her nieces and nephews went to court, arguing that Mary had not been married to Stuart and that children by that and previous liaisons were illegitimate. The family was divided, with Barbara's cousin William, an executor of the original will, defending Mary Taylor's rights. The dispute was conducted decorously, but the entire fur trade knew about it and senior HBC staff were tangentially involved. It was finally resolved in Mary Taylor's favour in July 1851 but, until then, men like Simpson were mindful of what they said, especially since the company feared a compensation claim because a third of the inheritance was eaten up in legal fees.[37]

When the Hardisty family and the various members of the HBC staff showed up at Rigolet in the summer of 1850, it became apparent that more than fur bearing animals were being pursued by the young clerks. Joseph McPherson was making eyes at Mary Hardisty and James Grant's requests from London, passed on through Donald Smith, included a gold seal with the initials ISH, as in Isabella Sophia Hardisty. As for Donald, he showed his usual courtesy to Mrs. Hardisty and discussed the business of the district with her husband. He was captivated by the Hardistys' youngest, Charlotte, whose quick smile and forthright charm easily won his friendship; and he was mindful of the feelings of young Tom Hardisty who would be sent away to school at Lennoxville, Quebec, when the *Marten* took her final departure.

Tom was an intelligent lad who had turned eight in June and, as his proud father reported to the governor, had been vaccinated, could read and write "pretty well" and could "do arithmetic, up to multiplication." Moreover, he had "always been made to say his prayers before going to Bed and his Catechism twice a week." Captain Dunn of the *Marten* had brought his young son with him on that voyage and the children were all of an age to play together in the late summer sun. It was a cheerful, family environment in which Donald found himself when his thirtieth birthday arrived in August that year, but, as he took stock of his life, he was forced to admit that, although he was the most senior man in the district after Richard Hardisty, he was also the most solitary.[38]

He would have had good reason to be pleased with himself had he seen Richard Hardisty's letter which went out with the returns that fall. He reported to Governor Simpson that he was

> highly satisfied with the conduct of Messrs DA Smith, McPherson, Grant & Connolly, Mr. Smith in particular. I would beg to recommend him to your most favourable notice as a Gentleman well deserving of it. He is an officer who is not sparing of his labor where the Company's interest is concerned. It is quite a common practise with him when heard of a Planter who is indebted to the Company having any furs, to set off immediately to the House — no matter what the distance may be, or what kind of Weather, and in this way he invariably secures whatever furs the Planter may have on account of his Debt to the Company. He is also deserving of much praise for the economy in which he manages the business of his Post.[39]

The allocation of staff for Outfit 1850 was to be as before, except that Joseph McPherson was assigned to Rigolet which had expanded its work load under Donald's management. Nothing came of this plan, however, for just before he was due to take up his new post, McPherson asked for Mary Hardisty's hand in marriage and her father revoked the appointment to Rigolet in order to allow the young people more time together. James Grant's situation in relation to Isabella Hardisty was more ambiguous because he was still a minor, but she had accepted the signet ring he had ordered for her.

Despite the distractions of all the visitors and the partying which inevitably accompanied the end of the shipping season, Donald was now working much more efficiently and he managed to make time to write a long and thoughtful private letter to George Simpson. Having said that he always communicated his views about the district to Richard Hardisty and consequently had nothing to add to his superior's communication, he proceeded to a thorough analysis of the business of Esquimaux Bay, setting it in its historical context. There was a feeling of hostility towards the company, he said, which had its origins during the management of Mr. McGillivray whose zeal was not matched by prudence or a knack for conciliation; his successor, Mr. Davies was petrified of Lachine and used this as an excuse for not doing anything. William Nourse confined himself to North West River and the interior posts, disregarding the salmon and seal fishing stations which resulted in maritime products of poor quality.[40]

With regard to the competition, Angus Brownson had quarrelled with Nourse and was therefore disinclined to have anything to do with his successor or with Donald either, but Donald thought he could be induced to sell his produce to the company rather than travel further to consign it to Hunt and Henley at Sandwich Bay, if only because he could make significant savings on transport by doing so. As for Nathan Norman, who was based at Brighouse on the outskirts of St. John's, and annually brought a trading vessel to Indian Harbour near the mouth of Hamilton Inlet, Donald acknowledged that he drove a good bargain, whether for cash or barter, but his goods were inferior and his prices were higher. Some pressure could be exerted on Norman since he only operated in the summer months and dealt primarily in cod. A small increase in staff would enable the HBC to encroach with advantage on Norman's cod fishery and the product would find a ready market in Quebec. In short, Donald proposed upsetting the equilibrium which existed among the larger companies working along the coast because he believed the HBC would come out the winner.

The fur trade, Donald argued, required better management, not more staff, and in this he disagreed with Hardisty. The planters were not a threat and, were Hardisty to make a winter tour of the posts, he would find that he could keep his staff up to the mark. Fewer men, but healthier ones who worked harder, was the solution, he suggested, indicating those who had been frequently ill and suggesting that one of the men was suffering not from "ague" but from venereal disease.

Next, he turned his attention to the running costs of Esquimaux Bay, and particularly to the benefits to be gained from a good vegetable garden.

> A considerable reduction in the importation of provisions might be effected by using more country produce, such as swedish turnips & potatoes than at present. Turnips and potatoes in any quantity can be grown at North West River and at no further expense than that of the seed. Here both soil and climate are unfavorable for cultivation but last year we had 15 barrels of excellent turnips, which by the bye, were sold to Esquimaux or Planters from 8/ to 12/ pr barrel, and these, besides causing a considerable saving of other provisions, conduced not a little to keep us in health. This year we shall have about 20 barrels of turnips, but if the same method is not followed at the other posts, it will be needless to persist in it here because it will but afford another cause for discontent. The rations at this post, during the winter, consist of pork or fresh meat, soup & abun-

dance of turnips for dinner, and bread & fish ad libitim [sic] for breakfast & supper.

By pork, the company referred to salt pork which, with bread, formed the staple diet for all classes at the trading posts, as indeed it did for sailors and for many in rural England who had neither sources of fresh produce nor adequate means of preserving food, except in brine. Donald had begun to experiment with vegetable gardens in the much more hospitable climate of Mingan, in part for reasons of economy and in part because he understood the relationship between the consumption of fresh vegetables and the absence of scurvy, which continued to be the scourge of fur trade posts long after the occupants knew how to prevent it.

Donald next raised the need for a Roman Catholic priest, observing that the Indians had asked him to make the request in the apparent belief that he was a more effective channel than Richard Hardisty. In this they may well have been right, since Donald shared their desire for a priest, albeit for different reasons. He added that he favoured Father Durocher whom he had met at Musquarro because he required the Indians to pay their HBC debts before receiving absolution!

Esquimaux Bay was a much more settled community than the King's Posts or Mingan and was populated by many more people with European blood and European ways. While items such as food, traps and ammunition were fairly constant whatever the post, clothing, domestic utensils and trinkets could vary considerably and the company needed to pay more attention to the tastes of the planters than it had hitherto. One of the reasons for the success of Hunt and Henley, he argued, was that the company's agent travelled to England each year to select the goods for the Labrador trade. If the head of the district were to go to Sandwich on the first vessel in the spring, he could collect the HBC goods and simultaneously see what the competition was importing with a view to amending the indent for the following outfit.

It is a measure of Donald's greatly improved self-confidence that, before closing his letter with thanks to Simpson for his inquiry about his eyes which were now completely recovered, he made a proposal to increase the efficiency of the accounting procedures. Salmon had been credited to the outfit in which it was shipped, rather than to the outfit in which it was caught and this had caused confusion in Montreal and Esquimaux Bay. In future, he recommended, it should be credited to the year in which it was caught.[41]

This long letter is distinguished by its coherent analysis of a wide variety of issues affecting the district. The capacity to produce such an assessment, with suggestions for improvements and ideas for solving problems, is presaged in the early part of the letter Donald wrote from Mingan in January 1845 when he surveyed the competition, and is a foretaste of later letters on the situation at Esquimaux Bay and on the company's transport system. They all stand out in the corpus of Hudson's Bay Company correspondence because they take the broader view and give evidence of strategic thinking of a sort which virtually never occurred at the trading posts, where men rarely saw beyond their own immediate horizons. A talent such as this was of great value to the company. This letter from Esquimaux Bay is the more remarkable for the reaction it prompted from George Simpson. In March, when he wrote Richard Hardisty, he passed on virtually every suggestion, from the turnips, to supplying Brownson, to changing the way in which the salmon returns were credited. He said nothing about the source of his suggestions and his silence both protected Donald and reinforced the notion that Simpson was omniscient.[42]

Having completed their last minute correspondence and fought back the tears as they said goodbye to little Tom, the Hardistys set sail for North West River and the men at Rigolet began to make their final preparations for the winter. Only a few hours after Hardisty left, however, a distraught Captain Dunn reappeared at Rigolet. Shortly after the *Marten* had departed on September 25, the wind had increased to a gale, fog had blanketed the inlet and it had begun to snow heavily. Dunn sought refuge in Tub Harbour near the mouth of Hamilton Inlet but the storm grew worse and the *Marten* began to drag at her anchor. At five the following morning, she struck a rocky island and now was slowly sinking. One of the sailors, who was drunk on his accumulated rum ration, had drowned while trying to go ashore on the twenty-eighth.

Joseph McPherson had not yet returned to North West River, and Donald immediately sent him off after Richard Hardisty while he himself hired a boat from Frederick Grove, a freeman, and headed for the wreck. He brought back the deerskins and feathers and gave orders for the rest of the cargo to be unloaded onto the island which the *Marten* had struck. Leaving Tom and Captain Dunn's son at Rigolet, he returned to supervise the work and to try to see if the ship could be salvaged. When it became apparent that hopes of saving her would have to be abandoned, Captain Dunn became so agitated that he interfered with the work which the men were desperately trying to accomplish before the ice clogged the inlet and made sailing impossibly dangerous. To relieve the tension and facilitate the work, Donald took Dunn back to Rigolet where, the following morning, the captain committed suicide in the cabin of the boat which had brought him back. "I cannot say," Hardisty reported to Simpson, "if the loss of the vessel was or was not owing to any mismanagement on the part of the Captain, but I am strongly of opinion that he believed himself to have erred in something or other, and that he did not expect that he would be able to answer satisfactorily some questions which might be put to him by any nautical man on his return to Canada." Moreover, he dreaded having to face Sir John Pelly, the company's governor in London.[43]

Added to the stress of the accident and the suicide was the fact that the *Willie* was overdue from Kibokok and until she came, there was no vessel to bring the cargo from Tub Harbour to Rigolet. The company could not afford to keep over the winter the men who were retiring and the accounts were required at Lachine as soon as possible. Donald was sent with the papers, the ship's crew and the retiring servants to Nathan Norman's station at Indian Harbour with a view to negotiating transport for the men to Newfoundland and thence to Canada. At one point, he was going to take the accounts to Lachine himself but he finally concluded that he could trust the ship's mate to do this for him. At Indian Harbour, Donald seized the opportunity to write a few lines to Simpson on the shipping requirements of the area, noting that if the *Marten* were to be replaced, the new vessel should be schooner or clipper rigged, as all Hunt and Henley's ships were. Such rigging would reduce the amount of dragging at anchor and allow the ship to be more easily worked among the "shoals and rocks with which the Labrador coast abounds." He also noted that the *Willie* was too small to do the work of the district.[44]

Having stowed away that portion of the *Marten's* cargo which they had managed to bring back to Rigolet, Donald settled into his winter routine. He had guests for Christmas, McPherson and Grant having arrived in the middle of December to get flint for trading at North West River and the inland posts. Outfit 1850 seemed set to be one of unexpected deaths, however, for in January 1851, George Lyall, the cooper at Kibokok, showed up at Rigolet with the news that William Cameron, having gone out hunting, had drowned on the eighteenth of December "while attempting to cross a bay that had but newly taken with ice." The water at that point was reported to be forty fathoms and the current was so strong that his body was never found. As Donald needed to go to North West River to fetch articles which were required for sale at Rigolet, he set out with Lyall to report the latest news to Hardisty. James Grant joined him on the return journey and then made for his temporary assignment at Kibokok.[45]

As spring came on, Simpson, Hardisty and Donald Smith turned their minds to the management of Esquimaux Bay. In the summer of 1850, Hardisty had written that the following year he intended to make formal application for furlough, the first he would have had since joining the company in 1817. He wanted to go to England in the autumn of 1852 to see about family matters, by which he meant that he had finally caved in to repeated requests from his son, Joseph, who was determined to go to Britain to study medicine when his HBC contract expired in 1852. Hardisty thought he should remain in the company's service and the combined pressure of family and Sir George Simpson ultimately did convince Joseph to renew his contract. Hardisty's other reason for an English visit was that his vision had deteriorated and he required spectacles. The question of his replacement at Esquimaux Bay needed to be settled before he could leave and, though it was obvious that Donald was the only person in the district qualified to take charge, Simpson needed to be sure that the additional responsibility would not precipitate another nervous collapse. "I have it in view," he wrote Richard Hardisty in July 1851,

> to appoint Mr. Smith to succeed you, but await letters from you before deciding on that point, not knowing whether he has had any return of a very distressing and uncomfortable complaint under which he labored at Mingan, which produced such depression of spirits as to incapacitate him for business. Let me request you will inform me frankly & confidentially your opinion of Mr. Smith's appointment and whether you are aware of any good reason for its not taking place.[46]

Donald knew that he was being considered as Hardisty's replacement, at least during the furlough year, and it is hard to imagine that he did not suspect Hardisty's motive when the question of his health was broached that summer. "In regard to the health of Mr. Smith," Hardisty wrote to Simpson,

> I am glad to say that I have not known him to be a day ill since he came to Esquimaux Bay, but thinking it possible that he might sometimes during the Winter Season while alone at this place [Rigolet] have been ill without my knowing it, I one day since receiving your letter, took the occasion of asking him without letting him know my motive in doing so, if, since his

> arrival in this quarter he had ever had a return of the illness he laboured under at Mingan. His answer was that he had not, and he said at the same time that he had never enjoyed better health in his life than he had since he came to Esquimaux Bay.[47]

Not only had Donald been physically well at Esquimaux Bay, he was also reaching a maturity which brought with it self-confidence and inner peace. At Mingan, he had been lonely, distraught at the death of his sisters, uncle and father, in pain because of the damage to his eyes and distressed because he knew in his heart that he was not measuring up to Governor Simpson's expectations. By contrast, in Labrador he had the companionship of the Hardisty family and of other clerks, his interest in his work replaced his homesickness, his eyes had healed and he was in good health, and he knew, without needing to be told by Hardisty or Simpson, that his work for the HBC was easily up to the mark.

"People speak of the solitude of Labrador," he reflected many years later. "It was n't a solitude for me. I knew everybody there, from the oldest white traders and fishermen to the youngest Indian hunters and Esquimaux, and even their dogs. I knew every turn in the coast-line and bend in the river, and every natural object had an interest for me. As for *ennui*, I can honestly say I did not know the meaning of the term."[48]

By the time Hardisty wrote Simpson, Donald was sufficiently sure of being appointed Hardisty's replacement that, in his own letter to Simpson, he requested permission to write the indents for the next outfit himself if he was to be in charge. Replacing Hardisty, however, meant a promotion and bound up in that was the availability of shares in the company's profit sharing scheme. When the HBC amalgamated with the North West Company in 1821, a Deed Poll, or contract between the senior officers and the Governor and Committee was drawn up to define duties and responsibilities, determine remuneration, establish the right to promotion, retirement and furlough, and generally regulate the relationship between the directors and the wintering partners. These latter were known as commissioned officers, of which there were two grades, chief trader and chief factor. The Hudson's Bay Company might have been English, but its personnel were primarily from Scotland where *factor* continues to be used to refer to a bailiff or land agent, managing property on behalf of its owner. The word, which also gave rise to the definition of some trading posts on the bay as factories, passed into the vocabulary of the amalgamated organization, replacing the North West Company's term *bourgeois*, though that expression continued to be used informally.

The Deed Poll of 1834, which modified the 1821 agreement, said that commissioned officers, who did not receive a salary, were entitled to forty percent of the clear gains and profits of the trade. That forty percent was divided into eighty-five equal shares. There were twenty-five chief factors, each of whom received two shares, and there were twenty-eight chief traders, each of whom received one share and one chief trader who only received a half share. The remaining shares were set aside to pay the officers' retirement interest. This provided a full share for the first year of retirement and a half share for the six succeeding years. A chief factor would consequently receive 2/85 of forty percent of the profit in his first year of retirement and 1/85 in the next six. In fact, retiring officers, generally managed to arrange a year or two of furlough, sometimes coupled with sick leave, prior to retirement, so that they had two or three years of full entitlement.

Promotion was by seniority and chief traders had to be selected from among the senior clerks, while chief factors had to come from among the senior chief traders. The Northern and Southern Departments' annual councils of commissioned officers advised on promotions but the Montreal Department, which included Labrador, had no council and it was up to George Simpson to look out for the interests of the men posted there when he attended the council meetings. However worthy a man might be, he could not hope for promotion if there was no vacancy in the grade to which he aspired. It would be unacceptable to have a district as large as Esquimaux Bay under the direction of a senior clerk, so Simpson's staffing arrangements were, in part, dependent on finding a chief trader's share for Donald Smith.

The appointment of clerks in Labrador was also to be governed by the love life of Hardisty's two eligible daughters. Mary married Joseph McPherson on the eighth of July and he was immediately posted to Kibokok to relieve James Grant. Hardisty had originally intended to send him to Fort Nascopie, but Donald objected, pointing out that the great improvements which had been seen at that post were Henry Connolly's doing and the system should not be disrupted. McPherson, he observed, was "a well meaning and good tempered young man, but far behind Mr. Connolly."[49]

Isabella, writing to her brother Richard ten days after Mary's wedding, confessed that she too was about to be married.

> I suppose I had better tell you, that there is a bit of a favourite of mine, who has really so overturned all my preconceived notions on the subject of single happiness that he has really convinced me I might be more than tolerably happy in the home he has prepared for me, so that after this month if no accident should intervene, I will have changed my name from Hardisty to Grant.[50]

Grant had turned her head and she was quite giddy when she thought of her intended, whom she described as "rather good looking, rather tall, and of a most amiable disposition." He was also rather young, only having attained his majority in May that year. He had charmed her father, who approved of his pedigree. He was a native of Montreal and his father, Charles, who had died in 1845, had been with the North West Company for many years. His grandfather, also Charles, had been a wealthy Quebec merchant and a senior partner in the North West Company. "He is of very good connexions," Hardisty reported to his son Richard the following year, "and I believe has very good expectations." James, who was a distant cousin of Donald Smith's, was sadly mistaken if he thought he was due to inherit a substantial sum from his father when he came of age. On July 28, two days before Bella's wedding, George Simpson wrote James Grant to say that his mother was seeking financial support.[51]

As Hardisty would not part with James Grant, the marriages effectively settled the disposition of staff for the winter, but Donald viewed the arrangements with a somewhat jaundiced eye. He felt that personal matters had taken precedence over the requirements of the company's business and that because "I alone, of the Company's officers in this quarter am left to represent the unblest," he was also alone in having to manage the lion's share of the work. He had matured since his days at Mingan, when he had suggested that a trading post was no place for women and the consequences of marital life; he had a real affection for the ebullient little Charlotte Hardisty and an unexpressed respect for the spunky Isabella, but there were no women in his life and he resented the fact that consideration of and for the Hardisty women seemed to get in the way of the efficient management of the business. He found it particularly galling that their interests led Hardisty to turn his back on the competition from Nathan Norman.

> While we are spending the honeymoon, projecting new & comfortable dwelling houses and capacious stores or it may be even building castles in the air, and coaxing ourselves with the belief of the great returns we are to make by & bye, [Norman] seizes time by the forelock, makes a trip to the north of Kibokok & returns to Indian Harbour with a goodly cargo collected from all & sundry.

Part of Norman's success derived from the respect which the planters accorded him in his role as a Justice of the Peace. Donald suggested to Simpson that the senior HBC officer should also be a JP and that, if the rumours that there was to be a customs collector on the coast were true, the company should try to secure that post as well. The Lloyd's agency could be helpful too, "in short, anything which might make us appear greater folks than our neighbors."[52]

In July, Donald complained to Simpson that Hardisty was not conversant with the way business was conducted on the coast and, when Brownson came into Rigolet, could not bring himself to speak to him about doing business with the HBC. "Even at the risk of appearing presumptuous, I must express my belief that my worthy Bourgeois, towards whom, as a private individual, I bear much esteem, is far better adapted to a quiet inland post than for the business of this quarter, which demands from a superintendent an amount of energy of which he is not possessed."[53]

Simpson was aware of how much more capable Donald was in the context of a competitive district like Esquimaux Bay and recommended that Hardisty consult him in all matters. This was an unheard of proposal from the head of an organization as hierarchical as the Hudson's Bay Company, but the chief trader had a good deal of respect for the younger man whom he saw as a worthy successor and said he was happy to comply. A cardinal principle of Hardisty's managerial technique was to avoid confrontation with either his superiors or the competition, and Donald hoped that Simpson would indeed appoint him to the charge of the district in Hardisty's absence so that he could grapple directly with the problems instead of being held back by the weaknesses of a senior officer.[54]

When the *Independence*, which had been chartered in place of the *Marten*, left at the end of September, taking Tom Hardisty to school and the returns to Canada, the men once more settled into their winter routines, hoping that the furs would be plentiful and their own lives peaceful. The hopes were short lived for the winter brought sorrow to the Hardistys and to all who had come to know the family. In February, just three months after her seventh birthday, Charlotte developed a pain in her side. With no doctor for hundreds of miles, the Hudson's Bay Company men and their wives were reliant on folk remedies and patent medicines at times like this. Castor oil was administered. Charlotte seemed to rally and when she declared that she wanted to go to the woods, she was allowed to do so. There, however, she got her feet wet and developed a cold and then a fever. She died at eleven o'clock on the night of February 27. The Hardistys were remarkably lucky to lose only one of their offspring in childhood, but this was little consolation to them now. For Donald, the news brought back memories of his own losses, but he also grieved for the little girl of whom he had become so fond. His next indent included flower seeds to plant on her grave at North West River.[55]

At the end of March 1852, George Simpson sat down at his desk to give orders for future arrangements at Esquimaux Bay. Richard Hardisty's leave of absence had been granted and Donald Smith was to replace him. In a letter to both men on the management of the district, Simpson advised that they grow more vegetables at North West River and also plant barley and oats. Taking up Donald's comments on the clustering of staff at the head of the inlet, he instructed that the men be spread throughout the district in order to keep an eye on the Indians and to ensure tougher competition for Brownson and Nathan Norman. Finally, he revealed that Donald's promotion to chief trader had come through and he was working on having him made a justice of the peace for Newfoundland and a Lloyd's agent. Nothing in the letter suggested that any of these changes might have been Donald's ideas in the first place.

To Donald, he offered congratulations on his promotion, but undercut the good wishes with a reminder that he did not expect a repetition of the chaos he found at Mingan. Simpson had no way of knowing how much of the Esquimaux Bay management was actually done by Donald, rather than Hardisty, and did not want to find himself disappointed in a year's time when the accounts were due.

In a friendly manner, he put the young man on his guard against a repetition of the "want of method and punctuality in your household arrangements, as well as the shipping office business," but then acknowledged that, in his official letter to Hardisty, he had accepted Donald's recommendations. He also agreed that McPherson's management at Kibokok had been weak. "A little more energy is required in the direction of the Company's affairs which I trust we shall witness under your administration."[56]

The same letter also explained to Donald that as a commissioned officer and therefore, in effect, a shareholder in the company, he was not entitled to draw on the fur trade account. From the beginning of Outfit 1852, he would no longer be receiving a salary and could not, therefore, ask the company to debit it with sums sent to his mother or used for services such as watch repairs. He could, however, sign a power of attorney which would allow Simpson to draw on his funds and act as his financial agent.

He could equally have given control to a senior staff man in London. Richard Hardisty had done this and, in his day, this was the common procedure. The younger men, however, had taken to signing over their funds to George Simpson because he had realized that Canadian investments were making substantially higher returns than the British ones which the company arranged. These Private Cash Accounts were quite distinct from official HBC business and were not meant to be managed on company time. In fact, of course, they were. Donald's first investment, made on his behalf by George Simpson, was two shares in the Bank of Montreal. Virtually everyone who had money in Private Cash had Bank of Montreal shares because they consistently paid a good dividend.

The summer of 1852 was a busy one as the Hardistys prepared to leave the district. Simpson had said that Hardisty was to complete the accounts for Outfit 1851, but that he could take the Hunt and Henley ship from Sandwich directly to England if he wished to do so. Hardisty declined the offer for several reasons. He wanted to settle Margaret in Lachine for the winter and to use that opportunity to see young Thomas. He also wanted an excuse to stay in North West River for as long as possible because both Mary and Bella had become pregnant very shortly after their weddings. The correspondence is all but silent on Mary's circumstances but either she miscarried or her baby was stillborn. Bella was more fortunate, giving birth to a healthy boy on the twenty-fourth of June 1852.

Donald spent much of the summer on the move: he was in Sandwich at the end of June to collect the shipment from England, and in North West River on the eighth of July when Hardisty officially handed over the responsibility for Esquimaux Bay. Thereafter, Donald would be based at headquarters at North West River and James Grant would winter at Rigolet. At the end of July, Donald returned to Rigolet where the *Independence* arrived on the twenty-fourth of August. In September, Richard and Margaret Hardisty, with all their possessions, appeared and Mary came from Kibokok to see them off. On Sunday the eighteenth the family gathered together as Donald christened Isabella's baby, naming him James after his father. His grandparents were his sponsors.

The shipping season was the busiest time of the year but it was also the jolliest, with news and gossip, dancing and parties to keep everyone in good spirits. The planters and the Inuit clustered around Rigolet to trade their salmon and seal oil and to catch up on the news of friends and relatives.

> There are varied out-of-door sports, and feasting on seal meat, young dog-meat, and salmon, smoked, boiled, baked and roasted. At night in the servants' room are uncouth dances and strange music — dances by the dim light of burning seal-oil and deer's tallow candles, energetic and fantastic — a strange commingling of dusky shadows that flit athwart the walls and ceiling and through the veiling smoke — a ceaseless thump and twirl, a Babel of tongues, and a suffocating permeation of perspiration and combined nameless stenches. There are no invitations to dance. Each one pulls his partner to the floor, willy nilly, *vi et armis*.[57]

The officers' pleasures may have been somewhat more subdued, especially in the autumn of 1852 with the imminent departure of Richard and Margaret Hardisty, but both Hardisty and Joseph McPherson had accordions and McPherson also had a flute. Dancing and singing formed part of their social life too.

On the Thursday and Friday before the *Independence* sailed, Donald finally made time for his correspondence. He sent George Simpson a letter which he had written the previous October in hopes of directing it to him via England. It drew attention to problems with Captain John Hoffman and the *Independence*. Hoffman had proved to be less than honest: he said his vessel could carry 700 barrels whereas she could only manage 613; he said she could carry six passengers with ease but there was scarcely room for one; the ship was thought to be inadequately manned and, far worse, Hoffman had been trading with the Indians at North West River. Captains who were prepared to charter for the Labrador coast were not easily found, however, and the *Independence* continued to be employed.[58]

In his official letter to Simpson, Donald explained that he had indented for fewer provisions because he wanted to encourage the officers to cultivate the gardens. The men at North West River ate scarcely any vegetables and had suffered from scurvy which prevented them from working through the spring and summer. He had asked Archibald Barclay, the secretary in London, to send seed potatoes and lime juice in case the carnivores suffered again in the spring. Other aspects of the indent such as children's clothes and a gold ring were likely to cause comment because such things had not been requested before but, Donald assured the governor, there were specific markets for these items. "Everything of this kind has been asked for by parties able to pay for them who if not accommodated in this way by us will naturally be led to seek them at Sandwich where, as the agent annually visits England, they have no difficulty in procuring them."

Donald had already seen both Brownson and Nathan Norman with a view to encouraging them to secure their supplies from the HBC. Norman had declined but Brownson had agreed to restrict his sales to two or three planters and half a dozen Inuit families. His *quid pro quo* was an annual payment of £50, two-thirds of which was to be in goods. In addition to the familiar request for a Roman Catholic missionary, Donald's letter also noted that he expected to divide his time between Rigolet and North West River. The new broom was already well at work.[59]

In his private letter, written the following day, the new chief trader acknowledged the admonition which Simpson had made with his references to Mingan, but he was so full of self-confidence and sure of his way forward that he left very little doubt about his capacity to manage Esquimaux Bay efficiently and effectively.[60]

The *Independence* sailed on Sunday, September 25 but Donald remained at Rigolet, dealing with details which inevitably cropped up after the ship had gone. The Hunt and Henley vessels generally left later and both they and Nathan Norman, who would return to Newfoundland for the winter, offered an opportunity for last minute correspondence. In 1852, Donald seized it to discuss transport arrangements with which he was dissatisfied, describing the *Charlotte*, the district's own boat, as "an overgrown whale boat not carvel but clinker built and that of green unseasoned wood."[61]

He was determined to take seriously his new role as a justice of the peace, but he embellished the truth when he observed that he was "an old Justice of the Peace clerk, having acted in that capacity for some time while studying law in Scotland in which study I spent two or three years to very little purpose." Luckily, the Forres town clerk was not at hand to contradict him! Nonetheless, he was committed to doing what was expected of him and asked for a treatise on his duties if such a thing existed. He also asked for the Newfoundland newspapers, for which he was prepared to pay, in order that he keep up to date with the colony's legal matters. He was already subscribing to one of the Montreal newspapers which, in yet another example of his efforts to keep on good terms with the opposition while fighting them, he lent to Mr. Brownson who was very interested in politics, an interest which Donald declared he did not share.[62]

This October letter also, though unintentionally, revealed where Donald's personal interests were beginning to be directed.

> You may perhaps not be aware that Mr. James Grant is a distant relation of mine, a Scotch cousin, I believe, a circumstance which, taken together with his being connected by marriage to Mr. Joseph E. McPherson, whose wife and Mrs. Grant are, as you are aware sisters, might render it quite as satisfactory to me were he transferred to another District, but so much has Esquimaux Bay suffered from the many changes which have taken place amongst its officers during the last ten or dozen years, that I cannot for a moment think of recommending it. He has 'tis true much to learn before becoming an experienced trader, his long residence at North West River having been anything but advantageous to him, as while there he had but little or nothing to do with the trade, and literally got no insight into the manner of keeping accounts which, beyond a Blotter or an Invoice he was rarely, if ever permitted to see. With his conduct however I am fully satisfied, as he is willing and anxious to learn he will soon be efficient.[63]

The implication that personal ties might make discipline difficult was not the only reason Donald would have been glad to see Grant posted elsewhere. He carried on to tell Simpson that he regretted Grant had "been persuaded" to marry when he was still so young. In fact, James Grant had not needed any persuasion. He had conducted his courtship with determination, quite unprompted by anyone, and certainly not urged on by Isabella's father wanting to see his daughter settled before his departure. Grant had ordered the young lady's signet ring before her father had applied for his furlough and he had married her nine months before his new father-in-law's leave was approved.

It is true that Grant was young and had married in defiance of the wishes of his relatives but Bella, who was five years older and had a wider experience of the world, had been swept her off her feet by Grant's good looks and charm and she had mistaken her infatuation for love. Bereft of her parents and with the responsibilities of a small baby, she had discovered that, at least from her point of view, the relationship with James Grant was superficial.

"It is just possible," Donald wrote by way of justifying his comments about Grant, that "these remarks might lead to the supposition that I myself have been an unsuccessful suitor, but the case is as far otherwise that up to the present time, I have not been so presumptuous as to aspire to the hand of any fair lady.[64]

Nothing in Donald's letter implied he had any personal interest in Bella — until he denied it, unwittingly revealing what he thought he was hiding. He had not been "an unsuccessful suitor," but now that her marriage was disintegrating, he could see that she needed tenderness and consideration and he wanted to provide it. If Grant left the district and took his wife with him, that temptation would be out of the way.

CHAPTER FOUR

CHIEF TRADER 1852-1861

A man who has been frozen and roasted by turns every year must be the tougher for it, if he survive it at all.
Lord Strathcona[1]

After the departure of the *Independence*, Donald spent a month at Rigolet in his new capacity as chief trader, attending to business at the post and in the neighbourhood and ensuring that James Grant was settled for the winter. When he returned to North West River on the twenty-eighth of October, his fellow passengers were Mary McPherson and Isabella Grant. Isabella had left most of her things at North West River, perhaps because there was not room enough for them in the boat which had also been required to carry her parents' possessions. The sisters provided companionship for each other and acted as each other's chaperone. The journey had the blessing of both young husbands, who appeared at North West River at the end of February to claim their wives. Mary went back to Kibokok but Bella declined to travel because her baby, Jamesie, was unwell and she was not willing to expose him to the stormy winter weather. The fact that she was enjoying her stay at North West River made it easier to take such a protective attitude to her child's health. "Oh my dear brother," she wrote to Richard eight months later, "you can have no idea how happy and comfortable we were. Mr. Smith was so very kind to us, had we been his own sisters he could not possibly have done more for us than he did, we can never be sufficiently thankful and grateful to him."[2]

Only one incident marred their happiness. Early in May, when the ice was beginning to melt, Donald took Bella and Jamesie for a ride in a komatik. The dog sled struck a patch of thin ice and went through, immersing them all in the water. In saving his passengers, Donald lost control of the komatik which struck him on the left side, breaking two or three of his ribs, according to Bella, though Donald's own account suggests only that he was badly bruised. Whatever the damage, he seems not to have wanted for nursing.[3]

In June, Bella returned to her husband at Rigolet. The population of Labrador may have been sparse, but it had its fair share of gossips and the fact that Bella had remained at North West River, living in Donald Smith's house, caused many tongues to wag. James Grant was greatly upset and felt none too warmly towards the cause of his embarrassment. Her sister later explained that "Mr. Grant did not at all act towards her as he should have done but treated her very badly so that she says it was impossible for her to live with him any longer." Bella herself reported to her brother Richard that she "found it impossible to live in any degree of comfort or happiness with him so we have mutually agreed to separate and live apart from each other."[4]

Perhaps Donald came closer to the mark when, in his private letter to George Simpson, he remarked that Grant's "marriage with Mr. Hardisty's daughter was unfortunate, as it has not been their lot to have even one day of comparative happiness since they have lived together, it seems impossible for them to live in peace. On this account she, at his request, spent the last winter at North West River, and he has again favoured a similar request to me this season. Unfortunately he has no command over his temper or passions, and perhaps her temper, but of this I have seen nothing, may be none of the most dulcet." James Grant's temper and passions were not the only factor in the separation. As Bella must have known when she went to Rigolet in June, and as Donald, and perhaps Grant, would have known by October, she was pregnant with Donald's child. Margaret Charlotte Smith was born on January 17, 1854.[5]

Bella was adamant that she would have nothing further to do with James Grant. "You can have no idea my dear brother," she wrote to Richard before returning to North West River that autumn, "what a good worthy excellent man Mr. Smith is, he was so fond of our poor dear lamented little sister Charlotte, he sowed some flower seeds all over her poor little grave some of them came up so nicely and it gave the little grave such a pretty appearance, a Headstone has come down from Canada this summer for our poor little sister's grave, and Mr. Smith intends having it put up as soon as possible after our arrival at North West River."[6]

Richard and his father were shocked at Bella's behaviour and insisted that she go back to her husband, but she would have none of it. "Nothing will ever make me return to him again," she declared. "It is impossible for you, or any other person who does not know how shamefully he has acted, to believe that anything in the shape of man could ever have allowed himself [to] act as he has done." As she was fully aware, she was not without blame herself, but her surviving letters make no mention of her second pregnancy and only gradually introduce references to little Maggie, making it hard for their recipients to gauge her age and therefore when she might have been born.[7]

Despite his emotional entanglements, Donald still had a business to run. He spent much of Outfit 1852 concentrating on raising the standard of living throughout the district and hoped that in doing so at Fort Nascopie where Henry Connolly was stationed, it might be possible for it to cease being regarded as a hardship post. Much of his effort went towards improving diet throughout the district, an interest which was becoming of increasing importance to him, in part because of the saving it allowed, in part because it increased the health of the people in the district and in part because he enjoyed the challenge of food production in a climate thought to be inimical to such activities. Gardens were cultivated at several posts, he reported to George Simpson in October 1853.

> A considerable quantity of both potatoes & turnips has been grown, indeed notwithstanding the unprecedented heat and dryness of the season, the result has been so satisfactory as to induce the hope that next year a sufficiency of both will be produced for the use of the people in the service. I may add that from the abundance of provisions received from Indians & other sources at a very trifling expense, not one pound of pork or other imported provisions save flour and the ordinary allowance of rice etc. was used at the mess table at North West River from October 1852, until September of the present year, and so much venison and other fresh meat was supplied to the men towards spring as to make them heartily regret the want of the salt meat, pork, of which from long use, they had become so fond. The result of this diet is found not alone in the smaller expenditure of pork and flour, but in the improved health of the men, not one case of scurvy having recurred amongst them, the past being the only spring for several years back in which some of them have not been incapacitated for duty from its attacks.[8]

He was so pleased with the first results of his efforts that he declared the condition of the HBC staff at Esquimaux Bay to be "much superior to that of residents on the Labrador in general and greatly in advance of what was the state of similar classes in England and Scotland some years since." It was particularly satisfying to be able to make such a report because in the summer he had received a letter from Governor Simpson advocating the course of action which he had already followed. "The comfort of the Company's servants, especially in respect to food," Simpson had noted, "depends much on the Gentlemen who have charge of Districts — when they are energetic & careful to improve to the utmost the resources at their command, the men fare well but when they are careless in that respect the reverse is invariably the case. I regard this as a better test of good management than the collection of furs, which fluctuate from causes beyond human control." In fact, the fur returns were down that year, so Donald found it especially satisfying to be able to report that he had passed the good management test with flying colours.[9]

Simpson had also eased his controls on what Donald was to do with his returns. Esquimaux Bay was beginning to produce more fish and seal oil than the *Independence* could hold and Donald was now permitted to make his own decision about whether he shipped everything to Canada, sent some items directly to England via Hunt and Henley's vessels or, as the least satisfactory option, sold it in Esquimaux Bay.

In the early months of 1854, Donald visited the Moravian missions on the northern coast of Labrador. He wanted to judge for himself the vigour with which the missionaries pursued their trading activities and to determine the benefits of providing some active competition. He said nothing about this when he arrived at Hopedale, half way up the Labrador coast, at the beginning of May, and in any event, there was no one to assign to such a post were he authorized to proceed. He did, however, discuss his desire for a resident missionary at Hamilton Inlet and invited the Moravians to visit him and assess the possibility of working in the area. In the face of George Simpson's annual refusal of his request for a Roman Catholic priest, Donald was exploring the possibility of a non-conformist alternative.

The journey to the north got off to a bad start when Donald failed to keep his rendezvous with Joseph McPherson, probably because he was caught in a blizzard. It was about that time that Lydia Campbell, who had briefly worked as a cook at Rigolet, and her daughter Margaret were roused from their beds towards eleven o'clock at night in the midst of a prolonged and heavy snow fall. Lydia's mother was an Inuit who had been rejected by her people when she was orphaned and, through her, her children and grandchildren had learned to fear the Naskapi, as all Inuit did.

Many years later, Margaret still remembered her fear that night.

> We woke up with a start, someone was knocking at the corner of our bedroom with an axe. I was afraid for I thought it was Indians. Mother called Susan [a daughter by Lydia's first marriage, who had gone to North West River as a child minder for Jamesie when Maggie was born] to light the lamp. She said, "Who can it be?" She thought of some starving person who had lost their way. She opened the door and in came a tall man, his coat was white with snow. Even his eyebrows and his whiskers were white. Mother asked him who he was. He said, "Mr. Smith." She helped him take off his coat and he sat in a chair. Tom [a son by the first marriage] took off his shoes and leggings. Susan got the tea ready, but he was too tired to eat. Mother asked him if he had come alone. He said that his Eskimo guide got behind; he left him a long way back. It had taken him a long time to get through the snow.[10]

The women's failure to recognize their visitor reveals how bad the storm was for the family knew Donald Smith; only that evening, Lydia Campbell had been reading a book which he had given her. In her account of the incident, Margaret says he was on his way to Rigolet with the mail but that is not likely. The preferred winter route from North West River to Kibokok was to follow Hamilton Inlet to Mulligan Bay, where the Campbells lived, before striking inland, thus avoiding Rigolet.[11]

At Kibokok, Donald instructed Joseph McPherson to re-establish the trading shop at Aillik, a seal fishing station at the mouth of Kaipokok Bay. George Simpson had earlier expressed misgivings about the management of Kibokok and the supervision of the little shop could indicate whether McPherson would be capable of handling the additional responsibility of supervising staff at an outpost.

While Donald was visiting the post, Simpson was writing him to reiterate his concerns about McPherson's management, particularly with reference to the prolonged detention of the *Independence* there and at Rigolet. "If the officer in charge there is so incapable or indolent as to be unable to get through the shipping business with more system & expedition than last year, it may be advisable for you to go to Kibokok in the schooner for the purpose of personally superintending the shipping arrangements." He also suggested a visit to the Moravian missions before establishing a Kibokok outpost, and Donald was pleased to discover that once again he was ahead of the governor.[12]

Simpson was also worried by the fact that the district had scarcely covered its costs in the previous year and thought that it could do better by improving its salmon returns. The fish was fetching good prices in Montreal and a new fisheries treaty with the United States would allow the export of fresh salmon from Labrador to the American market.

The winter of 1853-1854 started a month earlier than usual and was characterized by intense cold. The seal nets at Rigolet had to be brought in before a single creature was caught and for much of the winter, it was too cold for men to leave their houses. "So intense was the cold from the beginning of November until the end of February," Donald reported to Archibald Barclay in London, "the thermometer very rarely being above 40 and not infrequently falling to upwards of 50 degrees below zero, that the hunters found it impracticable to attend to their fur traps." As often happened in Labrador, however, the mice flourished, gorging themselves on the bait in the traps.[13]

The summer mails from England also brought censure from the Governor and Committee who, through Barclay, observed that "it is not creditable to your business habits to be so little acquainted with the contents of the packets forwarded by the Committee." Donald had asked for a priced catalogue for recent fur auctions and the Committee acidly observed that failure to do well in the fur trade could not be attributed to lack of catalogues. Donald had never been subservient in the face of such criticisms and was not so now. Richard Hardisty, he observed in his reply, had considered the priced catalogues to be private property and kept them to himself. The first Donald had ever received was sent in the same packet which contained the reprimand.[14]

His letter, which also contained the details of a petty squabble with Brownson and Hunt and Henley, was copied to Simpson who, in the spring, was at pains to point out that this was not the way to deal with the Governor and Committee. In a paternal tone, Simpson observed that a concise letter would satisfy London more "as neither the Secretary nor the Board have time to peruse a long argumentative letter such as yours." He also noted, again without rancour, that the report on the trade should be sent to himself and should be brief and to the point, "without flourish or circumlocution. When you want to bring a point strongly under notice it will have a better chance by putting it in a few clear and appropriate words than by opening out the theme so as to make it *look* important by the space it occupies on paper." Donald's letter had been unusually sloppy, and, though neither Simpson nor the board perceived this, it was indicative of his emotional turmoil.

He had written a private letter on October 28 in which he offered his views on the officers and the staffing arrangements which would work best in the district. It seems not to have survived, but in all likelihood it contained praise for Henry Connolly at Fort Nascopie and proposals for bettering transport arrangements and the fishing business in order to improve McPherson's returns. From Simpson's response to the letter, it is also clear that it drew attention to problems with James Grant, about whom the governor had been hearing from other quarters. In December, Simpson returned a cheque for £10, which Grant had sent to his brother Frederick in New York, because there were not sufficient funds in his HBC account to cover it. The company had a very low regard for men who could not manage their own finances, feeling that they would be liable to mismanage the company's as well.

Simpson had also heard from Richard Hardisty, who had been posted to Weymontachingue in the Southern Department at the end of his furlough. James Grant, it seemed, was spreading malicious stories about his father-in-law. Simpson had not heard these at first hand, but noted in his reply to Richard Hardisty that he would not "have attached any importance to them coming from that quarter, as I regret to say I have been under the necessity of ordering him up here next Autumn for the purpose of being discharged from the service for misconduct." Hardisty was sufficiently upset by what Grant had been saying and by Bella's leaving her husband that he had asked Simpson to authorize a passage for her on the *Independence* when it left Rigolet in the autumn; the governor agreed.[15]

In his letter to Donald Smith, Simpson presented the matter in a somewhat different light, saying that he did not think it right that Grant should remain in Esquimaux Bay and instructing Donald to send him to Canada on the *Independence* in the fall. "On his arrival here I shall consider whether he shall be discharged the service or otherwise disposed of. After he leaves we cannot keep his wife & children (if he has any) at the Company's posts. The lady, if she cannot live with her husband, must return to her father's protection. At all events the Company cannot be saddled with her maintenance."[16]

Neither Bella nor her husband were pleased with this news and both found ways of dealing with it. Bella simply declined to leave the district while Grant became petulant and ill tempered, saying he would not travel in the *Independence* and declaring that he would take his departure in the manner he thought fit. In some respects, he had reason on his side for, on September 4, the *Independence* was wrecked close to the point where the *Marten* went down; two men died in the accident. While the labourers did what they could to rescue the cargo, which had been on its way down from Kibokok, Captain Hoffman purchased another vessel; Grant took one look at it and refused to board, preferring to spend his own money to obtain a passage in the *Charlotte* to Newfoundland and from there to buy a place in a steamer to Montreal. In fact, he obtained passage in a ship going to New York and went there instead to see his mother who was ill. Late in December, he finally made his appearance at Lachine where he wrote a letter of resignation, explaining that he thought he was better suited to employment in the civilized world. Needless to say, Simpson accepted it.[17]

Reporting the encounter to Donald Smith, Simpson agreed that he was, "as you say, a weak young man on which account I am unwilling to credit all he said here in connexion with his own case, but on one point he appears firm which is to have nothing more to say to his wife." Simpson had already made up his mind about James Grant and did not intend to change it. He had also made up his mind about Isabella. "I agree with you that it appears strange she should be living with you at North West River when she has a sister in the district, with whom she might more desirously have taken up her quarters & prevented scandal," Simpson wrote, not suspecting that the arrangement was anything more than a matter of accommodation and certainly unaware of the fact that Mary and her son, Richard, who was born late in 1853, had spent much of the winter of 1855 living with Donald and Bella at North West River. Simpson repeated his instruction that Bella was to be sent to her father.[18]

Mary had reason to be glad that Bella chose to defy both her father and George Simpson and remain in North West River for in March 1856 she gave birth prematurely to another child which was either stillborn or died at birth. Were this not sorrow enough, the Esquimaux Bay gossips soon spread hurtful stories about the circumstances of the child's death. In a letter of condolence, Bella urged her to pay no attention to what was said.

> They can do you no harm by their dirty lies, how fortunate you are in having so good and kind a husband as Mr. McPherson how differently Mr. Grant would have acted under the same circumstances, don't you fancy because I say this that I think like that dirty crazy old Mrs. Thomas, how often do women have children at 7 months, John Miles for instance he was a 7 months child, and see what a fine smart fellow he is to[o].
>
> Never mind my dear Mary what they say, we know who are the fathers of our children look what was said and is still said about my poor unfortunate little Maggy, how I did suffer, and I used to feel oh so very miserable about it, but now I dont care one snap say what they like.[19]

Joseph had travelled overland to bring news of the baby's death, but as soon as the ice melted, Bella set out for Kibokok and spent two months there helping and comforting her sister.[20]

In the meantime, the men at Esquimaux Bay were having to deal with the consequences of the loss of the *Independence*. The insurance only covered the company's goods with the result that, for items ordered for Donald Smith and his family, there was no recompense. The unfortunate Peter Bell, who had been sent to replace James Grant, lost all his clothes and other possessions and, as he was already in debt to the company, could not afford to replace them.[21]

More widespread than these individual losses was the shortage of imported provisions on which the district depended. By the time Simpson heard of the shipwreck, it was too late to send replacements from Canada or to arrange for goods to be forwarded from New York. Donald negotiated for salt, molasses and flour from Hunt and Henley, but otherwise the men and their families had to manage as best they could. By the summer of 1856, everything was in short supply; the New York ship with flour and molasses was not due till early July, forcing Donald to negotiate with Hunt and Henley for three hundred pounds of biscuit, the salt-free, dried hardtack which provided the staple food and a flour substitute for the British army and navy and for people in out of the way places such as Hudson's Bay Company trading posts. Writing to London in June 1856, Donald noted that "notwithstanding the scarcity of fresh provisions such as has not been experienced in this quarter within the recollection of any person with whom I have conversed, we have succeeded in effecting a more than usually good trade.... I am further happy to say that the health of the men has generally been excellent, and that they have throughout shown the best disposition, taking in good part the privations which, but for the loss of our supply of Provisions, they knew they would not have had to suffer."[22]

The situation in the summer of 1856 was exacerbated by the late arrival of supplies from England and Canada and by the fact that items were missing from both the North American and the English shipments, though Donald was pleased with the quality of the flour when it finally did arrive. Two other problems marred the summer. The first was that illness, probably influenza which was prevalent throughout much of Labrador in the 1850s, attacked the canoe crew which was to take Henry Connolly's supplies to Fort Nascopie. One man died and the others were so weak that extra men had to accompany them for support. When Donald set out for Rigolet on September 12, there was no one to leave in charge at North West River. En route, he encountered the *Elzear* which had finally arrived with the Canadian goods. She got into the river with no difficulty but ran aground coming out of North West River in the dark. Captain David Irvine, the HBC skipper, who was married to Lydia Campbell's daughter, Susan, had been taken on board as pilot, but he spoke no French and a misunderstanding quickly ensued. It took eight days to free and repair the schooner.[23]

Despite these annoyances, life at North West River was beginning to take on a settled, domestic quality. Financially, Donald was doing well: Simpson was continuing to buy Bank of Montreal shares for him and had diversified his investment portfolio by buying Bank of Commerce shares; both banks were expected to pay eight per cent. This meant that he had no difficulties in contributing to the support of his mother and Jane, who had moved back to Forres in 1855, and he could provide for Bella and her two children without making undue strains on his pocket book.

Although his personal life was the subject of some tittle tattle, Donald conducted it with absolute propriety and in the manner which was deemed appropriate for the head of the district. His home was the centre of such formal entertainment as might be found at Esquimaux Bay and Bella was his hostess on those occasions. In true Scottish fashion, hogmanay was always observed. When she was twelve, Lydia Campbell's daughter, Margaret, was taken from her home at Mulligan to North West River for her first New Year's celebrations at the Smith house.

> Mrs. Smith sent for (us to go to) their kitchen where her girl was cooking. So (we went) through with our tea. She sent for us for we were the first womenkind that she had seen that winter. (Father) went out in the men's kitchen. Nearly all the men were out in the shop buying new caps and white shirts with pretty patterns, some with small stripes with little flowers running up it and others were getting black silk hankerchiefs [sic] to wear under their shirt collars. That night every one stayed up until 12 o'clock, waiting for the New Year. Just as the clock was striking the hour of 12, all the men went out with their guns. And then there was great firing, bell ringing and dogs howling. Mr. Smith was standing at his door with a bottle of rum in one hand and shaking hands with the other. When he had given them all a glass they came in and went to bed. We went out in the other kitchen to bed.[24]

People travelled with their bedding throughout Labrador in order to be able to spend the night outdoors or at whatever home they happened to reach at the appropriate hour. As a rule, they adopted the Naskapi practice and carried a sleeping bag made from animal skins with the fur turned inwards. A flap at the top protected the heads and faces of those obliged to sleep outdoors in winter. Food, however, was generally offered by the home at which the traveller happened to find himself, and at North West River, preparations for the New Year's festivities had clearly been under way for some days.

> The next morning, when we were ready, we went out in the kitchen to have our breakfast. We had chocolate, fresh milk, plum cake, potatoes and salmon. At 11 o'clock Mr. Smith sent for all hands. The men had been cleaning up, washing and dressing. Captain Irvin[e] went first, then T. Baikie, then William Spence, then all the rest and then all of us. Old Mr. Goudie and his sons were also there. There were chairs all around the house. Mr. Smith was standing at the table, and on the table were two decanters, one of wine and the other of rum and all around were wine glasses. There were three different kinds of cake, one sort was all shining with white icing and candies. There was a dish of raisins and one of candies. Mr. Smith handed a glass of rum or wine to each man and as the last man took his, they all wished him a very happy New Year. Then they all sat back on their chairs. Mrs. Smith went around with the cakes, James with the raisins and little Maggie with the candies. Thomas Baikie [the Scot whom Margaret Campbell was later to marry] asked Maggie to come to him. She went across but she couldn't look up, her face was red. She sat on his knee. She thought so much of him. When the weather was fine she would sit on his shoulder with her arm around his neck. He used to carry her down the bank and back again. She called him her horse.[25]

If the chief trader's house was the heart of much of the district's social and business life, it was also the medical centre for the region, though medicine was primitive indeed. With a mixture of common sense, folk remedies, patent medicines and occasional supplies of more sophisticated drugs, Donald and Bella did the best they could for those who applied to them for help. *Family Medicine*, a popular treatise of the period, and a *Materia Medica* were on the bookshelves at North West River and were regularly consulted. Margaret Campbell had not been well that autumn and, before she returned to Mulligan, "Father and I went to see Mr. Smith about my side. He took out his watch and took hold of my hand. Then he looked at my tongue. He said he would give me something that would make we well in a short time. I was very glad to think I would be well again. He spoke so kind and low."[26]

On another occasion, Thomas Baikie cut his foot badly while chopping logs "and Mrs. Smith sewed it up," his widow, Margaret, recalled in her reminiscences. "Then Thomas had to stop in bed for a while. Maggie and her brother, James, would carry him in a little kettle of chocolate, milk and cakes. Sometimes Maggie would give him candies, always asking if his foot was getting well."[27]

In April 1857, Brother Elsner of the Moravian mission at Hopedale finally paid his promised return visit to Esquimaux Bay. He travelled to Kibokok where he was joined by Joseph McPherson for the overland journey to North West River. A komatik with dog food went on ahead the day before, and on the morning of April 14, Elsner and McPherson set out at daybreak, accompanied by their drivers and an Indian named Louis. Spring was beginning to creep into southern Labrador, and they found that they frequently broke through the crust of snow, making every step twice as difficult and twice as tiring. It was Elsner's first such journey, and he breathlessly reported it to his English funders.

> Travelling through the forest, with a sledge and dogs, requires exertions, which none can understand but those who have made the experiment. In going down hill, the fore part of the sledge often penetrates the snow deeply, and must be dragged out by main force, if possible, before the dogs stop. Sometimes the team of dogs is divided into two parts, by a tree standing directly in their way [at which point his editor felt obliged to remind his readers that "every dog has a separate thong — a team of dogs in full speed having, consequently, something of a fan-like appearance"]; and, in this case, one part of the dogs must be dragged back, which is always a difficult matter, as a retrograde movement is quite contrary to the nature of these animals. Sometimes the sledge runs right against a tree, it being impossible, in the deep snow, to make a sudden turn, and the sledge is caught and wedged fast between the runners; the dogs pull with all their power, yet the sledge must be dragged back and turned. While engaged at this work, one sinks up to the arms in the snow, the dogs at last get the sledge away, and leave the traveller and driver half buried in the chilly mass. The latter must overtake the sledge as well as they can, and are pretty sure not to do so, till some new obstacle renders a repetition of their former exertions necessary.[28]

They spent the night, as Donald, McPherson and the other HBC men and planters must often have done, in a hollow scooped out of the snow, floored and roofed with overlapping fir or pine branches. Dinner was tea, bread and cold meat because they were too tired to prepare anything else. They rose at two o'clock the following morning and were on their way at five, but severe sunburn and a fever incapacitated Elsner and he was glad when they finally came to a halt at five that evening. When the men woke on the morning of the sixteenth, they found that the snow had frozen again overnight and they set out on snowshoes. Soon, however, it warmed to the point that they sank to their arms in snow and at four in the afternoon, it began to rain. Labrador was reaching that point when travel is impossible, it being neither cold enough for snowshoes and komatiks nor warm enough for sailing boats, kayaks and canoes. The dogs were unharnessed and the men, drenched to the skin, dragged the komatiks behind them. Happily, Hamilton Inlet was still frozen and they were able to use the komatiks again the following day. At noon they reached the home of a settler whom Elsner describes as David Campbell — almost certainly Daniel Campbell, who had taken his daughter Margaret to celebrate New Year's at North West River four months earlier.

Finally, at half past ten, the travellers were welcomed at the Smith house. "I suppose I must have looked very odd in my seal-skin clothes," Brother Elsner reported, "as a fine new, black cloth suit was brought to me, with the request that I would wear it, as long as I was here." Oddness was not the issue; the comfort of Donald's guest was what concerned him, and he was determined that any Moravian stationed at North West River should feel welcome.[29]

> It was Mr. Smith's opinion, that a Missionary (or rather a clergyman) should reside at this place, be considered to some extent a member of the family, and take his meals with them. This seems at first sight very feasible. But I did not omit to express my fears, that the proper object of a Mission-station would not be easy to be attained here, as the population is too thin. Not above fifteen persons, including children, reside at the settlement; while four settlers' families live at such a distance, that they could be reached in one day. But even these pass the summer at their fishing-places, at a still greater distance. Others could not be reached in a day. The Indians only come hither two or three times during the summer for a short period, for the purpose of trading. They belong nominally to the Roman Catholic Church, but would form the principal objects of any missionary efforts. They would not be allowed to settle here; nor indeed would it be practicable, on account of their hunting. This day (Saturday) I saw many of them, who came to barter away their seal blubber. Unfortunately, I could not converse with them; but their countenances wore an expression of good nature, and inspired confidence.[30]

In his capacity as a Justice of the Peace, Donald had been marrying people who requested him to do so, and in his capacity as head of the Hudson's Bay Company service in Esquimaux Bay, he officiated at baptisms and funerals and read a weekly Sunday service to those who wished to attend. Brother Elsner's English was far from perfect and his face was still inflamed from his sunburn, so he declined to lead the service, though he did, of course, attend it.

> It was very striking to me to see about thirty Indians, neatly dressed, come from their hunting-grounds, to attend the services of the Lord's day, in a language they did not understand. They remained till about four o'clock in the afternoon, in Mr. Smith's house. This gentleman, who appears to speak their language very readily, was kind enough to act as my interpreter, so that I was enabled to converse with them a little.
>
> The dress of the Indians has lost much that was peculiar, through their trade and intercourse with Europeans. They are

> however, distinguished for their preferences for the scarlet colour. The men wear coats of the European cut; the chief being distinguished by epaulettes, nearly resembling those of a Prussian lieutenant. The women appeared in jackets, like those of the Esquimaux, and high caps of scarlet cloth. They are very fond of rum, but get it only in small quantities, as *presents*. The *sale* of spirits to Indians is contrary to law.[31]

A glass of rum, some bread and butter or a piece of cake was used as an enticement to encourage the Naskapi to attend the church service, the intention being that, once the good habit was established, the bribe could be omitted. Donald and Bella also did their best to convince their parishioners that a religious gathering was a special occasion which required clean faces and "Sunday best," though the details of this message were not always clearly understood, as Donald remembered many years later.

> I call to mind an Indian woman with six grown-up sons. She was of somewhat large proportions, and, to her credit be it said, a regular attendant at our meetings. She tried to bring up her boys in the way they should go, and to attend our gatherings; but she would not let them go into the service unless properly clothed. On one occasion, one of the sons was anxious to attend, but his mother would not hear of it, because he had not what she considered the necessary attire; and I need hardly state that we were all rather surprised, and not a little amused, to see him come in later on after the service had commenced, wearing one of his mother's dresses, which, you will gather from what I have said, did not fit him anywhere![32]

Donald and McPherson spent much of Monday on business, giving Elsner an opportunity to browse among the books and select some to borrow. The visitors set out on their return journey on Tuesday, accompanied by Donald as far as Rigolet. Though North West River was free of ice, Hamilton Inlet was still frozen, affording good travelling to an abandoned fisherman's shack which the company kept in repair for use on their journeys between the two posts. On the following day, however, the ice gave way, pitching McPherson and Elsner into the water below. It was a bedraggled crew which came looking for a bed at Brownson's establishment at Snug Cove that night. The remainder of the journey was completed with difficulty, sometimes walking, sometimes riding and frequently carrying the komatiks over the slippery stones on the shore. At Rigolet, Brother Elsner discovered that only six men were in residence and that the fluctuating population of Naskapi, Inuit and planters coming to trade was neither large nor reliable in its attendance.

> Yet this would have to be the residence of a Missionary or clergyman for this district. Mr. Smith has a neat house, which he inhabits during the short time he remains here in summer, for purposes of business. This house he would place at the disposal

> of a Missionary, until a dwelling for the latter was ready. Mr. S. is of opinion that the Company would provide a church or chapel, as large as might be required. He also had reason to believe that the handsome annual contribution of £100 would be paid towards the support of the Mission, but had not been specially authorised by the Company to promise it.[33]

The sparse congregation scattered throughout the district, the difficulties of travel which he had already experienced and the fact that the Moravians were German speakers whose English was so shaky that their reports to their English funders had to be translated all conspired to convince Brother Elsner that a residency at Esquimaux Bay would not be a good use of the brethren's limited resources. This was confirmed by the mission board which reported in 1858 that the opening of new stations in Africa and India meant there were not sufficient men to send to Esquimaux Bay as well.[34]

Elsner's visit did, however, provide some support for Donald's long campaign to have a priest visit North West River, for it showed the lengths to which he was prepared to go to provide some form of religious instruction as an attraction to the peripatetic Naskapi. A request that summer from the Anglican Bishop of Newfoundland for support in visiting the region reinforced the suggestion that the Protestant churches were beginning to eye the vacuum created by the Roman Catholic absence. It could, George Simpson saw clearly, create an unseemly contretemps from which the company could hardly be the beneficiary. The issue was settled, however, when the Bishop of Quebec announced that he was sending a Catholic missionary, Father Charles Arnaud, up the Moisie River to Fort Nascopie and from there to North West River and Rigolet. Simpson acceded to his request for a return passage to Quebec in the company schooner. In a letter which sounds remarkably like those Donald had been sending at yearly intervals, Simpson explained that there was really nothing he could do to prevent the trip and, in any case, it would be impolite to thwart the plans of the Roman Catholic Bishop of Quebec. Additionally, he observed, "as the Nascopies are so bent on seeing a priest that they come out to the St. Lawrence for that purpose, it is better to meet their wishes in the hope that they may rest quietly at their hunting grounds, instead of wasting their time in travelling to the station at Mingan etc."[35]

What Donald said in private when he received this news may be imagined; to his credit, he had learned to manage his dealings with Simpson sufficiently well that he said nothing in his correspondence. In the event, it was many years before a priest finally appeared at Esquimaux Bay, and then it only happened because Donald arranged every step of the journey.

In 1857, however, matters of much greater import than missionaries at Esquimaux Bay were occupying the minds of George Simpson, the Governor and Committee and all those chief traders and chief factors who had learned the latest news from London.

Though the "Governor and Company of Adventurers of England tradeing into Hudsons Bay" had been granted their vast North American territory in perpetuity, they were still obliged to obtain a licence to trade and this alone gave the right to operate on the Pacific coast and in other areas not mentioned in the charter. The licence was due to expire in 1859, and in 1856, the company gave notice that it intended to seek renewal. It was not an opportune moment. The peace which followed the Battle of Waterloo allowed Britain to turn its attention to social and parliamentary reform, married to which was a general feeling against commercial monopolies which were perceived as contributing to the poverty and substandard living conditions of the inner cities. Foremost among the critics of the monopolies was William Ewart Gladstone, the Liberal politician whose power and influence was daily growing. To offset Gladstone's campaign against corporate oligarchies, the Hudson's Bay Company could call on but few friends among London's financial elite, most of whom perceived the company to be both secretive and snobbish.

Allied to the anti-monopoly movement was a developing imperialism which argued that the benefits of British parliamentary government should be more widely available to the nation's colonies. It also encouraged the settlement of unoccupied tracts of colonial land which had hitherto been exploited for commercial gain.

The British attitude towards the Hudson's Bay Company's monopoly of the plains between Canada and the Rocky Mountains was also affected by the rapid westward expansion of the republic south of the forty-ninth parallel and the knowledge that both the company and the British government were powerless to prevent American settlers from moving into British territory. Already, free traders were encroaching on the HBC monopoly, leaving dissatisfaction in their wake. In 1811, the company had allowed the idealistic Lord Selkirk to establish a colony at the confluence of the Red and Assiniboine Rivers but, by 1857, the descendants of those few men and women who had survived the horrors of the journey from Scotland to the bay and overland to Red River were beginning to complain about the HBC monopoly and the huge mark-up they were obliged to pay for goods obtained through the company stores. The American traders could offer goods manufactured in the US at a fraction of the HBC price and, because the interlopers were themselves from the region, they had a much better idea of what would be attractive enough to overcome the fact that dealing with them was illegal.

In such a climate, the repeated campaigns to call the company to account this time bore fruit. Henry Labouchere, later Lord Taunton, chaired a parliamentary select committee of very powerful men. It included Gladstone, Lord John Russell, who had been prime minister from 1846-1852, Lord Stanley, a future foreign secretary, the Earl of Derby, who had briefly been prime minister and was to serve as foreign secretary in the future, and Edward Ellice, the MP and son of Bear Ellice.

The select committee met for most of the first half of 1857 and heard evidence from twenty-five witnesses. On the whole, they agreed that the Hudson's Bay Company governed the people who came under its jurisdiction with tolerance and justice. Allegations were made that the company allowed the Indians to starve but these were countered by tales of the many instances when chief traders and chief factors had moved quickly to alleviate hunger. The crucial question was whether the territory was suitable for settlement but, because of its ignorance and because it could only interrogate those who could attend the hearings, the select committee heard disparate and often unrelated information which contributed to no coherent whole. At one moment, it received opinions and supposed facts about the shores of Hudson Bay and, a few minutes later, witnesses discussed the climate and agricultural potential of New Caledonia. In response to questions about whether the interior plain was habitable, the testimony was coloured entirely by whether the witness was in the employ or under the influence of the company.

George Simpson, as might be expected, did everything in his power to discourage settlement, which would drive out the fur bearing animals on which the company depended, and he did everything he could to help the company maintain its trade monopoly. Unfortunately, he did not feel obliged to tell the truth in support of his employers. He declared the Pacific coast to be "quite unfit for colonisation," despite evidence from an earlier witness that the company's farm at Fort Langley, near the mouth of the Fraser River, was flourishing. More damaging was his statement that the Red River district was not suited to settlement because the soil was poor, except on the river banks, and early frosts frequently destroyed the crops. To his embarrassment, one of the committee members, Arthur Gordon, son of the Earl of Aberdeen and his father's private secretary when he was prime minister between 1852 and 1855, then read back to Simpson his description of the district as published in his *Journey Round the World*. "Nor are the banks less favourable to agriculture than the waters themselves to navigation, resembling, in some measure, those of the Thames near Richmond," Simpson had written of the stretch between Lake of the Woods and Rainy Lake. "Is it too much for the eye of philanthropy to discern through the vista of futurity, this noble stream, connecting, as it does, the fertile shores of two spacious lakes, with crowded steamboats on its bosom and populous towns on its borders?"[36]

Simpson declared that he had "overrated the importance of the country as a country for settlement." But Gordon was not finished with him and his *Journey Round the World*. "The soil of Red River Settlement is a black mould of considerable depth," Simpson had written, "which, when first tilled, produces extraordinary crops, as much, on some occasions, as forty returns of wheat; and, even after twenty successive years of cultivation, without the relief of manure or of fallow, or of green crop, it still yields from fifteen to twenty bushels an acre." He had exaggerated then, just as he was now undervaluing the worth of the land and Gordon's questions severely damaged his credibility as a witness.[37]

Among the last to give evidence, and certainly the most significant, was old Bear Ellice who, once again, seized the lead in the company's negotiations, recognizing that change was inevitable and that it was in the company's interests to grant with dignity what could otherwise be rudely seized. Labouchere asked if it would be difficult to make an arrangement between the company and the Canadian government for the extension of settlement into the Northwest. "Not only would there be no difficulty in it," he replied

> but the Hudson's Bay Company would be too glad to make a cession of any part of that territory for the purposes of settlement, upon the one condition that Canada shall be at the expense of governing it and maintaining a good police, and preventing the introduction, so far as they can, of competition with the fur trade.

Did that mean, asked Labouchere, that "it would be more advantageous for the company to withdraw as it were to the more northern part of their territory, and to leave for gradual settlement the southern part of their territory?"

"I am of opinion that the existence and maintenance of the Hudson's Bay Company, for the purpose of temporarily governing this country, until you can form settlements in it, is much more essential to Canada and to England than it is to the company of adventurers trading into Hudson's Bay," Ellice replied, explaining that the area of settlement, whether under British or Canadian control, would require subsidy because there was no tax base to support the administrative infrastructure currently maintained by the company, nor would there be until the population increased.[38]

When the ships from London reached Hudson Bay and Rigolet in the summer, they brought news of the select committee's meetings and the testimony which had been presented, but they had sailed before the report was published. As a result, the chief traders and chief factors were left in the dark, uncertain whether they or the company to which they had devoted their lives had any future. Donald, with easier and more frequent links with Newfoundland and access to news from Montreal later in the season, was probably relieved of his concerns sooner than some of his more distant colleagues in the Northern Department.

The select committee recommended that the company's rule of Vancouver Island should be terminated and that a colony should be established incorporating it and the land between the Pacific and the Rocky Mountains. This came into force in 1858. It also said that the company should be prepared to cede to Canada those portions of the territory which Canada was prepared to govern and that this should be the subject of negotiations, followed by an act of parliament. As an interim measure, the license to trade was renewed for ten years.

In Labrador, the company's competitors did not appreciate that there was no comparison between the situation there and the monopoly which existed in the Northwest and assumed they would soon have *carte blanche*. Donald wasted no time in proving otherwise, as he reported to Simpson.

> Here under the expectation of a complete dissolution of the Company as a Corporation, the Messrs Hunt's agents and some others of our opponents began to lift their heads somewhat, giving us the opportunity of shewing them in a quick way that we intend being not a whit less active than formerly and equally tenacious of our rights, which on the Labrador at least, are quite as good as theirs.[39]

For Donald, one of the greatest effects of the select committee's deliberations was to encourage him to think about what the future of Canada might be and about what role the company could or should play in the Northwest. It was a subject which he had been reading about and mulling over for some time and on which he had already formed clear opinions. Some of these he expressed in a letter written in January 1857, before the select committee had begun to hear evidence. He addressed his thoughts to William Kernaghan, an Irishman who had established himself as a merchant in Chicago and who, like many other American merchants, believed that he should have unrestricted access to trade in the Hudson's Bay Company's chartered territory and should be able to establish transportation routes to make this possible. Kernaghan had spent some time at North West River and thought Donald was wasting his talents in the depths of Labrador.

> I have thought a great deal about your flattering proposal and you may depend upon it that if my prospects (or you would say lack of prospects) here induce me to retire from the service of the Honourable Company, I will not fail to write and let you know. It is possible that circumstances connected with the Company itself may make early consideration of such a step on my part necessary.
>
> I doubt very much now whether I shall ever be transferred to the West, but much depends upon what happens in this department in the course of the next few outfits.
>
> Your account of the city of Chicago and the opportunities it offers interests me extremely, and I have no doubt that one might make rapid headway there in commercial enterprises, such as shipping, which makes me regret all the more that this magical land of yours is not within the borders of the Queen's dominions.
>
> I myself am becoming convinced that before many decades are passed the world will see a great change in the country north of Lake Superior and in the Red River country when the Company's license expires or its charter is modified. Thousands of settlers are pressing forward into the Michigan Territory, where land, I gather, is not vastly better than that on the British side of the boundary. You will understand that I as a Labrador man cannot be expected to sympathize altogether with the prejudices against immigrants and railways entertained by many of the Western commissioned officers. At all events, it is probable that settlement of the country from Fort William westward to the Red River, even a considerable distance beyond, will eventually take place and with damaging effect on the fur-trade generally. Governor Simpson himself took a very favourable view of the character of the country for settlement.
>
> I shall prudently keep my opinion until it is asked for; I do not believe those in authority in London or elsewhere are well advised in thus shutting off the country and aspersing its character and that a Chicago is just as possible there as in Illinois.[40]

It is a remarkable letter, suggesting that from his reading in rocky Labrador he had a good deal more accurate information about Red River and its environs than many of those who were to testify before the select committee, and a much better capacity to see its potential than those such as Simpson who blindly defended the status quo.

In the meantime, Donald had his own, much more immediate concerns at Esquimaux Bay. First there were the all too familiar problems with shipping. The new schooner plying the route between Montreal and Rigolet was the *Helmina*. She was becalmed at Rigolet for a few days in September but then had to move from station to station, collecting the returns for amalgamation at Rigolet. Simpson had refused to allow the purchase of a ship to gather the returns in advance because of "a probability of some changes being made in the Company's arrangements for the posts below Quebec," so he and Donald were left to complain to each other about the frustrations of not being able to complete the shipping as promptly as they would wish.[41]

It was Donald's private life, however, which was the main cause of his uneasiness. He and Bella had decided, in the face of repeated demands from Governor Simpson and Richard Hardisty, that Bella should leave Esquimaux Bay for Montreal. She travelled in the *Helmina*, taking with her the two children, plus the McPherson's son, Richard, who was being sent to his grandfather, Murdoch McPherson, to be educated. As well, she had charge of Henry Connolly's son, James, who was going to school in Montreal. April Goudie, whose father had worked for the company for many years, went as a maid. In a letter carried out in the same vessel, Donald explained to Simpson what the financial arrangements were to be.

> I would also like to have £30 or £40 paid to Mrs. Grant who now proceeds to Canada with her children and from whom I have received many kindnesses during her stay in Esquimaux Bay. I trust they may be comfortable and happy, as I believe them deserving of being so. They have been at no expense whatsoever to the Company for the past year as I have charged myself with about six barrels of flour etc. besides other provisions, fully equal to what they would have used. Mr. Hardisty may have mentioned to you that he wished me to send to Lachine a note of any expenses incurred on account of his Daughter & her children, this I cannot for a moment think of doing, indeed as already mentioned Mrs. Grant has done me many kind offices and to Mr. Hardisty I have also been indebted, and I do not consider him under any obligation to me.[42]

Bella and the children were not long in Lachine before Simpson discovered that the "many kind offices" included being wife to Donald Smith and mother to his daughter. Better still, the governor approved of this intelligent and energetic young woman as a partner for his protégé and kept an eye out for her interests in Montreal. It was probably through Simpson that Bella found lodgings with a clerk in the Montreal office, almost certainly James Bissett. He was a native of Montreal, his father being the superintendent of the Lachine Canal, and quickly became, and remained, friends with the entire Hardisty and Smith families, welcoming them singly and jointly to his home throughout his life. When Simpson wrote to Donald in March, he noted that Bella seemed to be "comfortably situated" in a cottage near the office and considerately added, "I have heard nothing of her husband for a long time." His best news was in a postscript where he reported, "Mrs. Grant has applied for permission to return to Esquimaux Bay. It is probable she may be allowed to do so and that she will go down by the vessel of this season." "Probable" was Simpson's way of saying that she would be returning and the fact that he allowed it was his way of saying that she would henceforth be treated as Donald's wife.[43]

Bella and the children travelled to Esquimaux Bay in the *Helmina* in September 1858 and that October, Donald wrote Simpson about his dilemma. He wanted to marry Bella and regularize their relationship but presumed he was prevented from doing so by the fact that she was already married to James Grant. Not so, replied the governor.

> Her connexion with Grant was not in form, or any other respect, a marriage; it was merely such an union as the peculiar circumstances of the Indian country in former days admitted. Any authority, however, the Company's officers possess to solemnise marriages within the Company's Territory ceases beyond their limits, so that Mr. Hardisty could not legally unite his daughter to Grant within the colony of Newfoundland. Such an informal proceeding ought to have been legalised by the parties availing themselves of the first opportunity that offered of having the ceremony repeated by a clergyman. So far from taking that step, however, they separated by mutual consent, which was quite sufficient to annul any ties that existed between them as man and wife.[44]

In short, the company merely traded under license in Labrador whereas in the Northern and Southern Departments, it had sole control of the territory and made its own rules, which included the right of commissioned officers to marry people. The law in Newfoundland, like the law in Scotland, allowed couples to be married without benefit of clergy where none were available. It also required such marriages to be registered, whether or not they were later confirmed by a religious ceremony. Neither Bella's marriage to James Grant nor Mary's to Joseph McPherson, nor any of the marriages which Donald conducted as a Justice of the Peace, were reported to the registrar at St. John's.

Many years later, Donald said that he consulted several people about his right to marry Bella. One of these was probably Nathan Norman, the Newfoundland ship captain with whom Donald was increasingly friendly and whose descendants were under the impression that Norman had somehow been associated with the wedding. He, like Simpson, advised in favour of the ceremony for the simple reason that it put the seal on what was obviously a good match. "From what I have heard of her," Simpson wrote, "as well as from my personal acquaintance, I think she is qualified to make you an excellent wife. I should be really pleased to hear the marriage had taken place & should sincerely wish you both great happiness and comfort."[45]

The ceremony took place in June 1859, witnessed by some of the Orkneymen who were stationed at North West River. Because Donald was a JP and because the Anglican bishop of Newfoundland had approved of Donald marrying others in the absence of clergy, he was easily the most appropriate person in the district to conduct weddings. He therefore performed his own ceremony. Nothing in the colony's legislation governing marriages provided for such an option. Scottish law allowed a couple to make a formal declaration that they were married but required them to register this statement, but Scottish law could scarcely be said to extend to Newfoundland.

Whatever the legal circumstances, the arrangement satisfied both parties involved; it pleased the Hardistys and George Simpson, and it silenced the Labrador gossips.

Meanwhile, changes were afoot throughout Labrador. Donald had been thinking about the most efficient way of managing his district and it was becoming increasingly clear to him that the territory should be extended to increase the returns and to ensure that the company's operations from Ungava Bay to the St. Lawrence River worked in greater harmony than they presently did. His thoughts about northern Labrador had been reinforced in the winter of 1857-1858; more than thirty families who normally traded at Fort Nascopie did not appear that winter and before long news reached North West River that they were at the Moravian post at Nain where there was not sufficient food to ward off starvation. In a letter which captivated the Governor and Committee as a first hand account of a real life adventure, Donald explained what had happened.

> In April 1857 the Nascopies while prosecuting the Deer hunt came up with some Esquimaux by whom two or three of their number were introduced to Messrs. Hunts' station, and on return to their lodges, about 150 miles inland were accompanied by Messrs. Hunts' clerk with a considerable quantity of provisions, and which he exchanged for their furs and skins, informing them at [the] same time that in course of the ensuing summer he would procure for them abundance of rum and other supplies; promises which induced them to proceed to the coast in the autumn and winter, where being far removed from their hunting grounds and failing in procuring from Messrs. Hunts' people a supply of provisions, as they had no furs to give in return, many of their number, it is said upwards of fifty, including women and children died of starvation. At one time there were more than seventy of them at Nain in a state of utter destitution; but the missionaries not having even a sufficiency of food for the Esquimaux attached to their settlement who suffered greatly in consequence, were unable to relieve them to any extent.
>
> Immediately on becoming acquainted with this sad state of matters I proceeded to that station distant about 400 miles from North West River where I wintered, and 150 from Kibokok and fortunately arrived in time to rescue from certain death a few of their number. I have since been informed that the survivors had left on return to Fort Nascopie; but to provide against a repetition of the calamities of the past winter, we have established a post within a few miles of Messrs. Hunts' station under charge of an officer and two labourers.[46]

It was apparent that the HBC was going to have to pay more attention to activities in the north, not because of competition from the Moravian missionaries, though there was a long term plan to take over their trading operation in exchange for assistance with the missionary work, but because foolish or unscrupulous men could wreak havoc out of all proportion to their actions by not considering the greater consequences. The difficulty with Hunt and Henley arose in large measure from the fact that the company used sub-agents whom it did not actually employ and over whom it therefore had no control. Hunt's was prepared to say that it did not wish its people to have any dealings with hunters who normally traded with the HBC but it was unprepared to issue explicit instructions to that effect. The only way the HBC could hope to frustrate such activities was by establishing a post which, Donald suggested to George Simpson a year later, might eventually attract sufficient furs to pay for itself.

Hunt and Henley were not alone in extending their operations northward nor were they the only ones to use rum, though they denied that the amount supplied equalled their lavish promises. "Unfortunately," Donald explained to George Simpson in 1859, "owing to the great influx of traders, Newfoundland, Nova Scotian & American, within these two or three years back, who range along the Coast, even to the most northern settlement of the Moravian Brethren, intoxicating drinks, in almost unlimited quantity, can readily be obtained by all parties; an evil to arrest which missionaries and resident merchants are alike powerless." Nevertheless, if a small post could attract some of the furs, neither the Inuit nor the Naskapi would have anything to barter in exchange for rum and both they and the company would benefit from such an arrangement.[47]

Of greater concern was the difficulty which Esquimaux Bay continued to face in relation to the Hudson's Bay Company posts along the St. Lawrence. Simpson's persistent refusal to assist in the provision of a Roman Catholic priest, and his failure to do anything about it once he had capitulated, meant that Naskapi continued to travel south with their furs. It was only by developing the friendliest possible relations with his families that Donald was able to keep the majority of them at Hamilton Inlet, but every year he risked losing them.

The Montagnais and Naskapi observed only the loosest of territorial boundaries and ranged both north and south in search of game and good prices for their furs. It made sense for the company's management to reflect this reality. In 1855, Donald recommended uniting Mingan and Esquimaux Bay and building a post at the mouth of the St. Augustine River which flows into the St. Lawrence opposite Newfoundland's Great Northern Peninsula. There was already a tiny community and a Roman Catholic chapel there but few traders called. Simpson could see the logic but played a waiting game. "For the present, I think, we must continue to rub on as we are; if, as is not impossible, those of the King's Posts near Quebec, which are very unprofitable, be abandoned, and our operation concentrated to the lower posts & the Labrador coast, the appointment of one person to the whole management would very likely be made."[48]

In fact, the company was slowly inching its way towards acceptance of Donald's idea but had been distracted by the 1857 select committee and the negotiations with the British government which followed it. The Governor and Committee also wanted to put into effect another change before unifying Labrador and the posts below Quebec. From the beginning of Outfit 1859, Esquimaux Bay would no longer report through Montreal but would deal directly with London. Simpson was old, ill and tired; in confidence, he had penned his letter of resignation to take effect the following year, saying that it was time to make way for a younger man. In placing Donald Smith in direct communication with the Governor and Committee, he was allowing him to make his mark and allowing London to decide whether this was the younger man who might, in due course, succeed him.

In the meantime, Simpson and Donald continued their correspondence, devoting much of their energy to thoughts about the management of Labrador, Mingan and the King's Posts. Donald's last, very detailed letter on the subject was written at the beginning of October 1860, outlining transport routes through southern Labrador, making suggestions about the location of new posts and pinpointing them in relation to the richest hunting grounds. What he did not know and did not learn till the summer of 1861 was that Simpson had died a month earlier. He had fallen ill in Saint Paul in June, en route to the Northern Department council, and had been forced to return in easy stages to Montreal. In all likelihood, he had suffered a stroke. At the end of August, he arranged an elaborate entertainment with Kahnawake canoemen for the young Prince of Wales who was visiting Montreal to open the new Victoria Bridge, but two days later, he was hit by a massive stroke and convulsions and died on the morning of September 7. He had done much for Donald Smith, proffering admonitions, professional guidance and fatherly advice and Donald spoke from the heart when he said that he much regretted the loss of his mentor.

Simpson had guided him towards his professional maturity and the best tribute Donald could pay him was to work hard and work well. The efficient management of Esquimaux Bay, even if it was not enlarged, also demanded that something be done about the transport arrangements. Outwitting the competitors and increasing both the quantity and quality of the returns, especially by concentrating on salmon and cod, had driven up the profits of the region but this, in turn, put impossible pressures on shipping. In the beginning, it had been sufficient to send a boat from Quebec with goods and provisions from England and Canada. It unloaded at Rigolet and collected the returns which had been gathered there by the company's fleet of small boats. This meant that the early part of the trapping season was lost to them but there was compensation in the more efficient handling of the returns. When the schooner, *Independence*, was assigned to the route, it, being larger, had collected returns from Kibokok as well as Rigolet, but, when the number of employees was reduced to make savings and increase profitability, it became increasingly difficult to complete the trip in time because it was taking ever longer to load the vessel. The addition of the *Charlotte* to the local flotilla enabled the men at Kibokok and North West River to get their returns to Rigolet to await the schooner but by 1860, even the *Charlotte* was too small to collect all that needed to be sent out. On some occasions, even the schooner itself was not large enough for the task.

In October 1859, Donald wrote the Governor and Committee about the transport situation. Hunt and Henley were now responsible for carrying the goods from London to Cartwright in Sandwich Bay but it was up to the HBC to arrange transport from there to Kibokok, Rigolet and North West River and to find transport to the markets for the returns. The frequent dependence on Hunt and Henley, who put their own interests first and either overcharged or refused to make vessels available for local transport, caused innumerable problems and even more annoyance. To overcome these difficulties, Donald proposed to have the *Charlotte* considerably enlarged and, through Nathan Norman, to purchase a small schooner. This would give him the freedom to carry his own produce to Indian Harbour for sale to Norman or for transmission to Robert Prowse, a broker in St. John's. Alternatively, he could take it to Cartwright for forwarding to the HBC in England or for direct sale to Hunt and Henley themselves.

London approved the new arrangement and the purchase of the schooner in Newfoundland but neither the board nor Donald foresaw that their well laid plans would be wrecked by the weather. "From June until the middle of August," he explained to Thomas Fraser, the secretary in London, "we had the heat of the Tropics, the thermometer ranging from 80 to 103° in the shade, causing much sickness and many deaths among the natives and since the latter date there has been a succession of heavy gales with hardly an interval of fine weather." On the seventh of September, a hurricane tore up the Labrador coast, smashing docks and shipping as it went. At the narrow entrance to Lake Melville, the tide, which normally rose six feet, surged to twelve feet and nearly engulfed the houses at Rigolet. Nothing like it had been seen in Esquimaux Bay for fifty years. Donald had been forced to charter a vessel to bring the English supplies from Cartwright to Rigolet and she was driven aground in the storm. It was October before they were able to get her off and repaired and send her on her way. In the meantime, the *Charlotte* was battling her way up to Kibokok with the intention of collecting the salmon and taking it to Nathan Norman with whom a deal had been struck. Even before she returned, Donald knew she would be too late for Norman and that he would have to find some other means of getting the fish to Prowse in Newfoundland.[49]

As if the hurricane were not enough, the company's supply vessel the *Kitty*, returning from Hudson Bay was crushed by the ice off the north east tip of Ungava Bay on September 5. The chief mate and four crew managed to reach the Moravian settlement at Okak two months later but the captain and the remaining ten crew members in the longboat were blown away by the gales. London was forced to assume the worst, but it was only in July 1860, when Donald wrote from Cartwright, where he had encountered the mate and two of the men who were returning to England, that the Governor and Committee had their fears confirmed.

In the spring of 1860, before the proposed enlargement had taken place, the *Charlotte* was severely damaged and small schooners had to be hired locally. Donald's indent had arrived in England so late that the company had been obliged to estimate the provisions which would be needed. No sooner had they been shipped when the indent arrived and the additional goods were sent on the *Escort*, though it was feared she would reach no further than Francis Harbour, a long way south of Cartwright. Only after the *Escort* sailed did the company discover that the *Castilian Maid*, carrying the majority of the goods for Esquimaux Bay, had been lost at sea. In other words, there would be no imported British provisions to see the company's employees through the winter. The Moravians at Hopedale supplied Kibokok that winter and it is likely that a schooner brought supplies to Cartwright or Rigolet from Canada. Donald was presumably able to get flour or biscuit and some other essentials through Nathan Norman or Hunt and Henley.

That there was no comment on any difficulties occasioned by the lack of supplies is a silent tribute to all that Donald had done, by way of agriculture and animal husbandry, to raise the standard of living at North West River. The interest in gardens and food production had started in Mingan, where he had maintained a garden, and carried on to Rigolet, where he was proud of the potatoes and turnips he raised in an inhospitable climate. Initially, his motivation had been the prevention of scurvy and the reduction of the district's operating costs but, before long, farming in Labrador, with its short growing season and poor soil, became a challenge which he enjoyed for its own sake. In 1855, he acquired MacIntosh's *Book of the Garden* and Lindley's *Theory and Practice of Horticulture* but, even without them, he had already managed to create a flourishing farm. His self-satisfaction shows in the post journal entry he made one Sunday in 1855.[50]

> Our meals today consist entirely of "country produce" consisting of venison fish new & old potatoes, parsnips, cabbage carrots lettuce parsley onion leeks and green pease also rhubarb tart with pastry made of potatoes eggs milk — instead of the customary flour crust the only foreign or imported commodities used being sugar and by the people the dinner was pronounced to be the best they had ever partaken of.[51]

When Brother Elsner visited North West River in April 1857, he was impressed by the richness and variety of the diet, especially in comparison with what the Moravians experienced much farther north at Hopedale.

> The gardens produce potatoes, turnips, cabbages, beans, etc. in abundance. Mr. Smith has four head of cattle, besides sheep, goats, pigs, and fowls. He had also a fine dry cellar, in which there is room to store 200 barrels of vegetables, secure from the frost. Good water is supplied the year round, by a well, fifteen feet deep, provided with a pump. This was very interesting to me, as I had never before seen anything of the sort in Labrador. There was milk in abundance; and, for the first time in this country, I tasted fresh roast-beef, mutton, and pork.[52]

Frost proof cellars were essential to the preservation of root vegetables and similar commodities through the long winter months, but the night of February 9, 1861 was exceptionally cold and, in the company's store at North West River, produced some rather inexplicable consequences. The outside temperature was recorded at -33°F while the interior, because it was heated, showed -5° to -10°. There was no wind. Nevertheless, bottles of ale and porter were frozen and geraniums which had been wintered over in the cellar in previous years without difficulty were completely ruined. Obviously, it was much colder than indicated by the thermometers, which "were first class English made." The mystery was why they failed to record the true temperature, or why the mercury did not fall off the end or why they were not broken. It remained an unresolved puzzle, and more than twenty years later, Donald was still trying to find an answer to the enigma.[53]

In part, the generous harvest of the soil at North West River can be attributed to Donald's concern with fertilizers. He perceived that the fisheries along the coast were hugely wasteful, with large portions of the catch being thrown back into the sea or left on shore to rot. He thought fish fertilizer was a product which the company should produce and market, but in the interim, used it to good effect in his own garden, the richness of which surprised Charles Hallock who, with a group of companions from the Smithsonian Institution, travelled to Labrador to view an eclipse in the summer of 1860.

> Then the astonished ear is greeted with the lowing of cattle and the bleating of sheep on shore; and in the rear of the agent's house are veritable barns, from whose open windows hangs fragrant new-mown hay; and a noisy cackle within is ominous of fresh-laid eggs! Surely Nature has been remarkably lavish here, or some presiding genius, of no ordinary enterprise and taste, has redeemed the place from its wilderness desolation! Both are true. The climate is much warmer here than upon the coast, and there is a fair admixture of soil. Donald Alexander Smith, the intelligent agent of the post, is a practical farmer, and, by continued care and the employment of proper fertilizing agents, succeeds in forcing to maturity, within the short summer season, most of the vegetables and grains produced in warmer latitudes. He has seven acres under cultivation, of which a considerable portion is under glass. There are growing turnips, pease, cucumbers, potatoes, pumpkins, melons, cauliflowers, barley, oats, etc. Corn will not ripen, nor even form upon the ear. ... A bull, twelve cows, half a dozen sheep, goats, fowls, and dogs comprise his live-stock. There is no other place like Smith's in Labrador.[54]

August that year also brought a visit from HMS *Bulldog*, captained by Sir Leopold McClintock, the Arctic explorer who had been engaged to take soundings for a new transatlantic cable which it was proposed to lay in sections from Scotland to the Faroe Islands, Iceland, Greenland and Labrador. Fifty-five years later, McClintock remembered his tour of the farm and reported his conversation with its instigator, who had not yet been promoted to Chief Factor, though the captain recalled otherwise.

> "I had great difficulty at first," explained Mr. Smith, "in prevailing on the labourers to plough and dig. Few of them had done any farming, and hardly any of them had ever seen anything growing that required cultivation. Now each plants his own patch of root crops and it is quite surprising what a difference it has made. We have even turned to and built a good bit of a very fair road, as you see."
>
> "I see, Mr. Smith," said I, "you're not a man to be content with conditions as you find them in this world."
>
> "Who would be?" returned the Factor, smiling. "Who would be? The world would be a very sad place if we could n't make it a little better."

Donald, with Bella's help, was experimenting, pushing the demands on the soil enrichment and the greenhouses as far as they could go. They imported seeds from England but also brought them in from Orkney, looking for the hardiest varieties they could find. Not all the land was given over to food production, however, for, to the amazement of native and visitor alike, a colourful flower garden flourished in front of the house. "Most of the ordinary things grow very well, if they are well watered and manured," Donald explained to McClintock.[55]

For most people in Labrador, it was the first flower garden they had ever encountered. About 1861, Lydia Campbell was unwell and she, with her husband and children, travelled to North West River to seek medical advice, as her daughter, Margaret Baikie, recalled more than half a century later.

> Little Maggie Smith asked Helen [Margaret's sister] and I to have tea with her, down in her little Indian tent [as] she called it. She gave us cocoa and milk and currant cakes. She spread a cloth on the ground and we sat around. She said she had no pretty doll to show us, there were none in those days only wooden ones what they would make. After our tea we went back to the house. Mr. Smith asked us to go and see his garden. It was the first flower garden I ever saw, and such beautiful flowers of all sorts. He said he was busy all the spring, digging and planting carrots, cabbages, onions, cauliflowers and other things and he had lost his gold ring. It had a white stone in it and three letters. The letters were D.A.S., Donald Alexander Smith. I was very sorry about his ring.[56]

He never replaced the ring or wore any other sort of jewelery.

The road to which Donald drew McClintock's attention was a two mile carriage road ("strange sight in this roadless country!" Hallock observed) along which Donald used two of the farm horses to take himself and his family for a spin on a summer evening. It seems an odd thing to have done and any explanation he may have given has not survived. It may be that he decided he should learn to drive, in which case the road may be judged a failure for he drove as badly as he shot. What is clear, however, is that he had determined that if he was to be denied the opportunity to live in an urban environment, he would still provide for himself, his family and all those with whom he had contact as many of the benefits of civilized life as he could manage.

The suit to replace Brother Elsner's sealskins and little Maggie's tea party for Margaret Baikie and her sister show the family practising a courteous, considerate but somewhat formal hospitality. A rough and ready sharing of food and shelter was the Labrador norm but the local people came to value Donald Smith's courtesy and his belief that gracious living emanated from individuals themselves rather than from their surroundings.

"My most vivid impression of my old Bourgeois," one of the clerks recalled years later, "is that he was always the gentleman. None ever took any liberties with him. He was always referred to as *Mr.* Smith, even behind his back, when any other officer in Labrador would have been called *Smith*."[57]

One day, Donald observed that Captain Irvine, the skipper who had married Lydia Campbell's daughter Susan, was using more nails than necessary in putting up a cask. Irvine was told to use fewer, whereupon he lost his temper. This Donald never did. He simply told Irvine to do as he was told and to report to him later.

> At the hour appointed, he went and listened for half an hour to a stern lecture on his disobedience and insubordination. He was brought to reason and remorse. "And now," said Mr. Smith, shaking hands, "we'd better step this way." The man thought he was going to be discharged. A door was opened. "Mrs. Smith is waiting for us. She would like to offer you a little refreshment before you go." So they adjourned to the sitting-room where cake and wine were on a table and he was cordially entertained.[58]

Irvine instantly perceived that there would be no grudges and that the incident would never be referred to unless he transgressed in the same way again. He was treated as a friend and valued colleague and in turn became a steadfast supporter of the Chief Trader. This was reinforced when Donald began to help him with his financial affairs for Irvine, though he had a Private Cash Account in Montreal, could scarcely read or write. He signed his own business letters, but they were both composed and written by Donald Smith.

The men and women of Esquimaux Bay had grown accustomed to the restraint, the formality, the courtesy, the insistence on doing things nicely, but visitors such as McClintock were always struck by the incongruity of such behaviour miles away from what they conceived to be civilized society.

> Donald A. Smith as I saw him on the 26th August, 1860, was about forty years old, some five feet ten inches high, with long sandy hair, a bushy red beard, and very thick red eyebrows. He was dressed in a black swallowtail coat, not at all according to the fashion of the country, and wore a white linen shirt. Although the Factor's countenance could hardly be called handsome, it was distinguished, and his manners were irreproachable. His talk showed him to be a man of superior intelligence. He bade us enter the parlour, and after chatting a few moments on the weather and our trip up the river, he introduced us to his wife and two children. Mrs. Smith is a small, intelligent, rather attractive lady, who evinced the greatest curiosity concerning people and events in England and the States, the [civil] war, the fashions, and our own personal histories.
>
> We noted that the room was very well, even tastefully, furnished. There were several pictures on the wall, prominent amongst them a large engraving of the coronation of Queen Victoria.

Like most people who encountered Donald Smith in Labrador, McClintock was taken aback by how up to date he was on world news. "For a man situated off the beaten track as he is, he displayed a surprising familiarity with current events. He showed me a great heap of newspapers. I laughed and told him that when the cable came he could stop his subscriptions." In fact, McClintock did not expect the cable to come and said as much. There would be difficulties bringing it ashore at Greenland and he foresaw trouble with the ice at the mouth of Hamilton Inlet.[59]

As the *Bulldog* steamed down the inlet, life in Esquimaux Bay resumed its humdrum routine. Donald had dealt with most of the improvements needed in the district and those he had not managed to deal with were becoming frustratingly repetitious. The accounts were late, generally as a result of the many shipping problems he was encountering, though in the first year of his reporting to London they were presented in a manner which the accountants found unacceptable. New instructions and a blank account book were sent. On behalf of the district, Nathan Norman bought the *Lively* which was meant to resolve the transportation difficulties but Esquimaux Bay continued to face problems in getting furs across the Atlantic. In 1861, Norman agreed to forward them from Newfoundland, but they were still there when the Hunt and Henley vessels arrived in London. To Fraser's annoyance, the fact that they did not go via Hunt and Henley as usual almost vitiated the insurance as well.

When Donald paused at the end of 1861 to reflect on his life, his accomplishments and his ambitions, he felt a mixture of frustration and satisfaction. The transport business was still not properly sorted out and the question of enlarging the district had not been adequately addressed. There were rumblings from Canada and London about the future of the company and the inevitable collapse of its hegemony in the Northwest. This was bound to have a huge impact on the lives of the wintering partners and their families — but just what it would be and how it would affect them was still a matter of conjecture.

On the personal side, there was room for self-congratulation. The farm was a success; he was known and respected by virtually everyone in Labrador, whatever their background; while he would have liked a son of his own, he had a happy, healthy family and much to be grateful for in his domestic life. His investments were burgeoning, with profitable bank shares and a diversification into mortgages which were also yielding a steady, reliable income. His father-in-law had retired and he was able to make the occasional financial contribution to him as well as maintaining a regular allowance to his mother and Jane in Forres. His was a stable family life with much to commend it.

CHAPTER FIVE

CHIEF FACTOR 1862–1869

Time never hung heavily on my hands; I was always busy, and when I had no actual and definite task, I was planning.

Lord Strathcona, recalling his life in Labrador[1]

While Donald Smith was reflecting on the management of Labrador, the Governor and Committee were worrying about the management of the entire company. In particular, their attention focused on the King's Posts and Mingan which annually showed a loss. Finally, in February 1862, they determined that the leases at Mingan and the smaller post of Mille Vaches would not be renewed. Their decision was partly determined by Donald's proposal, made shortly before George Simpson died, of creating one or two inland posts which would intercept the Naskapi before they reached the St. Lawrence and thus keep the trade out of the hands of the free traders cruising along the north shore in search of furs.

The idea was that Mingan would either be reduced substantially or abandoned altogether and that in the interim it would be put under the charge of James Watt with instructions to make the post at least cover its costs. The intention was that Watt and Donald Smith would act in concert and agree the most effective way of handling the problem. Consequently the Governor and Committee were extremely angry when they read a letter from Edward Hopkins, who had been George Simpson's secretary and was now in charge of the Montreal Department, in which he referred to "the abandonment of the frontier as a protection to the interior Country" before announcing that he had renewed the Mingan lease. It was only a short term renewal and was probably necessary in view of the length of time it took for decisions to be reached because of the difficulties in communicating between North West River, Mingan, Montreal and London. Nonetheless, it indicated that Hopkins and the board did not see eye to eye on the future of the posts below Quebec. Nor was the board any more pleased when the accounts for Outfit 1861 arrived, showing that the Montreal Department made a loss at every post except Lake Huron, and revealing that the King's Posts and Mingan had made their greatest ever loss. Hopkins blamed the abandonment of the debt system but the board suspected unwarranted and extravagant expenditure. The fact that fishermen had legally had access to the north shore for anything but salmon since 1853 and that in 1858 the company lost its salmon monopoly must have contributed more to the deficit than either the final demise of the debt system or any extravagance, but for London, it was yet another reason to keep in mind Donald's suggestion of uniting Esquimaux Bay and the St. Lawrence posts.[2]

The financial situation for the entire company, and for the St. Lawrence and Labrador posts in particular, was exacerbated by the American civil war which upset that country's economic equilibrium, bringing about depressed fur prices, especially at the top end of the market, and interfering with salmon sales as well. Because the American market was stagnant, Nathan Norman declined to take salmon, except on commission, and Labrador was finally obliged to hold back some of the fish caught in the summer of 1862 in the mistaken hope that the market would pick up the following year. Donald did think he had found an entrée into the American market when Captain John Dodge, who had taken to running a tourist service from Boston to Labrador, agreed to try to place some Labrador salmon on his return to the United States in the autumn of 1862. He had made a favourable impression on both Donald and Bella and Donald thought it would be a good idea to use him in preference to Hunt and Henley, at least for some voyages. There was, however, as he acknowledged, the risk that Dodge might cease to make the journey if the travel business declined.[3]

> I am much pleased to find that on his several visits to the Bay he has refrained from having any trade with those connected with the Company. This may possibly in some measure have been in hopes of being employed by the Company in transportation ... but whatever the motives, the result is satisfactory and I think it probable an arrangement might be come to with him for introducing our supplies from New York or Boston which would be to our advantage, as he would I believe be willing to enter into a contract to this effect, for a lengthened period, say four or five years, the principal objection to employing him instead of Messrs Hunt & Henley being I believe the apprehension of being left after a year or two without a conveyance for our provisions.[4]

Dodge was the more attractive because the service provided by Hunt and Henley seemed to deteriorate every time the men at Esquimaux Bay made a call on it. The goods from England were delivered exceedingly late in the summer of 1862 and delayed the provisioning of the inland posts far beyond the point of safety. A year later, Donald was complaining that "our dependence on the Hunts again this year was a most unfortunate affair and landed us in great difficulties" and by 1864 he was referring to "an abject vassalage to our excellent friends and most active opponents Messrs Hunt & Henley or their people in this country for the good folks in England [the Hunt and Henley owners] manage so adroitly to excuse themselves for all shortcomings, as to make them appear almost victims. It is high time we should be at least to some extent, independent of these people."[5]

The Governor and Committee expressed sympathy for Donald's 1863 difficulties, but put off doing anything about finding an alternative means of transport because Hunt apologized and sent a strongly worded letter to his agent at

Cartwright. The HBC executive in London also knew that other matters would have a bearing on any decision they might come to.[6]

At the beginning of Outfit 1862, Donald received his commission as Chief Factor, a promotion which indicated the esteem with which he was beginning to be regarded by London. This showed as well in a letter which he received from Thomas Fraser, the secretary to the board, in the summer of 1863. He thought Donald should know about a topic which the board had been discussing and on which it wanted his views. The committee was considering re-opening the post at Ungava Bay which, prior to its closure in 1842, had been the responsibility of the Southern Department. It was abandoned because of the danger to the supply ship which had to detour to the bottom of Ungava Bay on its journey to and from Hudson Bay. The risk of being trapped in the ice or lost in the winter storms was deemed to be too great in proportion to the returns. London had also assumed that the trade would transfer to Hamilton Inlet or other Esquimaux Bay posts or to Great and Little Whale River in the Southern Department. In fact, it went to the Moravians. If Fort Chimo or some other post in the Ungava region were to contribute to the district's earnings, the independent transport which Donald was asking for would be economically viable.[7]

Donald's immediate response was to note that he had already suggested the re-opening of Fort Chimo to Governor Simpson and, in the winter of 1862-1863, had even gone so far as to prepare logs, boards and other building material to take north to repair the fort or erect a new one, North West River being the only adequately wooded post in the region and thus the carpentry centre, providing not only wood for building but also tables and chairs and any other furniture which might be required. Donald knew that Nathan Norman had been thinking of trading in the north and initially thought the Ungava area should be provisioned directly from London to avoid drawing Norman's attention to the company's moves, but the same thinking which saw the advantages of uniting the King's Posts, Mingan and Esquimaux Bay made him change his mind about Ungava.

> On more mature consideration I am now of opinion that it would be better it should be outfitted from and form a part of this district, believing that a divided charge would cause very great inconvenience owing to the propensity of the natives for wandering from one district to another, believing that by so doing they were relieved from the necessity of liquidating what on their return to either district had become old debts, the baneful effects of which I have too frequently seen while I was stationed at the King's Posts as well as in the relations between Mingan and Esquimaux Bay. I am of opinion that the business of Ungava should for some time at least be conducted on a more limited and consequently more economical scale than formerly, confining it in the first instance to Fort Chimo.[8]

Two other important factors also governed the future of Esquimaux Bay. The first was that the Northern Council, meeting in the summer of 1863, decided that Donald Smith was due for furlough and would be entitled to take it from the beginning of Outfit 1864. He had not applied for it and was unaware that the council had any say over his right to a year's leave of absence, but both he and the board saw immediately that it would give them a chance to discuss the management of Esquimaux Bay in person. It would also give Donald an opportunity to assess for himself the changes which were taking place within the company. These were significant and affected the entire operation, not just the wind-swept shores of Labrador.

In the summer of 1863, the mail in the company ship included a letter from one of Donald's friends, enclosing the prospectus of the International Financial Society which was offering for sale shares in the HBC's assets, its landed territory and its cash balance. In this way, through English letters and the English press, Donald and other commissioned officers, whose livelihood depended on the profitability of the company, discovered that it had been sold. They learned that the new committee proposed to open to European colonisation a large portion of what is now southern Alberta, Saskatchewan and Manitoba. As Donald read the document, "he trembled so that he could scarcely stand." "It is a little unfortunate," he wrote to Hopkins in Montreal when he had recovered his composure, "that the Directors have not seen fit to take us into their confidence. I have no doubt that they intend to deal with the wintering partners justly and loyally, but in the mean time what steps have been taken to ascertain our opinion or to safeguard our interests?"[9]

The answer, of course, was that it had not crossed anyone's mind to think of the men on which the whole enterprise depended. The sale had come about because the Grand Trunk Railway, which had been incorporated to link Toronto, Montreal, Quebec, and Portland, a transatlantic steamship port in Maine, was in financial trouble in 1862 and its British bankers had brought in Edward Watkin, an English railway manager, to suggest ways of resolving the problems. When he visited Canada, Watkin quickly learned that it was only a matter of time before settlers pushed their way into the Northwest. The Grand Trunk's problems could be solved, he decided, by building even more railway to take people across the continent. Returning to London, he sought a government subsidy which he believed would entice a group of capitalists to put up the remainder of the money needed for construction. He also persuaded the Duke of Newcastle, who was colonial secretary, to accompany him and the bank representatives to see Henry Hulse Berens, governor of the Hudson's Bay Company.

The crusty old Berens was outraged at the thought of the Grand Trunk ripping through the heart of Hudson's Bay Company lands, and when the proposal was put to him as a patriotic gesture which would ensure that the territory remained British, he retorted that if the Grand Trunk men were so patriotic, why did they not buy out the company. It was not as wild a statement as at first appeared: the 1857 select committee hearing had made it clear that time was fast running out for the monopoly and the governor knew that any influx of settlers would soon destroy the fur trade completely.

Newcastle asked the price.

About £1.5 million, Berens responded.

Watkin and the Grand Trunk bankers left to reconsider their position, giving Berens a chance to restore his equanimity and Newcastle an opportunity to put the proposition of state aid to the cabinet. The government flatly refused to support the scheme. Watkin and the bankers returned to see Berens at the company's headquarters in Fenchurch Street, not far from the Bank of England and the stock exchange. Painting and refurbishment was never high on the company's list of priorities, as the visitors discovered. "The room," Watkin recorded, "was the

'Court Room,' dark, and dirty. A faded green cloth, old chairs almost black, and a fine portrait of Prince Rupert."[10]

The company had considered the proposal, Berens informed the railway men, and was prepared to grant sufficient land for a road and a telegraph line. This, of itself, was no use because the Grand Trunk needed additional land adjacent to the railway line which it could sell in order to finance construction. The HBC would have none of it. Watkin reiterated a willingness to purchase the company in its entirety and on St. Patrick's Day, was allowed to see the account books — but not the balance sheet! On this scantiest of information, the men decided to purchase. It would, of course, be a cash sale, the company snapped.

The International Financial Society had been established in the spring of 1863 by a group of London banks as an investment agency and, attracted by the acres of land in the ownership of the HBC, it now put up the money for the purchase, paying £300 for every £100 share at par, to a total of £1.5 million. It then changed the company from a private one, controlled by a small group of men and women, to a public one, selling the shares far and wide to a multitude of small investors and creaming off a £300,000 profit for itself.

The new proprietors were indignant at the very suggestion that they had disregarded the interests of the commissioned officers. Alexander Grant Dallas, the resident governor who had replaced George Simpson, was at pains to assure everyone that the charter had not changed and there was no cause for alarm.

The new governor in London, Sir Edmund Head, had previously been lieutenant governor of New Brunswick and governor general of Canada and at least had some idea of what the country was like, but his letter to the commissioned officers was ripe with innuendo. The fur trade would be carried on as before, under the provisions of the Deed Poll. "Whatever collateral objects of a different character the Company may, hereafter, have in view, it is not intended that these pursuits should interfere with the fur-trade, or that the gentlemen connected with the Company should necessarily take part in them, so as to have their interests affected by them." If those "collateral objects" included the disposition of even a portion of the company's landed rights, how could they not affect the fur trade? Dissatisfaction simmered across the continent.[11]

The crux of the issue, as the wintering partners saw only too clearly, was that the old company had been a fur trading operation, to which the salmon and seal fisheries were an adjunct. The fur trade was inextricably linked to the land on which the fur-bearing animals lived and to destroy their habitat was to destroy the fur trade. The new proprietors seemed to think the land and the animals could be treated separately and that the wintering partners would be unaffected by the new arrangements because they were not being deprived of the fur trade and its profits. The new owners merely wanted the land; they wanted to open it to settlement and sell it as fast as they could for the greatest possible amount of money.

Donald had expressed his unease both officially and in private correspondence but he was delighted that his furlough would give him an opportunity to size up Sir Edmund Head and his colleagues for himself. Until he could travel, however, there was nothing for it but to keep his head down and work as efficiently and effectively as he could. In July, he proposed that the company should begin to tin salmon on the Labrador coast as an alternative to salting it as a means of preservation. He had discovered that salmon tinning was easily the most profitable part of Hunt and Henley's business in Labrador and suggested that a cannery be established at Ungava Bay where the fish could be stored for a year or two if the company ship had difficulty reaching Fort Chimo. He had learned, moreover, that the tinner who had worked for Hunt and Henley had left that company and might be available to the HBC.[12]

On the personal front, there was both good news and bad in the summer of 1863. Murdoch McPherson, Joseph's father and Donald's old bourgeois, died at his home in Nova Scotia. Among his last concerns were Joseph and his prospects in the company, understandably so, since Joseph seemed to have reached his plateau as head of one of the minor posts in Esquimaux Bay. The old fur trader died before news could reach him of the birth of yet another grandson, this one christened Donald Alexander by his namesake at North West River on August 10.

Of greater import to the Smiths was the decision that Bella should respond to her mother's plea for a visit; she was to travel in the *Nelly Baker* with Captain Dodge and his daughter to New England where she and the children would spend a month before carrying on to Lachine where the Hardistys had bought a retirement home. Maggie was nine and Jamesie was eleven and the trip was also intended to enable Bella to make arrangements for their education. The Smiths' thinking was that the family would stay in Montreal until Donald's furlough was completed and that they would return to Esquimaux Bay with a tutor who could also instruct the children of other HBC staff members in the district.

The fact that Donald could send Richard Hardisty £130 to support his family, as opposed to the £40 he sent in 1857 when Bella also had to pay rent, suggests that he was beginning to be financially comfortable, as does the fact that he asked Hopkins to invest £500 in mortgages that year. He and Hopkins had established a good working relationship; Donald was pleased with the investments which Hopkins, as manager of the Private Cash Account, had made on his behalf and the two men seemed to work well together to sort out the difficulties with the Gulf of St. Lawrence posts. As well, Hopkins was trying to make arrangements to send a Roman Catholic missionary to Esquimaux Bay. But Hopkins' judgement was not always sound, perhaps because he was sometimes concerned about his wife, the painter, Frances Ann Hopkins, who, though her most famous subjects were the Kahnawake canoes, did not like Canada, its climate or its people, and preferred to be in London with its art galleries and exhibitions.[13]

In July 1864, Hopkins sent Andrew Kenyon to Esquimaux Bay as a clerk, noting that he was very good and had had four years experience in the Montreal office. This was in lieu of Tom Hardisty whom, unknown to each other, both Donald and his brother-in-law, William Lucas Hardisty, had been trying to secure because he had established a reputation as a bright young man who was both intelligent and hard working. Kenyon, on the other hand, had already been a source of complaint, having been accused by Henry Connolly in October 1862 of treating his son James, who was boarding with the Kenyons, as "a regular slave."[14]

Since that unfortunate experience, Kenyon's wife had died, but sympathy for his circumstances was short-lived in North West River, as Donald was obliged to report to Hopkins in September.

> I have been placed in a very awkward position by Mr. Kenyon's arrival as he has already shewn himself to be a person in whom no confidence can be placed, and by his foolish and presumptuous manner & bearing he has already made himself disagreeable

> to most of the officers in the District. He has been drunk and disorderly over and [over] again and while in that state made a thorough fool of himself, both before the Hunts people at Cartwright and our own men here, so that they despise and ridicule him. In his cups he gave out that he came down to relieve me, and that on those conditions alone did he consent to come, and that he was to do so and so with all the — clerks. There has been much more than this, but quite enough has been said in writing regarding one who really appears to be not worthy of notice.[15]

The dash indicates profanity which Donald never used. For a man who was abstemious in his own habits — he admitted to having once had a glass of wine on his own after nearly drowning when a kayak overturned — Donald was notably tolerant of those who could not control their consumption of alcohol. Kenyon had been obliged to leave his young son behind when he accepted the Esquimaux Bay posting and Donald proposed that Bella bring him when she returned with her children. The three could be schooled together. Privately, Donald hoped that the boy's presence would induce more responsible behaviour in his father.[16]

In Bella's absence, Donald concentrated on establishing the first of the posts meant to deflect the Naskapi from Mingan and Sept Iles. He also turned his mind to housekeeping, clearing out the stores of goods which had not found a market in Labrador and were unlikely to do so. "Five barrels of buffalo robes which have been on hand here for twenty years" were packed off to Quebec, together with two barrels of knives and some mittens. There were more of the latter if Quebec managed to shift them. Also sent were 5,600 pounds of fish to test the Quebec market.[17]

The weather in October 1864 was stormy and wet on the southern part of the Labrador coast and the *Jacques Cartier* waited nine days to get out of Rigolet for Indian Harbour. She finally sailed on October 25 and two days later, Donald boarded one of Nathan Norman's ships heading for Newfoundland. It was a "boisterous passage" as he put it in a telegram to Hopkins at Montreal, but the phrase belies the beating the vessel took in the rough seas. At the beginning of the journey, waves smashed through the cabin, breaking the stove pipes and leaving a residue of three or four feet of icy water. The wind blew them three hundred miles out to sea, with the result that a passage which should have taken three or four days took two weeks; the men were cold and drenched throughout, being unable to either dry their clothes or warm themselves. Donald's feet were frostbitten. When they finally reached St. John's on November 7, he was carried to Nathan Norman's house and a warm bed. Frostbite is an extremely painful condition; when it happens, the affected extremities are numb but as the feeling returns with warmth, the inflamed tissues are unbearably sensitive and can remain so for many days. Sleep does not come easily in such circumstances and Donald found himself reciting the metrical psalms of his childhood and long passages of Livy's *History* which he had been required to memorize at school. The doctors were of little help.

Finally he was well enough to travel to Halifax, but as soon as he reached there on the nineteenth, he put himself under the care of Dr. Parker. By the twenty-fourth, his right foot was much better, though his left was still giving him too much pain to allow him to travel. At Halifax, he invested £100 in the cargo of a small steamer about to run contraband through the blockade and into the Confederate port of Wilmington, North Carolina. This was not his money — it could hardly have come from anyone other than Nathan Norman for virtually no one else knew that he was going to Halifax — and he entirely disapproved of the venture. "In the first place, the risk is too great, and in the second place, the whole enterprise is against my principles," he wrote. There were huge profits to be made from contraband, however, with returns of up to one hundred and fifty percent, and many in Canada and the UK made substantial fortunes from it during the civil war.[18]

The first week of December had passed before Donald was finally able to board a steamer for Montreal and it was not until the sixteenth of the month that he was at last reunited with Bella and the children at the Hardistys' house in Lachine.

Bella and Donald had much news to share and some important decisions to make about the children's schooling for the ensuing year. They agreed that Maggie would go to Mrs. Gordon's boarding school on St. Catherine Street in Montreal and that Jamesie would attend a school near Captain Dodge's home at Hampton Falls, New Hampshire. Donald would take the lad there on his way to England.

Besides occupying himself with more visits to the doctor, Christmas and hogmanay celebrations, and a party for Maggie's birthday on the seventeenth of January, Donald spent time at the Hudson's Bay Company offices which had been moved to Montreal from Lachine shortly after Simpson's death. Governor Dallas had re-established the Canadian headquarters at Red River, but the Montreal office retained much of the importance previously associated with Lachine because of the company's links with the business and financial community in the city and because it provided much superior communication with England, Quebec and other parts of Canada. Montreal was seen as a sort of alternative headquarters for the company in Canada and was the more important for the commissioned officers because the Private Cash was managed there.

Donald also took the opportunity of his Montreal visit to inquire about his cousin, George Stephen, who had moved to the city while Donald was in Labrador and was beginning to establish something of a reputation for himself. Stephen's mother was Elspet Smith, the sister of Donald's father, Alexander. A good twenty years younger than her brother, she had married William Stephen in 1828 and shortly thereafter had moved with him to Dufftown at the eastern end of the Spey valley. In 1847, William Stephen and his eldest daughter had emigrated to Montreal where William joined a cousin's wholesale dry goods business. The following year, the rest of William's family, except the oldest son, George, also emigrated. George was working for a similar company in London, but in 1850, he too sailed for Montreal and the family business. By 1865, George Stephen was well established as a merchant of some significance and his name figured among those who led the city's charitable activities. He had briefly been involved with a proposed transatlantic shipping line and was shortly to become a partner in the Rosamond Woollen Mill at Almonte, Ontario.

The cousins had never met but one day Donald asked one of the HBC staff who lived in Lachine if he had heard of George Stephen. Not surprisingly, he had and, long after, recalled what had happened.

> As Mrs. Smith had some shopping to do, we all went into the city together. I gave him Mr. Stephen's address and we parted company. A couple of hours later I met all the Smiths in St.

> James Street, loaded down with parcels, and Mr. Smith carrying a rather gaudy carpet-bag. He stopped to show me the bag, and asked my opinion of it. "It's just the thing for the Labrador," he said. "It'll make a great hit with the Indians there." I inquired if he had met his cousin, Mr. Stephen. "Oh, yes," he said; "I went in and had a few moments' conversation with him." "I suppose he was glad to see you, eh?" Mr. Smith seemed a little embarrassed at the question, but his wife exclaimed in her charming, sprightly style: "Really, why should Mr. Stephen be glad to see country cousins like us — all the way from the Labrador? I wish," she added slyly, — "I wish he had waited until he had met Mr. Stephen before buying that red carpet-bag. But he would n't let me carry it and the rest of us waited outside."[19]

Donald, with his sombre black suit, tangled eyebrows, long auburn beard and red carpet bag was doubtless an oddity in George Stephen's well-furnished office but pleasantries soon gave way to business and the men discovered they had a similar way of looking at things. The conversation turned on the provision of goods for the Hudson's Bay Company trade, and on the first of February, Stephen sent samples of Canadian made tweeds from the mill at Almonte to Mingan. They were sent care of Donald but were obviously meant to test the market.[20]

On February 6, Donald and Jamesie travelled to New Hampshire where the lad was deposited at school and his step-father proceeded to Boston and the ship which would take him to the long awaited reunion with his family. He had written his mother and his brother John to say that he had been delayed and explaining to his brother that he had been ill. He told them both he expected to be in Scotland by the end of January. By the middle of February, poor old Mrs. Smith was fretting, unaware that her son was still on the opposite side of the Atlantic. As early as 1854, she had asked her daughter Jane to write George Simpson to inquire if Donald might not be given leave of absence. The governor politely replied, explaining that he could not have it without applying for it and that her son knew full well what the regulations were with respect to furloughs. Simpson said nothing of the incident in his letters to Esquimaux Bay and the fact that the subject was never raised again suggests that Mrs. Smith might have decided to stay quiet about it as well. Now, however, with the prospect of a visit so close to hand, she was naturally eager to see her son.

When she returned to Forres, Mrs. Smith had first settled in rooms on the High Street, but she was now living at Milnes Wynd, one of the narrow lanes leading off it. Later, she would move to rooms in nearby Caroline Street. In Archiestown, Jane had been courted by the minister but, when nothing had come of the relationship, the two women went back to Forres where a number of their Grant relatives lived and where Jane could anticipate some help in caring for her eighty-one year old mother. John, who had married Eliza Cousins in Edinburgh in 1852, had retired to the Scottish capital ten years later, suffering from periodic, incapacitating recurrences of the malaria which he had picked up in India on his first foreign posting. He had two daughters, Margaret, who would remain a spinster, and Eliza Johana who was to marry Robert Grant and settle in Forres. With Britain's burgeoning railway system, John could take his daughters to visit their grandmother and aunt with comparative ease.

Twenty-seven years had elapsed since Donald and his mother had parted. She was no longer middle aged, but an old lady, and he was no longer a teenager, but a mature man with a family. He had read widely, whereas his blind mother was restricted to what others could offer her and, in any case, was principally interested in her church and her community. Though Donald was not yet a man of the world, he had seen a good deal more of it than his mother and Jane had ever experienced and his mind had grappled with complex issues of world commerce and international affairs. While it was a happy reunion, and Donald was delighted to visit his family, he also discovered that he had grown apart from them. His foot still troubled him, perhaps because he was experiencing the first attack of gout from which he suffered periodically in later years, so it was difficult to wander about Forres, reviving memories of his youth, and he was finally forced to confess that he had not much enjoyed his visit to Scotland.[21]

In his absence, Morayshire had acquired a little rail network and a station had been built at Forres. At the beginning of July 1863, a viaduct across the River Spey had been completed and the management of a collection of independent lines was undertaken by the Great North of Scotland Railway. Tales of idiosyncrasies abounded, the best of them concerning the Morayshire Railway, the engines of which, being more vertical than horizontal, were known as coffeepots. Reports suggested that they had neither lights nor brakes and were incapable of adhering to any timetable in the integrated system. Put sails on them, and Donald might have thought himself back at Rigolet trying to make his shipping business work efficiently. Nevertheless, places and relatives who, in his childhood, had been out of bounds because they were too far away were now close at hand and he undertook a rail journey. From Forres, he travelled to Elgin where Marianne had been to boarding school, then to Craigellachie at the eastern end of the Spey valley, Archiestown where his father had been born and his parents had moved after Marianne's death, and along the river to Grantown where his parents had first lived, returning from there to Forres. It was odd being a tourist in his own country but then again, he was no longer entirely Scottish: he was becoming Canadian too.[22]

After a visit with his brother in Edinburgh, Donald headed south for London, reaching there about the tenth of March. By the thirteenth, he had already met a Hunt and Henley director and agreed a price of £400 to buy out two of the firm's posts near Rigolet. More importantly, he had met the governor, Sir Edmund Head, and several of the senior directors, including Curtis Lampson and Eden Colvile. Lampson was an American and viewed with suspicion by the wintering partners who knew that he had once worked in the fur trade in opposition to the HBC. They also assumed that he would share Washington's views on issues such as the location of the international boundary west of the Rocky Mountains, a matter of some importance to the HBC which had both fur trading operations and an agricultural business south of the forty-ninth parallel. Donald was pleasantly surprised to discover his colleagues' opinions seemed to be ill-founded. Lampson had acquired British citizenship in 1849 and held patriotic views. "Moreover he has the highest possible opinion of the Company's officers and servants and a desire to do them justice," Donald wrote to Robert Hamilton. "He told me last evening that there never was a body of men in the service of any corporation in the world of higher intelligence, sobriety, and loftiness of character. His views on the Oregon Boundary question were at the time diametrically opposed to those of the American Government."[23]

Lampson had arrived with the International Financial Society takeover and was deputy governor. Eden Colvile, one of the few old shareholders to maintain his influence after 1863, was the son of Andrew Colvile who had served the company as governor or deputy governor for most of his working life. His son had grown up with the company and, between 1871 and 1889, would follow in his father's footsteps as both deputy governor and governor. When he encountered Donald Smith in March 1865, he was immediately impressed and arranged the dinner at which Lampson and the Labrador Chief Factor met for the first time. "He is just the sort of man you would like to meet," Colvile wrote to Lampson, "shrewd, and well-informed upon every topic relating to that *terra incognita* of the British Empire."[24]

At that gathering and on other occasions, Donald soon learned that the wintering partners could expect little sympathy from the new shareholders and the new board of directors. John Shepherd, who had been governor during the 1857 select committee inquiry, had said that changes such as settlement in the Northwest could not occur without the cooperation of the wintering partners and had stressed that their claims needed to be met. But his day had passed. "Unfortunately, our danger comes from the stockholders, who do not and will not trouble to understand the situation," Donald wrote to George Barnston, his old superior from Tadoussac days. "As Governor Shepherd said, 'they are of the usual class of investors, indifferent to any other question in the present discussion than the security of their capital and dividends'."[25]

By 1865, the Governor and Committee were beginning to discover that matters were not quite as simple as they had assumed. When the council of the Northern Department had met in 1864, it drew up a letter to London pointing out that profits were already decreasing and so reducing the officers' income. The proposals concerning the disposal of land would reduce their income even further. Two options were suggested: a minimum annual income of £350 for Chief Traders and £700 for Chief Factors under the existing Deed Poll or the abolition of the Deed Poll and the introduction of salaries for all staff. In the latter case, provision needed to be made for retired men who were still entitled to income under the Deed Poll. The Governor and Committee had responded with a compromise which guaranteed a lower minimum income and was to run for a fixed period of five years. By the time the General Court met in July 1866, however, the directors were convinced that they were on thin ice in proposing to open the territory for settlement. To do so would put at risk the "only source of actual income" with no guarantee that the land sales could actually be effected. A delay would help to win back the loyalty of the wintering partners and it would also mean that the company retained the option of selling the Northwest in a bloc to the British or Canadian governments as foreseen by the 1857 select committee. As John Shepherd had already observed, the security of their capital and their dividends was the shareholders' only concern and they voted overwhelmingly in favour of the fur trade.[26]

In reality, the proprietors and the wintering partners could do little more than wait in the wings while the stage was readied for the next act. As Donald Smith sat in the Houses of Parliament listening to the debates, toured the sights of London, and negotiated with the secretary and the directors about various issues affecting Labrador, two Canadians were locked in negotiations with the Colonial Office about the future of their country. They were John A. Macdonald and George-Etienne Cartier and their proposal was that all the British colonies in North

America should join in one federation. The agreement they eventually reached included provision for the entry into Confederation of the unorganized territories, by which was meant the Hudson's Bay Company lands in the Northwest.

In the meantime, as the crocuses came into bloom in the city parks, Donald concentrated on persuading the HBC management to accept his proposals for improving the profits of Esquimaux Bay. They agreed to his suggestion that a cannery be established and sanctioned the employment of tinsmiths and of Samuel Reeves who, having retired as head of the canning operation for Hunt and Henley, was persuaded to return to the Labrador coast for a year or two to teach his trade to the HBC men. On March 17, Donald returned to his brother's in Edinburgh and used his home as a base for journeys to Leith, the city's port on the Firth of Forth, where he learned enough about tinsmiths and their wages to engage men to work in Labrador.

He was sufficiently engrossed in visiting his brother, advising the board about navigation problems on the north Labrador coast, writing a memorandum on the Labrador trade and attending a Turkish bath in hopes of curing his foot that he paid little attention to the normal progress of life around him and had to be reminded by Thomas Fraser that there was little point in travelling to London on Easter Saturday in anticipation of seeing the HBC staff at the beginning of the following week. He did go to London at the beginning of May, then returned to Scotland, and finally headed back to London to select goods for trade at Esquimaux Bay and prepare for his return to Canada at the beginning of June. He had accomplished a good deal of work during his furlough, had had a valuable opportunity to size up the new proprietors, and had met the company's senior staff.

On Friday, the ninth of June, Thomas Fraser wrote to thank him formally and to put in writing all that had been agreed. Fort Chimo was to be re-established at Ungava to defeat the Moravian trading ambitions and was to report to Esquimaux Bay; Mingan and Sept Iles were also to be added to Esquimaux Bay and Donald was to spend part of each year on the St. Lawrence, wintering in Mingan, the lease of which he was also to sort out with the owners. He was to establish cod fishing and salmon tinning on the Labrador coast and to take over those Hunt and Henley posts which had been purchased. The letter reiterated that furs were to be sent to England but that otherwise he had *carte blanche* to dispose of his returns in whatever way was likely to produce the greatest profit. When the Governor and Committee agreed that Labrador should report directly to London, they began the process of creating a separate unit with almost no links to the old fur trade empire beyond those it chose to maintain; the new changes reinforced this separation and heightened the independence and the power of the district's chief. All he lacked was his own steamer.[27]

In the early days, the proprietors of the Hudson's Bay Company liked to visit the ship on which their fortunes depended before her departure for the inhospitable subarctic shores. They made sure the captain understood his instructions, looked the vessel over and wished all on board good luck for both the outward and the homeward journeys. This practice, motivated by curiosity, pragmatism and good will, transmogrified, like much else in the company's conduct of business, into a formal routine. It was an occasion when the directors could entertain important Canadian visitors and those in the British government or market place whose interests and influence impinged on HBC business. Any wintering partners who happened to be in London, and who could be relied on to bring a touch of the exotic, were also included. By 1865, it had become a day-long outing, starting with breakfast at Blackwall in the east end of London. From there, a steamer took the guests to Gravesend, the port near the eastern end of the Thames, where outbound ships dropped the London pilot before proceeding to sea. George-Etienne Cartier and John A. Macdonald, as well as men from the Foreign and Colonial Offices, declined the 1865 invitation, feeling they could not spare a Saturday for the excursion. Charles Brydges, General Manager of the Grand Trunk Railway, accepted, as did Alexander Grant Dallas, the company's Canadian governor. Dr. John Rae, the company surgeon and famous Arctic explorer, who had led several expeditions in search of Franklin, also attended and so did another doctor, William Cowan, who was based at Fort Garry where he served as one of the colony's four magistrates, besides providing a medical service for the community. The wintering partners included James Bissett, who had gone from Lachine to Honolulu and was now a Chief Trader at Victoria, and Donald Smith.

Dinner ended with a series of toasts, including the future of the company, the success of the voyage and the health of the commissioned officers. To the last, the Chief Factor from Labrador was asked to respond. The idea terrified him: this was not to be a passage of Livy in front of his school mates nor metrical psalms before the planters and Naskapi at North West River; it was not a conversation with the secretary or the governor where he could argue a case from intimate familiarity with his subject. In preparation, he made some notes, including a jesting allusion to Dr. Cowan residing in "the relative refinement of Assiniboia." He observed that he, himself, represented the company's interests in "an obscure and little known district" but that the men there were "animated by the same purpose, and inspired by the same spirit of loyalty to the Company and ... to one another." But when the time came for him to address his few words to the assembled guests, they found that he had vanished. As William Armit, then a young secretary in the London office, remarked many years later, "he had not the courage to face the music."[28]

He hated the thought of the Governor and Committee and their prestigious guests gazing at him while he stumbled through his efforts to be gracious, courteous, respectful, witty and brief — all qualities which he was capable of on paper or in private. The more he prepared, the more he thought he would forget. His mouth was dry, his brow was wet and his meal sat uncomfortably in his churning stomach. He had never spoken in public before and had concluded that his debut could wait for another day.

Donald was profoundly embarrassed at having balked at such a hurdle and when the ship called in at Deal on the Kent coast, he wrote to excuse himself, saying he was unaccustomed to public speaking and "had shrunk from making an exhibition equally painful to himself and his auditors." His composure was not yet restored, however, for he realized, once the *Ocean Nymph* was under way, that his worrying about the speech he had made him forget things in London. He compelled Captain Davis to pull ashore early on the morning of June 15 and the HBC secretaries were "somewhat startled" to see him later that day. "The vessel put into Portsmouth to enable him to procure his luggage," W.G. Smith reported to Donald's brother in Edinburgh, "which being done he left again in the afternoon and is now at sea in a much better state of mind than when he wrote to me from Deal." The captain was under the impression that they stopped "for necessary documents that was left behind," probably a more accurate explanation since, when he reached Labrador, Donald wrote to Fraser, observing that the secretary was "rather out of humour with me at the time I left England" but claiming that, in calling at Portsmouth, "I only did what was right under the circumstances." He softened the blow by sending a keg of cranberries "that you may have an opportunity of comparing them with those of Hudson's Bay, of which latter I had the pleasure of partaking at your hospitable board." Three pairs of native shoes and "a few trifling articles of Esquimaux ivory" further put the secretary in his debt.[29]

When Donald reached Portsmouth, he discovered that Captain Davis had seized the opportunity to ship another sailor as he judged those he had to be inefficient. Donald told him to let the least efficient go but Davis refused; it was the first of many disagreements.

The voyage started badly because, by Donald's calculations, it was already late if the schooner was to call at Rigolet to drop off him and the district's provisions, then continue to the north coast of Labrador to enable Joseph McPherson and his men to establish a post near the Moravians, and from there carry on to Whale River on the east shore of Ungava Bay with provisions for the Eastmain district. Then, the *Ocean Nymph* took seven weeks to cross the Atlantic. Captain Davis blamed the pumps which broke down but he had already decided against carrying out his instructions and knew that the later he arrived at Rigolet, the easier it would be to excuse himself from the voyage north.

It was July 29 before the guns at Rigolet finally sounded their welcome. Though he had supposedly repaired the pump, Davis announced the northern trip was impossible because the ship had neither suitable rigging nor an adequate crew. Furthermore, he complained that the cargo was poorly stowed, with packages for Ungava and Whale River in different parts of the hold which he perceived would cause difficulties and delays. An offer to relieve him of the Ungava stop if only he would take the provisions to Whale River was rejected. Davis' opinions were not shared by the first mate, and both he and Donald urged the captain on. He appeared to capitulate but the schooner was only part way up the coast when Davis announced that he was heading for England. Neither Joseph McPherson nor the mate could dissuade him, but they did at least get him to drop McPherson and his four labourers at Rigolet on September 18. It was a profoundly dissatisfying end to the furlough but very useful in reinforcing Donald's argument that his district needed a steamer which could become familiar with the coast and which, moreover, could be properly under the control of the company.

Offsetting these frustrations was a happy reunion with Bella and the children who came to Hamilton Inlet in Captain Dodge's ship. There was much to tell and presents from England and Scotland to delight the children and their mother. At some point, probably on this occasion, Bella received a simple ring which she wore as a wedding band. Another Scottish gift was a luckenbooth brooch which she wore for the rest of her life.

When they reached North West River to make arrangements for the winter, Donald fell ill. It was almost as though he had come home, could relax, had his wife to care for him and so had the luxury to be sick as he had not had, bar his frostbite, for the better part of a year. His illness, probably a severe cold of the sort which plagued him all his life, coupled with the length of the salmon fishing that year, meant they were late leaving Hamilton Inlet and it was nearing the end of October before they finally set sail in the *Jacques Cartier* for their new winter quarters.

At that point, they intended to stay at Mingan until the new year, so the mail for Montreal included letters and presents for Hopkins. Stuffed birds, deer antlers, a model kayak and a cask of locally grown potatoes accompanied a note which observed that Andrew Kenyon had been "excessively drunk for two or three days, in fact so much so as to have been falling about all over the place, cutting his face rather severely during his tumbles and requiring to be picked up by the men." Rigolet was left in charge of an experienced local clerk, something which would never have happened had Kenyon been able to control himself. Before the year was out, Kenyon was back in Montreal attempting to sort out his muddled financial affairs before trying to make a new life for himself elsewhere.[30]

It took less than two weeks to convince Donald that there was little to be gained from spending further time at Mingan and the sooner he could discuss future arrangements for the area with Hopkins, the better. He and Bella therefore set out for Montreal, arriving on November 12. It was fortunate that they did so, for when they reached Lachine, they learned that Richard Hardisty had died a month earlier. He had suffered increasingly from rheumatism and had not been well for the better part of a year, but his death was unexpected and so sudden that his wife only discovered it after he failed to answer when she spoke to him.

"His will, of recent date, is a strange one," Hopkins observed in a letter which did not reach the Smiths at Mingan in time. "All his property is left to his widow for life and at her death, almost everything is to go to Tom. The legacies to the rest of the family are very small." To further complicate matters, the house at Lachine was left jointly to Bella and her oldest brother, William. This was particularly unsatisfactory because Mrs. Hardisty wanted a new kitchen which Donald was perfectly happy to pay for, but it did not take much imagination to foresee the tangle which would ensue after her death should Bella and William try to put a value on improvements in anticipation of selling the house. Though Donald wrote both William and Richard to tell them of their father's death, he asked Hopkins to broach the subject of the house with William who was offered either cash or Bank of Commerce shares for his half. Initially, he accepted the shares and a price of $1,600 (£320) but he changed his mind and it was May 1867 before he settled with Donald for £400. "I consider Mr. Smith has behaved liberally," Hopkins wrote when the agreement was finally reached. "I should value the property at about $1900; and your chances of being entitled to one half within the next 5 or 10 years are slight, as your mother is strong and vigorous .... Smith gives you $1100 down, the interest on which, @ 7pct, is $28 a year, which he loses & you gain." Donald said it made no difference whether the second half was his or Bella's, a remark which suggests that their separations had done nothing to make them think of themselves as other than an indissoluble whole. The sale put the house entirely in her name, a transaction more common in French Canada where ownership of property by married women was familiar if not customary.[31]

One of the best things about the visit to Montreal was that Donald and Hopkins discovered how well they got along with each other, even though they disagreed about the future of Mingan. Hopkins thought even a restricted post would serve no purpose because there were now so many settlers along the north shore. It would be better, he thought, to have roving agents who would purchase furs as they encountered them. Donald disagreed, knowing the problems of shipping and understanding that both settlers and the peripatetic Indian hunters had to be able to rely on a post being there when needed. At this point the difference did nothing to undermine the friendship. Company correspondence, even among friends, generally started "Dear Sir" but by the end of November, when Donald was inspecting the St. Lawrence River posts as London had requested, the men were addressing each other as "My dear Hopkins" and "My dear Smith." From Quebec, when Donald wrote to acknowledge the arrival of blankets for Mingan, he thanked Hopkins "for throwing in 10 prs for nothing," the invoice having been incorrectly made out.[32]

At Quebec, Donald also had a long discussion with Father Durocher who was arranging the visit of a priest to Esquimaux Bay. It appeared that, eighteen years after first mooting it, Donald was finally to see his suggestion come to pass.

Before Donald set out on the trip down the river, Hopkins wrote London to say that the two of them had agreed that there was little to be gained by wintering at Mingan and, in view of the failure of the *Ocean Nymph* to carry out her intended voyage to Ungava, Donald could better spend his time in England preparing for next year's Labrador business. The Governor and Committee agreed, and the sooner they saw him, the better.[33]

Early in January, Donald and Jamesie boarded the *Peruvian* for a rough winter crossing to Liverpool. Friendship with George Stephen and his wife, Annie Kane, had flourished quickly. Though they eventually adopted the daughter of one of their servants, the Stephens had no children of their own, and Mrs. Stephen took a particular interest in Jamesie and Maggie, and was consulted on their education. She arranged for her uncle, John Plow, who lived in the Hampshire village of Alton, to take Jamesie under his wing and see to his schooling. While Donald's principal reason for being in the UK was business, the trip gave an opportunity to settle his step-son as well. They arrived at Liverpool on January 18 and that night, Donald was "in my old quarters The Queens Hotel St Martins Le Grand." He was just behind St. Paul's Cathedral and a fifteen minute walk from the HBC headquarters.[34]

The winter General Court was held at the London Tavern on the twenty-fourth of January, there now being too many shareholders to use the Court Room in Fenchurch Street. Preparations for it meant that neither the staff nor the directors had much time to discuss business with their Canadian visitor but they did pass on the welcome news that a five hundred ton steamer was being built at Sunderland for the Labrador coast.

As soon as the General Court was finished, the men turned their minds to the leases and other documents which gave them authority over Mingan and for several weeks there was much to-ing and fro-ing over where the documents were and what they did or did not say or mean. Donald ordered the trade goods for his newly enlarged district and had discussions with the directors about the Moravian mission. Fraser had written the brethren's headquarters at Herrnhut in December to say that the company would be establishing posts at Ungava and perhaps along the coast and acknowledged that this might conflict with the Moravians' activities. The essence of his letter was an offer to assist in the brethren's "philanthropic and religious objects" in exchange for which the missionaries were expected to restrict their trading activities. The company had not grasped that the Moravians needed the income from their trading activities to finance the missions and contribute to the costs of sending their own supply vessel to the coast.[35]

During this visit Donald "had the honor of touching fingers" with Governor Dallas, whom he had met at dinner on the *Ocean Nymph* seven months earlier. He also met John Rose, a Scot who exerted as much influence in Canadian affairs as Bear Ellice had done a generation earlier. In 1866, he was helping his friend, John A. Macdonald, work towards the confederation of the British North American colonies and would soon be serving as minister of finance in the Canadian government. For many years, he was one of the Hudson's Bay Company's most powerful shareholders.[36]

In addition to his business activities, Donald also spent time sorting out Richard Hardisty's estate and, though there are no references to it in surviving correspondence, he undoubtedly made a trip to Scotland, probably during the Easter break. It was a wet spring and Donald spent most of February "coughing away most lustily;" a trip away from the city's fog and pollution would certainly have done him no harm. Back in the city's, his shopping included the purchase of crystal and china in one of the city's more expensive and fashionable districts. This was not for use in Esquimaux Bay or the more primitive surroundings of Mingan; as he saw it, it was only a matter of time before his principal residence was in Montreal and the dishes could be stored there until he needed them. He left London on May 11 and sailed from Liverpool to New York on the *Cuba* on May 12. It was his first visit to the American city and he allowed himself a few days to explore it before heading back to Canada.[37]

The journey from New York to Montreal was more than usually interesting because the Fenians – Irishmen or sympathizers with the Irish cause who lived in the United States and believed they could promote independence for their homeland by attacking British targets such as Canada – were gathering to launch just such a raid. The Canadian and American authorities were obliged to treat the threat seriously, but Donald was pretty sceptical. "For my own part," he wrote to Fraser, "having met four or five hundred of the wretched Fenian troops on the way from New York to Montreal I formed so low an opinion of them as not to have been able to look upon the whole affair in anything like the same serious light in which it has generally been viewed by those who have not come so closely into contact with them."[38]

The first of June saw him back in Montreal again, admiring Mrs. Hardisty's new kitchen and hearing plans for a further extension on both the ground and first floors. The house, one of Lachine's older properties, had probably been rather poorly equipped when the Hardistys moved in but was now becoming a sizeable property. Mrs. Hardisty's sight was rapidly deteriorating but she preferred the disruption of the workmen and alterations to a place she knew rather than renting or buying a smaller house. With the Smiths coming and going, visits from the grandchildren, various company employees dropping by with news of her sons and daughters, and old fur traders calling in to reminisce, she was probably right. Besides, it pleased her to have the extensions made and, as far as Donald was concerned, that was justification enough.[39]

In Montreal, Donald was beginning to find doors opening and new acquaintances developing, partly as a consequence of his friendship with his cousin. George Stephen had set up his own dry goods business earlier in the year and was shortly to sell the family firm. Financially, he was very comfortable. "Now that he is possessed of some money, [he] is determined to enjoy life," Donald had written

Hopkins from London. "He can doubtless afford it, and I heartily wish him joy." Through him, he met Edwin King, the president of the Bank of Montreal, in which he now owned a considerable number of shares, and Hugh Allan, the Scot who had made himself fabulously wealthy first as a ship builder and then as the head of the Montreal Steamship Company, one of the world's biggest merchant fleets, familiarly known as the Allan Line.[40]

In July, the cousins attended what was, for Donald, his first political meeting. It had been called to protest the June budget which contained a proposal to reduce the tariff on imported goods. Though the tax had initially been imposed as a revenue measure, it had soon come to be seen as a protection for local manufacturers and they were reluctant to see it go. Men spoke of the risk of job losses and emigration to the United States; they pointed to the city's prosperity and noted that for five months of the year agricultural labour was impossible, but the factories still worked. Then, to the amazement of Donald Smith who had not yet found the courage to address even a Hudson's Bay Company dinner, his cousin rose to speak. Not only that, he bucked the trend and spoke in favour of the government's proposal. The reduction was merely from twenty to fifteen percent, he noted, and he felt satisfied that his companies in both Upper and Lower Canada could turn a profit with that degree of protection. "If they could not exist with that protection with the crippled resources and deranged currency of the United States, he thought it was a very blue outlook for Canada." Hisses and boos greeted his speech but it led to the creation of a local "free trade" league. It also made Donald think for the first time about the issues surrounding a government's fiscal policy and its impact on commerce.

July was an exciting month in Montreal that year for it also brought the first message from the new transatlantic telegraph cable. Donald instantly saw that telegrams would revolutionize the shipping industry because shippers would have a much more certain idea of the current state of the market for their produce. "It will have a powerful effect on ocean steamship stock, and the existence of ocean telegraph lines will probably bring about the substitution of steam for sailing vessels," he wrote.[41]

In the meantime, he had his own steamer on his mind. The *Labrador*, which had just been built for Esquimaux Bay and Ungava, was due in Quebec about the middle of June but when Donald arrived in the city to meet her, there was no sign of her and no news. Returning to Montreal, he discovered that she had been late out of London because the stevedores had first loaded her as though she were a coastal vessel, covering up the coal in the process. As a consequence, she was not due till the end of June. The Canadian supplies were gathered in Quebec, a mineralogist who was to investigate Donald's theory that there was mineral wealth in Labrador was prepared to embark, and lumber for the construction of a new post at Mingan was purchased and made ready for the voyage; at the end of the month, Bella arrived to join her husband on the journey back to Rigolet but, after waiting for a few days, went back to her mother in Lachine since there seemed no point in paying Quebec hotel bills for nothing. Donald was already annoyed because the original plan of sending the *Labrador* to Mingan had been overruled in favour of calling at Quebec, and it was with mounting frustration that he travelled back and forth between Montreal and the Quebec capital. Finally, he hired a schooner called the *Ripple* to carry the Canadian goods to Rigolet but no sooner was the ink dry on the charter party than the *Labrador* made her appearance. She had sprung a leak and was shipping four inches of water an hour. Her voyage across the Atlantic had been made at a snail's pace to keep the influx to a minimum and ease the job for the pumps and the crew, a number of whom deserted the moment the ship docked.[42]

The carpenters set to work to repair the *Labrador* but it was already apparent that the *Ripple* would be needed too, to carry all that was meant for the Labrador coast. That, at least, saved an argument with her owners. Bella rejoined Donald at Quebec and on the afternoon of the sixth of August they finally set off down the river. Three days later, they were at Mingan. With the help of John Rose, Hopkins had managed to reach an agreement with the owners of the seigneury and the men were able to lay out the site for a new post. The company was leasing a much smaller piece of ground and hoped that by reducing its expenses, the post could pay its way. The priest, who had spent several weeks waiting for them, had finally given up: it seemed as though the notion of a priest at Esquimaux Bay was as much a chimera as the idea of an efficient shipping service. No more encouraging was the mail from Rigolet which reported that many of the best men in the district, including Captain Irvine and Joseph McPherson, had been ill for much of the past winter.[43]

They left Mingan on Sunday the twelfth and on the following Friday, finally landed at Rigolet in the pouring rain. As soon as it was dry enough, the *Labrador* was unloaded and readied for the voyage to Ungava where McPherson was to reopen Fort Chimo. Happily, Captain Norbert Wood, yet another Scot in the company's service, was pleased with the new ship now that the leak was fixed and was, as Donald put it, "energetic." Better still, he was not intimidated when he learned that Fort Chimo was on the banks of the Koksoak River which rose forty or fifty feet with the tide. By the middle of October, the winter arrangements were finally in place. The schooner *Marie Anna* was loaded with the salmon and seal oil for the Canadian market and took as passengers Bella, Mary, Mary's children and a maid. They were joined by Henry Connolly's two daughters, Anne and Margaret who were being sent to the Sisters of St. Anne in Lachine, partly for their education but partly because one of the HBC officers had been making eyes at the elder girl. At Quebec, Bella helped Mary and her children transfer to the *Lady Head* which took them to Norway House at Pictou where McPherson's widowed mother still lived. She then returned to Lachine, expecting Donald to join her in a month or two.[44]

He, however, was having his usual shipping problems. He took the *Labrador* from Rigolet to Newfoundland but there discovered that the last ship of the season for Mingan and Quebec had already left. The fastest way to go to either place, let alone Montreal, was to go to London, and this he did, arriving on the tenth of November. Though this was an unscheduled visit, it had its uses in enabling him to keep his name and his face before the Governor and Committee and in helping him to keep their intentions and likely future plans in focus. Fraser was to retire as secretary and his place was to be taken by W.G. Smith, the son of the man who had arranged for both Donald and his father-in-law to enter the service, while William Armit moved up a notch to be assistant secretary.

Both Donald and Hopkins were concerned by the fact that the samples of tweed which George Stephen had provided had been rejected out of hand by the Governor and Committee. The view was that the wool was too good to be Canadian but the tweed was not good enough. Donald himself felt the tweed was not up to the standard which had been provided for Mingan and Esquimaux Bay but both men, together with W.G. Smith, felt the cloth had not been given an unbiased assessment. Stephen was very angry and, though he proved to everyone's satisfaction that the wool was indeed Canadian, he and other manufacturers were to face a long battle before they could convince buyers in either Britain or Canada that Canadian woollen goods could indeed be as good as British ones.

It was cold and foggy in London and Donald wasted little time in coming down with a cold and flu, though it did not lay him low till he arrived in Edinburgh shortly before Christmas. He spent the holiday in bed at his brother's but shortly before hogmanay he was "sufficiently recovered to be able to continue the journey to Moray where I am to spend a few days of the Christmas time with my good old mother." His news from Montreal was that neither Bella nor Mrs. Stephen was satisfied with the education that Maggie was receiving at Mrs. Gordon's and were making arrangements for her to travel to the UK at the beginning of May. She was far from pleased at the prospect, writing to her uncle Richard, "I do not like the idea of going at all, but there is no use me saying anything about it, because I know that I will be obliged to go whether I like it or not." She was, however, pleased at the thought of seeing her step-brother who reported that he was enjoying his school in Hampshire. According to Bella's letter to her brother, Maggie was going to a school "near Edinburgh" which was also attended by the daughter of Dr. Cowan, the magistrate and surgeon from Red River. Cowan's family were in Helensburgh, west of Glasgow, and Maggie spent time there as well.[45]

The summer of 1867 passed much as its predecessor had. The *Labrador* was late arriving in Esquimaux Bay from Montreal, though nowhere near as tardy as it had been the previous year. A priest, Father Bebel, joined her at Mingan and travelled with her as far as North West River. "At this post," he reported, "I found 32 Christian families, four of whom had never seen a priest, and 30 infidel Nascopies who had come down with the traders. I began the instruction of these pagans, but as each of them had left two or three wives at Fort Nascopie, I could do nothing for them until I had regularized their position according to the precepts of the Christian religion." The author of the North West River journal saw things in a rather different light. "The priest had some kind of ceremony together with the Indians in the Men's House," he sniffed on Sunday, July 21. "Prayers were read by Mr. Smith at 11 AM in the dwelling house at which Captain Wood together with the officers and men of the *Labrador* attended," he added, leaving no doubt about *his* own religious views. The Catholic services were the fulfilment of an ambition which Donald had conceived nearly twenty years earlier, but the achievement gave him no particular satisfaction. Father Bebel was no match for Father Durocher, and two years later was threatening to bring all the Catholic Indians down to Mingan, saying he would "have his own Canoe and not be humbugged by you and the old steamship," as William Church reported from Bersimis, adding that "Mr. Babel was drove from Les Escoumais, and the Rev Desore on the Ottawa and he is Detested all along this coast and but a few words to the Superior of his Order at Lachine would give him his walking ticket from here." In the summer of 1867, however, Donald just felt that it had taken too long to achieve his ambition and he was now much more involved with the problems of managing a greatly enlarged district.[46]

There was growing competition all along the Labrador coast from both the Moravians, who had stepped up their efforts, and the independent traders, especially those from Newfoundland. Donald was, as George Simpson would have noted approvingly, "active" and in October wrote W.G. Smith in London a long and energetic account of his summer, showing clearly that the *Labrador* had spent hardly a moment more than was necessary at any of the ports. They had called on the Moravians at Hebron, the most northerly of the brethren's posts where Donald was described as "very friendly, promising not to interfere in the mission in any way," though the missionaries were not convinced by these promises. The *Labrador* steamed north to Saglek Bay, the terminus of the shortest cross-country route to Ungava Bay. The trail, Donald reported,

> is undoubtedly used by the natives on their visits to the trading stations of the Moravian Brethren who finding that their request for permission to settle in Ungava was not acceded to by the Company had this season made preparations for building a post here and had already some timber on the ground for erection of buildings which they propose putting up next year. Fortunately we were in advance of them and were enabled to select the only really good site for houses to be found in the Bay which extends inland about thirty miles.[47]

At Hebron, the missionaries heard the news of the HBC construction from Salomo Lane, a fisherman who reported that the post was left in charge of Keith McKenzie, a southern Inuit named Thomas, "unbaptized" as the missionaries were obliged to observe, and "a sailor from Shetland." The Moravians feared, correctly as it turned out, that McKenzie and Lane would become friends and in their report to the Committee of the Society for the Furtherance of the Gospel also noted that thanks to Fort Lampson, as it was dubbed, the HBC took five hundred pelts which they estimated would otherwise have gone to Hebron.[48]

The *Labrador* encountered headwinds and "boisterous weather" off Cape Chudleigh (now called Cape Chidley) before she dipped down into Ungava Bay. London had been very concerned at sending Joseph McPherson and his companions to so forlorn a spot and Donald was at pains to assure everyone that they were "in good heart" and enjoying venison, ptarmigan and fish. Martens, foxes and wolves were plentiful and, he noted, in his letter to the secretary, Ungava was better off for fruit than Labrador.

> We found here the greatest profusion of cloudberries, cranberries, currants and three or four varieties of blueberries and in a small garden at the post were turnips and potatoes of fair size and in short it appeared to me that the only drawback to Ft. Chimo as an Inland Post and this applies generally to all other parts of Ungava Bay is the difficulty of communicating with it, owing to the great height to which the tide rises and consequent rapidity of the currents which on one occasion while we were anchored in South River ran at the rate of eleven knots an hour.[49]

Donald's enthusiasm for his work was given a further boost when he returned to Rigolet and found that the steamer was going to be able to take all the returns from all the posts between Mingan and Fort Chimo back to London. He, meanwhile, took the *Marie Valentine* to Quebec and carried on to Montreal to meet Bella.

She and her mother had spent a month in Pictou with Mary and Joseph's mother. Norway House was a large and impressive stone house on the outskirts of the little seaport and had sufficient land to enable the McPhersons to raise their own fruit and vegetables and allow them to keep a few animals. They were, however, having troubles making ends meet, in part because there were six children to feed and Richard, the oldest of them who might have been contributing to the family income had, as his grandfather had noted when he was a little boy, "crooked legs and a stammer." Nevertheless, there was a feeling that Mary's eyes were bigger than her pocketbook. When Donald said to Hopkins that Bella could have whatever she wished from his account, he knew that her demands would not be extravagant and than she had a basic understanding of how much she could comfortably spend. On occasion, Donald also passed on similar messages from McPherson, but Mary sometimes seemed to behave as though her husband's Private Cash Account were a bottomless pit. Little was said, but both Bella and her mother were concerned.[50]

The Smiths had barely a week together at Montreal and Lachine before they set off for Mingan where they were to winter. It was windy and bitterly cold and Bella found it impossible to shake off the nasty cough she had developed. Finally, her brother Tom brought her back to Lachine where she rapidly improved and was later able to re-join her husband. In the meantime, Donald was working on his plan to unite all the St. Lawrence River posts with Esquimaux Bay. In addition to Sept Iles and Mingan, he felt Bersimis should be included. The theory was that Montreal would look after supplies and transport while Esquimaux Bay would supervise the work. The board was interested in the idea, but Edward Hopkins was sure it was folly because Donald could not give personal attention to posts spread over such a distance and there was a risk that the person in charge at Montreal would contradict the orders or the intentions of the man in Labrador. It was Hopkins' territory which was being eaten away, but this concerned him less than the administrative issues. Their different views on Labrador and the King's Posts began to sour relations between the two men and they continued to deteriorate.

In part, Hopkins was right, for Donald was taking on more and more responsibility without the assistance which might ensure continued effective management. As usual, his accounts were late as were his personal expense claims for his trips to London in 1865, 1866 and 1867. On the other hand, he knew his staff and could rely on them; when he found he could not, he was quick to dismiss them.

In May 1868, Donald and Bella returned to Montreal. Though Donald had spent very little time in the city, it had been more than sufficient to establish a bond with his cousin, George Stephen, which went well beyond the courtesies of kinship. That spring, the two men devoted a number of hours to discussing the woollen business and Stephen determined to try to introduce Canadian-made blankets into the HBC trade. His view, which Donald was inclined to share, was that there was no reason why Canadian manufacturers could not match the standards set by the English suppliers. The source of the blankets was to be the Paton Company, established at Sherbrooke, Quebec by Andrew Paton in 1866. When he wanted to expand in the summer of 1868, he brought in Stephen, Donald Smith and Richard B. Angus to form a joint stock company. This enabled Paton to incorporate the neighbouring Lomas Woollen Mill and the men later purchased the Quebec Worsted Company.

The first board meeting of the new company was in July, but by the beginning of June, Donald was off on his travels again, checking on the posts along the river and then heading north in the *Labrador* to Rigolet, North West River and Fort Lampson. When he returned to Montreal in the autumn, he found a letter from London instructing him to winter in Montreal, replacing James Clouston who was ill. This was to be a temporary assignment and he was to be prepared to return to Labrador as soon as navigation re-opened. By December, however, the Governor and Committee had changed their minds and Donald was instructed to proceed to London as soon as possible in order to discuss some changes which were thought necessary in the Montreal Department.

The changes were that the entire Montreal Department was to be amalgamated with Esquimaux Bay and, in effect, be restored to the arrangement which had existed when Donald first went to North West River except that now there were more posts in Labrador and fewer along the river. All the posts between Tadoussac and Lake Superior were in areas where settlement was increasing daily and, under Hopkins' management, were consistently failing to make a profit. Hopkins had not been able to find a solution to this problem and, with his wife spending most of her time in London, felt increasingly ambivalent about his commitment to the company, especially now that it was changing so rapidly. Curtis Lampson thought Donald Smith was the man to replace him and persuaded Sir Stafford Northcote, who had succeeded Sir Edmund Head as governor, to go along with the idea. "I am glad you agree with me," he wrote in November 1868,

> that Donald A. Smith, Chief Factor of the Esquimaux Bay district, is the best man for the post and for the purpose. From what I have seen of him and know from his reports, he is really a person of extraordinary ability and judgment and may safely be relied on for any contingency which may arise. He has been in the Company's service about thirty years and it is entirely owing to him that our Labrador affairs have continued in a satisfactory state. Moreover, he enjoys in a marked degree the complete confidence of all those in the service with whom he has had relations.[51]

One of the problems in the Montreal Department was that the values fixed for furs had not varied for years. This was the figure which showed in the post accounts and did not necessarily bear any relationship to what a pelt had actually cost or what price it fetched at auction in London or Montreal. This was to be altered to bring the prices up to date. More radical, however, was the agreement reached between Donald and the board that he would appoint agents who, if they were not commissioned officers, would be on salary, to purchase furs. Though the letter of instruction makes no reference to future arrangements, this was clearly the first step towards either closing down uneconomical posts or converting them to sales shops.

The Governor and Committee had also been impressed by the efficiency with which the *Labrador* had been able to conduct business along the coast, despite teething troubles, and decided that steamers should also be introduced in the Northern Department, starting with one which was intended to ply along the shores of Hudson Bay among the posts reporting to York Factory. If the experiment succeeded, other steamers would be introduced and Donald was instructed to make inquiries in Canada about the kind which would be most suitable for the business. Although Toronto, Montreal and Quebec, where such information was likely to be found, were all accessible to the Commissioner of the Montreal Department, as Donald was to be called, this was clearly not Montreal Department business. The board had identified him as a man with a capacity to understand transport issues and had no intention of confining him to one area if he could be useful elsewhere.

In London, Donald was also able to persuade the board to consider the use of Canadian blankets for the trade. Two hundred pairs, conforming to the company standard for size and weight, were to be introduced at various posts, this too being an experiment.[52]

The only cloud on the horizon was the board's persistent annoyance about the failure to receive accounts on time. Those for the Labrador business in 1867 had still not been submitted in June when Donald was instructed to establish a system which would mean they would be supplied on time in future. They were Henry Connolly's responsibility now, but Labrador was short staffed and in November, London was still awaiting the 1867 accounts.

Early in May, Donald was back in Montreal, making plans to visit as many of the important posts in his new territory as he could manage. He was glad of the July first holiday on which Canada celebrated its incorporation as a dominion because it gave him some quiet time in the office to get caught up with his correspondence. That was soon interrupted, however, by news from Quebec that the *Labrador* had been rammed in the roads by a pilot. Like modern accountants and lawyers, the St. Lawrence River pilots put all their worldly possessions in the names of their wives or trustworthy friends and had nothing for which they could be sued. Donald spent weeks engaged in fruitless arguments.

It was customary for the man in charge of Private Cash to write those for whom he acted once a year with a statement of account and an indication of any important changes which might be in the offing. Private correspondence took place whenever an individual's specific investments or instructions required it. When Hopkins wrote to say that he was retiring, he announced that he would continue to manage the Private Cash Account, though he would be dividing his time between London and Montreal. As the investments were in Canada, this seemed odd indeed and many objected. Donald was nervous of taking on the responsibility himself; it was not a field in which he had any expertise but he was under mounting pressure from the officers in the field to take control. Under such circumstances, he explained to the board, he would do so until he received instructions from London.

He had not understood that "Private" meant just that and Secretary Smith was ordered to set him straight. "While the Governor and Committee are in no way opposed to your giving advice to parties who may apply to you, or even looking after their interests should you think there is occasion for it, they object most strongly to such a business being carried on by the officers or clerks in the service whose time should be occupied in their ordinary duties, and they cannot assume any responsibility in connection with the business." Donald wrote a suitably humble response, but in truth the business carried on as before, managed by the senior officer, in this case

Donald Smith, and administered by one of the clerks, with the half percent commission introduced by Simpson in 1855 applied, as before, to defraying costs.[53]

Donald's worry was perhaps justified in that he did not want to make a mistake with other people's money. He was, however, playing an increasingly important role in Montreal's business community and began to spend a part of nearly every day with George Stephen, sometimes discussing Canada's increasingly complex political situation but more frequently talking about financial matters and the many new investment opportunities which were becoming available. In the summer and autumn of 1869, they made their preparations to form the Canada Rolling Stock Company in which they would be joined by Edwin King, Sir Hugh Allan and his brother Andrew, and Robert Reekie, a man well-known for his Canadian railway interests.

That summer, the Smiths moved from Mrs. Hardisty's house in Lachine to their own home at 73 Mansfield Street in Montreal. It was logical that they should find their own accommodation now that they knew where Donald would be working, but the choice of Montreal rather than Lachine was a declaration that they were not intending to establish themselves among the mixed-blood HBC population which still clustered around the old headquarters. In choosing Mansfield Street for their first Montreal home, the Smiths were placing themselves firmly within the residential quarter in which clustered the wealthy Scots who, for generations, controlled the city's and, by and large, the country's economic life.

The ties with the Hardisty family remained close, however, and the summer and autumn months of 1869 also took on something of an air of a reunion. Tom was now living in Lachine and working in the HBC office in Montreal; early in the summer, William and his wife brought their eldest daughter down from the McKenzie District to attend the Wesleyan Female College at Hamilton, Ontario; and Richard Hardisty's furlough started in Outfit 1869 when he and his wife, travelling from Fort Edmonton with a maid, brought their daughter to the same college. Both the older brothers were meeting Bella's husband for the first time, but both quickly realized that they could count on him to look after their interests and invest their surplus money wisely.[54]

Joseph McPherson was on furlough in Outfit 1868 and he also was in Montreal in the summer of 1869. His visit, however, was not such a happy one. His year at Pictou seems to have done nothing to restore his financial equilibrium; his boys, except his oldest, were as idle as ever and neither his wife nor his mother seemed able to manage the farm or the house which was larger than they needed and expensive to run. He was of two minds about returning to work for the company: on the one hand, he needed the income, but on the other, he felt obliged to be in Pictou. For his wife's sake, Donald was patient but he felt increasingly irked by the indecision and by the fact that the dilatoriness which Simpson had suspected at Kibokok had surfaced again at Fort Chimo when McPherson revealed he was unable to provide the accounts for the post because he had no documentation beyond scraps of paper containing notes he had made while bartering. In the middle of June, McPherson finally made up his mind and wrote a letter of resignation, saying that "my private interests are at present of such paramount importance to me when compared with my position as Chief Trader of the Hudson's Bay Co that I am compelled however reluctantly in some respects, to beg that I may be permitted to decline returning to active service and respectfully request that the resignation of my commission be accepted from the 31st May last."[55]

Before he left Montreal, however, McPherson applied to his brother-in-law for a loan, offering his house as security. The situation at Norway House was not straightforward and it seems likely that Donald did not understand all the ramifications. McPherson certainly did not.

The story goes back to Edward Mortimer who came from Keith at the eastern end of the Spey valley. In 1788, at the age of twenty-one, he arrived in Pictou on a trading schooner from Halifax. His employers had sent him there to buy oak staves for the West Indies trade but he soon started business for himself as a timber agent and shipowner, confirming his dominance in the field when he married Sarah Patterson, the daughter of his main competitor. Before long, Mortimer was the richest man in Nova Scotia. His house is said to have taken two years to build and nothing but the finest craftsmanship was tolerated. It was finished in 1814 when it was insured for £3,000, though said to be worth £4,000. Mortimer died five years later but his widow lived in the house until 1835 when it was sold to Edward Smith. He had been a Chief Factor in the Hudson's Bay Company and it was he who named it Norway House.

Edward Smith had married, *à la façon du pays*, a native woman by whom he had five daughters, including Jane, who was born at Slave Lake in 1805. She, in turn, married Murdoch McPherson and was Joseph's mother. When Edward Smith died, he bequeathed the house to his son-in-law. Though Smith had the best intentions, it was a poisoned chalice he handed over for the house had been mortgaged to the rooftops. Besides obliging Murdoch McPherson to settle with his creditors, Edward Smith's will also required his heir to invest money for the care of Smith's two unmarried daughters, Eliza and Harriet. With the help of friends in Pictou, McPherson was able to clear the debts, but when he died, there was no money to care for his widow and nothing but the house to leave his son. To make matters worse, Joseph had eight children and a wife who seemed unable to economize.

Donald's loan was for $3,200 Halifax currency but it did nothing more than tide the McPhersons over for a while. In the spring of 1870, McPherson proposed selling the house and asked Donald if he would act as a trustee for an annuity which would be paid to Jane McPherson for the remainder of her life. Donald agreed, but McPherson was unable to find a buyer. Finally, in the winter of 1871-1872, he applied again to Donald for a loan, guaranteed by a mortgage on Norway House. McPherson fixed the value of the sum to be invested for his mother and that, coupled with the unrepaid loan and, presumably, the unpaid interest on the loan, was calculated to equal the value of the house. The document which the two men signed effectively sold the house to Donald Smith or at least gave him first refusal at the agreed price of $6,400. In the summer of 1872, when McPherson thought he had found a buyer willing to pay $14,000, Donald was obliged to remind him of their agreement and of the fact that he expected it to be adhered to. McPherson admitted that, in his dealings with his brother-in-law, he had fixed a price lower than that which he had hoped to get and that he had wrongly assumed that he was not expected to adhere to his side of the bargain. What he did not know was that Edward Mortimer, the poor Scottish lad who had made his fortune in Nova Scotia and built the house, was related to Alexander Smith, Donald's father. Mortimer's mother was Mary Smith, Donald's great-aunt. In buying Norway House, Donald Smith was acquiring a piece of his family's heritage.[56]

CHAPTER SIX

LOUIS RIEL AND THE NORTHWEST 1869-1870

The blame of having bungled the whole business belongs collectively to all the great and puissant bodies. Any ordinary matter-of-fact, sensible man would have managed the whole affair in a few hours.

William Francis Butler[1]

In March 1867, parliament in London passed the British North America Act which provided for the confederation of Nova Scotia and New Brunswick, and of Upper Canada, which was renamed Ontario, and Lower Canada, which became Quebec. On the first of July, when the act came into force, the new country of Canada came into being.

The legislation foresaw the inclusion of Prince Edward Island, which had been involved in the early negotiations, and of Newfoundland with her Labrador dependency. The British North America Act also made provision for the admission of the colony of British Columbia, which had been established in 1858 when Vancouver Island and the Pacific mainland were amalgamated, and, as foreseen by the 1857 select committee, it allowed for the incorporation of Rupert's Land, that area between Ontario and the Rocky Mountains which had been granted to the Hudson's Bay Company in the seventeenth century and was still governed by it.

In the early months of 1869, Canadian newspapers were full of stories about the future of the Northwest as negotiations between the HBC and the British government drew to a close. The Governor and Committee saw no need to brief employees in Montreal or Fort Garry. It was, as far as London was concerned, not a matter of the fur trade but of land and therefore need not concern the wintering partners. The fact that the head of the Northern Department, Chief Factor William Mactavish, was the governor of Assiniboia, the tiny settlement clustered in the vicinity of the company's post at Red River, and exercised what little civil authority there was over its inhabitants, appeared to the board to be of negligible importance. For their parts, the British and Canadian governments perceived the negotiations as relating to the smooth transition of power between one civil authority and another. They believed their actions to be in the best interests of the handful of settlers in the Northwest and of the immigrants who would follow in their footsteps, but they saw no need to explain themselves.[2]

The essence of the agreement was that on the first of December 1869, Canada would pay £300,000 to the Hudson's Bay Company, the money being provided through a loan guaranteed by the British government. In addition, the company would retain the one hundred and twenty posts which it presently occupied, together with the land around them, totalling a maximum of 50,000 acres; during the ensuing fifty years, the company could claim blocks of land in the fertile belt as it was laid out for settlement, the total not to exceed one-twentieth of the whole area. This would give the company seven million acres. The fertile belt was understood to extend from the US border west to the Rocky Mountains and east to Lake Winnipeg and Lake of the Woods. The northern boundary was the northern branch of the Saskatchewan River. It was believed that land outside the fertile belt could not be cultivated and was therefore not suitable for settlement. Ever a stickler for detail where money was concerned, the company also insisted that the Canadian government pay for the telegraph wire and other equipment which the International Financial Society had shipped into the prairies as a prelude to its plans to erect cable communication between the Northwest and eastern Canada. The fact that the value of the wire had not been ascertained before the deal was done was a minor hiccup when compared with the fact that the land which was the subject of the transfer, including those portions which were allocated to the HBC, had never been surveyed. Canada, for its part, was committed to governing its new acquisition even though, as Bear Ellice had pointed out twelve years earlier, there was no tax base from which to derive the funds to do so.

In anticipation of the transfer of power, the Canadian minister of public works, William McDougall, ordered the construction of a road between Lake Superior and Fort Garry. The Dawson Route, named after its engineer, Simon Dawson, was to be a bone-rattling corduroy road with more than forty portages and the dubious pleasures of a boat ride across Lake of the Woods. At the best of times, McDougall was both rash and arrogant and, in 1868, without bothering to consult the HBC or seek permission to trespass on its territory, he instructed the survey party to proceed to lay out the route, starting at Red River.

Some of the settlers in Assiniboia, at the confluence of the Red and Assiniboine Rivers, had purchased their land from the Hudson's Bay Company. Others were squatters who had established their right to the land by occupation over many years. The population was made up of Scots and English, many of whom had moved there with their families on retiring from the Hudson's Bay Company; the Métis, who were generally the descendants of Indian women and French or Scottish labourers who had worked for the North West Company; and Canadian immigrants — generally from Ontario — plus a handful of Americans who had migrated north. Among the English and Scots were families of mixed-blood, though the community recognized a distinction between a Scot, or English person, who had some Indian blood and a Scotch or English half-breed, the latter indicating a higher portion of native blood or a preference for a native rather than European way of life. Distinctions between the various sectors of the population were blurred, but as a rule, the English, Scottish, Canadian and American settlers were Anglophone and Protestant while the Métis were Francophone and Roman Catholic.

The Canadians and Americans were fairly recent arrivals at Red River. They owed no allegiance to the Hudson's Bay Company and, unlike the other settlers, could not look back over years if not generations of living amicably under the company's benign, paternalistic government. The old timers had their grumbles, but they rubbed along peacefully enough and were prepared to trust the governor who generally left them to get on with their lives. The newcomers, however, were a disruptive influence. They saw no reason to tolerate the company's monopoly and were loud in their complaints. They had compelled the company to allow them to open stores and if they could not trade furs publicly, many did so covertly. The Canadians had little time for the company's old fashioned, courteous ways and were impatient for change and the opportunity to make their fortunes.

The Métis led a somewhat nomadic existence, pursuing the buffalo hunt which provided the pemmican that sustained the fur traders on their long journeys. They were also the tripmen, carrying overland huge cargoes of furs and supplies between Saint Paul, south of the border in Minnesota, and Fort Garry, and between the fort and some of the HBC posts. Under the influence of the missionaries, the Métis were beginning to settle, clustering in the little community of St. Boniface, where a school had been established to provide the children with at least the rudiments of an education. In French, the word *métis* merely means half-caste but the Métis of Red River conceived of themselves as a separate nation, created out of their French and Indian backgrounds, and they were rightly proud of the discipline and skills which they brought to their work.

The decade of the sixties had been a harsh one in Assiniboia. Years of drought were followed by plagues of grasshoppers; 1868 was by far the worst year when the parched lakes and rivers yielded few fish, the grasshoppers ate what little wheat had struggled through the dry soil, the buffalo hunt failed and even the rabbits disappeared. McDougall conceived of the road survey as a project which, in addition to initiating the creation of the physical link between Canada and the Northwest, would help to alleviate distress by providing employment and therefore money to purchase imported provisions. However commendable his intentions may have been, he lacked the foresight to imagine the impact the surveyors would have on a community destabilized by contradictory rumours about what lay in store for it and suffering terrible privations through the failure of its natural resources. Governor Mactavish could not prove to the Métis or to anyone else in the community that the men had not come to steal their land or to force them to live elsewhere because he was as much in the dark as they were. He could make his own assumptions, but no one in authority had written him to explain the purpose of the survey and give him a tool with which to assuage the nervous settlers.

The survey party at Red River was led by John Snow and his paymaster was Charles Mair, a young protégé of William McDougall. The political leanings of Snow and Mair were evident as soon as they struck up a friendship with John

Christian Schultz, the leader of the Canadian faction in Red River. A doctor who had largely abandoned medicine for trade, Schultz was a big, brash, aggressive Orangeman of mixed Irish and Danish descent who had determined that the Northwest would be Canadian, a word which, as far as he was concerned, allowed little room for Francophone half-breeds. Mair, who lived with Schultz in the winter of 1868-1869, shared Schultz's conviction, as did Snow, that the Northwest should belong to people like them. Their crude disregard of local customs reinforced the growing suspicion among the Indians and the Métis that Canada, by which was meant the Orangemen of Ontario, intended to seize control of their land and destroy their way of life.

The English and the Scots were apprehensive in the face of the failure of Britain, Canada and the Hudson's Bay Company to provide information or reassurances, and somewhat fearful of the pugnacity displayed by Schultz and his friends, but they were generally passive, or at least willing to give the benefit of the doubt to those who controlled their future. The spice in this particular stew was provided by the Americans, both those who were resident and those who lived in the United States. It was obvious, they argued, that the North American land mass should be one unit rather than two. The United States was more developed and its merchants were playing an increasingly important role in supplying goods to all parts of Canada. Saint Paul was the centre through which the Hudson's Bay Company now shipped more and more of its indents and its returns, though the northern route through the bay itself had not yet been abandoned. Americans like Donald Smith's friend William Kernaghan believed that as soon as the company gave up its landed rights, merchants would trade on their own account and the US railway companies would extend northwards. Inevitably, the country would fall under American control and from there it was but a short step to American government. It was, so the argument went, America's manifest destiny.

The American option was never really a serious contender for the fate of the Northwest, though it could always be used to evoke a tremor of fear in Ottawa and London, for no one ever knew quite how seriously to take it. Occasional American calls for the use of force could generally be discounted but it was much harder to evaluate the psychological factors. For their part, the Americans never really grasped that the Anglophone communities north of the forty-ninth parallel did not want to be American, preferred the slower and more peaceful rate of development and felt an attachment to British culture and systems of government. The Métis knew that their society would be swamped much more rapidly if subjected to American influences but they, like the English speakers, were not above using a remark sympathetic to annexation if it seemed likely to help them get their way.

By the spring of 1869, a dangerous mixture of ignorance, Canadian arrogance and seeming American threats was brewing in the Northwest. Though wracked with tuberculosis, Governor Mactavish determined to visit London and Ottawa to find out what the government and HBC intentions were and to warn both the Canadian government and the company that tensions were growing in Red River, especially among the Métis, who perceived that their homes and their livelihoods were under threat. The governor arrived in London after the arrangements for the transfer were completed and was told he was unduly alarmed; in Ottawa he was assured that everything was under control. Though he was told that the transfer would take place, he was given no information about Canadian intentions with regard to land ownership or government and nothing with which to reassure the people of Assiniboia.

Donald Smith and Mactavish met each other in London and travelled back to New York together at the beginning of May. For several years, Donald had been thinking about the future of the Northwest. The select committee of 1857 had alerted him to the fact that the days of company dominance were numbered and the International Financial Society's plan to sell the land had prompted him to think still further about what might happen to those millions of acres and what role the company might play. In 1864, Hopkins had sent a copy of Sandford Fleming's pamphlet on the development of "Central British North America" and the need for a road to link it with British Columbia and Canada. It was, said Donald in his note of thanks, "a most masterly presentation of the Red River case very practical and avoiding the usual rhetoric for which we ought to be very grateful."[3]

The pamphlet was prompted by a series of public meetings at Red River and the views promulgated there were sent to Fleming, already known as a prescient surveyor who was familiar with the country, with a request that he prepare them for presentation to the British and Canadian governments. The people wanted a "line of road that would afford to that settlement free access without being dependent on a foreign country" and they wanted a telegraph line. They believed that a railway could be constructed between their settlement and British Columbia. "Canada would derive great benefit from the Overland Carrying trade, which would spring up immediately on the establishment of this route, and the constantly growing traffic of this district and British Columbia would thereafter be an ever increasing source of profit." In his remarks in support of this request, Fleming observed that the people of Red River were dissatisfied when they compared themselves with their "republican neighbours" whose population had steadily grown in conditions no more favourable than those obtaining in the Canadian Northwest. "Justly or unjustly," Fleming explained, "they attribute their backward condition to the sway of the Hudson Bay Fur company, and they clamour in a way that cannot be misunderstood, against a further continuance of a rule which they appear to believe is the chief hindrance of their progress."[4]

Fleming was very detailed and very accurate in his analysis of the country and its potential and he was clear in his explanation of the demand for representative government by a population which wanted to remain British but seemed to be being thwarted by the very nation to which it wished to adhere.

Having read this pamphlet and committed its information to his tenacious memory, Donald had a solid foundation from which to discuss the future of Red River with Mactavish. The governor, soured by his failure to convince the London board that it was on very thin ice and convinced that the Colonial Office had dictated an arrangement with no regard for the circumstances in Red River, was glad to have an intelligent listener to whom he could expostulate his frustrations and his fears. In their discussions, Donald learned much about the way of life in Assiniboia and began to appreciate how Schultz and his shrill followers had damaged the equilibrium which had kept the little settlement at peace under HBC rule.

In New York, the men encountered Richard Hardisty who had travelled out from Fort Edmonton on leave. Richard had passed through Fort Garry a few weeks earlier and now briefed his brother-in-law and the governor on the latest developments. The situation still seemed unstable but both Mactavish and Donald were certain that military intervention was to be avoided at all costs.

From Ottawa, Mactavish returned to his post, frustrated by his experience in both capitals and weighed down by the depression which so often haunts those who suffer from tuberculosis. The disease was making its final assault on his lungs and he was visibly weaker than he had been when he left Fort Garry in March.

In July, McDougall, who had learned nothing from the community's reaction to Snow and Mair, authorized another surveyor, Colonel John Stoughton Dennis, to proceed to Red River to lay out lots for the settlers who, it was anticipated, would rush in as soon as the transfer was completed. He and his crew arrived early in August and he too lodged with Dr. Schultz. Mactavish was appalled, warning the Governor and Committee that "as soon as the survey commences, the half-breeds and Indians will come forward and assert their right to the land, and possibly stop work till their claim is satisfied."[5]

That is precisely what happened. When Dennis failed to convince Ottawa to halt the surveys, he took his men to the border, keeping them, for the most part, out of the way of the Métis as they proceeded northwards. By October, however, they had reached the Métis settlement on the south shore of the Assiniboine River where they began measuring the hay privilege. Farms along the Red and Assiniboine Rivers tended to follow a pattern imported from Quebec where long, narrow plots allowed each family access to the river which provided both transport and fresh water. At the back of these farms was a two mile strip on which, by convention, each farmer cut his hay and grazed his animals; to those not familiar with the system, it appeared to be uncultivated and unfenced and therefore not owned by anyone. When Dennis' crew began to take measurements on André Nault's hay privilege, a group of Métis appeared. Led by Louis Riel and Baptiste Tourond, they stood on the chain while Riel explained that the land south of the Assiniboine belonged to the people of Red River and not to Canada. The survey would not be allowed to proceed any further. When Dennis took his case to Mactavish and the magistrate, Dr. Cowan, whose daughter had been at school with Maggie Smith in Scotland, Riel reiterated his position that the surveys could not proceed without the express permission of the people of Red River.

Louis Riel had been born in Red River in October 1844, the son of Julie Lagimodière-Riel, the first white woman to be born in wedlock in the settlement. His father, also Louis, was part Chippewa and had worked for the Hudson's Bay Company before taking up land at St. Boniface. Both parents were devout Catholics and each had considered taking religious orders prior to their marriage. Their first-born, too, had a profound faith. Both the Protestant and Catholic clergy were keen to find religious leaders within the native community and Louis was one of three boys sent by Bishop Taché to be schooled in Quebec in the hope that at least one of the lads would return a priest.

Riel attended the strict Collège de Montréal and, though he took some time to settle, proved himself an intelligent and willing scholar. In 1864, he was profoundly upset by his father's death and, like Donald Smith when his father died, by the knowledge that he was unable to help and comfort his mother to whom he felt particularly close. Riel's behaviour became erratic, rebellious and evinced signs of instability and four months before he was due to graduate in 1865, he abandoned his studies. He had been unable to concentrate on his books and was either unable or unwilling to conform to the rules of the college or of the Grey Sisters' convent where he briefly lodged.

He eventually found work in the law office of Rodolphe Laflamme where talk was all of politics in the advent of Confederation, which Laflamme vigorously opposed. The political conversations excited Riel but his attendance at the law office became as unpredictable as it had been at the college and in the summer of 1866 he left Montreal to work at various odd jobs in the United States before reappearing at Red River in July 1868. He was an unstable young man who was looking for an identity, looking for an ideal to which he could devote himself. The threat which his people apparently faced from an avalanche of Canadian colonists gave him a cause which he could champion.

By the autumn of 1869, Riel had sufficiently established himself as a leader of the Métis that Joseph Howe, secretary of state for the provinces, thought it wise to send him a message, presumably of goodwill, when he arrived at Red River. This was a curiously inept visit, ostensibly designed to enable Howe to discover for himself what was happening in the settlement and report his findings to his colleagues. Howe called on the HBC in Montreal with a request that Donald ask the forts along the route to facilitate his journey, but once in Red River, in order to preserve his independence, he stayed at one of the settlement's primitive hotels where he received all the old settlers who came to call. He got enough of Schultz's measure to know that he was a false friend to Canada's interests; already Schultz was scheming to try to prevent the introduction of a representative assembly until he was sure Canadian voices would predominate.

It was rumoured in Red River that Howe was ill and for that reason obliged to confine himself to his hotel. Whatever the explanation, he scarcely ventured abroad. Governor Mactavish found him a "shrewd clear headed man," which undoubtedly he was, but he made no public statements and did not consult the leaders of the various communities or broadcast reassurances concerning the intentions of the Canadian government. After a brief stay, he headed back to the comparatively civilized comforts of Ottawa.[6]

While he was in the Northwest, Howe did begin to grasp the need for absolute impartiality on the part of the Canadian government; it was essential that the new lieutenant governor should take no side. But the man who had been appointed, William McDougall, had been responsible for sending the survey parties which had allied themselves with Schultz and upset the Métis community.

McDougall, who was pompous and overly full of his own self-importance, had set out from Ottawa in September with an entourage and a baggage train more suited to an embassy at Washington than to a muddy little village on the prairies. Some of the furniture he took was so big that it would not fit into Silver Heights, the house which had been selected as the gubernatorial residence, while other pieces could serve no purpose in the Northwest.[7]

McDougall's instructions were to provide temporary government by means of an advisory council, to consult the people of Assiniboia, through the council, about their wishes for the future management of their territory, and to make no appointments until he had assessed the situation and discussed it with the Ottawa government. Nevertheless, he was accompanied by J.A.N. Provencher and Captain Donald Cameron, both of whom had already been given posts on McDougall's staff.

Howe met McDougall and his family in Minnesota Territory, not far from the border. Curiously, in view of the fact that Howe professed to have "a keen insight into the difficulties" which lay ahead and in view of his private conviction that the transition to Canadian government would not be peaceful, he offered McDougall no opportunity to discuss the situation. Blaming the fiercely cold wind, Howe promised instead to write him from Saint Paul. This he did, warning that Schultz and his friends were not to be trusted and that the populace, and especially the Métis, were nervous and very uncertain about what lay ahead. Great tact and diplomacy would be required. Unfortunately, these were qualities of which both McDougall and Cameron had but a very limited supply.[8]

Meanwhile, in Red River, the Métis had already begun to take matters into their own hands. They conducted the buffalo hunt under the direction of an elected council which brooked no opposition and this formed the model for a National Committee which was elected on October 19 to organize armed resistance to McDougall and his party. John Bruce was the president but the leadership rested with the secretary, Louis Riel. On the twenty-first, a blunt note was sent to McDougall instructing him not to cross the border without permission of the Métis council; coincidentally, a barrier was erected on the road between the settlement and the border. At a meeting after mass on Sunday, October 24, a group of moderate Métis engaged in a vociferous argument with Riel and his followers who were beginning to look like rebels. Finally, Riel's spiritual advisor, the Abbé Nöel-Joseph Ritchot, stepped in with a compromise. The conservatives could salve their consciences by remaining neutral.

On the Monday, Riel and Bruce were summoned to explain themselves before the Council of Assiniboia which was still the legal government of the country. Governor Mactavish was far too ill to attend and the meeting was chaired instead by Judge John Black. Riel explained that the Métis were perfectly satisfied with the present government and objected to any new system coming from Canada without prior consultation. Nothing could be said to dissuade him from his conviction that McDougall should not be allowed to enter the country.

On October 30, the *soi-disant* lieutenant governor and his party arrived at Pembina, the little frontier hamlet on the American side of the border. Here he received Riel's peremptory message to which he responded with vehement anger. Neither he nor Cameron had any intention of being cowed by what they perceived to be a posse of half-breeds, but both Cameron and Provencher were forced back at the barricade while Ambroise Lépine, Riel's trusted colleague, firmly escorted McDougall back across the line from the Hudson's Bay Company border post to which he had managed to make his way.

When they heard the news of McDougall's humiliation, Schultz and his friends assumed that the Métis were preparing for annexation to the United States; at the very least, they assumed that the Métis were conniving with the Hudson's Bay Company to ensure the prolongation of its possessory rights. It was obvious to both the Canadians and the Métis that they needed to control the community's source of supplies — food, guns, ammunition and cash — until they could gain reinforcements to impose their will or until they could force or negotiate satisfactory terms. That source of supply was the Hudson's Bay Company's Fort Garry and on November 2, Louis Riel and his men seized it.

It seems to have been Riel's intention to present a united front of Red River settlers who would then negotiate with the Canadian government and agree terms of entry into Confederation. The English and Scots were reluctant partners in this plan, especially after Mactavish issued a proclamation warning that the acts of military intervention had been illegal. After protracted discussion, it was finally agreed that a convention of delegates would meet under the aegis of the Hudson's Bay Company government. But the English delegates wanted to bring McDougall into the country and to negotiate with him the bill of rights which the Métis had drawn up. To Riel, that would be tantamount to accepting Canadian rule and then discussing the terms. He refused.

In the meantime, McDougall had been contributing to the deterioration of peace in the settlement. He had been instructed to travel to the Northwest as a private person and not to assume authority until he received official notification from Canada that the transfer had actually occurred. As soon as he had learned that Fort Garry had been seized, Prime Minister Macdonald had instructed the British government not to hand over the money, arguing that Canada was entitled to take over a settlement at peace. In Red River, however, there was great fear of a power vacuum into which Riel might slip, and Dennis, Schultz and their friends urged McDougall to ensure that the transition to Canadian rule took place as scheduled. It suited McDougall's vanity to comply and he therefore drafted an entirely illegal proclamation; with a few supporters, he quietly crossed the border on the night of November 30 and read his fine words to the windswept, frozen prairie. This might have remained an empty gesture had he not also sent an advance copy of his proclamation with Colonel Dennis to Red River. There, it was printed and plastered all over the settlement.

A few days later, Schultz provoked further trouble. At his warehouse at Winnipeg, a little village about eight hundred yards from Fort Garry, he was storing the salt pork which was to feed the survey party for the winter. Food was scarce enough during the winter in Red River and the food shortages of the previous years meant that few families had anything in reserve. If it came to a fight, victory could well go to the side with the most provisions. The Canadians therefore established an armed force to protect the pork. Inevitably, this provoked Riel who threatened a small but bloody battle if the men did not give themselves up, and on the seventh of December his men imprisoned Schultz and his garrison.

On the eighth, Riel issued a Declaration of the People of Rupert's Land, establishing a provisional government which he said was needed after the Hudson's Bay Company had abandoned the people of Red River and handed them over to Canada which would impose "a despotic form of government."[9]

News of the events at Fort Garry reached Ottawa, Montreal and London by a variety of circuitous routes. All communications had to go via Saint Paul where they were forwarded by mail to their destination and it would therefore take about two weeks for a letter to reach Montreal from Red River. Sometimes it took much longer. On October 12, Mactavish wrote the Governor and Committee in London. They in turn sent extracts of his letter to Donald Smith in Montreal and he, receiving them on November 24, forwarded them, as requested, to the Canadian government. When he wrote, Mactavish had been concerned about the surveys but, by the time Donald took up his pen to communicate with Joseph Howe, it was known that McDougall had been turned back and that the situation had deteriorated. In addition to offering assistance to facilitate the surveys, as instructed by London, Donald offered "the assurance that the Governor, Factors, and officers generally will use their influence and best efforts to restore and maintain order throughout the Territory."[10]

As there were no government agents in the settlement, there was no one with authority to communicate directly with the prime minister and his colleagues, who consequently found themselves dependent on the HBC and the newspapers. The press in Ontario and Quebec carried stories of varying reliability. Joseph James Hargrave, the son of one of the HBC's most senior officers and a future historian of Red River, sent letters to his friend, Tom Hardisty, who then arranged for them to be published anonymously in the *Montreal Herald.* Charles Mair sent his account of events to the Toronto newspapers while the Saint Paul press picked up information which, once published, was cabled to the newspapers of eastern Canada. The man who most successfully cut through the morass of often contradictory evidence emerging from the Northwest was Sir John A. Macdonald who quickly perceived that Riel was not a rebel but a man who wanted to negotiate the terms under which his people would enter Confederation. Macdonald had brought his own negotiations with the British government to a successful conclusion less than three years earlier and Riel's demands struck a familiar chord.

Macdonald therefore determined to send men who might be respected in Assiniboia to explain the intentions of the Canadian government. He chose the Grand Vicar Jean-Baptiste Thibault, who had just retired after serving for thirty-six years as a missionary in Red River, and Colonel Charles de Salaberry, who had been quartermaster to a Northwest exploration party twelve years earlier and was considered to have "considerable experience in dealing with French half-breeds."[11]

As the most senior Hudson's Bay Company officer outside Red River, Donald Smith found himself increasingly in conversation or in correspondence with the Canadian government. He spent all of the first week of November in Ottawa and Sir George-Etienne Cartier, the minister of militia who, with Macdonald, had led the way to Confederation, had called on him in Montreal to talk about "this Red River affair," as Tom Hardisty expressed it. "He remarked that it was all a mistake and appeared not to be pleased at the way the government officials have been conducting themselves at Red River."[12]

On November 22, Donald was back in Ottawa for another meeting with Cartier on "the unfortunate state of matters now existing at Red River," as he reported to London. "I was in possession of little further information on the subject than he himself had. I strongly recommended that resort should not be had to force in the present condition of affairs, believing that it would be unwise to introduce any armed force whether Regulars or Volunteers in the present excited state of the Territory."[13]

Donald was keen to provide the government with whatever reliable information came his way and urged Norman Kittson, the company's agent at Saint Paul, to keep him briefed as best he could. Mactavish's deteriorating health was equally a cause for concern. "I grieve to learn how very ill Governor Mactavish is," Donald wrote to Kittson, "and his latest private letter to me unfortunately gives very little hope of his speedy recovery, and on public grounds as well as regards the Company's business, his illness at this moment is a great misfortune."[14]

Mactavish's "latest private letter" contained sufficient new information to warrant sharing it with the government and on the afternoon of Saturday, November 27, Donald called on George Stephen whom he knew to be friendly with Sir John A. Macdonald. The proposal was that Stephen accompany Donald on the night train to Ottawa and introduce him to the prime minister the following day. Stephen was not free to make the journey but he wrote Macdonald a somewhat inaccurate letter in which he described his cousin as "an old & intimate friend of McTavish [sic] at Fort Garry with whom he is in almost daily communication." If Macdonald wanted to see Donald Smith, he should cable on Monday and Donald would take the evening train to Ottawa.[15]

The prime minister was glad of all the information he could get, though, in his reply to Stephen, he remarked that it was his opinion "that the insurrection or riot will die out of itself." Macdonald had hoped that Donald would arrive armed with a solution to the problem in the west. "I was very glad to see Mr. Smith who seems a clever man; at the same time I am exceedingly disappointed at the apparent helplessness of the Hudson's Bay authorities," he wrote to Stephen on the first of December. On learning that two French Canadian commissioners were about to set off for Fort Garry, Donald's only proposal had been that the government might also send a Protestant who was known to be an independent man of business. He suggested George Stephen. As Macdonald anticipated, Stephen declined. But Macdonald thought that sending an influential Protestant was a good idea and decided that the man should be Donald Smith.[16]

Donald explained to the Governor and Committee that the Canadian government believed that "it rests with the authorities of the Hudson's Bay Company to put down the insurrection, before the Dominion can assume the Government of the Territory, to which I replied that the rising had its origins not in opposition to the Company's rule but to the measures ... which they either believed or professed to believe would be introduced by the incoming Governor and his Council."[17]

Macdonald and Cartier urged Donald to stay in Ottawa while the privy council considered the situation. If the influential Protestant was also a senior figure in the Hudson's Bay Company, they reasoned, there was a chance that he might gain the confidence of the disaffected Métis and persuade them that they would not be worse off under Canadian rule. The councillors might also have considered the alternative: if the mission failed, it could always be blamed on the fact that the emissary worked for the HBC.

At his meeting on the first of December, Donald further proposed that the government consider "how far the malcontents could be appeased by assuring them the Dominion Government had no intention of extending to the North West Territory for two or three years the Canadian tariff but would with the view of encouraging immigration and developing the resources of the Country admit all goods duty free with the sole exception of spirits."[18]

The greatest beneficiary of such tax exemptions would, of course, be the Hudson's Bay Company which had the staff and facilities to take advantage of it. Undoubtedly Macdonald perceived this too, but it only proved that his proposed new commissioner had a sophisticated mind which could grasp a complex situation and perceive it from many different perspectives.

Macdonald instructed Sir John Rose, the former minister of finance who was now the Canadian government's agent in London, to inquire if the HBC would authorize Donald's journey. In response, the Governor and Committee noted that they were aware that Donald had never been to Red River and could not see what influence he might have. It would be better, they said, to send Mactavish's brother, Dugald, who was then in London, a proposal which suggested they had no idea of the developing urgency. On the same day, the second of December, they wrote Donald to complain that they had not heard from him since November 12 and to discuss the quality of George Stephen's blankets, seven hundred and fifty pairs of which he was to order for the Northern and Southern Departments.[19]

On the third of December, Donald was formally asked to go to Red River and cabled London for permission, which was granted. On the fifth, he sent a confidential telegram to Curtis Lampson, the deputy governor. It began with a note that an exemption of duties in the Northwest had been granted for two years at least. Little wonder that Lampson called on John Rose on December 9 with a message for the Canadian government to the effect that, after full consideration, the board had decided that Donald Smith would be a better delegate than Dugald Mactavish.[20]

Back in Montreal, Donald took advantage of Richard Hardisty's furlough to have a detailed conversation with him about people and circumstances in and around Red River. After all, Richard had been at school in the settlement, had travelled from Fort Edmonton to Saint Paul on horseback in 1862 and had recently passed through the community on his way out on furlough. Friends and colleagues there kept him posted on political, social and economic developments. It soon became apparent to Donald that he should take Richard with him. In addition to his familiarity with the place, the people, and their customs, he also spoke Cree which would be of great value if the Indians allied themselves with the Métis as many people feared. The government accepted the proposal and agreed to defray his expenses.

The men were back in Ottawa by noon on Saturday the eleventh. Donald was given documents which outlined his authority, including the right, if not to negotiate on behalf of the government, then to create the circumstances under which negotiations could take place. In this respect, he had considerably more power than the grand vicar and the colonel who were only authorized to persuade. Donald was also provided with letters or copies of letters from the governor general and various government officials, all of which contained assurances that the people of Red River would be treated fairly.

His other authority took the form of a highly confidential letter from Macdonald in which the prime minister recommended that he "talk over with McDougall the best means of buying off the Insurgent Leaders or some of them. ... Employment might be found for the most active of the half breeds of the different races."[21]

At seven o'clock on Monday morning, Joseph Howe and Sir John were at the railway station to see off the new commissioner and his brother-in-law. The two were joined by Charles Tupper, another father of Confederation and a prominent Conservative member of parliament. Tupper was a man much given to helping others, especially if they were members of his own family, and was quick to draw his good works to the attention of those he assisted. His only daughter, Emma, was married to Captain Cameron and had accompanied him to Pembina. She was in an "interesting condition" and Mrs. Tupper had insisted that her husband, a doctor, bring her home to Halifax where she could be cared for, at least until she had given birth. For Donald Smith and Richard Hardisty, Tupper was excess baggage but since he was going anyway, Macdonald asked him to bring back whatever news he could on the situation at Red River.

The men arrived at the Sherman House in Chicago about ten o'clock on the night of the fourteenth and the following morning, before they set out for the train station, Donald seized an opportunity to write the Governor and Committee. He was authorized to make concessions to the insurgents, he reported, but had suggested that these should be phrased as the original benevolent intentions of the Canadian government. "Of course I am permitted to spend lots of money, but will be as sparing as possible of going far in this way but a few thousand dollars may do good." He assured the board that he would consult Mactavish and try to benefit from his experience. "You know that he and I understand each other thoroughly so that we shall get on capitally as far as that goes." He also observed that he thought he would be able to persuade the government to let the company be exempt from duties for two years after they came into force for everyone else in the territory. In essence, he saw himself as a company employee, looking out for HBC interests, even though he went in the guise of a Canadian commissioner. "They say they have very great confidence in me personally, are willing to adopt my views, and much more that is fine and flattering but just at this moment they want to use the Company." The prime minister, by contrast, viewed the commissioner with a politician's eyes. "Your friend Mr. D.A. Smith is rather lucky," he wrote to George Stephen. "He will go up there on an important mission, will succeed beyond a doubt & will get a good deal of praise therefor."[22]

A story had been planted in the *Montreal Gazette* to the effect that Donald was going to help Governor Mactavish in view of his illness but anyone looking at the trio as they worked their way west must surely have doubted this tale. Their conversation, when they could talk privately, focused on what options might face them when they arrived and what course of action might most effectively defuse the situation. The nub of it, whatever they found at Red River, was what power Donald could legitimately exercise and what he could acceptably offer the insurgents. Canada's intention remained as it had been when McDougall was sent a few months earlier. The territory would be governed by the nominated Council of Assiniboia until Canada understood the situation better and could make arrangements for representative government both within the region and in the federal parliament. It would not immediately become a province.

In Ottawa, it had initially been proposed that Donald be authorized to assume the government for Canada. It was quickly realized, however, that this would completely undermine what little authority was left to McDougall. Furthermore,

Canada intended to adhere to its insistence that it would not take possession until peace was restored and therefore would not sanction anyone to take over on Canada's behalf. Macdonald did, however, want to be sure that if Mactavish died, Donald would immediately be able to take over the duties of resident governor. He too was worried about a power vacuum.[23]

From his experience in Labrador, Donald knew that the more authority he had, or appeared to have, the easier it would be to carry the day. It was a view which Mactavish shared, noting in a letter to London that at least one of the commissioners should have been "of such influence as to render any stoppage of free intercourse between them [the commissioners] and the people impossible." When they reached Saint Paul on the evening of December 16, Donald suggested a compromise which would not conflict with McDougall's authority but would reinforce his own: he should be made a member of the privy council. Tupper reportedly thought it was a good idea and regretted that it was not considered in Ottawa. Donald immediately cabled the prime minister proposing it. He also mentioned it to Norman Kittson who, many years later, admitted, "For a gentleman comparatively so unknown as Mr. Smith to demand a Privy Councillorship fairly took my breath away." Macdonald would have none of it: Donald Smith was going to Red River as a Hudson's Bay Company employee with sufficient authority from the Canadian government to make some commitments on its behalf, but he would not be allowed to muddle the company's authority with that of the government.[24]

The men stayed at Saint Paul long enough to gather the latest news and attempt to winnow truth from rumour. Donald wrote Tom, who was temporarily in charge at Montreal, to arrange the purchase of blankets from George Stephen and he almost certainly wrote Bella; family tradition has it that he rarely missed an opportunity to correspond with her when they were apart and those occasions when he failed to write are signalled by a request to a business colleague to tell her he is well and will write by the next mail.

Kittson arranged for Donald, Richard Hardisty and Tupper to travel eighty miles north to Breckenridge, the end of rail, and purchased stage tickets for their journey to Fort Abercrombie, after which no public transport was available. He gave Richard Hardisty $400 and made provision for him to acquire another $100 at the end of the stage line. He also packed a picnic hamper with "potted chicken, tongue, etc., brandy, whisky, and wine, with bread, biscuits and cake etc.," as the rotund Tupper remembered nearly fifty years later. At their last stop before Fort Abercrombie, the homesteader with whom they stayed served them broiled moose and from him they bought a hindquarter from which they cut chunks to fry with potatoes as they travelled north. When the moose was finished, they substituted fat pork. At Fort Abercrombie, they acquired a pail of new milk which they left out to freeze at the fort and from which they then cut chunks to put in their tea. "The ozone we were breathing constantly was so stimulating that we wanted nothing stronger than tea by way of stimulant," Tupper recalled. What was old hat to the fur traders was an exciting new experience for the politician.[25]

From Abercrombie, they proceeded by canvas covered, horse drawn sleigh, driven by Antoine Girard at whose home they stayed on the night of December 22. The day before, they had encountered McDougall, who had had enough of waiting in a log cabin at Pembina and had decided to return to Canada. He had little to offer by way of advice or encouragement and less by way of news.

Like Joseph McPherson and Brother Elsner, Donald and his companions broke camp early in the morning, stopping for breakfast about half past eight and for another meal when they made their camp at night. Sometimes, they continued travelling after their main meal and did not finally lay down their blankets and buffalo robes in the snow until nearly midnight. When the horses were exhausted, the men, who were scarcely less tired, walked.

On Christmas Eve, they finally reached Pembina and Tupper was united with his daughter who could not imagine why her father had made the effort to come to her. Colonel de Salaberry was still there, having been persuaded by Cameron and Provencher that a military man, and one who was not as well known in Red River as the grand vicar, should not rush into trouble. Thibault himself had been obliged to remain in Pembina for the better part of two weeks because he had been unable to find a guide to take him across the prairie to Fort Garry. After presenting Emma Cameron with Kittson's picnic hamper, Donald and Richard Hardisty, whose usefulness was daily more apparent, carried on to the Hudson's Bay Company post just across the Canadian border, while Tupper was requested to stay behind at Pembina with a promise that he would be sent for at the opportune moment.

It was not in Tupper's nature to stay put and he set about making his own arrangements to get to Fort Garry. It led to an altercation at the HBC post on Christmas Day when Tupper discovered that his erstwhile travelling companions were still there. According to Tupper's account, Donald said it was dangerous to proceed to the fort because Riel had seized it and thus controlled the arms, ammunition and alcohol. This news may have come from McDougall whom Donald had spoken to on his own, or he may have heard it in Saint Paul. In either case, he had not shared it with Tupper but revealed it now in hopes of discouraging him from continuing his journey. Donald claimed, in Tupper's version, that it was "simply courting death to go there at present." In Tupper's mind, this was evidence of Donald's cowardice, an opinion which the prime minister shared with John Rose in London. "Dr. Tupper who accompanied him from Ottawa to Pembina, says he seems to be a very good man but exceedingly timid. In fact the Dr. has told me confidentially that he is incapacitated from usefulness by the most wretched physical cowardice."[26]

Tupper, it seems, chose to misinterpret Donald's warning about the dangers in Fort Garry when he reported to the prime minister in Ottawa. Yet by Tupper's own admission, Donald had withheld the information about the seizure of the fort because he knew Tupper was impetuous and feared, correctly as it transpired, that he would do something rash. Tupper set out from Pembina with a young guide who did not know the way and lacked the foresight to travel with either matches or an axe. They got lost and only managed to recover their direction when Tupper remembered childhood lessons about finding the pole star. When he finally did reach the fort on December 28, ostensibly in search of his daughter's possessions which had been confiscated from Captain Cameron, Riel and his companions made short work of him before sending him back to Pembina en route for Ottawa. Tupper justified himself by arguing that he had paved the way for Thibault and de Salaberry and claimed that he had seen enough of the situation at the fort to be certain that Donald would not be able to accomplish the mission on which he had been sent. On both these points he was wrong.[27]

Donald and Richard Hardisty reached the gates of Fort Garry on the evening of December 27. They asked the armed guards to take them to Governor Mactavish's house but were obliged to wait while one of them fetched Riel. Donald, probably in company with Hardisty, was taken to a room where Riel introduced him to members of his "provisional government." The phrase was the most concise way to refer to the group of men who had seized control but Donald was careful, in both his correspondence and his official report, to use quotation marks to indicate that he did not accept this claim. It was a subtle distinction, but an important one, the more so since it was one the Francophone commissioners failed to observe.

In response to Riel's question about the purpose of his visit, Donald explained that he was connected with the Hudson's Bay Company but also held a commission from the Canadian government to the people of Red River. He offered to show his credentials as soon as the people were willing to receive him. With these words, he established the first strand of the rope with which he hoped to bind Riel. His mission was to the people of Red River as a whole, and not to Riel and his unrepresentative advisors. He refused to promise not to upset Riel's regime but did agree that he would give him prior warning if he intended to do so. Finally, the men were taken to Dr. Cowan's house where they were to be quasi-prisoners for the next two months.

Here, they discovered that a few hours earlier, John Bruce had resigned as president of the National Committee and had been replaced by Louis Riel. They also learned that, on three occasions, Riel had asked Governor Mactavish for a loan of £1,000 from HBC funds and had thrice been denied. On December 22, at the third refusal, Riel and his Irish-American side-kick, William O'Donoghue, had seized the cashbox, the contents of which were used to pay off the Métis supporters. The ultimate beneficiary, however, was Dutch George Emmerling at whose saloon, above which flew an American flag, the men squandered their money, leaving their womenfolk and children to go to midnight mass on Christmas Eve without them. In addition to the safe, which contained Hudson's Bay Company notes, American currency and various pieces of gold and silver, the Métis had helped themselves to provisions from the company stores, always with an assurance that they would pay for them.

Cowan also told Donald that, on the tenth of December, Riel had pulled down the HBC flag at Fort Garry and replaced it with a fleur-de-lis and shamrock, symbols which were sure to further discourage any cooperation from most of the English speaking community. The Irish emblem reflected Riel's collaboration with O'Donoghue who considered himself a Fenian.

Grand Vicar Thibault had arrived at Christmas and had taken up his residence in the archbishopric at St. Boniface. Here, his companions were the priests who sympathized with Riel's ambitions and who could, perhaps, foresee the day when their flock would form but a tiny proportion of an Anglophone, Protestant population. The grand vicar, having worked as a missionary among the Métis and the Indians for nearly forty years, felt a natural empathy for the men who had put themselves outside the law. He convinced Riel to allow de Salaberry to enter, which he did on the fifth of January. On the sixth, Riel confiscated their papers from which he learned that they were powerless and could safely be disregarded.

The French speaking commissioners served to distract Riel's attention while Donald Smith and Richard Hardisty quietly enquired into the sympathies of the various sub-groups which inhabited the settlement and discovered that within the company's own ranks there were some people who were altogether too supportive of Riel's ambitions. Most notable was John McTavish, a very good accountant but not clever enough to combine his work with his political and personal interests which he nonetheless pursued vigorously for many years. He had many friends in the Métis community and was always happy to share a drink, or several, with them. In January 1870, for example, he hosted a "dancing spree" at the home of Roger Marion, Norman Kittson's brother-in-law. Some within the HBC felt that McTavish's greatest crime was to be a bit high spirited and prone to being friends with everyone, a view which Donald came to share in later years.[28]

As was customary on New Year's Day, many people in the settlement paid calls on each other and on the fort's residents. Dr. Cowan's visitors were equally keen to meet the new arrivals who, in turn, were glad of an opportunity to size up those who came to offer their good wishes for the new year. Many others took the opportunity to call on the doctor in the ensuing days and, at night, James Anderson, the store-keeper at Fort Garry, used to slip in through a back door which Riel's men did not know about and pass on the day's news. From these visitors, Donald learned of their conviction that an armed force would be required to restore order. From his own point of view, Donald explained in a letter to the prime minister, the most important thing was to create a common front among those "well-affected to the British Crown," but he had modified his views on military intervention and now believed that the Canadian government should be prepared to "throw in a sufficient force to crush an insurrection" in case matters got out of hand. If Canada did not do this, he warned, the people of Red River would call on the Americans for assistance, with inevitable consequences.[29]

While Donald assessed the situation from within the confines of the fort, Hardisty was able to move about the settlement, ensuring that the support of the majority of the English speakers could be depended on, quietly persuading some influential Métis that it was in their best interests to back a peaceful transition to a Canadian government, and promising financial rewards when this proved the best way of winning allegiance.

Among the Métis he would have met were Pascal Breland and Pierre Falcon. The former was a wealthy farmer whose appointment to the Council of Assiniboia in 1857 had been engineered by George Simpson after he had joined other Métis in a challenge to the company's monopoly of trade in Red River. The latter was well-known as a Métis poet, one of whose most recent compositions, sung to the tune of "The Wandering Jew," was used to taunt McDougall who, according to the song, substituted a commode for the vice-regal throne.[30]

Better known was Falcon's "Ballad of Seven Oaks" which lauded a skirmish in 1816 in which a group of Métis killed twenty settlers and lost one man on their own side. The unplanned exchange of fire was an incident in the quarrel between the North West Company and the Hudson's Bay Company, the latter having permitted the establishment of the Red River settlement at the most important junction on the Montrealers' trade route. The Métis leader at Seven Oaks was Donald's relative, Cuthbert Grant, one of whose daughters had married Pascal Breland and whose younger sister had married Pierre Falcon. Grant, of mixed

Scottish and Indian blood, was born in the Northwest in 1793 and had been educated at Montreal and in Scotland where he and his brother James were cared for by his, and Donald's, Stuart relatives. The executor of Cuthbert Grant's first will was John Stuart, Donald's uncle.

On the sixth of January, Riel called on Donald for the first time since his arrival at the fort. The two men were beginning to take each other's measure; Donald, for his part, found himself confirmed in the opinion that his negotiations would have to be with the people of Red River and not with Riel's council, even were he willing to acknowledge its authority. "Should we arrive at the point of negotiating, half our difficulties will have passed," he commented in a letter to the prime minister. In the meantime, Donald and Riel waited to see how Thibault and de Salaberry would play their hands. On the thirteenth, the two men appeared before the Métis council, delivered themselves of their platitudes, and were politely dismissed. At that point, it was clear to Riel that if anyone was going to change the course of events, it was Donald Smith. Indeed, he appeared already to have done so because Riel was discovering that some of his most influential allies had withdrawn their support and taken others with them.[31]

On January 14, Riel again visited Donald at the fort, but this time the interview was specifically about Donald's authority as a Canadian commissioner. Riel became agitated when he discovered that Donald had left his papers behind at Pembina, a precaution he had taken precisely because he had been warned that the Métis leader would seize them. Donald knew better than to accede to a request that he provide a letter authorizing one of Riel's men to fetch them, and the two finally agreed on a compromise whereby Richard Hardisty would be sent to bring them in; Riel faithfully promised to ensure that they were delivered to their owner who would then be allowed to communicate their contents to the people at large. At that point, Donald was made prisoner and denied oral or written contact with anyone.

As soon as Mactavish got word of this deal, he was sure that Riel would not uphold his part of the bargain and that Richard, on his own, would be powerless to ensure that he did. Clearly, Riel wanted to judge Donald's authority for himself, but it was equally clear to Mactavish that if he did not like what he saw, he would confiscate the papers. The governor therefore sent three Métis, Pierre Léveillé, John Grant and Angus McKay, after Hardisty to provide an armed escort back to the settlement. McKay carried the papers since it was obvious that Hardisty would be the first to be molested.

On their return, they spent the night of January 17 at the home of Laboucane Dauphinais. At the age of seventy-five, he had just taken to wife a woman some forty years his junior and the family had arranged a celebratory dance. A party at such a moment of crisis in the community tended to confirm the outsider's view of the Métis as feckless, but dancing was firmly rooted in Red River custom and was no less odd on this occasion than the fact that the fortnightly mail continued to arrive and depart as normal throughout the insurrection.

After supper that night, one of Riel's men came to claim the guard whom the insurgent had sent with Hardisty and who was now a prisoner. On learning who had sent the messenger, Léveillé retorted that if Riel wanted Hardisty or the papers he should come for them himself. He shut the door in the man's face, and in Riel's too, for he was waiting in the shadows. Next morning, Dauphinais sent word to his neighbours who joined the escort bringing Richard and Donald's commission to the fort. At every farm they passed, more joined them until finally there were between sixty and eighty men in the procession.[32]

Mactavish knew his business when he sent the men after Hardisty, as Alexander Begg, a Winnipeg store keeper and future historian of the settlement, recorded in his journal on January 18.

> As the party drove along they were overtaken by Riel in a cutter by himself — he tried to pass them putting his horse at full gallop — but he was prevented from going ahead. Before reaching La Rivière Salle [sic] they met Rev. Mr. Richot [sic] who stopped the party to speak to Laveiller [sic] but the latter told the Rev. gentleman that the road was not the proper place to speak that they were going to the Fort and he could see them there. The party then proceeded as far as La Rivière Salle where it was proposed to have a meeting at Jos. Hamlins House. Riel here attempted to pass and go on but a man sprang before his horse and he was ordered to stop — he refused whereupon Laveiller told him he would make him. Riel on this jumped out of his cutter and told them that he would die first before they would compel him. Laveiller on this went up to him (Riel) and took him by the throat. Riel struggled with him — when Laveiller drew his revolver and was in the act of putting [it] at Riel's head when one or two stepped in and prevented it. Riel then said that he would not stop for a meeting there but would go on with the party as a friend and not as a prisoner. This all consented to and the party proceeded.[33]

Most of the men turned back at the gates of the fort, but Léveillé stood his guard and continued to do so. The interference by loyal Métis provoked arguments and recriminations between the Métis factions, but Father Lestanc, who had consistently backed Riel urged everyone to place their confidence in him now.

At that point, Donald suggested what the local newspaper, referred to as "a grand mass meeting of the inhabitants of the Settlement." It was convened for January 19 and *The New Nation*, so called because that was how the Métis perceived themselves, provided such detailed and accurate accounts of the public debates that all sides confidently sent off copies as the most efficient way of telling Saint Paul, Washington, Ottawa, Montreal and London what was afoot in the settlement.[34]

Before the meeting could take place, however, Father Lestanc had other work to complete. In the early hours of January 19, he and the Grand Vicar Thibault went calling on the Métis who had been persuaded to withdraw their support from Riel. In the unpublished version of his official report, Donald suggested that Thibault did so against his better judgement "for I believe him to be a truly honorable man, but wanting in resolution to withstand the pressure put upon him." It is generally assumed that Lestanc and Thibault confined themselves to persuasion, but on January 22, the grand vicar wrote Joseph Howe to report that he and de

Salaberry had been obliged to call on the HBC for $1,000 in addition to the $1,000 with which they had been supplied before their departure. In total, de Salaberry received $2,367.10 for his fee and expenses while the vicar general was paid a round $3,000.[35]

There was no place in Red River big enough to contain all those who turned up for the meeting and it was therefore necessary to hold it outdoors. On the sixteenth of January, the thermometer had fallen to -35°F and seven men had frozen to death. By the nineteenth, it had risen to -20°. At noon that day, upwards of a thousand men, many of them armed, met in the pale wintry light of the court yard in the fort. They stamped their feet and clapped their hands to keep their blood circulating in the frozen air. Impatiently, Donald waited for Colonel de Salaberry and the grand vicar to arrive. Finally, he sent a messenger to the colonel and after that a note, urging him, by his presence, to countenance the proceedings on the part of Canada.[36]

Finally the other commissioners appeared and the men climbed the staircase in the middle of the block which accommodated the clerks and junior officers of the HBC. Together with the dignitaries of the settlement, they stepped out onto the balcony facing the cold, tense crowd below. Thomas Bunn, an English half-breed, was elected president of the meeting, while Judge Black served as secretary. Donald asked Colonel de Salaberry

> to act as interpreter, so that the contents of the several documents and any observations in English might be faithfully translated to the French party. He readily promised to do so, but, perhaps, feeling some diffidence in himself, which I endeavoured to overcome, he proposed that Mr. Riel should be appointed interpreter, and this was carried before the meeting had time to reflect on the import of the motion. This had a most damaging effect on the cause of order.[37]

Thibault and de Salaberry wanted to dissociate themselves from the grand mass meeting, for their presence on the platform would send a message contrary to the one they had been delivering in the middle of the night.

Finally, it was time for Donald to present his arguments. The last time he had been called on to make a speech, nearly five years ago in front of a sympathetic group of Hudson's Bay Company officials and their guests, he had flinched. How now was he to manage before a much larger and less homogeneous crowd on an occasion where so much depended on his powers of persuasion? He was no orator and never would be. What he could do, he decided, was to take them into his confidence and read them word for word the documents which conveyed both the mission with which he had been entrusted and the government's intentions towards the settlement.

He started with his letter of commission from Joseph Howe and followed with his letter from the Governor General, Sir John Young. In addition to translating, Riel constantly interrupted with questions such as whether the letters were private or public and why the Governor General had signed his name rather than "Governor." After five hours of reading, translating and arguing, during which the people of Red River were assured on several occasions that the Canadian government intended to respect their land, their languages and their religious persuasions, the meeting broke up with an agreement that it would reconvene the following day.

The twentieth was slightly warmer, but hardly a temperature to encourage standing around out doors for hours on end. Nevertheless, even more people attended the meeting. Judge Black declined to continue as secretary and was replaced by Andrew Bannatyne, Alexander Begg's business partner. Part of the previous day's negotiations had centred on papers which Riel had confiscated from Thibault. They included letters from the Canadian government to Governor Mactavish and Robert Machray, the Bishop of Rupert's Land, which reiterated yet again the government's good intentions towards the people of Red River. By referring to them, and allowing the crowd to demand them, Donald was able to bring out into the open information which Riel had known and kept secret, and was able to demonstrate before the crowd that this had been the case.

As the second day proceeded, Donald began to feel more confident about his role. True, he was aware that some of Richard Hardisty's work had been undone but he felt that progress of a sort was being made and the people at least had some facts on which to make their judgements. It gave him courage to interject some personal information. Since reference had frequently been made in the correspondence to McDougall, he said, he thought it best to point out that he did not know the man or any in his party and had never spoken to them except for a few minutes on the road from Pembina. Neither was he writing to them. The news brought cheers from the men who, anyway, were inclined to shout and jump about to keep themselves warm. "My commission is simply alone, from the Government of Canada," he went on.

> Though personally unknown to you, I am as much interested in the welfare of this country as others. On both sides I have a number of relations in this land (cheers) not merely Scotch cousins, but blood relation[s]. Besides that, my wife and her children are natives of Rupert's Land (cheers). I am here today in the interests of Canada, but only in so far as they are in accordance with the interests of this country (hear, hear, and cheers). Under no other circumstances would I have consented to act (cheers). As to the Hudson Bay Company, my connection with that body is, I suppose, generally known: but I will say that if it could do any possible good to the country, I would, at this moment, resign my position in that Company.[38]

Governor Mactavish was himself of the opinion that no one connected with the company could carry weight with Riel and his colleagues and the offer of resignation in part took cognizance of this point of view. It also reflected Donald's early discussion with the prime minister when it had been suggested that he could take possession of the country for Canada, a course of action which would necessitate his abandoning his Hudson's Bay Company career, at least temporarily.

When Donald finally finished his reading, the meeting was in danger of stagnating. Riel recognized the chance to reassert his influence and took advantage of it, proposing a convention at which twenty representatives from the English community would meet twenty from the French. It was agreed and the meeting broke up with a general feeling of good will.

Even the dour Governor Mactavish thought things might have taken a turn for the better, but his optimism was short lived. On the morning of January 22, Riel "entered Dr. Cowan's house," as the governor wrote to London

> and in the presence of a number of people, a few of whom were opposed to him, violently abused the Hudson's Bay Company, and its officers, and among other things said that the Company must be struck down; demanded the keys of the shop, which he said hereafter must remain in the hands of one of his people, though I think as yet he has not enforced his demand, but he may do it at any moment.[39]

On the French side, elections to the convention were acrimonious because Riel did all he could to ensure that all the parishes were represented by those who were sympathetic to his cause. While he managed to prevent Pierre Léveillé from gaining a seat, three others who were, in the words of the English, "well affected" did win places and so held the balance of power. Riel evidently tried to retain control of himself, but was increasingly inclined to lose his temper, particularly when he failed to have his own way. As Donald Smith observed, the personal magnetism and the instability made a dangerous combination.

> Riel may have his faults, but he is decidedly a man out of the common. In the first place, his appearance is striking; he is swarthy, with a large head, a fine brow, and a piercing eye. His manner is very restless, and his assumption of dignity and coolness is constantly interrupted by explosions of temper, which as quickly subside again. He seems fairly well-educated and on the whole is regarded here as a remarkable but an ill-balanced man.[40]

On the twenty-seventh, Donald was invited to address the convention. He repeated the assurances that when the settlement entered Confederation, it would be given all the "rights, privileges, and immunities enjoyed by British subjects in other parts of the Dominion" but he declined to comment on the list of rights which Riel had drawn up in December. It was agreed that a new list should be prepared by a committee of six representing equally the two communities. It was not, in fact, a list of rights but a set of terms under which the people of Red River would be prepared to enter Confederation. It dealt with duties and taxation during the transitional period and with the need for steam communication with the rest of Canada and the establishment of a line of rail to the American border as soon as the Americans ran a line to the border from their side; other issues included the expenses of government, the continuance of rights and privileges hitherto enjoyed, the establishment of representative government, Indian treaties and the supposed size of the new territory. It called for a bilingual court and legislature and demanded an assurance that the territory would not have to contribute towards the £300,000 which was to be paid to the Hudson's Bay Company.[41]

The full convention argued at length over each point. On the third of February, Riel proposed that entry into Confederation should be as a province rather than a territory. Provinces have greater powers of self-government but the system assumes a sufficiently large population base to provide both the administration and the revenue. The convention rejected the idea. Riel then proposed that the arrangement between Canada and the Hudson's Bay Company be replaced by a new agreement between Canada and the Red River settlement. This required the convention to accept that Riel's rule had legally supplanted that of the HBC and threatened to re-open the question of responsibility for the £300,000. It too was rejected.

In both cases, the outcome was determined by the three Métis who were opposed to Riel. On the second vote, he exploded with anger. "You must remember that there is a Provisional Government, and, though this measure has been lost by the voice of the convention, I have friends enough, who are determined to add it to the list, on their own responsibility." Democracy was fine, as long as it provided what Riel wanted.[42]

Riel's belligerence was not satisfied by shouting at the members of the convention. He blamed the Hudson's Bay Company for his reverses and that night stormed into Governor Mactavish's sick room and,

> heaping reproaches and insult upon him, declared he would have him shot before midnight. Riel then sought out Dr. Cowan, the officer in immediate charge of Red River District, upbraided him for his persistent opposition to "the people," the insurgents, and declaring that his name would go down with infamy to posterity for the part he had taken, demanded that he would immediately swear allegiance to the "provisional Government," or prepare for death within three hours, giving him a quarter of an hour for consideration. The Doctor immediately replied that he knew no legal authority in the country but that of Great Britain to which his allegiance was due, and that he would not take the oath required of him. He was then seized and put in confinement along with the prisoners taken in December last.[43]

Riel was cannier with Donald Smith. True, he was a Hudson's Bay Company officer and undoubtedly shared the responsibility for persuading some of the Métis to change sides. On the other hand, he was a representative of the Canadian government and, though Riel too often let his urge for personal power get in the way of his ultimate objective, he was trying to negotiate the terms under which the settlement would enter Confederation.

At eleven o'clock on the morning of Monday, February 7, Donald was given the list of rights which the convention had drawn up; two hours later, he was called, together with the other commissioners, to comment on it. Once more, Thibault and de Salaberry trotted out their message of good will in a demonstration of their powerlessness. The session then quickly became a sparring match between Riel and Donald Smith.

The original list of rights, hastily drawn up by Riel and his cohorts at the beginning of December, had been incorporated in one of Donald's letters to

Ottawa and he had received Macdonald's comments on it. Insofar as the new list repeated some of these demands, he could safely make observations in line with the government's views. He also had a fairly clear idea of how the federal system was working and what official policy with regard to the admission of this new territory was likely to be. Consequently, he could say, because Macdonald had written to that effect, that the federal government would defray the expenses of government *pro tem* and that the claims of Indians and those half-breeds who lived as Indians would be equitably dealt with. On questions such as the payment of the £300,000, however, he could only say what he believed to be the case. Moreover, he had no authority to commit the government to anything. This was the hook on which Riel caught him, and he wriggled uncomfortably.

"I want some certainty," Riel insisted at the beginning of their altercation, "and not merely an expression of opinion on what we desire. We are now in a position to make demands. How far is the Commissioner in a position to guarantee them on behalf of the Canadian Government?"

When he wanted to, Donald could spend a lot of time saying nothing in order to avoid saying succinctly what he preferred not to reveal. "While I might have power in regard to some of the articles, to assure you, so far as assurance can be given to anything which has not yet occurred, I could not, at the same time, do so equally in regard to the whole."

Riel persisted and Donald again showed that he had studied enough philosophy to know that anything in the future is only probable. "I believe that the nature of my commission is such that I can give assurances, full assurances, so far as any such guarantee can be given, that the Government of the Dominion would so place the right guarantee before Parliament that it would be granted."

"So you cannot guarantee us even a single article on that List?" Riel interjected.

"I believe my powers to be sufficient to admit of my guaranteeing, so far as anything can be guaranteed which is not yet passed by Parliament, certain articles in this List."

Riel kept pushing and Donald kept refusing to admit that his word would not bind the Canadian government. Finally, the young Métis felt that he had gained his victory and could be magnanimous.

"You are embarrassed," he said. "I see you are a gentleman, and do not wish to press you. I see that the Canadian Government has not given you all the confidence they ought to have put in your hands. At the same time, we will hear your opinion, although we are satisfied you cannot grant us, nor guarantee us anything by the nature of your Commission."[44]

After the convention had inched its way through the list, Donald invited the people of Red River to send a delegation to Ottawa to agree the terms of entry into Confederation. He had had authority to do so for some time, but refrained from saying anything until he knew the time was right to play his ace. On the following day, the convention issued its formal acceptance. To Riel, it appeared a victory, but in truth it was a hollow one for, had anyone bothered to convey the information to the people of Red River a year earlier, McDougall's instructions as lieutenant governor in transition were effectively to give the people of Red River what Riel had achieved by more strenuous means.

Having reached what to everyone seemed a satisfactory conclusion, the convention then proceeded to debate Riel's suggestion that yet another provisional government be established to run the settlement until terms were agreed and the link with Canada was established. To the English delegates to the convention, this smacked of illegal rule again, but it was blessed by Mactavish, who was eager to see some form of stable government return to Red River. What the men who consulted him failed to report to the convention was that Mactavish had said that under no circumstances would he abandon his responsibility as governor of Assiniboia. Having gained approval for his intentions, and an agreement to hold fresh elections for a governing council, Riel then bullied his way into the post of president and announced that he would free the prisoners.

The convention finally broke up at eleven o'clock on the night of February 10. The fort's cannon boomed in celebration and numerous bullets rang through the stormy winter night. "A regular drunk commenced in which everyone seemed to join," Begg observed in his journal; O'Donoghue and the HBC accountant, John McTavish, went to Winnipeg from the fort to join the merriment which "was kept up till about four O'Clock in the morning."[45]

Had Riel freed the Canadian prisoners that night, Red River might have sobered up and gone about its business. Unhappily, he did not. On the ninth of January, twelve of the Canadian inmates, including Charles Mair and a young hothead named Thomas Scott, had escaped and made their way to Portage la Prairie, a hamlet on the Assiniboine River about forty miles west of Winnipeg. On the twenty-third, John Schultz had used a pocket knife smuggled into the prison by his wife, to cut his buffalo robe into strips from which he formed a rope to let himself down from his window. The escaped prisoners were in hiding, but they were also plotting.

On the twelfth of February, Riel did release a few of the Canadian prisoners, but this was not what the people had been led to expect. At Portage la Prairie, Scott's account of his imprisonment had excited indignation and men in sympathy with Scott and Schultz began to make plans to seize the fort and release the remaining prisoners. Captain Charles Boulton, who had been with Dennis' survey party, tried to discourage such talk in Portage la Prairie, but this merely drove the others to secrecy. Only when their decision was irrevocable did Scott and his fellows reveal their intentions to Boulton, who agreed to lead them, not because he approved of their action but because he hoped to be able to prevent the worst excesses and, with any luck, divert the attack altogether.

In the meantime, Schultz was gathering a similar force in the Scottish parishes along the Red and he had no doubts whatsoever about the righteousness of his cause.

When rumours of the planned attack reached Fort Garry, emissaries were sent to try to persuade the Canadians to desist but the men were too caught up in the excitement to be willing to pull back. At that point, Riel released all the prisoners, but it was too late: the men intended to complete the business on which they had set out. Then, through a series of blunders, a frightened young Métis, Norbert Parisien, shot and killed Hugh Sutherland, a young man whose family was among the oldest in the Scottish community. Parisien was caught and beaten so badly that he died a few days later. On bended knees, young Sutherland's mother and the women of the Scottish parish of Kildonan begged Schultz and Boulton to disperse their men. With tearful voices, they implored them to take the braver step which would avert civil war between the English and French communities. Mactavish and Riel joined forces to the same effect. Slowly, Schultz's little army disappeared back to their homes. The Portage party also agreed to return.

At this point, Boulton suggested his men should spend a few days among the English community and then disperse singly to avoid arousing suspicion. But his followers would have none of it. They had come boldly and would return the same way. The plan had been ill-considered from start to finish but to set out for home on the Portage road, which led through Winnipeg and within a few hundred yards of Fort Garry, was the ultimate folly.

Riel, meanwhile, had prepared to defend the fort. All his armed followers were ordered in, as *The New Nation* reported to its readers.

> Men were gathering in hot haste. Cannons mounted, grape and canister laid in order. Five hundred men and more, we are informed, were told off to man the bastions, ramparts, etc. Shot and shell were piled around promiscuously. Everything that could be done, was done to make a bold stand to strike terror into the hearts of *les anglais*.[46]

On the morning of the eighteenth, the men in the fort saw the Portage party heading their way. Two horsemen, Ambroise Lépine and William O'Donoghue, followed by about fifty men on foot, set out to meet them, anxiously watched by everyone in the fort and by the male population of Winnipeg, the women and children having been sent away to safety. Boulton had ordered his men not to shoot for any reason and when the Métis instructed them to drive into Fort Garry, they did so. Forty-eight men were disarmed and imprisoned, among them Boulton and Thomas Scott.

Riel was determined to show that the brash Canadians could not impose their will; a court martial such as those the Métis used on the buffalo hunt quickly condemned Boulton to death, a sentence which Riel would only reprieve if Schultz were captured and executed in his stead. But Schultz, despite injuries sustained during his escape, was making his way to Canada by snowshoe and sleigh. The Sutherlands, the Bishop of Rupert's Land and the Catholic clergy all pleaded for Boulton's life but their supplications fell on deaf ears.

Shortly after eight o'clock on the evening of Saturday the nineteenth, four hours before Boulton was due to meet the firing squad, Donald called on Riel whom he found rifling the mail bag.

> Riel was obdurate and said that the English settlers and Canadians, but more especially the latter, had laughed at and despised the French Half-breeds, believing that they would not dare to take the life of anyone, and that, under these circumstances, it would be impossible to have peace and establish order in the country; an example must therefore be made, and he had firmly resolved that Bo[u]lton's execution should be carried out, bitterly as he deplored the necessity for doing so.[47]

Donald's counter argument was simple and, besides being true, appealed to the concerns which Riel had himself expressed. The execution of Captain Boulton would inflame the English and Canadian communities and set them against the Métis. In such circumstances, there could be no united front in the negotiations with Canada and no collaborative interim government. At about ten o'clock, Riel agreed to spare Boulton's life on condition that Donald helped to pacify the English community and convince them to continue the elections to the new governing council. As soon as the council met, all the prisoners would be released.

The following day, Donald and Archdeacon McLean set out to visit the English parishes. For eight days, they travelled throughout the settlement, explaining that the council was purely provisional and persuading the English speakers to collaborate with their French neighbours in the ensuing months. It was exhausting work, but the elections were finally completed and, by the twenty-sixth of February, Donald was able to write the prime minister that his travelling had had "the best effect in restoring order and as I sincerely hope and believe paving the way for the peaceful and speedy union of this country with Canada."[48]

Donald and Richard Hardisty were beginning to contemplate packing their bags when Father Lestanc called on March 4. Bishop Taché, the influential and widely admired head of the Catholic church in the Northwest, was shortly expected in Red River, having been summoned from the ecumenical council in Rome by Sir John A. Macdonald. Lestanc had been requested to ask Donald to delay his departure so the two men might meet. Lestanc then added that "the conduct of the prisoners was very unsatisfactory, that they were very unruly, insolent to the 'soldiers' and their behaviour altogether so very bad, that he was afraid the guards might be forced to retaliate in self defence." A man named Parker was particularly violent and obnoxious.[49]

Donald's next visitor that morning was George Young, the Methodist minister, who arrived with the news that Thomas Scott was to be shot in less than an hour's time. It was Scott, not Parker, who was obnoxious, as he had been ever since he arrived in Winnipeg to work on the road construction crew. A big, young, Irish Protestant, he had led a strike in the summer of 1869 and, when work stopped for the winter, had devoted his time to drinking and fighting. He came under the influence of John Schultz, sharing his arrogance but not his intelligence. In prison following the Portage debacle, he had insulted his guards to such an extent that they dragged him outside and were only prevented from killing him when one of Riel's advisors passed by. On the following day, March 1, Riel visited the prison to try to convince Scott to moderate his behaviour lest it lead to bloodshed. Scott sneered at him and made fun of what he considered to be his racial inferiority. Riel had him clamped in irons while his Métis followers insisted that he be punished. Scott derided them as cowards which he justified by pointing to the fact that Boulton had not been executed. He was convinced that Riel would avoid bloodshed at all costs and would not dare shoot him. How wrong he was. A tribunal, at which Scott was given an opportunity to defend himself, found him guilty of insubordination and agreed by a majority vote that he should die at noon the following day.

The Reverend Mr. Young had wasted many hours trying to persuade influential citizens to plead with Riel on Scott's behalf before making his way to the fort to plead with Riel himself. On the way, he called on Donald Smith to tell him what was happening. The commissioner was as incredulous as Scott himself but, when Young failed to persuade Riel to be lenient, Donald undertook the same task. Riel would not budge. He believed he needed to set an example which would oblige other impetuous and bigoted young men to curb their tongues and their tempers. He rejected Donald's argument that bloodshed might imperil negotiations with Canada and insisted that this display of force would win Canada's respect.

Shortly after one o'clock, Scott was led from his room in the Hudson's Bay Company's office building which was serving the Métis as a prison. The firing party consisted of six men, all of whom were said to be more or less drunk. Donald said later that he thought Riel was not quite sober either. It appears that only three muskets were loaded and one man failed to fire. Scott was wounded and the *coup de grâce* was delivered with a revolver. His body was interred inside the walls of the fort in an unmarked grave.

At this point, there seemed little reason for Donald and Richard Hardisty to remain at Fort Garry. The delegates who were to negotiate with Canada were preparing for their departure, a form of interim government had been established with Mactavish's approval, and the killing of Scott had provided the example which would, in the short term, curtail the excesses of other foolish and belligerent young men. Bishop Taché had returned to Red River bringing a letter from Macdonald saying that if the HBC government was restored, a general amnesty would be granted for any illegal acts. When it was written, Scott had not been killed but Taché had warned the government that bloodshed might ensue and that the promised amnesty would have to cover such an eventuality. The letter also said that the government would compensate the Hudson's Bay Company for stores which had been taken by the Métis. Though now distrusted by Riel, who saw him as another Canadian emissary, the bishop soon re-established his customary friendly relations with the Métis and was able to exercise a moderating and beneficent influence throughout the community.

Donald sought permission to leave, Riel having insisted that a pass was necessary, and on the nineteenth of March, he and his brother-in-law set out with a dog train. Blizzards swept across the prairie, obscuring the trails while the bitter winds hurled arrows of icy snow at even the tiniest fraction of exposed skin. Most wise men and their dogs were indoors. At Elm River, however, the travellers encountered another dog sled heading north. It was driven by James Hill, a young friend and colleague of the Hudson's Bay Company's Saint Paul agent, Norman Kittson. Curiosity and an eye for a potential business deal in the independent community had prompted him to suggest to the Canadian government that he take a quick trip to Fort Garry and report on his findings.

Donald passed on the latest news and said that he was going to recommend that a military force be sent to the territory as soon as the weather permitted. Men were worried about how the Indians further west would respond to the imposition of Canadian rule and it was felt that some protection should be offered the settlers until Indian claims had been dealt with. The travellers also talked about the need for better transportation between the Atlantic seaboard and the new Canadian territory. Immigrants could not be expected in large numbers if rail transport was not provided and businessmen now and in the future had the right to demand a better means of conveyance than wagons and canoes for themselves and their goods. The conversation revealed a remarkable meeting of minds under exceptional circumstances.[50]

At Saint Paul on March 30, Donald cabled London and Ottawa to say that he would be going directly to the Canadian capital to make his report. There, he briefed the Governor General, Sir John Young, Prime Minister Macdonald and Joseph Howe, the minister of the interior.

As soon as the Hudson's Bay Company learned that delegates from Red River would be negotiating with the Canadian government, the governor, Sir Stafford Northcote, proposed that he go to Ottawa to look out for the company's interests. The other directors were against it, believing that such a visit might imply that the HBC was prepared to take responsibility for the situation in the Northwest, but Northcote argued that greater familiarity with the situation and with Canadian ministers and businessmen would better enable him to represent the HBC's case to the British government and in parliament where he sat as an MP. At one point, he even thought he might go to Red River with Bishop Taché. On April 5, the board agreed that he could go.

No one in Canada wanted Northcote's intervention in a complex situation, the intricacies of which he could not possibly grasp after being in Canada for such a short time, and Donald and the governor general found themselves keeping him at bay while the negotiations took place. Both Macdonald and Cartier declined to communicate until an agreement had been reached and Northcote was intelligent enough to recognize that he could best serve the country and the company by not forcing himself on the Canadian government.

Donald spent considerable time briefing the government on the circumstances in the settlement so that discussions with the Red River delegates could be as informed as possible and he and Judge Black also kept Northcote informed of what was being said and what progress was being made.

The delegation had brought a list of rights which had been altered by Riel without consultation and now included the demand that the settlement enter Confederation as a province. At Riel's suggestion, it was to be called Manitoba, a word meaning "Spirit Strait" in Cree and "Lake of the Prairies" in Assiniboin. What few foresaw was that the new province was to comprise only one hundred square miles. Even then, it took considerable pressure to convince Macdonald to stretch the western boundary to include Portage la Prairie. The rest of the vast land mass was to be the North West Territories, administered from Ottawa and by the lieutenant governor and an advisory council in Fort Garry. While the Manitoba Act provided for a local government and federal representation much as enjoyed by the other provinces, it placed all unoccupied land under federal control for the purpose of constructing railways and government buildings. This also meant that it would be with the federal government that the HBC would have to negotiate for the acres which were promised as part of the price for giving up the territory.

When William McDougall had returned to Ottawa in January, he had submitted his resignation as lieutenant governor of what was now Manitoba and the prime minister was only too happy to accept it. There was much discussion concerning who might replace him and Howe suggested Donald Smith. Macdonald agreed with the idea and put it to Stafford Northcote who in turn undertook to make enquiries. Donald and the governor talked it over in confidence. The crux of the matter was that Governor Mactavish would be leaving Red River as soon as the weather improved and Dr. Cowan was departing on furlough. Someone would have to take charge and, if it were to be Donald, he could not combine his HBC duties with those of the lieutenant governor. It was not a difficult decision for him to make. "The sacrifice of my liberty and of all my present plans which it would entail, made my rejection of it, had it been formally offered, unavoidable," he wrote in response to Northcote's flattering letter which put in writing the proposal they had already discussed. "I could not, as matters stand, have continued my connection with the Company without incurring opposition so violent as to undo any good my mission may have done."[51]

Northcote and Donald spent much of their time together considering the future of the HBC. Donald was of the opinion that the land would prove an encumbrance but he was more concerned about the general state of trade and the attitudes of the men who were supposed to be conducting it. "He thought that if we had the men we might reorganise our machinery and place our business on a footing which would render it far more profitable than it had been of late," Northcote noted in his diary after he first met Donald in Montreal on April 21, "but he did not know where we were to find the men to do it." Hopkins also shared the view that there were few highly capable men among the Chief Factors. He attributed this to the policy of admitting half-breeds into the service while Donald was of the opinion that Simpson had been lax in later years and had not insisted on a higher standard of education among the company's recruits. The HBC was now paying the price, as Northcote recorded after his conversation with Donald.

> In short, the fur trade as hitherto conducted, is ceasing to be the remunerative business it used to be, and unless some vigorous measures are taken, and that soon, the whole will collapse. On the other hand the Company has still a great position, and if it knows how to use it, may turn it to excellent account. Its business should, he thought, be of a more general character, and it should cease to depend on the fur trade alone. It might constitute itself the great organ for the supply and development of the new Settlement and thus possess itself of a highly lucrative business. He said the difficulty would be in finding a man to put at the head of the concern; that Governor M'Tavish had told him he did not know of a single servant of the Company who was fit even to take charge of Red River, much less had we anyone competent for such functions as he contemplated. I asked if he thought we could find such a man in England; he said no, it would be more likely that we would find one in Canada. (I don't know whether he had any idea of suggesting himself.)[52]

Donald also warned Northcote that the earnings of the wintering partners were declining and the men were very dissatisfied. Three days later, when the two met again in Ottawa, Donald pressed Northcote to communicate with the

Northern Council which was to meet in June. "Looking to the condition of the country, and the wretched prospects of the fur trade for the coming outfit, he thought it quite possible that when the Council meet they might throw up the business unless they received some assurances from us which would satisfy them as to the future."[53]

Northcote revealed that a letter for the Northern Council was on its way from London and said he would show it to Donald when it arrived. "It may be sufficient to stave off the mischief which he apprehends, & give us a little time for consideration," Northcote wrote to Curtis Lampson, but I am strongly inclined to think that we ought to go further, & to promise the Council that we would at our next meeting of Shareholders recommend to them to continue the guarantee for another year so as to keep the business alive." He asked Lampson to cable his views and then added a further recommendation. "I think D Smith should preside at the Council, & should be in a position to assure our officers of our readiness to take their interests into our especial consideration. It is very probably that the next outfit may prove an unremunerative one, and it would be for the real interest of the Shareholders to take the loss upon themselves & to prove to their out partners that they have liberal employers."[54]

The outcome of these discussions was that Donald was appointed President of the Northern Council and instructed to attend the June meeting at Norway House. Thereafter, he was to go to Fort Garry and take care of the company's business there.

Between the meetings with Northcote in Ottawa and Montreal, Donald had to deal with the usual problems of indents and returns, though the support, in the Montreal office, of Dugald Mactavish, brother of the governor of Assiniboia, did much to relieve the daily pressure. William Mactavish, in the meantime, travelled to New York where there was some doubt that he would even be well enough to make the journey across the Atlantic. He finally did so, but died at Liverpool two days after his arrival there in July.

Much of Donald's time in Ottawa and Montreal was spent in briefing Colonel Garnet Wolseley who was preparing to take a small force of British regular soldiers and a larger number of Canadian militiamen to Fort Garry as soon as the Dawson Route was passable, it being impossible to send armed men and munitions through the United States. At that time, and for many years to come, Canada had no military force of her own but was allowed to maintain a voluntary militia, though its senior officer was always a seconded British soldier. Garnet Wolseley, had become friends with the Stephens whom he had met as fellow passengers on his first voyage to Canada in 1867, and through them, the colonel and his wife got to know the Smiths as well.

The decision to send the expeditionary force was partly prompted by fear of an Indian attack. Sitting Bull and his Sioux warriors had sought refuge in the Canadian prairies after the 1862 Minnesota uprising and there was widespread concern that they or others influenced by them might attack the settlers in the Northwest. This worry was partnered by the fact that no one in the east could be certain that Riel's men would not turn to violence again. News of the death of Thomas Scott had prompted great excitement in Ontario and all manner of threats were bandied about both publicly and privately. Two of the Red River delegates were even arrested briefly and more sensible minds feared that this might provoke the Métis to retaliation. In fact, the little community was reverting to its normal rhythms; most of Riel's supporters had gone back to their families and their farms and others had fallen away when they discovered that he had settled into Fort Garry in quarters made comfortable by William McDougall's luxurious furniture.

Near the end of June, Donald set out for the west, combining the inspection of some of the posts on Lake Huron and Lake Superior with inquiries to ensure that the company could assist the troops when they passed through in July. For at least part of his journey, he was accompanied by Colonel Wolseley; they took a steamer to Fort William but separated at Shebandowan Lake, about thirty-five miles further west. Donald headed north through the network of lakes and rivers which brought him to Fort Alexander on the south eastern shores of Lake Winnipeg. He carefully avoided Fort Garry, having been advised that his reappearance there might precipitate unwanted trouble. He then sailed north to Norway House, the traditional meeting place of the Council of the Northern Department on the northern shores of the lake.[55]

The official business of the meeting, attended by all the chief factors of the district, focused primarily on transport and food. There was, he noted in his report, "an increasing spirit of mutiny among the men" because they were tired of coping with unsatisfactory shipping arrangements. A steamer was urgently needed on the Saskatchewan River and there were difficulties with freighting in other parts of the district as well. The Americans were building a railway between Saint Paul and the border and "in the presence of facilities which will then be offered it appears to me very inadvisable we should persevere in the use of the long, difficult and most expensive route by York Factory."[56]

As for food, the fur trade had, almost since its inception, been dependent on pemmican which was prepared by the wives of the Métis hunters. Strips of buffalo meat were dried in the sun, then pounded with berries before being placed in sacks of green buffalo hide and sealed with melted fat. It was light to carry on long journeys and, boiled with the ubiquitous biscuit, provided a nourishing if unattractive meal. The buffalo hunt had not failed in 1869 or the spring of 1870, but the traders recognized that the animals were becoming increasingly scarce. The company could not allow itself to remain dependent on pemmican nor on the Métis to supply it —and this was yet another reason for the urgency of placing a steamer on the Saskatchewan.

In his report to the Deputy Governor and Committee, Donald reiterated what he had said earlier to Northcote: circumstances in the Northern Department had now completely changed and staff and the way of doing business would have to be totally restructured. In a letter written the same day to the secretary, he warned of the need for men with "commercial knowledge and habits" to take the business forward.[57]

At Norway House, Donald conveyed the reassurances of the Governor and Committee concerning the future of the commissioned officers, but they carried little weight with the men. When the official business was completed, they asked him to represent them in negotiations with London. This Donald agreed to do and the wintering partners set about gathering the powers of attorney which he would need in order to be able to speak on their behalf.

Colonel Wolseley and his troops, meanwhile, had struggled their way over the incomplete Dawson Road, attacked by swarms of blackflies and mosquitoes as they built bridges and cut poplar poles to form the surface of the corduroy roads which linked the multitudinous lakes. At Lake of the Woods, they headed north through Rat Portage and English River to Fort Alexander. In the meantime, Donald had instructed the Hudson's Bay Company men at Fort Garry to built a cart road from the fort to the North West Angle of Lake of the Woods to facilitate the soldiers' return journey.

On the tenth of August, Donald arrived back at Fort Alexander to await the arrival of Colonel Wolseley. Here, he heard rumours that Riel had called a meeting of about 600 Métis "the purpose being to oppose the entrance of the troops until an amnesty should be granted covering the shooting of Scott and all other acts done by the insurgents. It appears that the meeting pronounced against resistance," Donald reported to London, "and were not sparing in their abuse of 'President' Riel and the other members of the 'Provisional Government,' his more immediate followers." On the eighteenth, the first detachment of regular troops, men of the 60th Rifles, arrived at Fort Alexander and were soon joined by the rest of the regulars and their commanding officer.[58]

At three o'clock on the afternoon of the twenty-first, the soldiers set sail for Lower Fort Garry, the Stone Fort, on the shores of the Red River, close to the point where it empties into Lake Winnipeg. "It has been arranged that Colonel Wolseley shall take passage with me in one of our Boats and it is my intention to go with him to Fort Garry," Donald reported with more than a tinge of pride and excitement in his voice.[59]

"I hope Riel will have bolted," Wolseley wrote to his wife, who was staying with the Stephens in Montreal, "for though I should like to hang him to [sic] the highest tree in the place, I have such a horror of rebels and vermin of his kind, my treatment of him might not receive from the civil powers that be that amount of approval which in these puling times of weaknesses and timid policy, is only accorded to the mildest policy."[60]

His attitude was shared by the HBC journalist at Lower Fort Garry, who noted on the twenty-third, "This morning Mr. Smith with Colonel Wolseley with the long looked for troops arrived here amidst the cheers of the settlers. After stopping for breakfast the Colonel with all his detachment left here with their boats etc. for the Upper Fort to dislodge the rascally rebels and to establish law and order in the country."[61]

Wolseley's wish was granted. The government had been equivocating over the promised amnesty and Cartier, the source of much reassurance, had found that he had less influence in the cabinet than he thought. Without a formal, written amnesty, and with the volunteers in the militia bent on avenging Scott's death, Riel knew that his life was at risk. He and his closest confidants fled with so suddenly that they left their breakfast of cold meat on the table, much to the satisfaction of Wolseley's servants who made short work of it.

Despite their attempts to dress their arrival in Fort Garry in the language of a glorious military exercise, the officers were obliged to admit that they were not an inspiring sight. It had poured rain on the night of the twenty-second and, though the following day was clear, rain streamed down on the night of the twenty-third and throughout the twenty-fourth as the soldiers squelched through the gumbo towards Fort Garry. "We were like drowned rats," Wolseley confessed to his wife. George Young, the Methodist minister who had accompanied Thomas Scott to his place before the firing squad, was only moderately more eloquent.[62]

> This triumphal entry was not attended by such "pomp and circumstance" as have attended many events recorded in history. The rain fell too fast; our native mud, so celebrated for its adhesiveness and slipperyness, was too abounding, and the loyal people, who were aware of what was about to take place, were too few and too widely scattered for that.[63]

Inside the walls of the fort, the men found the square covered with water and more mud. The 60th Rifles, assuming they were entitled to the spoils of war, set about pillaging the Hudson's Bay Company stores until they were told that it was private property. This was not the first time the men had got out of hand. At the HBC post at Sault Ste. Marie, where Lake Huron meets Lake Superior,

> the troops broke open all the stores, burned & stole everything they could lay hands on & used the fence rails for fuel ... & on leaving they even pulled down & sold fixtures, stalls put up in the barns & left the warehouses used for stables full of manure and filth.[64]

Collecting the compensation for this and other damage was to be one of Donald's jobs in the coming months.

In the meantime, the troops, finding there was no excitement to be had at Fort Garry, took themselves to Winnipeg where the citizenry, in anticipation of their deliverance had been celebrating since the previous evening. The Reverend Mr. Young found it a painful sight.

> It was most distressing for me to see, on that first night especially, so many of these men — soldiers, voyageurs and Indians — who had abstained from all intoxicants so advantageously to themselves and the entire force, now so crazed with the vile stuff they were buying at very high rates from these abominable rum shops, as to be actually rolling and fighting in the miry mud holes of Winnipeg.[65]

Lieutenant William Butler, who served as an intelligence officer with the expedition, observed that

> the miserable-looking village produced, as if by magic, more saloons than any city of twice its size in the States could boast of. The vilest compounds of intoxicating liquors were sold indiscriminately to every one, and for a time it seemed as though the place had become a very Pandemonium. ... It is almost to be considered a matter of congratulation, that the terrible fire-water sold by the people of the village should

> have been of the nature that it was, for so deadly were its effects upon the brain and nervous system, that under its influence men became perfectly helpless, lying stretched upon the prairie for hours, as though they were bereft of life itself.[66]

It had been intended that Adams Archibald, the new lieutenant governor, would already be at Fort Garry when the troops and militia arrived. A peaceful transition to civilian power would swiftly be effected and the regulars would be on their way out of town well before they had a chance to drink it dry. Instead, Wolseley and Donald discovered that no one exerted civilian authority: Riel's provisional government had vanished with him and the Council of Assiniboia had ceased to function when the HBC gave up its civilian authority in the area. As Donald explained to London,

> Colonel Wolseley having declined to accept the Government of the Country either for the Imperial or Canadian governments and having intimated to me that the only authority he could recognise in the Settlement was that of the Hudson's Bay Company, I have felt myself compelled to make provision for the maintenance of peace and order, until the arrival here of Lieut. Governor Archibald.[67]

He felt extremely uncomfortable about assuming the responsibility and he wrote Bishop Taché to let him know the reluctance with which had accepted the government of the settlement. Personally, he disliked being singled out in this way; the whole tenor of his thinking and plans had been to reposition the company so that it became associated with business rather than with government and so that it was seen to be concerned with the whole community rather than one particular segment.

Though the responsibility was Donald's, Wolseley worked with him closely. He posted a picket at Winnipeg which reduced the drinking and violence among the 60th Rifles and on the twenty-sixth, Donald issued an order closing all taverns from seven in the evening until six the following morning and forbidding the sale of alcohol for consumption off the premises. He swore in a force of special constables to try to enforce order in the community, but this in itself caused suspicion because many of the men were those same Métis who had helped him during the winter. Riel's supporters, unnecessarily, feared the worst. The greatest violence was promulgated by the volunteers from Ontario, who had determined that they would avenge Scott's death by killing Métis without discrimination. The militia remained in the country after the regulars departed and several men died at their hands before September was out.

Late on the night of September 2, Adams Archibald finally made his appearance at Fort Garry. He was a guest in Governor Mactavish's old quarters which he shared with Donald who had both his office and his residence in the fort's main building. On the following day, all the regular troops except Colonel Wolseley and Lieutenant Butler left for eastern Canada. On Monday, the fifth, Donald hosted an informal dinner for Archibald, Bishop Taché, the Bishop of Rupert's

Land, Colonel Wolseley and various local dignitaries. On the following day, as a formality, the Council of Assiniboia met for the last time. At one o'clock, Archibald read the proclamation commissioning him to be lieutenant governor of Manitoba and of the North West Territories; oaths of office were administered, Donald read an address from the Council of Assiniboia and the long and stormy transition to Canadian government was finally over. Now it was time to build the future.

CHAPTER SEVEN

A REPRESENTATIVE MAN 1870–1871

I will know no difference as regards creed, race or party. What I honestly believe to be for the good of the general public, that I will advocate to the best of my ability.

Donald Smith[1]

"BAH!" declared *The Manitoba News-Letter* in disgust. "We notice that some people here, and a good many of the newspapers of Ontario spell the name of our Province with a final 'h'. They should go the entire swine and spell the name of the Dominion 'Canadah'."[2]

The little community may have entered Confederation as a province but it was scarcely more than a frontier hamlet and uncertain about a good many things, including its name. Winnipeg now had a weekly mail service which went to St. Cloud, Minnesota by horse in the summer and dog train in the winter. The first stage, running to Fort Abercrombie, the end of the American stage line, was not introduced until 1871 but proved so popular that, before the year was out, it increased its service from once to three times a week. The timetable was not particularly convenient, for it arrived at Winnipeg about midnight and departed again about four o'clock in the morning. In November 1871, telegraph communication via Pembina finally allowed the people of Winnipeg to communicate by cable with the east.

The infamous Winnipeg mud, described as late as 1885 as being like "a mixture of putty and bird-lime," was a perennial problem to housewives and servant girls who had to fetch water from the river in pails. It was good drinking and cooking water, so the locals said, but had to be filtered, preferably twice, to remove the visible impurities. By 1872, two wells had been dug and in July that year a water delivery cart was introduced. Two years later, hoses were used to transfer water from a tank to domestic containers "without the pail system," as the newspapers reported.

While Roman Catholics had had the benefit of a cathedral at St. Boniface for many years, those who adhered to the Church of England had to make do with the Red River Hall, a room above W.H. Lyon's store. If too many people attended the service, the floor sagged and Lyon and his friend, Alexander Begg, spent Sunday evenings propping it up with poplar poles. When the danger became too great, Holy Trinity Church was built.[3]

The summer of 1870 found the community with virtually no money. Hudson's Bay Company notes valued at £5, £1, five shillings and one shilling had been legal tender but these had been usurped by Riel's men or used to pay the troops. Most of the silver had found its way across the border and as early as the beginning of March the saloons had been obliged to issue tickets for one shilling in lieu of giving change. London sent more HBC notes and, to the great annoyance of the Governor and Committee, others were printed in Red River without approval. At the end of the year, the Canadian government sent in $30,000, with a further $10,000 not long after. The HBC notes were still used for the majority of the military expenses and for public works but the completion of the road to Lake of the Woods and the intention of withdrawing most of the militia in the spring meant that there would soon be a limited demand for the company's currency. Towards the end of the year, Donald Smith initiated its gradual withdrawal, starting with those notes which had been printed without London's sanction.[4]

Because there were no banks in the settlement, the company acted as banker to the provincial and federal governments and sometimes to private individuals as well. It was convenient for the government to do business with the company because provisions for the militia, for example, could be supplied in Manitoba while the invoices were dealt with between Ottawa and Montreal. The company soon discovered, however, that the government found it very inconvenient to actually settle its account.[5]

Government of the North West Territories, as opposed to Manitoba, was by an Executive Council which advised the lieutenant governor. Towards the end of October, Donald, together with Judge Johnson, the new provincial recorder, and Patrice Breland, son of Pascal, was sworn in as a councillor. The men's most immediate concern was a smallpox epidemic which was rapidly spreading through the plains. The Americans had refused to permit the company's furs to cross the border for fear of infection but a much greater concern was the number of deaths among the Indian and half-breed population. By the end of September, at least 1,500 Indians were thought to have perished.[6]

A board of health was set up and vaccine was urgently requested from the east. A doctor with the militia volunteered to attend the sick along the Saskatchewan River, but his commanding officer refused to allow him to go. A private doctor offered his services at $1,000 a year plus expenses, but this was far more than the little government could afford. In October, Lieutenant William Butler, who had come in as an intelligence officer with Colonel Wolseley, indicated his willingness to take "a good supply of medicines, with printed instructions for the treatment of the disease." He also had "lymph for the purpose of vaccinating the people at the several stations." Dr. McDonald of the Ontario Volunteers followed later, but news of his scandalous behaviour soon reached Winnipeg via outraged letters from the HBC posts. McDonald was reported to be "never quite sober," to have shared his alcohol with the Indians and to have bedded some of the women when he and they were drunk.[7]

Before he set out, Butler had a long conversation with Donald who gave him some advice on winter travel, based on his experiences in Labrador. "Under his direction," wrote Butler in *The Great Lone Land* which recounted his journey,

> I had procured a number of the skins of the common cabri, or small deer, had them made into a large sack of some seven feet in length and three in diameter. The skin of this deer is very light, but possesses, for some reason with which I am unacquainted, a power of giving great warmth to the person it covers. The sack was made with the hair turned inside, and was covered on the outside with canvas. To make my bed, therefore, became a very simple operation: lay down a buffalo robe, unroll the sack, and the thing was done. To get into bed was simply to get into the sack, pull the hood over one's head, and go to sleep.[8]

In this way, the Naskapi sleeping bag made its appearance on the prairies and, thanks to Butler's book, soon found its way to Europe and to campsites around the world. In *Travels With a Donkey in the Cevennes*, Robert Louis Stevenson claims for himself the invention of the "sleeping sack" in 1878, six years after Butler's volume was published in London.

Butler's assignment served several purposes, for he was also able to assess any potential Indian aggression and to report on the need for military posts in the North West Territories. A military or police presence in the Northwest was something which Donald had been seeking for some time: he had raised it in his report to the federal government on the Red River disturbances, had discussed it with Wolseley in September and had both written and spoken to Lieutenant Governor Archibald on the same subject. His hand was further strengthened when he received a copy of a letter addressed by Richard Hardisty to his colleague, William Christie, both of whom briefed Butler. Hardisty warned that the Indians were unsettled and regarded the white men as trespassers and the source of the smallpox which had afflicted them. Europeans were also held responsible for the disappearance of the buffalo. The Indians had been upset by the disturbances at Red River and were being worked upon by half-breeds who had lived among them, sowing the seeds of discord.

"It is my opinion," Hardisty concluded, "that as soon as an influx of whites comes to the Country," by which he meant the western part of the North West Territories in which he was based, "and especially of miners and if there is *no protection speedily* sent into the Country, or *law* enforced, which will be wanted as much for the Indian as the white man, and even more so, the Country will be embroiled in Indian troubles which none of us may live to see the end of."[9]

To Donald's considerable satisfaction, Butler's report recommended the establishment of "a well-equipped force of from 100 to 150 men, one-third to be mounted, specially recruited and engaged for service in the Saskatchewan." The force was to be distinct from the Hudson's Bay Company and its posts and was to uphold the authority of a representative of civil government which he also called on the government to establish. Donald Smith and others spent months pestering the federal government before it agreed to create the police force. It was called the North West Mounted Police, later changing its name to the Royal Canadian Mounted Police.[10]

Donald's service on the advisory committee of the North West Territory was, in many respects, an extension of his responsibilities as temporary head of the

Northern Department. Northcote had asked him to stay on at Fort Garry after the Northern Council to try to disentangle the confusion which had been created by the insurrection, the virtual stoppage of HBC business and the death of Governor Mactavish. The company urgently needed to address the way in which the Northern Department would be run in future but it also needed to get its business back to some semblance of normality.

In September 1870, Donald restarted the company brewery as there was a good deal of barley on hand and both the troops and the settlers provided a market. He asked George Stephen to arrange a supply of "fancy goods" since there were none in the vicinity, and the company imported furniture for the new barracks and a piano for Dr. Schultz. Many hours were occupied in trying to assess the losses which had occurred when the fort was seized. The usual inventory had been taken on May 31, 1869 and the company's calculation assumed normal business throughout the country from the start of Outfit 1869 until September that year when all business came to a halt. On April 9, 1870, a second inventory was begun. That one occupied just over a week — long enough to suggest that Riel's men had left quite a mess behind them. In addition to the losses thus revealed, the company had been obliged to "lend" Riel and his men £5,000 at the end of March. The damage to buildings, houses and furniture was estimated at £1,500 and actual loss on trade was fixed at £19,729. The total for Fort Garry was just short of £30,844. Direct and indirect losses throughout out the country brought the total closer to £70,000. Determining the figure, however difficult it may have been, was easy compared to the long slow process of obtaining compensation for the loss, since neither Britain nor Canada was prepared to acknowledge responsibility.[11]

Donald also started to put his mind to the question of land titles at Red River, but when he opened the Land Register, he discovered that

> nothing could be more unsystematic and irregular than the manner in which entries have been made, a number of them being merely pencil memoranda, while in many cases of lands occupied for several years, no record has been kept. The whole thing in short is a tangled web to unravel which will be very difficult if not utterly impossible and to complicate matters we are at present without the surveyor's plans of the settlement which in the early part of this summer were demanded from Mr. John McTavish by John Bruce a member of the "Provisional Government."[12]

In 1857, Francis Johnson, the Assiniboia recorder, had written to George Simpson to say that someone would have to spend two or three years to sort out the land records; this had not been done and, in the intervening years, the muddle had grown worse.[13]

In addition to trying to tackle the specific problems of accounts and property documents, Donald was concerned about the general way in which business in the Northwest was managed. It seemed remarkably old fashioned after the more commercial operations of Labrador and the St. Lawrence River posts. "Our trade must be conducted on the most liberal terms," he wrote to Archibald McDonald at

Qu'Appelle, "and in a spirit of the greatest fairness to those with whom we have to transact business, but we must entirely get rid of the ruinous system of indiscriminate debt giving for which, in many instances, there were excuses more or less plausible which now that we have got rid of all responsibility of governing the Country, no longer exist."[14]

Donald's main preoccupation, however, was the improvement of the Northern Department transportation system which had not substantially changed in two hundred years. Goods were distributed from the north, via York Factory. From there, brigades of canoes would transport bundles through the rivers to Lake Manitoba where they would be transferred to large, shallow draft York boats which sailed down the rough waters to distribution points leading either west or south. With the extension of the railway network, some goods were being shipped via Montreal to Saint Paul but transport overland, whether between Saint Paul and Fort Garry, or from Red River to Fort Carlton and Fort Edmonton at the foothills of the Rocky Mountains, was by Red River cart. These were large boxes with one pair of wheels about six feet in diameter, driven by Métis and pulled by oxen. They contained no nails or iron of any sort and, where binding had to replace the joiner's skill, shaganappi — rope made of buffalo hide —was used to tie sections together. Because the only way to keep the axles from clogging up with dirt was not to grease them, they squealed and screeched like souls in torment. The noise "must be heard to be understood," exclaimed a novice to the Northwest, Jean d'Artigue. "A den of wild beasts cannot be compared with its hideousness. Combine all the discordant sounds ever heard in Ontario and they cannot reproduce anything so horrid as a train of Red River carts. At each turn of the wheel they run up and down all the notes of the scale without sounding distinctly any note or giving one harmonious sound. And this unearthly discord is so loud, that a train of carts, coming towards you can be heard long before they are seen." Wide trails were gouged into the prairies by the wagon wheels and have left their memorial in Winnipeg's Portage Avenue, once part of the trail, where wagons could pass four abreast.[15]

The boat and cart brigades might once have suited the company's business but they were too slow and uneconomical for the last quarter of the nineteenth century. Far too many people were employed in transport and it took far too long to turn a profit either on the furs exported or on imported goods.

In 1869, just after he moved to Montreal, Donald was asked to inquire into the kinds of steamboats which would be most useful for the company's business in the Northwest and once he had some experience of the country, he became convinced that the company should put a steamer on Lake Manitoba in time for the shipping season in Outfit 1871. He was also convinced that one should be able to ply the Saskatchewan River.

Other improvements could be made to freighting arrangements but it was at least as important to recognize that life and business in the Northwest had irrevocably altered. "The circumstances of this Province and of the Territory generally are rapidly changing and we must either adapt our business to these or be content to see others go in advance of us. The former course I believe to be quite practicable and such as will have the hearty cooperation of every officer whose services are worth retaining," Donald wrote to London in September.[16]

If the Governor and Committee of the Hudson's Bay Company had failed to inform the commissioned officers and servants in Rupert's Land of the changes which were imminent when the land was sold to the Canadian government, they were even more remiss in making no plans for the management of the company once the sale had taken place. Northcote had perceived this when he was in Canada in the spring and had discussed with Donald the possibility of sending Alexander Galt, a Montreal businessman and former finance minister, to prepare a report on the future management of the business. The company should have commissioned it in 1868, with a view to implementing it as soon as possible after the handover of power was completed, but the HBC and most of its commissioned officers were conservative in outlook and it took them a long time to perceive the need for a new way of thinking. Many of the wintering partners never did accept that the old way of life had gone for good.

By the autumn, Northcote had convinced the board that it needed a survey of the company's future requirements and a set of recommendations for the conduct of business. Galt was not appointed, probably because the committee could not bring itself to trust someone who did not live in England, but as he had insisted on travelling with a valet and an amanuensis, he may not have been the right man for the job anyway.

In November, the Governor and Committee decided to appoint Cyril Graham who was familiar with the political situation in Canada, having been private secretary to Lord Carnarvon who, as colonial secretary, had been responsible for piloting the British North America Act through parliament. The board wanted Graham to convince the Canadian government that it was obliged to compensate both the company and the settlers in Red River for losses incurred during the 1869-1870 insurrection and, from his visit to Red River, the committee wanted an outsider's eye on future arrangements. Knowing that Donald was sometimes quick to take offense if he thought he was being disregarded, Northcote made a point of telling him that Graham's appointment was temporary, adding, "He knows nothing of trade but you will find him intelligent and of good judgment."[17]

It is perhaps an indication of his good judgement that Graham's report mirrored Donald Smith's views so closely. In his first letter to Northcote, sent in January 1871, he warned of the extent of the unrest among the wintering partners and urged that Donald travel to England as soon as possible to negotiate their claims. He noted that the men at the Northern Council had initially been suspicious of Donald and thought he had an "undue bias in favour of the shareholders. But the high reputation he enjoys, and his good tact, soon secured their confidence; they listened to his appeal to do nothing rashly; & not to have recourse to a mode of action which could only terminate in bitterness, & the destruction of those interests in which they had so long laboured." Graham outlined the issues at stake and alerted the Governor and Committee to the fact that businessmen in Montreal would be willing to back a new company if the HBC did not reach a satisfactory arrangement with the commissioned officers. Northcote had discovered this for himself in May, when Donald introduced him to George Stephen, who said he thought there would not be much difficulty in finding capitalists to buy out the HBC if the company was inclined to sell.[18]

In another letter, Graham repeated Donald's advice concerning placing steamers on Lake Manitoba and the Saskatchewan which "would relieve you from the enormous outlay at present incurred upon servants who are becoming every year more and more unruly and untrustworthy." In his report, he also suggested that steamers could be placed on the Mackenzie and Peace Rivers and advised relying on North American experience to determine the type of vessel most appropriate for inland navigation.[19]

He shared Donald's view that the officers undervalued the land grant which accompanied the settlement with the Canadian government and pointed out that the company could profitably turn its hand to tree farming or to raising cattle.

Graham advocated the abolition of the debt system, another point raised in one of Donald's earlier letters, and pointed out that the prices which the company was using for trade goods in Rupert's Land had not altered since the amalgamation with the North West Company in 1821, with the result that the HBC was now selling articles such as tea for less than they cost to purchase. He also commented on the expense of the rationing system which allowed a man to receive sufficient food to feed not only himself but his family. The buffalo shortage meant that pemmican was now very expensive and supplying it to families was no longer an economical proposition for the company. "It might be necessary to maintain the system in some outlying posts," he said, "but otherwise proper wages should be paid and men should be responsible for feeding their own families." It was a revolutionary suggestion, for the company had always paid its employees in a mixture of money and provisions. As a rule, there had been nowhere for them to spend cash and issuing supplies to a man's family had ensured a much more stable workforce. The changes which were in the offing in the Northwest, however, would do away with the barter society but it would not be an easy transition for either the company or the men.[20]

Donald had already written sharp letters about the quality of employees which had been provided from England and he also recognized that many of the more experienced fur traders would be unable or unwilling to adapt to the commercial competitiveness which would now be required in Manitoba and the North West Territories. A means had to be found to promote more flexible younger men to senior positions. Graham's report advocated four new classes of officer: inspecting chief factors, factors, chief traders and traders. There would be more men at the lower grades and these could be selected from among the officers most likely to comport themselves well in a commercial environment.

For all that the two men got along well together, Graham's presence caused difficulties which Donald felt obliged to point out to Curtis Lampson. The commissioned officers did not believe the stated reasons for Graham's presence in Red River and, since they had empowered Donald to act on their behalf, deduced that Graham was working on the part of the shareholders to oppose their claims. Because his report was confidential, neither Donald nor any of the other wintering partners knew how strongly Graham would support their demands; in the absence of specific information, Donald could only issue reassurances which he knew were not being believed. He recognized that Graham genuinely wanted to do his best for the company but

> any information he could get here in respect of the means of transport and necessities of the country generally, are already in our possession, while on the other hand his mission has been

> taken by the settlers, or at any rate a large portion of them, who are industriously schooled by the extreme Ontario party, to import a design on the part of the Company to pay some portion of the losses sustained last winter. This idea will doubtless appear to you as it does to all of us, very absurd, but it is not the less true, and it appears to me that the matter of indemnification, or compensation and other points affecting the interest of the concern, could have been more satisfactorily settled in a quiet way, without the intervention of a special agent, as the personal influence we had already gained would have stood us in good part in dealing both with the Provincial and Dominion Government.[21]

In fact, Graham's discussions with the federal government about rebellion losses were to be no more than a gracious introduction to an argument which went on for years.

It was inevitable that Donald, as the senior HBC official in Canada, would be appointed to the Executive Council of Manitoba which, for a brief period at the end of 1870, advised the lieutenant governor while preparations were made for an elected legislature. To establish an electoral roll, a census of the Manitoba population was ordered, and revealed that there were 1,565 whites, 558 Indians, 5,757 Métis and 4,083 English half-breeds. Catholics and Protestants were almost evenly divided, with 6,247 owing allegiance to Rome and 5,716 subscribing to the Church of England or the non-conformist sects. Nominations for the provincial legislative assembly took place on December 27 and voting followed on the thirtieth.

Except for a handful of men such as George Simpson, the staff of the Hudson's Bay Company had never been in a position where they might have been tempted to run for elected office. Commissioned officers were always instructed to maintain good relations with the civilian authorities but very often the HBC men were the government themselves. With the creation of Manitoba and the North West Territories, however, there arose the possibility of taking part in the democratic process or of influencing it, and several commissioned officers put themselves forward for election. The company eventually established a policy requiring neutrality on the part of all its employees but turned a blind eye on the occasions when men exerted pressure in favour of a particular candidate or party, providing it was done with sufficient subtlety.

From the beginning, Donald Smith was an exception to the company's rule. Formally, he sought no advice and obtained no permission to become a candidate in provincial or federal elections but the company was aware of what he was doing and approved. He may have discussed the possibility of standing for the federal parliament with Stafford Northcote when the two met in Montreal and Ottawa in the spring, though Northcote's diaries are silent on this point. The argument would have been that the company needed someone who could be in a position to influence those government intentions which affected the company's welfare. It was not an order or a request — either man could have proposed the idea — but if it seemed to Donald that it was a course of action which could usefully be followed, he was to understand that the company would not stand in his way.

He did not make any effort to offer himself for the provincial elections, but he was nominated for Winnipeg and St. John's, a parish close to the confluence of the Assiniboine and the Red. "The people would insist on putting me in and I thought it well to remain passive," he explained to George Stephen. His opponent, John Schultz, conducted a lengthy campaign, but Donald entered the fray less than a week before nominations closed. When the results were announced at four o'clock on the afternoon of December 30, it was found that seventy votes had been cast for him and sixty-three for Schultz. According to a press report sent to London, the total number of people entitled to vote was seventy-three. The secret ballot had yet to be introduced in Canada and it was sufficient for a man to say he was entitled to vote in a parish for him to be able to do so. On voting days, populations shifted according to electoral necessities.[22]

Schultz was livid. Donald Smith had foiled his ambitions while Riel was in control of Fort Garry and had done so again. He insisted that more men said they had voted for him than the results indicated and he and his followers burned Donald in effigy.[23]

Extremists such as Schultz were kept at arm's length by Lieutenant Governor Adams Archibald who was a quiet, confident, rather unassuming man and, as such, just what the province needed. He had helped bring Nova Scotia into Confederation and understood the way power structures worked and how to achieve a consensus. He had become fluent in French as part of his commitment to the new, federated nation and in his Manitoba Executive Council had carefully balanced Catholic and Protestant, English and French. For the opening of the provincial legislature, however, he decided that a bit of pomp would impress on the populace the seriousness of the business they were about to undertake, even if it was to be largely advisory in the first instance.

The only buildings in Winnipeg and its vicinity which were big enough to house the legislature belonged to the Hudson's Bay Company and, besides being needed for its business, were quite inappropriate now that the settlement was no longer governed by the company. Andrew Bannatyne owned one of the largest houses in the village and he generously put it at the disposal of the new government until a legislative building could be erected. The ground floor parlours provided space for plenary sessions while the attic accommodated the committee rooms. The Bannatynes lived on the floor between, though as the kitchen and laundry facilities could not be moved, it seems likely that laws were sometimes made with the smell of baking bread in the nostrils and the sound of the scrub board in the ears.

The ground floor was carpeted and festooned with red drapery, while a flag pole was erected on the roof. On the fifteenth of March, the Union Jack fluttered over Mr. Bannatyne's house while a hundred men from the Ontario militia marched out from Fort Garry behind the regimental band and formed a guard of honour along the snow packed Main Street. At three o'clock, resplendent in the Windsor uniform required of British ambassadors and other representatives of her Majesty on very formal occasions, Adams Archibald stepped from his sleigh at the Bannatynes' front door while the troops presented arms and the band played "God Save the Queen." "All proceeded as formally and decorously as if the eyes of Westminster had been upon us," Donald reported to Stafford Northcote. Ladies displayed their finery and Hudson's Bay Company visitors, including Robert

Hamilton, Donald's old friend from Musquarro and now based at Norway House, tugged at their unfamiliar collars and ties. A plethora of clergymen represented the spectrum of Christian denominations. It was a prettier sight than might have been expected a mere two months earlier for, in February, Winnipeg had acquired its first barber and there was now no excuse for a scruffy haircut or a straggling mustache.[24]

The day after the speech from the throne, in which Archibald urged the people of Manitoba to show that they were worthy of the liberal institutions they had acquired, the legislature was called upon to decide on Donald Smith's request for a leave of absence for the rest of the session and on Schultz's protest at his electoral defeat. As the province had no electoral law, neither request was easily dealt with.[25]

Donald's leave of absence was sought because he had also been elected a member of parliament, it then being permitted for men to sit in both federal and provincial assemblies, and his presence was required in Ottawa. He had not looked for a role in the provincial legislature but the federal parliament was another matter entirely, and he campaigned as vigorously as his normally diffident manner would allow. There were occasions when it was easy to be passionate for Schultz, who was standing in another riding, kept appearing at Donald's election meetings, spoiling for a fight. Earlier he had approached Donald with a request for £2,000, saying "on this depends whether the hatchet shall be buried as concerns the Hudson's Bay Company" and, in the autumn, he proposed that Donald support him for a senate seat, in exchange for which he would ensure that Donald would be elected unopposed. On both occasions, Schultz was rebuffed and he was now determined to show his mettle.[26]

On November 17, the *Manitoban* carried the announcement of Donald's nomination and his letter of acceptance in both English and French. The same copy appeared on the front page of every issue until the election on March 2, 1871. William Coldwell and Robert Cunningham had been appointed the Queen's Printers in 1870 and at the same time established the new paper. The *Manitoban* was sympathetic to Donald and the Hudson's Bay Company, but paid advertising such as the nomination and acceptance letter undoubtedly helped to secure its financial future and, in turn, helped to ensure its support for those causes in which Donald believed. That support was reinforced in April 1871 when Donald lent them $2,800, repayable two years later.[27]

In his letter accepting his nomination, Donald pointed out that there were as yet no political parties and no defined issues in the province, so he could make no pledges. He promised to "do my utmost on all occasions, to the best of my conscience and judgement, to promote the interests of this vast country without distinction of race, party or creed."

Donald Smith was raised in a white, Presbyterian environment, one which believed that friendship with Roman Catholics might lead to religious contamination, and which experienced people of other races only on those rare occasions when the mixed-blood progeny of men who had worked in Canada or India were sent back to Scotland to be educated. But, in this respect, Donald was no longer a product of his upbringing. He had learned to judge men and women by their actions and not by the colour of their skin or the god they worshipped and in this he was much more tolerant and more liberal than his friends among the wealthy, white businessmen of Montreal and London. He was very much in love with a woman who had Indian blood and his child by her was part Cree too. He had enjoyed the company of Catholics in the fur trade and had a growing respect for priests such as Bishop Taché who had devoted their lives to working among the Indians and mixed-blood people of the Northwest. Years later, he reflected on his religious opinions.

> I am a Presbyterian because I was born one. I was born in a Presbyterian environment. Suppose, however, I had been born in India — I would have been a Hindu or a Mohammedan. A mere accident you see.
>
> Now, as a Hindu or a Mohammedan I would have been doubtless a firm believer in my faith, and have accounted all the rest wrong. Should this consideration not make us tolerant of those who differ from us, seeing that it is simply accident, birth and environment which make up what we are?[28]

Addressing the electors of St. James' Parish on the evening of November 28, he forced them to consider their attitude to the mixed-blood people of Manitoba.

> Who are these Half-breeds? They are, let me say, men having in their veins blood of some of the best families in Scotland, England, France and Ireland. You will remember that besides the Hudson Bay Company, there was once another great organisation here, the North West Company. It was formed mainly of the descendants of those who had bled in what they believed to be a just cause, that of the Stewarts. The grandsons and great-grandsons of such men are now stigmatised as something very low. They are such men as the Macdonalds, MacGill[i]vrays, Mackenzies, Mactavishes (and here I do not allude simply to the late Governor's family). We have here too men of such fine old families as the Macdermots, the Deschambeaults, the Bourkes.[29]

He carried on to refer to the Grants and others on White Horse Plain, north of Winnipeg, who differed "only in the point of religion." Had his listeners the key to unlock the history underlying this impassioned statement, they would have discovered that it was autobiographical. His family, especially his uncle John, had played a prominent part in the North West Company; on his mother's side he had Stuart blood and on his father's side, an ancestor had fought for the last Stuart pretender, Bonnie Prince Charlie, in 1745; the Grants on White Horse Plain were his Catholic, Francophone, Scottish kinsmen.

He told his audience he was in favour of reciprocity and free trade, by which he meant that he approved of the termination of the HBC monopoly, and wanted to see a market for home produced manufactured goods created in the Northwest. Manufacturing and trade meant little to most voters but land rights were a major issue throughout the campaign. The federal government had agreed to reserve land for Indians with whom it would negotiate treaties and had also agreed to reserve 1,400,000 acres for the half-breed population. The English and Scots felt that they too were entitled to a land grant and Donald admitted that he sympathized with them and would do what he could to ensure that they also received an allocation. He did attempt to do so, but was unsuccessful.

On the fifth of December, another meeting was called at St. James' Parish but Schultz and his followers arrived at the school house first, obtained the key and, once everyone was inside, locked the door. The doctor then ensured that he was elected chairman by refusing to allow anyone else to be nominated. Donald was sick with his usual winter cold and bronchitis but nevertheless managed to expound his views, most of which were already well known. Schultz asked for questions, though he had refused to answer those put to him at his own electoral meetings, and when there were none, closed the meeting. Andrew Bannatyne objected. There was further business, he said, and that was to confirm the parish's support for Donald Smith's candidature. His motion in support of Donald's nomination was seconded. Schultz refused to countenance this because he had closed the meeting, which he demonstrated by leaving the chair. The men then elected as chair William Tait, the man whom they had intended to fill this role in the first place. At this point, Schultz resumed the chair and called for a vote on whether the meeting had been adjourned. Clearly, he had not brought enough cronies, for only thirty-one supported him while thirty-eight sided with Andrew Bannatyne. Schultz and his men marched out and the meeting resumed with Tait in the chair.[30]

The doctor caused trouble, again in St. James' Parish, when he tried to force Donald to sign a petition in favour of retaining the militia, the majority of whom were to return to Ontario as soon as navigation opened. It was a cause with which the candidate sympathized and for which he had been working for several months, putting pressure on the lieutenant governor and writing Wolseley, but he was not willing to sign a petition which unfairly blamed the lieutenant governor when he knew that Archibald also wanted the troops to remain. The upshot of that argument was an "impromptu" election meeting, "large and well attended" in the offices of the *Manitoban*. It produced a revised petition which did not blame Archibald for Ottawa's decision, and Donald was happy to sign it and deliver it to the lieutenant governor.[31]

In the meantime, the federal election came close to being derailed without any help from Dr. Schultz because the election writs had not appeared. The Hudson's Bay Company was blamed; for some it was an autonomic response when something went wrong and could be seen, by whatever abstruse logic, as being beneficial to the company. Others preferred to blame the Canadian government or the lieutenant governor. In fact, the culprit was an American postman. The writs had been put into a bag with newspapers and the mail carrier left it behind somewhere between Fort Abercrombie and Pembina because it was too heavy.[32]

Finally, on the second of March, the voters were called to make their choices. In Selkirk, Donald's riding, the day passed peacefully but in Lisgar, where Schultz was standing against Colin Inkster, a Hudson's Bay Company man, protests were entered on the grounds of intimidation, bribery, and illegal voting, and also on the grounds that the returning officer declared the poll closed at twenty minutes past nine in the morning. In Selkirk, John Taylor, who had ridden with the Portage la Prairie crowd and had been imprisoned with Boulton and Scott, stood against Donald Smith, almost certainly on advice from Schultz, and entered a protest when he lost. He did nothing to pursue his complaint which nevertheless briefly baffled the Canadian parliament which had not yet produced a law to deal with contested elections in Manitoba.

With both elections out of the way and his leave of absence approved by the legislature, Donald made a dash for the east. It was nine months since he had parted from Bella and he wanted to see her, to tell her all that had happened and to hear her news. She had been to Scotland to collect Maggie from her school and place her with Charlotte Geddes, a Scottish woman in Dresden who taught languages, manners and all the qualities which "finished" a young lady.

On the twenty-first of February, the Hudson's Bay Company's new secretary, William Armit, had sent a cable via Montreal and Saint Paul, instructing Donald to leave Fort Garry immediately and proceed to Washington to see Governor Northcote and to carry on from there to London. With the federal election only ten days off, Donald ignored the telegram. On the tenth of March, Dugald Mactavish in Montreal received an impatient query about Donald's whereabouts. The deputy governor, Curtis Lampson, had written in January saying that the board hoped "to hear soon that you have succeeded in your elections" but the Governor and Committee had clearly not grasped how long it took to accomplish things in a land which still had no telegraph line.[33]

Donald finally managed to leave Fort Garry on March 17 and, using relays of horses, was able to reach Pembina twelve hours later. His baggage included a parcel of patterns and instructions to a milliner and dressmaker in London who, using silks purchased through the Hudson's Bay Company, were to make up hats and dresses for the lieutenant governor's wife and daughters. Donald would look after bringing the finished products to Fort Garry, together with a water filter, a croquet set, sheets, carpets and lace. Winnipeg was growing by leaps and bounds, but not quite fast enough for the Archibald ladies.

In Saint Paul, Donald spent time with Kittson and with J.J. Hill, whom he had met on the trail out of Fort Garry the previous year. The men went over business matters, primarily the arrangements for shipping goods into the company's depot in Winnipeg, but their conversation was tinged with the conviction that there had to be improvements in the company's clumsy transportation arrangements.

Donald did not go to Washington as instructed or to Montreal as he wished. Rather, he went straight to Ottawa, checking into the Russell House hotel on the evening of the twenty-eighth. A man, and especially a journalist, spending a week in the foyer of the Russell House when parliament was in session, could be assured of seeing most, if not all of the members of the cabinet and leading opposition figures, the majority of backbenchers (who either lived there or called on those who did) everyone who was lobbying for a piece of legislation or a contract, a bevy of society hostesses and a variety of young women who were almost certainly not married to the gentlemen who escorted them. If an MP were a tippler or a trencherman and was not to be found in the bar or the dining room of the House of Commons, he was likely to be discovered in the smoke filled public rooms of the Russell House. The cigars, the noise, the smells: all were things Donald disliked but he had no choice but to grit his teeth and put up with them.

On the twenty-ninth of March, he made his first appearance in the House of Commons. Opposition members invited him to sit with them and he was about to do so when, amid laughter, George-Etienne Cartier rescued him and led him to a seat with the ruling Conservatives. He had campaigned on the premise that he belonged to no party but no one doubted that the senior Hudson's Bay Company officer would be a Tory. Insofar as Donald saw himself as a representative of the people of Manitoba, he knew that he would secure what he believed those people needed from the government and not from the opposition. Similarly, the interests of the HBC would best be served if he allied himself with the policy makers. Political parties were in their infancy and were more loose coalitions which gathered around a leader and shifted, sometimes according to principle but often according to the perceived benefits to a constituency, a friend or an MP's pocketbook. Despite this fluidity, aligning himself with any political grouping was a compromise for Donald and not always a comfortable one.

Like many new MPs, Donald took his responsibilities seriously. The principal debate at that time concerned the admission of British Columbia into Confederation and he felt obliged to hear out the arguments and to speak when he thought he had something useful to add. He was in favour of expanding the dominion to the Pacific Ocean and supported the proposals for the construction of the Canadian Pacific Railway, a proviso which British Columbia had demanded in its treaty of association but which was clearly in the interests of his own constituents too.

He managed a long weekend in Montreal at the beginning of April but was on the night train back to Ottawa on Tuesday the fourth. On the following day, he introduced Pierre Delorme, the member for the Manitoba riding of Provencher, and on the tenth rose to defend Delorme against charges of having collaborated with Louis Riel. In the meantime, Northcote was sending increasingly anxious telegrams from Washington where Donald's presence was long overdue.

Just as British colonies were not allowed to maintain their own armies and navies, so also they were not permitted to determine their own foreign policies and conduct their own relations with other countries. The mother country took care of these things for her children. As a result, when the 1854 Reciprocity Treaty with the United States expired in 1866, the rights of Americans to fish in Canadian waters became liable to renegotiation and this issue was packaged together with the question of free entry for Canadian goods into the United States, access to waterways such as the St. Lawrence River, and a dispute over the *Alabama*, which had been built for the confederate states in British shipyards in contravention of the UK's neutrality during the civil war. The American government claimed compensation for the losses the vessel had inflicted on the north's shipping. Northcote had returned to North America as one of five commissioners who were negotiating the *Alabama* claim and simultaneously dealing with the other issues on Canada's behalf. Because the Gladstone government was inclined to some rather radical ideas with regard to the colonies, Sir John A. Macdonald was also invited to be one of the commissioners, but he was given to understand that he was there as a British representative and not as a Canadian.

Primarily, Northcote wanted to see Donald about Hudson's Bay Company business, but he was not reluctant to discuss the fisheries questions with him either. Donald had, after all, twenty years' experience of fishing on the Labrador coast. For Donald, the Washington visit was a tricky one. The four British commissioners, some of whom strongly disapproved of an upstart Canadian prime minister appearing as their equal, were keen to settle the questions promptly. The balance of power was shifting in Europe and Germany was now a vigorous, united nation. Britain could not afford to be without her American ally in time of trouble and Canadian fish were but a small price to pay to improve transatlantic relations. Not surprisingly, Macdonald thought differently and was generally at loggerheads with the other commissioners. It became a test of Donald's diplomatic skills as he shared their confidences and made suggestions when he thought he could. He also produced a report on the negotiations for Robert Cunningham at the *Manitoban*.

> After dinner Sir Stafford explained to me broadly the results he hoped might accrue from the proposed treaty, apart from its definite object in removing all present causes of friction between the two great powers immediately concerned. If Great Britain and America would agree on a definition of contraband of war, and agree to the principle of a joint tribunal to settle disputes, other powers might be brought in and represented on such a tribunal, which would permanently fix the rights and duties of neutrals. I agreed that this would be a great gain, but that we as Canadians could hardly be expected to centre our attention on ulterior advantages, when we had so much directly and immediately at stake.[34]

Macdonald was so distressed by the untenable position in which he was being placed by the other commissioners and the Colonial Office, that he seriously considered resigning, as Donald reported to Curtis Lampson.

> Sir Stafford at once exclaimed upon the unwisdom of this course, to which Sir John replied that as the representative of Canada he owed a duty to his own people; that his colleagues would repudiate him if he acted otherwise; that no Englishman could possibly be expected to share his feelings; and that if Canadian interests were to be sacrificed, it would be political ruin for him to appear as a party to the sacrifice. ... I pointed out to him that in my judgment his action would be most unwise, because the whole treaty would certainly be carried through, and that it was by no means too late to affect its ultimate character for our benefit, and that he must contest the articles inch by inch. He retorted that he liked fighting in the open and not "struggling in muddy water with sharks." He did not appear at dinner, and I feared he had actually carried out his threat. The next morning, however, he announced that he had reconsidered his decision. Sir Stafford and I were in consequence greatly relieved.[35]

Donald had clearly discovered where his own interests lay. "We as Canadians" is not a phrase he would have used in Labrador, but speaking on behalf of the Canadian government at Red River and guiding the men and women of the Northwest towards Confederation had made a Canadian of him.

He was also able to make a small contribution to the contents of the treaty itself, for when navigation of border rivers was discussed, he pointed out that there were rivers in the west which flowed through both Alaska and Canadian territory and that Canadians needed access to them just as they needed to be able to use the St. Lawrence River. Macdonald acknowledged his contribution in a letter to Charles Tupper.

> Then it happened that Donald A. Smith mentioned to Sir Stafford Northcote and myself that it was of great importance to the North-West to secure the free navigation of the three rivers mentioned in Item 8. He says that the use of the Yukon is absolutely indispensable. That American vessels from San Francisco carry goods via the Yukon into our country at rates much cheaper than they can be conveyed by any other route. The Stickine [sic] River, he says, goes through a gold country, and its navigation is of importance. The Porcupine is a branch of the Yukon. As the Americans contended for the general principle, they were obliged to consent with respect to these three rivers.[36]

The discovery of gold in the Dease Lake region in the 1870s and the Klondike gold rush of 1898 were to prove just how important it was to have free access to these waterways.

Stafford Northcote's main reason for summoning Donald to Washington, however, was to discuss the wintering partners' grievances which both the board and the staff recognized as being extremely serious. Northcote needed to reach an agreement with Donald, as the partners' representative, in order to present it to the General Court for approval in the summer.

In some respects, the wintering partners' discontent stemmed from the sale of the company to the International Financial Society in 1863. Prior to that time, there had been a relatively small body of shareholders who understood the symbiotic relationship between the company and the chief factors and chief traders. Any new shareholder or director soon came to appreciate the delicate equilibrium and cooperated in the gradual evolution of the company. The brash new shareholders who flooded in after 1863 had been attracted by the prospect of a quick return on their money and, because they outnumbered those more familiar with the old arrangements, it was much more difficult to make them understand the extent to which the fur trade depended on the commissioned officers and the land which supported the fur bearing animals. Eventually the new directors began to comprehend the arrangement, guided by senior London staff such as W.G. Smith and William Armit, and helped by senior Canadians such as Donald Smith who, though a wintering partner dependent on the company profits, had gained his experience in the competitive environment of Esquimaux Bay.

The guaranteed minimum income which was agreed in 1864 assured wintering partners of £275 for each 1/85 share, meaning that chief factors would receive a minimum of £550 and a chief trader half that amount. The agreement ran for five years and any sums payable under the guarantee were to be computed at the end. For the first three years, income was in excess of the minimum but, for the last two, it was well below. In Outfit 1868, it came to a little over £77 and in the following year the figure was just over £166. The commissioned officers claimed their guarantee for these two years but were denied it because the Governor and Committee had added a clause which said that the guarantee was only payable if the *aggregate* for the five years was below the total minimum of £1,375. Because profits had been better for the first three years, the aggregate for the five years was slightly over £1,671. In addition, there was a dispute over whether the accounting period was the calendar year or the Outfit. To make matters worse, the Governor and Committee had announced they had no intention of extending the guarantee beyond June 1, 1869, despite Northcote's recommendation to the contrary.

A further point which Donald was required to address on behalf of the wintering partners related to the company's headquarters on Fenchurch Street in London. For years it had appeared in the company's books at a fixed valuation but in 1865, prior to its move to Lime Street, the company re-assessed the worth of the building and discovered an increase of £36,000. As the headquarters at their old value had always appeared on the books of the fur trade, the wintering partners insisted that they were entitled to their share of this sudden boon. It took a friendly suit in the Court of Chancery before the fur traders could prove their point but negotiations over the value of the property delayed its sale until August 1870.

Another source of disagreement which Donald had to deal with originated in the Oregon Boundary Treaty of 1846. The North West Company had traded as far south as the Columbia River in what is now Washington State but was then known as Oregon Country. The Hudson's Bay Company acquired possession following the 1821 amalgamation and pursued both the fur trade and, through its wholly owned subsidiary, the Puget's Sound Agriculture Company, it conducted a small but profitable farming operation. Because Britain had more important domestic and foreign policy considerations than a minor dispute over twenty thousand square miles nearly half way around the world, she signed a hastily drawn boundary treaty with the United States in 1846. The treaty recognized the HBC's possessory rights below the forty-ninth parallel but did not define them. From 1850, the US government tried to prevent the fur trade in the area and George Simpson went to Washington on several occasions to negotiate with the State Department. Long after his death, the farm land and trading posts were purchased by the US government from the two companies for $650,000, the sum Sir George had proposed in 1855.

When the agreement over the Oregon property was reached in 1869, the General Court was told that the usual forty percent would be handed over to the commissioned officers, but a shareholder objected. Lawyers were consulted and found in favour of the fur trade but the decision was again challenged by Thomas Skinner, later to be governor of the company and Lord Mayor of London. At the General Court in November 1870, he argued, "If we now acknowledge their claim as proposed, when we come to deal with a large quantity of land by arrangement with the Colonial Government, we shall be met with precisely the same proposition, and the Traders will expect to share in whatever we may get for our property." His view carried the day and the Governor and Committee sought legal opinions on this point as well. Counsel advised that the commissioned officers had a strong moral claim but no justification in law since the trading posts and other possessions had never appeared as fixed assets in the statements of account.[37]

What worried the wintering partners above all else, however, was the fact that the shareholders clearly intended to place all of the £300,000 which had been received for Rupert's Land in the general account rather than the fur trade account. The men in Canada would see none of it. What they certainly would see was the disappearance of their livelihood as the influx of settlers drove the foxes, the muskrats and the martens closer and closer to extinction. The buffalo were disappearing first, but the other animals would soon follow. Moreover, if the fur trade were to be reorganized, as everyone understood it would be, what was to become of the retiring interest? If they were not to receive on retirement the portion of shares which they were allowed as a pension, Donald argued, they were entitled to have it purchased from them immediately.

There was also the matter of the trading posts which the company was retaining. The annual accounts had always included an inventory valuation in the fur trade account so it was clear that the fur traders had a share in the worth of the shotguns, kettles and traps. Their right to the one hundred and twenty posts themselves or the 50,000 acres surrounding them or to the seven million acres in the fertile belt was much less explicit. As far as the Governor and Committee were concerned, none of these assets except the trade goods would show in the fur trade account.

As he discussed these issues with Donald Smith, Northcote began to understand that they would not easily be resolved. Donald had admitted in the spring of 1870 that the wintering partners clearly had no right to a share in the £300,000 "but the men had good ground for dissatisfaction at the reduced amount of their gains coupled with the advance in the price of necessaries." Their insistence on sharing in the purchase money was based not so much on the legality of their claim as on its worthiness. Northcote tended to agree that the officers deserved more consideration than the board had shown them hitherto and appreciated that, quite apart from any moral justification, there was the risk that they would withdraw their services, either to go into business for themselves or simply to ensure that the entire fur trade collapsed. Both courses of action were improbable, but, like the threat of American annexation of Rupert's Land, the uncertainty had a great psychological impact.[38]

To pursue the negotiations, Donald travelled to London where he and Bella arrived on the tenth of May. He immediately presented his letter of commission from the wintering partners at Hudson's Bay House. Two days later, he had dinner with William Cowan, with whom he had stayed at Fort Garry, Chief Factor James Anderson, and the Yukon explorer, Chief Trader Robert Campbell. Though the three were on furlough and not authorized negotiators, they had agreed to brief Donald on the details of their case. In November, they had attended the General Court where they were "perfectly disgusted with the greed and selfishness they [the shareholders] evinced in their speeches," but, in Donald's absence, they were able to do little except worry. His arrival did not immediately push matters forward because many of the directors were out of town and none of them would do anything until Stafford Northcote came back from the United States. Campbell was pleased to observe to his friend Roderick MacFarlane that Donald "repeatedly said to us that he was determined to keep to the letter of his instructions, and would not back out till the matter is brought to an issue."[39]

Northcote returned to London about the fifth of June. Negotiations with the Governor and Committee later in the month were intense, for although the governor was largely in sympathy with the demands of the wintering partners, the other board members were not. Chief Factor Joseph Fortescue, who was also in London at the time, said the board "declined any compromise whatever, and it was only by holding over them *in terrorem* the possibility of our throwing them over altogether in a body that they consented to consider the case and lay the affair before the shareholders."[40]

In a written statement of the wintering partners' claim, Donald warned of the consequences of failing to meet the demands of the commissioned officers.

> I consider an acknowledgment of the right of the wintering partners to share in the proceeds, not only of the present sale of lands, but of all future sales, as the only certain means which you possess of attaching permanently to your service the class of experienced officers and servants the Company has always commanded in Rupert's Land. Moreover, if their claim to a share of the indemnity paid by Canada is rejected, they are advised to take steps to test their claim by the process of law.[41]

Donald could not make the Governor and Committee budge on sharing the £300,000 which had been paid for Rupert's Land, nor could he change their mind on land sales, and the committee flatly refused to consider including a guarantee in whatever new Deed Poll was concluded with the wintering partners. He was, however, successful in persuading the board to buy up the retiring interest and he compelled the Governor and Committee to hand over a portion of the Oregon Treaty money in exchange for the wintering partners' acceptance of a figure lower than Donald had originally proposed for the abrogation of the Deed Poll. To ensure that the board complied, Donald pointed out that if the Oregon money were not included, he would insist on contesting every claim the wintering partners had against the company.

The sum finally allocated to the abrogation of the Deed Poll was £75,255 while the Oregon money was forty percent of the sum received, less expenses, and came to £31,800. The money was to be divided among the factors and traders according to seniority.

Though most board members could not be said to be happy with the arrangements which Donald had negotiated, they accepted that a compromise had to be reached. The more difficult battle was to convince the shareholders to ratify the agreement. The General Court was called for June 28 and Stafford Northcote explained that the directors wanted to reorganize the company in view of its new circumstances. This required cancelling the present Deed Poll and negotiating a new one in which the commissioned officers would have a share of the general business, including the fur trade, the saleshops and anything else, other than land, in which the company might become involved. He explained that the officers had legally enforceable rights which had to be taken into account.

The shareholders were incensed. One group advocated that the company give up the fur trade altogether and confine its business to the land but most concentrated on retaining the Oregon money, in defiance of Graham's report which advocated that the officers be allowed a share in virtually all the company's interests.

The one shareholder to speak up on behalf of the wintering partners was Alexander Kennedy Isbister, a man of mixed-blood who gave up his career in the HBC when he saw he had little chance of advancement. Having obtained a B.A. from King's College, Aberdeen, an M.A. from the University of Edinburgh and an LL.B. from the University of London, he set himself up as a school teacher in Dr. Johnson's old house, just off Fleet Street in London. His friends in the legal profession had advised him, he said in a paper circulated to the shareholders, that there had been

> a breach of contract on the part of the Company, who agreed to give the Wintering Partners (who are really servants) a share of the profits of a monopoly, and who by selling their territory and privileges, have disabled themselves from continuing such monopoly or trade; we are, therefore, of opinion that the so-called Wintering Partners are entitled to give up their employment, and to sue for damages for such breach of contract.[42]

After lengthy argument, one of the shareholders proposed that a decision be postponed until a committee, to be appointed, could confer with the directors, examine the books and report to an extraordinary general meeting. Thomas Skinner also called for additional information. The resolutions prompted further excited debate and culminated in a ballot, the results of which were to be reported the following day.

When the meeting ended, Donald wrote a short but very explicit note to William Armit. "In the event of the amendment being carried by the majority of the shareholders, I request you will notify the Governor & Committee that it is the intention to withdraw from the Company the balances belonging to the officers and servants who have entrusted me with powers of attorney." The reference was to the money which the commissioned officers kept on account in London. As a rule, most of them transferred it to Montreal every year or two for investment in the Private Cash Account which Donald administered, but men also kept money on hand in London to cover their expenses when on furlough, to support infirm parents in the UK or to pay for educating their children in England or Scotland. The company invested this money in order to be able to pay the men interest on it and made a small profit for itself, by way of an administration fee, at the same time. The sudden withdrawal of the money on deposit would create major financial problems for the company and would considerably damage its reputation on the stock exchange and in the money markets. It was a very serious threat to the company's stability and reputation.[43]

On June 29, the reconvened meeting broke up in confusion after some people claimed that they had been voting on the proposed amendment which called for

House by the Mosset Burn where Donald Smith was born.

John Stuart

Alexander Smith

Donald Smith, 1848

Sir George Simpson

Margaret and Richard Hardisty

William Hind, Donald Smith at North West River, 1860.

Richard Hardisty

Donald Smith, 1871

Louis Riel, 1865

Fort Garry

John Schultz, 1876

James J. Hill, 1878

Norman Kittson, c. 1878

Isabella Smith, 1871, a photograph taken when she was in Dresden while Maggie was at finishing school.

Maggie Smith in Scotland, 1867.

Mary McPherson

Joseph Hardisty, 1906, shortly before his death.

Sir John A. Macdonald, 1883

Sir William Van Horne, 1886

George Stephen, 1871

R.B. Angus, 1874

On the steps at Silver Heights, October 31, 1885; Donald Smith and John McTavish, the CPR land agent, in the middle. The photograph was almost certainly taken by Sandford Fleming.

Grand Central Hotel, Field, B.C., November 3, 1886; John McTavish, first left; Donald Smith, fourth left. The man second from the left and the man fifth from the right are also in the previous photograph. One is probably George Harris, an American director of the CPR. Sandford Fleming almost certainly took this picture as well.

Donald Smith at the driving of the last spike of the CPR, November 7, 1885; the tall man in the stovepipe hat and broad white beard is Sandford Fleming; William Van Horne is to his right; John McTavish, in a bowler hat, stands behind the boy.

Isabella Smith, 1878. She had been ill for most of the year, as shows in her face.

Isabella Smith. She wears a luckenbooth brooch at her throat.

Smith house on Dorchester Street, Montreal.

an investigation by a shareholders' committee while others thought they had been voting on the main resolution which called for the acceptance of the governor's report, including the deal which had been done with Donald Smith. It was agreed that a further meeting would be called.

The company's charter allowed one vote per share and required shareholders to be present in person if they wished to exercise their votes. Attendance at General Courts was always poor and the Governor and Committee were worried that busy men and women with other responsibilities would not bother to show up for more stormy arguments about the Deed Poll and the Oregon Treaty money; they sent letters to all the major shareholders whom they thought would vote with the board, urging them to attend.

The day fixed for the Special General Court was July 12 and the notice calling it contained the information that the amendment calling for a postponement had been defeated. The meeting began with the resolution by Northcote that the report of the Governor and Committee be accepted. He added that if it were rejected, the vote would be interpreted as one of no confidence and he and the board would resign. The threat did nothing to abate the vigorous arguments and, once more, an amendment calling for a postponement was proposed. On a show of hands, it was defeated and on a second show of hands, the report was accepted. Then, a ballot on both the report and the amendment were demanded. Having learned nothing from the previous experience, the directors issued only one ballot.

When the shareholders met the following day, it soon became apparent that, yet again, some had thought they were voting on the amendment while others thought they were voting on the report. Thirty-four shareholders, representing 3,152 shares, had voted on the amendment and, of these, a clear majority had favoured a postponement. Three hundred and two shareholders had voted on the report and the results proved that the committee's letter-writing campaign had been a success. There were 19,557 shares in favour of the report and only 7,711 against accepting it. Northcote agreed that there should have been two ballots but would brook no opposition to his insistence that the report had been accepted and that was that.

On the twenty-fifth of July, a sub-committee of the board gave Donald a draft of the new Deed Poll. He accepted it, subject to the approval of the wintering partners. When six had signed, the £107,055 was to be paid over. By the middle of October nearly all the wintering partners had signed, though Donald did not get around to requesting that the money be placed to their credit until April the following year. The shareholders accepted the Deed Poll at the General Court in November.[44]

The new arrangement allocated one hundred shares to the wintering partners and created the new categories which Graham had recommended. There were to be four inspecting chief factors receiving three shares each, eight chief factors receiving two and a half shares, twenty factors with two shares, ten chief traders with one and a half shares, and eight junior chief traders with one share. The five remaining shares went into a fund for the officers' benefit, but there was no retiring fund.

Most of the officers were pleased with the results of the negotiation. James Lockhart at Little Whale River thought the terms had given "almost universal satisfaction. For my own part, I think them more liberal than many of us expected." Robert Hamilton felt that "Mr. Smith fought a hard battle for us, and I do not believe there is a man in or out of the country who would have secured us such terms."[45]

When Donald returned to Montreal, he was feasted at a "Grand Spread" attended by all those chief traders and chief factors who happened to be in town. The men expressed their satisfaction with the deal which had been done on their behalf, but some other wintering partners were less pleased. Joseph Fortescue believed that the new Deed Poll indicated that the company intended to reduce the fur trade while Roderick MacFarlane complained repeatedly for the rest of his life about the arrangements of the new Deed Poll. The other person who was dissatisfied, though he kept his thoughts to himself for many years, was Donald Smith. He felt the wintering partners should have had a share in the land which the company had retained in the fertile belt. The men he represented disagreed with him, largely because they were and wanted to remain fur traders and found it difficult to see far enough into the future to put an accurate value on the land. "I ought to have pressed it on them," Donald confessed to James Anderson a long time after, "but really, it seemed such up-hill work and I had so much to do."[46]

CHAPTER EIGHT

CHIEF COMMISSIONER 1871-1873

I quite recognize ... that the old order is past and that the Company is not the same as it was in our young days, but my old allegiance survives and I am not yet without hope that we may once again work in unity and with success.

Donald Smith [1]

Before Cyril Graham had left England to report on conditions of business in the Northwest, Stafford Northcote had taken him into his confidence to the extent of explaining that the company would have to appoint someone to have overall responsibility for the management of the HBC in Canada. As the company no longer provided the government for the Northwest, the title would not be governor, but no suitable alternative had yet been determined. Donald Smith was a candidate in the board's eyes but there were other possibilities, including William Mactavish's brother, Dugald, and perhaps James Grahame who was in charge in British Columbia. Alternatively, the company could do as it had done in the past, most notably with George Simpson, and choose an outsider with no experience of the company and the fur trade.

The most revealing observations in Graham's letters and report, which, apart from his recommendations on the treatment of the wintering partners, was adopted almost in its entirety, concern his views on Donald Smith. They had previously met in Canada but in Fort Garry they shared a portion of the governor's house and consequently met daily. "I am much struck by his judgment, and his good sense, & his intimate knowledge of valuable details; & from all that I have heard of him, both in Canada, and since I have been here, he seems to be regarded as amongst the most efficient, the most zealous, & the most trustworthy of your officers," Graham wrote.[2]

He had no hesitation in recommending Donald to be the new man in charge, as he explained in a fulsome postscript to a letter to Northcote at the end of

January 1871. "Mr. Donald Smith greatly grows on one by acquaintance. His reserved manner & his shyness prevent him from doing himself justice in the eyes of those who only meet him casually, but it is impossible to be daily with him as I am without becoming aware of his great worth." Graham was taken by the fact that, like many other officers, Donald had a small but good library and had read widely. "He constantly surprises me with his knowledge of general subjects."

> From yr officers both here, and at a distance, & the many persons with whom circumstances have recently brought him in close contact I hear but one unanimous expression of regard, and during the critical period of last year, I believe that to his discretion & temper is due, the immunity of the colony from a great disaster.
>
> I am inclined to counsel you to see him once more, before you definitively name your Governor for I cannot help thinking, that, with his qualities, his intimate knowledge of the details of your business, & the trust which all your servants seem to place in him, you would not find it at this particular moment easy to select a better or perhaps so good a chief.[3]

Graham's advice that the governor see Donald again before making up his mind suggests that Northcote preferred another candidate, possibly one who was more extrovert, but Graham's recommendation was undoubtedly in the governor's mind when he discussed HBC business and the fisheries treaty with Donald in Washington that spring. The facts Donald proffered concerning the Yukon and Stikine Rivers demonstrated clearly both the attention to detail and the breadth of knowledge which Graham had admired. Northcote and Lampson, if not all the board, must equally have borne Graham's opinion in mind when they heard Donald argue the case for the wintering partners in the summer of 1871. Luck also played a part, for Dugald Mactavish died suddenly and unexpectedly of a heart attack in May 1871. Consequently, when the Deed Poll negotiations were completed, the Governor and Committee offered Donald the post of Chief Commissioner, as they had decided to call the senior resident officer, with an annual salary of £1,500 and expenses. Coincidentally, he would cease to be a wintering partner and lose his entitlement to shares under the Deed Poll. The Governor and Committee also offered a single payment of £500 in recognition of the fact that he had served as *de facto* governor in the year following the death of William Mactavish.[4]

Donald's new salary was nearly three times the amount he would have received under the old minimum of £275 per share and it was well above anything he had ever received when the company was flourishing. It gave him financial security at a time when the HBC was undergoing great changes which would inevitably affect the company's profitability and destabilize the income of the commissioned officers. It was not, however, his sole source of income. His shares in the Bank of Montreal had steadily increased and when a new rights issue was declared in January 1872, he increased his holding to 109 shares. The Canadian economy was very buoyant in the early 1870s and the bank experienced a phenomenal growth between 1870 and 1873, to the benefit of George Stephen,

Donald Smith and their friends, as well as to the many Private Cash clients who also had shares in the bank. The new rights issue was so successful that in December of the same year, the bank issued a further $4,000,000 of new stock at twenty percent and the existing shareholders made a handsome gain. In September that year, Donald was elected a director unanimously and in absentia which suggests that he was held in high regard by his fellow shareholders.[5]

Donald also had a growing business as a private banker. On June 21, 1872, he lent $1,100 to Francis Johnson, the Manitoba recorder who also shared the house at Fort Garry. Interest would have been at seven per cent as it was on a seven year mortgage of $32,000 granted in December 1871 to the Reverend F.A. Toupin on a substantial parcel of land in Montreal. In August the following year, he gave Tom Hardisty a mortgage on land at Lachine and in December 1873, he lent $25,000 to Pullman's Palace Car Company, taking as security $35,000 in seven percent bonds. On this deal, he had an option of purchasing the bonds at eighty-five percent of par plus the accrued interest instead of taking the interest on the loan.

He continued to develop his investment portfolio, buying 2,100 shares at $5 each in the Thunder Bay Silver Mining Company in September 1871, one hundred and twenty-five shares at $10 each in the Manitoba Brick and Pottery Company in January 1873, two hundred shares at $50 each in the London and Canadian Loan and Agency Company in March 1873, fifty shares at $100 each in the Mitchell Line of Steamships two months later, and one hundred shares at $100 each in the Cold Brook Rolling Mills in Saint John, New Brunswick in September 1873. New companies frequently required only a percentage of the shares to be paid for initially, so he was able to stagger his investments. The very fact that he could be making such purchases, however, indicates the extent to which he was not dependent on the Hudson's Bay Company for his income. It also suggests that his shares in the Bank of Montreal alone were making him a wealthy man.

During this period, Donald continued his investment partnership with George Stephen. Together with Hugh Allan, they established the Canada Cotton Manufacturing Company in Cornwall, Ontario in January 1872 and in July of the following year, Donald paid for his thirty shares at $500 each. In the same month, he increased his holding in the Paton Manufacturing Company by thirty shares at $500 each. The cousins also applied successfully for a number of railway charters but nothing came of these ventures because the government, not wishing to create competition for its own railway plans, declined to promulgate them.[6]

The investments over this three year period formed a pattern which was to be replicated again and again for the rest of the century. First, there was the solid, well established financial institution, represented by the Bank of Montreal. Secondly, there were mortgages. In a developing nation such as Canada, there was bound to be a demand for land and as long as he judged his clients and their property carefully, Donald took little risk on these transactions. Developing nations also needed transport and the Pullman cars, the rolling stock and the rolling mills all represent an investment in rail travel which was growing rapidly in both Canada and the United States. The textile companies acknowledged the need to clothe a burgeoning population and provide it with bedding and furnishing fabrics, while the brick and pottery investment recognized the fact that, although Winnipeg might still be a collection of plastered log cabins, it would soon be a metropolis of brick houses with indoor plumbing. In fact, the brick and pottery company failed, but the other ventures were all highly profitable.

In Montreal, the house at 73 Mansfield Street was almost certainly rented; the Smiths gave it up, probably in May 1872, and moved to 100 University Street. A year later, they were at number 284 on the same street. These moves brought them closer to the developing McGill University and kept them firmly within the square mile which housed the city's prosperous merchants. They were, however, rarely at home; after the trip to London in 1871, Bella had gone to Dresden to be with Maggie, and Donald was more likely to be in Red River or Ottawa than he was to be in Montreal.

He spent barely two weeks in the city when he returned from negotiating the new Deed Poll. By the second of September, he was on the road to Fort Garry, escorting Governor Archibald's daughter, Joana, and taking in his baggage the hats and dresses which had been made for her and her mother in London.

He had scarcely unpacked his bags before he was involved in another property deal. The Carlton Trail started in Fort Garry and followed the banks of the Assiniboine before heading north to Fort Carlton, the HBC post on the North Saskatchewan, and thence to Fort Edmonton and the Rocky Mountains. About five miles along the trail from Winnipeg, John Rowand had built a log house in 1856. Called Silver Heights, it was large by local standards, but appropriately so since Rowand was grossly fat. When he died in March 1865, the house was inherited by his son, also John, who died the following July at the age of five. It was this house which John Stoughton Dennis had selected as the residence for the new lieutenant governor and for which McDougall had brought furniture which was too big. When Adams Archibald arrived, he and Donald went out to look at the house, but the new lieutenant governor was unwilling to live there because it was too far from the centre and, in those unsettled times, he felt it was also too exposed to dangers. He did spend a brief period there in the spring and summer of 1871, but Margaret Donaldson, Rowand's widow who had taken for her second husband a captain who came out with the Red River expeditionary force in 1870, demanded possession.

In September 1871, the house was sold by public auction on the instructions of Bishop Taché and James MacKay, the administrators of the estate. MacKay was married to one of John Rowand's daughters as was John McTavish, the HBC accountant. McTavish secured the house, perhaps thinking that he and his wife Maria would live there. He soon realized, however, that he could not afford the house and at the end of October asked Donald to take it off his hands. This he did, paying £905 which was considered to be a good deal more than the house was worth. On the same day, he bought adjoining land which had been bequeathed to another Rowand son who had also died.

The purchase of Silver Heights helped to resolve a problem. The governor's house in Fort Garry, designed to house one family, was currently accommodating the lieutenant governor, his wife and family, and was also serving for all official business which Archibald and his staff needed to transact. Judge Johnson was living there and so was Donald Smith for whom the house was also the headquarters for all the Hudson's Bay Company business in the Northwest. It was too crowded, it appeared to outsiders that the company and the government were hand in glove, and it was very difficult for either Donald or the governor to conduct business with any discretion. Donald consequently negotiated office space for himself in the building and leased the rest of it to the government, taking himself out to the country to live.

The log house had a living room *cum* dining room on the ground floor, with a lean-to kitchen where the caretaker lived. There were four bedrooms upstairs but there was no "closet" and no drainage. Silver Heights seems something of a misnomer for a house on the flat prairie but the land was sufficiently above the flood plain to be dry when the Assiniboine overflowed its banks in the spring thaw. "Silver" is thought to have referred to the underside of the leaves in the clumps of poplar trees blowing in the incessant prairie wind or to the buffalo grass or other silvery vegetation.

With the house came one hundred and twenty-three acres, primarily of wild land, much of it swampy. Within a year, Donald had established a kitchen garden, the profusion of which took visitors by surprise. "A walk in the garden at Silver Heights was sufficient to prove to us the wonderful richness of the Assiniboine valley," the Reverend George Grant observed in 1872. "The wealth of vegetation and the size of the root crops astonished us, especially when informed that no manure had been used."[7]

It was important for Donald to be able to provide adequately for himself and his guests, for Winnipeg, though it was growing rapidly, offered few provisions in its shops. Julie-Cimodocié Casault, arriving at Fort Garry early in December 1870, was appalled at what she found.

> In the way of provisions it is the most destitute place with nothing but beef and rarely pork no vegetable of any kind not even an onion to flavour the meat, potatoes are very scarce. There is not a pound of butter to be got in the place people cook with what poor canadians would make candles of.... I forgot to say there was no eggs or milk. I use preserved milk.[8]

Ten years after the initial purchase, Donald added a further 192 acres, this time paying $9,500, and in 1890, he bought just over 200 acres more for $7,000. The land was drained, a farm was established and the vegetable garden was extended. Stables and a greenhouse were built and six further bedrooms were added to the house. Donald's HBC account for 1874 shows the payment of freight on furniture and a disbursement for making a bath. A buffalo run was created and Scottish longhorn cattle were introduced. In part, Silver Heights was managed as an experimental farm with a view to discovering what crops would flourish best on the prairie soil, but it rarely received the close attention which Donald had been able to give his farm at North West River.[9]

Silver Heights was in St. James' parish where Donald had conducted some of his more successful election meetings, but it was considered to be a good way out of town. In summer, when it was dry, the roads were rough and when it was wet, they were all but impassable. "It took several hours, if you got mired, to get the wheels out," Donald remembered years later. The purchase was made quickly and without much consideration; "it was a bagatelle, a mere nothing, looking to how I was occupied at the time."[10]

One of the things which had been occupying Donald and most of the other inhabitants of Fort Garry and Winnipeg in the autumn of 1871 was military drill for, on the first of October, news reached the settlement that a Fenian invasion was to be expected any day.

William O'Donoghue, Louis Riel's Irish-American colleague in the winter of 1869-1870, was a true annexationist and had allied himself to the Métis cause because he believed he could achieve his own goals through collaboration with the French half-breeds. He had fled Fort Garry with Riel and travelled with him to the United States. They had already quarrelled bitterly over the question of annexation and when it finally became apparent that Riel had no intention of supporting O'Donoghue, the Irishman set off for Washington where he supposed he would win the sympathies of the American government. President Ulysses Grant quickly rebuffed him and he turned instead to the Fenian Brotherhood in New York. Donald Smith had scorned the scruffy remnants of the Fenian "army" which had tried to invade Canada in 1866 and an attempted invasion in 1870 had been no more successful. The Brotherhood would have nothing to do with O'Donoghue's plans to "liberate" the people of Manitoba. Had they seen his draft constitution for the Republic of Manitoba, they would have been even more sceptical: O'Donoghue had modestly reserved for himself the positions of president, chief justice and commander-in-chief.

One Fenian, John O'Neill, did respond to O'Donoghue's appeal and together the men managed to secure a few rifles and to gather a handful of "soldiers" at Pembina on the American border. This was to be no secret attack. O'Donoghue had instigated stories that he was coming with an army of a thousand men and all sorts of wild rumours about his Fenian army had been circulating in Red River for weeks.

On the second of October, O'Donoghue sent word to the Métis of Red River, confident that they would rally to his cause. In fact, they had already had a secret meeting with Louis Riel and loosely agreed that they would not collaborate, though two men went to investigate O'Donoghue's strengths and intentions.

On the fourth, Archibald issued a proclamation calling on the people of Manitoba, "irrespective of race or religion, or of past difficulties" to rally to the defense of the province. The officers and employees of the Hudson's Bay Company were the first to enroll, Donald proudly reported to William Armit.[11]

Early on the morning of October 5, O'Donoghue and O'Neill led about thirty-five men over the border and seized the little Hudson's Bay Company post where Donald had had his contretemps with Charles Tupper in December 1869. According to Donald's friend Robert Hamilton, the trader, William Watt, "seized O'Donohue [sic] by the throat and tried to make him prisoner, but the Fenian scoundrel was too much for poor Watt with his one arm." Having plundered the post's provisions, the Irishmen waited for their Métis supporters. Then horsemen appeared outside the trading post: Captain Lloyd Wheaton and a detachment of American soldiers, who had been posted at the border since the troubles of 1869-1870, had arrived to sort things out. The Fenians skedaddled, as Watt reported, but most were quickly captured. O'Donoghue was taken by two Métis who turned him over to the American authorities.[12]

Fears of further trouble kept the HBC staff on "active duty" in the fort and they anticipated being sent out to support Major Acheson Irvine who was leading a company of soldiers and volunteers through the pouring rain and mud to the American border, unaware that the US cavalry had galloped to the rescue. Two hundred men and twenty teams set off from Fort Garry at five o'clock on Friday, October 6, but were immediately held up by the river ferry, "a curious looking contrivance, half wharf, one-third scow, and the remainder raft," which was pushed by the current of the river and controlled for direction by a wire fastened to either bank. Its load was two teams and twenty or thirty foot passengers per trip.[13]

> In the pelting rain the men had to stand for nearly three hours waiting for the whole to cross that abominable ferry. The Winnipeggers had only fifty-five blankets for eighty-eight men, and these were wringing wet, so that the comfort of the first night's campaigning was not very agreeable. But the men were in the best of spirits. The roads were nearly impassable, and we had scarcely marched two miles ere the teams got off the road, so we threw out a line of skirmishers to find it, and when they came to a ditch, they shouted out to the driver "right" or "left," as they were unacquainted with the teaming phraseology of "gee" and haw."[14]

After three wet and unadventurous days, they turned around and slogged their way home without ever having reached the border. "Thus," as the Reverend George Young, Methodist chaplain to the expedition, observed, "ended the farce that followed the fizzle."[15]

It nevertheless took some time to discover how inconsequential O'Donoghue's little raid had been and on the fifth, Archibald had assured Louis Riel that he would not be molested should he provide a body of Métis to help defend the province. On the following two days, Riel assembled companies of men from each of the Métis parishes and on the eighth, Archibald went to St. Boniface to review them.[16]

The meeting between Archibald and Riel was not without repercussions, as Donald reported to London.

> Headed by L. Riel and L'epine [sic] some 250 of them met Governor Archibald in view of and within a few hundred yards of this Fort, a proceeding on the part of the Governor which, although dictated by considerations for the best interests of the Province, has given great umbrage to a portion of the English, Upper Canadians principally, who entertain bitter feelings of resentment against the French.[17]

With a federal election due to take place in 1872, the fate of Louis Riel soon became a political football, pitting the English of Ontario against the French of Quebec. Neither Sir John A. Macdonald nor Sir George-Etienne Cartier wanted to see all their work to establish Canadian Confederation dissipated at the first properly contested election and they cast around for a solution to their problem. When Taché, now an archbishop, visited Ottawa to press the case for an amnesty,

Macdonald was forthright about the political problem he faced and explained that the Liberals would use it as a stick to beat the Conservatives. On the other hand, a strong Conservative victory would make it easier to reach agreement on the amnesty. For all he was a priest, the archbishop was a man of the world and understood the arguments. Cartier suggested that Taché persuade Riel to leave Manitoba until passions had died down. That, said Taché, would be "extremely difficult." Riel was poor and his mother was a widow with young children and no means of support beyond the labours of her eldest son. "I do not think it is fair to ask him to leave his home without some compensation or some means of travelling." Cartier agreed and shortly thereafter, the archbishop received a confidential letter from the prime minister, enclosing a bank draft for $1,000 "for the individual that we have talked about."[18]

An Ontario warrant for the arrest of Riel and Lépine, coupled with a Métis promise of armed "protection", made Archibald fear the worst. Riel himself was aware that his life was at risk and was not averse to disappearing for a while, but he pointed out to Taché that $1,000 would not suffice to keep him and Lépine in the United States for a year and also take care of their families.

On February 6, a messenger at the provincial legislature asked Donald to call on Governor Archibald. He did not leave immediately because the legislature was dealing with tax and land issues which directly affected the HBC but he soon received a note explaining that the matter was urgent. At Fort Garry, the governor and the archbishop asked if he would add £600, the equivalent of $3,000, to Macdonald's $1,000. Archibald explained that there was not that amount of money available in the provincial treasury — or so Donald reported to a federal select committee two years later. In reality, a loan from the HBC could be a discreet transaction whereas Archibald would have been obliged to account publicly for provincial government money and might even have been compelled to take members of his legislative council into his confidence. Macdonald had taken his contribution from the secret service account which was not open to public scrutiny.

Donald did not see either Riel or Lépine, but he knew what the money was to be used for. "I cannot remember whether anything was said about subsisting their families," he reported to the select committee, adding, "I think it was mentioned that they were to remain away, or promise to remain away, for a year, but they should not, under any circumstances, return until after the elections were over." Donald was also assured by Archibald that the money would be repaid by the dominion authorities, and so the $3,000 was added to the growing federal obligation to the HBC and became yet another irritant in the relationship between the company and the government.[19]

When not involved with provincial government business, Donald tried to sort out the store at Fort Garry. He was dissatisfied because it still offered for sale goods people did not want and could not supply them with things they needed. Early in 1873, he was able to send a man from the Northwest to London to help select stock for the trade but he could not afford to release anyone to choose products for 1874. Staff in London could scarcely be expected to guess local demand, but it remained the company's policy that they should do so. A detailed report on the goods chosen in 1873 would not suffice, he explained in November 1873, because it could not "take the place of the knowledge which a person perfectly conversant with the quality and description of goods required for the Trade, would bring to bear in going in person to choose them in the best markets, and I feel convinced that until the Company have such an individual to assist in making their purchases, they will not stand in the same favorable position as that of other merchants in the North West, and in this country generally, who invariably send to Europe some of their best and most experienced hands" as buyers for the coming season. Obviously there would be high initial costs to restock the stores in the Northwest but there would also be more business and higher profits to offset the declining income from the fur trade. The Governor and Committee disagreed and refused to change their ways.[20]

Transport, however, was Donald's main concern. The Governor and Committee had authorized a steamer for Lake Manitoba but Donald and Cyril Graham had agreed that construction should not be started until the arrangements for the new Deed Poll had been settled, reasoning that if the negotiations were unsuccessful there might be no need for steamers or any other form of transport. The first vessel, to be called the *Chief Commissioner*, was built in the winter of 1871-1872.

In November 1871, shortly before he left Fort Garry for Montreal, Donald had received a very interesting letter on shipping from James J. Hill, the man whom he had met on the prairies when returning from Fort Garry after dealing with Riel. He generally saw Norman Kittson, the HBC agent in Saint Paul when he passed through and, as Hill and Kittson often collaborated, he sometimes saw Hill as well. He made a point of it after receiving Hill's November letter.

In Saint Paul, Hill had been involved in warehousing and had worked as a coal merchant before going into partnership with a civil war veteran, Colonel Chauncey Griggs and a steamboat captain, Alexander Griggs, who was no relation of the colonel's. In the spring of 1871, they had launched a steamboat, the *Selkirk*, on Red River. Hill knew that the rail connection to the river was soon due to be completed and foresaw a profitable business taking passengers and freight from the railhead north to Winnipeg.

The Hudson's Bay Company had been running its own paddle-wheeler, the *International*, on the same route for a decade and had grown lazy in enjoyment of its monopoly. Hill brought the company up short when he discovered that all vessels entering Canadian ports from the United States had to be bonded and further, that foreign vessels were not permitted to operate in American waters. The *International* was halted at the border while the *Selkirk* sailed through, making a substantial profit for her owners on her first voyage. Donald fought back when he was in Washington discussing the fisheries treaty with Northcote and Macdonald. He transferred the *International* to Norman Kittson who, though born a Canadian, had taken out American citizenship by 1871.

Once the bonding matter had been sorted out, the *Selkirk* and the *International* ran in competition with each other for the remainder of the 1871 season, cutting rates to the detriment of both operators. Hill's letter proposed that they amalgamate their interests, charging an agreed rate for freight and passengers. Donald saw at once that it would be to the company's advantage, the more so since it was agreed that the HBC would be charged \$1.00 per hundredweight while its competitors would pay \$1.50. Today, unpublicized deals on travel, accommodation and other services are commonly negotiated with customers who can promise a large volume of business and similar bargains were struck as freight transport developed in the nineteenth century. What distinguished this particular deal, however, was that the company, as a partner, was also entitled to a share of the profits made on hauling its own freight.

On January 19, 1872, when he was in Saint Paul on his way back to Red River, Donald signed the shipping contract which was to last for one season. Knowing what Schultz and his loud mouthed friends would make of the monopoly, Donald insisted that the company's participation be kept secret and Kittson, who would also suffer if the contract was disclosed, was only too happy to agree.[21]

So committed to the confidentiality of the arrangement was Donald that he sent only the barest outline to the board. He made a quick trip to London in April to settle the details of the new Deed Poll and explained the shipping arrangements then, but nothing was put on paper. The Governor and Committee were very uneasy about the creation of a partnership for which there was no documentary evidence and insisted on a formal, written agreement. This was prepared at the end of 1872 and brought Kittson's Red River Transportation Company into being. The new company was jointly owned by the Hudson's Bay Company, Norman Kittson and J.J. Hill, though the terms and the HBC involvement remained a secret to secure the silence of those who objected, with or without justification, to anything the HBC did. Two-thirds of the gross earnings were to go towards costs and the remaining third was to be distributed at the end of the shipping season according to the carrying capacity of the vessels which each partner contributed to the business.[22]

Any doubts the Governor and Committee may have entertained about the verbal agreement were set aside when Donald wrote in January 1873 to say that Kittson estimated that the profits for the 1872 season would be in the neighbourhood of $35,000 to $40,000. With the refurbishment of the existing vessels and the construction of a new paddle-wheeler, the *Dakota*, this dropped to $25,253.14, still a tidy sum for one year's work.[23]

In the spring of 1874, the arrangement was changed from a partnership to a limited company with the creation of the Red River Transportation Company in which shares were issued according to the value of the partners' contributions. By this time, the *International* was so battered as to be virtually worthless but a new steamer, the *Alpha*, was acquired to replace it. Donald held the HBC shares in trust and wrote a formal letter to the board stating clearly that the company was the owner and that the shares could be transferred to another company nominee at any time.[24]

Controlling the steamer line between Saint Paul and Fort Garry was important, but it was not the only link in the chain to import consumer supplies into the Northwest and take out the furs. River transport was governed by the seasons for it could not operate during the frozen winter months and, despite their shallow draft, the steamers risked being left high and dry in the summer when there was insufficient water. What could make the transport easier, however, was the removal of the obstacles along the Red River and in parts of the Saskatchewan. As early as October 1871, Donald wrote Lieutenant Governor Archibald to say that work should be started as soon as possible, while the water was low and before it froze, on removing the obstructions at the rapids twelve miles north of Fort Garry, adding that he would be prepared to support at Ottawa, "by our votes or otherwise, as may be required," whatever course of action Archibald favoured. In February 1872, he raised the subject in the provincial legislature and in 1876, he brought it up again in Ottawa. As late as 1878, problems still existed: there were boulders to be removed from the Saskatchewan River, he told the House of Commons, and large bodies of water such as Lake Manitoba had yet to be surveyed. A railway, of course, would ease the problem, but that did not exist either.[25]

In the spring Donald was obliged to negotiate the freight rates which would have to be paid to bring goods from New York or Montreal to Saint Paul and, on the basis of those figures, could begin to calculate what the fur posts at the western end of the Saskatchewan would have to charge for their trade goods. This was a process which was further complicated by the fact that some transatlantic shippers were prepared to offer a through rate to Minnesota. Moreover, they sometimes quoted different rates to the secretary in London and to Donald in Montreal and this too needed to be sorted out in the most efficient way. Another factor which had to be taken into account was the date at which goods might arrive at Saint Paul, for the sooner they reached their intended market, the higher the price they would fetch.

For Outfit 1873, however, the goods meant for the west would have to come in through York Factory again, much to everyone's chagrin. The *Chief Commissioner* which had been launched in the spring of 1872, sank on the Saskatchewan River that August. She had surmounted the rapids, which were seen to be the greatest obstacle to her journey, when she struck a rock. There were numerous accusations of blame but it appears that the crew either disobeyed or misunderstood the captain. The steamer was not as solidly constructed as she might have been and her hold rapidly filled with water. The tea was lost and the tobacco damaged, but Robert Hamilton arranged for the sugar to be boiled down and declared that it was "almost as good as new." Nevertheless, the captain's report showed a loss of $28,466.71 on the steamer and nearly £3,528 on the cargo.[26]

What with his duties in Manitoba and the Northwest, his obligations to the provincial legislature and the federal parliament, and the never-ending negotiations with the federal government over land issues and Ottawa's growing debt to the HBC, Donald was rarely at home in Montreal. Bella was in Dresden and London with Maggie until the spring of 1872 but Jamesie was rather at loose ends and sought out the company of James Bissett and his family on several occasions. In September 1871, his uncle, Joseph Hardisty, had arrived from British Columbia on furlough and had taken the lad travelling in Ontario and the United States. On their return, Joseph set sail for England on a journey which introduced him to Elizabeth Kate Dance, a young lady who lived in Whitby, the Yorkshire fishing port. In October 1873, Donald granted Joseph a leave of absence on what Bissett described as "urgent private business." Joseph returned a married man and, since he was then posted to La Cloche on Lake Huron, his young wife spent the winter with Bella in Montreal. The arrival of a house guest cannot have pleased Jamesie who, perhaps prompted by the frequent absences of his step-father, was turning into a rather self-centred young man.[27]

In June 1872, Canada's first government came to the end of its five year term of office and parliament was prorogued. Elections were called for September and there was no question but that Donald would stand again for Selkirk. Towards the end of February that year, knowing an election was in the offing, Donald's campaign supporters had decided on hosting a dinner as a way of demonstrating enthusiasm for the candidate and contradicting what they considered to be the many false statements made about him and his position in the country. Almost all the influential men in the province, except the lieutenant governor and John Schultz, attended the dinner which was held in the Opera House but catered for by the Queen's Hotel.

Robert Cunningham of the *Manitoban* was in the chair. He reiterated a point which Donald had made in an earlier campaign speech when he argued that the Northwest was British because it had been controlled by the Hudson's Bay Company and had not been open to all comers. He is "a representative man," Cunningham said, adding that "we all require a clear-headed business man like Mr. Donald A. Smith to watch our interests at Ottawa." In reply, Donald said that he was proud of his association with the HBC and, through his ancestors, with the North West Company. "It is a somewhat singular coincidence that I should see the last of the old regime of the Hudson's Bay Company; and have been empowered by that Company to aid it in taking up a new lease of prosperity," he told his listeners, adding that it was a prosperity which greatly concerned all the present and future inhabitants of the Northwest. It was a grand speech, full of optimism for the future and, as he jestingly reported to Bella, it was his "greatest oratorical effort" to date. He was never to become a notable public speaker but at least he had overcome the worst of his stage fright.[28]

Campaigning for the 1872 election was very subdued in Manitoba. Most candidates had made their views known just a few months earlier and no one was inclined to hear them all again. It was a blistering hot summer, with the thermometer just a shade under 100°F on July 9, and indoor political meetings held little appeal. Donald confined himself to being helpful and agreeable. When the Provincial Agricultural Association elected him in absentia as its president, he was quick to cable his thanks from Montreal. He accepted the honour of being vice patron of the Manitoba Rifle Association, the patron being the lieutenant governor, and he chaired the Selkirk St. Andrew's Society.

Though he was inclined to keep silent about his charitable giving, it was known that when the Winnipeg St. Andrew's Society made a collection for the victims of a fire which devastated Chicago in October 1871, the largest contribution, $50, came from the Chief Commissioner. The following spring, he negotiated an arrangement with the company to enable him to give, without reference to London, up to £200 a year to worthwhile causes in the company's name. In general, he directed it towards such things as the purchase of seed when crops failed through drought or plagues of grasshoppers.

Women's education concerned him, in part because he was aware that he had been to school while his academically inclined sister, Margaret, had not, and in part because he could see how Bella had benefitted in comparison with her uneducated sisters. As early as 1871, he headed a committee to establish in Winnipeg the Ladies Higher Boarding and Day School to give girls the equivalent of the

Red River Academy which the Hardisty boys had attended. To both the school and the nascent Manitoba College which opened its doors in the autumn of 1871, he gave $250 and he was later to sit on the college's management committee. After it amalgamated with colleges of other denominations to form the University of Manitoba, he became a substantial donor.

At the end of July 1872, the first missionary conference west of Lake Superior was held at Fort Garry. It was a splendid occasion for the non-conformist proselytisers, who included Richard Hardisty's father-in-law, the Methodist missionary, George McDougall, and Richard's brother-in-law, John McDougall, who was ordained a minister at the gathering. To ensure that the special guests, the Reverend Dr. William Morley Punshon and John Macdonald, were well taken care of, they were accommodated at Silver Heights, "to which hospitable home we were all invited for a visit and dinner one afternoon," John McDougall recorded. "Sir Donald, even in the early seventies, was noted for his princeliness of hospitality, and he, as also the great company he represented, did honor to our conference in many ways."

As Grace Church in Winnipeg was far from big enough for the crowds who were expected to hear one of Dr. Punshon's famous lectures, Donald arranged for one of the large warehouses on the banks of the Assiniboine to be cleared out for the occasion. "Having handsomely decorated it with cloth and bunting, and arranged it with improvised seats, 'Daniel in Babylon' was listened to by a mixed multitude which had gathered in from the whole country." Donald was chairman for the event and the lieutenant governor joined him on the platform. What either man thought of the lecture, which was one of Punshon's frequently repeated favourites, was not recorded, but Archibald was glad of the opportunity to question the McDougalls closely on the Northwest for which he was responsible but about which he knew so little.[29]

Sandford Fleming, sent out by the government to establish a route for the proposed Canadian Pacific Railway, arrived in Winnipeg while the missionaries were there and he and his colleagues were also entertained to a meal at Silver Heights. The lunches and the lectures meant little in themselves, but they demonstrated to any voter who chose to think about it that the candidate was well connected and quite capable of using his influence on behalf of the people of Winnipeg.

The elections themselves, however, were another matter altogether. Selkirk was divided into three districts, Headingly, Winnipeg and St. Boniface. At the latter, which was a Métis community, the polling station was in the house of Roger Goulet. It was attacked by people who claimed to have just arrived from Ontario, though they appear to have been Canadians from the settlement who had prepared for their task in the Winnipeg saloons. At that point, the polling book showed eighty-four votes for Donald Smith and one for his opponent, so the attackers seized the book and tore it up. When Donald attempted to quieten them, they responded with mud and axe handles, driving him back into his carriage. The mob then directed their attentions to the Winnipeg polling booth but, finding that it was in the police station, they turned instead to the offices of the *Manitoban* and *Le Métis*, the local French language paper. Schultz was delighted, describing the *Manitoban* office as "a perfect pandemonium of printers' ink — windows smashed — press ditto. The *Métis* office as near as I can hear went bodily out of the window, and it will be some time before Jean Baptiste can express his grievances in print." It was December before the *Manitoban* reappeared, and even then it was printed on the *Manitoba Free Press* equipment. Despite the violence, Donald was returned with a handsome majority, gaining 256 votes to the opposition's 62.[30]

Not all of Donald's supporters were happy with the result, not least of them his old friend Robert Hamilton. "Of course I am glad that since he did come forward he was victorious, but I would much rather see him retire now from Political life, as the business of the Fur Trade is sufficient to give full occupation to any one man who holds the position of Chief Commissioner." In addition to the fur trade, of course, there were the land issues and the government's debts. Donald had hoped to get to Ottawa to deal with some of these by the second week of October but was involved in a serious carriage accident which injured his spine and caused concussion. "I am told he came very near being killed," Hamilton reported to his friend Roderick MacFarlane, adding that both he and Inspecting Chief Factor William Christie "often warned him that he would some day come to grief as he drove a very skittish pair of grey Mares that he was utterly unable to manage, being without exception the worst driver I ever saw in my life." A two mile road in Labrador was probably not the best place to learn to drive.[31]

CHAPTER NINE

THE PACIFIC SCANDAL 1873

For being so eager to mix in Politics, [he] was called a *Renegade & Traitor* by Sir John A, for which there was to have been some blarney that night.
Henry Hardisty [1]

As soon as the Hudson's Bay Company had calculated the costs of the insurrection at Fort Garry in the winter of 1869-1870, it began to seek compensation. Just as both governments and the company denied responsibility for the failure to ensure that power was transferred smoothly, so also they refused to bear the costs which were incurred when it did not. It fell to Donald Smith to try to extract compensation for the HBC from the Canadian government.

In April 1871, a committee of the Canadian privy council investigated the matter and concluded that it would be impossible to obtain a vote of money in parliament that year because public opinion was against it. Ontario's demand for the blood of Louis Riel and Ambroise Lépine would suffice to ensure that there would be a popular outcry if the tax payers were asked to foot the bill for the trouble these Métis had caused. The committee, in a report sanctioned by the governor general, further argued that, when Canada consented to pay £300,000 for Rupert's Land, there was no expectation of also having to pay for a military expedition.

In addition, the committee noted that

> there is a wide spread feeling in Canada both in and out of Parliament that the Hudsons Bay Company are chiefly responsible for the success of the insurgents in the Red River Settlement in 1869/70 and so long as this feeling remains unchanged it would be useless for the Government of the Dominion to submit to Parliament any claim for compensation on the part of the Company. It must moreover be borne in mind that large claims have been made on the part of loyal inhabitants who were imprisoned and expatriated during the ascendancy of the insurgents.[2]

One such claimant was John Schultz who received $35,000 for his losses, a remarkably large sum for a man who contributed more to the creation of the troubles than to their solution, though it was only half his original claim of $71,581.62.[3]

Besides seeking compensation for its losses, the company expected to receive interest on the £300,000 from the time it was to have been paid until the time it was actually received. As well, there was the cost of constructing the road from Fort Garry to the North West Angle of Lake of the Woods for use by the expeditionary force in the summer of 1870 and there were more straightforward debts such as rental of the governor's residence at the fort and accommodation and supplies for the troops and militia.

None of these sums was easy to collect. On January 12, 1872, Donald wrote London to say that, "On a visit to Ottawa last week I presented for payment accounts from Fort Garry amounting to upwards of £29,000." He was promised prompt payment. On April 11, 1872, he sent the government an invoice for $14,425 for rent on HBC property occupied by troops at Fort Garry, Lower Fort Garry and Pembina. At the end of January 1873, he wrote the Governor and Committee from Ottawa to say that Hector Langevin, the minister of public works, had promised an immediate settlement of the outstanding amount. Things looked better on the fourth of April when he was able to report that $20,000 would be paid at once and a further $60,000 when the estimates were approved. In June, however, he was again invoicing for the $14,425 outstanding rent and a further $3,750 for rent on the lieutenant governor's residence from September 1870 until May 1, 1871. In November 1872, he was once more explaining that he had not yet had the money from the government for rental of company property in 1871. His letter to William Armit on October 24, 1873 reported, "Yesterday I saw Sir John Macdonald in relation to monies due to the Co. for rent, and he assures me that the whole will be settled without further delay. I am again to see him on this subject next week." The correspondence is consistently courteous and even tempered but Donald's patience was sorely tried, the more so since he was piggy in the middle with Sir John, Old Tomorrow as he was often called, procrastinating on the one side and, on the other, the company pressing him to have the claims settled.[4]

The obligations which were most difficult to deal with, however, were the $2,500 earmarked for the "loyal French" and the $3,000 which was used to keep Riel and Lépine out of the country in 1872. The former was, at best, a gratuity while the latter was clearly a bribe and parliament could not be expected to assent to such expenditure without comment. Furthermore, any discussion of the money for Riel and Lépine would inevitably disclose the fact that a further $1,000 had been paid to them from secret service funds. Macdonald temporized, trying to find a budget in which he could hide the payments, but the parliamentarians' habit of picking through the estimates looking for trouble meant he could not find a way of dealing with the problem.

For Donald Smith, the failure to provide the money for the "loyal French" was an embarrassment: promises had been made in his name and were not being honoured. As for the money given to Taché for Riel and Lépine, it was a genuine disbursement for which repayment had been promised. The company and the two governments could argue about the principles of compensation for losses during the uprising but the $3,000 was a different obligation altogether.

When he had arrived in Ottawa on March 8, 1872, at Archibald's request Donald told Cartier, Langevin and Macdonald about the cash which had been given to Riel and Lépine and both the prime minister and Cartier had assured him that the money would be repaid. That sum and the money for the "loyal French" were frequently discussed; the subject came up again in the autumn when Archibald was in Ottawa and received assurances that at least one of the sums would be forthcoming. When Donald went to see the prime minister about it, however, he was told that "it would not be convenient to have it paid until after the Session of Parliament. All the discussions were in the same sense; such discussions and assurances were repeated also in the spring session of Parliament in 1873." Both men were irked, the one by the constant demands and the other by the constant evasion.[5]

In other respects, the two Scots got along tolerably well though their personalities were very different. Macdonald drank, often to excess, while Donald, though not teetotal, was abstemious and always in complete control of himself. The prime minister, generally a solitary drinker, was otherwise a very sociable man whose understanding of the complexities of human personalities usually enabled him to handle his political opponents skillfully and keep his own colleagues in line. Donald was less interested in the foibles of human nature and so less calculating when it came to determining a particular course of action. He assumed that people would behave honourably and that business and political decisions were governed by straightforward economic considerations. Politics as a game which men played for its own sake held no interest for him. Both men were well read and in the breadth of their knowledge more than made up for any deficiencies in their formal education. On a professional level, they were also united by a firm conviction that a railway should be constructed to link western Canada with the east.

Donald did not especially care whether the railway was built by the government or by independent companies. What mattered to him was that it should be built. He recognized that the 1871 bargain which brought British Columbia into Confederation demanded a line of rail to the Pacific coast, but his greater interest lay in getting an effective and efficient transportation system into Manitoba and the North West Territories. The Hudson's Bay Company needed to replace its labour intensive and therefore expensive shipping network with rail transport which would bring in supplies for its trading posts throughout the Northwest and ship out the furs which accumulated at those posts; settlers needed a decent means of travel to bring them to the Northwest just as much as they would need the goods in the HBC stores when they got there; and the people of the Northwest would soon need a way of sending their produce to market. He accepted the argument that it should be a Canadian line, though he was not such a patriot that he preferred jolting along the mosquito infested Dawson Road to the more comfortable rail travel through American territory. The risk of the American route for immigrants, however, was that they could be induced to stop short of their intended destination in the Canadian Northwest. The upshot was that Donald voted with Sir John on most railway matters, as he did, by and large, on other issues as well, though he felt no iron-clad loyalty to the man and his political views.

Macdonald and his cabinet colleagues intended not merely that the railway should traverse only Canadian soil but also that it should be constructed by a company which was primarily if not entirely Canadian. The foremost contender for the contract was Sir Hugh Allan, who had partnered George Stephen and Donald Smith in the Canada Rolling Stock Company, the Canada Cotton Manufacturing Company and various other ventures. A poorly educated Glaswegian of immense wealth acquired through his transatlantic shipping line, he had been advocating the construction of a railway by a private firm ever since the spring of 1870 when the acquisition of the Northwest made it possible for the government to grant land to a railway company.

Though he denied it, Allan's backers in the bid for the Canadian Pacific Railway contract were Americans, including George McMullen, a young man who was born in Picton, Ontario, but who, before his thirtieth birthday, had established himself as a Chicago businessman of few principles beyond lining his own pocket. McMullen brought other Americans into the scheme, notably William Butler Ogden and General George Cass, senior figures in the Northern Pacific Railway, and, most importantly, Jay Cooke, the Philadelphia banker who exercised financial control over the US line. Cooke was an annexationist who firmly believed that it was the manifest destiny of the United States to control the whole of the Northwest, and the Americans' intention was that the Canadian railway would be a feeder for their own transcontinental system then under construction or, better still, would be part of a network entirely owned by them.

Before Donald left for the Northwest in February 1873, rumours concerning the Pacific Scandal, as it was being dubbed, or the Pacific Slander, as it was called by the government's supporters, began to appear in the press. The stories suggested that Hugh Allan had made such generous contributions to Macdonald's election campaign that they could only be explained as bribes, in exchange for which he was to be granted the railway contract.

Allan was not one of nature's innocents but neither had his previous business dealings been marked by wholesale corruption. Nevertheless, as Donald was to learn, Allan and his American friends had been misled by Francis Hincks, Macdonald's naive minister of finance, who, supposing that any call for tenders to construct the line would be a charade, encouraged Allan and his American partners. But in July, as the 1872 election campaign in Ontario and Quebec entered its final stages, Hincks finally grasped that the cabinet really was firmly against any American involvement. The opposition of Sir George-Etienne Cartier, especially, stood firmly in the way of Allan and his colleagues receiving the charter. Cartier controlled forty-five votes in the house, sufficient to bring down the government should he choose to do so, and he was adamant that he would resign before he would let "a damned American company have control of the Pacific."[6]

Macdonald, who was campaigning in Ontario, had hoped to create a compromise company which brought together Allan and Senator David Macpherson who also wanted the railway contract, but the men refused to cooperate on the question of the presidency. "Under these circumstances," Macdonald wired to his Quebec colleague on July 26, "I authorize you to assure Allan that the influence of the Government will be exercised to secure him the position of President." For Allan, this was essential because he needed to be in a position to satisfy the demands of his friends in the Northern Pacific. Indeed, it was so important that he wanted the promise in writing.[7]

Unhappily, Cartier was suffering from Bright's disease, a degenerative kidney ailment which impairs the judgement, and he agreed to a written promise. Allan had already made financial contributions to the election battle on behalf of the Conservative party from which he expected so much, but the party coffers were very low and Cartier indicated that more would be welcome. That, too, should be in writing said Allan.

Dissatisfied with the government's draft, Allan composed his own letter which said, "The friends of the Government will expect to be assisted with funds in the pending elections, and any amount which you or your Company shall advance for that purpose shall be recouped by you." Neither Allan nor Cartier believed the line about repayment; in an era when votes could be, and regularly were, sold to the highest bidder, election campaigns were frequently about money rather than principles. What distinguished the business between Allan and Cartier is both the unsubtle manner in which it was conducted and the high stakes for which Allan was playing.[8]

The note proposed $25,000 for Sir John A. Macdonald, with an additional $10,000 included further down the list. For Hector Langevin, the minister of public works, the figure was $15,000, with an additional $10,000. Cartier himself was down for $20,000, with a further $30,000. When Macdonald learned of the letters, he was furious and cabled that his telegram of July 26 was to form the basis of the agreement with Allan. For his part, Allan consented to the withdrawal of the letters, comforted by the fact that the prime minister had acknowledged the agreement. Later in the campaign, Cartier asked for and received another $20,000 and there was also a positive response to Macdonald's cable, "I must have another ten thousand. Will be the last time of calling. Do not fail me."[9]

Macdonald, who was returned with a handsome majority, used none of the money in pursuance of his own campaign but employed it instead to assist his colleagues who needed support. As the prime minister was later to explain, there was no central political office which could raise money for election expenses and candidates were obliged to find resources in whatever way they could.

> There is what they call the legitimate expenses, which every candidate has to undertake — the expenses of canvassing, printing and advertising —those are the legitimate expenses. There is also a very large expenditure, which is very common in this country, although it is contrary to the Statute. It is, however, I believe so universal that I have never known any serious contest before an Election Committee on that ground. I refer to the expenditure for teams to bring the voters to the polls. My experience has been, with respect to this item, that you cannot get the voters to come to the polls on either side unless some effort is made to provide conveyances for them.

In addition, there was the cost of what was known as "treating" which included "dinners and things of that kind, all of which are contrary to Statute, but they generally prevail in Canada."[10]

In Montreal, the money had effectively been wasted, for Cartier was soundly defeated, many of the votes being cast against him coming from the very men who had been bribed with Allan's money to support him. Macdonald immediately asked the Manitoba lieutenant governor to arrange for Cartier's election in that province where voting was not due to take place for nearly a month. Both Lieutenant Governor Archibald and Archbishop Taché saw that they could use this plea to increase the pressure for Riel's amnesty and, in their desperation, Macdonald and Cartier agreed to do their best. Louis Riel, who had been intending to stand in the solidly Métis riding of Provencher, stepped aside for Cartier who was elected by acclamation.

With the elections out of the way, Macdonald put his mind to sorting out the railway problem. When it became apparent that he could not effect a compromise between Macpherson and Allan, he had determined that a new company would be chartered to build the Pacific railway and that it would have directors who reflected the interests of each of the provinces. On November 3, 1872, he asked Donald Smith to be the Manitoba representative. Macdonald could see that it would be useful to have the Hudson's Bay Company as an ally when the government sought money from the London banks and was also aware of Donald's burgeoning interest in railways. For his part, Donald accepted, explaining to the Governor and Committee that it would be to the advantage of the company to have a voice on the board. He said he would not have felt justified in declining. Indeed, a year earlier William Armit had written to enquire whether he could "make arrangements" in relation to the railway in order to advance the company's own interests.[11]

In November, Donald was able to report that the government was to provide grants of both land and cash to the proposed new railway company which was to lodge a nominal capital of $10 million with the government which would pay interest on it. In his conversation with Donald, Macdonald had added that the HBC concerns were so bound up with the opening of the Northwest and the construction of the railway that the company should put up the deposit itself. The prime minister was right about the railway being closely linked to the company's interests but he clearly had no understanding of its nervous, tight-fisted shareholders.[12]

When the structure of the proposed company came before parliament in May, the MPs insisted that none of their fellows should sit on the board of the new railway, a move which Donald supported with his vote. He and several others were replaced by different geographical representatives. In the case of Manitoba, the choice fell, at Donald's suggestion, on the old free trader, Andrew McDermot.

Between the Manitoba federal elections in September and the first sitting of the new House in March, Donald busied himself with Hudson's Bay Company business, Bank of Montreal meetings and the Manitoba legislature. The provincial law makers had moved from Andrew Bannatyne's house to a room over the jail, in the court house on Main Street; they entered and left by the outside fire escape. At formal state openings, the sergeant-at-arms, "bearing the mace, walked backwards before the Lieutenant-Governor, bowing at frequent intervals, an agile performance which was applauded with joyful derision by the populace."[13]

In February 1873, there were acrimonious debates about the incorporation of Winnipeg as a city. The bill allowed taxation on all lands within the proposed limits and would significantly increase the HBC's tax liability. Donald argued that, in fairness, the company should have been consulted and pointed out that members should have been given an opportunity to read the bill before being called upon to discuss it. Despite the logic of this position, he was subjected to a considerable amount of vituperation and, along with several others, was burned in effigy on Main Street. Old animosities had not disappeared with the loss of the HBC monopoly and many Winnipeggers believed Donald was acting in the company's interests rather than in those of the people he represented. Naturally, he was concerned about any legislation which affected the HBC and, in this case, about the huge increase in taxes which would follow, but his opposition to incorporation also derived from a belief that the introduction of taxation on unimproved lands, which had hitherto been tax free, would discourage businesses from moving to Winnipeg and so slow down the development of the area.

Donald Smith was still in Fort Garry when the new governor general, Lord Dufferin, opened the second Canadian parliament. Donald had been late setting out for Fort Garry because the winter was so severe, bringing all travel to a halt while blizzards raged across the prairies. It was the seventeenth of February before he had left Montreal and the twenty-second of March when he set out on his return, taking the usual route by sleigh to the head of rail in Minnesota, and then by train to Saint Paul, where a network of railway systems took him to Chicago, where he changed to another system which took him to Toronto. He arrived in the capital on March 28.

Donald had persuaded the government not to bring Manitoba's taxes up to the level operating in the rest of Canada for a minimum of two years after the province joined Confederation, but Ottawa now intended to put the province on a par with the rest of Canada. The provincial legislature had petitioned to have the existing four percent level retained for a further period and Donald had been authorized to negotiate on its behalf. Simultaneously, he was ensuring that the HBC got an adequate supply of wine, spirits and tobacco into the province under the old rate. When he returned to Ottawa from Montreal on March 31, he found that he had been successful: a year's extension of the four percent rate had been granted, except on alcohol.

For Macdonald, however, the tariff in Manitoba was an insignificant irritation when compared to the stories which were now common parlance in Ottawa, Toronto and Montreal. It was impossible to pick up the Toronto *Globe* or to walk through the foyer of the Russell House in Ottawa without hearing tales of Hugh Allan's bribes. As Donald was beginning to suspect and Macdonald was beginning to realize, many of the stories contained a good deal more than a grain of truth.

The prime minister had not conducted the election in complete sobriety and was not sure what promises had been made by Cartier or what agreement he had referred to in his telegram or, indeed, whether he had meant *agreement* at all. He was not even sure how many cables he had sent. Moreover, the Liberals were saying that huge sums of money had changed hands and rumours were thick in the air. Finally, Allan acknowledged to Macdonald the extent to which Cartier and the Conservative Party were indebted to him. Then Cartier, who had gone to London to seek medical treatment, confirmed that he had been as indiscreet as Allan had said.

Allan had paid out $343,000 in gold and a further $13,500 was still owing when he had reported on his expenditure to McMullen in September 1872. This was cash, not promises of shares, and it was more than seven times the figure agreed on for bribes. McMullen was horrified. Allan seems to have assured him that Cartier's promises were in writing and could be counted on but, not long after, Macdonald at last convinced Allan that the government really would not assign the contract to a predominantly American alliance and Allan was finally forced to tell McMullen that the deal was off.

Hugh Allan had never before been so unsophisticated in his business dealings but he appeared quite convinced that he had bought the government and bought the contract to build the Pacific railway. As far as he could see, though the Americans were out of the picture, he personally had nothing to worry about. Perhaps he had never before done business with a man less honourable than himself.

When Allan refused to put himself in the same position as the Americans by withdrawing from the contract to build the railway, and also refused to have anything further to do with McMullen, Cass, Cooke and their friends, McMullen took a little trip to Ottawa. He arrived at the door of the prime minister's office on New Year's eve and read Macdonald some of the more compromising paragraphs of Allan's letters. He explained that Allan had paid off a member of parliament who was close to the prime minister. If Macdonald's insistence that he had not agreed to give the contract to Allan were true, said McMullen, Allan was a swindler who had taken the Americans' money dishonestly. He urged Macdonald to accept the original contract — which the prime minister could not do because of the American interests — or to deny Allan the contract — which he could not do because he was obliged to honour the commitment which Cartier had so foolishly made. The prime minister explained that parliament could not possibly give the contract to a company made up as the Canada Pacific Railway Company was. Allan should have understood this and been "more frank with you," he said to McMullen.[14]

Macdonald never wanted to see McMullen or any of his friends again, but he knew that something would have to be done, and soon. He buckled under the pressure and asked Hincks to speak to J.J.C. Abbott who, besides being Allan's solicitor, was the lawyer the government and big corporations used to smooth things over behind closed doors. He proved to be a proficient haggler, knocking McMullen's pay off down from $200,000 to $37,500. He handed over $20,000 and gave Allan's cheque for the remainder to Henry Starnes who worked at the Merchants' Bank which Allan had founded. In another envelope Abbott placed the correspondence which had caused so much trouble and this too was given to Starnes. Ten days after the end of the spring 1873 parliamentary session, the banker was to give McMullen the remainder of the money and Allan the letters. With this transaction, Abbott believed he had purchased the letters and McMullen's silence.

On the evening of April 2, 1873, Donald joined the crowd of MPs in the House of Commons. The press gallery was packed and everyone in Ottawa who might conceivably be interested in government or railways was crammed into the visitors' gallery. Two days earlier, Lucius Seth Huntington, a Liberal member for Shefford, in the Eastern Townships of Quebec, had indicated that he would request a select committee to inquire into the Pacific railway. A lawyer, Huntington had taken an interest in rail transport and was acquainted with Jay Cooke. Now, everyone wanted to know how much he knew and what he was going to do with that knowledge.

Silence descended as Huntington called for a parliamentary committee of inquiry to investigate charges that Hugh Allan's Canada Pacific Railway Company was financed by American capital and that the government knew this; he charged further that Allan had paid out large sums of money, some of it from his American backers, to aid the Conservatives in their election campaign and that Allan was to receive the railway contract in exchange.

When he was finished, all eyes turned to Macdonald. He ignored the visitors' gallery and the members opposite; he said nothing and had compelled his front bench to silence too. Finally the speaker broke the tension by calling for a vote on the motion for a parliamentary committee. Donald Smith and others who were loosely attached to the Tories went into the lobby with Macdonald who found himself with a comfortable majority of thirty-one.

While the Liberal committee rooms were filled with indignant assertions that Macdonald was corrupt, the men in the cabinet office were concluding that their victory of silence looked too much like sweeping the allegations under the carpet. Whether or not Huntington knew more than he said, he had certainly blundered by making no political capital from his call for an inquiry. If the government itself set up a committee of investigation, people would assume there was no dirty laundry to wash. On the eighth of April, Macdonald announced a select committee, despite the fact that his true preference was for a royal commission for which he would be entitled to select the members.

At this point Macdonald knew that McMullen had received the first installment of his bribe; he also knew that McMullen had double-crossed Allan by retaining copies of his correspondence with Allan and selling them to the Liberals for $25,000, substantially more than the sum remaining to be paid to keep them out of circulation. A percentage probably went to the go-between, Senator Asa Foster. Foster was to have been one of the beneficiaries of Allan's Canada Pacific Railway Company, and his motive, like McMullen's, was now not money but revenge.

As far as Donald could tell, the correspondence and the cheating unquestionably reflected ill on Allan and the scoundrel McMullen, but it only tangentially touched Macdonald and others who had been named by Allan. These included men who figured on a list of those whose support would have to be secured through a gift of shares. Among them was Donald Smith, the most influential man in the Northwest, who was down for $100,000 worth. There is no evidence that Allan discussed his proposed bribes with Donald or with most of his intended recipients, but, as Donald laconically observed to Stafford Northcote, "anyone is at liberty, I suppose, to put down any one else's name for a sum of money in a memorandum, a last will and testament, or any other document."[15]

The prime minister, meanwhile, took comfort from the fact that the correspondence which incriminated him and Cartier had been safely removed to Abbott's office.

As soon as the select committee was announced, it ran into technical problems of the sort which beleaguer newly created nations. The first problem was that committees of the House of Commons could not sit after parliament was prorogued. The ice in the St. Lawrence had broken on the first of May and spring was fast approaching. The summer recess would soon have to be called so that the members could return to their constituencies the moment the roads dried. Macdonald overcame this technicality by suggesting, to everyone's satisfaction, that parliament would not be prorogued but adjourned. When the select committee had finished its deliberations, a handful of members who lived near Ottawa would assemble to vote for the prorogation.

Old Tomorrow, whose policy was always one of delay in the face of trouble, then argued that the committee should be allowed to adjourn since neither Cartier nor Allan could testify until they returned from England, where the former had gone to seek medical help and the latter to negotiate financial backing for his railway company. It was only fair to give them an opportunity to speak in their defense. Donald and a majority of other MPs agreed and voted in favour of the motion.

The other technical problem facing the government was that the committee was unable to take evidence on oath. A select committee which could neither compel people to attend nor oblige them to tell the truth was effectively emasculated.

Parliament met through most of the rest of May and Macdonald continued to gain a majority when any railway issue came to a vote. They were uncontroversial motions and, in each case, Donald supported the government.

In London, Allan's efforts to raise backing for his railway enterprise were failing miserably. News of the Pacific Scandal was in the British press and Allan was proving himself to be "about as bad a negotiator as I have ever met," in the opinion of Sir John Rose. Rose's next communication was much more distressing for it recorded the death of George-Etienne Cartier who, with Macdonald, had been the architect of Canadian Confederation. Macdonald wept and sought solace in the bottle.[16]

Parliament finally adjourned on May 23 and Donald left for Montreal the following day. He was back on the first of June to try to sort out the refund of the $3,000 paid to Riel but the prime minister was "too unwell" to see visitors.

Finally, on the seventh of June, he sailed from Quebec on the *Polynesian*, known by her sailors as the Rolling Polly. He had not been long in Britain when the papers began reporting that the Canadian press had got hold of Allan's correspondence and was publishing it. Hugh Allan was held up as a fool and McMullen as a blackmailer and a charlatan. Once again J.J.C. Abbott was brought in, this time to write an "explanation" for the humiliated Allan to send to the newspapers. Macdonald, however, was still in the clear.

On the seventeenth of July, three Canadian papers published McMullen's retaliation. He commanded little respect for the farrago of lies he produced to explain himself and his misdeeds, but tucked away at the end of his justification were the letters and telegrams from Cartier and Macdonald, making it perfectly clear that they had sought money from Allan for their election campaign. While Abbott had been in England with Allan, his private secretary, George Norris, assisted by Alfred Cooper, had copied the incriminating documents and sold them to the Liberals for $5,000. The legal office which served as the Liberals' intermediary, as Abbott was doing for the Conservatives, was headed by Rodolphe Laflamme, the man who had once given the young Louis Riel a job.

Macdonald disappeared for several days to seek liquid consolation but, at the beginning of August, about the time that Donald returned from the UK, the prime minister pulled himself together and returned to Ottawa. The adjourned parliament was to reconvene on August 13 and it was Macdonald's intention to have it prorogued immediately. This would axe the select committee which had done virtually nothing since it was formed and would enable Macdonald to revert to his original plan of establishing a royal commission, composed of sympathetic judges whose "sittings would be prolonged and the public mind would be wearied of the subject before the Session, which he then thought would be held in December or January."[17]

Donald was among the MPs who felt that parliament should not be prorogued. Four months had elapsed since the Pacific Scandal had broken and not a thing had been done about it. Richard Cartwright, who had once hoped to be made minister of finance instead of Hincks, organized a petition calling on the governor general to keep the house in session. Ninety-two members signed it, Donald among them. In response, Lord Dufferin said he owed it to members from more distant constituencies not to recall parliament and he said that he felt obliged to prorogue parliament because his ministers had advised him to do so. Were he to disregard their advice, he would be obliged to dismiss his ministers and find new ones. He also noted that the signatories did not represent fifty percent of the House. When the Commons met that afternoon, August 13, the disgusted Liberals, together with those Conservatives who had signed the petition, remained in their places while the prorogation ceremony took place in the Senate. Ten days later, Donald was on his way west.

In Ottawa, the prime minister and the leader of the opposition mustered their arguments and their parliamentary forces for the forthcoming battle over the Pacific railway contract. In September, Macdonald cabled Fort Garry to urge Donald to return for the opening of parliament. The royal commission had discovered that all the principal players in the Pacific Scandal had lost their papers and their memories or were unavoidably detained abroad and unable to attend. Neither had the commissioners felt themselves constrained to inquire too closely into the evidence which they were able to extract from the witnesses. Nevertheless, while clearing Macdonald of personal corruption, selling the charter to the Americans and dealing improperly with Allan, the commission had found Macdonald and his ministers guilty of receiving money from Allan for illegal election purposes. The consequences of this charge would have to be brazened out in the House and Macdonald needed all the supporters he could muster.

Donald, who had little patience with the formalities involved in the speech from the throne and the political posturing which accompanied it, had planned to return to Ottawa in time to influence the legislation in which he was interested. He was committed to an autumn visit to Swan River and Fort Carlton to sort out problems with indents and to "introduce a system more in consonance with the present greatly altered condition of the country than heretofore followed." Finally, after some telegraphic negotiations, Donald agreed to be in Ottawa before October 20.[18]

What he could not say on the open telegraph line was that he had been delayed because once again he had been trying to make peace in the Métis community. Mayor Francis Cornish and several troublemakers of like mind had persuaded a magistrate, Dr. John O'Donnell, to sign a warrant for the arrest of Louis Riel and Ambroise Lépine. Riel was shrewd enough to keep out of the way, but Lépine was dragged off to prison at Fort Garry. On September 20, *Le Métis* published a letter from Riel calling the arrest a violation of the good faith of the government and on Monday the twenty-second, a mass meeting brought together a seething and angry crowd. The arrest united all the Métis and brought men such as Robert Cunningham of the *Manitoban*, the merchant Andrew Bannatyne, John McTavish of the HBC, and Donald Smith to their support. The meeting drafted strongly worded resolutions and the four Anglophones helped turn them into a form which might enable the government to act. Lieutenant Governor Morris, who had replaced Adams Archibald the previous December, received the petition but, as he privately admitted to Prime Minister Macdonald, though his sympathies were with the Métis, there was nothing he could do. Beyond assuring Morris that the arrest had not been instigated by the federal government, there was little Macdonald could do either. Indeed, it made the likelihood of an amnesty seem even more remote. Nor was an amnesty at the top of the prime minister's agenda that autumn.[19]

Donald was at last able to set out from Silver Heights on September 24 and, on October 7, was inside Chief Factor Laurence Clarke's house at Fort Carlton before Clarke and his family even realized the Chief Commissioner had arrived. It had not been an easy journey. Snow fell in the middle of September and lasted until the third of October and there were sharp frosts throughout these weeks. It was the time of year when there was neither sufficient snow for sleighs nor soft, dry ground for horses, and wise men avoided travelling if they possibly could. "He does not look at all well," Clarke glumly reported to Richard Hardisty, "and I fear is not long for this world unless he takes more care of himself."[20]

On the eleventh, Donald was off again from Carlton, so exhausted from travel and overwork that he strapped himself to the buckboard to keep from tumbling out if he fell asleep. Relays of horses were posted along the Saskatchewan Trail and, whenever the animals were changed, a company officer would thrust a mug of hot tea into Donald's hands and answer questions about business at his post. The return journey took five days which, as Henry Hardisty exclaimed, speaking for all who heard of it, was "quick travelling at that time of year."[21]

By October 23, Donald was in Ottawa where he saw the prime minister "in relation to monies due to the Co. for rent, and he assures me that the whole will be settled without further delay," he wrote to Armit. He also raised the question of an amnesty for Louis Riel as well as the money for the "loyal French," while Macdonald, himself, brought up the matter of the repayment of the money given to Riel. The men agreed to meet the following week to talk about these matters and about the terms under which the police would occupy Lower Fort Garry.[22]

In the speech from the throne that afternoon, Lord Dufferin said that the report of the royal commission would be tabled and that the charter for the Canada Pacific Railway would be withdrawn because financial backing had not been found. It was the commission report and, to a lesser extent, the failure of the railway which worried Macdonald, not the irritating and long postponed payment of Hudson's Bay Company debts. Earlier in the month, he had calculated that he had a majority of twenty-five and his friend, Senator Alexander Campbell, the minister of the interior, and leader of the Tories in the upper house, was confident of twenty when the speech from the throne was read. Had a vote been taken almost at once, Campbell believed, the Conservatives would have won. As it was, their numbers began to ebb away.[23]

Donald returned to Montreal on Friday, October 24 and spent a difficult, thoughtful weekend trying to decide how he should vote.

> For two days and nights I struggled with myself over the course I should take. On the one hand were my admiration for Sir John Macdonald, my grateful sense of his services to the country, my confidence in his ability and statesmanship. On the other hand was a clear perception of the terrible political mistake which had been committed and the evil effect which it might have on the community. But the chief reflection which led me to vote as I did was that I had been sent into Parliament to represent my constituents, and I soon had ample reason to know how they regarded the affair. I had therefore only one course to take; it was a severe wrench to my personal feelings, but I took that course, let the cost be what it might.[24]

The note was sent the following spring to William Buckingham who had founded the *Nor'Wester*, which was published in Red River for ten years from 1859, and who was subsequently to become private secretary to Alexander Mackenzie. Though it was written with hindsight, it suggests that Donald's decision to vote against Macdonald was not easily reached and that, for him, it was primarily a moral dilemma. The problem, as he saw it, was not that Macdonald had accepted Allan's contribution to his party's electoral expenses. It was that Allan had believed the money was not a donation but a bribe; he believed he was purchasing the railway contract and Macdonald disregarded this fact, either because it was convenient for him to do so or because he was too drunk to recognize how others would interpret the transaction. This, in Donald's view, was a grave error. It was not enough for a prime minister, especially of such a new nation, to be honourable: he had to be seen to be honourable.

On Monday, he was back in Ottawa. At the end of that week, he saw his friend, Inspecting Chief Factor Colin Rankin, who had been to Labrador to try to get the accounts there sorted out; before that, he was invited to meet some of the prime minister's supporters in the speaker's room. Hector Langevin, now Cartier's successor as leader of the party in Quebec, Alexander Campbell, and Donald's friend, Henry Nathan, wanted to persuade him to cast his vote in Macdonald's favour. "No, I cannot do so; I cannot possibly do so; I cannot conscientiously do so," he recalled telling them when the subject came up in the House five years later.[25]

The proposition before the House was an amendment to an amendment to the proposed acceptance of the speech from the throne. The first amendment, put forward by Alexander Mackenzie, the Liberal leader, censured the prime minister and the government while a subsequent Tory amendment expressed continued confidence. In the speaker's room, Donald proposed an alternative to the Conservative amendment which he said he would support. "The Government should frankly confess their fault to the House, and then if the country condoned it, and Parliament condoned it, it would be a very different thing. That is what I proposed to the hon. gentlemen, and this was reduced to writing at the time." Once again, it was an opinion based on moral principles but requiring popular support.[26]

As the week had progressed, the men on whom the Tories thought they could count had begun to drift to the opposition. The Conservatives were not helped by the fact that Macdonald was never sober, nor by the fact that his habitual policy of delay was, in this case, exacerbated by the conviction that during an unguarded, inebriated moment in the election campaign, he had sent other cables which had not yet surfaced and of which he now had no recollection. Campbell was frank about the effect this had on the party's attempt to survive.

> I do not believe up to the last moment that he felt sure, or now feels sure, that all he telegraphed during the Elections has come out. From the time he left Kingston, after his own election, to go West, I am very much afraid he kept himself more or less under the influence of wine, and that he really has no clear recollection of what he did on many occasions at Toronto and elsewhere during that period.
>
> I am very sorry to say that the same reasons which impeded his management of the elections was operating during the whole of the days the Parliament remained in Session, and we never had the full advantage either of his abilities and judgment or of his nerve and courage. A night of excess always leaves a morning of nervous incapacity and we were subjected to this pain amongst others.[27]

Donald spent the next week in Ottawa, listening to the arguments and waiting to discover how the prime minister might defend himself. At last, at nine o'clock on the evening of November 3, Macdonald rose to speak. His cabinet colleagues calculated that they had a majority of about six at that point and the speech, if it went well, could confirm them and perhaps bring other errant MPs back to the Conservative fold.

Before he started to speak, Macdonald asked his friend, Peter Mitchell, to provide him with gin and water. Mitchell, who had served in the coalition government which had been in power for the first five years following Confederation, had decided that he could not follow a man with Macdonald's drinking habits and was intending to declare himself an independent, but remained by the prime minister for the duration of the Pacific Scandal. He was unwilling to comply with a request to compound the behaviour to which he objected but reluctantly did so. After three drinks, Mitchell noted that the effect of the alcohol was beginning to show; when the fourth was requested, he told the messenger boy to reduce the amount of gin. Macdonald complained that it was too weak, whereupon Mitchell slipped up to the visitors' gallery to seek advice from Lady Macdonald. She was deeply upset by his drinking but finally said he had better have what he wanted. When the speech was over, Mitchell discovered that two others were also providing gin, each of them under the impression that the other two were bringing water.

Despite these circumstances, the speech was widely judged to be the best Macdonald had ever made and cheers resounded throughout the Commons when he took his seat nearly five hours later. Even the opposition had good words to say about it, despite the fact that he had delighted in attacking the Liberals. "They have spies and thieves and men of espionage who would pick your lock and steal your notebook," he declaimed. He made accusations about the vast sums some men had spent on their election campaigns and when David Blain objected, hinted that Blain's electoral expenses had been met by his wealthy wife.

The core of Macdonald's speech was an emotional appeal to his listeners, couched in the slightly histrionic language of late nineteenth century Canadian politics. He reiterated that no illegal expenditure had taken place and that the railway charter had not been sold to any foreign body. Whether his conclusion drew on the advice which Donald had given the previous week or whether he even saw the memo or was able to grasp it is now impossible to say. But he did ask parliament and the country to condone what had happened. "Sir, I commit myself, the Government commits itself, to the hands of this House, and far beyond this House, it commits itself to the country at large." There were loud cheers. "I throw myself upon this House; I throw myself upon this country; I throw myself upon posterity, and I believe that I know, that, notwithstanding the many failings in my life, I shall have the voice of this country, and this House rallying round me." There were more cheers.

"I leave it with this House," he concluded, "with every confidence. I am equal to either fortune. I can see past the decision of this House either for or against me, but whether it be against me or for me, I know, and it is no vain boast to say so, for even my enemies will admit that I am no boaster, that there does not exist in Canada a man who has given more of his time, more of his heart, more of his wealth, or more of his intellect and power, such as it may be, for the good of this Dominion of Canada."[28]

It was true that Confederation owed more to Macdonald than to any other man and, with this impassioned address to the fore in everyone's minds, the Conservatives might well have won the day had the vote been taken at once. But the battle was not over. Though it was nearly two o'clock in the morning, Edward Blake, the Liberals' fact-obsessed deputy leader, rose to speak. It was he, in his brief career as premier of Ontario, who had engineered the outcry after Louis Riel and Lieutenant Governor Archibald had shaken hands during the abortive Fenian invasion in 1871. He had no sense of humour and was devoid of the common touch but he knew how to marshal his arguments and to ensure that everything he said was backed up by an army of facts. Unfortunately, he also felt an obligation to say absolutely everything which might conceivably be relevant and to pile every scrap of supporting evidence into his long-winded speeches. He also had no mercy. "It was not to these high and elevating sentiments that Sir John had appealed during the election," he declared as the cheering died down; "it was not upon the intelligent judgement of the people he relied, but upon Sir Hugh Allan's money!"[29]

Blake spoke for a little less than an hour, but returned to the attack for four hours the following day. He believed that they were about to see the end of corruption and the re-establishment of standards of public virtue. The shame had been discovered, he said, and the perpetrators should be given their just reward.

At three o'clock that afternoon, November 4, Donald Smith was due to speak. Blake's speech had detached one more Conservative and it was entirely possible that the member for Selkirk could remove the remaining five. If Donald could be persuaded, the Tories reasoned, if Macdonald would show him a little courtesy and some of his easy charm, perhaps the balance would tip in their favour. About two o'clock, Sir Charles Tupper and Senator Campbell approached Peter Mitchell whom they knew to be friendly with Donald. Would he persuade Donald to delay his speech until he had met the prime minister and then persuade Macdonald to agree to the meeting? Mitchell had a way with Macdonald and was judged the best man for this delicate task.

> I went and saw Mr. Smith who was just waiting for the speaker to take the chair to commence his speech. I told him what my mission was. He said to me, "Mr. Mitchell, I don't desire to defeat your Government, but Sir John has acted in such a shameful way to me that I will put up with it no longer, and if he desires to make amends for it, if you arrange the interview I will meet him." Mr. Smith put off his speech till the evening session of the House at eight o'clock.

Mitchell went to Committee Room Number Five where he found the prime minister "lying on the sofa in a state of intoxication." He said that he had been asked by Macdonald's colleagues to arrange a meeting with Donald "to see if you cannot settle your differences."

> His only answer to me was, with a half broken utterance, "Damned scoundrel! Damned scoundrel!" and he turned over with his face to the wall to go to sleep again. I said, "Sir John, he may be all that you say, but I think, from the manner in which your supporters have stood by you throughout your troubles, that something is due to them on your part, and that you ought to see Mr. Smith." In reply to that he said, "Come to-morrow." I answered, "To-morrow you won't be a minister." He then said, "Give me a couple of hours," which I thought the only sensible remark he had made since I had entered his room.

At five o'clock, Mitchell escorted Donald to the meeting, saying by way of opening remark that Donald was "an old friend" who had come to see him. "I hope you will reconcile your differences," he said cheerfully before withdrawing to the lobby to await the outcome of the manoeuvre. Donald knew better than to raise the overdue repayments at such a juncture, but Mitchell's recommendation that the two men reconcile their differences, probably intended as a reference to their political views, prompted Macdonald to raise the subject himself. Several months later, Donald reported him as saying, That matter should have been arranged long ago, but it will be arranged now, if you will just merely, as a matter of course, write me a note now, stating (in order that we may have something to show) that it was paid to Archbishop Taché, at the instance of Governor Archibald, and you shall receive a cheque, or rather the money, to-morrow morning." Perhaps it was the fact that the irksome business of the money for Riel would not go away, perhaps it was because he was not sober; whatever the cause, Macdonald lost control of himself. Twenty minutes later, Donald returned to the lobby and Mitchell

> could see by the expression and color of his face that he was very much excited and I feared it was all up with us. Mr. Smith came along to where I stood and said to me, "Mitchell, he's an awful man that's done nothing but curse and swear at me since I went into the room." Mr. Smith said, "I did not want to vote against your Government, and particularly on your account, Mr. Mitchell, because you have always treated me very fairly — but there is nothing else for me to do, and I will have to do it."[30]

It was one o'clock on the morning of November 5 when Donald Smith finally began to speak. Like others in the House, he was tired; they had all kept themselves going by a mixture of curiosity, adrenaline and a belief in the importance of the issue they were debating. Many Liberals thought their party would lose the vote; most of the Conservatives and a good many of the public who had crowded into the chamber believed it could go either way; only Mitchell, Tupper, Campbell and a few of their close colleagues knew what was going to happen. Tupper had begged Donald not to be offended by Macdonald's language, saying he was in no state to tell right from wrong. But Donald had had enough.[31]

The House fell silent, eager to catch each nuance which might influence the vote. The sombre clothes, the auburn beard and light red hair, now threaded through with white, bespoke a man with no political flair, a man who did not care to score points, a proud man certainly, but one who did think about the difference between right and wrong and who was prepared to make his judgements accordingly.

In his delicate Scottish accent, he began by praising Sir John for his great contribution to the creation of the dominion. The Conservatives were delighted. He condemned the opposition for stealing the documents on which it had founded its case, saying that the sanctity of private correspondence should never be violated. Again the Tories were pleased. The directors of the Pacific railway should be British subjects, he stated, making it clear he had no sympathy with Allan's American backers. Moreover, he did not believe that Macdonald had taken the money from Sir Hugh Allan with any corrupt motive. Indeed, he did not believe that the prime minister was capable of taking money for corrupt purposes. The Conservatives were cheering; some, it is said, had already headed to the bar for a celebratory drink.

He would vote for the government, he said, if he could do so conscientiously. At this last word, the Liberals pricked up their ears. He deeply regretted that he could not vote for the government but "to take money from an expectant contractor was a grave impropriety. For the honour of the country, no government should exist that has the shadow of a suspicion of this kind resting on them" and for that reason he could not vote in their favour. The Liberals cheered jubilantly and shortly thereafter, the House adjourned.[32]

CHAPTER TEN

LAND COMMISSIONER 1874–1879

> As I stood in twilight looking down on the silent rivers merging into the great single stream which here enters the forest region, the mind had little difficulty in seeing another picture, when the river forks would be a busy scene of commerce, and man's labour would waken echoes now answering only to the wild things of plain and forest.
>
> *William Francis Butler* [1]

The day after Donald Smith's speech in which he said he could not vote for the government conscientiously, Sir John A. Macdonald resigned and the governor general asked Alexander Mackenzie to form a government in his stead. National elections were called for February 1874 and Donald stood again for Selkirk, having resigned his seat in the provincial legislature when a law was passed prohibiting simultaneous membership in both provincial and federal parliaments. He won by a comfortable majority of one hundred and four, the campaign having concentrated on the Pacific railway. Some committed Conservatives were unwilling to accept that he had voted according to his conscience when the Pacific Scandal erupted but the sharper criticism came from opponents who argued that he was the "member for the Hudson's Bay Company" and concerned with its interests rather than those of Manitoba. There was an element of truth in this claim but, for Donald, the two were inseparable in most instances: what was good for the company was good for the province and vice versa. He rarely spoke in parliament except on issues affecting the Northwest, and then his concerns were the provision of an adequate police force, support for natives who were ill or hungry and, above all, transportation, all matters of concern to both the HBC and the population at large.

The people of Manitoba were increasingly vociferous in their demands for a railway connection with the east and during the election campaign Donald's opponents argued that he would oppose the construction of any railways in order to protect the Hudson's Bay Company's interest in Kittson's Red River Line. Donald's response to the Red River allegation was somewhat disingenuous as he claimed that the company had no interest in it when, in fact, its steamer was part of the package which Kittson was managing. The arrangement was legal but secret because it was designed to circumvent American customs regulations. He was franker, however, when he added that it was to be reorganized as the Red River Transportation Company, an enterprise in which the HBC would have a large shareholding.

Before the year was out, he had demonstrated just how keen he was to see railway communication between the province and the rest of Canada. On the last day of July, he was among those attending a meeting at St. James' Restaurant in Winnipeg for the purpose of establishing the Manitoba Southern Railway Company, and was elected its president. Nothing came of this venture, as nothing had resulted from the various railway companies in which Donald and George Stephen had been interested, because of the government's overriding concern to ensure that the national railway encountered no competition. His participation did, however, make it clear that he did want a railway link, and the sooner the better.

Following the collapse of Hugh Allan's railway company, the new Liberal government announced that it would take on the construction of the Pacific railway itself. Mackenzie had always argued against assigning railway charters to private companies, not least because he believed that it was a means by which Tories dispensed patronage. Now that he was in a position to apply his principles, he declared that the great national work would be undertaken by the government for the national good. Mackenzie expected it to be his memorial.

Though there had been frequent disagreements about whether construction should be by a private company or a national enterprise, the survey had always been a government undertaking. The engineer-in-chief, Sandford Fleming, had selected the route which he believed would be most cost effective, taking into account distance and the construction problems to be encountered on the way and not considering the needs or wishes of the few established centres of population between Ontario and the Pacific coast. As a result, he had proposed that the tracks cross the Red River about twenty miles north of Winnipeg at a point which was eventually to be called Selkirk. Here, the risk of spring flooding was considerably less than it was at Winnipeg where both the Red and the Assiniboine habitually overflowed their banks when the snow melted.

Donald Smith demonstrated his commitment to Winnipeg and to transnational railway communication by becoming one of the leaders in the lobby to have the route moved south, and he urged the city to speak with a united voice. On November 13, at Winnipeg's first civic dinner, his response to the toast to the Dominion and the House of Commons "alluded to the petty squabbles existing among the different wards of the city, and recommended the citizens of all parts of the town to drop such miserable jealousies and animosity and to join amicably together, hearth [sic] and hand to work for a matter which was of equal importance to all and would require their utmost energy to secure — viz: the passing of the Pacific Railway through Winnipeg itself instead of its being allowed to cross the Red River at any [other] point."[2]

In October 1874, he was collaborating in another effort to persuade Mackenzie to change the route and, five months later, he was working with a delegation which was trying to persuade the government to get a move on with the Pembina Branch which would connect Selkirk, via Winnipeg, with the American border. There it would meet a branch of the Northern Pacific which, though in receivership, was due to be pushed north to Pembina. Mackenzie, a rather dull, prudent Scot, would build no more than the nation could afford and saw no reason to hurry the Pembina Branch, while Fleming saw no reason to bow to political expediency and urged the prime minister to adhere to the Canadian Pacific's northern route preferred by the surveyors and engineers. The railway was being built in bits and pieces, when it was built at all, and in the meantime, Manitoba, and Winnipeg in particular, seethed at the government's failure to provide a satisfactory connection with Canada and the rest of the world.

Railway communication with Manitoba was only one of many concerns demanding Donald's energies in the early 1870s. He found himself with more work than he could cope with and London had not been slow to notice it. Part of the difficulty stemmed from his inability or unwillingness to delegate. He had brought Labrador to profitability by personally supervising every detail of the outfits and returns. There, he had kept his eye on everything: the management of the outlying posts, the packing of the salmon, the men's diets and their health, the minutiae of each shipping arrangement; all came under his scrutiny. The effect of this personal attention showed as soon as he left North West River when the system, and, ironically, especially the keeping of accounts, began to deteriorate.

As Chief Commissioner, his geographical responsibilities were far wider and the problems which demanded his attention were much more complex than they had ever been in Esquimaux Bay. To this he added his activities as a member of parliament and a member of the council of the North West Territories. His personal financial portfolio and the administration of the Private Cash also required his time. It was much more than one man could do single handed. In July 1872, the board complained that it was "dependent upon newspapers for scraps of information with regard to the affairs of the Company in the North West." Donald was told to instruct the officer in charge at Fort Garry to communicate fully in the Chief Commissioner's absence and not merely confine himself to financial information. That officer was John McTavish and, while he was excellent in many ways, he lacked Donald's sophisticated appreciation of the circumstances and was something of a political maverick. It could be dangerous or misleading to allow him too much authority, but neither did Donald suggest any alternative. Nor had he the time for more detailed reporting on the company's business there himself.[3]

In December that year, the complaint was about Norman Kittson whose integrity was not in doubt but who had proved to be very lax when it came to accounts. The Governor and Committee insisted that there should be "a different system adopted from that of the past as regards the advices of drafts, shipments and other matters, to which some one approved by the Company should give his time and attention as Mr. Kittson's assistant, if that gentleman, with other engagements, cannot conveniently do so." Donald pointed out that Kittson was receiving a pittance for his work for the company. "Considering the trustworthy position occupied by that gentleman," Armit responded on behalf of the board the following July, "and the growing importance of the duties devolving upon him they are of opinion that the salary of £450 per annum fixed many years ago is quite inadequate and they authorise you to arrange with Mr. Kittson the terms and conditions on which it is considered advisable that the business at that place should be carried on. The amount of salary should not exceed $5,000 gold per annum including the services of a clerk."

At one stroke, Kittson's HBC income was more than doubled, but it did not make him much more inclined to produce the detailed reports the company wanted.[4]

Donald had paid increasingly little attention to his responsibilities as a member of the provincial legislature but, even after his resignation, he still had more work than he could handle and the board was very concerned. In December 1873, Governor Northcote wrote. It was a considerate, private letter, sent from his home, but it nonetheless reflected the views of his colleagues.

> It seems to us that you must require help in order to keep all the details of the business in proper order. You have an enormous amount of work upon your hands, more than one man can be expected to do without assistance. I was cross-questioned at the [shareholders'] meeting as to the land sales and was rather embarrassed by the fact that we had received so little information from you. I did, however, give some particulars, which had for the most part been gleaned from the newspapers. I hope they were substantially right.

Northcote was also worried because the Dominion Lands Act seemed to contain clauses detrimental to the company yet no protest had been entered. As Donald was a member of the legislature which had passed the act, the company could now scarcely complain.

> The matter is not of great consequence in itself, but I mention it because it has given occasion for the renewal of some remarks, which have been made before, to the effect that your position as a Member of Parliament may be a cause of embarrassment to us sometimes. I have always held that on the whole your being in Parliament was advantageous to the Company; and I still think so, but there are no doubt some drawbacks to be considered; and as I am writing you freely and confidentially I think it as well to notice the point.

There were also concerns that Donald might occasionally feel obliged to hold his fire on the company's behalf.

> Again, let me tell you of one other remark which I have heard: some fears have been expressed that you may be deterred by political circumstances, from pressing our claims upon the Dominion Govt. as strongly as you would do if you were in an independent position. I am sure that this will not be the case; but I would press upon you the importance of getting some of the matters, which are now open, settled as early as possible.[5]

Shortly after Christmas, Northcote wrote again with a list of the outstanding points which needed clearing up. "It is useful now and then," he chided, "to make a note of this sort, as one is apt to forget one point while one is thinking of others. I have often found in official life the advantage of calling periodically for a return of 'questions undisposed of.' I daresay that you have by this time written to us upon several of them, but there is no harm in sending the list."[6]

Donald had indeed written, but in high dudgeon, for despite the friendly and sympathetic tone of his letters, Northcote had contrived to insult the Chief Commissioner by suggesting he should have an assistant. The idea was that Samuel Parson, whose work on accounts was particularly admired, should give Donald a hand. Donald had never learned to accept correction, however well meant or however much it might have been in his interest to do so. Bella was the only person who could tell Donald what to do and she tended to confine herself to his health and domestic affairs. Unsought advice from other quarters implied dissatisfaction and Donald, intelligent, widely read, highly principled and with a good memory, found it hard to accept that he could not do everything, understand everything and give universal satisfaction in his work. He did not solicit praise but he found it hard to stomach even kindly suggestions for improvement.

Eden Colvile, the deputy governor, tried his hand in February, saying that Donald had "misapprehended our suggestion with respect to Mr. Parson's appointment. It was never intended that he should be subcommissioner but merely your own Private Secretary." He followed some comments about the amount of correspondence Donald had to keep up with by explaining the duties of a private secretary and drawing a flattering comparison between Donald and a high government official who would be expected to have such an assistant.[7]

The Governor and Committee were right, of course, to want to be kept abreast of what was happening in Canada and Donald was too hot-headed in his response to the suggestion that he should get help and delegate some authority. Had he taken some time to analyze the situation, he might have realized that much of the information which London wanted was of the sort in which he had little interest. If he had delegated the financial reporting and the details of the requisitions and returns to others and kept for himself the broad sweep of policy issues as they related to transport and land, his life would have been easier and the board happier. In truth, he was often too busy to reflect.

On the other hand, the board seems not to have grasped the extent to which the company's business had changed when Rupert's Land was sold to Canada. The fur trade was diminishing and new systems had to be devised to make it economical. Trading posts had to be converted to stores which would meet the demands of new settlers and the entire accounting procedure had to be revised accordingly. New transportation systems needed to be put into place, but it was not in the company's power to establish railways or build roads over land where it no longer exerted absolute authority. And prolonged and difficult negotiations with the government would be required to settle the major differences about the land to which the company was entitled as a consequence of the 1870 surrender. Whenever one issue was given priority, others were neglected and the board complained.

The staff had all been trained to be fur traders and few were possessed of the skills now required. Delegation was difficult, not only because of Donald's temperament but also because there were so few men capable of taking on the new responsibilities; one of the results was that Donald and the board bickered over the quality of the men being sent from England to work for the company. Patience was required but there was not sufficient time to be patient.

The board's patience ran out in the summer of 1873. On the eighth of July, it passed three resolutions.

> 1. That it is undesirable that any of the Company's officers, connected with the management of the Fur Trade, should sit in the Dominion Parliament or in any of the local legislatures, or connect themselves with any business or occupation in which the Company have no direct interest, except with the written permission of the Committee.
>
> 2. That the Governor and Deputy Governor communicate with the Chief Commissioner with the view to give effect to the foregoing resolution not later than the 31st May 1874.
>
> 3. That it is expedient to separate the duty of managing the sales of Land and arrangements connected with the management of land from the Chief Commissionership, and to appoint an officer with proper assistance to manage the land business from the 1st June 1874.[8]

The intention was that from the beginning of Outfit 1874, Donald Smith was to be responsible for the land business and for all dealings with the government concerning legislation which might affect the company and with regard to the government's unpaid bills. In the past, the company had distinguished the fur trade from all its other financial activities; it now made its Canadian land a third category and this, in turn, enabled the company to make regulations which applied to everyone else in Canada except Donald Smith.

It suited the HBC to have a free-wheeler who was, at the same time, genuinely committed to the interests of the company, but the committee was only prepared to tolerate one such figure and wanted him to be the exception and not an example for others. The board had been worried about its employees' extra-curricular activities for some time. As early as December 1872, Armit had written about John McTavish and J.J. Hargrave who were involved in the formation of the Bank of Manitoba and the Manitoba Insurance Company. "At the outset the Committee wish it to be clearly understood that they cannot allow their officers or clerks to be engaged in any other business than that of the Company, and they direct me to request that you will accordingly inform the gentlemen to whom I have referred, that while in the service they cannot be allowed to take an active part in connection with these or any other undertakings."[9]

By 1872, Donald's parliamentary and business career was already an acknowledged exception to this general principle; the 1873 resolution merely expressed formally the company's determination that, from the beginning of Outfit 1874, he would be officially exempt from the rules which were to apply to everyone else. As well, Stafford Northcote and William Armit probably guessed that if the regulations were made to apply to Donald too, he might just choose the alternative and leave the company altogether.

It would be wrong, however, to think that the enforcement of the policy on extraneous business and political interests was the only, or even the principal, reason for making Donald responsible for land. The decision was motivated by the need to split the work load and it recognized that in dealing with the government over land issues, Donald's position was strengthened by his being an MP and having a role in the business community.

The board appears not to have consulted Donald on its intentions, for he arrived in London the day after the resolution was passed in July 1873. Stafford Northcote and the deputy governor, Eden Colvile, discussed it with him a few days later and he accepted the proposal, modifying the definition of the new post slightly to include "all other matters unconnected with the Fur Trade and commercial business of the Company." The arrangement gave him an office in Montreal, the same salary of £1,500 a year plus expenses, and made him the company's official conduit to the government not only on land matters but also on any other issue, even those relating to the fur trade. In short, the only significant change was that he would no longer have to concern himself with the indents and returns, with the shopkeeping or with the steamers on the rivers.[10]

The title for this new post proved something of a problem since the 1871 Deed Poll restricted the title of Chief Commissioner to the management of the fur trade. The best the Governor and Committee could come up with was Land Commissioner which they felt was unsatisfactory because it erroneously suggested that Donald's responsibilities had somehow been diminished, and it failed to convey his close connection with the management of the company. The board did its best to ensure that Donald knew he had not been demoted, despite the implicationns of this new title, writing to tell him that "The management and realization of the Company's lands are matters to which the Governor & Committee and the shareholders attach much importance and which greatly concern the future prosperity of the Company, and in entrusting to you these and such other confidential affairs as may from time to time arise, the Committee feel that they may rely on the same zeal and interest which have hitherto marked the discharge of the duties about to be transferred to Mr. Grahame."[11]

James Grahame, the new Chief Commissioner, had made his career in British Columbia. He had objected to being made subordinate to the Chief Commissioner following the Deed Poll of 1871 and was allowed to continue to run the Pacific coast business independently. In view of the difficulties of communicating across the Rocky Mountains and the impossibility of shipping goods in or furs out via that route, his objections were justified, but Grahame was a prickly character who had not taken kindly to the idea of having a superior officer.

In many respects, promotion to the Chief Commissionership now elevated Grahame beyond his abilities. He was a meticulous man, fastidious about the tiniest detail, and much inclined to whine when things did not proceed exactly as he wished them to. In matters of business, he lacked courage and always tried to adhere to the old ways, whether or not they were appropriate in changing circumstances. His son, James Ogden Grahame, also worked for the company and came to Fort Garry with his father to act as his secretary. To his father's capacity for complaint the younger man harnessed his own arrogance.

Donald Smith, himself, was not always an easy man to get along with; he was quick to take offence at criticism, however well intended, and resented being offered advice he had not sought. His *amour propre* was easily slighted and he retaliated vigorously if he thought his honour had been impugned.

Donald and Grahame were almost bound to come into conflict, a fact the board recognized when it made the new arrangement. In June, Eden Colvile wrote Grahame, warning him that what he was about to say was private and not to be quoted to third parties. "We have done all we can to prevent any clashing of authority, but still I think it will require considerable tact on your part to get things to work easily," he observed, rightly implying that tact was not Grahame's strong suit. Equally, he was aware that Donald frequently failed to recognize where his own responsibilities ceased. He did not set out to meddle, but he sometimes did and where he could see that a course of action would benefit the company, he followed it, whether or not he exceeded his authority in doing so. Grahame alone was in charge of the fur trade, Colvile wrote, and "must put a stop to any interference with this authority on the part of Donald Smith or anyone else, should such be attempted. But while this should be done with firmness it should also be done in such a manner as will avoid giving offence, and with a person of Donald Smith's temperament this will require tact and management."[12]

Although the board knew it was taking a risk with this combination, its attractions were obvious. In Donald Smith, the company had a man with vision who could grasp new ways of doing business and devise new strategies for new circumstances. In Grahame, it had a man who took pleasure in tidy accounts and in the smooth and repetitious order of things. The fur trade officers were pleased to think that their business might be less chaotic under Grahame's management and looked forward to a prompt and more efficient handling of the indents and returns. Within a year, however, there were complaints, especially about his handling of transport arrangements. Worse, there was an incipient feeling that he did not have the interests of the wintering partners at heart.

Donald Smith was finding it equally difficult to establish a *modus vivendi* with James Grahame. Their first disagreement centred on the fact that Donald had rented the main residence at Fort Garry to the lieutenant governor and had taken himself out to Silver Heights to live. There was no place for Grahame. Donald quickly offered to share Silver Heights and Grahame was obliged to accept, but it was not a satisfactory arrangement and he soon moved to Winnipeg where the company eventually consented to build him a house.[13]

From Donald's point of view, the friction was created by Grahame's incessant whining, by his brusque way of expressing himself, his habit of assuming that all problems were caused by other people, and his frequent lack of courtesy.[14]

While he was in Montreal in February 1875, Grahame wrote a very peculiar letter which he handed to Donald when he returned from England a few days later. The letter outlines, in the numbered paragraphs of which Grahame was fond, twelve problems which he faced in Manitoba. There are no social formalities by way of introduction nor is there any request for Donald to do anything about most of the problems, though that is clearly the intention of the letter. When he does request assistance on the very important issue of the Canadian-American boundary in the Alaska panhandle and the freedom of HBC ships to travel along the coast of British Columbia without being intercepted, he baldly states, "I want you to get the Canadian government to ascertain from the United States Authorities at Washington" whether the Americans could impede such journeys.[15]

Grahame was undoubtedly right to raise a number of issues, including the fact that Charles Tupper's son-in-law, the arrogant Captain Cameron, who was now leading the survey party locating the Canadian-American boundary in Manitoba, was illegally selling his duty-free surplus supplies in the vicinity of the company's establishment at Pembina and undercutting the company in the process. The difficulty lay not in Grahame's drawing attention to such problems but in the manner in which he did it.

Grahame was also trying to clear up outstanding debts from the 1869-1870 insurrection and wanted to settle a suspense account in Donald's name. It came to $3,228.31 and consisted of hotel dinners and the like. In part, its very existence reflected Donald's insouciant attitude to bookkeeping but it also indicated some ineptness on the part of both Grahame and John McTavish at Fort Garry. In reply to Grahame's letter, Donald said that he would have been happy to have seen the account settled long ago, "but as I informed you before it had never come before me until last autumn and in respect of many of the items I know nothing whatsoever. You will recollect that when we met in January you promised to send me the details of the large amount of some $11,000 odd charged I believe to my acct in England." The Fort Garry debt, a mixture of personal expenses, including those incurred when he was Canadian Commissioner in 1869-1879, election expenses and loans or land purchases, would be paid when he knew what the figures represented.

Ill feeling between the two men was exacerbated when Grahame furnished for payment by the government accounts which contained substantial mistakes, including the inclusion of some large sums twice. Donald had lectured the government on the meticulous accuracy of the company accounts, only to be embarrassed when the gross errors were pointed out. The relationship with Grahame was worsened by the government's continuing to hesitate over the payment of all bills, whether relating to the insurrection or to the rental of company property or to expenses incurred by the mounted police force.[16]

The difference which caused Donald the greatest dismay, and which most clearly revealed Grahame's unwillingness to be involved with anything out of the ordinary, occurred in 1876 when the North West Mounted Police sent a contingent to Edmonton. The government proposed that the company act as bankers to the force and the Bank of Montreal agreed to support the operation and supply the cash. In October, the Governor and Committee wrote Donald to say they approved of the proposal but Grahame demurred. As a consequence, the contract, at two percent, went to I.G. Baker and Company, an American firm based at Fort Benton, Montana. Inevitably, Baker also secured the police provisions contract. A year later, the HBC was offered a similar opportunity to supply the Fort MacLeod Indian treaty requirements and once again it was rejected by Grahame, this time on the extraordinary grounds that he did not have the $40,000 when it was obvious that the Bank of Montreal would agree to provide the cash. Yet again, the business went to Baker.[17]

Grahame proved equally unable to perceive the dangers of allowing competitors into the transport operation on the Saskatchewan and, having no business experience, was clearly frightened of the simple obligations implied in holding in trust the company's shares in the Red River Transportation Company. Nevertheless, the Governor and Committee did not ask for Grahame's resignation until 1883.

Though his letters betray his disgust at Grahame's turning down business, Donald generally kept his feelings about Grahame to himself. He helped Grahame find accommodation in Montreal and, having a soft spot for all young children whatever he thought of their parents, was genuinely delighted with news of

Grahame's youngsters. For the most part, however, he had more to occupy him than Grahame's irritable personality.

The 1870 Deed of Surrender incorporated what those who drafted it undoubtedly thought were clear provisions for the disposition of the land in the Northwest. The entitlement to a portion of this land was considered to be of the greatest importance by the HBC because it believed that the £300,000 paid in compensation for the loss of the remainder was far from adequate. In addition to being allowed to keep the posts it occupied, whether in Rupert's Land or other parts of British North America, the company was also granted the right to select a specified number of adjoining acres at posts indicated in an annex to the deed. This included land around some Esquimaux Bay posts such as Fort Nascopie and Fort Chimo but excluded land in Ontario and Quebec, then occupying much less territory than they do today. Recognizing that the situation in Red River did not admit of such an easy solution, the annex declared that, there, the number of acres and their location was to be agreed between the company and the Canadian government. A separate memorandum confined the total land around the posts to 50,000 acres.

In the fertile belt, the land allocated to the company was to be determined by lot and the HBC had up to ten years after a township was laid out to make its claim; all land claims had to be settled within fifty years. The company was obliged to share with the Canadian government the costs of surveying this territory. Land along the Saskatchewan River was perceived to be particularly valuable and the deed provided for an equitable sharing between the government and the company. The government could claim a portion of land chosen by the company for the construction of roads and bridges but was required to pay compensation if that land was found to be farmed or otherwise occupied.

The government was required to confirm all titles of land conferred by the company prior to the surrender and, in a most important clause, agreed to allow no exceptional tax on the company's land, trade or employees. It was also agreed that the government would deal with all Indian land claims.[18]

The first thing required to make these clauses enforceable was an act admitting Manitoba into Confederation. All other provinces were given control over their own lands but the tiny province of Manitoba and the North West Territories beyond it were obliged to allow the federal government control over their lands, in part to permit the terms of the Deed of Surrender to be honoured and in part to facilitate an allocation of land to construct the railway to the Pacific.

The second requirement was the Dominion Lands Act which, in effect, served to ratify the Deed of Surrender. It also served to change it. The deed had said that land in the fertile belt would be laid out in oblong blocks with river frontage but, like so much else in the transfer of the Northwest to Canada, the proposal appears to have been based on ignorance and supposition rather than knowledge of the area derived from consultation with the people who lived and worked there. With the exception of settlements such as Red River, where people were already living on long narrow farms facing the rivers, the surveys in the Northwest followed, with minor changes, the American system of marking out land in sections, each of one square mile or six hundred and forty acres. Each section was divided into four. A township was defined as thirty-six sections or six square miles. The southern base line for the survey was the forty-ninth parallel, though that had yet to be accurately surveyed, and the eastern was the Fort Garry meridian which was drawn about eight miles west of the confluence of the Red and Assiniboine Rivers. The surveyors had been working on the eastern base line, moving from the border towards Fort Garry, when Louis Riel and his colleagues brought their work to a halt in 1869.

Donald spent much time in 1871 and 1872 ensuring that the differences between the Deed of Surrender and the Dominion Lands Act would be to the benefit of the Hudson's Bay Company. In accordance with a proposal put by Donald to the prime minister in April 1871 and adopted at the end of the year, the act did away with the notion of allocating the land in the fertile belt by lot. As a rule, the HBC was to receive all of section eight and three-quarters of section twenty-six, but in every fifth township, it was allocated all of section twenty-six as well as section eight.[19]

Most importantly from the company's point of view, Donald's intervention introduced a clause allowing the HBC to exchange land found to be worthless for land elsewhere. Donald also insisted on the right to substitute other land for any property found to be occupied. He attempted to force through an amendment giving the company three years to consider whether it would accept particular sections in any township but was finally obliged to settle for a year. He also negotiated a clause "permitting the Company to re-convey to the Government any portion of the lands allotted to them within twelve months after the title of the same has passed to them." In that way, it could hand back land of little value, thus avoiding paying tax on it, and still retain the option of selecting other, more suitable land at a later date. He used the act to clarify an understanding that the company would not be liable to "undue" tax in unorganized townships and to restate the condition in the deed of surrender which exempted the company from "exceptional tax."[20]

The Dominion Lands Act, passed in June 1872, could not come into force unless agreed by the Hudson's Bay Company which finally approved it early in 1873. The survey of Manitoba, which proceeded in accordance with an order in council passed in April 1871, was completed in 1873 and in April that year, Donald urged the House of Commons to undertake the survey of the North West Territories as soon as possible. Thereafter, he said little about the survey because as soon as land was accepted by the company, it became liable to tax.

The question of exceptional taxation came to a head in January 1878 when the Manitoba legislature introduced an act to try to raise money for an education fund. It defined the company as an absentee landowner and, as such, required to pay five times as much tax per acre as resident owners. Virtually no other company or individual would be placed in the same position and the act appeared, in spirit if not in letter, to be aimed specifically and spitefully at the Hudson's Bay Company. Donald calculated that the tax burden would be about $25,000 a year. He also worried that it would set an example which other parts of the Northwest might follow.

He lodged a petition which reached Winnipeg too late and spent much of the rest of the year in a two pronged effort to have the legislation reversed. On the advice of the company's solicitors in Winnipeg, he launched an appeal, the effect of which was to give the company a year's grace. He also lobbied in Ottawa, arguing that the act should be disallowed since it transgressed the exceptional tax provision of the Deed of Surrender. The minister of justice pointed out that the legislation could not be disallowed since provinces had the right to tax real property in any way they chose, but the prime minister and the minister of the interior accepted Donald's point and agreed to put pressure on Manitoba to treat the company as resident. It finally came to a court case which decided in the company's favour at the end of September.[21]

In the drafting of the Dominion Lands Act, Donald had insisted on the removal of the clause compelling the company to select unoccupied land in the *same* township in exchange for land found to be occupied. It was a change which proved to be of tremendous importance to the company and one which the Mackenzie government regretted. "I need hardly say," Donald wrote to London in 1876, "that the value of this privilege of selecting land is very great and the Government would now gladly find almost any reasonable means for avoiding it." It meant that the company could select as replacements those lands which it thought most likely to increase in value.[22]

When the land proved to be of reasonable quality and unoccupied, the process was simple, but every time the reverse was found to be the case and every time a township was fractional because a portion of it was set aside for some other purpose or had settlers on it, or was broken by lakes, or was otherwise uninhabitable, the negotiations and arguments began. This was especially true, and especially important, in the townships which were made fractional by the old, oblong river lots where settlements were obviously growing and land values increasing. Allocations in fractional townships were meant to be by lot but in reality were generally by negotiation as Donald pushed for more valuable land in the vicinity of settlements or more fertile sections or land near railway routes in agricultural areas.

Difficulties in settling land allocations were made worse on some occasions by ministers refusing to approve selections without the prime minister's agreement which, whenever he was absent, delayed resolution of the land question yet again. In 1876, the government decided to resurrect the argument about whether alternative land had to be in the same township. They squabbled over quality and quantity, with Donald constantly having to keep his eye on the railway route and the possibility of timber, coal or other valuable minerals, in addition to assessing the fertility of the soil. Some timber land was set aside for use by settlers while other stretches were retained by the federal government which sold leases to cut timber. Donald had agreed with Alexander Morris, who had piloted the Dominion Lands Act through parliament, that the company would have the right to select alternative lands if it was found that the land initially chosen infringed the timber rights. Morris did not ensure that his commitment was enshrined in the act, a failure which created innumerable difficulties for Donald and the Liberal government and caused a degree of friction between Donald and Morris when the latter was appointed lieutenant governor of Manitoba.[23]

The land negotiations were tedious and the results were slow to materialize. In an uncharacteristically personal letter to William Armit in the summer of 1876, Donald observed, "It is very uphill and most unsatisfactory work this necessity for being constantly on the defense in protecting the Company's rights as against the attacks by the government in favour of whom the surrender of the territory was made and the duty is anything but a pleasant one."[24]

It became even more unpleasant when David Mills, recently appointed as minister of the interior, decided to challenge the entire basis of the agreement between the government and the Hudson's Bay Company. He queried the allocation of land around the company's posts, and the way in which land in the fertile belt was being chosen. He countered Donald's rather spurious argument that land reserved for Indians was land marked out for settlement to which the company was therefore entitled to one-twentieth and he disagreed about the date from which the occupation of lands should be reckoned. Despite the surveyors' encounter with Louis Riel on André Nault's hay lands in 1869, the plans still showed this common land as unoccupied and some of it had been granted to the HBC. Mills objected to the company requesting alternative land when it was asked to return the hay privilege. He disagreed with decisions which had been reached over the company's farm lands at Portage la Prairie and various other places in Manitoba.[25]

It was a hugely annoying letter, prompting Donald to call in the company's solicitor to advise, and forcing both Donald and the Governor and Committee to rehash all the agreements which had been reached in the previous seven years. Fortunately, the frustrations were relatively short lived, for the Liberals' term of office expired early in 1878 and they lost the election contest.

North American business had flourished in the first years of the decade, largely as a result of rapid developments in railway and steamship construction in the United States. But by 1873, many financiers had over extended themselves and in September of that year, Jay Cooke, who had backed the Northern Pacific, suspended payments; the shock waves, reverberating among the many interdependent companies, brought ruin to thousands of banks, brokers and railway enterprises. In the spring, the Prussian boom had collapsed, dragging many European firms into serious financial difficulties. Europe's problems reverberated in North America and vice versa. The Great Depression of the 1870s bankrupted Canadian banks, ruined Canadian farmers who lost the market for their grain and brought the country's lumber trade to a standstill.

As the depression deepened, Donald began to perceive that the HBC would not benefit to any great extent even if it did clear up all the land problems and put its property on the market. It would do much better to bide its time, waiting for prosperity to return and the price of land to increase. Land close to the railway would be of much greater value when the government actually got around to constructing the railway line and land near settlements would be worth much more when those settlements were more mature. As the government was giving away land to immigrants, provided they occupied it and made improvements, the HBC could hardly expect to compete, even if it charged moderate prices for its acres in the Northwest.

Donald had warned Northcote in April 1870 that the company could find its land "an encumbrance" and recommended parting with it "at any price we can get from the Canadian Govt." He thought the government would be glad to have it if it took up the idea of providing a land grant to a company prepared to construct the transnational railway. The subsequent tiresome and problematical negotiations he had had with the government seemed to prove his point and Donald was therefore willing to listen to offers to buy all the company's lands except the 50,000 acres around the trading posts. The first proposal came in

1874 from a consortium which intended to seek a charter as the North West Land Company. Its argument was that a colonization company should be Canadian, not British, and that it was best suited to the job, though it intended to collaborate with the HBC. In view of the fact that the government was giving away land, the prospects of a colonization company seemed bleak and the proposal soon fell by the wayside.[26]

Early in 1875, another consortium, based in Three Rivers, made an offer of seventy-five cents an acre for five million acres, but the HBC lost interest when it became apparent that the men only wanted an option for a year.[27]

The men from Three Rivers continued to press their case, however, while much more discreet negotiations were taking place with the Canadian government. An order in council in June 1875 authorized Alexander Mackenzie to broach the subject of acquiring the HBC land and, on the eighth of June, he and Donald sailed from Quebec on the *Sarmatian* to discuss the sale with the Governor and Committee. The company was not particularly keen to sell and negotiations carried on throughout the summer. They were haggling over price, but they were also trying to determine precisely what land would be left to the company. At the end of July, Donald found himself back in Edinburgh working on both price and land details with the prime minister who was insisting that, except at Fort Garry, the land to be retained could only be used for farms or for HBC trading operations. If it was not to be used for either purpose, it was to be sold within twelve months of finalizing the contract.

The company and Mackenzie reached agreement on August 18 and the prime minister reported confidentially to the privy council on his return to Canada. The government would pay £500,000 in cash, or £550,000 in government bonds, for six and a quarter million acres.

To many members of Mackenzie's cabinet, the bargain bore no relation to the realities of Canada's economic life. At least three banks had folded while the prime minister had been in the United Kingdom and the government had even found itself strapped for cash to pay for a shipment of rails; Mackenzie was forced to concede that the deal with the HBC could not be implemented until the economic climate improved. By the time the depression ended, the Liberals were no longer in power and the HBC, aware that it could get more for the land by selling it piecemeal, let the agreement lapse. At forty cents an acre, the government had concluded a considerable bargain, both in the light of the offer from the Three Rivers consortium and in view of the fact that by 1910, the HBC had made a profit more than three times greater than the price agreed with the government.[28]

While Donald was in England and Scotland negotiating the land sale, Bella had opted to spend the summer at Fort Coulogne with some of George Stephen's family; Colin Rankin, an inspecting chief factor with whom the Smiths were friendly, kept an eye on her and made sure she and her friends were comfortable. His son, Jamie, was a favourite with the Smith family and while in London, Donald tried to see if he could find any medical treatment for the boy's deafness. In the company of the prime minister on this trip, he also found himself mixing in rather more exalted society than usual. The Dufferins were in London on leave and there was an "at home" for the governor general on the first of July, while on the seventh the Canada Club gave a dinner. "Having an invitation, I may perhaps go to see the great folks," Donald wrote to Rankin with tongue in cheek, "and get a plate of turtle soup which of course will be plentiful on such a grand occasion." When he was in Edinburgh, he bought Rankin a portable desk, much like his own.[29]

The London visit also allowed Donald to make his first investment as a shareholder in the Hudson's Bay Company. Through William Armit, who had power of attorney for the dispersal of his English funds, he acquired one hundred shares for himself and a further hundred for Sandford Fleming with whom he had become friendly, despite their disagreement about where the Pacific railway should cross the Red River. It was a risky time to be making such an investment; the 1875 dividend was only slightly larger than that of the two previous years and there were to be no returns to shareholders at all between 1877 and 1880. It seems likely that both men hoped they were buying at or near the bottom of the market and that both believed that when the depression ended and rail transport with the Northwest was achieved, land values would soar, taking HBC shares up as well.[30]

The agreement with Mackenzie to purchase all the company's lands was sufficiently confidential that other businessmen felt able to make what they saw as advantageous proposals for acquisition of the land. In May 1877, when the market was even further depressed, George Laidlaw, a Canadian entrepreneur with whom both Donald and George Stephen had collaborated on railway ventures, proposed acquiring the land and setting up a colonization enterprise which would include a railway. The following month, a more interesting idea was put forward by Colonel John Stoughton Dennis, the surveyor general. He suggested that the government take responsibility for selling the land in the settlement belt, irrespective of whether it was owned by the company or the government, and simply hand over one-twentieth of the profits. Dennis was referring to the lands along the Red and Assiniboine Rivers where settlements were already established and were likely to grow. The attraction of his proposal lay in its simplicity but Donald advised the Governor and Committee against complying because he believed that, if the company were going to sell piecemeal, it should bide its time and sell when the government's land had been occupied and the company could see more clearly how Winnipeg and the other villages were going to develop and what effect the long awaited railways were going to have on the patterns of settlement. At that point, the company would reap a much higher reward.[31]

The need to extinguish by treaty the Indian right to land in the Northwest complicated land sales but so too did the block of 1,400,000 acres in Manitoba which was guaranteed to the unmarried children of the Métis population. The significant difference between the Indian and Métis grants was that the latter was not inalienable. Rather, the children and, after 1877, the heads of families, were issued with scrip entitling them to occupy the land. Confirmation of their ownership came with a patent which was issued by Ottawa after a title search to confirm that the land did not belong to someone else.

Many opposed the introduction of scrip. The racists among them argued that the Métis would only settle to farming and the raising of cattle if they were obliged to occupy the land, but men like Donald Smith believed that the half-breeds, whether English, Scotch or French, should be given specific parcels of land outright. "My own opinion," he told an election meeting in 1870, "is that it ought to be held in fee simple — so that the owners could dispose of it as they thought proper. But, on the other hand, I hope the iniquitous scrip system will not be introduced. It has done great evil in the States." As he was aware, scrip was open to abuse because it was traded and, as it flooded onto the market, its value declined. This is precisely what happened in Manitoba, despite the government's efforts to hedge the scrip with protective barriers in the interests of the Métis. Like many private individuals, the HBC benefitted from the devalued scrip. As it settled its land claims, it also purchased adjoining lots, sometimes in its own name but often using Donald Smith's friends as trustees, a procedure which quietly enabled the company to build up blocs of land throughout the settlement belt. When the HBC finally received the patents for the adjoining land, a process which generally took years, it paid for it in scrip whenever it could, thereby reducing the cost by a third.[32]

As Land Commissioner, Donald was also obliged to deal with the land to be retained in the vicinity of the company's posts, in accordance with the Deed of Surrender. Though the number of acres for each post, except Fort Garry, had been agreed, it was virtually impossible to proceed with identifying precisely which land the company meant to claim until the area had been surveyed. That, in turn, was the responsibility of the federal government. In 1872, while he was still Chief Commissioner, Donald discovered that Pembina had been omitted from the Deed of Surrender. The post, established by Norman Kittson, was in fact south of the border but the boundary had yet to be established. Donald was sure the omission was an oversight "as Pembina is one of our principal frontier trading posts, and where the Company have for many years had an extensive Cattle Farm;" he began to barter the land in the Peace River district for a comparable plot at Pembina.[33]

At Fort Garry, the entire allotment had to be negotiated. In an ideal world, there would have been 4,840 acres which would have brought the total to the maximum of 50,000 acres set out in the memorandum which accompanied the Deed of Surrender. In reality, however, much of the land in the vicinity of the fort was occupied and title to that property had to be ascertained before the company could determine whether or not it might lay claim to it. When it became clear that there was not sufficient land in the neighbourhood of Winnipeg to fulfill the company's entitlement, Donald compelled the government to negotiate over land in other areas.

The Governor and Committee did not authorize the engagement of a surveyor for Fort Garry until April 1872 at which point Dennis, the surveyor general, was recommended by the board. Even then, identifying and securing the land was a tortuous business; under the Conservatives, the processing of patent applications was exceedingly slow and it was not much faster under the Liberals.[34]

Once the company had clear title to the land, it was Donald's duty to sell it. In May 1872, he received the company's power of attorney to enable him to do so, but London was unable to send him a copy of the company's common seal which had to be attached to the land deeds in order to complete transactions. Purchasers refused to make their final payments unless the sale could be completed and objected to having to wait for what they perceived to be weeks of uncertainty while the documents were sent to London where the seal was affixed and the papers posted back.[35]

Sales and the occasional gifts of land had to be handled in such a way as to enhance the value of unsold land. As Winnipeg developed, it began to grow away from Fort Garry and Donald used the donation of a number of acres for a lieutenant governor's residence and the provincial legislature as a means of drawing the momentum back towards the fort. He offered land for a post office, customs house and land office as well, but his old sparring partner, John Schultz, succeeded in countering this and these government buildings were erected closer to the stores of Schultz and other Winnipeg merchants.[36]

The depression delayed the influx of immigration on which the land sales had been predicated and the relative stability of the population, coupled with the financial climate and the grasshopper plagues of 1874 and 1875, meant that there was little spare cash for land purchases. Most people's money was tied up in possessions which they either needed or could not sell. Donald organized land auctions in July 1872 and October 1874, but economic conditions and the excuse of the absent corporate seal meant people often failed to meet even the first payment on their purchases. By 1877, the situation was much worse. "Sales of town lots and of landed property generally can hardly be effected on any terms," he reported to London, advising against offering any of the company's lots at auction.[37]

As for himself, Donald took very little personal interest in the lands of Manitoba and the Northwest. His investment policy generally favoured projects which would make a continuing return for his capital and his money therefore tended to go into banks, manufacturing, transport and the rather riskier field of mortgages and personal loans. Much of his landed property was acquired when borrowers defaulted. After 1874, his Manitoba investments were handled by Sedley Blanchard, the Winnipeg lawyer, and there were many instances when Donald was not even consulted about mortgages, providing the loans were adequately secured.

In an 1878 election speech, Donald remarked that he had never owned any scrip and a month later, he told another crowd of voters that he had not purchased as much as an inch of public land since the Mackenzie government came to power at the end of 1873. Prior to that, he did buy public land, but in each case, he was acting on behalf of others, generally one of the railway companies with which was associated. In some cases, when the railways did not materialize, he seems to have retained the land for himself, only selling it in 1900 when other companies finally pushed the lines through. In 1879, he pointed out to the Governor and Committee that, as Land Commissioner, "it would have been improper for me to have made any purchases of the company's lands either for myself or for others."[38]

Apart from Silver Heights, which was by far his most valuable property in Manitoba, Donald owned several lots in Winnipeg, the most important of which was a block purchased in 1874 by a man named McVicar who defaulted on his $5,000 mortgage. It was in an excellent location and Donald led a group of Canadian businessmen to establish the Canada Pacific Hotel on the site. It was badly constructed and the hotel began to fall down almost as soon as it was up. In 1881, Donald bought out his associates and enlarged the hotel, buying land from the company to enable him to do so. He also persuaded the company to give him three lots since the construction would benefit the HBC by helping to attract business to its part of town. For its part, the company quibbled about the quality of the plans. "The largest drawing room is only 14 x 14. A first class hotel should have a good sized well furnished room for ladies to sit in, and in which a reception could be held." In 1902, it was replaced by Fort Garry Court, an apartment block which incorporated stone from the walls of Fort Garry and which, in 1907, was producing rents of $1,000 a month.[39]

One of the largest borrowers for land purchases in Manitoba and elsewhere was the surveyor general, but he succeeded in repaying all his debts to Donald Smith and George Stephen by the end of 1879. Andrew Bannatyne, the Winnipeg merchant in whose house the first provincial legislature sat, was another borrower though he had his money when both land prices and interest rates were high.[40]

The land boom of the early 1880s drove up taxes as well as prices and when the bubble burst, men found themselves unable to afford the taxes, let alone the payments on their land. Henry Clarke, a Manitoba member of parliament, mortgaged land in St. Boniface for $40,000, but the lender, A.S. Mallock, sold the mortgage to Donald Smith for a mere $12,000. In 1887, when the taxes far exceeded the value of the land, which had been subdivided into town lots, Donald paid the taxes and prepared to bide his time until the land reached its true value.[41]

Though the decade of the 1870s saw many altercations with the government over unpaid bills, one obligation was at last settled. At the beginning of June 1875, Hector Langevin wrote Lieutenant Governor Morris to say that $2,500, to be paid to the "loyal French" in accordance with "the representations made by the Honble D.A. Smith, when acting as Commissioner at Red River for the Dominion Government, in the Winter of 1869-70," was now to be handed over. The top payment, as Donald wrote to Morris in December, was to be $250 and was given to each of John Grant, Angus McKay and Pierre Léveillé, the three men who had escorted Richard Hardisty to Pembina to collect Donald's papers. Two others were put down for $200 each, while six were each given $100. It left $750 to meet other claims, only one of which came in. It was from Joseph Hamelin, never a Riel supporter, who sought recompense for feeding ten men who were involved in the Pembina journey. The surplus makes it clear that the men on Donald's list had been assured they would not be out of pocket and would receive a token of gratitude but no hard bargains had been struck and no specific cash promises made. It is likely that the majority acted out of conviction rather than in anticipation of financial reward. At the beginning of 1876, when the recession was beginning to bite, the money from the government was welcomed as a windfall, not as overdue payment for services rendered.[42]

Honouring his commitments to the Métis was not Donald's only unfinished business from his time as Canadian Commissioner. There was also the matter of the promised amnesty to Louis Riel. In the bye-election in February 1874, Riel had won Provencher, the seat he had given up to George-Etienne Cartier in 1872 and which had become vacant in May 1873 when Cartier died. In March 1874, to the astonishment of the clerk of the House, Riel had been sworn in and signed the roll without being detected. He then quickly disappeared. On the thirtieth of March, his supporters in parliament demanded a general amnesty but were defeated. On the first of April, Donald moved that a select committee be established to inquire into "the causes of the difficulties which existed in the North-West in 1869 and 1870, and into those which have retarded the granting of the amnesty announced in the Proclamation by the late Governor General of Canada, Sir John Young."[43]

The Orangemen of Ontario were gunning for Riel. Either he was to take his seat, in which case a warrant for his arrest would be applied before he reached the sanctuary of the chamber, or he was to be expelled from parliament. A motion, supported by Donald Smith and many others, to delay consideration of Riel's expulsion until the select committee reported, was defeated and Riel was ousted. Most of the MPs voted in favour of rejecting Riel, Donald among them. Though he frequently disapproved of Riel's methods, Donald recognized that the Métis leader's intentions were honourable. Indeed, he is said to have given quiet support to Riel's election in the first place. But Donald was also a peace maker and, with the Orangemen baying for Riel's blood, peace and an amnesty were more likely to be brought about by avoiding confrontation.

The select committee heard repeatedly that an amnesty had been promised. Donald, who chaired the committee, testified that Archbishop Taché "assured me over and over again, that such a promise had been made to him. I know that the Archbishop made the same statement to various other persons at various times, and continued to make it consistently."

Donald's testimony also captured Macdonald's equivocation over the amnesty. "I have heard members of the Government at Ottawa frequently speak of an amnesty, but I was never given to understand that any amnesty would be given although it was said that it was most desirable that these things should be settled, and that there should be an amnesty. I heard these sentiments frequently in conversation, both from Sir George Cartier and Sir John Macdonald; in fact they were always made a subject of conversation whenever I was in Ottawa." In commenting on Macdonald's statements, the archbishop was rather more blunt, saying he "lied (excuse the word) like a trooper."[44]

The evidence of a commitment to an amnesty was sufficiently strong that it gave Mackenzie the justification for introducing a motion, in February 1875, calling for an unconditional amnesty for everyone, except William O'Donoghue, Riel and Ambroise Lépine. O'Donoghue's Fenian shenanigans had put him beyond the pale and in the case of Lépine and Riel, the amnesty was to be conditional on five years banishment.

Lépine had been sentenced to death following his arrest in Winnipeg but Governor General Dufferin had proposed to the imperial government that the sentence should be commuted. When Lieutenant Governor Archibald had accepted the Métis support against the Fenian invasion, Dufferin contended, he had, in effect, wiped out the obligation to pursue charges in relation to any previous felonies. It was a felicitous argument which pleased the colonial secretary. The sentence was commuted to two years imprisonment and permanent loss of political rights.

The amnesty motion enabled Mackenzie to walk on both sides of the street; he had campaigned in the 1873 election on an anti-Riel platform, accusing Macdonald of having promised an amnesty. Now, as prime minister, he declared that the Liberals were bound to honour the promises of their predecessors. The Conservatives objected and the House divided on party lines. Donald Smith would clearly have added his support to the Liberals, but he was in England discussing with the new HBC governor, George Goschen, a renewed effort to claim rebellion losses.

Donald also made a sad journey to Scotland that winter, for the previous April, his mother had died in Forres at the age of eighty-nine. With his brother John, now a widower, he erected a memorial stone in the graveyard of St. Laurence parish kirk, commemorating their father, Alexander, who had died in Archiestown in 1847; their mother, Barbara; their oldest sister, Margaret, who had died of small pox in January 1840 at the age of twenty-six, their youngest sister, Marianne, who died of a fever in December 1841 not long after her sixteenth birthday; and their little brother, James M'Grigor, who was only three when his parents followed his coffin to the churchyard. No reference is made to their sister Jane, either as a contributor to the stone or as having died, and her name never occurs in surviving correspondence after 1850 nor does she appear as a beneficiary of the financial support which Donald continued to provide for his relatives, especially the unmarried women.[45]

Four months before Barbara Smith died, Joseph McPherson had died in Pictou, raising again the problem of his finances and Norway House. Donald continued to honour his promise not to disturb Jane McPherson and simply disregarded the fact that the mortgage on Norway House was now due, but he and his brother-in-law, Thomas Hardisty, became increasingly alarmed at Mary's level of expenditure. Tom wrote stern letters on several occasions, warning her that she had to live on $600 a year from her father's estate and whatever her sons might contribute, but his admonitions seemed to have had no effect on Mary's spending. Shortly after Joseph died, Tom had been to visit her and concluded that "she does not appear to be very comfortable where she is." The house was large, expensive to heat, and had no indoor plumbing, but the impression created by the family's letters and their accounts of their visits to her is that she was uncomfortable because she lacked friends and companionship. She may have found it difficult to share the house with her mother-in-law; equally, her loneliness could have resulted from the people of Pictou keeping their distance because both women were of mixed-blood.[46]

On the first of November 1875, Tom Hardisty's "now old enemy," tuberculosis, caught up with him and he too died, leaving money to Mary. Scarcely had the family begun to recover from their distress at losing the youngest and much loved son when Margaret Hardisty also passed away. "She died at Lachine on the 2nd April last after only a few days illness and the blow coming so soon after the death of poor Thomas has fallen especially heavily on my wife and indeed all of us," Donald wrote to Colin Rankin.[47]

Mrs. Hardisty had sent Mary what money she could afford but Mary continued to spend without regard to the morrow. In October 1878, when Donald returned to Montreal from Manitoba, he found Mary's eldest, Richard, in the city, perhaps thinking he might find work. He returned to Halifax, "I trust to find some profitable employment," Donald observed. It may have been this comment which sparked a response from Mary, complaining that Donald did not care about her and her family and that this was proved by the fact that he had not been to see them. It was not a request for closer family ties but yet another demand for money.

"I am sorry you have not all the money you could wish to have for the use of yourself and your family," he wrote, "but it [is] not in my power to furnish it to you." There were other calls on his money "much larger than you appear to have any idea of," he explained, without adding that he believed it his duty to care for his female relatives and the duty of the Hardisty brothers to care for the female members of their family. Were Mary truly indigent, his attitude might have been different but, as he lectured her, she had spent $1,150 in 1876, in addition to whatever her mother had sent; in 1877, she had had $1,200 and in 1878 she had already had $500 and was to receive the same amount by the cheque which he was sending.

"Now my dear Mrs. McPherson," he wrote, "I am afraid you understand but little about money matters," for, despite Tom's letters saying that she must confine herself to an annual expenditure of $600, "you have received and I presume have spent double that amount yearly since his death all of which comes from the portion falling to you from your father & brother[']s estate of which *very little* now remains and when it is exhausted, which it would be in little more than another year at the same rate I surely do no know where you are to find the means of living. All your brothers have families of their own to support & educate except George and his earnings are not more than he requires for himself." Indeed, George was lucky to have finally secured employment as a purser on the HBC steamers travelling the Pacific coast.

Donald was willing to join with Mary's brothers in making up any shortfall so that she received $600 a year, but he was not prepared to pay for her extravagances. Equally, she ought to be aware that her brothers were now struggling to make ends meet. "Your brothers in the Hud Bay Co service have got actually *no dividends* for a couple or three outfits back and the dividends on Private Cash and other securities are so low compared to those of former years." The effects of the depression on short term deposits with the Bank of Montreal meant that interest had been cut from sixteen per cent to ten percent.

In the midst of these financial difficulties, Bella returned from her summer visit to Pictou with what seems to have been meant as a gift of silver plate. For public consumption, the Smiths were claiming to have been married in March 1853 so it might have been a silver wedding present; it seems more likely that Mary simply wished to make the Smiths a present or was sharing a McPherson family inheritance. Whatever the reason, it was not a gift Mary could afford to make; if she did not want the silver, she should have sold it. "By the way," Donald added at the end of his stern letter, "I have told Isabella that she must keep a correct account of the Plate you gave her as we cannot have it except by paying for it its proper value and I shall take care that credit be given to this extent." Unfortunately, the letter did more to sour the relationship with Mary than it did to help her understand her financial circumstances.[48]

Donald's private letterpress book for 1878, the only one to have survived, contains not a single letter to his wife; by then he had established the habit, which lasted throughout his life, of sending cables at frequent intervals when they were apart. Her cable address in the early years bears witness to his affection and his protectiveness: telegrams were sent to *Bellefeuille*, beautiful leaf.

Margaret Hardisty's death in April 1876 was not the only occasion when the beautiful leaf trembled that year. Richard Hardisty, her brother, was confined to his bed at the end of May with severe rheumatism, a weakness inherited from his father, and Maggie, who was only twenty-two, was suffering from the same complaint in June, while her father was troubled with lumbago. It was Bella's turn in the autumn when she was seriously ill with another of the bronchial infections which dogged her winters and were growing increasingly hard to shake off. In September, Henry, nearly two years short of his fortieth birthday, died suddenly of heart failure. He had been unhappily posted at Cumberland House where neither his wife nor his children had been able to accompany him, but had succeeded, perhaps through the influence of his brother, Richard, and his brother-in-law, Donald Smith, in obtaining a transfer to Edmonton. "It appears to be ordained for our family," William, the eldest son, wrote from Fort Simpson, "that the youngest shall be taken first, while the elder ones are left to mourn their loss." Henry's wife, Maria Rolland, seems to have been Francophone, for her brother-in-law, Richard Hardisty, who kept her in supplies immediately after Henry's death, took a son and a daughter into his care to teach them English before sending them to school. Both Thomas and Henry died intestate as did their mother and it inevitably fell to Donald to disentangle their finances and to ensure that money was safely invested in the interest of those for whom it was intended.[49]

The gloom of the mid-1870s was briefly relieved when the wintering partners determined to honour their former Chief Commissioner for all that he had done on their behalf. The idea took root in Outfit 1874 and was intended as a leaving present, since Donald would no longer be responsible for the fur trade, but it was also a mark of gratitude for the work he had done in negotiating the Deed Poll of 1871. Just as it took months to communicate with the distant posts on questions of indents and returns, so also it took a long time to canvas the views of the chief factors and traders. William Armit was then entrusted with the task of selecting something appropriate and ensuring that each man's account with the company was debited accordingly.[50]

The arrangements for the testimonial were in the hands of James Bissett who was managing the Montreal office and who had become a close friend of the Smith and Hardisty families. It was all meant to be a secret and if word leaked out between the autumn of 1874 and April 27, 1876 when the presentation was finally made, Donald nevertheless assured the friends and colleagues who gathered at Hudson's Bay House in Montreal that he was surprised. The date was chosen to enable James Grahame to attend, a somewhat ironic decision in view of the relationship which was developing between the Chief Commissioner and the Land Commissioner. Other guests included Henry Connolly who had replaced Donald as chief of Esquimaux Bay and George Barnston, his old bourgeois from Tadoussac, as well as George Stephen and the company's Montreal solicitor, Thomas Ritchie.

As well, there was a reporter from the *Montreal Herald*, the newspaper to which many of the wintering partners east of Red River subscribed. The paper told its readers that the presentation was a "massive service of silver plate, comprising full dinner and tea services." The centrepiece, meant to grace a formal dinner table, was engraved with Donald's crest and an inscription to which the names of the donors were to be added. Donald was just beginning to evolve his personal insignia, the central feature of which would always be a beaver gnawing at the base of a maple tree with the motto "Perseverance" above. The beaver, the tree and the motto are all North West Company images and their presence in Donald's own arms indicates the extent to which he saw his involvement in the

HBC as an extension of the career of his uncle, John Stuart, and of the many other relatives who had also been partners in the North West Company. The plate, he said, would be "a souvenir of great kindness experienced at the hands of the donors, and of much that often made life pleasant, even when the surrounding circumstances were not otherwise calculated for enjoyment."[51]

The presentation indicated the gratitude of the donors and it commemorated Donald's association with the fur trade, but it certainly did not mark the end of his links with the wintering partners. If anything, it drew attention to the fact that Donald had served the interests of the fur trade officers and could do so again.

That moment arrived in October 1878 when he was asked to take up their grievances with London. The depression, coupled with the push of settlement further and further into the territory of the fur bearing animals, meant that there were fewer furs and less money with which to purchase them. The fur trade had earned no profit in Outfit 1875 and the wintering partners were consequently not eligible for any payments under the terms of the Deed Poll. At the Council of the Northern Department in the summer of 1877, the officers had addressed a letter to James Grahame, asking him to make known to London their concerns for their future but Grahame, though he forwarded the letter, did not support the officers and prided himself on remaining neutral.

In response, Governor Goschen had pointed out that he and the Committee, like the wintering partners, were bound by the Deed Poll which could not be changed without the authority of the General Court. Instead, he had proposed a "temporary expedient" which would guarantee £100 per share for Outfit 1876 should the fur trade again fail to make a profit, as everyone expected would be the case. The majority of this money was to come from the fund created from the five shares set aside for the benefit of the wintering partners in the Deed Poll of 1871. Grahame had accepted Goschen's offer on behalf of the officers and at the General Court in June 1878, the plan was approved with little discussion. Another "temporary expedient" had been required for Outfit 1877 when the company paid no dividends at all and was clearly going to be needed in Outfit 1878. But, at £100 a share, officers were receiving less than their clerks and could see no end to their difficulty.[52]

In the spring of 1878, a group of worried officers, centred around John McTavish at Red River, had discussed what they might do to alter the Deed Poll of 1871 in order to ensure that they received a guaranteed minimum. McTavish who, with his brother George, energetically supported Donald Smith's political activities, argued that Grahame had no proposals to make and appeared to be the mouthpiece of the Governor and Committee. It was therefore up to the officers to nominate their own spokesman, not to antagonize the shareholders but to "arrive at some conclusion that will be satisfactory to all parties." The officers knew Donald Smith's weaknesses as Chief Commissioner, but they also knew that he had succeeded in acting on their behalf before and that he had the ear of the Governor and Committee. Moreover, it was apparent from correspondence and conversations that he genuinely cared about their well being. Two officers, J.J. Hargrave, who had written the Fort Garry letters which the *Montreal Herald* had published in 1869, and Alexander Christie, based at Fort Garry, disagreed, arguing that "Mr. D.A. Smith is always *too late* for everybody's business but his own."

They proposed that John McTavish should share the responsibility for representing their case to the board.[53]

When the Northern Department Council met at the beginning of July 1878, the McTavish brothers had secretly broached the idea of Donald negotiating with the Governor and Committee on their behalf. Laurence Clarke, who was based at Fort Carlton where the council met, was implacably opposed to working through Donald and remained so, believing that the only acceptable approach to the Governor and Committee was through the Chief Commissioner who was, after all, responsible for the fur trade. Richard Hardisty was inclined to agree with this point of view but ultimately fell in line with the others. When the Council had completed its deliberations, the officers had set about gathering powers of attorney in favour of Donald Smith and McTavish had also written James Bissett in Montreal who became an active supporter of the movement and brought in the Southern and Montreal Departments.[54]

Both Grahame and his son were carefully excluded from these secret conversations, but they cannot have failed to notice that something was afoot and on July 19, Grahame wrote London to say that he had heard confidentially that Donald Smith was to represent the interests of the wintering partners to the Governor and Committee.[55]

McTavish discussed the movement in a general way with Donald in Fort Garry in the autumn, and on October 7, just after Donald set out for Montreal, a number of officers met and constituted themselves as the Fur Trade Party. At this point, they articulated a threat which had been implicit in previous discussions. If they failed in their objective, the men resolved to resign *en masse*, but Donald was only to use this threat "in case of manifest expediency and urgency."[56]

Just before Donald left, Grahame also spoke to him about the movement. In a letter to Armit, written a week after his return to Montreal, Donald explained that he had been told by the officers that Grahame had said that his position as Chief Commissioner "precluded him from giving any assistance in communicating with them on the subject." He had also been assured that nothing hostile to Grahame was intended and that, for his part, he would act "with the most correct and friendly feelings towards the Company as well as towards Mr. Grahame."[57]

In fact, Grahame was, with increasing discomfiture, trying to sit on the fence, saying one thing to people's faces and another behind their backs. In essence, he was attempting to dissociate himself from the Fur Trade Party while telling the board that he was perfectly willing to cooperate with the officers. In reality, he was offended by the wintering partners' refusal to take him into their confidence, even though he had declined to help them, and insulted by their preference for Donald Smith as their representative.

When Grahame arrived in Montreal in October, Donald found him "tired and out of sorts," so he waited a day or two before broaching the subject with him. Grahame complained that the officers had shown "a want of confidence" in him, which Donald thought odd since he had been told by George McTavish that Grahame had said he could "take no part in the matter." Grahame was also waspish about John McTavish, who clearly felt about the Chief Commissioner much as Donald did, for Donald had no compunction in sharing Grahame's comments with McTavish. Grahame went "on & on" about how he had got John

McTavish his commission as chief factor and said that Donald would lose his position as Land Commissioner "for meddling with" the Fur Trade Party. No doubt Grahame was recalling Eden Colvile's letter of four years earlier. Donald retorted that the charge of meddling was "an unwarranted assumption amounting to impertinence on the part of Mr. Grahame" and observed that Grahame had assumed he wanted to remain as Land Commissioner, a position which he did not need to hold "for pecuniary reasons."[58]

In fact, though he said nothing about it to Grahame or McTavish, he had already made up his mind to resign.

Grahame's letter prompted the Governor and Committee to believe that Donald was meddling in the officers' concerns and they wrote him, through Armit, to say that he "must have been misinformed" about Grahame's unwillingness to act on behalf of the wintering partners as Grahame's communications "entirely negative such a supposition." The phrase is not Armit's and almost certainly came from Governor Goschen who was less accustomed to the more mellifluous phrasing favoured by the officers and senior staff. It also covers up the fact that at no time did Grahame explicitly offer to represent the interests of the Fur Trade Party and when asked for his assistance with the letter written in 1877, had declined to give it. As he wrote to the board, he kept reminding the officers of Goschen's response to that letter, believing that to do so was to demonstrate his concern for their welfare.[59]

In London, however, the conviction remained that Donald was being discourteous in usurping the Chief Commissioner's authority. Armit wrote again on behalf of the board.

> I would also call your attention to the anomalous position in which you as a salaried Officer of the Company, — unconnected with the Fur Trade — would be placing yourself both towards the Board and the Officers by undertaking to represent the interests of the latter. The Committee cannot but think that on consideration you will yourself see that every such representation should come through the Chief Commissioner, and that it would not be courteous to him, and would tend to subvert the proper discipline of the Service to encourage it through any other channel.[60]

The very formation of the Fur Trade Party had subverted "the proper discipline of the Service" and the Governor and Committee were as yet ignorant of the seriousness of the threat they faced. In his efforts to make peace among the various factions, Donald pointed out that "the position appears to me to have become very grave" without specifying any details. He would, however, have known that George Stephen had just received a letter from John McTavish who was beginning to scout for financial backing should the wintering partners be forced to abandon the HBC and set up their own company. Stephen had promised to do all he could to help.[61]

In a more detailed letter repudiating the board's charges, Donald pointed out that in some respects the Fur Trade Party represented unfinished business from 1871 when the Governor and Committee had refused to comply with a request for a guaranteed minimum. He was surprised that the board had responded as it had, given that the "representations from the officers to the Board were totally of a friendly character" and pointed out that, as a shareholder, he was "interested in seeing the fur trade prosper." Again, he stressed that he had been repeatedly told that Grahame had "declined to consider the question."[62]

In a letter in which he attempted to pacify Grahame, Donald also held a mirror up to the truth when he said that he "distinctly understood from these gentlemen you had, if not actually in so many words, at any rate virtually declined being the medium of presenting their views and wishes ... and that you left on the minds of those who had spoken to you on the subject the impression that you could hold out to them no hope of an amelioration of their condition, at least in the immediate future." It was precisely what Grahame believed, as he had said, not only to the officers but also to the Governor and Committee. Donald reiterated that no discourtesy was intended.[63]

Through Donald's letters, a kind of peace was restored with Grahame and the board but Grahame remained resentful of the Fur Trade Party's decision to exclude him and was increasingly aggressive in his dealings with John McTavish as a result. Not content with belligerence, Grahame implied that the Fur Trade Party, which he did not know by that name, was in fact a nascent trade union. Nothing could have been further from the truth, nor could anything have been better inspired to instill fear in the Governor and Committee. "How is it that you, an Officer in so high a position and in instant personal communication with myself should have been in any way mixed up in a combined movement?" he wanted to know. McTavish should have discussed it frankly with his chief, said Grahame, adding that senior officers "might be expected to set an example of loyal sincerity."[64]

In response, McTavish politely explained that Donald Smith was his attorney in these matters and Grahame should seek an explanation from him. Grahame's letter also hinted that an offer would be coming from the board, news which prompted members of the Fur Trade Party in the vicinity of Red River to agree that they would use the same tactic of referring Grahame to Donald Smith if, as they correctly anticipated, they individually received offers of a guarantee. The decision was rapidly sent to other districts to ensure a united front.[65]

On December 13, Donald arrived in Fort Garry, partly to receive specific instructions from the Fur Trade Party and partly to try to improve relations between Grahame and McTavish. The Chief Commissioner had not yet received Donald's letter trying to make peace and still had a rather shadowy notion of the objectives of the wintering partners. When he saw Donald's letter, Grahame found that it clarified some points and members of the Fur Trade Party wrote an explanatory letter on the fourteenth. This was almost certainly prompted by a recommendation from Donald that their interests would be better served by briefing Grahame in an effort to reduce his hostility. It may well also have been his advice that John McTavish should not be a signatory; a strong letter signed by others would demonstrate that the men were firm in their resolve and that the movement would not collapse without McTavish. In their letter of explanation, they said that "various indications incapable of being misunderstood, given to individuals of our number" had convinced them that Grahame would not approve of any approach to the board. They had intended that Grahame should tell the board about the plan, but the Governor and Committee had been informed "through some channel unknown to us." That channel, of course, was Donald Smith's October letter.[66]

The officers' letter served its purpose in placating Grahame and he, in turn, wrote a conciliatory response. On the eighteenth of December, he started to send out the board's offer of a guaranteed minimum of £150 for Outfits 1877, 1878 and 1879. The Fur Trade Party, however, sent special couriers off in December with both news of the offer and a copy of the recommended response which directed Grahame to the wintering partners' attorney, Donald Smith. It is unlikely that the board felt disposed to send Donald a copy of the offer but he would have been shown it by James Bissett or one of the other officers with whom he was on good terms.[67]

Donald sailed for London on January 11, 1879 and on the thirtieth presented the Fur Trade Party's proposals to the Governor and Committee. The board discussed the suggestions throughout February and on the twenty-sixth conceded virtually every demand. The insistence on a permanent minimum guarantee of £200 was modified to £150 but this was extended to five years rather than the three offered at the end of 1878. It was only to be applicable if the fur trade profit was less than £60,000 per outfit. If it was greater, the guarantee would go up to £200. Donald had modified a request for "full salary" for the first two years of a man's retirement to £200 for each year but the board declined to give any assurances about retirement payments. With these two exceptions, all the concessions were granted as were some additional points relating to the management of the company.[68]

Grahame had been summoned to London and, with Donald, had worked on the framing of the final version which the board approved on February 26. Donald was not entirely pleased with the results of his negotiations but recognized that the board's hand was constrained by the economic circumstances in which it found itself. On February 27, he wrote that he would explain the offer to the officers "although I am not without fear that the terms proposed by the Governor & Committee will be received with disappointment by the officers, yet they are such as under the actual circumstances appear equitable to me and I shall recommend their cordial acceptance by the gentlemen who have accredited me to act on their behalf." In particular, John McTavish's acceptance was needed, for the Fur Trade Party had given him a power of veto after Grahame had prohibited him from travelling to London.[69]

Donald immediately cabled the results and McTavish equally promptly rejected them. On March 17, the day before his ship docked in New York, Donald sent a telegram requesting the McTavish brothers to meet him in Chicago on the twenty-third. En route to Chicago, he collected James Bissett from whom he expected a briefing on all that had happened in his absence. They had less than ten hours in Chicago, during which Donald had at least one other meeting, and were back on the train to Montreal shortly after five o'clock on the afternoon of their arrival.[70]

George and John McTavish were both dismayed to find that a permanent guarantee of a minimum of £200 had not been accepted, though Donald explained that he had pushed the board as far as he could. There was no point in gaining concessions from the Governor and Committee which would be rejected by the shareholders in June. On March 26, George McTavish returned to Red River but his brother, with authorization from the Fur Trade Party, proceeded to Montreal to see whether George Stephen and his friends might make a specific proposal about providing the capital to set up a separate company. Because of the depression, no one was able to better the board's proposition and McTavish recommended that it be accepted. The shareholders approved the measures in June.[71]

With variations, the guarantee remained in force until 1894 when the Deed Poll of 1871 was abolished and all officers were placed on salary. In only two years between 1879 and 1894 did the fur trade earn enough to meet the guarantee; in every other year, the company had to make up the amount from other earnings and in four years, it was obliged to contribute the entire sum. Except for 1879, the guarantee was £200 each year.[72]

The members of the Fur Trade Party wrote to say they were grateful to Donald for all that he did on their behalf and, some months later, wrote James Grahame to express their confidence in him as Chief Commissioner. As quickly as the movement had flared up, it died down again.

Donald, in the meantime, was starting to think about drafting the letter in which he told the commissioned officers that he was leaving the HBC, though he would continue to look after their Private Cash interests.

His resignation may have been hastened by a number of sharp letters from London, calling his attention to the fact that he had been dilatory. "Looking to the small amount of work connected with the accounts of the Land Department," Armit wrote in June 1878, "it was hoped that the details would have been promptly and regularly rendered, but as the Committee are again disappointed in this respect, they direct me to state that a minute was passed directing your special attention to the matter and calling upon you in future to render the accounts in question regularly."[73]

But Donald had finally accepted that he had taken on more than he could do well. As he admitted in a letter to Campbell Sweeny at the Bank of Montreal's Winnipeg office, he had been doing too much and his "office duties" had suffered. A letter to John McTavish on political matters said much the same thing.[74]

He was also dissatisfied with Land Department policies. "It is full time it should be understood by the Company whether or not the Canadian government intend assuming the one twentieth of their township lands under the agreement with Mr. Mackenzie in August 1875; as if not, it will certainly be to the interest of the Company to dispose of a considerable portion of their lands which I believe could next year be done at good prices." As he admitted in the House of Commons in 1880, he had "always thought it would have been infinitely better had the Canadian Government — and I wish this to apply to both Governments — extinguished the landed rights of that Company [the HBC] altogether, and purchased its lands for the public, when it had an opportunity of doing so." In 1878, however, it was apparent that a major change was in the offing in the Northwest and that if the company was going to sell, it should be prepared to do so soon. He also thought that someone else should handle the sales.[75]

He had intended to go to London to discuss his situation in December 1878 but postponed the journey to accommodate the needs of the Fur Trade Party. When he was in England in February 1879, he wrote his formal letter of resignation, explaining that he had "come to this determination from the consideration that my private affairs now require my personal care more than formerly, making it impossible for me to continue to give to the Company's landed interests that close attention which their great importance demands on the part of the officer administering them."[76]

The "private affairs" which had been demanding so much attention were the construction of railway communication with the Northwest, a subject which had concerned him since his first journey there in 1869.

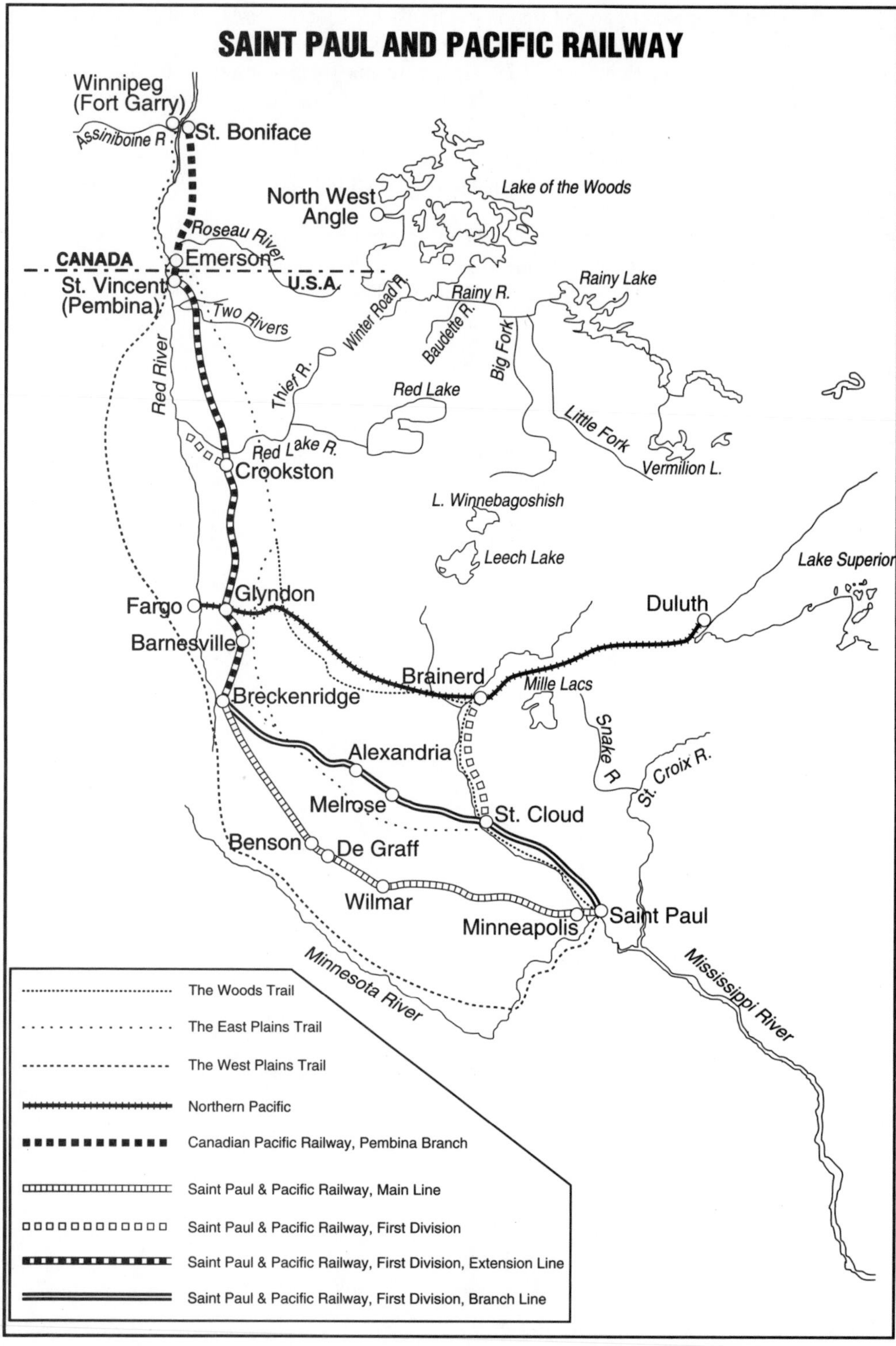
SAINT PAUL AND PACIFIC RAILWAY
Winnipeg
(Fort Garry)
St. Boniface
Assiniboine R.
North West
Angle
Lake of the Woods
Roseau River
CANADA
Emerson
U.S.A.
St. Vincent
(Pembina)
Two Rivers
Winter Road R.
Rainy R.
Rainy Lake
Baudette R.
Big Fork
Red River
Thief R.
Red Lake
Little Fork
Red Lake R.
Crookston
Vermilion L.
L. Winnebagoshish
Leech Lake
Lake Superior
Fargo
Glyndon
Duluth
Barnesville
Brainerd
Mille Lacs
Breckenridge
Snake R.
Alexandria
St. Croix R.
Melrose
St. Cloud
Benson
De Graff
Wilmar
Minneapolis
Saint Paul
Minnesota River
Mississippi River
The Woods Trail
The East Plains Trail
The West Plains Trail
Northern Pacific
Canadian Pacific Railway, Pembina Branch
Saint Paul & Pacific Railway, Main Line
Saint Paul & Pacific Railway, First Division
Saint Paul & Pacific Railway, First Division, Extension Line
Saint Paul & Pacific Railway, First Division, Branch Line

CHAPTER ELEVEN

THE SAINT PAUL, MINNEAPOLIS AND MANITOBA RAILWAY 1870–1880

On again the iron horse sped, keeping at the pace of twenty-five miles an hour.
Manitoba Free Press [1]

Throughout the years that he served the Hudson's Bay Company as Chief Commissioner and Land Commissioner, Donald Smith was also occupied with achieving a rail connection between eastern Canada and the Northwest. From the beginning of his association with the Red River settlement and the lands beyond it, he had perceived that the future prosperity of both the HBC and the community at large lay in achieving a rail link which would bring in manufactured goods and settlers and take out the produce of the land, whether furs or grain, or undiscovered riches such as coal and oil.

No one could doubt that decent transportation was needed. The Dawson Road was impassable in winter when the lake and river sections were frozen, it offered absolutely no facilities for travellers and expected men, even though they had paid their passage, to contribute to the labour of driving, portaging, rowing and carrying what little baggage travellers were allowed on that inhospitable route.

The rail and wagon journey via Saint Paul was remarkably civilized, but only when compared to the mosquitoes, the jolting, the wet and the cold of the Dawson Road. In November 1870, Julie-Cimodocié Casault, the wife of Lieutenant Colonel Louis-Adolphe Casault of the Second Quebec Rifles, set out to join her husband at Fort Garry, accompanied by Colonel Jarvis, also of the militia, and his wife. They had only reached Sarnia, at the tip of Lake Huron, when Mrs. Casault found things so dirty she was reluctant to eat but, "if I judge from Colonel Jarvis we shall get over this feeling before we get to Fort Garry."[2]

The route from Montreal, via Toronto and Sarnia, led over the rails of the Grand Trunk and its American allies to Chicago. In December 1871, Donald noted that he was late back to Montreal, "the Grand Trunk trains having been as usual far behind time." The journey from Chicago to Saint Paul was often no better: it took Mrs. Casault twenty-seven hours in 1870 and in January 1872, Donald was reporting that "owing to innumerable delays on the Grand Trunk Road and an accident by which several carriages were thrown off the track, about 100 miles east of St. Paul, instead of our accomplishing the trip as usual in three days we did not arrive here till this morning." In other words, it took six days from Montreal to Saint Paul.[3]

The trains, for all their problems, were vastly better than the coaches, Red River carts and dog sleds which travellers were obliged to use from the railhead north of Saint Paul. There was no snow when Mrs. Casault travelled at the end of November but the incessant prairie wind was bitterly cold. At Benson, she spent the night in a house which was "little better than a shed a single plank house & the wind blows through it at night as if it were a cardboard house," while the next night she slept in a room with seventeen other people. It was followed by a night in tents and another "crammed in a room."

> Our appearance is anything but neat or stylish. We have given up *chignons* hoops, *bustles*, collars & cuffs & almost washing our faces & combing our hair we have to do it under such difficulties. I must say it takes some time to get over cleanly habits. I caught Mrs. Jarvis going behind the carriage to use her pocket handkerchief she was ashamed of its colour & really we could not get to any of our trunks.[4]

As Colonel Jarvis maltreated his Métis drivers, who responded by taking their time and ignoring his requests, Mrs. Casault set out on her own for Pembina where she was relieved to be able to undress for the first time in ten days.

Snow did not necessarily mean the travellers had a faster or smoother journey. Cyril Graham reported to London that his trip from Fort Garry was "very difficult and very slow. During the first portion of it the snow was so deep that 25 miles was a good 16 hours work, & during the last part I was glad to make 55 miles in 21 consecutive hours." Years later, Donald noted that on his journeys north, he had been glad to encounter the railway construction gang's caboose where he could get warm and have a hot meal. "I have also been detained for days together blocked up at Wilmar during snow storms."[5]

Though the trains travelling on the few miles of track north of Saint Paul were regularly snowed in, they were still faster and more efficient than the Red River carts and the dog sleds, especially when it came to the transport of freight. In 1870, freight arrived by rail in Saint Paul, was transferred to carts which hauled it north to a landing stage on the Red River, where it was put on a barge or steamer and carried north to Winnipeg. Every transfer brought labour charges, an opportunity for theft, loss or damage, and the risk of bureaucratic delays: the idea of loading a shipment of Hudson's Bay Company goods onto a train at Montreal or New York and not touching it again until it reached Winnipeg was immensely attractive.

In 1870, there appeared to be two ways in which a through route might be achieved. The first was by means of the Saint Paul and Pacific, a railway created by reorganizing the bankrupt Minneapolis and Pacific Railroad in 1862. Its Main Line was slowly being constructed from Saint Paul towards Breckenridge on the Red River, where it was meant to connect with the steamboats, while the Branch Line was following the east side of the Mississippi River towards St. Cloud, where the East Plains Trail and the Woods Trail merged. If the Saint Paul and Pacific were extended to the border and a Canadian line was constructed from Winnipeg to meet it, the problem would be solved.[6]

The other option was the Northern Pacific which was building from Duluth to the Pacific and would have to cross the Red River at some point in the vicinity of Saint Paul. It was likely that it would establish a branch to the Canadian border. Indeed, the reason the Northern Pacific directors were attracted to Hugh Allan's Canada Pacific scheme was precisely because it would enable them to funnel traffic to and from the Canadian prairies via the Duluth line and its connections to the east. Foolishly, the Northern Pacific directors intended to bypass Saint Paul, which had originally developed as a transport hub and distribution centre for the Northwest because it was at the head of navigation of the Mississippi River. The Saint Paul and Pacific, on the other hand, acknowledged the importance of the city and the freighting and forwarding infrastructure which had been developed there.

The progress of the American railroads was often a topic of conversation in London for English financial houses underwrote many bond issues in the great US railway boom and influential shippers such as the Hudson's Bay Company were always in search of new routes which might be more advantageous for their businesses. In October 1870, Donald wrote Secretary Smith in London to say that he had drawn Norman Kittson's attention to the Saint Paul and Pacific route through Benson (and, eventually, Breckenridge) which would be faster than the one via St. Cloud. He promised to discuss shipping routes when he got to Saint Paul.[7]

In May the following year, Kittson was able to report that the Northern Pacific would cross the Red River at a point thirteen miles south of Georgetown. "This place will therefore become the head of navigation of the river," he wrote.[8]

In November 1871, when Kittson, Jim Hill and Donald Smith established Kittson's Red River Line, the forerunner of the Red River Transportation Company, they envisaged a short-lived, profitable operation which would provide efficient cargo shipment along the river route until 1873 when it was widely assumed the Saint Paul and Pacific, in alliance with a Canadian line, would have linked Fort Garry and the Minnesota capital. The line to Breckenridge had already been completed by the time Donald reported to London at the beginning of November.

Indeed construction on the American side was moving so quickly that it seemed sensible to ensure that there would be a Canadian road to meet it at the border. In December, the *Canada Gazette* announced that an application would be made in the next session of parliament for a charter to build the Manitoba Junction Railway from St. Vincent or Pembina on the border to Fort Garry. The men seeking the charter were Donald Smith, his cousin George Stephen, and several other Montreal businessmen, including Daniel Torrance, a Bank of

Montreal director, and George Laidlaw who was later involved in a bid to buy the Hudson's Bay Company Lands in the Northwest. The charter also allowed them to put steamers on Lake Manitoba and the Saskatchewan River and to clear obstacles in the waterways. The men represented sufficient capital to ensure that the line would be built, but Sir John A. Macdonald refused to have the charter proclaimed in order to protect the trans-Canada scheme. The failure to have the charter brought into force delayed the opening of the Canadian Northwest to settlement but it also threw the onus of developing water transport back onto the HBC.[9]

The company's interest in securing a rail link was sufficiently well known that Jay Cooke, the Philadelphia banker who had invested heavily in the Northern Pacific, felt no compunction about claiming the company's involvement in his railway when he issued a prospectus in order to raise money on the London market at the beginning of 1872. Not surprisingly, the Governor and Committee objected: they knew nothing of Cooke's claims. Cooke, who was unaware of the tight control exercised by London on all the HBC's Canadian activities, insisted that freight negotiations were taking place and that a dock had been leased in Duluth. "The opening of the Northern Pacific Railroad from Duluth to the Red River changes all this; and one of the immediate consequences is the transfer from St. Paul to Duluth of the business hitherto conducted by the Hudson's Bay Company at the former place." It was true that Kittson had been negotiating freight rates, but neither he nor Donald had ever favoured sending cargo through the Great Lakes because this route increased freight handling and could significantly delay the arrival of goods in Manitoba if breakup on the lakes was late. Cooke was guilty of wishful thinking.[10]

In the summer of 1872, it appeared that the Canadian government was on the verge of starting construction of the Pembina Branch, the link from Fort Garry to the border, but hopes that a through line would be completed the following year diminished in October when a section of the Saint Paul and Pacific was placed in the hands of trustees.

Nineteenth century railways in North America were established by government charter which gave the right to construct the line and also provided land grants, sometimes of enormous proportions. The idea was that the railway company would sell the land and use the capital to finance the construction. Initially, unscrupulous developers sold the land and ran off with the money, not bothering to build a railway. Subsequently, land grants were allocated gradually in accordance with the number of miles completed but even that arrangement did not prevent greedy or incompetent railway builders from looking out for their personal interests first. In the case of the Minneapolis and Pacific, only ten miles of road had been constructed by 1860 and the rest of the money had found its way into the owners' pockets.

When the Minneapolis and Pacific was restructured in 1862, two companies were created, the Saint Paul and Pacific and the First Division of the Saint Paul and Pacific. When issuing the charters for the two new companies, the Minnesota authorities added yet more land to the original large grant. It was used to secure mortgages which, in turn, underpinned three bond issues totalling $11,800,000. By 1870, a large portion of the money raised by the bonds had been siphoned off by the directors.

In 1871, yet another bond issue was floated on the European market, this one worth $15 million. At about the same time, Edwin B. Litchfield was brought in to take over the construction of the railway and, in part payment, received all the common stock of the First Division. This he conditionally sold to the Northern Pacific which wanted to control the line because it wanted feeders for its east-west route and because it wanted to incorporate the Saint Paul and Pacific line to the border into the Canada Pacific plans it was hatching with Hugh Allan. Litchfield, an established railway contractor, backed by Northern Pacific financing, appeared to give the Saint Paul and Pacific security and the rapid northward construction of the Main Line and the Branch Line seemed to justify the optimism which everyone felt in 1870 and 1871.

The divergent goals of the Saint Paul and Pacific and the Northern Pacific, however, soon provoked a split, much to the alarm of the bondholders, most of whom were based in Holland. In the autumn of 1872, as soon as the interest on the bonds was six months in arrears, they called into force a provision of the mortgage securing their loan and placed their trustee in charge of the company. The trusteeship was held by the New York merchant banking house of John Stewart Kennedy and it was one of the partners, John Barnes, who now took responsibility for the company. As Donald noted glumly in a letter from Fort Garry in October 1872, work had been halted for the season and the stoppage was likely to discourage construction on the Canadian side. The HBC would probably have to rely on steamers for another year.

On the twentieth of October, Donald left Fort Garry for Ottawa, spending the better part of a week in Saint Paul en route. Much of his time was taken up with discussions with Norman Kittson and J.J. Hill about what needed to be included in the formal agreement required by the HBC for the creation of the Red River Transportation Company but inevitably some conversation focused on the mess the Saint Paul and Pacific was in. It was apparent that Hill knew a good deal about the line, and Donald began to appreciate his potential as a collaborator in resolving the HBC's transportation problems.

Born in the Quaker village of Rockwood, Ontario, in 1838, Jim Hill was the son of Irish Protestants, and was married to a staunch Catholic, though he developed no particular interest in religion himself. Following the death of his father, his mother had moved the family to Guelph, Ontario, but early in 1856, Hill had packed a suitcase and set off to explore some of the American cities. In July that year, he "took a notion to go and see St. Paul" where he found steamboats and the beginnings of the railway system which would be his life's passion.[11]

Hill, who had lost the sight in his right eye following a childhood accident, was a great talker and loved the excitement of the burgeoning frontier town, but his enthusiastic "booming" was not all hot air. It was founded on facts and on the minutely detailed information which he absorbed whenever something interested him.

Like Jack Sprat and his wife, Donald and J.J. Hill were opposites which complemented each other. Where Donald was always carefully groomed, Hill generally needed a haircut. Hill's suits were fashionable but inevitably rumpled while Donald wore conservative black coats and sombre trousers, scarcely changing the style throughout his life. His trousers usually looked freshly pressed, but that was easier for him because he was thin and wiry while Hill tended to be chubby as a young man and was fat in his maturity. Hill was gregarious while Donald was reticent, but the contrast which mattered most in their relationship was that Donald was very good at broad concepts such as the way in which the HBC transport could be reformed while Hill was superb at the multitude of details which could make a concept work. What they shared was a belief that the Northwest, whether Canadian or American, faced a prosperous future to which they could contribute and from which they and a great many others could benefit.

Hill's older colleague, Norman Kittson had been born in Chambly, Quebec, in 1814 and was the grandson of Alexander Henry, one of the early explorers of the Northwest. Kittson, whose middle name was Wolfred in honour of Wolfred Nelson, a family friend who was one of the 1837 rebels, became a fur trader and was a vigorous opponent of the Hudson's Bay Company before being subsumed by it. He had many friends and relatives in the Red River Métis community, including Ambroise Lépine, Riel's associate, who was also one of Alexander Henry's grandchildren. Kittson's first wife was a Métis, one of the Marion family who were opposed to Riel's insurrection, and when she died in 1868, he took her body back to St. Boniface for burial among her family and childhood friends. A sartorial elegance and a love of race horses set Kittson apart from his two younger friends but the three were already united by a trust which enabled them to work together, as they had done throughout the 1872 shipping season, with no more than a verbal agreement.

Transportation seemed to be on everyone's mind as the winter snows set in: there were days in December when the storms were so bad that the mail could not get through to Montreal; in January, travellers froze to death on the prairies; importers such as the Hudson's Bay Company were engaged in the usual round of negotiations to find the fastest and cheapest route from Europe to the North American farmlands; Canadian and American politicians and pressmen were alert to every new nuance in the emerging Pacific Scandal; and Jay Cooke, the great American railway banker, kept making large and very risky short term loans to the Northern Pacific. As the snow melted and the grass grew green again in the spring of 1873, some bankers may have guessed that that autumn's fruit would be rotten.

Some of those bankers were the Dutch who held the majority of the bonds in the Saint Paul and Pacific. When things had begun to go wrong, most of the bankers and some other owners had assigned their bonds to a trust, Associate Casse, in order to protect their interest. Certificates representing the bonds were traded on the Amsterdam exchange and a committee, drawn from the bankers, was formed to manage the precarious business. Its spokesman was Johan Carp, a manufacturer from Utrecht.

Late in August 1873, Carp and a colleague sailed to New York in hopes of discovering whether the Saint Paul and Pacific might have a future and whether the bankers might recoup any of their investment. On September 5, John Paton, the New York agent of the British Bank of North America, who was a friend both of the banker, John Kennedy, and of Lieutenant Governor Morris, wrote Morris seeking information on the progress of the Canadian Pacific. The Dutchmen, he said were "anxious to learn what encouragement you hold out, if they run their Road out to Pembina to meet the proposed Road from Fort Garry." Was there anyone they might meet in New York or Saint Paul with whom they might discuss the Pembina Branch?[12]

When the letter arrived, Donald Smith was at Fort Garry, attending meetings of the Executive Council of the North West Territories and dealing with HBC business. Morris discussed Paton's letter with him and a correspondence between Donald and Carp ensued. The Dutchman wanted to know whether Donald, but more likely the Hudson's Bay Company, could finance the extension to the Canadian border.[13]

Carp and John Barnes, who was an experienced railway banker, travelled to Saint Paul to assess the situation at first hand. Barnes wrote to Morris on the twenty-fifth of September.

> The Hollanders hold about $15,000,000 of the bonds upon the lines — and as none of the land grant which constituted the chief security of these bonds has as yet been secured to them, and as the railway in its present condition is of little value as a railway, you will understand that they are in a very disagreeable position particularly as by the 30 of December next the land grant will be forfeited if the road is not completed by that time, none of it having yet been completed to the standard imposed by its charter.[14]

On the eighteenth of September, Jay Cooke's financial bubble had burst, revealing to Carp and Barnes that the situation was worse than they had anticipated. Neither Edwin Litchfield nor his brother, E. Darwin, who had reclaimed from the Northern Pacific his brother's shares in the First Division, nor the people they had appointed to manage the railroad were in any way competent and Cooke had been throwing his money away. So too had the Dutch, as Barnes discovered.

> The management of this enterprise by the Northern Pacific Co and its appointees, who have controlled its destinies by being the owners of its share capital, has been simply disgraceful. The means furnished so liberally by the Dutch public have been squandered and wasted and misapplied. We shall proceed against the responsible parties with all the power of our law courts & hope to bring them to a speedy accounting.[15]

From Saint Paul, Carp and Barnes travelled to Ottawa where they hoped to see Prime Minister Macdonald and Senator Macpherson. With the Pacific Scandal moving towards its climax, neither man had either time or sympathy, least of all for men who had, however unhappily, associated themselves with the Northern Pacific.

Donald's correspondence with Carp, and the fact that the bondholders seemed to want to pursue the extension of the Saint Paul and Pacific to the border, despite Cooke's bankruptcy, made Donald think that there just might be some chance of achieving the rail link the company and the Northwest so badly needed. When he stopped at Saint Paul on his dash from Fort Carlton to Ottawa for the Pacific Scandal debate in October 1873, he asked Norman Kittson and J.J. Hill what they knew about the railway. Ever since he had come to Saint Paul, Hill had been observing the road and analyzing its prospects. "I showed him," Hill recalled, "that the line to St. Vincent [on the border], running as it did for most of its length through unsettled country, could not possibly be made to pay for several years to come and any investment looking to a future success would have to consider the property as a whole."[16]

Donald asked Kittson and Hill to see what they could discover about the railway, its finances, the quality of the construction which had already been completed, and the work which still needed to be done. They were also to keep an eye on the plethora of lawsuits which were developing. Initially, Donald's dealings were primarily with Kittson who, as the HBC agent, was paid to do such work. But Hill had been all but obsessed by the railway for years, keeping a weather eye out for the moment when he might take control of it and enable it to fulfill its promise. He was delighted to have an excuse to do what he wanted to do anyway.

The federal election consequent on the collapse of the Macdonald government after the Pacific Scandal brought Donald back to Winnipeg at the beginning of February 1874 and on his way out, he spent a little time in Saint Paul where Kittson introduced him to Frank Delano, the superintendent of the First Division. Delano recommended controlling the Branch Line which went from Saint Paul to St. Cloud. Its mortgages were smaller and, once it was in hand, it would be easier to negotiate for the Main Line, which went to Breckenridge, and for the Extension Line, which went from Glyndon on the Northern Pacific road to Crookston, a village which had grown up at the point where the East Plains Trail crossed Red Lake River. Though Crookston was, as far as the railway men were concerned, in the middle of nowhere, it was, as far as Donald was concerned, on the way to the border and it was the Extension Line that mattered to him.

Delano said he thought the Saint Paul and Pacific would be "an excellent road to acquire;" he, Hill and Kittson were under the impression that the stock was of no value and that the bonds could be available cheaply. Donald asked Kittson to continue to supply him with as much information as possible "as failing to get the road through in any other way, I should have been glad to have been able to induce others, along with myself, to take it up, if it could be got upon such terms as these gentlemen thought it could be obtained; that was very little as they thought at that time."[17]

Back in Ottawa, Donald began a delicate exploration of the possible sources of funding. Mackenzie, who was responsible for railways as well as being prime minister, assured him that he wanted to have the Pembina Branch of the Canadian Pacific Railway completed "without delay." The two men discussed the possibility of the Canadian government buying or leasing the line through to Glyndon and they also talked about the possibility of getting the bondholders to authorize construction of a continuous line right through to Fort Garry. A collaboration between the Canadian government, Darwin Litchfield as the major shareholder in the First Division, and the Dutch bondholders briefly seemed to offer a glimmer of hope, but it was quickly extinguished as the depression took hold.[18]

In March, Kittson reported that about a million dollars would be required to complete and equip the line between Glyndon and the border so that the Canadians could use it to import rails, engines and other material needed to construct the Pembina Branch. Failure to meet its December 1873 deadline should have meant that the Saint Paul and Pacific forfeited its land grant, but the American trustees had applied to Congress for additional time to build to the border, Kittson noted, adding that without the land grant, it would be impossible to raise the money to finish the line.[19]

As he explored these various options for completing the railway, Donald kept the Governor and Committee briefed. If both the Canadian government and the agents for the bondholders did as they said, he reported to London at the beginning of April 1874, "the probability is that the whole Line of Railroad will be opened through to St. Paul and further within twelve months from this date." On one level, he was merely passing on information because it was to the company's advantage to know what was happening and to be on friendly terms with a firm which might soon be required to carry its goods; equally, construction of the railway would affect the company's interest in the Red River Transportation Company. On another level, however, he was also creating a basis of knowledge from which the HBC might perceive that it was in its own interest to invest in the railway and ensure its completion. If the board members were tempted, they did not let it show and they too were beginning to feel the effects of the depression which would lead to four years without a dividend.[20]

Donald also discussed the circumstances of the railway with George Stephen. When the cousins were both in Montreal, they tended to meet daily and "consulted together with regard to anything and everything of importance." Donald's returns from the Northwest always meant he would talk enthusiastically about the country's potential and about the Saint Paul and Pacific lines "and the important part they were likely to play in securing a railway connection between the older provinces of the Dominion of Canada and these new territories of the Northwest." For his part, Stephen was quite uninterested. "In the first instance," Donald later explained, "he thought of Minnesota, as many others did, that it was at the North Pole somewhere."[21]

The only one to make any progress in 1874 was J.J. Hill. He arranged to get regular information on Saint Paul and Pacific bond prices in Holland from a Dutch newspaper called *The Financier* and he persuaded John Barnes to authorize construction of a very short spur from Breckenridge to Fisher's Landing on the Red River. It was built in the summer of 1875 with financial support from the Red River Transportation Company and meant that the steamers could collect their cargo in much deeper water and so carry much larger loads. In some cases, the volume went up from thirty tons to three hundred tons and the profit increased accordingly.[22]

By the end of the summer of 1875, the Saint Paul and Pacific was still no more than bits of iron rail, often rusty, going from Saint Paul to nowhere in particular; other bits of rail went from nowhere to nowhere and there appeared to be little chance that these links would ever be connected to form a coherent and useful railway system. The Dutch committee ran out of patience in August and foreclosed on the 1871 mortgage of $15 million, forcing a section of the Saint Paul and Pacific into receivership. The following March, the Dutchmen appointed as their receiver Jesse P. Farley who had also been made general manager of the portions of the railway controlled by the trustees. It made sense to have the same man responsible for both companies but Farley was dull, unimaginative, badly educated and poorly read. The complexities of the court cases and the financial dealings which had brought the road to its knees were quite beyond his grasp.

When foreclosure proceedings were instigated, it quickly became apparent to Darwin Litchfield that the Dutchmen's next move might well be an aggressive one in the direction of his shareholding in the First Division. To forestall this and retain his control, Litchfield invited the bondholders to join him on the board and offered to allow them to select the president and take charge of the management of the company. Litchfield proposed yet another bond issue and, to sweeten the deal for the Dutch, suggested that the land grant, which had been confirmed to the company, be used to retire some of the debt to the bondholders. It was a scheme which would mollify the Dutch while simultaneously protecting the First Division, which was vital to the Saint Paul and Pacific, from other predators.

Details of the negotiations between Litchfield and the bondholders began to appear in Saint Paul's *Pioneer Press* at the end of August and more information was published in October, but it was not until February 1876, shortly before Farley's appointment as receiver, that Hill felt he had reliable information on the compromise which had been reached. Like the first tiny movement which indicates a knot is loosening, the deal between Litchfield and the Dutch suggested to Hill that there might be an opportunity to unpick the financial and legal tangle of the Saint Paul and Pacific. But they would have to move quickly since Litchfield's offer to involve the Dutch in the management of the First Division was due to expire at the end of August 1876.

On the sixth of March 1876, another precondition for unpicking the Saint Paul and Pacific knot fell into place when the Minnesota legislature passed a law allowing companies which were sold as a result of foreclosure to be reorganized without losing their land grants. It meant that if the Saint Paul and Pacific were acquired, it would come with its valuable territorial possessions still intact. (Previously when the railway had come to grief, it had been repossessed by the state rather than being sold as a consequence of foreclosure.)

Late in March, when Donald was in the House of Commons for debates on both CPR legislation and the amnesty for Louis Riel, J.J. Hill sent in his card from the visitors' lobby. Ostensibly, Hill had gone to Ottawa to negotiate the details for carrying rails for the Canadian Pacific Railway from Saint Paul to Fort Garry on the Red River Transportation Company's steamers, but his real purpose was to brief Donald on the latest Saint Paul and Pacific developments. That evening, Donald could only manage a few minutes' conversation, but the men agreed to meet for breakfast the following morning.

In March 1874, the directors of the Bank of Montreal had approved an arrangement whereby the bank's Ottawa manager would have the use of a house on O'Connor Street, next door to the bank and a few yards from the Houses of Parliament, "it being understood that certain suits [sic] of rooms in the building may be used by the Executive officers while in Ottawa on bank business or rented by Directors while temporarily residing there in attendance upon parliamentary duties." The arrangement gave Donald, who was the only director with "parliamentary duties," the privacy which the Russell House lacked and made it vastly easier to conduct confidential conversations such as the one he had with Hill that March morning in 1876.[23]

Over breakfast, Hill explained that if the arrangement between Darwin Litchfield and the Dutch bondholders were confirmed in August, the chances of anyone else getting control of the Saint Paul and Pacific would be slim. The legislation allowing retention of the land grant following foreclosure meant that persons controlling the debt, say the Dutch or those who acquired their bonds, might raise money to complete the line, using the land as security. Donald again reiterated that he was only interested if the package included the Extension Line to the Canadian border.

Not knowing that the HBC land had provisionally been sold to the Canadian government, Hill was under the impression that Donald wanted the railway to facilitate HBC land sales by providing access to them for settlers. This, coupled with his concern for the company's transportation problems, had been true a year earlier, but now Donald's intentions were both altruistic, in the sense that a great many people would benefit from the opening of the Northwest, and personal, in the sense that he was thinking of investing his own money in the railway. It was now obvious that neither the Hudson's Bay Company nor the Canadian government was going to take a financial interest in the American line but it was equally obvious that even Donald's growing wealth was not sufficient to bankroll the project. He suggested that John Rose, the former finance minister and now Canada's unofficial high commissioner in London, might be interested in financing the deal. Morton Rose, his firm of merchant bankers, had interests in other North American railway projects and a New York office through which they could be pursued. Before an approach could be made to Rose, however, the price of the bonds would have to be determined. Donald asked Hill to try to find out what Johan Carp and his associates would accept.

In December, Carp was back in Saint Paul where Hill and Kittson chatted to him about their interest in the Saint Paul and Pacific and indicated that Donald Smith had implied he might finance an acquisition of the bonds. At that point, Carp had no authority to negotiate their sale and had been told by Barnes that the interest in the line shown by Hill and his friends made no sense since it would be in direct competition with their Red River steamers. Nevertheless, Carp could see that the men in Saint Paul were in earnest and he knew from his previous correspondence that Donald Smith was sincere in his desire to see the line completed to Winnipeg.

Hill made a tentative offer for the bonds, designed to test the water. Carp was interested but was "a little troubled as to the way he shall be able to convince his committee that the offer is one which Mr. Hill & Mr. Kittson have the ability to perform." Barnes, who was obliged to share information with Farley, though he seemed not yet to have grasped his incompetence, admitted to the receiver that he had "only some general notion that some Canadian gentlemen stand behind them, & who are able & willing to furnish the large sum mentioned" but he thought it might be an idea if Hill and Kittson offered some sort of guarantee. Neither Carp nor Barnes appear to have realized that Hill was on a fishing trip.[24]

In February, Hill landed his catch when Carp returned to Saint Paul with enough figures to enable Hill to calculate just how much money they would need. This progress also enabled Donald to provoke a glimmer of interest in George Stephen's eye and in May, Hill and Kittson were invited to Montreal to meet him.

Kittson was ill, but signed a power of attorney which Hill carried with him to Montreal.

The two cousins listened intently as Hill presented his calculations. He valued each class of bond and estimated that $4.3 million would be required to purchase them, with a further $300,000 to buy those bonds not held by the Associate Casse and to foreclose the various mortgages. A further $910,000 would be needed to complete the Extension Line to the border. With lawyers' fees and other miscellaneous expenses, the total would come to $5,540,180. It would buy track and equipment worth $12,200,000, plus $400,000 worth of surplus property which could be sold off, plus $200,000 worth of townsite land on the Main Line. In addition, there was the land grant which, according to government property valuations, was worth $6,700,000. In fact, Hill undervalued the property but as far as he was concerned it was neither the land nor the track and equipment which was worth acquiring but the railway itself. A modest assessment of the earnings showed $600,000 a year, rising to $800,000 as the country was settled.[25]

In Montreal, the three men reached several tentative agreements. The first was that their course of action would be to acquire the bonds and then foreclose. Hill would return to Saint Paul via New York with a view to sounding out Litchfield on the price he would accept for his shares in the First Division. They also agreed that George Stephen, who was planning to go to London in the autumn, would undertake to find financial backing for the proposed purchase of the bonds. Like Donald, he thought Morton Rose a likely bet. The third understanding was that Stephen could not undertake to try to find the money until a price had been agreed with the Dutch committee, but no formal agreement could be made until the money had been secured. That placed Hill in the unenviable position of having to devise an offer which appeared to be firm but from which they could escape if Stephen's London trip failed to raise the cash.

A letter went off to Carp in Utrecht before the end of May and by the end of June, it had been sent to John Barnes with a request for comment. As he wrote to Jesse Farley, "We are inclined to advise our friends to take the matter into consideration, and have mentioned prices which would, in our opinion, be more in accordance with our ideas of the value of the property, altho' it can not be expected that parties will buy these bonds except with a pretty sure prospect of a large profit; & except these Canadians, there would not be found persons ready to give any such sum in these times as is now offered."[26]

At the end of July, Donald, accompanied by Maggie, was in Saint Paul where he raised Hill's hopes still further. Hill reported to Kittson, who was in Rhode Island trying to recoup his health, that Donald thought "the money matters will be very easy in England, in fact I think he said it was about arranged."[27]

The optimism added a nice glow to the preparations Donald and Hill were making for the governor general's visit to the Northwest and Donald's pleasure was increased because, for the first time he was able to show his attractive young daughter the land which had increasingly occupied his thoughts.

Bella's propensity to travel sickness had not diminished and she had consistently declined opportunities to travel west in trains unequipped with decent springs or any of the other mechanical refinements which would prevent her from being thrown about the carriage. She was more than happy for Maggie to serve as her father's hostess on this occasion. Donald's first intention was that the governor general should enjoy himself, but Lord Dufferin was coming to the end of his Canadian assignment and it would do no harm to have him return to England, keen on the Northwest and its economic opportunities which would best be fulfilled when rail communication was complete.

Hill helped sort out the railway transport and assisted in getting the vice-regal party to the Red River where they boarded the *Minnesota* for Fort Garry. The steamer was part of the Red River Transportation Company's stock but it had been built for the ill-fated Merchants' International Line which had been established in the winter of 1874-1875 to fight the Red River company's monopoly. On June 4, 1875, the Merchant Line's other paddle wheeler, the *Manitoba*, was rammed broadside by the RRTC's *International*. The crash happened just before midnight as the *International* rounded a tight bend which, at the best of times, was likely to skew a steamer travelling with the current, but contemporary evidence also suggests the *Manitoba* was in the wrong lane. The *Manitoba* was rebuilt, but the additional expenditure, coupled with the vigorous competition from Kittson's line, soon meant that the Saint Paul and Winnipeg merchants who had backed the Merchant Line were glad to sell out to the RRTC.[28]

Donald and Hill seem to have enjoyed fussing over arrangements for the Dufferins that summer. Together with their various servants and aides-de-camp, the governor general and his wife were to stay at Silver Heights and Hill kept an eye on shipments of furniture which Donald brought in for the occasion and arranged the purchase of a pair of carriage horses to allow the Dufferins' host a bit of modest showing off. "I had them tried both single and double before sending them, and also had them driven up to the Railway cars, so that I think they are safe, however I do not know how they would act in the presence of bands of music etc. etc., but from the gentle disposition they showed alongside of the cars I think they will be quite reliable. Your man might drive them a few times at first until you get to know them." A wise precaution, in view of Donald's record as a driver.[29]

Hill also "found some California fruit which looked very nice" and sent a small case to Silver Heights for the delectation of Donald's guests. The house had been extended to accommodate the visitors, as the marchioness reported to her family. "A fine reception-room, and two ante-rooms, carpeted, papered, and furnished, have been added to the house for us, which we regret, as the place is really too far away to entertain in; nor have we the china, or the knives and forks, wherewith to give a ball or a dinner!"[30]

Lord Dufferin was equally unaware that his host was deriving considerable pleasure from his hospitality.

> It is impossible to describe to you all that Donald Smith has done for our comfort. Had he been a great Duke in the old country receiving the Queen he could not have made greater exertions, — in fact I am quite vexed about it as the expense of his preparations must have been very considerable, and they quite exceed what we needed, for instance he has built a large Reception Room, and two offices for the Colonel and myself which are quite equal to those at Rideau [Hall, the governor

> general's Ottawa residence], and in the minutest details has forgotten nothing, and at the same time is so quiet and unassuming about it all that I scarcely know how to make him understand how sensible we are of his kindness and fore thought.[31]

The sports day, the "grand classical concert" and the Citizens' Ball at which Lord Dufferin danced all the dances except the Red River Jig (with a "genuine Red River fiddler, specially engaged for the occasion, moccasins and all") offered a brief respite to the tension which mounted as the Saint Paul and Pacific negotiations pressed forward.[32]

An important little congregation gathered at the Merchants Hotel in Saint Paul on Saturday, the first of September. George Stephen and Richard Angus, the general manager of the Bank of Montreal, had been in Chicago on bank business at the end of August and had travelled from there to Saint Paul. Donald came down from Winnipeg for the weekend and Norman Kittson returned from Rhode Island. On Sunday, Jesse Farley produced the pay car, the best the railway could offer, and the men set out for a tour of the line.[33]

The partners in the Red River Transportation Company were well aware of the attractions of the prairie and the need for a decent railway service. The very fact that they had enticed Stephen to Saint Paul suggested that he was beginning to appreciate their arguments but Donald knew his cousin well enough to realize that the entire venture could stand or fall on this one little journey to Benson. If Stephen was not convinced of the future of the territory, he would certainly not be able to convince British bankers to finance the purchase and would probably decline to try. As they rode out into the hot, uninhabited prairie, Donald could see by Stephen's face that the dust, the wind and the grasshoppers were conspiring to defeat his ambitions. These would not provide business for a railway. But then they reached De Graff, a village named after a troublesome railway contractor. Dozens of families in their Red River carts and farm wagons were trundling in for morning mass. Hill seized the opportunity and carefully explained that Bishop John Ireland, long a friend of his wife and family, had been planting colonies throughout the region. The flourishing scene in De Graff had been but a mote in the prelate's eye a year before. It did the trick, as Donald cheerfully admitted to an election meeting in Winnipeg the following year. "They [Stephen and Angus] were looked upon at home as sober, serious men, but when they returned from the West, they were almost beside themselves, and advised everyone to 'go west'."[34]

Meanwhile, Barnes and the Dutch bondholders had established the prices they wished to achieve for their bonds and were prepared to negotiate. In September, Donald and Stephen, together with Hill and Kittson, hammered out the details of their proposed agreement with Barnes in Montreal. It took a day and a half of intense discussion; on the part of the bondholders' committee, the aim was to increase the price on certain classes of bonds in order to ensure that the owners would agree to the sale; for George Stephen and Associates, as they were beginning to be known, the goal was to retain the price they had originally set, no matter how it was distributed among the various bond issues. In the end, the associates' price was increased by only $1,252 to a total of $4,331,232. It was almost exactly the sum Hill had forecast in the spring.

During those few days, the associates also discussed briefly how they would divide the shares in the company they would soon be forming and agreed that they were all in it together and equally. They also agreed that Stephen should take as many shares as he needed to induce banks to supply the investment capital they would need. Privately, the cousins agreed that a five-way split, directing the additional fifth to the merchant banks, seemed the best basis on which to move forward. In the midst of these negotiations, Donald hosted a dinner party, inviting about a dozen of his Montreal friends to meet Kittson and Hill. It was probably no more than an instance of the expansive social gesture of which he was becoming increasingly fond but it also served as an indication of the economic strength on which he and George Stephen could call within the Montreal financial community should they need to.

Scarcely had the associates wiped their lips than they were off to oversee the next stage of their venture. Donald was back in Winnipeg on September 21 to host the Dufferins on their return from their camping trip. On September 29, Lady Dufferin drove the spike which, at last, inaugurated the construction of the Pembina Branch of the CPR. Winnipeg was delighted, but the town was positively ecstatic when the first railway engine arrived on the eighth of October. Aptly named the *Countess of Dufferin*, she had been mounted on a barge and pushed upstream from Saint Paul by the *Selkirk*. Ironically, this was the sternwheeler Jim Hill had constructed in order to trap the HBC in the bonding dispute at the beginning of the decade; this was the steamer which provoked the creation of the Red River Transportation Company and now she was the agent by which the associates were working for the construction of the railway line to the border. Another steamer pushed a barge carrying a caboose and flatcars.

The little *Countess of Dufferin* was decorated with flags and bunting and festooned with evergreen branches. "The whistles of the boat and locomotive continued shrieking, the mill-whistles joined in the chorus, the bells clanged a young lady, Miss Racine, pulling manfully at the ropes; and the continuous noise and din proclaimed loudly that the iron horse had arrived at last."[35]

While the iron horse enchanted the people of Red River, things began to go wrong for the associates. On the twenty-sixth of October, the *Pioneer Press* in Saint Paul published on its front page a detailed and generally accurate account of the negotiations with the Dutch bondholders. It appeared that Hill believed the deal was all but done, that Stephen would return from London with the necessary capital, and that he could safely let the people of Saint Paul know about the great changes which were in the offing. It was boyish enthusiasm rather than a desire to gratify an inflated sense of self-importance which loosened his tongue. Indeed, to the horror of both Donald and R.B. Angus, he gave the credit to George Stephen, "president of the Bank of Montreal."

When a copy of the story reached Montreal, Angus and Donald consulted each other and both immediately took action. Angus wrote to the bank's New York manager.

> Fearing lest the Bank's name should in any way be mixed up with the St. Paul & Pacific Railway Scheme I resolved to have no part in the negotiation and for that reason also I requested you not to shew the papers which had been left in my hands to

> anybody. J.J. Hill one of the parties connected with the affair at St. Paul has I understand published an account of the negotiation, which he alleges has been completed by Mr. "Stephen, president of the Bank of Montreal." I don't know whether this is correct or not, but should the Bank's name be associated with the matter in New York I wish you would take prompt means of disclaiming any participation on the part of the Bank.[36]

The story contravened all of Donald's business instincts: his inclination to secrecy, his preference for keeping his negotiations verbal until the deal was done, his knowledge that publicity now could scupper his cherished plans. The Bank of Montreal's general manager was privy to the cousins' secrets so that he could advise them, so that he would understand the nature of any risk the bank might undertake if called on to support their investments or invest itself, and so that a clear line could be drawn between George Stephen in his capacity as president of the bank and in his capacity as the leading financial negotiator for the associates. Donald wrote urgently to Kittson, advising him to issue a "personal denial" and adding that the statement should be "scrupulous by avoiding to mention in any way either Mr. Stephen's name or the Bank of Montreal in connection with the affair."[37]

In the meantime, messages from George Stephen in London were disproving the optimism conveyed by the press article. The banks were not willing to risk their capital in a bankrupt railroad on the empty plains. The deal Stephen was offering was £800,000 at five percent, backed by his own personal security and an interest in the profits of the line. Only John Rose was tempted. He knew Stephen and was aware that the Northwest held untapped riches. Whether Morton Rose should invest in the American line, however, was a different matter. His company asked its New York correspondent, Morton Bliss, to investigate and it, in turn, sent the civil war hero, General Edward Winslow, out to have a look. He was distinctly unimpressed, being much more interested in his own railway schemes, and advised against investment.

But George Stephen had been thoroughly entrapped that Sunday morning at De Graff. He was not going to be defeated by the general. As president of the Bank of Montreal, he knew precisely what security a loan would require and he knew how much he and Donald could offer and could make a shrewd guess about what Kittson and Hill might provide by way of collateral. On November 29, while Stephen was still in Europe, the other three associates met in John Kennedy's New York office, the Dutch committee having charged the firm with negotiating on its behalf. Stephen had come up with a new proposal which called for the money to be found in North America, though the details were not to be settled until his return. Carp, breathing a sigh of relief, assumed the money was to come from the New York market and was quite prepared to take Barnes' assurances that payment would be made. Quite how, Barnes did not know, but for the time being, it seemed best not to disturb the equilibrium which had finally been achieved.

On Christmas Eve, while Donald Smith was attending the Bank of Montreal's bi-weekly directors' meeting, George Stephen was disembarking at Halifax and J.J. Hill, together with his lawyer, Ruben Galusha, was climbing into a train to head east, collecting Norman Kittson in Chicago en route. The men were gathering in Montreal to re-assess their position with regard to the bondholders and to agree a new way forward.

Two more Bank of Montreal board meetings and a hogmanay dram interrupted the conversations but on the first of January 1878, Stephen outlined the proposal and the deal he and Donald had negotiated with the bank. The following morning, Hill, Kittson and their lawyer were in New York for a day of discussions with John Kennedy and John Barnes. That evening, Hill and Galusha retired to their hotel rooms to draft a memorandum of agreement on the new purchase offer and, when Donald and his cousin arrived on the Thursday the third, they were briefed for the negotiations which continued that day and all Friday. On Saturday, the new offer was sent to Holland.

The old agreement had assumed that money would be raised to enable the associates to purchase the bonds outright. It was a tidy arrangement which would leave no loose ends. The new proposal was a good deal more complex and placed a much heavier burden on the resources of the associates. To begin, they offered to make a deposit of $125,000 gold as a guarantee of their good faith. The sum would be handed over with no strings attached should they fail to honour the rest of their commitments. The money, deposited with the Bank of Montreal in New York, was in fact a loan from that bank, with personal securities from the associates as collateral. In the short term, it meant that the four men were obliged to earmark some of their other investments to secure the loan and to find the interest payments. None of them would find that exceptionally difficult.

The associates would purchase the Dutch bonds for cash if the owners insisted but offered a much more attractive deal in the form of bonds in a new company. By foreclosing on the various mortgages, the associates would acquire all the assets of the Saint Paul and Pacific which would then be formed into a new company in which the new bonds would be issued. While the foreclosure suits were proceeding and the new company was being formed, the associates would pay the Dutch committee seven percent interest on the full amount of the old bonds. If they were lucky and only had to pay two slices of the biannual interest, the associates would still be required to find about $280,000.

In addition, they pledged themselves to complete the road to the Canadian border and to push on a bit of the Branch Line, taking it from Melrose to Alexandria. Both sections could probably be built with receiver's debentures which Kennedy was prepared to instruct Farley to have authorized by the district court, but the associates would have to be prepared to find about half a million dollars to pay for Litchfield's stock as well as cash for the expenses of court cases, to buy bonds from those Dutchmen who were unprepared to take bonds in the new company, to buy out the Red River Transportation Company which would cease to operate when the line was completed, and to meet other related costs. At least a quarter of a million dollars would be needed for these additional expenses. At an absolute minimum, each man would have to be able to find $300,000 in cash or securities amounting to at least that.

Hill and Kittson were aghast. In Saint Paul terms, they were wealthy men but, even if they sold all their investments, they were unlikely to be able to raise such a sum. Hill was not in the room as Donald and Stephen were about to leave Kennedy's office for the train station, though Kittson and probably Galusha were. Kennedy or perhaps Barnes, made a reference to the financial commitment the men were undertaking and Kittson balked. Galusha seems to have compounded the gaffe. Somehow someone glossed over this breach in the confident front the men were presenting, but the cousins were severely shaken. The older man had very nearly cost them the entire deal by one incautious, if honest, remark.

Donald gave himself a day or two to allow his anger to subside before sending a dismayed letter to Saint Paul.

> The little episode just as Mr. Stephen and I were leaving Mr. Kennedy's office for the train on Saturday last greatly surprised and I must add not a little pained me, as I felt there must be some grave misunderstanding, the cause of which I could in no way account for and I regretted extremely that it should be made to appear to our friends Messrs J.S. Kennedy & Barnes that there existed between ourselves any thing other than the utmost cordiality; when we had one and the same interest to serve.

He added that he knew Stephen had written the day before and that he agreed with what had been said in that letter.

> I am still ignorant of what may have occasioned the misconception and hope to have from you an explanation which I know you will give in the most candid manner. You and I are equally aware that in such an enterprise as that we are desirous of embarking on it is of vital importance that we should have implicit confidence in each other.[38]

To what extent the contretemps really did reflect a misunderstanding is hard to say without knowing what was said in Kennedy's office. It fell to Hill to handle most of the correspondence from Saint Paul and the suggestion that there had been a misconception provided just the key he needed to assuage his Montreal colleagues.

> I am very sorry indeed that our time was so short on Saturday P.M. in New York which prevented our more fully explaining the matter to Mr. Galusha and having the whole thing chased up at the time, and am especially sorry that yourself and Mr. Smith or either or you, should have got the impression that I differed from you in any way, or that I thought for one moment there was any want of mutual confidence, personal cordiality, or good faith, for, I beg to fully assure you that I have no such feeling, and I trust that nothing that has occurred, will be allowed to disturb the absolute confidence and mutual trust necessary in an affair of the kind we are endeavouring to carry out.[39]

His hesitation, he explained, resulted from the knowledge that neither he nor Kittson could meet the full financial obligation the proposal required, though they were quite prepared to risk everything they had.

Before the end of the month, there was more to make Hill and Kittson nervous. Kennedy had suggested his clients be allowed to retain the deposit in order to cover various expenses they had incurred. These came to $280,000 and that was the sum the Dutch expected to receive. In addition, they wanted to be paid for the construction which they had undertaken on the Breckenridge-Barnesville link and wanted seven rather than six percent interest on the new bonds. They also wanted assurances that the extension to the border would be completed for they, just as much as the men in Montreal and Saint Paul, could see that the profit which would repay their original investment was going to come from running a through line.

While the Dutch were determining their response to this latest offer, George Stephen was pressing Prime Minister Mackenzie to come to an arrangement over the Pembina Branch. It appears that Donald and Stephen were not merely trying to secure a lease to operate the railway, they were trying to establish a joint venture agreement for the construction and operation of the line from Winnipeg over the border to Crookston where the Extension Line had come to a halt. "I can make a capital arrangement with the Govt that cannot but add enormously to the future value of the St. Paul & Pacific proper," Stephen wrote enthusiastically to Kennedy. "This will be all the easier done from the fact that the St. Paul way are to have only a 2/5 interest in the concern." The scheme would give the Canadians a much needed line, the Canadian government would recoup its investment by taking three-fifths of the profits from operating it, and the Saint Paul and Pacific would get a cash injection for the construction work. In responding to the Dutch demand for assurances that the Extension Line would be completed, Stephen pointed out that there could be none better than the agreement with the Canadian government.[40]

The deal with the government was typical of the way the cousins worked. Donald, because of his public position, made introductions, smoothed the way, and briefed the politicians and Stephen. Then Stephen stepped in to handle the negotiations. It enabled Donald to maintain his public persona, saying that he had done nothing beyond making an introduction or arranging an appointment, yet their colleagues knew that a word to George Stephen was as good as a word to Donald Smith and vice versa.

Thinking their deal with the bondholders was virtually a *fait accompli*, the associates met in Chicago on January 19 to sign a draft agreement between themselves. Drawn up by Hill, it acknowledged their intention of taking over the railway and issuing $5 million worth of common stock, bonds to the value of $12,000 per mile of finished road and six percent preferred stock up to $3,000 per mile of finished road. By the agreement, all the profits and losses were to be shared equally, with each man taking one-fifth and George Stephen having at his disposal an additional fifth "for the purposes of securing the cooperation of an associate or associates in said enterprise through whom the financial aid necessary to enable us to complete such purchase may be obtained as understood between us in New York at the time of making our said offer of purchase."[41]

The extra fifth was to go to John Kennedy. As one of the best railway bankers in late nineteenth century America, he would inevitably want an interest in the Saint Paul and Pacific. As the agent for the Dutch bondholders, however, he seemed to place himself in an ambiguous position by accepting Stephen's offer.

His duty to his clients was to get the best possible price for their bonds and the highest recompense for their outlay. His one-fifth interest in the company, however, meant that he should be keeping the price as low as possible. Stephen's timing in involving Kennedy was impeccable for the bond prices had already been negotiated with John Barnes and all the other essentials of the agreement were largely in place when the offer was made. The fifth rewarded Kennedy but it also provided him with a good reason to ensure that nothing went amiss between then and the formal acquisition of the company by the associates. It also acknowledged the role he would have to play in arranging finance for future construction. All the parties to this agreement recognized that, should it ever become public, the money to Kennedy would be construed as a bribe and long and expensive court cases could well follow. A few people, including R.B. Angus and the New York lawyer, John Sterling, who were intimately bound up in the associates' financial affairs in later years, were aware of Kennedy's interest but could be counted on to keep it to themselves. In 1908, Stephen acknowledged in a letter to King George's private secretary that Kennedy had received the fifth: he was using the information as an example to support his argument that self-interest would encourage men to support the charitable fund for which he was then raising money. That letter remained buried in the royal files until 1971.[42]

In response to the Dutch letter demanding a deposit of $280,000 and various other payments, Donald and his cousin drafted a new agreement which they sent to Kennedy, noting that it was subject to the approval of Kittson and Hill. The cousins arrived in Saint Paul on the first of February 1878 and by noon the following day had completed their discussions about the new deal and were on the east bound train.

The modified arrangements meant that although $280,000 was to be handed over to the bondholders, the funds in the hands of the trustees, amounting to about $300,000, were to remain as part of the railway property. Payment for the link between Barnesville and Breckenridge was postponed until the purchase of the Saint Paul and Pacific was completed. Interest on the new bonds was accepted at seven percent but it would not be payable in advance. More comforting to Hill and Kittson, however, was the knowledge that "if we should want to sell our contract the Milwaukee road would pay $1,000,000 *cash* for it and let us step out."[43]

The associates would also benefit from the fact that the Saint Paul and Pacific was, after a fashion, a functioning railway; it was Kennedy's suggestion that they use the profits from the Barnesville-Breckenridge link to pay the interest on the bonds outstanding on the Extension Line. As well, there was the comforting knowledge that Kennedy, with his substantial resources, could also be called on to tide the associates through a sticky patch.

Agreement with the majority of the bondholders was finally reached on February 24, but on the eighteenth, the associates were already signing the demand note for the $280,000. Foreclosure was completed on the thirteenth of March and on the twenty-seventh the associates put their signatures to their partnership agreement. It was virtually the same as the January agreement of intent, but now included arrangements to be brought into force in the event of the death of any of the signatories before the reorganization was complete, provision for approval by the signatories before any shares could be sold in advance of completion and arrangements whereby shares in the Red River Transportation Company were taken over by the associates at sixty percent of their par value. RRTC shares owned by others, primarily Winnipeg businessmen, would be taken over by the associates at the price which was paid for them, a procedure which could prevent difficulties when the full extent of the associates' activities became known. When the Extension Line was completed, transport on the Red River would be passé and the best thing Hill, Kittson and the HBC could do with their shares was to convert them into shares in the new company. This procedure also enabled the associates to apply the RRTC's earnings to railway construction. The HBC board was briefed and Stephen set up a separate trust to protect the company's shares.

In March, the Bank of Montreal authorized a loan of $700,000 and in June, Stephen was organizing the signatures on another demand note for $140,000 to cover the first installment of interest. The Bank had developed a policy of rarely, if ever, taking a lien on capital assets; preferring instead to see its loans backed by first class collateral. For a project such as the Saint Paul railway, which was also earning money, it made sense for the borrowers to support loans with bonds and shares in totally separate enterprises. Interest and principal could be repaid from railway earnings, leaving the securities available to underpin another loan when it was needed. For the associates, especially Kittson and Hill, the problem was to find sufficient collateral.

Among Donald's most valuable shares in 1878 were his 223 in the Bank of Montreal which had weathered the depression better than many less conservative institutions. His one hundred Hudson's Bay Company shares were worth more in the japanned box in which he kept them than they were on the open market since the company was not earning enough to pay dividends. The Bank of Toronto, the Montreal Investment Association and the various insurance companies in which he had invested were healthier than the HBC, as were the textile mills and the railway related enterprises such as the Canada Rolling Stock Company. Nevertheless, it would require skillful financial management to ensure that the associates remained solvent over the next eighteen months.

The importance of the railway to the Northwest and the fact that cities like Saint Paul and Winnipeg were small and gossipy inevitably meant that stories about the changes in the Saint Paul and Pacific were rife long before any formal agreement was reached. Jesse Farley was garrulous at the best of times and, as both Hill and the press knew, a little flattery to his inflated self-esteem quickly brought forth information of varying reliability. Before Kennedy was incorporated into the associates' fold, Barnes customarily provided the receiver with summaries of the situation with the bondholders; these, shared, were fairly trustworthy, but Farley's own ignorance — for example, he thought George Stephen had gone to London to seek financing from the Bank of England — meant that he could also be the source of some wildly inaccurate stories. Other information about the Saint Paul and Pacific developments came to light when the Minnesota state legislature dealt with issues which affected the railway. Hill himself contributed to the publicity when he gave an interview to the Saint Paul *Daily Globe* which took a sentimental view of the proceedings, headlining its story "St. Paul To Join Hands with Winnipeg and Also to Clasp Alexandria and Intermediate Points in Fond Embrace."[44]

The Toronto *Globe*, never a friend of Donald Smith or of any manifestation of the CPR, picked up stories from the Saint Paul papers, especially those which suggested that a lease on the Pembina Branch had been agreed between the Canadian government and the capitalists who were now in control of the Saint Paul and Pacific. John Schultz, with whom Donald had repeatedly quarrelled in the House, went on the attack. On the twenty-eighth of March, he observed that "a lease of the Pembina Branch for a term of years was contemplated to parties connected with the notorious Kittson Red River line. To do this was simply to create a monopoly on land instead of the monopoly on water, which now existed, and to throttle the best interests of the Province."[45]

On the fourth of April, parliament was asked to approve a modification to the CPR bill which would confer "powers regarding the leasing and working of the Pembina Branch of Railway." Parliament was not asked to approve a specific agreement for leasing or working the railway but to accept that such an agreement could be made. It was not the principle of the lease which mattered, Schultz thundered, but the terms.[46]

Many people thought the Red River Transportation Company's rates were too high and feared a railway link, run by the same people, would similarly penalize settlers in Manitoba and the North West Territories. It was claimed that the Dutch bonds had been purchased for $520,000 to enable the RRTC men to preserve their monopoly on transport in the Red River Valley.

At this point, silence would have been Donald Smith's best friend but he would not, or could not, adopt such a course, even though he was laying himself open to well justified charges of conflict of interest. Though he was now nearly fifty-eight years old, he still bore the characteristics of the young man who vigorously defended himself in January 1845 after complaints about the detention of the *Otter*, and of the mature HBC trader who fought back when the Governor and Committee spoke slightingly of his request for a priced fur catalogue in 1854; he was still very much the Canadian Commissioner to Red River who insisted that promises such as the repayment of loans and the amnesty of Louis Riel be honoured. Now Schultz was belittling his years of efforts to achieve a rail connection between Manitoba and eastern Canada.

No other American company was prepared to build to the border, Donald assured the House and neither had the bonds been purchased for the "trifling sum" mentioned. "He could not state the exact amount, nor was it necessary that it should be given, but it was a good many millions of dollars." The Red River Transportation Company rates were high, he agreed, but passengers and goods were charged at a through rate, most of which went to the Northern Pacific. He cited passenger rates and freight charges for wheat, noting what portion went to the railway and observing that the greater expense was born by the RRTC which made a proportionately lower charge. He gave altogether too much factual information for a man who was supposedly unconnected with the steamboat line or the railway.[47]

Schultz demanded that Donald reveal the names of the Canadians backing the Saint Paul and Pacific and was quickly supported by Sir John A. Macdonald and his Tory colleague, the unfortunately named Mackenzie Bowell. Bowell cited a paragraph in the *Pioneer Press* which named the associates and pointed out that it had twice been read in the house and had not been denied. The House therefore had every reason to believe it was true.

> It mattered not to the House how much these gentlemen had paid, but, if what was stated in the paragraph was matter of fact, then they had the extraordinary spectacle in that House of the champion of this proposed lease using his power and influence as a very humble and obedient supporter of the Government to secure to himself and his partners in the transaction the advantage of a lease. Either this was true, or it was not.

His voice dripping with irony, Donald replied that he was humbled by Bowell's correction but consoled by the fact that Bowell had numbered him among the millionaires. He reiterated, as Prime Minister Mackenzie had done, that it was an enabling bill "to empower the Government to make some arrangements for the completion of the American line to Pembina" and had nothing to do with specific leases. The opposition had the bit between its teeth but it was concentrating so hard on the notion that Donald's advocacy of the bill was one of self-interest that no one caught the reference to the completion of the *American* line or guessed that it might imply indirect Canadian government support for the construction of a US railway.

Macdonald sprang to his feet, claiming that the member for Selkirk had admitted being a partner in the concern and that the House had a right to know about it.

"I have admitted no such thing," Donald insisted as the debate took on a tone reminiscent of his sparring match with Louis Riel when the Métis leader wanted to know precisely what Donald had the power to approve on behalf of the Canadian government and Donald was equally determined not to tell him he had no power at all.[48]

Macdonald assured the House that he did not impugn Donald's word; his complaint was that he would not give it, to which Donald observed that he found it neither necessary nor desirable to satisfy the curiosity of the former prime minister.

The dinner recess cooled tempers and the fracas died down temporarily. "You will see by the newspaper that the Govt Bill was the cause of a lively debate on Thursday last," Stephen wrote to Hill. "*Between ourselves* Mr. Smith brot it on. Had he held his tongue or been out of the House, there would not have been a word said. It is however no matter, we shall get all we want & the opposition critics will feel '*sold*' when they find out that I wont have a *lease* & that they have been 'barking up the wrong tree'."[49]

It was not long, however, before the Pembina Branch was back in the news. On the eighth of May, the Senate, still dominated by Tories whose antipathy to Donald Smith had not diminished, rejected Mackenzie's enabling bill for the Pembina Branch and on the ninth, Macdonald praised this "constitutional action" which "put a stop to their [the government's] bargain with the hon. member for Selkirk, to make him a rich man, and to pay him for his servile support."[50]

Federal elections were in the offing and, on May 10, the day after Macdonald's speech, parliament was to be prorogued and electioneering would begin in earnest. The carriage bearing the Governor General, Lord Dufferin, in his ceremonial uniform had already clattered up Parliament Hill when Donald Smith rose on a question of privilege. At any moment, Black Rod would be tapping on the door and requesting the presence of the "faithful Commons" in the Senate for the prorogation ceremony, but this did not deter Donald who wanted to get something off his chest. He had been absent the previous day and had not known of Macdonald's remarks until he read them in the newspaper. He denied the Tory leader's assertion that he had admitted being interested in the Saint Paul and Pacific and defended his record in trying to achieve railway communication for the Northwest. What had really upset him, however, was the allegation that the Pembina agreement was to have been a pay off for his support for the Liberal party.

"I would ask the hon. member if I have ever received one sixpence of public money or one place, either for myself or any other person connected with me, and if at this moment there is one single person related to myself who receives one sixpence of the public money." He stressed his independence, asking the Liberals if he had ever sought favours.

"This unwarrantable attack of the right hon. gentleman is but a continuation and a repetition of what he and his friends have been saying of myself both inside and outside this House for some time back. The hon. gentleman who sits on his left, the hon. member for Cumberland [Sir Charles Tupper], has not been slow to use my name, as I find by another public print."

Ontario Conservatives liked to conduct their summer electoral campaigns at political picnics where brass bands blared and long tables offered a feast of cold meats, fancy cakes, seasonal fruit, lemonade and something a little stronger for the gentlemen. A picnic was a popular social gathering with a punchy political ending when cabinet ministers shouted praise for Tory policies and abuse of their Liberal opposite numbers.

Tupper had recently spoken at a picnic at Orangeville where he had been slighting of those who had not supported the Conservatives during the Pacific Scandal debate in 1873. He claimed that Donald had defected because he was "a representative of the Hudson Bay Company and he had been pressing a claim on his right hon. friend for public money; Sir John had been holding back and Mr. Smith came to the conclusion that it would be just as well to jump the fence if there was to be a change of Government."

It was just the sort of slur to rouse Donald's anger. "I give it the most positive denial," he asserted and launched into a detailed account of his interview with the prime minister and the efforts the Tories had made to gain his support in November 1873.

By this time, members from both sides were shouting abuse or supporting the speaker in his calls for order. Black Rod tapped politely, requesting admittance so that he could deliver his invitation to join the upper house but his knocks went unheard as the honourable members bellowed at one another. Undeterred, Donald continued his account of what Macdonald had said that night five years earlier.

"There is not one single word of truth in that statement —not one single word of truth," Macdonald shouted. The hon. gentleman is now stating what is a falsehood."

At that point, Donald struck below the belt. "The hon. gentleman says he did not say so; certainly the spirit within him said it; for the words came out of the gentleman's mouth."

Amid more shouts for order and, according to the memories of many who were there, amid imprecations which *Hansard* thought it best not to record, Donald twisted the knife. "The hon. member for Cumberland the same evening told me that the right hon. gentleman was not capable of knowing what he said."

Now it was Tupper's turn to be incensed. He did not mind being two-faced, but did not like being caught at it. He accused Donald of a cowardly abuse of privilege when he knew that Black Rod was at the door and there was no opportunity to respond to the allegations which he was now making. The speaker pointed out that Donald was defending himself against very serious charges and had a right to do so.

More shouts and interruptions were hurled across the chamber until Tupper was finally able to make it clear that he wanted to contradict Donald's assertion that he had never asked for a favour. Now it was Tupper's turn to play dirty.

"The hon. gentleman begged of me to implore the leader of the Government to make him a member of the Privy Council of Canada. That is what he asked for, and he was refused; and it was the want of that position, and that refusal which, to a large extent, has placed him where he is today." It was true, of course, that Donald had suggested such an appointment might reinforce his position in Red River and, as Tupper had conveniently forgotten, it was also true that he had been in favour of the idea. What was not true was that refusal of the councillorship had had any affect on Donald's decision not to support the prime minister in 1873.

Shouts of "coward" and "order" resounded as the Sergeant at Arms tried to convey to the speaker that he had a message from the governor general. The speaker's response was more of a dumb show, his words being drowned by the unparliamentary language which flew around the House. "That fellow Smith is the biggest liar I ever met!" Macdonald exclaimed. At last, the men rose from their seats, still shouting abuse, and it was only the hurly-burly of the confused crowd and the restraining hands of a few wiser and more cautious men which prevented an eruption of fisticuffs as they made their way to the Senate.[51]

This disgraceful violation of parliamentary procedure is the more remarkable for having at its centre a man who, only thirteen years before, had been afraid to respond to a toast to the Hudson's Bay Company's wintering partners. Not only had he gained the courage which kept him from flinching as the insults flew back and forth, he had actually enjoyed himself! Thirty years later, he declared it to have been one of the most exciting experiences of his life.[52]

Despite the Senate's rejection of the enabling legislation and the storm in the House of Commons, Donald and George Stephen quietly continued their negotiations with Alexander Mackenzie. Their technique was one which Donald had used successfully on several previous occasions; they would obtain an order in council which the government could defend in parliament later if it had to. Reaching agreement was now urgent, however, for there were only a few weeks left before parliament was dissolved; a new government, if the Liberals won the election, would not necessarily pick up the threads of the negotiations while a Conservative government would not even consider doing so.

Negotiations lasted throughout June and it was only on July 25 that Stephen went up to Ottawa to sign the papers on behalf of the associates. He had been prepared to compromise on the original proposal which gave the Saint Paul and Pacific access to the Pembina Branch for ten years but as early as the sixth of

June, Donald was able to persuade the prime minister that "it should remain ten years as formerly as the agreement proposed was a perfectly equitable one." Mackenzie seemed not to be taking much interest, not surprisingly in view of the looming election campaign and the fact that he was obliged to attend the multitude of dinners and official receptions which marked the end of Lord Dufferin's term of office. Nonetheless, Donald stressed that it was important to have a decision without delay.[53]

The agreement gave the associates running rights over the Pembina Branch for ten years and provided them with a grant of $15,000. For their part, the associates contributed running stock and some maintenance and pledged themselves to have the through road finished by the end of 1878, a mammoth task in view of the fact that they had scarcely gained control of the American line.[54]

The land grant for the Extension Line which would meet the Pembina Branch was only payable if the line were completed by the end of the year and the associates were therefore desperate to get the road through to the border as soon as possible. As the line was in receivership, Farley was obliged to request the court's permission to extend it and to issue receiver's debentures by way of payment. Unfortunately, the judge, John Dillon, was in bad odour for having favoured previous owners of the Saint Paul and Pacific who had lined their pockets at the expense of the company and he was now inclined to be very stringent in what he would allow. Hill's plan was that Farley would ask the associates to complete the construction and that the Branch Line, which they were purchasing as part of the deal with the Dutch bondholders, would then lease the Extension Line and operate it. Certainly, the associates would not quibble at being paid in receiver's debentures for their construction costs and, by being in control of the route, they could start to earn the money they would need in order to acquire the other parts of the line and meet the mounting interest payments.

Farley was too foolish to be conniving. Hill carefully gave Judge Dillon enough information to prompt him to suggest Farley should give the associates the contract for construction of the Extension Line, at which point the old man piped up that he could build the extension better and more cheaply. There was little to do but accept the verdict. Where debentures were accepted they had to be backed by yet more personal guarantees from the associates but where cash was needed, Kennedy stepped in; his word was sufficient guarantee for any loan that might ever be needed on the Extension Line. Certainly Kennedy's good name would be required, for Farley's intervention had prompted the judge to decree that the court would only authorize payment of the debentures when the line was completed and full receipts were presented.

The fact that the associates now controlled the Extension Line and had instructed Farley to build to the border as fast as he possibly could did not perturb the receiver in the least. He conceived that he was still in charge and would plod along at his usual pace, taking time off to recuperate at his Iowa home whenever the summer heat or the pressure of work became too much for him. All the associates were worried, but Hill, being closest to the problem, was most concerned. Finally, he could stand it no longer and forced Farley to subcontract to David Robbins who had been Hill's first choice to do the work.

Farley, of course, complained, saying that the price had escalated as a consequence and excusing his own insufficiently detailed accounts on the grounds that

Robbins had caused confusion. "The only change Mr. Robbins made," Hill explained, "was to reduce the force and double the work but in order to do this he had to discharge one of Mr. Farley's favorites who had full charge north of Crookston and who spent half his time in Crookston with a strumpet, and took her over the road with him on the Engine, or at times would take the engine off the work in the middle of the afternoon to run down to Crookston in order that he could keep some of the other employees out of his preserve."[55]

Farley and the Crookston floozie were not the only problems the associates faced that summer and autumn. The Red River was the lowest it had been in living memory and many of the steamboats were unable to transport the rails and other material needed for the Canadian line. When finally it rained, work had to stop on the Extension Line because the tracks were under water.

Meanwhile, there was precious little evidence that the Canadians had any intention of finishing the line to the border by the end of the year. The contractors claimed they were losing money and were not prepared to meet the extra costs of working in bad weather. For Hill and Donald Smith, that was no excuse. Hill arranged for another contractor, a man in whom he had some faith, to buy out one of the Canadians for $15,000 and, as soon as the Extension Line was completed on November 10, he sent tracking cars and flats to carry rails for the Canadian work. While Hill pushed from his end, Donald placated the customs officials, encouraged the workers and did his best to get the troublesome contractor out of the way. When the road was finally completed early in December, both men had to use every ounce of charm they possessed to convince the Canadian government inspector to approve the line, despite his long list of work which had yet to be done.

At last, on December 3, twenty Manitoba ladies lifted the last rail into place and the through line from Saint Paul to St. Boniface finally existed. It would take a good many more arguments and further investment before a bridge was constructed to enable the train to cross the river to Winnipeg. But that problem lay in the future and thoughts of it did not mar the pleasure of the Red River settlers who excitedly boarded the train for the inaugural trip. The *Manitoba Daily Free Press* engaged in some of its most flowery prose to celebrate the occasion.

> On again, the iron horse sped, keeping at the pace of twenty-five miles an hour, the ride, notwithstanding the cars were not Pullmans, and the track unballasted, not being an unpleasant one, the road-bed being solid, the jolting of the cars very slight, and not rough — like that experienced even in first class Grand Trunk passenger coaches a few years ago. On past Arnaud the snorting monster carried us, and as we whirled along through the chequered space to the left was seen the wigwam of an Indian and the thought irresistibly pressed itself upon one that this occasion, so replete with high expectation for us, was simply another seal set upon his hopeless life, another mark of the red man's disappearance before the white.[56]

The *Free Press*, ever inclined to let the air out of its own bombast, discovered that the occupant of the wigwam was in fact one of the construction workers who had been employed to haul wood for the cross ties.

The thrill of having rail access to the outside world momentarily blinded travellers to some of their discomforts. "There were no palatial sleepers or high-toned parlor cars in those days on the road, and the primitive train consisted of several not very comfortable flat cars and a box car in which were some rude benches, a lot of straw carpeting, and a small wood-burning heater," George Ham recollected. The Saint Paul and Pacific supplied a first class passenger carriage for the inaugural journey and, when teething troubles with the Pembina Branch were over, also provided one for the regular trips.[57]

There were one or two other inconveniences in the early days of the Pembina Branch. A roundhouse had yet to be built at St. Boniface, so trains went forward to Winnipeg but had to travel in reverse for the return journey. Sandford Fleming was just beginning to develop his concept of universal time and until it was accepted as the now familiar set of time zones, cities and villages throughout the world used their own time, often determined by a church clock or a time piece in a jeweller's window. The through line, managed by the Saint Paul and Pacific, ran on Saint Paul time which was twenty minutes ahead of time in St. Boniface. When station managers in Manitoba failed to publish an adjusted timetable, they found themselves faced with irate would-be passengers who were on time by their watches but twenty minutes late by the engineer's.

Completing the Extension Line was a great relief because, after yet more difficulty with Judge Dillon, the associates were finally able to claim $800,000 in receiver's debentures. More should have been available, but Farley had failed to keep the receipts. In addition, there were earnings to the border; north of the forty-ninth parallel the situation was a good deal more confused.

In helping his preferred contractor, H.B. Willis, buy out one of the Canadian contractors, Hill had failed to get the change approved by the Canadian government. The original Canadian contracting partnership then insisted on its right to be paid and, further, on its right to run the line for a year, despite Mackenzie's agreement with the Saint Paul and Pacific to the contrary.

The associates' problems in Canada grew worse when Mackenzie and his Liberal Party lost the autumn 1878 election and a new government was formed by Sir John A. Macdonald. Though Donald retained his seat by a narrow majority, the furore in the final hours of the last parliament ensured that the dying embers of the 1873 Pacific Scandal had been fanned into a bright new fire to which the fuel of the Saint Paul and Pacific agreement had been added. Donald Smith was not the most popular man in Ottawa, least of all with the Conservative party.

In February 1879, while Donald was in London negotiating with the Governor and Committee on behalf of the Fur Trade Party, George Stephen went to Ottawa to assess the new situation and try to settle the arguments over the contractors on the Pembina Branch. He reached an arrangement with the government whereby the Saint Paul and Pacific would operate the line, using its own trains and giving the government twenty-five percent of the gross earnings from local business. The tariff for traffic between the border and Selkirk would be set by the Canadian government which would also be responsible for maintaining the road bed and other Pembina Branch property, while the Saint Paul and Pacific would be responsible for the cars and stations. No trackage would be paid by the Saint Paul and Pacific for local business. Sandford Fleming, chief engineer of the CPR, was proving to be on the side of his fellow Scots and agreed to hand over the line as soon as possible.[58]

No sooner had the ink dried on Stephen's letter than he discovered that Jesse Farley, together with Joseph Upper, the Canadian contractor, had been nobbling Charles Tupper, the new minister of railways and canals. Less than a month after that news, a source in Ottawa cabled Stephen to say that Tupper had done a deal with Upper, John Schultz and some others to run the line for five years after the necessary ballasting and other work had been completed. Stephen was incensed by "this attempt at swindling" and declared that "the whole thing looks to me just now as if Tupper and Schultz had put their heads together to devise a plot for injuring Donald Smith and perhaps feathering their own and their friends [sic] nests." Donald was on his way to Ottawa with advice from his cousin to take no notice of the conniving and to remember that the Saint Paul and Pacific could take care of itself.[59]

The next day, Stephen exploded that it was "now clear that the two doctors are trying to bleed us. Tupper is about as big a rascal as Schultz & you know the extent of his infamy." The plan, Stephen thought, was to "put us to all the trouble and expense they can to punish D.A."[60]

Any attempt to deprive the associates of the rights to the Pembina Branch could be offset by the use of the Red River Transportation Company for yet another season, a fact which prompted Schultz and Tupper to insist that the collector of customs apply the existing regulations which required goods carried in Canadian waters to be conveyed by Canadian vessels. Less than a decade after the same provision had been used by Jim Hill against Donald Smith and the Hudson's Bay Company, it was now being used by the Canadian government against them. The associates had not forgotten earlier lessons and promptly transferred two of the steamers to Canadian ownership.

Schultz had been encouraged in his moves against the Saint Paul and Pacific by disgruntled voices in the Northern Pacific. That railway had been resuscitated and, in the summer and autumn of 1878, had been ready to quarrel with the associates' road. The Northern Pacific's intended competition took the form of a line of rail west of the Red River going north from Saint Paul to the border where Schultz intended to meet it with his own Manitoba South Western Colonization Railway. It took weeks of Hill's belligerent arguments and more weeks of pacifying negotiations by Stephen before a truce was finally reached and, for the moment at least, it was agreed that the Saint Paul and Pacific was a north-south line and the Northern Pacific an east-west one. With that principle established, the NP also agreed to sell its shares in the Saint Paul and Pacific to the associates, though a series of foreclosures would have to be gone through first.

The agreement with the Dutch committee, the frantic construction and the negotiations with Judge Dillon were not all that occupied the associates in 1878. Even before the men had settled with Carp and his friends, it became apparent that they might also need to acquire a majority of the bonds held in other hands. This would be especially necessary if the wily and uncooperative Darwin Litchfield refused to sell his shares in the First Division — and all the evidence suggested he would be troublesome.

Many of the bonds were traded, primarily in Holland, and because they could be exchanged for the railway's land grant, a syndicate had been established in

Saint Paul to purchase those bonds in Europe and re-sell them in the United States at a comfortable profit. The leader of the syndicate was Henry Upham of the City Bank of Saint Paul. Upham had long been one of Hill's friends and they were neighbours besides.

In January 1878, Hill decided it was time to call in a favour from Upham. The deal with the Dutch committee had included a clause allowing the bonds to be withdrawn from the Amsterdam exchange. Hill offered Upham the opportunity to sell the associates' bonds in Saint Paul for less than the syndicate had been charging while retaining an appropriate return for Upham. That, in turn, broke up the syndicate and drove down the prices on the Amsterdam exchange, enabling the associates to purchase bonds there at a fraction of their earlier price. The Saint Paul sales also allowed the partners to earn cash with which to offset some of their expenses while the conversion of the bonds to land had the effect of proportionately increasing the associates' majority holding in the remaining paper. In addition, the sales placed settlers on the land to raise the crops on which the railway would soon be dependent.

Even if the deal with the committee in Amsterdam and the sale of the independent bonds had been sufficient to enable the associates to control the company, it was increasingly apparent that they also had to get Litchfield out of the way. Hill had begun negotiations with him in 1877 but Litchfield was not to be swayed from his position that he had agreed to the trusteeship of the First Division and that it was still in effect. The only alternative was that he might be an equal partner with the associates. The Red River would freeze in August before Donald, Hill or Stephen would consent to ally themselves with a man they considered to be irrevocably corrupt. A year later, Litchfield indicated he could be bought out: his price would be a million dollars. The Red River would flood in January before the associates would agree to that price.

When the associates signed a protocol of agreement with the Northern Pacific in November 1878, its president, Frederick Billings, revealed that Litchfield had offered to sell his First Division stock to the company. The protocol precluded the NP taking up this offer, even had it been able to afford it, but Billings did offer his services as a negotiator on behalf of the Saint Paul and Pacific. Litchfield had clearly made up his mind to sell and was now playing hard to get. His coyness would have turned to genuine reluctance had he seen the earnings figures from the First Division and grasped what his stocks and bonds were soon to be worth. Hill's evidence of the rapid increase in the company's earnings gave an urgency to the associates' negotiations which they needed to complete before the interest on Litchfield's bonds was due.

George Stephen took over the negotiations, discussing each move in his regular meetings with Donald Smith. On Stephen's instructions, Billings carefully took the associates up from their initial offer of $200,000 and brought Litchfield down from his million dollar demand. Copyists were kept busy sending the lengthy correspondence to Saint Paul and New York and Stephen, whose public persona pretended to be unconcerned by Litchfield's procrastination, let off steam in his correspondence and conversation. "Here is a fresh instalment of the Litchfield-Billings correspondence which I hope you will be able to read without losing all the equanimity and calmness derived from your Thanksgiving services," he wrote to Kennedy. "Litchfield is a wary old bird full of suspicion."[61]

At the beginning of January 1879, Stephen and Donald, went to New York for the final negotiations with "the old fox" as Stephen tended to call him. They met him at noon on the tenth and when they had dinner with Kennedy that night, it seems likely that they reported that they had reached agreement at $500,000. Though the negotiations through Billings had broken down, they had known for a month that Litchfield would settle at this price and in January had merely been required to let him force them up from $400,000. While Donald sailed to England for the Fur Trade Party negotiations, his cousin settled the details and then sent Hill a cable to say that the negotiations had failed.

The associates had not yet sorted out a telegraphic code for their confidential communications and Stephen assumed that Farley and others would quickly hear the news from the telegraph office. At the end of the month, Kennedy sent a similarly discouraging letter to Farley, observing that "Mr. Litchfield has intimated ever since the trustees took possession, from time to time, that he would like to settle; but, whenever he was seen on the subject, his demands were so unreasonable, and he was so impracticable, that nothing could be done with him, and I do not believe now that any settlement can be made with him except through the courts."[62]

Hill was dejected by the news from New York but his spirits revived when he received George Stephen's letter, written when he had returned to Montreal, and learned the truth.

> We shall have to meet in New York the week after next to execute the agreet. We have to pay Litchfield $100,000 down on his turning the company over to us. Once we get the reins the Trustees will leave the road to us & old Farley will have to confine his duties to his Receiver's roads & these he will very soon be relieved of.
>
> Now not a word about a settlement must be said, & no one in St. Paul must know about it, except of course Mr. Kittson, not even the Lawyers. The old rascal's idea is to bring Bigelow & Becker [the one a lawyer; the other a trustee who favoured handing the Saint Paul and Pacific over to the Northern Pacific] to N.Y. to *make* an agreet. They must not know or have an idea that we have made one already or all the fat would be in the fire. Old L. wants to cheat both of them, & it is not our policy to interfere. You better be quietly getting ready for a trip to N.Y. without saying a word to anyone that you have such a thing in view.[63]

Donald was back in New York on January 30 where his cousin met him with the latest details. Hill and Galusha joined them there on the third of February when the men sat through the charade of negotiations with Bigelow and Becker before returning to Litchfield's office in the evening for the formal resignation of the Litchfield board and the election of the associates' board to replace them. John Barnes, representing the trustees, was the new president and it was his company's cheque which completed the deal.

On the seventh of May, a little group of men dodged the mud puddles in the streets of Saint Paul. For several days, spring thunderstorms had been crashing down on the prairies, lighting up the nighttime skies and leaving dirty, wet souvenirs to inconvenience morning walkers. A passing pedestrian, should he have looked up from his own precarious course, might have recognized Jim Hill and the Saint Paul attorney, George Otis, in the group but the other two were strangers and, to judge by their dress, city folk from down east. In fact they were George Stephen and John Barnes and they were making their way to the court house in front of which Sheriff King was to sell the bit of the Saint Paul and Pacific which went up to St. Cloud. As the *Pioneer Press* explained to its readers, the sale was "ostensibly to satisfy the claim of the plaintiffs and others, but really to transfer the route to the bondholders under the amicable arrangements made between the contestants." The price, $200,000, had already been agreed and Barnes handed over a certified cheque made out on his company's account. A week later, Barnes filed a notice naming the purchasers of the Branch Line as Donald Smith, George Stephen, J.J. Hill, Norman Kittson and John Barnes. As the law required, he also announced that a reorganization meeting would be held on May 23.

On the evening of May 16, Donald Smith's carriage rattled its way over the cobbled streets of Montreal to the Grand Trunk station. The horses had been there so often in the past year that they could probably have found their way unaided and their master had boarded the train for Chicago and Saint Paul so frequently that the stewards knew his wishes without having to ask. This time, he was going to Saint Paul to witness the birth of a dream. Reorganization of the railway meant a new name and, for Donald, that meant that the word Manitoba had to feature in the forthcoming christening. His friends agreed and so it was that in the offices of Bigelow, Flandreau and Clark, Solicitors, the Saint Paul and Pacific became the Saint Paul, Minneapolis and Manitoba Railway. George Stephen was the new president and there were to be two managers, for Jim Hill was joined by R.B. Angus who had been persuaded to leave the Bank of Montreal for the riskier pleasures of the railway business. As the cousins' confidant in the Saint Paul takeover, Angus already knew much about the company's financial dealings and he had handled the loans and the management of the bond acquisitions with great delicacy, taking care to protect both the bank and his directors.

The new railway directors soon discovered that Carabosse, the wicked fairy who was not invited to Princess Aurora's christening, had been reincarnated in the person of Jesse Farley. He complained that he should have been made a director and alleged that he had been promised a share in the company. If Farley had, as he was to claim, misrepresented the value of the company in order to persuade the Dutch bondholders to sell, he was in dereliction of his duty as the agent of the trustees and as a receiver. He was quite prepared to sully what was left of his reputation in order to fight for a stake in the company and initiated a court case which dragged on for years; he died before the last round went against him.

Stephen had intended to recommend offering Farley a "bonification," one of Johan Carp's linguistic inventions which had seized the associates' imagination. Farley cannot be said to have deserved it; his refusal to accept instructions from his new principals, his secret collaborations with opposing railway lines and his unauthorized deal with the contractors on the Pembina Branch made that plain, but it was the complaints leading to the court case which quickly froze Farley out of any consideration at all.

Having taken Lord Elphinstone, a Scottish peer who was keen on the Northwest and investing in its future, to Manitoba and out onto the plains, Donald returned to Montreal at the end of May. Scarcely had his shirts been laundered before he set out for Saint Paul again. Kennedy was there as well for a series of meetings to sort out the shares and the bonded debt of the new company.

At the reorganization meeting, Donald proposed that the capital be $15 million, each share being worth $100. He also proposed that two million be issued immediately. The four associates, together with their lawyers, Bigelow and Galusha, and John Barnes, each took five shares while the remainder were held in trust by Barnes who required Donald's signature to release them. They were to be used to underwrite the Bank of Montreal loans and other obligations, easing the burden on the securities which the associates had been providing.

In June, the directors' first step was to authorize the seven percent bonds which were to pay the Dutch committee for their old bonds. The issue was to total $8 million and in 1879, they actually issued $6,780,000, the majority of which were sent to Holland. Most of the remainder were sold through Kennedy's merchant bank to meet a variety of other costs, most notably the Bank of Montreal loans and the receiver's debentures which had paid for the completion of the Extension Line. As early as August 1879, when gossip about the Bank of Montreal loans began to surface, Angus was able to write "that the amount advanced to Stephen and his associates towards the western enterprise was never in my opinion excessive, was always secured, was made remunerative to the Bank and was, every dollar of it, repaid."[64]

At the June meeting the directors also issued the rest of the shares, assigning 125,500 to Barnes in trust, a mechanism which allowed them to put something aside for themselves which they would look at again when they had a clearer idea of the financial picture. They still had to bring foreclosure suits to enable them to control other parts of the company and countless other costs would nibble away at their purses.

The men met again at the end of September when they agreed to a second mortgage which would total $8 million in six percent bonds. The original deal with the Dutch had promised a bonus in preferred stock for those who accepted bonds in the new company rather than insisting on cash. As the directors subsequently decided against issuing preferred stock, Kennedy suggested they offer the second mortgage bonds to the Dutch instead. This was good news in Amsterdam where the old investors were beginning to realize that they were finally on to a good thing. All the remaining second mortgage bonds were bought by the associates who immediately lent nearly $3 million in bonds back to the company to pay for further construction.

At both the June and the September meetings, the directors attempted to settle their affairs with the Hudson's Bay Company by replacing its eight hundred shares in the Red River Transportation Company with five hundred in the new railway as had initially been agreed. An alternative of $24,000 plus interest was offered on condition that a reply be received by the end of October. Grahame was distinctly nervous about a business he scarcely understood and did not know how to advise the Governor and Committee,

> but judging from common report I fear that, in consequence of the larger amount of Mortgage Bonds that have been floated than was at first contemplated, and which are a first charge on the profits, there will be very little prospect of dividends for some time, while the completion of the Canada Pacific Railway to Thunder Bay which will likely be attained in two or three years will to a great extent take away business from the St. Paul Road. I can only say that in the conversation I had with Mr. Stephen about it he seemed to think the offer of $24,000 & Interest was a very liberal one and the impression left on my mind was that he thought it had better be accepted.

Donald supported Stephen's argument, saying that "he considered $50,000 Stock fully worth $24,000 Cash and in fact if it were his he would not sell it at that price." To this, Grahame timidly observed, "It may however be deemed prudent to take the $24,000 Cash so as to terminate a transaction which has always been very peculiar."[65]

While the HBC dithered, Angus and others pressed Grahame to accept the stock. By November, Donald had to step in to take the pressure off his erstwhile colleague, but Grahame's nervousness only slightly abated.

> In the meantime Mr. Donald A. Smith has undertaken to have all action suspended until Mr. Stephen goes to London, which by present appearances may not be before the end of the year. I shall feel greatly relieved to have this transaction finally wound up being very anxious that the history of the Steamboats from the beginning should not transpire as involving interests and questions of international law that might end in serious complications. The dread of anything of the kind is the reason for Mr. Kittson always being so reticent on the subject & constantly anxious.[66]

The dithering played into the HBC's hands for when the company sold its five hundred shares in May 1880, it grossed a tidy $40,000.

Hill had rejected Stephen's suggestion that they should sell all the remaining stock on the open market, arguing that they should retain it at least until there were some earnings to demonstrate its true worth. On November 22, each associate received a certificate for 29,995 shares, with double that number going to Stephen who held Kennedy's portion in trust for him. As a bonus to Angus for all his support, each man made him a gift of 1,100 shares, Stephen, as usual, contributing double.

In May 1880, with the last of the foreclosure sales out of the way, Kennedy totted up the earnings and expenditure in the associates' account and discovered a surplus of $278,044.18. Donald was not short of uses for his portion. Kittson sold his shares in 1881 and the remaining associates, with Kennedy, formed a syndicate to buy his entire allocation at $60 a share.

In the summer of 1880, Angus decided it was time to sort out the associates' accounts and tie up all the loose ends. As a meticulous banker who was at least as careful with other people's money as he was with his own, he was astonished at what he found — or rather at what he did not find. For help, he wrote to John Kennedy Tod who had joined his uncle's bank, replacing John Barnes who left after a difference of opinion with the senior partner.

> When I first essayed to check the account of George Stephen's Associates I found no books had been kept by them and few useful data preserved. The matter was therefore remitted to Mr. Hill who expected to be able to supply from memory and from documents to which he had access all that was needed for an audit of the transactions. He has only lately been able to render assistance and together we have succeeded pretty well, but the business having been conducted rather unfortunately in Montreal we shall have to trouble you again for some additional details and explanations.[67]

In one case, there was an unexplained disparity of about $161,000. There was no suggestion of dishonesty or deceit. The men had trusted each other so completely that they had undertaken the entire negotiation without feeling the need of regular and detailed accounting. That trust had allowed them to put at risk all they owned; they had gambled the investments on which their wives and families depended without asking for receipts and without doubting that each of the associates was equally committed — and it was a commitment in which each partner was obliged to make good the failure of any or all of the others. It was an enormous investment, but one which was about to ride high on the wave of prosperity which was returning to the United States. For Donald Smith, it was the foundation of an immense fortune.

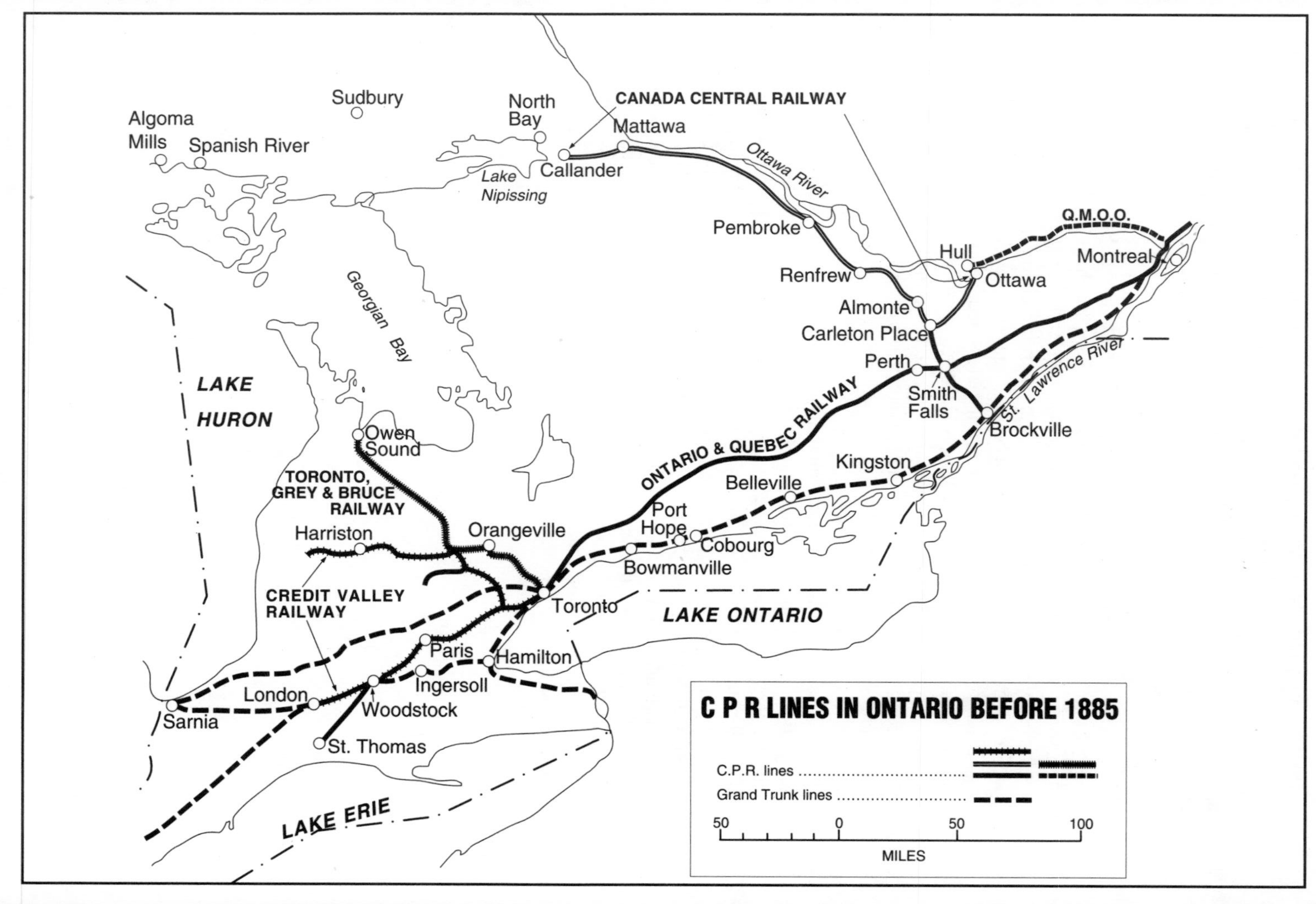
C P R LINES IN ONTARIO BEFORE 1885
C.P.R. lines
Grand Trunk lines
50
0
50
100
MILES
CANADA CENTRAL RAILWAY
Q.M.O.O.
ONTARIO & QUEBEC RAILWAY
TORONTO, GREY & BRUCE RAILWAY
CREDIT VALLEY RAILWAY
Algoma Mills
Spanish River
Sudbury
North Bay
Callander
Mattawa
Lake Nipissing
Ottawa River
Pembroke
Renfrew
Almonte
Carleton Place
Hull
Ottawa
Montreal
Perth
Smith Falls
Brockville
St. Lawrence River
Kingston
Belleville
Port Hope
Cobourg
Bowmanville
Toronto
Orangeville
Owen Sound
Harriston
Georgian Bay
LAKE HURON
LAKE ONTARIO
LAKE ERIE
Hamilton
Paris
Ingersoll
Woodstock
London
Sarnia
St. Thomas

CHAPTER TWELVE

THE CANADIAN PACIFIC RAILWAY 1880–1885

What Smith and I have done and are doing individually, is simply absurd on any kind of business grounds. I venture to say that there is not a business man in all Canada, knowing the facts, but would say we were a couple of fools for our pains.

George Stephen [1]

The acrimonious quarrel in the House of Commons in May 1878 left Sir John A. Macdonald feeling so bitter that he was determined to be rid of Donald Smith. He cast around for the most powerful Tory he could find to oppose him in the Selkirk electoral contest and lit upon Alexander Morris, the erstwhile lieutenant governor of Manitoba. It was scarcely a welcome opportunity for Morris who could hardly be expected to grace a soap box, having so recently stepped down from the formality of his vice-regal throne, and his position was not helped by the fact that Winnipeg lacked a strong newspaper with Tory sympathies. He could only console himself with the fact that Donald was not a brawler either and would share his wish to preserve as much decorum as possible when they met on the electioneering platform.

Although the two men did not get along particularly well, there were no real bones of contention between them and they had little to bicker about when addressing the voters. Morris thought Donald had not been sufficiently vigorous in pushing for a southern route, through Winnipeg, for the CPR and, not knowing of Donald's intended resignation as Land Commissioner, suggested he might not be able to serve both the Hudson's Bay Company and the people of Manitoba.

Donald's people complained that Morris imported a private secretary from Ottawa when he was lieutenant governor because he claimed he could not trust anyone in Manitoba and there were some arguments about land. On this latter point, Donald was by far the stronger, having at his fingertips all the points at issue, knowing precisely who owned which piece of disputed land and what steps were being taken to resolve the disagreements. He had a phenomenal memory for figures and details and had read most of the relevant information.

Voting in Manitoba was scheduled for September 26 but in the older provinces, it took place on the seventeenth. To Donald's surprise and Morris' delight, Mackenzie's government was decisively overturned in the east. It had been blamed for the depression and was about to see the Conservatives reap the benefits of the turn around in the economic climate. Ironically, Macdonald himself was defeated and both Liberal and Conservative candidates in the Manitoba riding of Marquette stood aside to allow him to be returned by acclamation there. The same honour was accorded him in Victoria and he chose to sit for the latter, knowing that a compliment to British Columbia would scarcely be amiss at a time when the province was still without its promised railway.

In his election speech on the twenty-fourth, Donald admitted that "it was true that a person entirely in accord with the Government had a readier access to the departments; but at the same time it was indisputable that a man, thoroughly independent, looking to, and working for the interests of his constituents, would be heard, and have influence no matter what Government was in power."[2]

The decisive factor, however, was that a good many people in Manitoba, having experienced Morris as lieutenant governor, did not like him and did not want him as their representative. This was especially true in the rural parishes where his inside knowledge of intended Métis reserves had enabled him to purchase some better plots for himself and forced the Métis to accept inferior land. There was also a feeling that he might have done more to try to secure an amnesty for Riel and Lépine. In Winnipeg itself, where the effects of the depression had been more widely felt, commercial interests tipped the balance towards Morris.[3]

This was the first dominion election in which ballots were used, and the *Free Press* took great care to instruct its readers in how to place their crosses, using the Selkirk ballot as an example, with the cross very firmly marked by Donald Smith's name. Voting was peaceful, although, despite regulations prohibiting the sale of alcohol, one voter was so drunk that he posted his ballot in the YMCA collecting box.[4]

When the ballots were counted, they revealed seventy-one votes for Morris in Winnipeg, compared to only thirty-one for Donald. But Donald won a majority in all but two of the outlying parishes, scoring particularly well in St. James, which included Silver Heights, and in the Métis parish of St. Charles. The final result gave him a slim overall majority of ten. His men hired the band which exultant Morris supporters had engaged after the Winnipeg count, and a party quickly ensued.

Morris requested a recount and readdition and Donald riposted with a request for a recount, claiming he was entitled to two more votes in St. Charles. Donald's case was heard before Judge Louis Bétournay on October 1 when he lost one ballot, reducing his majority to nine. Two days later, Morris appeared before Judge McKeagney who found himself unable to conduct a recount because the returning officer, Sheriff Colin Inkster, a former Hudson's Bay Company officer, had parcelled up the ballots after the first recount and sent them off to Ottawa as the law required.

On November 6, a protest was entered, accusing Donald of "bribery, treating, undue influence, hiring and promising to pay and paying for horses, carriages, etc. to convey voters to and from the poll" and also "corrupt practices." Judge Bétournay also heard this case, a fact which incensed many Winnipeg voters who knew that he was indebted to Donald Smith. When the preliminary round of the protest was heard in February 1879, Nicholas Flood Davin, the colourful Irish writer and future MP, was persuaded to write the Prime Minister, outlining the "facts" and saying that "it was a flagrant indecency that a Judge having such pecuniary relations with Donald A. Smith should preside over an inquiry which might issue in Mr. Smith's losing his seat for Selkirk & even in his disqualification for a seat in parliament during a number of years."[5]

Though the newspapers published the information, claiming the mortgage was for $10,000 or $15,000, Macdonald made no response to the allegations until May when Hector Cameron, an MP from Ontario, raised the matter in the House. Donald was absent, but on the seventh of May, rose on a question of privilege. The mortgage was for $4,000, he said, and had not come from him but from his agent "who had acted in this case, as with every other with which he had been connected in Manitoba, simply as his agent to invest moneys, and in most cases without his personal knowledge. In many cases he did not know the parties dealt with or the sums handled. The particular transaction spoken of in this instance took place in August 1874, when his agent, Mr. Blanchard, a barrister of Winnipeg, was put in charge of his (Mr. Smith's) personal affairs in Manitoba, and who had invested for him to a considerable extent, on his belief that the security given was ample." In fact the judge's property was worth $8,000 or $10,000 and Donald spoke, he said, because he wanted the judge to be free from suspicion.[6]

Despite the publication of this information, Bétournay had not felt himself disqualified to hear the corrupt practices case which turned on a man named Murray who wanted to bribe voters and who was refused the money with which to do so. There was also a mortgage to John Grant which, though demonstrably separate, became entangled in the election campaign and there was a carriage, hired and paid for by Elias Conklin who also had a mortgage with Donald Smith, though that did not come out in court. The evidence was weak and, for the most part, easily controverted. Morris himself manipulated events from a distance, keeping Macdonald briefed. A lawyer by training, Morris drew attention to the fact that the best chance of gaining their objective was in reference to the hire of the carriage but, as Bétournay pointed out, that disqualified Conklin from voting and made him eligible for a fine, but it did not void the election.[7]

With the revelation of the judge's debt to Donald Smith, however, the Tories had little difficulty in appealing and in May 1880, the case went before the Supreme Court in Ottawa. All the charges were thrown out save that of Conklin's hiring a team to bring electors to the polls, but that was sufficient to overturn Bétournay's verdict. A bye-election was called for September.

Donald promptly announced that he had no intention of standing. He had other commitments that summer, including being in London for the HBC General Court, and could not devote himself to an election campaign. Selkirk then found itself in the curious position of having no apparent candidate of any political stripe. Finally, Donald yielded to persuasion and agreed to stand. It appeared for a time that he would be unopposed but Thomas Scott, a former Winnipeg mayor, put himself forward for the Tories.

In his election speeches, Donald concentrated on land policy and the encouragement of immigration. He took a much broader view than he had in previous elections and appeared to be less interested in Manitoba's more immediate concerns. The land regulations were "obnoxious" he said. Too much was charged for government land and most of it was up to a hundred and fifty miles away from Winnipeg "and you know how difficult it is for an emigrant to get to these places. They feel it enough to get to the end of their railway journey, but then their great difficulties are just beginning. In spring the roads are all but impassable." When they found there was no railway communication, between a quarter and a third of them went to Dakota where tracks had been laid, he said, carefully adding that the Saint Paul, Minneapolis and Manitoba Railway did not go to Dakota.

The government excused its land prices, saying the money was needed to finance the CPR, but the railway was not being built. The Saint Paul road had constructed two hundred miles in the previous year; why, he asked, could the dominion government not do the same?

> There is I believe, a great deal of ignorance among our public men, and, as in every Government, there is also a great deal of influence, of one kind and another, which must be attended to; and under all the circumstances I really do think it will be a happy deliverance for the country when by a syndicate or in any other satisfactory way the Government are enabled to disburthen themselves of the work of railway construction and railway running as well. But the most stringent conditions should be made with any company permitted to take up this great work — one of which conditions should be that the land should be open to settlement at the very lowest prices — lower even than the Government land could be got. The great object should be to get settlers on the land.[8]

The people who build the road, he argued, should expect to make their profit from running it, not from selling the land.

The broad pattern of voting proved to be much the same as it had been in the 1878 election, with the difference that Donald slipped badly in Winnipeg north and in his own parish of St. James. He also made a poorer showing in St. Boniface where he had only scraped through in the past. The upshot was a resounding defeat, with Thomas Scott gaining a majority of one hundred and twenty-seven.[9]

The attempt by Macdonald and Charles Tupper to unseat Donald Smith had finally been successful but neither man realized how little the defeat meant to Donald. He did not share their passion for politics and had not wanted to stand in the bye-election. Had he won, he would probably have resigned before the end of his term because the Canadian Pacific Railway legislation which Macdonald and Tupper had pushed through parliament in 1874 specifically forbade shareholders from being members of parliament and their victory in ousting Donald from his parliamentary place now left him free to join the CPR syndicate to which he had alluded in his campaign speeches. It was, moreover, a syndicate which the Conservative government was eager to work with; British Columbia was threatening to pull out of Confederation unless the railway was built and something had to be done, and done soon.

In the autumn of 1879, Macdonald, Tupper and the finance minister, Sir Leonard Tilley, had gone to London to seek a loan for the line but found that the depression, having come later to Britain, was also later in lifting. The banks thought any attempt to construct a railway north of Lake Superior or through the Rocky Mountains was a recipe for bankruptcy and the politicians had returned without either a British government guarantee for a loan or the loan itself.

Forced to do something to pacify British Columbia, the Conservatives had found themselves obliged to follow the Liberal policy of building piecemeal and had given contracts for four sections in BC to the young American builder, Andrew Onderdonk, who would lay tracks from the Pacific coast through the Fraser Canyon to Kamloops on the Thompson River. Perhaps the fact that he had sound financial backing and nothing whatsoever to do with the Northern Pacific was sufficient to excuse his nationality.

Both Tupper and Macdonald had been convinced by Donald's arguments about the need for a railway to bring immigrants to the Northwest and Macdonald now proposed to satisfy the demand by authorizing the cheapest, scrappiest railway line he could get away with. Tupper, however, had other ideas.

By the spring of 1880, stories of the financial success of the Saint Paul, Minneapolis and Manitoba Railway were beginning to circulate. When the report was published for the first annual general meeting in August, it would reveal that net earnings for the first year were sixty percent in excess of the bonded debt, or a total of $1.58 million. Nor was this a fluke, prompted by the exceptionally rich harvest in the autumn of 1879. In September 1880, newspapers reported that the gross earnings of the line in July had been $272,089.05, an increase of $30,749.88 on the previous year. Gross earnings for August showed an increase of $43,638.72. Clearly the owners were men who knew not only how to build a railway, but also how to run one. Moreover, most of them were Canadian.[10]

In June, Tupper's *volte face* with respect to Donald Smith, George Stephen and their colleagues on the Manitoba road was completed when he wrote a memorandum for the cabinet in which he noted that, "owing to the great interest at present excited in relation to the North West, the value of land there, and the great success which has attended the St. Paul, Minneapolis and Manitoba Railway Company," it would be quite practicable to complete the railway from Winnipeg to Kamloops by providing twenty-five million acres of land and $12,500,000. To build from Lake Nipissing to Winnipeg would require $45,500,000, he estimated, and asked for authority to negotiate with "capitalists of undoubted means." The size of the cash subsidy and the reliability of the men seeking the charter would be the crucial points and the cabinet gave Tupper permission to see what he could do.[11]

Capitalists and would be capitalists of both doubted and undoubted means began to court Tupper but the only proposal of any interest came from Duncan McIntyre, another immigrant Scot, who was building the Canada Central from Ottawa to Lake Nipissing. Clearly this railway would be essential to the CPR's through route and just as clearly the letter was written by George Stephen, even if McIntyre signed it. Like Jim Hill's early letters to the Dutch bondholders, this was another fishing trip. It asked for $26.5 million and thirty-five million acres which was more than the government could agree to. For the moment, the matter was closed. Except it was not.[12]

When the confederation of Ontario, Quebec and the maritime provinces was being negotiated, Nova Scotia and New Brunswick made the construction of a railway linking them with the Canadas a condition of their participation. The Intercolonial Railway went from Halifax through eastern New Brunswick and then followed the Matapedia River in Quebec to the south shore of the St. Lawrence River where it linked up with the Grand Trunk Railway at Rivière du Loup, the Fraserville of Donald's early days in Canada. When it was completed, accommodation which had been built for the senior construction staff and engineers was sold. Some of the best houses were to be found in Quebec where the Matapedia ran parallel to the St. Lawrence and these were purchased by George Stephen. All his life he had been a keen salmon fisherman and the shimmering rock pools of the Matapedia came close to his idea of paradise. Stephen sold the other houses to friends, arranged to purchase the fishing rights in the river, and set up a fishing club. John Kennedy, the New York banker, was an enthusiastic member as was R.B. Angus, and another house, originally occupied by the engineer, Peter Grant, was bought by Donald Smith.

As a man who had spent thirty years catching and salting Atlantic salmon, and as a man who had never demonstrated either enthusiasm or skill for any sporting activity, Donald is unlikely to have been eager to fish for pleasure. He did appreciate Canada's scenic beauties but often said that winter was his favourite time of year. He loved the clear, crisp, sunny days and the dry air which made the cold so much more acceptable — but there was none of this in the salmon season. What was important about Matapedia, and would have been the only reason for Donald's buying a house there, was that it provided an informal gathering of business associates where, over a drink on the verandah as the sun set, a good deal of dreaming and a judicious amount of planning was done.

Both the cousins were there at the beginning of July 1880 and so were Angus and Sandford Fleming who, following a prolonged campaign of vilification, had recently been ousted as chief engineer of the CPR. Together, the four Scots considered the options for building the railway and tried to decide what was practicable and what Stephen should tell Sir John. He, Tupper and John Henry Pope, the minister of agriculture who shared responsibility for the CPR, were sailing to London to assess British offers to build the road and were to make another attempt to raise the capital which would have to be offered to the successful contractor. Stephen had promised to send a letter to the ship when it passed Rimouski. In view of the quarrel with the prime minister, Donald's name was not mentioned, but both Sir John and his ministers were perfectly aware that he would be party to any deal that was done. It is less likely that they would have guessed that Fleming had been consulted.

The letter was casual, as most of Stephen's business correspondence was, and nonchalant in a way which suggests he and his friends did not care one way or the other whether their offer was accepted. It is precisely this disinterested tone which makes the letter so seductive. Stephen begins by saying he is quite sure Macdonald will find men "on the other side" who will courageously take up the railway scheme because they do not know the difficulties and will "adopt measures for their own protection which I could not avail myself of."

> There are two ways by which you can get the road built and operated: one by getting up a financial organization such as Allan contemplated and such as Jay Cooke & Co. got up for construction of the Northern Pacific Railway — with what result I need not remind you. A scheme of this nature involves the issue of a large amount of Bonds, just as large as an attractive prospectus will float (and you have capital material to offer for a very "taking" prospectus): the outcome of a plan of this character is that the real responsibility is transferred from the Company to the people who may be induced to buy the Bonds, while the Company or the projectors pocket a big profit at the start out of the proceeds. This, in the rough, is I fear the method any English financial organization is likely to follow. The risk to the Government and to the country of allowing the matter to be manipulated in that way is sufficiently obvious. It would indeed be a disastrous affair to all concerned if the English public were induced to invest in a bond issue which the road could not carry — that is on which the interest could not be paid. The other plan, and the one I should have followed, had we been able to come to terms, would have been to limit the borrowing of money from the public to the smallest possible point, and if we issued a bond at all to take care it did not much exceed $5000 —(Five thousand dollars) a mile — to have looked for the return of our own capital and a legitimate profit entirely to the growth of the country and the development of the property — after the work of construction had been fully accomplished. I could not be a party to a scheme involving a large issue of Bonds on a road which no one can now be sure will earn enough to pay working expenses. I am more willing to risk my own means in the venture than those of the English public. It would be quite useless my going over to London; we are certain to be outbid there, and for the reasons I have given. No English or American organization could really do the work as advantageously and at so little cost as we could, nor could they so readily develop the earning power of the property; but, while we should wait for our profit and take the risk of its coming at all, they would inevitably pocket theirs at once.
>
> When I met Pope in Montreal on Saturday he told me that the Government had *decided finally* to give no more money than twenty millions, and as I could not see my way to do the work for a less cash bonus than twenty-six and a half millions, I though it better to end the negotiations, leaving you perfectly

> free to make the best bargain you could on the other side. Pope was disappointed and not very well pleased with me, but I thought and still think it was the right thing to do. Mr. Angus has been with me all the week, and we have done little else than discuss the matter, the salmon being few and far between. We are both satisfied of our ability to construct the road without much trouble, but we are not so sure by any means about its profitable operation; but in regard to this, if we cannot operate it successfully no one else can. We think, as I explained to you at Ottawa, that we could immediately utilise the Thunder Bay branch for our Lake traffic and in this, and other ways, earn enough to secure the payment of interest upon such indebtedness as we might incur. Our experience of settling lands in Minnesota would be a great help to us in the management of the lands granted to the Road. We are also clear on the point that the Canada Central and the Quebec roads would have to be incorporated. Nipissing is nowhere. Montreal or Quebec must be the starting point. Although I am off the notion of the thing now, should anything occur on the other side to induce you to think that taking all things into consideration, our proposal is better upon the whole for the country than any offer you get in England, I might, on hearing from you, renew it and possibly in doing so reduce the land grant to some extent. Here let me say that, so far as I am able to gauge public opinion, I think most people and especially the opposition (if we may judge from the utterances of the "Globe") would prefer limiting the grant of land and increasing the cash subsidy — that is, they would prefer giving 30 millions cash and 20 millions acres of land to 50 million acres of land without any cash; but as to this you can judge much better than anybody else.[13]

The letter was immensely attractive and Stephen's offer became even more desirable when Macdonald discovered that the English proposals were insubstantial. Duncan McIntyre had travelled to England with the ministerial party, a carefully arranged "co-incidence" which enabled him to enter into negotiations, cabling Stephen with information and seeking his approval. The associates were in Winnipeg, together with Lord Elphinstone, early in August and later in the month were in Saint Paul for the annual general meeting of the Manitoba road. The CPR could not be a project for the associates alone, though they agreed to form its initial core. They accepted a slight compromise on cash, down to $25 million, and, as Stephen had hinted in July, complied with the government offer of twenty-five million acres of land. Duncan McIntyre signed the agreement in principle on September 4.

Even before Macdonald and McIntyre reached Canada, before the deal was approved by the privy council or the contract drafted, the associates began raising funds for their project. They agreed to pool some of their shares in the common stock of the Manitoba road and to place them on the New York market. The intention was partly to establish a trading value for the shares in order to determine how they might be used to secure loans for the CPR and partly to raise cash for the new venture. They were hoping to sell at seventy cents on the dollar. "The stock will be well worth the money especially if we get hold of the Canada Pacific," Angus exulted. It rather caught Donald on the hop, however, and he suggested that "*all* the cash proceeds should not be absorbed in the new venture. 'Could you not (he said at last) give me $50,000 cash' — I told him there might be that coming to him but I could not say, and I supposed he must be getting more money than he knew how to dispose of — but he says that is not quite the case." As Angus eventually discovered, "Mr. Stephen gave Mr. Smith to understand he might count on receiving some portion of his stock about this time, and in expectation of that Mr. Smith made advances to a mutual friend of ours in Montreal."[14]

More cash was raised on the twenty-eighth of September, when the Bank of Montreal approved a six month loan of $600,000 to Donald and George Stephen. It was secured by second mortgage bonds on the Saint Paul, Minneapolis and Manitoba and in January, Stephen used stock in the same line to secure an advance of $625,000.[15]

The fundraising was designed to enable the syndicate to move as quickly as it could on the network of existing and partially built railways which would be eastern feeders for the main transcontinental route. Stephen personally gained control of the Credit Valley Railway which linked London, Ontario, with Toronto and had a northern branch pushing towards Lake Huron; his first motive was to help his friend, George Laidlaw and it would be several years before the line was incorporated into the CPR system. Most important, however, was control of Duncan McIntyre's Canada Central which was acquired by taking over its $1.8 million mortgage. Its western terminus at Callander on Lake Nipissing was the point from which the Canadian Pacific construction proper would begin. First, however, the Canada Central had to build to Callander.

Soon after Macdonald and McIntyre returned to Canada, J.J.C. Abbott began to draw up the CPR contract and J.J. Hill came east to study the draft. His main concern was to ensure the safety of the Saint Paul, Minneapolis and Manitoba Railway but he warned that a clause requiring the difficult eastern section, north of Lake Superior, to be completed could put the whole enterprise at risk; he also advised that the land grant should be tax free. Hill was keen to see the road built because he wanted an east-west line which would enable the Manitoba road to compete with the Northern Pacific, now close to completing its line to the west coast. Offsetting this desire for a transcontinental link was a belief that it was folly to construct north of Lake Superior and a fear that, by not going south of the Great Lakes, the CPR would have no need of his facilities in Saint Paul or of the Manitoba road.

The contract, which was signed on October 21, but subject to the approval of parliament, required the cash and subsidies to be earned as construction proceeded. The land grant was to be taken from a strip of land, forty-eight miles wide, running along the railway line between Winnipeg and Jasper House, the Hudson's Bay Company trading post on the Athabasca River in the Rocky Mountains. It was to be "fairly fit for settlement" and Donald's experience with HBC lands and the constant haggling over their value ensured that the contract also provided for selection of land in other areas should that bordering the railway prove unsuitable. The company was authorized to issue land grant bonds against this territory.

Another clause said that all the sections which the government had already undertaken to build would be completed and handed over to the company. These included the Onderdonk lines in British Columbia, the Pembina Branch and the line which was being built from Thunder Bay, at the west end of Lake Superior, to Manitoba. The company was also allowed to take over other lines, a condition which enabled it to secure feeder lines and a terminus in Montreal. All railway material was to be admitted to Canada free of duty and, thanks to Hill, the land grant was to be tax free for twenty years or until it was sold. Stations, workshops and other railway premises would be free of tax forever.

Clause fifteen proved to be the most contentious. It became known as the monopoly clause and gave the syndicate sole control over the Pembina Branch while prohibiting any other company from constructing south of the CPR to within fifteen miles of the American border. John Schultz and others in Manitoba had been itching to build a line competing with the Pembina Branch, there was antipathy to the associates and their freight rates, and there was a genuine need for lines which would connect settlers and their produce to the markets in the east. Unfortunately, both bloody-mindedness and genuine transport needs could divert traffic to the American lines which would rush to the border to connect with any Canadian railway built south of the CPR's main line. Siphoning off southern traffic would kill the CPR and Stephen was adamant that he would not allow this, but the clause proved deeply worrying to J.J. Hill. "The only reason for going into the scheme was for the purpose of benefitting the St. P. M. & M. Ry," he wrote to Angus in October, "but now it assumes the position of a deadly enemy. I sincerely hope I am all wrong but I fear the result much more than I can tell you."[16]

The men who signed the contract were George Stephen, Duncan McIntyre, R.B. Angus, J.J. Hill, John Kennedy and representatives of Morton Rose, the English merchant bank which had nearly invested in the Manitoba road, and Kohn, Reinach and Company, a Franco-German banking firm which Macdonald had insisted on in the interest of keeping Francophone Quebec happy.

Noticeably absent from the signatories was Donald Smith. He was in England when the contract was signed but his name was left off because it was felt better to keep quiet about his involvement in order to reduce the chances of a ruction in the House. Stephen could be brusque on occasion and did not think to mollify his cousin with a simple, considerate explanation. The omission of his name wounded Donald's pride. He did not seek fame but neither did he wish to disguise his involvement with the most important project to be undertaken in Canada since Confederation. By publicly associating himself with a great national enterprise, he would be able to demonstrate that he truly did care for the future of the Northwest, but George Stephen denied him this.

"I have had a terrible bother with D. Smith because his name is not printed in the papers submitted to the House," Stephen wrote to John Rose in December. "It was not necessary to have it then and both Angus and I thought we were doing him a good turn by keeping him out. He has been like a baby over the thing." In a letter to Macdonald, he observed, "He is excited almost to a craze and so troublesome that I do not care if he does withdraw though his money and cooperation would be useful, so would his knowledge of and influence in the Nor West."[17]

Stephen explained to his cousin that they had wanted to avoid discussion in the House which had been specially reconvened to get the CPR bill through before spring so that construction could start as soon as possible, but Donald suspected that the true motive had been the prime minister's dislike of him. "I must not and do not complain of Sir John Macdonald's prejudice against me, which I trust time will tend to abate;" he wrote in a rare letter to his cousin, "but I shall not the less on that account exert myself to the utmost consistent with the conditions which that prejudice imposes." It would, however, be some time before he could be a director in fact, though from the beginning, he was one in all but name.[18]

In answer to Stephen's letter, Macdonald indicated that he was quite content for Donald to be involved in the syndicate. While Donald Smith's role in bringing down his government in 1873 continued to rankle, the prime minister was fully aware that that one incident was no reason to exclude Donald, or his money or his knowledge of railways and western transportation at this vital juncture in Canadian development. Donald, who was inclined to square up to problems rather than pretending they did not exist, felt the same way. "The fact is that he is most anxious to make friends with you," Stephen replied, "that I could see from the way he expressed himself when I told him what you said to me about his being in the syndicate, and he is terribly put out with Blake and Cartwright, especially the latter, and says he thinks they have alluded to 1873 in order to prevent any rapprochement between you and himself, how far that may be the case I do not know."[19]

Edward Blake and Richard Cartwright were only two of the Liberal MPs who argued against the CPR contract. Nearly everyone on their side of the House had objections, as did a good many Conservatives. The press, too, was howling for blood. It was too big a scheme, too risky and cost too much. It would never be completed, they shouted.

In introducing the bill on December 14, Tupper tried to explain how the government had come to be convinced the railway could be built.

> One of the causes which led to the great change in the public sentiment in relation to the value of land in the North-West, and of railway enterprise in the North-West, was the marked and wonderful success that was published to the world as having resulted from the Syndicate who had purchased the St. Paul, Minneapolis & Manitoba Railway, and become the proprietors of that line. The statements they were enabled to publish showed not only the rapidity with which railway construction in private hands could be carried on, but it showed the value of prairie lands in the North-West, and the extent they could be made valuable for the construction of such lines.[20]

The enthusiasm for the Saint Paul associates rang false notes in the ears of those who knew Tupper had been conniving against them on petty political grounds only two years earlier. Blake pointed out that one of these welcome Saint Paul men was Donald Smith whom Tupper had called a coward in the stormy scenes as parliament closed in 1878.

"His name is not there," shouted a loyal Conservative backbencher.

"I know you do not see it, but it is there for all that, and you know it well," Blake snapped back.[21]

Cartwright's speech was much more bitter and far more personal than Donald gave it credit for being. He had lost his political sympathy for Macdonald in the late 1860s and the Pacific Scandal had crystallized his dissent. Rather than give up politics and apply his energy and intelligence to another field, he became a bitter Liberal whose eagerness to wound the other side sometimes allowed him to attack without consideration for the truth or effectiveness of what he said. He read from the *Hansard* account of the 1878 parliamentary uproar when Macdonald had called Donald a liar and contrasted those opinions of him with the ones now put forward by the government.

> It is perfectly well known that one of the most prominent members of this St. Paul and Manitoba Railroad Company, and, by consequence, of the Syndicate, is that honorable gentleman, termed by Ministers, the late Member for Selkirk. I entertain for him, as I always entertained of his friends with him in this contract, a very high opinion indeed. But I really think that unless the statements made last night by the hon. gentlemen opposite are intended to be received as, perhaps, they will be received by that gentleman, as a full and ample apology — considering that he and they are now to be entrusted with sovereign power — some formal apology ought to be made to them, or those pages should be expunged from the *Hansard* of 1878.[22]

Despite his professed regard for the members of the syndicate, he also implied that they had bribed the Conservatives in order to enable the Tories to repay Hugh Allan for his 1873 contribution to the party's electoral funds. Even Cartwright's friends found it difficult to sympathize with this nonsense and the debate reverted to more conventional parliamentary abuse.

A filibuster designed to allow the Liberals time to manufacture their own syndicate to bid for the contract took up hour after hour of the House's attention, but the phoney alternative bid was finally disposed of and the third reading passed on the first of February 1881. Macdonald, exhausted, sick, but sober, argued convincingly and took his Tory majority with him. Two weeks later, royal assent was granted; on the following day, February 16, the CPR was incorporated. George Stephen was elected president and McIntyre, because of his Canada Central line, became vice-president. Hill and Angus were on the executive committee and Charles Drinkwater, who had been Prime Minister Macdonald's secretary for nine years, was appointed secretary and treasurer. J.J.C. Abbott was nominated counsel. Having deposited a guarantee of a million dollars with the government, the company was ready for business. Donald Smith and George Stephen were about to embark on the most harrowing five years of their lives.

The company was authorized to issue common stock, preferred stock, land grant bonds, and mortgage bonds to a total of $90 million and was obliged to issue common stock worth $5 million and to have received payment for a third of it in order to validate the contract. On February 17, Donald Smith, George

Stephen, Richard Angus, Duncan McIntyre and James Hill each signed for five thousand shares with a par value of $100 each. Morton Bliss took 7,410 shares, John Kennedy's firm bought 5,000 and Kohn, Reinach acquired the rest. On March 3, a further 11,000 shares were issued, primarily to friends who had been promised an opportunity to be involved. These included Lord Elphinstone and Henry Northcote, the son of Stafford Northcote, the former HBC governor, and husband of Stephen's adopted daughter.

In August, the first of the land grant bonds were issued. The underlying principle was that the bonds represented the land subsidy and were therefore worth a total of $25 million, the land being valued at a dollar an acre. A fifth was deposited with the government as a guarantee and the remainder was available for sale. Money earned from the sale of the bonds had to be handed over to the government which then doled it out as the land grant was earned. Sale of the land would enable the company to redeem the bond. As the land grant was meant to be adjacent to the railway, it was assumed that the presence of the road would enhance the value of the land and so enable the company to earn a profit which would help to pay for the expense of construction. The great weakness of this arrangement was that a very long time elapsed between the sale of the bonds and the receipt of the money by the company. The scheme did, however, support the syndicate's contention that it intended to make its profits from carrying freight and not from land sales or mortgage bonds which would throw the financial risk of construction onto the public. Donald had been saying for ten years, on the hustings, in parliament and among his friends and business colleagues, that the richness of the Northwest could only be tapped by populating it and land grant bonds were a means by which the railway could be built and this goal achieved.

The first issue of $10 million at ninety-two was immediately taken by the Bank of Montreal and J.S. Kennedy who spread their purchase over thirteen months and took options on a further $5 million at ninety-five and another $5 million at ninety-seven and a half. The price of the Bank of Montreal's involvement in underwriting the CPR's bonds was George Stephen's resignation from the bank's executive. His presidency of the CPR had provoked attacks on the bank which had never been prepared to associate itself with such controversy. Donald remained on the executive and the following June was elected vice-president.

Before 1881 was out, the company had made major changes to the route which had been surveyed by Sandford Fleming and approved by parliament. Winnipeg, by dint of offering to build a bridge and provide free land for a station and other buildings, had convinced the company to cross the Red River at the Manitoba capital, and John Macoun, who had explored the southern prairies west of Winnipeg, had persuaded the company that a more southerly route was practicable there as well. In preference to the Yellowhead Pass chosen by Fleming, the company would now pierce the Rocky Mountains through Kicking Horse Pass, but it still had to find a way through the Selkirk Mountains, immediately to the west of the Rockies.

For want of anyone else with intimate knowledge of railway construction, Jim Hill had taken over responsibility for hiring senior staff. To the job of finding a pass through the Selkirks, he assigned the irascible, cussing Major A.B. Rogers, promising him that he would receive $5,000 and have the pass named after him if he succeeded. In the autumn of 1882, Rogers, with his wild whiskers and rough clothes, burst in on an elegant dinner party at George Stephen's Montreal mansion to report that he had indeed found the pass which now bears his name. He put up with being stuffed into one of Stephen's evening suits so he could join the dinner guests; he tried to hide his disgust at the quantity of food on offer, his own belief being that a man only needed a few beans and a plug of tobacco to survive; he did his best to keep his profanity under control. There was, however, one thing he refused to do and that was to cash the $5,000 cheque. Framed, it hung in his brother's house in Minnesota, admired by his nephews. In that form, as far as Rogers was concerned, its price was beyond rubies.

Having determined on the southern route, the syndicate rushed into the construction of the line. As any land speculator knew, the railway would require stations along the way and divisional points where larger administrative centres would be located. The speculator's trick was to guess or otherwise discover where stations would be and therefore where towns would develop, to acquire the land before the railway arrived and to sell it on at a vastly inflated price. A fantastic boom in land prices in Winnipeg and west along the supposed route erupted in 1881 and 1882 and some senior CPR staff used their inside knowledge to speculate in land.

In November 1881, Hill persuaded the CPR to hire as its general manager an American railroad man who would put a halt to such wholesale corruption and energetically push the construction work forward. William Cornelius Van Horne was a giant of a man in every sense of the word. Tall and broad, he consumed gargantuan meals with evident pleasure — and made sure the railway crews were well fed too. His strength was phenomenal and he cheerfully spelled off navvies, swinging a sledge hammer with apparent ease. An avid collector of fossils, he discovered several new types which were named after him. He sketched and painted, designed buildings, bred roses, and collected Chinese porcelain. He thought nothing of sitting up all night playing poker, smoking his huge cigars and drinking brandy. Without a thought for bed, he would be back at work early the next morning, scornful of men who needed sleep. He had great respect for Hill whose meticulous attention to detail and unwavering commitment to his railway work matched his own; he respected and worked well with Stephen, with whom he shared a passion for salmon fishing; and he developed a warm, almost protective affection for Donald Smith who was quiet where Van Horne was loud; formal and gracious where Van Horne was sometimes casual and raucous; abstemious where Van Horne verged on gluttony.

The CPR's policy was to build the prairie section as rapidly as possible and afterwards deal with the more difficult sections such as the line north of Lake Superior and the route through the Rockies. The prairie route could quickly be put into service and earn money for construction elsewhere and, since all the land grants were going to be in the Northwest, the sooner there was a railway to bring in settlers to occupy this land and supply the railway's future cargo, the better.

Before the year was out, however, it was apparent that financing even this comparatively easy stretch of the road was going to present problems. Not having been informed that any of the land grant bonds had been sold, the Department of Finance declined to authorize payments on land which had been earned. On the sixth of December, Donald and his cousin went cap in hand to the Bank of Montreal, offering their New Brunswick Railway Company bonds as a security for a short term loan of $300,000.

In March 1882, they were back again, this time with Saint Paul, Minneapolis and Manitoba shares as collateral for a $1.5 million short term loan, again because the proceeds of the land grant bonds were slow to materialize. Donald, Kennedy and Hill each put up $500,000, receiving as collateral for their contribution half a million dollars worth of CPR common stock and the same amount of preferred. In the parcel with his own Manitoba road stock, Hill sent $2,300,000 of Donald's which could be used to shore up the CPR. In the short term, the money was needed to purchase rails before the price escalated but the CPR also had to find nearly half a million dollars in cash as a deposit on the purchase of the Montreal to Ottawa line of the Quebec, Montreal, Ottawa and Occidental Railway. Of this, $200,000 came from Donald Smith.[23]

This cumbersomely named line went from Quebec city, along the north shore of the St. Lawrence to Montreal where it branched north to the capital. It guzzled money and its owner, the Quebec provincial government, was desperate to offload it. Ten years earlier, Cartier had promised it would be incorporated into the CPR and Quebec MPs had made their support for the 1881 charter conditional on Macdonald's finding a way of getting the railway off the province's hands. What goaded George Stephen and his cousin into action, however, was news that Quebec was negotiating with Henry Villard, the new president of the Northern Pacific. It was obvious that, under the pretence of being a Canadian line, the Northern Pacific would then build from Ottawa through Ontario to Sault Ste. Marie where it would connect with its own projected American line going to Saint Paul. If this happened, there would be no point in building north of Lake Superior and the dream of a Canadian railway, spanning the country, would vanish.

The Northern Pacific had launched a two-pronged attack. It had acquired control of John Schultz's 1879 charter to build the Manitoba South Western Colonization Railway going from Winnipeg down the west side of the Red River and southwest to the Souris coalfields, its main objective being to continue the road south from the coalfields towards the US border. The Northern Pacific seemed to assume that the CPR's monopoly clause could be circumvented, perhaps because Schultz's charter had been granted prior to the CPR's, and proceeded to build north from Dakota to connect with the Manitoba South Western. The intention to was revive Jay Cooke's scheme of taking Canadian traffic south of the Great Lakes and bringing it north into Manitoba.

The CPR men managed to have the monopoly regulations enforced and the Northern Pacific called a halt to construction work both north and south of the border. Both the NP and Schultz's line, however, posed a latent threat to the CPR, so the Manitoba road, partly from self-interest and partly from goodwill, bought both of them, even though there was no provision in its charter allowing it to acquire foreign railways. The Canadian line had been purchased at the behest of George Stephen who needed somewhere to park it until the CPR could afford to pay for it. Hill, who was increasingly identified with the Manitoba road, was initially happy to do a favour for the Canadians but, by March 1883, he was complaining to Angus that the SPM & M had $1.25 million tied up in the Manitoba

South Western line. In July that year, he was writing to Kennedy to point out that the deal had been undertaken at the request of George Stephen as president of both roads but his fellow CPR directors had declined to allow Stephen to honour the commitment to take the Manitoba South Western off his hands.[24]

It was little wonder the CPR board declined to hand over more than a million dollars to the Manitoba road. It did not have the money to give to Hill or anyone else.

By the spring of 1882, it was evident that Tupper's estimate that the CPR could be built for $45 million was a pipe dream. Even if the syndicate had not been obliged to meet unforeseen expenses such as the acquisition of the QMOO, it was still obliged to make payments much in excess of the original estimate. Building from east to west across the prairies was proving to be far more expensive than following a north-south river valley as the Saint Paul, Minneapolis and Manitoba Railway had done. And building quickly in order to finish the prairie section and put it into operation meant doubling shifts in the summer months and paying for huge volumes of men, supplies and equipment. Such a policy carried its price which was the more noticeable as the government dragged its heels in paying out the land grant moneys and the cash subsidy.

The initial plan of issuing a small amount of stock and keeping a tight control on the company had to be abandoned and in May, a further 190,000 shares were issued. The par value was $19 million, but the company struggled to raise a quarter of that. Most of the purchasers were men who had already subscribed to the company's stock. Few others were willing to undertake what the Grand Trunk assured them was a foolish risk.

In the previous decade, it had been easy to dismiss attempts to build the great Canadian railway and the Grand Trunk had grown accustomed to ignoring them. Its directors, safe in their English boardroom, were convinced that construction through the Precambrian Shield, that inhospitable region north of Lake Superior, was impossible and would soon be irrelevant since their own line was about to reach Chicago and obviate any need for a competitor on Canadian soil. But as the CPR syndicate seized control of feeder lines in Ontario and Quebec and energetically pushed construction forward, the Grand Trunk's president, Sir Henry Tyler, his Canadian general manager, Joseph Hickson, and their colleagues panicked. They launched a crusade of vituperation designed to poison the CPR's reputation in British and American financial circles. It was argued that the climate was so inhospitable that settlers would never take up land in the prairies where men and cattle regularly froze to death during the long winters. BC was worthless, being nothing but mountains. The CPR company was a financial bubble which would burst, taking its investors with it.

In the summer of 1881, Lord Lorne, the new governor general, who was married to Queen Victoria's daughter, Princess Louise, had taken a party of English journalists to Manitoba in hopes of persuading them that the reality was not as their colleagues had painted it. Lorne and some of his staff stayed at Silver Heights though Donald, having picked them up at the train station, left the following evening for Montreal. The public excuse for his unexpected and rapid departure was that he had been called to England on urgent business. His evident pleasure in providing hospitality, especially for such important guests, suggests that the business was very urgent, though no information about it now survives beyond the fact that on August 4, he and Bella left Montreal for Quebec where they boarded the *Polynesian* for England. In all likelihood, it was family matter which took them to the UK, quite possibly a dangerous recurrence of his brother John's malaria.

The exuberance of Lorne's welcome in Winnipeg, the clear air and obvious fertility of the prairie soil, and the fun of discovering new towns in the throes of being born, convinced both Lorne and the pressmen that Canada did indeed have a rich future in this uninhabited land. But while the newspaper reports and Lorne's enthusiastic lectures did controvert some English opinions, they carried little weight in the face of the Grand Trunk's many powerful allies.

In 1882, as Canada prepared for another federal election, the Grand Trunk quickly discovered more friends among supporters of the Canadian Liberal party who were glad to use the British railway's views about the Canadian Pacific as ammunition against Conservative policies. American railway interests, especially the Northern Pacific, found it useful to draw attention to the Grand Trunk's campaign. In England, both Baring Brothers and Glyn Mills and Company, the influential London merchant banks, were closely allied to the Grand Trunk which they had originally helped to finance; it was not in their interests to speak well of the CPR.

In Montreal, the Merchants' Bank had Grand Trunk men on its executive. One of these was Charles Brydges who had been the Grand Trunk's general manager in Canada before replacing Donald Smith as the HBC's Land Commissioner. It was clear from his letters to the HBC board as early as December 1880 that he was opposed to the CPR and Governor Eden Colvile felt obliged to bring him into line. "You have doubtless a strong opinion on the subject," Colvile admonished, telling him to keep his thoughts to himself and not let people think the HBC took sides in the matter. "The course I have pursued in any conversation with Donald A. Smith & George Stephen," Colvile explained, "has been to express no opinion, one way or another, on the policy of making the Railway in the manner proposed by John A. McDonald [sic] & at the same time to express a desire, if the contract is confirmed, to work harmoniously with the syndicate."[25]

One of the ways the CPR attempted to deal with criticism in the Canadian press was to gain control of the papers. In Manitoba, the *Free Press* had always been sympathetic to Donald Smith and his interests and in August 1879, he provided a mortgage on the company's buildings and presses, an investment which may have encouraged the paper to speak well of the CPR, whatever it thought about Conservative policies generally. Essentially, however, the *Free Press* valued its independence and refused to be prompted by its creditors. The CPR was no more successful with the Manitoba *Standard* in which Donald had invested in 1875, being joined in a small way by several men whose Private Cash Accounts he managed, though the investments were made at their request and not at his suggestion. The paper never had any significant political impact and, in financial terms, it was a total failure. It was sold in the spring of 1883 and Donald reimbursed men such as the old fur trader, Roderick MacFarlane, who had put $500 into the original venture. Donald himself lost $8,000, in addition to the money he returned to the Private Cash investors who, being wintering partners, were having trouble making ends meet.[26]

In Toronto, the *Mail* had been established as a Tory paper by John A. Macdonald and his colleagues in 1872 and could thus be counted on to be sympathetic to the CPR. In January 1874, Donald bought a bloc of ten shares but outside investors had little influence and the newspaper's policy continued to be discreetly dictated from the prime minister's office in Ottawa.[27]

The most vigorous and persistent attacks on the CPR in Canada came from the Toronto *Globe* which described the railway charter as a "monstrous bargain." It led the attack on the employment of Americans in the construction of the road, quietly ignoring the fact that there were no experienced Canadians available to do the jobs. By November 1883, Macdonald was so exasperated that he wrote Stephen, suggesting that Donald might try to sort out an arrangement with the paper. The prime minister was confident that *The Globe* was struggling financially and therefore liable to be tempted by a suitable offer. "It should keep its character & position as a Liberal organ," Macdonald argued, except where the CPR was concerned.[28]

Not long before his death in 1880, *The Globe*'s founder, George Brown, had financed new presses and other developments with loans from his brothers-in-law, William and Thomas Nelson, the Scottish publishers, giving shares in the paper as collateral. They wanted to sell the shares and were impressed when Donald, visiting them in Edinburgh, told them that he was interested in acquiring their interest, but "so long as the Globe kept on attacking the C.P.R. there was no chance of him or anyone connected with the CPR taking further pecuniary interest in the Globe." Donald and Stephen attributed *The Globe's* silence on CPR matters at the beginning of January 1884 to the success of this ploy but the Nelsons had alerted the party faithful to the conditions which would have to be fulfilled before they could accept Donald's generous offer to acquire their shares. Quickly, the Liberals raised the cash to buy out the Nelsons and *The Globe* returned to the attack.[29]

Unable to turn its enemies, the CPR was forced to rely on its friends. In the summer of 1882, it instigated the formation of the Canada North West Land Company. This was an Anglo-Canadian venture, chaired by Thomas Skinner, a London-based financial journalist and HBC shareholder. In Canada, the principal figures were Edmund Osler, a Toronto banker who was active in railway affairs in Ontario, and William Scarth, who had previously worked in the Toronto office of the North British Canadian Investment Company. Donald invested in the land company as soon as it was formed and was one of the Canadian directors. The company agreed to buy $13.5 million worth of land grant bonds from the CPR and to purchase five million acres of land. The company was also to hold in trust all the townsite plots and station sites between Brandon, Manitoba, and the Rocky Mountains. The trustees for the townsites were Donald Smith and R.B. Angus for the CPR and Scarth and Osler for the land company. When townsite lands were sold, the income was divided equally between the two companies. Land was transferred to the company as it was needed because as soon as it changed hands, it became liable to tax.

The market for Northwest land collapsed almost before the CNWLC was set up and as early as November 1882, it was appealing to the Bank of Montreal for a loan of $2.7 million, security being the land grant bonds and a guarantee from the CPR. By December 1883, it was apparent that energy and ambition were not sufficient and the project had to be scaled down. About half the land and half the land grant bonds were once again on the CPR's hands.

Land which the CPR retained was sold in competition with the Canada North West Land Company's allocation but, because the land company was essentially a railway offshoot, little conflict actually occurred. The CPR's land commissioner was John McTavish who had been lured away from the HBC with offers of a better and more interesting post, while in London, the land agent was Alexander Begg, Manitoba's first historian and a friend of Donald's since 1870.

In August 1881, senior CPR men had met in Winnipeg to define the company's land policy. They determined to encourage settlement by a rebate scheme which refunded fifty percent of the purchase price if the land was occupied and tilled. By 1882, however, land was proving to be a problem because about eighty percent of the sections in the railway belt were found to be unsuitable for settlement and alternative sections had to be discovered elsewhere. Unfortunately, "elsewhere" had not been surveyed and Begg and McTavish found it more than a little difficult to persuade intending settlers to purchase land which had not been identified. If it had been located, neither railways nor roads led to it, and until they were built, the land could not provide the CPR with much needed freight business.

In the summer of 1882, with the land company just formed, there was an air of optimism in the CPR's Montreal offices, despite the growing concern about the location of the land grant. With McIntyre and Angus, Donald travelled over the eastern section of the line in July and found that track had been laid on the Canada Central route almost to Lake Nipissing. That month the syndicate "came to the conclusion that we should occupy a stronger position towards the public and the Government in case of any inquiry" and so paid in full for their allocation in the spring share issue. Even though they only paid twenty-five percent of par, the men were each obliged to find $300,000 to add to the deposit of $200,000 which they had paid a few months earlier.[30]

In August, Donald was on the train heading for Pile o' Bones Creek which was to be the new capital of the North West Territories. Pile o' Bones lacked the implications of grandeur which might properly attach to such a city even if, for the present, it was no more than a cluster of tents on parched prairie. At Macdonald's suggestion, the choice of name was left to the Governor General, Lord Lorne, who decided to honour his mother-in-law and name the future city Regina. The men of the Northwest were unimpressed by this "double-barrelled forty-horse-power fool of a name" but there was little they could do about it and the capital was duly christened with a toast in Van Horne's private car. It was not a public occasion; none of the settlers was invited to join Donald, Van Horne, Duncan McIntyre, John McTavish and their guests, and the ceremony seems to have been an excuse for a junket by senior staff and shareholders who wanted to have a look at the territory at the end of the line. If nothing else, it would help them appreciate the nature of their land grant problems.[31]

The summer interlude may have been pleasant but it did not disguise the fact that construction in 1882 had consumed a vast amount of money. By September, members of the syndicate had been obliged to find $5 million from their own resources. Some of the money came through completing payment on their shares but Stephen was obliged to sell all his Bank of Montreal stock to make up his contribution. There is no evidence to suggest how Donald raised his portion of the $5 million but it is unlikely that he sold shares. Throughout the 1880s, his Bank of Montreal holding remained steady and he continued to invest in other enterprises during this decade. In all probability, his contribution was a mixture of cash earned from other investments and a loan from the bank. By the end of the year, the cousins and their friends had invested a colossal $14 million of their own money in the CPR, a sum which more than five times exceeded the line's gross earnings for 1882.

Desperate for money, Stephen persuaded the government to return the million dollar deposit in exchange for his debentures in the Credit Valley Railway. Though the company was eventually to be incorporated into the CPR, it was not at this time and the debentures were Stephen's own. To protect the shaky reputation of the transnational line, he quietly let it be understood that the company owned the paper.

Even this million dollars from the deposit was not enough to make a significant dint in Van Horne's anticipated expenditure for 1883. Costs were due to rise astronomically as the company finally got down to building the dreaded section above Lake Superior. At the beginning of November, the cousins, McIntyre and Angus met John Kennedy in New York. In a day of meetings, Donald, Stephen and Kennedy agreed to the formation of a pool to maintain the level of Saint Paul, Minneapolis and Manitoba stock and to ensure that the associates retained control. In the spring, Donald had sold stock in the Manitoba road to finance an English investment and in October, when he and George Stephen were again scrabbling around for money for the CPR, they both released further Manitoba shares. These late autumn sales had confused the market and Kennedy felt obliged to set up a pool to steady the price. "Mr. Stephen & Mr. Smith ... have both agreed to contribute $1,500,000 each to it, you and I doing the same," he wrote to Hill, "which will make $6,000,000 in a pool for 5 years and with the stock you and I have left say $3,000,000 will give us absolute control of $9,000,000 and I will always be able to get control of at least one million more any time I want it and that will make us perfectly sure of the control." They also wanted to stabilize the price of the stock since all of them needed to use it to underpin other investments.[32]

The bulk of the day, however, was occupied with "long and serious discussions over Canadian Pacific Rd matters." At an extraordinary general meeting on the twenty-eighth of November, stock was to be increased from $25 million to $100 million. Kennedy was optimistic about the syndicate which he formed to purchase $10 million at fifty with options on a further $20 million at slightly higher prices because "there are so many people who expect & desire to be 'counted in' when a stock syndicate is made up." He cheerfully predicted it selling at sixty on the exchanges in Montreal, New York, London and Amsterdam. He was only partly right: it was listed on the New York exchange in January when both the cousins bought five thousand shares. It made no mark at all in the other markets.[33]

The cousins sailed for Liverpool late in December but found it quite impossible to create a market for the stock in London. What they did do was to promote it among their friends and acquaintances who could then purchase shares on the New York exchange. About $3 million was sold that way. Donald bought

$14,000 worth, giving shares to William Armit's wife and his six children as well as buying for the women in the M'Grigor family. Stephen sold another $4 million through a Dutch syndicate established for the purpose. It was clearly going to be a long time before the CPR could make a market for its stock in London.

At many of the cousins' daily meetings in Montreal they discussed how they were going to meet Van Horne's pressing demands for more money, but they also explored how they were going to establish control over the little railways of southern Ontario and Quebec and create out of them the network which would be essential if the CPR was to do any eastern freight business worth talking about. They had an ally in Edmund Osler, whose Ontario and Quebec Railway was building from Montreal to Toronto where it would link with the Toronto, Grey and Bruce and the Credit Valley which Stephen owned. The Credit Valley extended to London from where the CPR could build to Detroit without much difficulty; a deal had already been done with William Vanderbilt's Michigan Central to carry traffic from there to Chicago. This would give them access to the lucrative American market and deprive the Grand Trunk of its monopoly in that respect.

At its eastern end, the Ontario and Quebec linked with the little Atlantic and North Western, a railway which was valuable because it had the right to bridge the St. Lawrence and, from the south shore, the CPR could build both to Portland, a warm water port in Maine, and to Saint John, New Brunswick. In June of 1882, Donald put $40,000, soon followed by a further $20,000, into the Ontario and Quebec and in April the following year he bought a thousand shares for $50,000. In July 1883, Donald and George Stephen, together with some of their colleagues, gave their personal guarantees on a Bank of Montreal loan of $900,000 to enable a take over of the Toronto, Grey and Bruce Railway which connected Toronto with Owen Sound on Georgian Bay and would thus give them access through Lake Huron to Lake Superior, allowing construction supplies to be dragged by dog teams over the frozen lakes and deposited along Superior's north shore in winter and a small fleet of steamers to carry the equipment in summer. Quietly and assiduously, Donald and his cousin brought the lines under their control.

Sir Henry Tyler, president of the Grand Trunk, and his general manager, Joseph Hickson, were furious and at the end of March 1883, Tyler made an open and direct attack on the CPR, his belligerence masking the fact that he was deeply worried by the CPR's aggressive moves in Ontario. He would have been even more angry had he discovered that Stephen considered him "nothing but a bottle of stale ginger pop."[34]

While the Grand Trunk's bitter campaign to prevent the CPR from raising funds in England took on a new vigour, Donald was obliged to deal with another divisive problem on the home front. Van Horne's energy and enthusiasm for the Canadian railway was matched by Hill's for the Manitoba road and as the CPR completed its stretch from Winnipeg to Thunder Bay, it posed an increasing threat to the Saint Paul, Minneapolis and Manitoba. It was now possible, by a combined rail and water route, to ship into and out of the Northwest without going through the United States. The Thunder Bay section came into operation earlier than Hill had understood it would and Van Horne had felt no obligation to alert him to this fact. The men quarrelled, each determined to obtain the best advantage for his own line. Hill was temporarily persuaded not to sell his CPR shares, a procedure which would have caused a major failure of confidence in the line, but he did resign from the board, using as an excuse the fact that he was too far from Montreal to attend meetings. Donald replaced him.

At the end of May 1883, Hill went to Montreal to see Donald and Angus, hoping that they would bring Van Horne into line. "They expressed themselves to me as somewhat surprised, that the opening of the Thunder-Bay line would make any material difference to the Manitoba company," Hill wrote to Kennedy. "The position by Mr. Van Horne, that we had no more right at Winnipeg, than any other local station on the C.P. I think will not be supported by the C.P. board, this position of itself is simply folly, and I think both gentlemen in our interview so considered it."[35]

Scarcely had Donald turned from the first of many attempts to make peace between Hill and Van Horne when new trouble broke out, this time at the foothills of the Rockies. As early as March 1882, Richard Hardisty had sent a memo, warning Donald that the projected railway route across the Bow River in what is now southern Alberta would cut through the Blackfoot reserve. For the same reason, a townsite at the river crossing would also be impossible. Donald passed the letter to Angus who in turn gave it to Van Horne. The CPR appears to have acted on Hardisty's letter because the dispute which did arise over the location of Calgary had to do with land set aside for grazing mounted police horses and not with infringing the rights of native peoples. The railway line itself, however, was another matter. The re-surveyed route still crossed the reserve, implying to the Blackfeet that, yet again, the white man was going to steal Indian land.[36]

The CPR contract included a clause in which the federal government agreed to extinguish Indian rights to any land which the railway might need and to provide compensation, generally in the form of other land. Lieutenant Governor Dewdney, who was also Indian Commissioner, had apparently slipped up. The young Blackfeet were determined to remove the railway forcibly and sought authority from their chief, Crowfoot. One of the most intelligent and sagacious of Indian leaders, Crowfoot had early understood that he could bring his people to destruction by opposing the Europeans who were moving onto the prairies in increasing numbers or he could negotiate a *modus vivendi*. Famous as a brave warrior who had survived many battles, he generally counselled peace, but he too was insulted by the railway's transgression and sympathized with the aggressive intentions of his young men. Father Doucet, the Oblate missionary to the tribe, did his best to defuse the situation and sent an urgent message to Father Lacombe, then priest at St. Mary's, Calgary.

Albert Lacombe was the finest example of Christian charity ever to appear in the Northwest. Born in Montreal in 1827, he was ordained twenty-two years later and immediately headed west where he dedicated his life to helping the native people and the Métis. Occasionally, his superiors would send him to hopelessly unsuitable tasks such as serving as priest to the railway gangs, but his heart was among the people of the Blackfoot Confederacy. He nursed them, offered guidance, prayed with them and for them, and acted as an intermediary between the native peoples and the advancing white population. Noted for his wisdom and gentleness, Lacombe was not blinded to the ways of the secular world by his saintly nature. When Major Rogers, fresh from discovering the pass through the Selkirks, found himself with spare cash after paying for his supplies, he offered it to the priest for his mission school at Blackfoot Crossing. Rogers was struggling to control his profane tongue while the priest was his usual modest, reticent self. Rogers' temper was always on a very short leash and burst forth as he shoved the money into Lacombe's hands.

"Here, take it. If you can't use it that way then buy yourself some cigars. Blue Jesus, what in hell's the use of me toting it across these damnation prairies." Tom Wilson, who worked for the mountain exploration and construction crews, observed the scene and recorded that Father Lacombe's whoop of laughter was so loud it could be heard in Fort Calgary, sixty miles to the west.[37]

Father Lacombe and Crowfoot were natural allies, but Lacombe also knew Dewdney and Van Horne and had been friends with Donald Smith for many years. "But ah, he was determined behind that pleasantness," he observed of Donald, saying that he was "smooth but so firm!" In response to a cable from Lacombe, Van Horne ordered a halt to construction on the Blackfoot reserve while Donald responded to his own telegram from the missionary by asking him to intervene. The priest, equipping himself with tea, sugar and tobacco rushed to the reserve, handed over his presents with a ceremonial flourish, and advised the Blackfeet to allow the railway to pass, assuring them that other land, adjoining the reserve, would be provided in compensation. The cable he had already sent to Dewdney would ensure that his promise was honoured.[38]

The CPR's gratitude was expressed that summer in Calgary when Donald, Stephen, Van Horne, and Angus took Baron Pascoe Grenfell, who represented Morton Rose and also Kohn, Reinach, over the road. They were joined by Prince Hohenlohe who was interested in a scheme for German emigrants. Father Lacombe was invited to join this distinguished group for lunch in Van Horne's private car. Accounts vary, but it appears that Angus proposed that Father Lacombe be made president for an hour and the priest, in turn, appointed George Stephen rector of St. Mary's. Some stories claim that the pious president voted himself a lifetime pass on the railway, free use of the telegraph wire and free transport of Oblate mission materials. He was far too self-effacing for that but a proposal may have come from Van Horne or Donald Smith as an expression of their appreciation for Lacombe's help. However it happened, both Crowfoot and Father Lacombe received passes over the line and the Oblates never paid freight charges.

In the summer of 1883, as part of the peace-making process with Jim Hill, Donald had found the money to acquire Hill's interest in the Manitoba South Western, which he held in trust for the CPR. Before the year was out he had contributed to the purchase of the Ontario and Quebec Railway bonds and to buying back a substantial part of the land grant bonds sold to the Canada North West Land Company. All in all, 1883 was a year to suck money from the pockets of Donald Smith and his friends.[39]

Van Horne had spent $30 million in 1883, quite apart from the money Donald and his cousin had committed to the other lines, and the demands in 1884 would be much greater. Knowledge of what was in store might have been easier to bear had North American railway shares not entered a period of depression: CPR stock nosedived, pushed further down by Kennedy's resignation from the board. Then an early frost on September 7 killed the wheat crop, depriving the prairie section of a chance of making a little money on its freight business. Cash had to be found somewhere and it had to be found quickly.

At this point, the company still had unissued stock with a par value of $45 million and a market value of less than half that. Offering shares on the New York exchange at that juncture would merely have invited a further depreciation. It was not unusual for governments to guarantee the interest on railway bonds, especially if they wished to encourage companies to undertake construction for the national good. Stephen, perhaps following conversations with Baron Grenfell and Prince Hohenlohe and certainly after discussions with his cousin, came up with the notion of having the government guarantee the dividend on CPR shares. The company had regularly paid five or six percent biannually, as was normal for railway shares at the time. A government guarantee would challenge the depressed market and help to raise CPR share prices.

The proposal was to provide a ten year, three percent, government guarantee for all the stock which had been issued, the company to find a further two percent from its own resources. Rather than release the entire remaining stock, only $10 million would be let onto the market in order to reduce the amount of dividend to be guaranteed. The government's guarantee would in fact be covered by the company which would deposit nearly $16 million in the federal account. This was to be made up of an immediate deposit of just over $8.5 million, with a further deposit of just under $3 million due in February 1884 and the remainder following later. Assets, including the postal subsidy which the railway was earning, could form part of the deposit due in February and land grant bonds could serve as security.

To raise the first slice of the deposit, the syndicate borrowed $5 million from John Kennedy, using the new stock issue as security. A further $2.5 million was borrowed from C. Unger and Company, the New York bankers who, ironically, borrowed the money in turn from the Bank of Montreal. Again, CPR stock was used as collateral. Unger also took Manitoba road stock owned by Donald, Stephen and Angus as security.

Initially, the price of CPR shares rose on the New York exchange but press speculation attributed the guarantee to a new wheeze by which the directors would line their pockets and the price quickly fell again. Yet another bankruptcy of the Northern Pacific depressed railway shares even further. The guarantee scheme had proved a disaster.

To December 1883, the CPR had spent $58,695,377. In cash subsidy, it had earned $12,289,211. The earnings from the land subsidy were about $9 million gross and $6 million net. The syndicate had found through loans and the sale of shares a total of $37,377,155. Net earnings in 1883 were just over half a million dollars and the company's total debt, most of it guaranteed by shares owned by Donald and his cousin, totalled roughly $15 million.

Donald was in London attending Hudson's Bay Company meetings when the CPR mustered the remainder of its big guns for a journey to Ottawa to persuade the prime minister that a government loan was essential. The thought of trying to cram such an unpopular piece of legislation down parliamentary throats was more than Macdonald could bear. He refused.

It was late at night and the Montreal train did not leave till four in the morning, so Stephen, Angus, McIntyre, Van Horne and their lawyer, J.J.C. Abbott, resorted to Bank Cottage. Following Donald's electoral defeat, the suite had been rented to John Henry Pope who was acting minister of railways since Tupper had been despatched to London as Canada's high commissioner. On discovering the reason for the men's gloomy looks, Pope asked them to wait and at one in the morning called for a carriage to take him to the prime minister's residence. Rousing Macdonald from his bed, he delivered a simple home truth. "The day the Canadian Pacific busts the Conservative party busts the day after."[40]

The following day, the syndicate's gloomy looks were replicated on the faces of the senior cabinet ministers. Some wanted to turn their backs on Stephen and his colleagues while others wanted the government to take over the CPR. None of them relished the parliamentary fight which would ensue when they sought authority for a loan and Charles Tupper, one of the company's greatest parliamentary allies, was summoned home to pilot the bill through the House.

It was not, however, a solution to the short term problem. The company needed $3,850,000 by the first of January 1884 to pay off immediate debts. Nearly the same amount was needed to pay off a short term loan due on the eighth of January and the next installment to cover the dividend guarantee was due to the government on the first of February.

Donald arrived back in Montreal on January second and went straight to a Bank of Montreal board meeting. The bank was already carrying a CPR debt of $1,950,000 and had insisted the government provide a written guarantee that it would pick up the pieces if the syndicate defaulted. It was to be signed by Macdonald, Tilley who was the minister of finance, and Tupper. Only Tupper was prepared to comply with such a demand. Despite opposition within the bank's board, it authorized an overdraft which was not to exceed $3.5 million. Donald gave his personal guarantee for the full amount in addition to the amount Stephen, Angus, and McIntyre had already guaranteed. A million dollars in land grant bonds was lodged with the bank, as were $1.3 million worth of South Eastern Railway bonds. As well, the syndicate was required to provide "a letter undertaking to transfer to the bank when required certain shares of the Canada North West Land Company and a letter from Sir Charles Tupper, Minister of Railways and Canals, to pay on behalf of the Dominion Government all sums earned or to be earned by the CPR under its contract with the government whether out of cash subsidy or land grant bonds until the $3.5 million is fully repaid." Having stuck its neck out that far, the bank was less inclined to balk when Tupper asked if it would lend a further million dollars to stave off the railway's creditors until the government loan received parliamentary approval.[41]

The government loan was to be for $22,500,000 and was due to be repaid on May 1, 1891. In addition, the company requested the government to defer for five years the deposit of the next $7 million on the dividend guarantee and asked that the remaining cash subsidy and that part of the loan not needed to cancel debts be handed over on the basis of work done as a proportion of the total remaining to be done rather than on the mileage basis which had been used hitherto. It also sought the return of the land grant bonds which had been deposited as a guarantee that the company would honour the contract. In return, the company mortgaged the entire railway, including the land it had yet to claim. As well, it pledged to complete the road by May 1886, five years earlier than the contract specified.

The conditions, which had been proposed by George Stephen following at least one meeting of the company's executive committee in New York and undoubtedly following private discussions with Donald Smith, were dangerously flawed. If the men had in any way underestimated what it would cost to complete the railway, they would have no resources left within the company to provide collateral for a loan. Everything was to be mortgaged to the government, but some of the most difficult sections were yet to be built. Forty-five miles of barren rock had to be traversed north of Lake Superior and there was a gap of two hundred and ninety miles from Kicking Horse Pass, through the Selkirks to Kamloops where the Onderdonk line ended. The mountains, glaciers and thick forests of British Columbia could hold any number of costly surprises for the construction gangs. Yet without these stringent conditions, there would be no loan. Even with them, Macdonald could not be certain of his own party's support.

On the first of February, Donald was in the House of Commons' Visitors' Gallery to hear Tupper introduce the Railway Relief Bill. It was a strange sensation, looking down on the scene in which he had so recently played an active part. In the Press Gallery, the reporters nudged each other and pointed him out. The elegant man with him was his cousin, George Stephen, the older men whispered to the new recruits. The fat one was Van Horne. *The Globe* snidely observed that Donald was there to "hear the man who in 1878 denounced him in the most infamous manner in the same chamber labouring hard to show the company of which Mr. Smith is a leading member is composed of men of great wealth, enterprise, unblemished honour and undoubted integrity. Time certainly brings its revenge."[42]

The HBC's land commissioner, Charles Brydges, still a champion of the Grand Trunk, was found to be drifting through the Commons corridors as the debate got under way. Ostensibly, he was in Ottawa to settle problems with land patents but Stephen was certain he was briefing Cartwright and the Liberal Party on CPR matters. "He professes to be extra friendly to CPR but that does not deceive me. I know he is busy sewing 'tares among the wheat' and as he always is — fool enough to imagine no one sees it."[43]

The cousins scurried back and forth between Montreal and Ottawa, listening to the debates and ensuring that the government front bench had all the facts and figures necessary to counter the virulent criticism from the other side. It seemed increasingly silly that Donald and the prime minister were still not on speaking terms, the more so since each man had expressed to Stephen a desire to break through what was now a highly artificial barrier. Early in February 1884, Stephen offered to arrange a reconciliation. Both men agreed and on the ninth of February, Donald called on Macdonald at his office in Ottawa. When the men parted, they were friends. George Stephen was delighted.

> I must send you a line to say how grateful I am for your kind and cordial reception of Smith yesterday. He said nothing, but I know he *felt* a good deal and I know without saying it that he is today a much happier man. The pluck with which he has stood by me in my efforts to sustain the credit of the C.P.R. made it

> almost a duty on my part to try and restore friendly relations between one who has stood so courageously by the Company in its time of trouble and you to whom alone the C.P.R. owes its existence as a *real Canadian* Railway. I hope some day this fact will become more generally known than it is now.[44]

The restoration of cordial relations between the two Scots was the highlight of an otherwise depressing month. The daily newspaper attacks not only threatened the passage of the bill through the House but also damaged the company's credibility in the London financial market where the reprinted Canadian stories were compounded by Grand Trunk slanders. The British railway's owners were increasingly vengeful both publicly and privately. Letters were sent to the governor general who felt obliged to point out to Lord Claude Hamilton, a director of the Grand Trunk, that the English company had badly misjudged Canadian sentiments. "I should say with regard to portions of your letter and of Mr. Tyler's letter (those I mean in which you point to the consequences which the C.P.R. must expect unless it is able to propitiate your friends) that Mr. Hickson had done more harm than good by the minatory tone of his letters and public utterances. He is represented by his opponents as the mouthpiece of foreign shareholders who are endeavouring for selfish ends to thwart a great national enterprize."[45]

As the ponderous parliamentary wheels ground their slow way towards the CPR loan, the cousins fought daily battles to keep their enterprise afloat. On the evening of February 27, McIntyre went to New York "to raise by way of a loan for a few days $300,000 which we think will keep us out of the sheriff's hands till Tuesday or Wednesday." He was successful in finding the money, but he appears not to have raised a loan. "Manitoba stock dropped on Thursday [February 28] to 90 or 91%," Kennedy wrote to Hill on the first of March, "and as I could not understand the cause I went to work to trace it out and found that Duncan McIntyre came down here from Montreal on Wednesday with an order from Mr. Donald A. Smith for 2,500 shares of his stock which was immediately thrown on the market. He tried to conceal his movements by having his brokers who were really the sellers appear as buyers but I have been too long in the Street to be fooled in that way." Towards the end of March, Stephen wrote Hill a disingenuous letter saying he did not understand the fluctuations in the Manitoba road stock and offering assurances that both he and Donald would continue to hold a large amount.[46]

With the government loan in place, Stephen tried, and failed, to raise money in London that April to continue the construction of the Manitoba South Western which had attracted its own land grant which could be used as collateral. Again, the directors turned to the Bank of Montreal, requesting an overdraft of $1,250,000. This time the bank's demands were much as they had been in January: power of attorney enabling the bank to draw on the government for the monthly estimates, a deposit of South Eastern bonds and Canada North West Land Company stock and the personal guarantee of Donald and Stephen for $500,000 and of Stephen for a further $250,000.[47]

In May, McIntyre was so convinced that the CPR's days were numbered that he withdrew from the company. Van Horne replaced him as vice-president, and, to keep the matter quiet, Stephen eventually bought McIntyre's shares as he had done those which Kennedy and Hill had sold. Stephen was inclined to see things, especially where the railway was concerned, in black and white and could rarely bring himself to forgive what he perceived as betrayal. His anger with McIntyre boiled over eighteen months later.

> He has been so coarsely selfish & cowardly all through these 5 years. Ruthless in disregarding the interests of others whenever he could advance his own that I am bound in justice to my own self respect to avoid him in every way I can. Now that the CPR is finished I cannot help calling to mind that last year in our darkest days he was the first to refuse to credit the Coy and to threaten to sue it unless his firm's a/c for dry goods was at once paid.... When McIntyre deserted the Coy he made up his mind that it would "*burst*" and that Smith & I would lose every dollar we had, in the collapse. I think he is ashamed of himself now.[48]

McIntyre was followed in December by Baron de Reinach and, again, Stephen bought his shares. In July 1884, Stephen was back in London, using land grant bonds to obtain a four month loan from the British Bank. Even that was only approved after Angus and the cousins also provided their own personal guarantees.

The gloom lifted briefly in October. The balance sheets showed that the company was making a comfortable operating profit on all its divisions; there was over half a million gross in the first nine months of 1884, and when Stephen approached the National Provident Institution in Edinburgh, he raised £50,000, roughly a quarter of a million dollars, by pledging $385,000 worth of Toronto, Grey and Bruce bonds owned personally by himself, Donald and Angus. Their personal guarantees were also demanded in what was beginning to seem like a routine pledge. So cheered was he by the success of his Scottish mission that he hastened to a telegraph office and cabled to Donald the rallying cry of their clan. *Stand Fast Craigellachie!* There was fight left in George Stephen and his renewed vigour inspired his fellow Scots. Even the big, bluff Dutch-American, William Van Horne, took courage from the exhortation.

In November, the $5 million loan from John Kennedy was repaid and the stock which he had held as collateral was returned. Yet again, it was the cousins who put up the money, but they risked defaulting on the British Bank loan and on the 1883 Bank of Montreal loan which had been secured with Toronto, Grey and Bruce bonds. By December, Stephen was depressed again, warning the prime minister that "the credit of the Company both at home and abroad is at the moment gone and the ability of Smith and myself to sustain it is about exhausted."[49]

In January, the New York Stock Exchange authorities threatened to suspend CPR shares if the exact dividend was not announced. The three percent government guarantee was all very well but if, as everyone believed, the company was on the verge of bankruptcy, it could be forced to reveal its hand by announcing, or admitting that it could not announce, the dividend. Between them, Donald and

Stephen raised $650,000 to enable the usual five percent return to be declared. Early in February, Prime Minister Macdonald, Pope, the acting minister of railways, and Sir Leonard Tilley, the finance minister, in both their personal and government capacities guaranteed a five month Bank of Montreal loan for a million dollars. It was payable not to the CPR but to the cousins who made it over to the company to keep it going for a few weeks longer. In a letter which suggests he was unaware of the ministers' involvement, Stephen told Macdonald what he and Donald had done, adding, "It is necessary you should know this as in some quarters there is a feeling that we do not do as much for the Coy as we might. The real truth being that what Smith and I have done and are doing individually is simply absurd on any kind of business grounds. I venture to say there is not a business man in all Canada, knowing the facts, but will say we were a couple of fools for our pains. But as long as we are able to save & protect the company against its enemies who seem bent on its destruction we shall not grudge any risk, or loss that may occur. Personal interests have become quite a secondary affair with either of us."[50]

Years later, Van Horne liked to reminisce about the CPR's hour of crisis, sometimes adapting his stories to fit his audience. He recounted a board meeting early in 1885 when the company faced imminent bankruptcy. "If we succumb," said Donald turning to his cousin, "that must not be as long as we individually have a dollar." In one version of this story, Van Horne attributed the line to George Stephen while in others, he credited it to Donald. The statement has none of Stephen's casual language and use of slang and is much more likely to have fallen from Donald's lips. The personal responsibility implied in the phrase is entirely in line with the young Hudson's Bay Company clerk's obligation to account for each bullet and each mitten in the company store and it is allied to the stern sense of moral rectitude which old Mrs. Smith had inculcated sixty years before. When the last trumpet sounded, Donald did not want to be found wanting.[51]

Initially, financing the CPR's debts from their personal resources had not been especially difficult. Donald and his cousin had substantial holdings in the Saint Paul, Minneapolis and Manitoba Railway which they could use as collateral for loans while living comfortably on the handsome dividends the company paid. Earnings from other investments such as the cotton and woollen mills into which they had put their money many years before had enabled them to purchase companies such as the New Brunswick Railway which in turn provided further collateral for bank loans. The CPR paid five percent dividends twice a year on the face value of shares for which investors had, in some cases, paid only a quarter of par. This income enabled Donald and his cousin to buy more shares or to consolidate their ownership of the network of lines in Ontario and Quebec which would ultimately feed into the CPR. As long as they could roll over their debts, paying off one loan, claiming back the collateral and using it to support a subsequent loan, the men were comfortable.

Though the Grand Trunk's malicious campaign was at first little more than vexatious, it became highly damaging the moment it took hold and prevented the sale of shares at anything approximating their true market worth. The general depression in railway stocks exacerbated an already difficult situation which was made still worse when construction costs were discovered to be far in excess of anything anyone had calculated. It became progressively harder to roll over the debt and, as the company scrabbled for money, it was forced to take high interest, short term loans which merely compounded the financial problem. By the beginning of 1885, the men had virtually nothing left to use as collateral. Had the Bank of Montreal and one or two other creditors acted simultaneously to demand the men honour their personal guarantees, Donald Smith, R.B. Angus, George Stephen and the CPR would undoubtedly have found themselves calling in the receiver.

It was becoming more and more apparent that the solution to the company's problems could only come from the government's resources. On the fifteenth of January, two days after he arrived back in Montreal from London, Donald was on the train to Ottawa with Stephen and their lawyer, J.J.C. Abbott. He had spent the previous day discussing the options with Stephen, looking particularly at the proposal that they give up ten million acres from the land grant. Donald feared the adverse effect on the company's credit and persuaded Stephen that a sale of the company's lands, even at the government's current valuation of $1.25 an acre, would be preferable. It would be a purely paper transaction for the $10.25 million earned by the sale would immediately be used to wipe out nearly half the company's 1884 government loan. Reluctantly, they also agreed that if the government would give up its lien on the railway, they would cancel the remaining $35 million worth of authorized stock, replacing it with four percent mortgage bonds for which they sought a government guarantee. The money earned from the sale of the bonds would enable them to extinguish the government debt and pay for expenditure such as the acquisition of the Canada Central which had not been foreseen in the original contract. In the end, the government took land grant bonds worth ten million acres but otherwise, this was the deal which was accepted. The trouble was that it took a very long time to reach agreement.[52]

The cabinet was horrified at the prospect of coming to the rescue of the CPR yet again and initially refused to accept Stephen's proposals. Old Tomorrow bought time when there was none to buy by pushing through a franchise bill in which he was especially interested. Stephen fretted, daily sending urgent messages to Macdonald. Late in February, Donald found some more CPR shares to use to shore up American loans which, surprisingly, were renewed early in March.

On the eighteenth of March, the company officially applied to the privy council for a $5 million loan. In Ottawa on the twenty-sixth, Stephen received what he was obliged to consider the final rejection of his request for government aid. Dejected, he was about to check out of the Russell House when George Campbell, a CPR lobbyist, and Senator Frank Smith, one of the few remaining Tory railway enthusiasts, deduced what had happened and impelled Stephen to postpone his departure. While Campbell stood guard to prevent the president's escape, Smith and Mackenzie Bowell, now a convert to the CPR, drove to the prime minister's residence. Yet again, it was a midnight call. Macdonald agreed to reconsider.

In the meantime, the construction gangs, exasperated by the prolonged absence of the pay car, went on strike. There were nasty riots at Beavermouth, on the Columbia River. In desperation, Stephen begged John Henry Pope to urge Macdonald to action and once again, Pope delivered his dire warning. The collapse of the CPR would bring down the government, but this time it would take a huge number of Canadian businesses, all CPR creditors, down with it. On the twenty-fourth of April, Macdonald asked the Bank of Montreal to lend $5 million to the CPR and the bank flatly refused. It had no intention of figuring on the list of companies destroyed by the CPR. On the first of May, Macdonald finally gave notice that he intended to introduce relief measures and that was enough to persuade the bank to part with $750,000, enough to stave off the worst trouble while the franchise bill dragged on. Donald and Stephen signed the promissory note.

Though Macdonald had straightforward financial concerns about the relief bill, he knew that the attitude towards the CPR among the government and the general public had dramatically changed that spring. Suddenly, the railway had become a steel ribbon binding the nation together instead of a leech sucking the country's treasury dry and it was this which convinced him that he could persuade the House to authorize more financial support. The catalyst for this remarkable change was none other than Louis Riel, the man responsible for introducing Donald to the Northwest in 1869.

Riel had passed the majority of his banishment in the United States though he had also spent time in a mental hospital in Quebec. When he was committed, there was every evidence that he was mentally ill, but he subsequently claimed that he had been pretending and his followers accepted this account. He moved west to live and work among the Métis in the United States and, in 1884, travelled north from Montana to Batoche in what is now Saskatchewan, convinced, as he had been fifteen years earlier, that he had a mission to help "his people."

Riel had not long been in Batoche before he was calling for a united front among the Anglophone and Francophone settlers whether or not they were of mixed-blood. He wanted, by peaceful protest, to secure free land for the settlers, provincial status or at least a voice in the Dominion parliament for Saskatchewan, Alberta and Assiniboia (the southern half of Saskatchewan), and a revision of the land laws to encourage and facilitate settlement. Riel grew increasingly excited and unwilling to listen to the moderating voice of the church. In March 1885, the mounted police ordered a detachment from Regina to reinforce Fort Carlton but exaggerated accounts of this move convinced Riel an attack was imminent. He took prisoners and seized guns and ammunition. On the twenty-sixth of March, a scuffle between police from Fort Carlton and a group of Métis escalated into a half hour gun battle. Twelve police and militia men were killed and eleven wounded. The Métis, who were in a much superior position, lost five men and one was slightly wounded.

From the CPR's point of view, trouble in the Northwest was worrying because it took the government's mind off the railway's looming bankruptcy. But while George Stephen waited with growing despair for a reply from Macdonald to his proposal for the second railway relief bill, Van Horne stepped forward and offered to transport troops west on the CPR. There was a little matter of four interruptions in the line of rail north of Lake Superior but sleighs took men over two of the spaces and they marched over two twenty mile stretches. In the national emergency, the construction gangs found new energy and drove the line forward at a furious pace. The last rail was in place before the last of the troops passed on their journey west.

Donald, in the meantime, obtained for the Hudson's Bay Company the contracts to provision the troops and provide transport from Qu'Appelle on the CPR line to the junction of the North and South Saskatchewan Rivers. There was virtually no one in Ottawa with any knowledge of the Northwest and Adolphe Caron, the minister of militia, had no experience of troop movements or commissary needs. True, Canadians had never fought a battle apart from flurries with invading Fenians, but the Militia Department had never even given a thought to rations. Donald and Joseph Wrigley who had replaced Grahame in 1884, decided the men should have vegetables with their beef and hard tack and so cakes of dehydrated and compressed vegetables were sent out from Winnipeg. It was weeks before Caron announced that vegetables were not part of the approved rations. The department had not even provided for a telegraph cypher and had not even considered using one till Wrigley suggested it. As late as April 5, Wrigley was cabling to Donald, "Fear trouble from want of military organization and apparent incompetence," but between them, Donald, Van Horne and Wrigley managed to sort out transport and supplies for over three thousand soldiers.[53]

On May 12, a four day battle at Batoche came to an end, bringing the final defeat to the Métis. Three days later, Louis Riel surrendered. Among those who died of wounds received at Batoche was Private Richard Hardisty, the eldest son of William Lucas Hardisty, Bella's eldest brother.

Shots were still being fired at Batoche when Van Horne suggested that some of the directors might like to travel over the newly completed section of the line. Donald and Sandford Fleming had HBC work in Winnipeg and it seemed a good idea to essay the Lake Superior route. Angus, Van Horne and Osler accompanied them to Fort William. The road had been built as cheaply as possible and large sections were unballasted. Speed was impossible. On Saturday the sixteenth, they proceeded at the stately pace of four miles an hour. On Monday, when the last rail was laid over the final gap in the line, they were preceded across it by the Montreal garrison heading west, not knowing that the fighting was over. After Fort William, however, the CPR directors travelled quickly and reached Winnipeg on the twenty-first.

Hudson's Bay business was interspersed with social calls and dinner parties. Donald and Fleming attended the Scots Presbyterian church on Sunday morning and in the afternoon attended the funeral service for young Richard Hardisty and two of his comrades. "No such gathering had ever before been seen in Winnipeg or in the Northwest," the *Free Press* reported to its readers, trying hard to replace the excitement it usually conveyed when describing new experiences with a solemn demeanour more fitting to the occasion. "The presence of the Montreal Garrison Artillery in full force added an important feature to the occasion, their band delighting all listeners with its strains; and the firing party at the grave completing the appropriateness of the military character of the demonstration."[54]

The trip to Winnipeg, and a visit with Jim Hill on the return journey via Saint Paul, offered a brief respite to the incessant worry about the railway's future. True, Macdonald had publicly said he would do something but he had not devised the legislation and time was running out. It seemed likely that Macdonald would be able to win the support of his cabinet since the CPR's prompt action in transporting the troops had completely revolutionized the way people thought of Canada and the railway. The British government, preparing for the possibility of war with Russia, now viewed the railway as a national asset and had asked if the CPR could transport British troops to the Pacific coast. Finally, at the end of May, with Van Horne and some of his colleagues desperately trying to eavesdrop in an ante-room, the cabinet agreed to back another million dollar loan from the Bank of Montreal. It was "quite illegal," Macdonald explained to Stephen but at least it would mean the company could meet the interest on the Ontario and Quebec bonds due the following week.[55]

Macdonald finally brought the CPR Relief Bill before parliament on June 16. That it would pass was a foregone conclusion but Blake nevertheless seized the opportunity to attack in another of his long and turgid speeches. Though they would not have realized it, the more he and others on his side of the house talked, the closer they brought the CPR to collapse. On July 14, the company's obligation of $400,000 to the Dominion Bridge Company was due and others were to come up at weekly intervals till early August. The bill passed the Commons on July 10 but still needed the approval of the Senate and royal assent. On the thirteenth, Van Horne took a special to Ottawa and sought out Macdonald. If Dominion Bridge called in the payment, the company "would burst;" he thought only the Bank of Toronto and the Bank of Montreal would survive the crash which would ensue. Macdonald could do nothing to hurry the Senate and the bridge company, seeing its money coming, allowed a few days' grace. Royal assent was given on July 20.[56]

Donald and George Stephen were sufficiently confident of the government's support that they permitted themselves a week at the fishing camp at Matapedia at the beginning of July. No doubt there was fishing but the conversation was of the mortgage bonds which they were planning to launch in London. On the eleventh the men, together with Bella and Maggie and doubtless Annie Stephen as well, boarded the *Servia* for Liverpool.

The day royal assent was given, the CPR board approved the new five percent mortgage bond issue and the Stephens and Smiths arrived in Liverpool where they were met by Thomas Skinner, who had already prepared the bonds. Charles Tupper, back in London as high commissioner, had effectively done a deal with Baring Brothers which only needed the cousins' approval. This they cabled and the bonds were up for sale before the travellers reached London. The Canadian government took $15 million worth of bonds as a contribution towards its loan and another $5 million as collateral for a $5 million loan which was also secured by the postal subsidy. Barings bought the entire remainder at ninety-one, much to the disgust of John Rose who had been preparing a syndicate to take them at seventy-five. So grateful was the CPR to the London bank that the little town of Farwell where the line crossed the Columbia River was renamed Revelstoke in honour of the bank's chairman. In fact, only about half the bonds sold to investors, "Barings and their friends taking the other half," as Stephen wrote to the prime minister in October. "Mr. Smith & I have done what we can to build up the sale by buying between us £100,000." The important point, however, was that the company had broken the Grand Trunk stranglehold and established itself on the London market as a Canadian security worth investing in.[57]

Leaving Bella at the spa in Carlsbad, Donald and Maggie returned to Canada on the *Parisian* in the latter part of August. Soon after his return, his Toronto, Grey and Bruce bonds were again in use as collateral for a $640,000 loan from the Bank of Montreal, almost certainly to meet the next dividend payment. On the eighteenth of September it was the cousins' Ontario and Quebec debentures which underpinned an advance of a million dollars to enable the railway to build a bridge across the St. Lawrence. A few days later, a government enforced deal with the Grand Trunk gave the CPR control over the North Shore Line, formerly the Quebec, Montreal, Ottawa and Occidental route between Montreal and Quebec. Financially, it was not plain sailing yet, but at least the loans were containable. The fear of failure had subsided, to be replaced by growing excitement as the line neared completion.

In September, Lord Lansdowne prepared for a trip west. He would visit the territory newly opened by the railway and had accepted the company's invitation to drive the last spike. Van Horne's concern for creature comforts meant the governor general travelled in style and much appreciated the chance to do so. "Your new sleeper has put us a little out of conceit with the old 'Cumberland' which rattles like a London 4 wheeler," he genially complained to George Stephen. Unhappily, by the end of September, he had reason to feel less cheerful for streaming rain had delayed construction work and he was obliged to return to the east for the opening of parliament.

Late on the night of Tuesday, October 27, Donald and Van Horne boarded the CPR at Montreal. Their first stop was Ottawa where they picked up Fleming who had been elected a director of the railway in June. Two private cars made the journey west, the *Matapedia,* named in recognition of the role the fishing camp had played in the instigation of the railway, and the *Saskatchewan* which acknowledged both the role of the recent rebellion in the completion of the railway and the place which the entire Northwest had played in the development of the cousins' commitment to rail communication. The next private car was to be called *Earnscliffe* after the prime ministerial residence and in honour of the support Macdonald had given the company.

On Thursday the twenty-ninth, the travellers were delayed by two sinkholes and wise they were to wait. When the government had constructed the section of track west of Fort William, it had filled in numerous of these slime covered bogs only to find a few weeks, or sometimes a few minutes, later that the muskeg at the bottom had melted and the holes were greedily sucking in everything that weighed more than the ubiquitous mosquito.

Saturday brought them to Winnipeg and dinner at Silver Heights with John McTavish, the land agent, George Harris another director, and J.J.C. Abbott, the company's lawyer. "It seems difficult to realize we left Ottawa so short a time back & did not travel two nights," Fleming noted in his diary. Donald had been unwell in the days before he left Montreal and now took the opportunity to stay close to home, resting and harnessing his resources. No doubt he wrote Bella who had gone from Carlsbad to London where she was probably the Stephens' guest at their new home in St. James's Place. She had recently been to a dinner party at the Armits' and would shortly be off to Edinburgh to visit Donald's brother and to see Richard, son of her favourite brother Richard, who was at school in the Scottish capital. How far apart they were, but how close, despite the miles which separated them. And what stories would he have to tell when they met in London at Christmas![58]

The first regular CPR train from Winnipeg to Montreal departed with passengers and freight at eight o'clock on Sunday night. Twelve hours later, Donald and Fleming were seated in Donald's carriage, ready for the drive from Silver Heights to the station in Winnipeg. At half past nine, the train pulled out for the first journey to the Pacific.

They were already past Medicine Hat when they woke the following morning and travelled at the astonishing speed of fifty miles an hour for the first ten miles west of Calgary. Then began the slow pull up to Kicking Horse Pass and the exhilarating views as they snaked their way down towards the Columbia River. The air was clear and the snow crested mountains looked their best in the crisp, late autumn air. At Field, they stopped to take on water and fuel and the men lined up outside the tent hotel to have their photograph taken. As they headed towards Donald, the first crossing on the Columbia, the driver pushed his engine to sixty miles an hour.

The next day's journey through the Selkirks brought back happy memories to Fleming who, at Van Horne's request several years earlier, had checked Rogers' pass to confirm that it really was as feasible as the explorer claimed. To the delight of his fellow passengers, Fleming pointed out his old camping grounds and recalled the early days in the mountains before the arrival of the construction gangs.

They had plenty of opportunity to admire the mountain scenery at Revelstoke where the air remained cold but clear. Ahead, the rails had still not been laid because of the heavy rain and there were reports of a foot of snow further west. At three the following afternoon, having collected Sam Steele of the North West Mounted Police and others from the west, they headed for Eagle Summit in the Gold Range where they spent the night.

At six o'clock the next morning, Saturday the seventh of November, navvies began to lay the final mile of track and an hour and a half later, the special headed west from Eagle Summit. As Donald recalled many years later, "It was a dismal, dreary day in the first week of November, but we soon got out into the open country, and presently it was one of those bright, pleasant, bracing days of the autumn summer." There was much joshing and chafing among the workmen as the gentlemen stepped down from their cars. Van Horne they knew and some had encountered the tall man with the white spade beard. He was Sandford Fleming. The thin, rather quiet one was Donald Smith, the Scot who had risked his fortune to bring these two pieces of steel together.

There would be no fancy ceremony, the general manager had declared. "The last spike will be just as good an iron one as there is between Montreal and Vancouver, and anyone who wants to see it driven will have to pay full fare." He was not quite as good as his word, for his own tribute to the men who had sounded their clan's rallying cry and brought the railway back from the edge of disaster would soon be nailed to the junction box. This was Craigellachie.[59]

A maul was handed to Donald who, in the absence of both the governor general and the railway's president, was to drive the last spike. The men crowded around him. To his right were Van Horne and Fleming, behind him were Michael Haney, general manager of the Onderdonk section and Henry Cambie, the section's engineer. John McTavish, the erstwhile HBC accountant and now in charge of the land office, and John Egan, the railway's western superintendent, also gathered to watch the scene as did over a hundred of the men by whose labour the road was pushed across the prairies and through the mountains. They froze while the photographer captured the scene, changed poses and froze again.

The task of driving the last spike more than made up for Donald's having his name left off the original contract, but had George Stephen thought about his cousin's physical skills rather than his financial and emotional commitment to the Canadian Pacific Railway, he might have had second thoughts before he asked him to do the job. Major Rogers held the tie in place and Donald swung. He missed and bent the nail. Quickly, it was pulled out and replaced. With some rather more delicate taps to get it started, he succeeded in driving the nail home. Writing of the occasion for the *Canadian Alpine Journal*, Fleming observed that

> the engineers, the workmen, every one present, appeared deeply impressed by what was taking place. It was felt by all to be the moment of triumph. The central figure — the only one at the moment in action — was more than the representative of the railway company. His presence recalled memories of the Mackenzies, Frasers, Finlaysons, Thompsons, McLeods, MacGillivrays, Stuarts, MacTavishes, and McLoughlins, who, in a past generation had penetrated the surrounding mountains.[60]

To reach this point, Donald had twice crossed the Columbia River in which his uncle, Robert Stuart, had drowned while saving his colleagues. The train would shortly descend the Fraser Canyon which Robert's brother, John Stuart, had explored with Simon Fraser so many years before. Indeed, it was because of John Stuart and all these men from the North West Company who crowded in on their thoughts that Donald now stood at Craigellachie.

> The spike driven home, the silence for a moment or two remained unbroken. It seemed as if the act now performed had worked a spell on all present. Each was absorbed in his own thoughts. The silence was, however, of short duration. The pent-up feelings found vent in a spontaneous cheer, the echoes of which will long be remembered in Craigellachie.[61]

Called on to make a speech, Van Horne for once was lost for words. "All I can say is that the work has been well done in every way." It was the right thing to say at the time, but hardly the truth. Large sections of track had been left unballasted to save money. For the same reason, huge trestles had been made of wood and would have to be replaced by steel ones. Some gradients were too steep and there would be a prolonged wrangle over the quality of work on the Onderdonk section where corners had been cut to save costs. Still, the Canadian Pacific was now an accomplished fact and had been completed well ahead of the deadline specified in the original contract.

In the scramble for souvenirs which followed, Van Horne's secretary picked up the discarded, crooked nail, but Donald asked him to hand it over. A portion of it, ringed in diamonds, made a gift for Bella. They had not spent much time together for the last ten or fifteen years. Donald's duties in Ottawa, Winnipeg and London and Bella's need for warmer climates to keep chest infections at bay, and summers in Carlsbad to minimize the rheumatic pains which plagued many of the

Hardistys, had forced them apart more often than either of them wished, but the absences had not diminished the love they felt for each other. They were bound together by experiences of which their city friends knew nothing and those were unbreakable ties. With a diamond encrusted nail, Donald could express his gratitude for her love.

"All aboard for the Pacific!" a voice shouted and the directors and their guests scrambled onto the train which headed along the Thompson River Valley. The *Matapedia*, the *British Daily Colonist* noted, was "an elegant and luxurious affair" but Sam Steele, travelling at the end of the train in the private car of the traffic manager of the Onderdonk section, was proud to note that he, the traffic manager and James Dickey, the dominion engineer, were the only ones in their car who were not sick as the train whipped around corners at an average of fifty-seven miles an hour. Modern brakes and coupling systems would be needed before the journey could truly be luxurious.[62]

They spent the night at the western end of the Thompson Valley, joining the Fraser early the next morning so the passengers could enjoy the canyon's scenic splendours in daylight. A few hours later, at half past eleven, the train pulled into Port Moody where the passengers boarded the *Princess Louise* for a tour of Burrard Inlet and English Bay. The provincial government had recently handed over six thousand acres of thickly forested land in order to induce the railway to move its terminus from Port Moody to the little village of Granville on the southern shores of the inlet. The trees were beginning to be cleared and a street plan was being drawn up; Van Horne had decided to call this new place Vancouver.

The steamer took the men across to Vancouver Island for congratulatory speeches in the provincial capital before returning to the mainland, travelling up the Fraser River to New Westminster. Late on the morning of the twelfth, they were back on the train. They may well have felt pleased with themselves, but thought otherwise when they reached Eagle Pass again. There were twenty-one inches of snow in the Selkirks and the engine was thrown off the line. It took twelve hours to clear the tracks and reset the engine, but once they were under way again, they made good time. Close to noon on Sunday, the fifteenth of November, the train was running parallel to the Assiniboine River, heading towards Winnipeg and a celebratory party at Silver Heights. Van Horne, always fond of a practical joke, was probably the author of the account of what happened next.

> We were all engaged in conversation, and Mr. Smith apparently did not notice that the engine driver had reversed the engine. At last he looked out of the window.
>
> "Why, we are backing up," he said; and then, "Now, there's a very neat place. I don't remember seeing that farm before. And those cattle — why, who is it that has Aberdeen cattle like that? I thought I was the only one. This is really very strange." Suddenly the house came into view. "Why, gentlemen, I must be going crazy. I've lived here many years and I never noticed another place so exactly like 'Silver Heights'."

> "Silver Heights," called the conductor. The car stopped and some of us began to betray our enjoyment of the joke. After another glance outside he began to laugh too. I never saw him so delighted.[63]

While the directors had been in the west, a railway crew, on Van Horne's instructions, had used spare rails and ties to lay a spur from the main line along the edge of Silver Heights, bringing passengers almost to Donald's front door. It was a splendid gesture and gave a happy fillip to the journey's end.

The only thing to mar the day was news from Regina that Louis Riel had been hanged that morning. He was a difficult and complex man, prone to extreme behaviour but with much in his character that Donald had found admirable: his death brought a tinge of sadness to an otherwise joyful day.

By noon on Thursday, Donald was back in Montreal, completing in two and a half days a journey which had taken him two weeks fifteen years before. On Saturday the twenty-eighth, he sailed from New York with a bent railway spike in his pocket. It would be a fine Christmas.

CHAPTER THIRTEEN

THE CANADIAN SUB-COMMITTEE 1880–1889

If there ever was a fool's paradise, it sure was located in Winnipeg. Men made fortunes — mostly on paper — and life was one continuous joy-ride.
George Ham [1]

In the autumn of 1878, Donald Smith had made up his mind to retire from the Hudson's Bay Company. He rightly anticipated that Sir John A. Macdonald would not wish to honour Alexander Mackenzie's commitment to purchase the land which the company had retained and he perceived that a market for that land would be created when the Saint Paul, Minneapolis and Manitoba Railway was completed by the end of 1879. The Land Commissioner's job would substantially change and Donald was not especially interested in the work which would be entailed in selling plots to intending settlers. The policy of the company's Land Department and the general principles to be applied to settlement of the Northwest were of great importance to him, but he hoped to avoid being involved in the details of their implementation. Even without the heavy returns from the Manitoba road, his investments were producing sufficient income to enable him to live comfortably and, much as he cared about the HBC, he felt no obligation to remain as an employee.

In January 1879, he discussed land policy with the Governor and Committee, suggesting ways in which it should be developed in the light of what he knew would soon happen. At the same time, he indicated his intention of resigning, formally writing to this effect on the twenty-fifth of February.

The board initially thought it would appoint a clerk to manage land sales and Donald probably recommended John McTavish, who subsequently became the CPR's land agent. The change would provide an opportunity for the Governor and Committee to revert to a more direct involvement in the management of the company, something which it had always found difficult to do with Donald. The board undoubtedly thought itself sufficiently knowledgeable to exercise its judgement: Eden Colvile, the deputy governor had first hand Canadian experience and was to refresh his knowledge of the Northwest with a visit there in 1880, and John Rose, who was well connected with many Canadian businesses, was also on the board. Donald and Sandford Fleming, now both shareholders, could also be called on for information should it be required.

Early in February, Charles Brydges, then living in Montreal, learned of Donald's resignation, probably in a letter from John Rose, and wrote to Prime Minister Macdonald to seek his help in getting the job for himself. Brydges was a loyal Tory and long time supporter of the prime minister, though he was not as influential as he believed himself to be.

In 1879, however, it happened that Macdonald owed Brydges a favour. As general manager of the Grand Trunk Railway, Brydges had been keen to find a Canadian warm water port as a terminus for his financially ailing line and in 1868 conceived that this could be achieved through the Intercolonial Railway, then being built to link the Maritime provinces with the rest of Canada. To facilitate Brydges' ambitions, Macdonald, at the recommendation of John Rose, had appointed him to the Intercolonial's board of commissioners from which vantage point he persistently harassed the chief engineer, Sandford Fleming, whose standards of construction and safety were considerably higher than those generally adhered to by railways such as the Grand Trunk. Though it was never proven, Fleming was accused of corrupt practices in the construction of a portion of the Intercolonial and a contribution to Tupper's election fund was said to have ensured that Tupper would side with Fleming whenever possible. For whatever reason, Tupper did back Fleming in most controversies and Brydges opposed both men, constantly alluding to their supposed corruption.

Brydges himself was no saint. His charitable work on behalf of churches and hospitals in Montreal and Winnipeg laid a veneer of respectability over a somewhat slippery morality which allowed him to favour himself, his family, friends and political allies, sometimes at the expense of those to whom he owed a professional allegiance. He was a highly capable and experienced, if autocratic, manager with whom it was well to be on good terms but not wise to trust absolutely.

In 1874, Brydges resigned from the Grand Trunk when Mackenzie appointed him general supervisor of government railways but in 1879, when the Conservatives returned to power, he was immediately dismissed by Charles Tupper. Tupper and Brydges could not have been expected to collaborate on a railway policy which would entail the construction of the CPR, especially since Fleming was then the chief engineer and Brydges was understood to have continued his sympathies and support for the Grand Trunk: Macdonald had no alternative but to agree to Tupper's request for his dismissal. But it did place Macdonald under an obligation to find Brydges other employment.

In accordance with Brydges' suggestion, Macdonald wrote John Rose and, shortly after, Brydges sailed for London, though, at Rose's insistence, he kept the real reason for his journey a secret. Rose, in the meantime, set about convincing his fellow HBC directors that Brydges should be appointed as Land Commissioner. It was not an easy task, for Brydges had made a good many enemies and did not have the reputation for financial probity which the Hudson's Bay Company normally expected of its employees. As a concerned shareholder observed at the General Court in June, "He is, no doubt, a man of great ability, but he has also the reputation of taking great care of himself." Investigations concerning some of his past dealings found him blameless and even Donald, who had heard the stories, could see the advantages of having a man of his experience in the post and supported Rose in his advocacy.[2]

Rose, who never had any qualms about discussing the HBC's confidential business with the prime minister, wrote to explain that it was intended that Brydges should eventually replace Grahame as well, but this would have to be done gradually, not only because Brydges needed to familiarize himself with the work but also because the wintering partners disapproved of bringing in an outsider as Chief Commissioner. Placing Brydges in overall responsibility is unquestionably the kind of plan Rose would have liked to have seen put in place but whether it was HBC policy is doubtful. Nothing in company correspondence ever refers to it, even obliquely, and the idea that "a gentleman should be selected and placed over the whole of the Company's affairs in the Dominion" would be specifically rejected in March 1883.[3]

It had been arranged that Donald would help Brydges over a two year transition period and receive £250 a year for doing so. Donald would naturally have supported his successor insofar as his time and Brydges' needs demanded it and payment for doing so, which was decreed by the board without consultation, was rather demeaning. When £250 was credited to his London account with the company in May 1880, he returned it, asking that it be donated to "the Fund for the benefit of the families of officers connected with the Home Service requiring assistance, which was established by Mr. Potter & which has been found to be of great service in several instances." A second gratuity was not offered.[4]

Now that he was no longer a company employee, Donald was obliged to establish an office and staff for himself. He had been using Chief Factor James Bissett as his attorney and had taken on a man to keep the Private Cash Accounts. Bissett was on furlough in 1880 but working most of the time for Donald; before the year was out, he had resigned his HBC commission and set up Donald's Montreal office in the HBC building. To the company's annoyance, in 1881 Donald also secured offices for himself in the company's new building in Winnipeg. The Governor and Committee sensed that, though he was no longer on the payroll, he had no intention of letting go and, in that, they were entirely correct. His loyalty to the company was a deeply personal one: he perceived his lineage as stemming from the North West Company in which his uncles and other, more distant relatives had been partners and he neither could nor would turn his back on this heritage.

When land fever broke out in Winnipeg as the CPR steel got closer and closer, speculation was not confined to the railway staff; almost everyone was buying land in the Northwest as fast as possible and reselling it at a vast profit. A land madness gripped the prairies in 1881 and 1882: in Winnipeg, HBC reserve lots sold for an average of $295 in June 1880 but soared to $813 in April the following year. By August 1881, the average price had doubled to $1,502, a tiny increase compared to the jump to $6,425 which was recorded at the beginning of 1882. In February, it was up to $8,576, but the bubble had burst by May when the price was down to $2,750.[5]

At the beginning of the boom, the HBC had still not disposed of much of its land reserves, including a large portion in the vicinity of Fort Garry, and this gave the men in the land office considerable power both as sources of information about land sales and as partners in speculative deals. As early as June 1879, warnings from Donald and Sandford Fleming prompted the board to pass a resolution forbidding officers or servants to engage in land speculation and in July that year, Armit wrote Brydges to warn him that "the Governor & Committee have a strong objection to any land speculation on the part of the Officers of the Company." Brydges and Grahame were requested to "discourage any such practice by every means in their power."[6]

It was, however, easy to shelter behind others and very tempting to do so when the rewards could be so great. Staff joined syndicates, frequently organized by Arthur Wellington Ross, one of the most active speculators in the Northwest, and used other names to disguise their activities. Both Charles Brydges and Alexander Galt used their sons as fronts in deals done with Ross.[7]

At the beginning of December 1881, James Grahame wrote William Armit, observing in the course of his letter that "everybody is speculating and getting rich except myself." "Did you mean anything in particular?" Armit responded, adding that Grahame "need not be afraid of mentioning the *name privately*." It should be sent in a coded cable and not be copied to Brydges, he explained, noting that the head of the Land Department "does not strictly confine his attention to said matters, but sometimes goes into other peoples [sic] provinces with or without their leave."[8]

En route to and from Nice that winter, Donald called at the HBC's London offices where he revealed his concern about land speculation, especially with regard to the HBC's Winnipeg town lots. Sandford Fleming had discussed his worries with Donald in Montreal in the middle of June, pointing out that the situation was complicated by the fact that land sales were secret and known only to Brydges and his intimates. Rumours of favouritism were rife. London's alarm increased when Grahame observed in January 1882 that "it is quite impossible to get our employees to refrain from speculating in Real Estate."[9]

Donald and Fleming discussed the situation in the Northwest on several occasions in the spring of 1882; Fleming had been elected the HBC's first non-resident director and was conscientious in his duties, worrying particularly about the company's reputation in the light of the stories which were circulating. On the ninth of June, shortly before Donald left for London and the semi-annual meeting of the General Court, Fleming briefed him again on the situation in the Land Department.[10]

By May, the Governor and Committee were well aware of stories that a syndicate had purchased lots at the old Fort Garry site and had re-sold them at a substantial profit. Colvile wanted the names of the syndicate, just as he wanted the names of another group which had been buying town lots in Edmonton. "You should be most careful in these stirring times, to give no handle to a lot of speculators to accuse you of favoring connections or relations," he warned Brydges. "You must be like Caesar's wife above suspicion."[11]

In the Northwest, old settlers and men seeking a stable future for themselves and their families often found themselves in conflict with land sharks. In the HBC land office, this created an obligation, as the governor had said, to be above suspicion while, at the same time, obtaining the highest possible prices for land. In London and Canada, there were growing doubts about the land office on both counts.

Matters began to come to a head in the summer of 1882 when a delegation of shareholders called on the Governor and Committee in advance of the General Court to express their concern. The board seems to have expected trouble at the meeting but forestalled it by telling the dissatisfied shareholders that Armit would be assigned to investigate the complaints, with assistance from Fleming who knew the land in the Northwest so well. Donald may have been among the delegation of shareholders and certainly had already raised the matter with the board, for Colvile wrote him on June 20 to point out that the Committee had a duty to protect officers from false accusations but "it is equally their duty to investigate charges made on the authority of gentlemen of standing, & having a large share in the Company like you."[12]

Donald's "large share in the Company" was of very recent standing. In April he had sold about $200,000 of his Saint Paul, Minneapolis and Manitoba shares in order to buy fifteen hundred HBC shares from stockbrokers William Bennett and Sydney Scott. To the one hundred shares he had bought in 1875, he had added three hundred and seventy-five in October 1879 and a further twenty-five in April 1880. His total was now a highly respectable 2,000 shares.[13]

In August, Fleming, Armit and Donald were all in Winnipeg where dinners at Silver Heights introduced the English visitor to local dignitaries. Undoubtedly there were also private conversations as Armit began to dig in the HBC's Winnipeg offices. He soon discovered that Grahame, rather than being the innocent observer of other people's land speculation, had himself been a party to a purchase arranged through the company's (and Donald's) lawyer, Sedley Blanchard. The proposition had come from Blanchard and the syndicate also included John Balsillie, a clerk in the land office. Before it was known publicly that parts of the Fort Garry reserve were for sale, the three bought fifty-six lots there for $280,000 and a few days later sold eleven of them for $270,000. Both Grahame and Blanchard reported that Brydges had also been a partner in the syndicate, though Blanchard subsequently denied having said so. Sir John Rose, who took it upon himself to investigate the same allegations, found that Brydges was not guilty of this charge but, as Rose confided to Sir John A. Macdonald, he had been guilty of nepotism.[14]

Armit also discovered that the men surveying the company's land were allowed to purchase it. They shared their assessments of the quality of the land with clerks in the land office who showed the information to others in the company's employ, enabling them to acquire land with a good idea of its value and without the general public being informed that the land was for sale. Brydges saw no harm in private sales, providing he was able to achieve the price he had set, but only a public sale would prove it was the best possible price.

The question of land prices blown out of all proportion was a dead one by the time Armit and John Rose arrived in Winnipeg that summer. In April, land sales at Edmonton, which was little more than a fur post and a few houses, had failed, with a knock on effect that rapidly depressed prices across the prairies. Also in April, the Red River burst its banks. The river frequently floods in spring, spreading black alluvial soil across the valley and enriching the farms. But in 1882, it flooded as it had not done since 1856.

Heavy snowstorms at the beginning of March were followed towards the end of the month by blizzards so severe that rail traffic in and out of Winnipeg was halted for the better part of two weeks. A rapid thaw with torrential rains south of the city ensued in April. The river began to rise two feet a day as the flood moved inexorably north towards Winnipeg. On the thirteenth of April, Donald was closeted in Van Horne's office with Angus, McIntyre and Hill, discussing the CPR's May share issue, the threat from the Northern Pacific and the formation of the Canada North West Land Company. On Monday, the seventeenth, the others left for the east, but Donald remained.

On the eighteenth, the rising waters and broken chunks of ice swept away the bridge at Emerson on the Canadian side of the border before rushing on to Winnipeg. By noon on the nineteenth of April the ice was packed against the piers of the newly completed Broadway Bridge and hundreds of men, women and children lined the shores of the river in ghoulish anticipation. As the *Free Press* explained to the few readers who missed the sight, "about one o'clock in the afternoon the vast field of ice commenced to move, and in a few moments the river was covered from bank to bank with the advancing avalanche." It "dismembered" the bridge and the waters flooded the city streets. The March snow blockade which had stopped the trains was replaced by a blockade of water. South of the city, trains went off the track or found that their fires had expired because the fuel supplies were under water. Tracks were washed out and service was suspended on both the Pembina Branch and the Manitoba road. In Winnipeg, food and supplies of all sorts either ran out or reached such exorbitant prices as to be unaffordable.

Finally, on Monday the twenty-fourth, a passenger train set out for the south. Donald, together with a Montreal friend, Alex Davidson, joined it, along with about three hundred others, all eager to make their escape from the water and the mud. The bridge over the St. Joe River near the American border was doubtful and the passengers were obliged to disembark and walk in the dark across the open tie bridge, following a brakeman with a lantern. Davidson's foot struck the heel of the man in front of him and he slipped. Normally the surface of the river was thirty feet below the bridge, but one leg went down through the ties and Davidson was wet up to his thigh.

When the travellers reached the south end of the bridge, a paddle wheeler came into sight. It offloaded north bound passengers and collected Donald and the others. "For an hour the steamer proceeded over the prairie farms until we reached the Pembina upgrade, where a freight train was partly under water. A cable from our steamer was secured to the rails, and the boat slowly pulled alongside the embankment. Then we crept along the edge of the embankment keeping as close as possible to the freight cars, until we reached the passenger train near the station. There we found Pullmans & comfort." Donald's travelling companions remembered "his simplicity and his genuineness" on that journey; for his part, he must have recalled the Findhorn fish boats sailing over Scottish farms in the great Morayshire flood of his boyhood.[15]

The rains may have drowned land speculation in the Northwest, but they did not wash away the problems which the land boom both caused and revealed. In the autumn of 1882, the company issued a reminder that speculation in lands was forbidden and in March 1883, the Governor and Committee asked Grahame to resign though it would be over a year before they could actually be rid of him because they had great difficulties in finding a suitable replacement. When he was finally dismissed, Grahame responded spitefully, sending a letter to Colvile and copying it to all the wintering partners who had held commissions in 1869 and were still active. He alleged that their interests had not been taken care of as Donald had promised in 1871 when he renegotiated the Deed Poll. Rather, he claimed, compensation for company losses in 1869 had finally been received and had been retained by the stockholders instead of being shared with the commissioned officers. In fact, the company had, at last, received the interest earned between the date the £300,000 compensation for the company's landed rights was due to be paid and the date it was actually handed over. None of it was owed to the wintering partners and Grahame merely succeeded in ensuring that his former colleagues thought even less well of him.[16]

Fleming's report to the board in October 1882 explained clearly that private sales would inevitably bring Brydges' judgement into question and give rise to complaints, whether well founded or not. Public advertising of sales and regular auctions would allow the prices to be determined by the market place and simultaneously rid the HBC of the taint of favouritism. Armit, in his report, contended that many plots had been sold prematurely, especially those which Brydges had disposed of before the railway had reached them. As a result, prices were much below what could have been expected.

Both Fleming's and Armit's reports were hard for John Rose to swallow for they made it clear that his protégé was lining, if not his own pockets, then his son's; that he had failed either to curtail or to report his staff's contravention of the rules regarding land speculation; and that he had not obtained for the shareholders the best possible return on their investment. Rose tried to persuade Armit to modify his report but the secretary declined, citing specific instances which proved his point, comparing prices which others had achieved for similar land and quoting the views of Alexander Begg, the CPR's agent in London.[17]

Donald was both too unwell and too occupied with CPR business to attend the General Court in November, when the reports by Fleming and Armit were treated as confidential and not revealed to the shareholders. Soon after he arrived in London at the beginning of January, however, Donald wrote Fleming to say that, although he had had little opportunity to discuss the November meeting with Armit, he had learned from others that it was "not considered very satisfactory by most of the shareholders and for reasons which both you and I fully recognize," adding that "it will be a most difficult matter under existing circumstances to regain the confidence of the proprietors."[18]

The HBC's policy, enunciated by Eden Colvile in November 1881, was to sell its land gradually when prices were high and to hold its land in reserve when they were depressed. While the government needed to sell or give away its land to attract settlers and the railway needed settlers to provide freight, the company could derive no further value from its agricultural land once it was sold. It was therefore of paramount importance to judge the market carefully. The shareholders in November 1882 were not told that, while the company had made a sizeable profit from the land boom, it had not made as much as it could have. Neither was any mention made of the numerous rumours concerning Blanchard's syndicate and the involvement in it of senior HBC officers.

More disconcerting, however, had the shareholders known it, was the fact that the Governor and Committee did not then direct their attention towards establishing a policy to guide the Land Commissioner in the future. Whether land should be sold, when it should be sold and how the price should be determined were points which needed to be clearly enunciated. More immediately important, however, was what should happen when purchasers were unable to complete their payments. Some men turned their profits quickly but a great many others, both genuine settlers and speculators, were caught by the collapse of the land market and found themselves unable to make the second and subsequent payments on their land or even to meet their interest payments, and the HBC needed to determine how these people should be treated.

In December, the Governor and Committee did instruct Brydges to hold auctions when he thought it appropriate to do so but he was also to continue sales by private contract. He was told to improve relations with the CPR and, above all, to ensure that he neither said nor did anything which might lead the public to assume it would be treated unfairly. The board wanted to hear nothing "which in the remotest way might give occasion for remark reflecting upon the Management of the Company's Land Department." Coincidentally, the board attempted to exert a tighter control over Brydges by requesting that he communicate more frequently with London and with Fleming in Canada.[19]

This general policy statement offered no rules for dealing with arrears and more and more people fell behind as they discovered that they could neither sell on their land, especially the town lots, at the price which they had paid nor could they keep up the payments which they were required to make after the initial deposit. In a great many cases, they could not even afford the interest on the overdue principal or the tax which the land attracted as soon as the HBC sold it. Moveover, Brydges, who resented being asked to comply with instructions from London or Montreal, did not shake himself free from stories that he had been profiteering, nor did he desist from criticism of the CPR.

Freight rates which were proposed by the railway company and sanctioned by the government in the spring of 1883 were publicly objected to by only one person. That was Charles Brydges, speaking in his capacity as president of the Winnipeg Chamber of Commerce. George Stephen complained to the HBC and, Colvile, in admonishing Brydges, observed that he was "unable to say whether a similar irritation exists in the mind of the Dominion Government official who sanctioned these rates." As that official was Charles Tupper, Colvile could have been fairly certain that a "similar irritation" did indeed exist. Yet again, the governor was compelled to remind the Land Commissioner that the company wanted to remain on good terms with the CPR and that Brydges should think twice before allowing himself to accept positions which could require him to make statements against company policy.[20]

By that time, Donald was becoming increasingly annoyed by the HBC's failure to make Brydges comply with instructions and by Brydges' failure to collect the growing mountain of arrears. The board had decreed that, without its permission, sales could not be cancelled and down payments could not be transferred to other property, enabling purchasers to complete the transaction on a smaller number of lots while freeing the rest for sale. Though administratively tidy, such a scheme would entail the loss of the substantial revenue which had so nearly been within the company's grasp.

Having got through the summer General Court without significant trouble, the board sought to deflect further complaint by again assigning Armit to investigate. His report revealed that although Brydges had asked Blanchard to take steps to recover arrears and interest, he had failed to mention that Blanchard himself owed the company $60,000. Worse was Armit's discovery that many of the sale agreements had not even been signed, a circumstance which meant that the company had no legal right to claim for arrears on principal or interest and the published conditions of sale could be ignored with impunity.[21]

Armit's report demonstrates that the board was aware of specific problems in the land office but was doing nothing to rectify them, while keeping the shareholders in the dark. To strengthen his own position, in April and May Donald bought a further two thousand shares, all from his regular stockbrokers, Bennett, Payne and Company. He now owned four thousand shares in the company, far from an absolute majority but more than anyone else and certainly sufficient for him to be able to compel attention to his views.[22]

Shortly before the November General Court, Donald sought an interview with Governor Colvile and told him that, "if certain information was not given or certain things were not done," his action at the General Court would be against the board. Colvile offered to take Donald into his confidence, presumably to reveal the contents of the reports by Armit, Fleming and Rose. As Fleming and Donald were close and Armit sympathized with Donald's concerns, it seems likely that he already knew the substance of their reports; he had even been present at most of the inquiries Rose had made in Winnipeg. But it was not information in confidence which Donald sought. He approved of dealing with problems discreetly but there was no evidence that changes had been effected in the management of the land office. It might be difficult to acknowledge in public the problems in Winnipeg, but bringing them out into the open would at least distinguish fact from rumour and satisfy those who had invested in HBC stock that efforts were being made to conduct their business more satisfactorily.[23]

When the shareholders met at the Cannon Street Hotel near Saint Paul's Cathedral on November 22, they were informed that arrears on land sales amounted to £132,000 but few buyers had been taken to court in order to avoid a dangerous panic. Colvile's speech was bland and so were the questions until Matthew Robins, a shareholder who had lived in Toronto, said what must have been on many people's minds. The Land Commissioner, he claimed, should feel humiliated by the arrears which he had allowed to accumulate. He accused Brydges of a want of impartiality and referred to the rumours about the syndicate in which Grahame had participated; he demanded that Armit's reports be published and called for the formation of "some local board of supervision over your officers, so that there may be an absolute guarantee to the proprietors that the business of the Company will be conducted on true business principles."

Donald, who was suffering from a cold and had difficulty speaking, reiterated Robins' demands and said that the CPR had sold land near Brandon for $3,000 an acre while the HBC had only managed $10. Land on the CPR route should have brought the company "many hundreds of thousands of dollars more than you will ever receive from them now, owing to the conditions on which they have been sold," he told the crowd, adding that the commercial business, which was Grahame's responsibility, had also been badly handled. Information about the mismanagement of the business in Canada had been "as well as ignored." He called for "a direct and thorough investigation and inquiry ... into all those matters so as once and for all ... to clear them up to the satisfaction of everyone; not only for the satisfaction of those gentlemen here, the proprietors, but also in the interest of that very valuable and highly respectable body of gentlemen you have in that country — your officers throughout the whole country."[24]

In response, Sir John Rose observed that there had been many complaints, all of them anonymous or confidential. No one was prepared to name names and make specific charges. He had gone to Winnipeg where he and Armit had discovered a mare's nest, as Donald knew perfectly well. Rose explained that all inquiries into the controversial sale had indicated that Brydges himself was not involved. Furthermore, it appeared that Blanchard's syndicate had been unable to collect the money when it sold on the land at the much higher price. In response, Donald reverted to Grahame's initial claim that Brydges was part of the syndicate to purchase the Fort Garry lands. Though Brydges denied it and no evidence had been found, Donald and others were inclined to believe Grahame's allegation.

The meeting began to deteriorate into a squabble about whether Donald and Brydges were "at daggers drawn" as Sir John Rose's son, William, claimed, while Donald pointed out that he had helped to disprove allegations against Brydges in 1879 in order to facilitate his appointment as Land Commissioner. Colvile told the disputants to settle their differences elsewhere and the board's report was adopted.

At that point, most of the shareholders left, there remaining but the routine business of adopting the directors' slate of candidates for the new board. One director had retired and the remainder offered themselves for re-election, together with the board's nominee for the vacancy. The company's rules did not permit voting by proxy but it was assumed that the election would be a mere formality. When the ballot box was opened the following day, however, it was discovered that Donald had proposed a new board. His list retained Eden Colvile as governor but did away with Sir John Rose who was replaced by the Earl of Dunraven as deputy governor. The earl was a military officer and sportsman who knew the Northwest from hunting expeditions and was increasingly conscious of Canada's strategic importance in the global defence of the British empire. Sandford Fleming remained, as did Herman Hoskier, and Edward Hamilton, a treasury official who was Gladstone's private secretary and who had been involved in an investigation into the company's trading business in 1879. Donald replaced the others with Thomas Dakin, Thomas Reynolds, and Charles Russell, a barrister and member of the UK parliament who later became Lord Chief Justice of England. His own name was also included.[25]

As Donald admitted to George Stephen before the votes had been counted, he had not considered that most of the other shareholders might leave; his gesture was meant as a protest which he assumed would have no validity because he had not sought the agreement of his nominees. But the protest itself was important. Something had to be done to regularize the situation in Winnipeg and his ballot demonstrated that if the Governor and Committee were not prepared to take action, he had the power to vote them out of office and replace them with men who would address the problems.[26]

Initially, it was thought that the company was obliged to accept the changes since Donald had such a preponderance of votes. Consultation with a lawyer, however, revealed that Donald's list could not be recognized because it had not first been offered to the shareholders for comment and discussion. Rather than risk a more serious confrontation, however, the board thought it wise to seek a compromise and offer places on the board to Donald and perhaps others of his choice "in order that he may have an opportunity of making good his charges against the management in Canada," as Rose explained to the prime minister, adding that he believed Donald should simply have asked for places on the board "in a manly way" or should have made clear and specific allegations against Brydges.[27]

As always, Rose misunderstood Donald because he failed to grasp that while the man enjoyed the esteem which came with influence, he did not seek power in order to achieve that recognition. He was quite happy to remain in the background unless he perceived that his interference would halt a wrongdoing or prevent a dangerous conflict from escalating. If the majority of the Hudson's Bay Company shareholders had elected him to the board, he would have been hugely pleased; to seek inclusion on the board's list of nominees "in a manly way" was not merely demeaning, it suggested he wished power for its own sake.

Rose's observation that Donald should have brought specific charges against Brydges was quite right in the sense that there can be no trial without a clearly articulated complaint, but it overlooks the fact that Donald was consistently careful of men's reputations and would protect a person rather than make a false claim. Rose also missed the fact that Donald believed that corruption and mismanagement should be dealt with quietly and efficiently by the board and not flaunted before a shareholders' meeting and, as a consequence, before the general public. Had the original reports by Armit, Fleming and Rose produced a significant change in the way the land office was managed, had the board even acknowledged that it was trying to address the problems in Winnipeg, Donald might have been satisfied. As it was, it seemed that the board was sweeping everything under the carpet or was shielding a man who did not deserve its protection. This was not behaviour to be tolerated in a company which Donald cherished: his only alternative had been to force the issues out into the open.

Though the house list was declared to be the only legal one, and its members took their oath of allegiance, the directors immediately set about creating vacancies to allow Donald and one of his nominees, Charles Russell, to join the board. This they did at an extraordinary meeting of the General Court on December 7. Shortly before Christmas, the Governor and new Committee met for the first time. Rose, who was devastated by his wife's sudden and unexpected death a few days before, prepared a letter to be considered at the meeting, though he also managed to attend it, despite his grief. He made three explicit points. The fur trade was unaffected. Grahame's resignation had been requested; he was not convinced that the company could carry on a large, general business profitably but acknowledged that this certainly could not happen without good staff. If there were other problems in this department, "I trust Mr. Smith will not hesitate to lay them before his colleagues in a shape which will enable the Board practically to deal with them." His last point, concerning the Land Department, was that "the Company should not retain in its service any one in whose integrity, reliance could not be placed."

Equally, he would insist, as he said in a letter to Macdonald, that any inquiry into Brydges' behaviour "be of open and impartial character."[28]

Rose was not at all pleased with the changes and wrongly predicted that the new board would soon fall out. He believed Donald was vindictive and failed to take into account that there were many others both within and outside the HBC who felt that Brydges was not trustworthy; certainly he was not as compliant or as meticulous as most of the company's chief traders and chief factors, but neither did most of them have the flair and business acumen which could take the company into the future.

Rose was an intelligent man who worked hard to ensure that Brydges was treated fairly and that the HBC flourished, though CPR supporters perceived as a threat his championing of the Grand Trunk's former manager. This seemed to be confirmed in July 1884 when his banking firm, Morton Rose, concluded that it could no longer provide financial support for the CPR, though this is more likely to be due to the influence of Rose's son than to Rose himself. In August, the Bank of Montreal was sufficiently doubtful about Rose's capacity for independent judgement that it asked him to resign his directorship and cease his connection with its London committee.[29]

A year later, at the winter General Court of 1884, tempers had cooled. In part, Rose was subdued by both his wife's death and his dismissal from the Bank of Montreal and in part he was beginning to perceive that Brydges was his own worst enemy, cockily refusing to comply with the regulations which were finally being established for him.

At the end of January 1884, the Governor and Committee asked Donald and Fleming to inquire into the general shop trade and indicate whether they thought changes might usefully be implemented. A week later, on January 29, they were requested to inquire into the land sales, particularly those at Fort Garry, Regina, Edmonton and along the CPR route, all of which had been the subject of dispute at the General Court. Brydges was instructed "to attend at said examination and assist therein." "This seems curious," Fleming noted in the margin of his copy of the instructions. "The resolution practically puts the land commissioner on his trial & he is directed to assist in trying himself."[30]

Both Donald and Fleming were in London in April when they discussed with the governor a need to formalize arrangements in Canada. In their conversations, the three men developed Matthew Robins' idea of a Canadian supervisory committee. While Donald slipped south to Nice to collect Bella and Maggie, Fleming put on paper the recommendation that a three member Canadian sub-committee be established. It was no longer possible, he said, to run the Hudson's Bay Company on fur trade lines. A sub-committee should "simply be a section of the general Board domiciled in Canada and in entire harmony with it. That its duties should be to see the wishes and intentions of the General Board carried out in the most fitting manner by the officers of the company, and to advise the General Board on all matters affecting the Company's interests." The theory was that it would have no powers separate from those of the board and would act under its authority. One of the men, Fleming explained, should have "sound commercial experience."[31]

The phrase "sound commercial experience" was probably meant to describe Donald; with his knowledge of business, though not of shopkeeping which was of growing importance to the HBC, and with both his and Fleming's knowledge of western land values, they had the essential requirements for the sub-committee. They were the only two directors resident in Canada, however, and it is hard to imagine how the board, when it accepted Fleming's recommendation on the first of May, could have appointed anyone else. The third person never materialized for that very reason.

The special meeting of the Governor and Committee which established the Canadian sub-committee also determined that "any further inquiry" into "the recorded disapproval by the Governor and Committee of certain land transactions to which exception has been taken by shareholders" would be "inexpedient and undesirable." A further resolution specifically annulled the request made at the end of January that Donald and Fleming investigate those land sales. The undercurrent of the meeting was clearly that there was nothing to be gained from dwelling on past errors. What was needed now was a way of disentangling the mess which had been created in the land office and re-establishing the tight controls through which the company had successfully managed its Canadian business in the past.[32]

The sub-committee began operations in June. Initially, Donald and Fleming conducted their meetings formally, as their minutes record. Soon, however, they were more casual and allowed their correspondence to stand as a record of their discussions and decisions. Arranging meetings was not always easy as both men had other obligations and Donald was especially distracted as he sought to keep the CPR from bankruptcy. Brydges was much inclined to tell London that he had seen Donald "for a few minutes" or that he would communicate with the sub-committee "when I can reach them," phrases which were clearly meant to be subversive and which indicate both his dislike of being fettered and the constraints which the new arrangements put on his management of the land business. Matters were not helped by Brydges' determination to go his own way. This flared up most glaringly in March 1885 when Donald and Fleming decided that they would go to Winnipeg to discuss some points with the land commissioner only to discover that, without telling them, he had set off for Ottawa, ostensibly to deal with land patents but in fact to lobby against the grant of a government loan to the CPR.[33]

The sub-committee's main concern, however, was to establish a policy for dealing with arrears. The men needed to take into account whether the defaulter was a speculator or a genuine settler, whether there was any evidence that the purchaser did intend to pay for the land when he could, whether the land had been sold on, whether the costs of pursuing a claim through the courts would lead to a Pyrrhic victory, and whether any action would expose the land to seizure by the courts for non-payment of taxes. If the municipal authorities stepped in, the land would be sold, the taxes and a further ten percent deducted, and any remaining cash handed over to the nominal owner. Even if he in turn handed over all the sale money to the HBC, it would not meet his obligation to the company because the bottom had fallen out of the land market. If the company repurchased its land at the tax sale, it would be obliged to pay tax on it as long as it owned it, and would be unlikely to sell it again quickly, given the depressed state of the market. In the meantime, the company's accounts would show a loss, reflecting the difference between the high price for which the land had been sold and the income which had actually been achieved.

While the company's failure to declare a dividend between 1877 and 1880 can be attributed to the general depression throughout the western world, the failure to declare a dividend in 1885 and 1888 was largely prompted by weaknesses in the Land Department. Otherwise, through the depression which lasted for about ten years from 1885, the company managed to declare at least a modest return for its shareholders each year. Dividends in 1886 and 1887 reflect the trading surplus achieved primarily as a consequence of the government supply contracts awarded during the uprising in the Northwest.

The policy for dealing with arrears also had to take into account public attitudes to the HBC; as Brydges rightly pointed out, the company could not be seen to be less generous or less tolerant than its competitors, even though its underlying purpose in selling its lands was significantly different.

Though discussions had taken place with Brydges in June, no policies had been formulated when the Governor and Committee, including Donald, discussed land arrears on July 8. At that meeting, it was decided "to avoid taking legal measures except against those who can but will not pay." The company did not want to acquire a reputation as a litigant. The same meeting asked the Canadian sub-committee to consider replacing Blanchard as the company's solicitor in Winnipeg. Knowledge of the board's misgivings did not affect Donald's own relations with Sedley Blanchard to whom he lent $12,000 in September 1884 on the security of his shares in the Manitoba Cartage and Warehousing Company, nor did it alter relations with Blanchard's partner, John Bain, to whom Donald lent $12,000 in November that year on the security of property at Shoal Lake.[34]

The Governor and Committee had instructed that no sales were to be cancelled without the approval of the Canadian sub-committee and all cases were subject to review. For his part, Brydges was understandably pressing for decisions, warning that legal proceedings would be required to regain possession if decisions were not taken soon. Bringing men before the magistrate was contrary to both the spirit and the letter of instructions from the board and the sub-committee and, as Fleming put it succinctly in marginalia on of one of Brydges' letters urging a court case, "Why press legal proceedings now if it can be done equally well when there is some demand for property in the future?" Though Brydges had done a deal with Blanchard on fees for cases in Chancery, he had not taken into account where the money would come from to pay either the lawyers or the taxes if he could not resell the land.[35]

By October, Donald and Fleming had at last decided that cases should not be judged by their individual merits but that the same regulations should apply to all. It would be the most equitable. Together with the board, they worked their way towards a set of rules to govern Brydges' future transactions and were finally able to enunciate these in February. Every effort was to be made to be lenient, provided interest and tax payments were maintained. Cancellations would require the forfeiture of the first installment but subsequent payments could be applied to a smaller number of lots in order to complete at least some sales. Where land had been sold on, the original purchaser was still bound to honour his contract with the company.[36]

Brydges immediately responded that the rules would be "hopeless" to implement and it took some effort to force him to agree to comply with them. The Governor and Committee did, however, acknowledge his arguments about the disadvantages which would ensue if the local authorities instituted tax sales and conceded that the rules were not necessarily applicable to every case. Brydges was to consult the sub-committee when he thought he could not advantageously apply them.[37]

A few days later, meeting in Montreal, Donald and Fleming noticed that recent legal expenses in the Land Department had exceeded $4,000 and decided that they must again "impress on him as fully as we possibly can to extend the time for payment of Instalments rather than have recourse to legal measures for the recovery of the debt, this being the best means, as we believe, for keeping down similar expenses in future, as well as ensuring to the Company the greatest advantage from such sales as have been made.[38]

At the beginning of June, with Blanchard's land dealings still not sorted out and his income from HBC court cases still on the increase, the board cabled that the company's legal business in Winnipeg was to be handed over to Stewart Tupper, son of the high commissioner and railway minister, and Hugh John Macdonald, son of the prime minister.[39]

When Donald and Fleming went to Winnipeg following the end of hostilities in Saskatchewan, one of their purposes was to make inquiries at the Land Department in anticipation of the report they were preparing for the Governor and Committee. Fleming wrote the first draft and observed in his covering letter to Donald, "I daresay you will think my language a little strong but I have left it to you to tone down as much as you like;" he had correctly guessed that Donald would rewrite it to make it less belligerent. Their concern was primarily with men who had been caught short by their speculations rather than with genuine settlers. They noted again that they favoured leniency as long as taxes and interest were met and repeated that legal proceedings were undesirable. "The subcommittee were greatly surprised when they made an investigation at Winnipeg to discover that the Land Commissioner had not carried out the instructions given him," they reported. What particularly disturbed them was that Brydges "had issued letters in most cases peremptorily demanding payment of all arrears and threatening, if such payments were not at once made, that legal proceedings would be taken."[40]

On discovering that legal costs had reached $15,000 or $16,000 a year, the men asked the CPR and the Canada North West Land Company what they had spent on court cases and discovered their expenditure was minuscule. Interestingly, Donald also sought information from the Canada Land Company with which he had decided not to ally himself nearly fifty years earlier. The CPR, being protected by a well-worded contract, had not instituted any legal proceedings and the others had brought only one or two cases, again because their contracts protected them. Stewart Tupper and the HBC's Montreal lawyer, J.J.C. Abbott, thought the HBC contract was in itself sufficient, though they suggested one or two minor changes which might improve it.

John Rose chaired the board meeting which considered the report. He and some of his colleagues found it hard to accept that Brydges had been spending unnecessarily on legal fees, despite the evidence which suggested otherwise and finally resolved to call on Brydges for "full explanations." At the same meeting, the directors were irked to discover that full information on land transactions had yet again not been provided, despite several requests that this should always be done, and were very annoyed to discover that Brydges had written the minister of the interior about policy issues without authority or even consultation with the board or sub-committee. He had sent the sub-committee a cable seeking authorization but had received no response, probably because Donald anticipated discussing its contents in London. Brydges, however, had not waited for a reply and the Governor and Committee found no excuse for his independent action. "As already intimated to you, they desire you clearly to understand that any proposals involving a change of policy in dealing with the Company's Lands should be first addressed to the Board and the Canadian SubCommittee and not be undertaken executively by the Commissioner," Armit wrote.[41]

In December, Donald was invited to address the General Court on the quality of land in the Northwest and the company's prospects for the future. He was full of enthusiasm, having just come from the last spike ceremony at Craigellachie, and took the opportunity to reiterate the general land policy which Colvile had enunciated to the General Court in 1881. The company owned excellent lands for growing wheat and for grazing, he said. "You have a very fine property there which must go on increasing in value. If you do not get a great deal of money for it this year, and next year, and not much more the year after, still it is a property which ultimately must become of great value." Like Eden Colvile, he looked much farther into the future than Charles Brydges and some of the shareholders who wanted to see results a good deal sooner.[42]

After 1885, bickering about arrears on land sales died down but was replaced by a feud between Brydges and Joseph Wrigley, the Trade Commissioner who had replaced James Grahame. The HBC was the main shareholder in a railway bridge across the Assiniboine River, the principal individual shareholder being Donald Smith. Though intended for public use, the bridge was primarily built to allow access to a mill on company land and to permit goods for the company's stores to be brought into its warehouse. In the interests of HBC earnings, Brydges believed tolls should be as high as the market would bear while Wrigley felt they should be as low as possible because he had a duty to keep his department's expenses to a minimum. Wrigley, who had previously been president of the Chamber of Commerce in Huddersfield, did his best to retain his equilibrium in the face of Brydges' ill-mannered contempt, but the two men were scarcely on speaking terms. Donald brought in Van Horne to decree a rate, which he did without full knowledge of all the circumstances, but his decision at least established a temporary truce.

In 1886, the board also began to articulate its dissatisfaction with the expenses being incurred by the Land Department. Brydges was in the habit of making an annual tour of inspection of western lands and the costs were proving to be out of proportion to the returns. In January, the Land Commissioner was instructed to seek approval for such "large expenditure" and was asked whether, under the circumstances, it was really necessary to keep horses all year round. Later in the month, the board noted that expenses in November had exceeded income by $2,000, largely as a consequence of the continuing outlay for legal fees. The board also looked to the fur trade to cut its costs and in July, accepted Wrigley's recommendation that the number of commissioned officers be reduced.[43]

The Canadian sub-committee was an awkward way of trying to assert control over the company's business, though it worked well enough with Wrigley and with Brydges' successor. It would never have been instituted had not Brydges' speculations with Arthur Wellington Ross, his failure to allow the public equal access to land purchases during the boom, and his lack of control over speculation within the land office itself not alerted the Governor and Committee to the fact that some form of supervision would be necessary. Had Brydges accepted that he did not have the independence he had enjoyed in previous positions, conflict with the sub-committee and with the Governor and Committee in London would have been minimal and he would have earned the freedom he wanted. As it was, he continued to pursue his own way in defiance of instructions; his course of action may well have been the wiser in many cases, but every time he erred and was found to have been acting contrary to established policy, he incurred the enmity of more and more HBC directors. His arrogance did not help his cause.

For the Governor and Committee, the last straw was Brydges' defiance over land for the Northern Pacific terminus. In Manitoba, strident agitation against the CPR's freight rates put pressure on Macdonald to negotiate the cancellation of the company's monopoly clause while Stephen, needing to float more land grant bonds on the London market, was driven to bargain abolition of the clause in exchange for a government guarantee for the bonds. As soon as the clause was revoked in March 1888, the Manitoba government authorized the construction of the Red River Valley Railway — a reincarnation of Schultz's North Western Colonization Railway — to the border where it was to meet the Northern Pacific. Construction and management of the line was entrusted to a subsidiary called the Northern Pacific and Manitoba which sought land for a station and other facilities in Winnipeg.

Brydges had determined a year earlier that he wanted to see a railway terminus located on the old Fort Garry reserve and had been negotiating with the provincial premier to arrange it. "He is very persistent," Donald observed in a note to Fleming, "but happily for the Company's best interests in this case not successfully so." When the monopoly clause was revoked, Brydges saw his chances renewed and began negotiations with the Northern Pacific early in 1888. Having been told in January that "no grants of the Company's land shall be made [to railways] without their authority being first asked for & obtained," Brydges wrote London in May, seeking permission to grant land for the terminus without having to make explicit and detailed reference to London or the sub-committee. If he were successful, he anticipated an increase in the company's land values in the vicinity, and benefits to the HBC store and the Broadway Bridge across the Red River.[44]

Discussions about the terminus took place in London early in June while Donald was still in Canada and Armit wrote to say that the board objected to Brydges' proposal to let the railway company have as much as twenty acres. A plan showing the precise location was to be sent. At the beginning of July, Armit both wrote and cabled to reiterate that Brydges could not grant any land without reference to the board. Further conversations took place in London in July, probably late in the month because Donald, whose participation would have been sought, was seriously ill for most of the first two weeks; on August 2 the board sent a cable indicating that it wanted the station to be located at the company's end of town and giving permission for the railway to have ten acres. John Rose wrote to the same effect on August 7, adding "if more land is wanted why could not the Railway Co. buy it at a fair price." This was a private letter, not discussed with his colleagues on the board. On August 27, Brydges formally offered the ten acres of land and, at the same time, agreed to the sale of a further ten acres for $10,000. James McNaught, the Northern Pacific's president, was sufficiently uncertain about the extent of Brydges' jurisdiction that he specifically inquired if he had authority to enter into a contract and the Land Commissioner gave assurances that he did.[45]

Brydges did not reveal what he had done until September 21, the day after his arrangements had been confirmed by the Northern Pacific board in New York. At that point, he had already sold an additional $10,000 worth of land.

Armit was instructed to send a sharp telegram of remonstrance. "Board distinctly decline to recognize suggested arrangement which is contrary to Board's authority," he wrote, adding that the board would neither give to the railway nor sell to it land north of Broadway Street. The company's store was on Main Street, a block north of Broadway and the reason for having the station south of Broadway was to bring people past the store on their way to and from the station. Brydges' arrangement entailed the railway company constructing not only the station but also a neighbouring hotel several blocks north of the HBC store. The Governor and Committee winced when they saw that the Northern Pacific would be spending $60,000 to buy about an acre of land adjacent to the HBC's for the station and hotel while its own twenty acres had brought a mere $10,000. Furthermore, the plan called for the city to cut off certain streets which would do away with several level crossings but would also deny access to unsold portions of the Fort Garry reserve.[46]

The board was angry that its regulations requiring consultation prior to sales of this nature had once more been flouted and doubly distressed because Brydges' independent negotiations had resulted in a very poor deal for the HBC. Donald was in Canada when Brydges revealed his arrangements with the railway and in transit between Montreal and London when Armit wrote expressing the ire of the Governor and Committee but he agreed to try to re-negotiate the arrangement. Apart from withdrawing some riverside lots from the agreement, he was able to make very few alterations to Brydges' deal, partly because the board had determined to avoid a court case and partly because the Northern Pacific, having purchased land for the station and hotel and having been misled by a company employee, was in no mood to bargain any further. Even if Brydges had made the best possible deal under the circumstances, his failure to wait for authorization to do so was a grave error in the eyes of the Governor and Committee. New problems erupted when a dispute arose between the city and other property holders about the precise location of a street which, in turn, had been used to define the land which the company was granting to the railway company. By the time that was settled, the Northern Pacific was bankrupt and in the hands of the receivers. The land was not finally transferred until 1897.[47]

John Rose died suddenly in August 1888, and when Donald returned to London in October that year, he was asked to replace him as deputy governor of the HBC. At the General Court on December 4, he was confirmed in this position. The meeting was not without controversy because a shareholder, Robert McLean, claiming to represent an association of shareholders, demanded the resignation of the governor, Eden Colvile, and the right to appoint five new directors, including the deputy governor. The nub of his complaint was that the company was not presenting sufficiently detailed accounts, was not making as much money as it could and was not managing the Land Department properly. Negotiations, including a session on New Year's Day, revealed that McLean could not muster the number of votes he claimed, but Eden Colvile nevertheless offered to step down as governor and the board agreed to bring Walter Morgan onto the board as a representative of McLean's views. As a consequence of McLean's arguments and Colvile's resignation, Donald was propelled into the governor's chair less than a month after the General Court had confirmed him as deputy governor. An extraordinary meeting following the General Court in July 1889 confirmed him as governor and the Earl of Lichfield as deputy governor.

McLean did have a point about the Land Department as the board well knew. A letter to Donald was prepared on December 18, when he was still deputy governor, and approved at a board meeting which he attended three days later. It observed that the costs of the department were too high and requested that he take action to reduce them. The Governor and Committee "consider that the remuneration of the Land Commissioner is altogether out of proportion to the business transacted and have come to the conclusion that the time has arrived when the services of Mr. Brydges must be dispensed with. They have the more readily come to this conclusion after looking to other good sufficient causes with which you are familiar." Donald was asked to find a temporary replacement. On January 17, Armit wrote Brydges about the expenses of his department, explaining that "changes" would be made to the Land Commissioner's salary and to his direction of the post. As Wrigley had health problems and wanted to leave, the board hoped to find one person who could take responsibility for fur, land and stores.[48]

Donald arrived back in Montreal on January 29 and had hardly had time to read his accumulated mail before he discovered that Brydges had sold six hundred and forty acres to the North West Coal and Navigation Company at $20 an acre. Donald and his colleagues on the board felt the company would only be interested in the land if it was confident that coal would be found on it and that it was therefore worth a good deal more. Again, Brydges was instructed to refer to the sub-committee in Montreal and again he objected. He believed that, following Sir John Rose's death, he was being spitefully harassed. In a letter to the prime minister, he asked for help and Macdonald agreed to ask Charles Tupper, who was still in London as high commissioner, to raise the matter with Donald. There was no need for that, however, for on February 16, Brydges was taken ill at a meeting of the Winnipeg Hospital Committee and died the same day.

In March, Donald was in Winnipeg to try to settle some of the land issues and see if there were ways in which economies could be made. He proposed to dismiss one man and reduce the salary of another. "A very considerable saving can also be effected in concentrating the work of the office by giving up the addition made to the building three or four years back no part of which is required for the work now being done. It consists principally of a large Room used for meetings of the Winnipeg Hospital Board, the Episcopal Synod etc. and is designated, by a Plate on the door, as the Board Room, and another Room which is used by the Ladies of the Town as a Sewing Room for charitable purposes. This Room is furnished with 2 or 3 sewing machines used by the Ladies which I presume belong to them. This addition cost within a fraction of Ten thousand dollars, and to keep it up requires an additional Furnace the Coals alone consumed in which cost upwards of Two hundred dollars annually." Turning over unused space to a good cause is commendable, but heating it and losing the potential income from renting it cost a man his job.[49]

Wrigley and Brydges were replaced by Clarence Chipman who had been the accountant for the great Colonial and Indian Exhibition which celebrated Queen Victoria's golden jubilee. He had also served as secretary to Sir Charles Tupper during the early years of his tenure as high commissioner in London. An able and intelligent administrator, Chipman had the great fortune to be appointed at the beginning of a long period of prosperity.

Though the Canadian sub-committee was never formally wound up, Donald's election as governor of the Hudson's Bay Company effectively marked the end of its operation. The collaboration with Fleming had brought a new friend into Donald's small inner circle of men with whom he could feel at ease. Fleming could gently tease him and Donald was able to respond in kind in a way that only friends, secure in each other's affection, can do. "Dear doctor" began Fleming's congratulatory letter when Donald received an honourary doctorate and Donald's note of thanks continued in the same spirit. When Fleming's wife died in March 1888, Donald was unfailingly considerate, not just in the weeks immediately following the bereavement, but for years after.[50]

Early in September 1887, Fleming's diary records that he made a sketch of Donald after a CPR board meeting and two diary entries at the end of the month indicate that they sketched together. Fleming drew him again in November 1889. Fleming had an engineer's skill with a pencil but Donald's capacity to miss his prey when shooting and bend the CPR's last spike suggest that his eye-hand coordination would have been ill adapted to drawing. The very fact that he spent a few hours on consecutive days playing at something he could not do well reveals how comfortable he felt in Fleming's presence. Similarly, when he needed to find accommodation in Ottawa in 1889, Donald had no hesitation in asking Fleming and his daughter to look out for something for him. He knew many men and women in the capital, but it was to Fleming he could comfortably turn for a personal favour. Fleming happily reciprocated. It was a friendship which would last the rest of their lives.[51]

CHAPTER FOURTEEN

A MAN OF SUBSTANCE 1886–1896

Is it not positively amazing what the Scot can grow to imagine, undertake and accomplish if caught young enough and transplanted to the stimulating climate and conditions of Canada?
Andrew Carnegie, in reference to Lord Strathcona [1]

In Montreal, leases on domestic accommodation expired at the end of April and May 1 was moving day, when all the horses and carts in the city were busy taking families to their new quarters. In the early 1870s, Donald and Isabella Smith never spent more than two years in a house, though with each move they improved the quality of their home and its surroundings. In the spring of 1875, they took up residence on Côte des Neiges Road, close to the Collège de Montréal where Louis Riel had been educated. There were few houses on the road and gardens and fields surrounded the college, while a short distance to the north, the parks of Mount Royal offered clear, fresh air. The move might well have been made in hopes that a cleaner atmosphere would help the family's winter colds, but it seems to have had little impact on their health.

In November 1876, the Smiths finally purchased a house in Montreal. It was at 1157 Dorchester Street, at the south western corner of the square mile which was occupied by the city's wealthy elite. At that point, Professor Robert Bell, head of Canada's geological service, was living in the house, though spending a good deal of his time in Philadelphia where he was occupied with the Canadian contribution to the American centennial exhibition. The two families saw each other socially — Bell arranged a hotel for Donald, Bella and Maggie when they went to the exhibition in October, and Bella and Mrs. Bell travelled to the United States and Scotland together in April 1877, just after the Smiths moved into their new home.[2]

The Dorchester Street house was a grand stone mansion built in 1869 by Jean-Baptiste Auger, a shipbuilder and manager of the Montreal and Ottawa

Forwarding Company. Donald paid Auger's widow $18,000 and agreed to pay a further $5,000 at six percent to the Sulpicians from whom the land had been bought. Like many religious orders in Montreal, the priests found they no longer needed the farms and pastures which had once been essential and consequently were selling the land to finance their religious work. In 1881, Donald bought another plot from the Sulpicians and added more land in 1889 when he also signed a covenant to build a house on it within two years.[3]

When the Smiths moved into the house, their neighbours were Duncan McIntyre, who would soon be a partner in the CPR venture, and Angus Ogilvie, scion of the flour milling family. George Hague, of the Merchants' Bank, was another neighbour. McIntyre's home was a duplex, the other half of which was acquired in 1882 by Van Horne who in turn sold it to Thomas Shaughnessy, initially the CPR's purchasing agent and eventually its president. In the summer of 1888, McIntyre sold his half of the house to Donald who wanted the extra space for guests, but the Smiths were not especially happy with the arrangement and eventually sold it to James Cantlie who was married to George Stephen's sister Eleonora. Before long, R.B. Angus was also a neighbour and in 1887, Donald sold the house he had built on land bought from the Sulpicians to Charles Drinkwater, the CPR secretary: the western end of Dorchester Street became something of a CPR enclave.[4]

At the end of 1884, Donald signed contracts for improvements to the house, including the construction of a conservatory. At this point, he had the exterior faced in red sandstone imported from Port Credit, Ontario, and he built another house on adjoining property which he had acquired on Dorchester Street. In due course, he owned many of the residences surrounding his own. In some cases, he sold them to friends and colleagues, but there were six houses on Baile Street, running parallel to Dorchester, which had tenants, as well as a further three in a neighbouring street and eight in a less salubrious area a few blocks south.[5]

In 1887 and 1888, the Smith house was substantially renovated, and became one of the most talked about residences in Montreal. It spread over three storeys with a mahogany double staircase so well constructed by master cabinetmakers that no nails were used. The house had central heating and hot water systems as well as elaborate fireplaces with carved wooden mantles and tile and stone facing. Initially, it was lit by gas, but electric lights were later installed. From the vestibule, visitors passed to a large reception room, hung with silk and lined with rosewood wainscotting. Adjoining the reception hall was the conservatory, a popular feature amongst the Montreal gentry in the late nineteenth century because it allowed fresh flowers all year round. Built of glass, wood and stone, it had tiled floors with mosaic pavements and marble work. Throughout the public rooms, ornamental plasterwork decorated the ceilings.

After their years in Labrador, the Smiths appreciated good plumbing and bathing facilities, electricity and telephones, and Dorchester Street was equipped accordingly. But they also followed the fashion of the day which led wealthy North Americans to adopt what they understood to be the style of the renaissance for their residences. The Smith's dining room was hung with a tapestry from Pau, the birthplace of Henry Bolingbroke, though it depicted rural scenes from the vicinity of seventeenth century Berne. A portrait of Donald by William Walter Ouless, a British Royal Academician, also hung in the dining room which had three bow windows into which had been let stained glass portraying Samuel de Champlain, Henry VI and Louis XIII.

The grand staircase led to a picture gallery from which the oriental carpets could be lifted to convert it to a ballroom. Above the light oak wainscotting, the walls were covered with silk, patterned with large acanthus leaves and other foliage. There was a minstrel gallery at one end and a skylight, shaped, according to one reporter, like a huge wagon wheel while another recorded that it was oblong and ran nearly the full length of the room.[6]

It was deemed appropriate in the last half of Victoria's reign that men of wealth should acquire a collection of pictures and Donald, J.J. Hill, Van Horne, Angus, and Stephen all complied. Conservative artistic taste of the time looked back to the old masters of the seventeenth and eighteenth centuries and distrusted the artistic concerns of the impressionists and their followers. The arbiters of taste at the Academies in London and Paris, and the European and North American collectors who followed their dictates, favoured representational works with a bias towards portraits, landscapes and sporting pictures. Donald shied away from sporting subjects, having had enough of that in real life, but his collection showed a tolerance of Roman Catholic themes which was typical of the man but not of his class.

Initially, Donald set out to collect old masters, as did many of his contemporaries, but these were rarely what they seemed to be. A portrait, said to be of Cardinal Gian Carlo de Medici, was attributed to Raphael but since the painter died ninety-one years before the prelate was born, it was clearly by another artist or of another cardinal. A portrait of Philip II was said to be by Titian but was later re-attributed, as were works supposedly by Rubens and Rembrandt. A Canaletto was later thought to be by Francesco Guardi. But Turner's *Mercury and Argus* (1836) was legitimate. It had previously been owned by the Scottish collector, John Graham and was sent to Christie's auction house in London for sale in April 1887. The Glasgow dealer William Laurie purchased it and sold it to Donald in the autumn that year. Acting for both Donald and Angus, Laurie also bought other parts of Graham's collection that spring when Donald's bill came to £2,600.[7]

Wealthy buyers, whose critical faculties were sharp when they bought shares or lent money, tended to be guided entirely by dealers when it came to the purchase of works of art and the advice given to Donald regarding many of his old masters was, at best, optimistic. Even when advisers were scrupulously honest, the possibility of error was great when the provenance of an old picture was not meticulously documented and, in the last quarter of the nineteenth century, the need for such information was just beginning to be understood. Because they could not be sure what they were paying for when they purchased old masters, many collectors diverted their attention to works by contemporary painters. Donald soon followed suit, buying pictures by Alma Tadema, Benjamin Constant, Rosa Bonheur, Millais, and a charming Tissot, then called *Lady in Black* but now generally titled *October*. By far his best known picture, however, was Jules Breton's *The Communicants*, sometimes called *The First Communion*. Exhibited at the Paris Salon of 1884, it depicts a group of French country girls in their white communion dresses, walking towards a village church. Breton's nostalgic rendition of unchanging values in a changing world appealed to urban sophisticates who took comfort from this reaffirmation of moral certainties and his work enjoyed great popularity at the end of the nineteenth century. The critic of the *Montreal Gazette*, visiting Donald's gallery in 1888, was ecstatic. "The faces of the girls are sweet and pure. They are true village girls of the best type, into whose minds the vain thoughts of the world of cities have never entered. What nobleness of feature, what velvety softness of tone. In their pious contemplation they seem as they move along to be wrapt in some vision celestial."[8]

The Communicants had been bought by Mary Jane Sexton Morgan, a wealthy New York widow who spent large sums on works of art in preference to conserving her late husband's money for her step-children whom she did not like. They had the last laugh, however, for the Breton, for which she had paid $12,000 in 1884, was bought by Donald in March 1886 for $45,500, then the largest sum ever paid for a work by a living artist.

Donald bid through Walter Watson, the Bank of Montreal's New York manager, unaware that one of the would-be buyers who was driving up the price was J.J. Hill, also cloaked in anonymity through his dealer, Samuel Avery. As soon as he discovered who his competitor was, Donald had the painting shipped to Saint Paul with his compliments but Hill as swiftly sent it back. With his own daughters making their first communions, Hill found a resonance in Donald's painting but he was not prepared to accept as a gift a picture which he had been unable to afford to buy.[9]

While Donald's pictures reflected the taste of the period, his Japanese collection, housed in a room off the gallery, was decidedly unfashionable. There were miniatures — probably *netsuke* — *inrō* and other lacquer, sword guards, bronzes, vases and manuscripts. One vase, Sir Henry Tyler reported in astonishment to his wife, cost eight hundred guineas. He later acquired suits of armour and the furnishings of a Buddhist temple. Family tradition claims that a box of miniatures, unopened, was discovered after Donald died, a report which has given rise to a suggestion that at least some of the items were acquired as a subtle means of providing financial assistance to collectors who were down on their luck.[10]

Donald enjoyed his collection, which he continued to build for many years, as an outward manifestation of his success in other fields, but he derived much more satisfaction from the pleasure he was able to give those who inspected the pictures. His guests never failed to express their delight and recommended connoisseurs were always granted a private view, whether or not Donald was at home. Angus believed, in 1885, that Donald intended his pictures to be donated to a public collection but the discovery that the old masters were not what they were purported to be seems to have put paid to that idea and Donald's last will contained no reference to any work of art.[11]

News of the driving of the last spike had barely crossed the Atlantic before Lord Elphinstone initiated the process which would lead to honours for Donald and George Stephen. Elphinstone wrote his friend, Lord Lansdowne, the governor general, to suggest that "a mark of appreciation would be gratifying — not so much to themselves personally — as to the whole of the Canadian people — for they have done more for Canada — if not for the world at large — than any two men living." Friends at court had bruited the notion with Queen Victoria who agreed, a view which was supported a week later when the Duke of Connaught also had a word with his mother. The proposal was that Stephen, who had shouldered the greater responsibility, should be offered a baronetcy and that Donald should be made a Knight Commander of the Order of St. Michael and St. George, the order generally used for service to Britain's overseas interests. Both men would be entitled to the prefix Sir, but Stephen's honour was heritable, had he had a son.[12]

The proposal could not be seen to have been initiated in the UK, so Lansdowne wrote Macdonald who was in London. There was some concern that an honour for Donald might lead to other claims for preferment but Lansdowne felt that he had made "personal sacrifices, or rather perhaps run personal risks which have not been encountered to the same extent by anyone else."[13]

Neither man was prepared to accept. Stephen felt that the future of the CPR was not sufficiently secure and wanted to wait until he felt more confident before agreeing to any honour, but pressure from Donald, Annie Stephen and the prime minister persuaded him to change his mind. "Though she has not said anything to me I find Mrs. Stephen is woman enough to rather like the distinction," Stephen wrote by way of excusing his acceptance. A few years later, when Van Horne agreed to a knighthood, he also blamed his wife whose republican principles had suddenly vanished.[14]

It took longer to find Donald, who was in transit between the Pacific coast and England, and, when the prime minister finally was able to speak to him, Donald was reticent. Macdonald urged him to accept, pointing out that in 1872 the governor in council had written that Donald's services in Red River merited a knighthood. As a mark of appreciation for his efforts nearly fifteen years earlier, Donald agreed to accept the honour.[15]

He then realized that this might be impolitic, given that Ontario and Quebec were at each other's throats as a consequence of the execution of Louis Riel, so wrote the governor general to say that if reference to the Northwest was going to cause difficulties, he would be content if nothing further were done. In avoiding mention of the CPR, he explained, he had been hoping to prevent any resuscitation of the Pacific Scandal and the quarrel of 1878.[16]

Two weeks sick in bed gave him a chance to think the matter over still further and when he had recovered at the end of February, he wrote Macdonald again. He could appreciate, he said, that such an award could be important to politicians, senior civil servants and military officers but it could be "of no consequence to businessmen like myself in private life." Any friend worth having would not disdain him if he remained plain Mr. Donald Smith, he said, before adding that the one thing which he had done which he thought appropriate to such an honour was his mission to the Northwest. "Given as an acknowledgment of these services, I should as already mentioned, accept and appreciate it, but in connection with anything I may since have done, would unhesitatingly but respectfully decline it."[17]

The dithering looks like false modesty but Donald was apt, when ill in bed, to review his moral principles. What, after all, had he done for the CPR? He had not conceived the idea, surveyed the line or reconnoitred the passes through the mountains. Neither had he taken the lead in the negotiations with the government or the banks. True, he had risked his fortune but many men led useful lives on a fraction of the income he enjoyed and so, he hoped, could he. The old paraphrase he so often recited when he was ill reminded him that the rewards of celestial wisdom were those he should seek and if he were to accept earthly honours, he preferred them to acknowledge his role as a peacemaker.[18]

The governor general sent a reassuring note, the recommendation went off to London where it was delayed by a change in government, but in May, Queen Victoria gave her assent to Donald's knighthood.

In addition to caring for his wife and children, Donald had continued to play an important role in advising and giving material help to Bella's family and to his own. His brother John was often prostrate for months at a time, suffering from recurring attacks of malaria. John's first daughter, Eliza Johana, had married Robert Grant of Forres, but his second, Maggie, remained at home to nurse her father. Donald sent money to ease their financial burden, a kindness which was particularly important after the collapse of the Caledonian Bank in which both John and their mother had placed their savings. Donald also looked after some investments for Robert Grant.

Of Bella's family, Hannah, the eldest Hardisty child, was a widow who had difficulty making ends meet, but her large family helped to provide for her until her death in 1891. Bella's oldest brother, William Lucas, took a year's leave of absence at the beginning of Outfit 1878 and retired the following year. He spent the winter of his furlough at Silver Heights where he gave splendid parties, according to the stories which rapidly spread among the HBC fraternity. The following year he was at Lachine, but his brother Richard was hoping that he would settle in some rural area. "By all accounts it will be better for him to be away from any place where he can get liquor for I hear he goes into it pretty freely." Richard had the same worry the following January when he learned that William intended to join him in Edmonton. "I cannot say that the place will suit him if he is still given to drink — for large quantities of the abominable stuff is brought in these [days]." William had no opportunity to try it, for he died of erysipelas on January 16, 1881. His widow, Mary, later remarried.[19]

Joseph resigned from the HBC at the beginning of Outfit 1884, in preference to accepting a posting to Labrador. He had had several disagreements with James Grahame and felt his services were undervalued, a point of view with which Donald likely agreed for he engaged Joseph to handle all the paperwork for the Canadian sub-committee. When James Bissett retired as Donald's secretary and attorney, Joseph replaced him, continuing in that role until his death in 1906.

Richard continued his HBC career at Edmonton, though he too quarrelled with James Grahame and went as far as submitting his resignation at one point. There were arguments about the prices Richard charged soldiers and the police for goods but he provided invaluable information about the movements of Indians and Métis during the 1885 uprising, quickly cutting through the exaggerations and hysterical rumours which flew across the telegraph wires from other quarters. As well as running the company's operation effectively, Richard made sensible investments on his own account in land and small businesses such as saw mills. With Donald and Joseph, he also shouldered the burden of Bella's less responsible or less able siblings.

In 1887, Richard agreed to stand for parliament, though he knew himself well enough to realize that he had spent too long on the Canadian frontier to be altogether comfortable in cities and the parliamentary milieu. Thinking Richard would be unopposed and certain that his knowledge of the Northwest would benefit the House, Donald encouraged the candidature, with the proviso that Richard stand as an independent. I.G. Baker, the company's principal competitor in Alberta, threw its financial weight behind an opponent but Donald refused to break HBC rules and provide money to back Richard. His failure to win the seat embarrassed Richard, Donald and Prime Minister Macdonald, who provided compensation with the offer of an appointment to the Senate. Knowing it would be churlish to decline, Richard accepted, but spent as little time in Ottawa as he possibly could.

In the autumn of 1889, he and another HBC officer, Archibald McDonald, were at Broadview, about a hundred miles east of Regina, in connection with the visit of the governor general, Lord Stanley, who had taken up his appointment in June the previous year. On the morning of the second of October, as Richard's democrat crossed the CPR track, the jolting of a wheel against a rail dislodged a loose seat. Both he and McDonald were hurled to the ground. Richard landed across one of the rails, breaking his back. He was completely paralysed. Sir James Grant, an Ottawa doctor who was following close behind with the vice-regal party, tended Richard and when Dr. Hutchinson arrived from the little town of Grenfell, about twenty-five miles away, the two medical men agreed that Richard should be conveyed to the General Hospital in Winnipeg. Initially, the telegrams to Montreal wavered between the optimistic and the pessimistic but when Richard's wife arrived in Winnipeg on Wednesday the eighth, Wrigley cabled that "if his affairs require attention delay is not desirable." At the beginning of the following week, the news was much worse and Joseph set out from Montreal. Richard was conscious and able to speak and Wrigley said he was cheered by news of Donald's concern, expressed in daily cables, and asked after Bella. She had been absent from Montreal but as soon as she returned, on the fifteenth, Donald cabled her love and his warmest wishes. Wrigley rushed to the hospital to deliver the message but was too late. Bella's first and only journey west, for Richard's funeral, was a doubly sad one, for a week before she lost her favourite brother, Mary McPherson, too, had died.

After Donald's sharp letter about her financial management and the need to live within her means, Mary had taken some control over her life but Donald still paid her a regular annual allowance. After old Mrs. McPherson died, Mary made plans to move with her family to the Northwest in the autumn of 1880; Richard agreed with Donald that he would pay his share of her expenses and help her find a place to live. In November 1880, Donald foreclosed on the mortgage on Norway House but Mary and her family continued to live there until the spring of 1882 when they at last set out for the Northwest. Donald arranged with James Grahame for the HBC to assist with transport.[20]

The intention then was that Donald, perhaps in conjunction with Joseph and George, would continue an allowance until such time as the boys could look after their mother themselves. In 1885, however, Richard's account of the McPhersons was, as Donald expressed it in his response, "certainly most unsatisfactory and if you feel that by continuing to aid their mother encouragement is given to the Lads to lead an idle and as regards at least one of them, a vicious life, you are of course right in withholding help. At the same time please understand that I am perfectly willing to continue to Mrs. McPherson an allowance of Five hundred dollars yearly as heretofore: this to be furnished entirely at your discretion." Mary, who seems not to have succeeded in finding much happiness in her life, was only fifty-six when she died.[21]

George, the youngest of Bella's surviving brothers, appeared to have settled to a satisfactory career as a purser on the HBC's steamer, *Princess Louise*, which plied the Pacific coast. Nothing in his behaviour seems to have caused comment when he visited Montreal on leave in 1879 but at the beginning of February 1884, he was forcibly removed from a train at Saint Paul and declared insane. He was en route to Montreal at the time and, according to the doctor who cabled Donald, had "valuable papers" with him as well as a draft for $400 on Montreal. Joseph immediately set out for Saint Paul with Donald's letter asking Jim Hill to provide any financial or other help which might be necessary. The doctor's letter indicated that George would have to be confined to an asylum, at least temporarily, and Donald guaranteed to meet all the expenses.[22]

Joseph was unable to place his brother in the recommended hospital in Batavia, just west of Chicago, but found him a place in Cincinnati. By the end of March, he was reported to be much improved, both physically and mentally, but at the beginning of May, Joseph wrote to Richard to say that the news was discouraging. By September, George was in the Montreal General Hospital, "on his back with rheumatism," a condition from which Richard also suffered. Though the Canadian sub-committee did not keep Joseph fully occupied, he felt he could not absent himself to visit his brother and, when he wrote Richard in September, had not seen George since May when he had fetched him from Cincinnati. Such a gap suggests the two brothers had little in common — indeed, George does not seem to have been close to any of his siblings, or to anyone else. In Joseph's view, "it would be best to remove him to the Northwest where he would be among his own friends or relatives & where he could *be compelled* to work or take exercise if he wouldn't do so voluntarily or without urging."[23]

In October that year, Richard cabled Donald that he wanted to see him — probably on a question of investments — but he took George back with him to Edmonton. Richard found himself responsible for the more difficult members of his family partly because, with Joseph, he was the man most capable of looking after them and partly because he lived in the Northwest where land and living were cheaper and where the opportunities for new beginnings were greater. Whether it was the right place for George is another question, but at a time when few advances had been made in the amelioration of rheumatism and the care of mental illnesses such as schizophrenia and manic depression, it is hard to imagine where George might best have settled. Donald and Joseph contributed to George's expenses and were gratified to learn, in the autumn of 1885, that he was "apparently somewhat better mentally than when he first went up to the North West," but Joseph felt that the improvement in a year was not sufficient to warrant believing that he would ever be truly well again. A diligent man himself, Joseph was convinced that "if he can only be induced to give up the indolent life he leads and be made to do *some work every day* and regularly so as to have something to engage & occupy his mind I would not give up hope of his ultimate entire recovery."[24]

As if George and Mary were not sufficient worry, Donald and Bella were also concerned about Jamesie who seemed unable to settle. Though Donald cared deeply for the young man, he had taught himself to keep his feelings under tight control and had difficulty in expressing his affection. He was very fond of young children, as his official HBC correspondence makes clear whenever it diverts to discuss the welfare of his colleagues' little ones. When the girls matured, he found them relatively easy to deal with because he treated them with the same old fashioned courtesy he proffered their mothers. Young men, however, were something of a mystery to him, the more so since he had had little guidance from his own father and had effectively been on his own, with a little advice from HBC officers, since he was eighteen. He was not quite sure what to do with Jamesie, beyond providing financial support when he needed it.

Jamesie had little contact with his natural father who had remarried and settled in New York where he became a commodities broker, specializing in metals. At one point, he is reported to have met his son and asked why he did not use the Grant surname, to which Jamesie responded that the man who had acted as a father towards him all his life was named Smith and he saw no need to change this name. Donald tried to do his best by Jamesie, but the young man's whims may have been indulged more than was good for him; certainly Richard Hardisty found him spoiled. In November 1887, when he was in Montreal on leave, he reported to his wife that "just before D.A. left the office he asked me to go and have a plate of soup with him. Jamesie did not like this as the dinner was got up for my benefit."[25]

Jamesie had married Emma Davis of Montreal and Donald had hoped that the couple would take over Norway House where Jamesie could prove himself by managing the property and making its thirty acres turn a profit. In 1884, Donald paid for extensive repairs to the house, providing a much improved scullery and kitchen and laying on a water supply and indoor plumbing. Having made Norway House a going concern, Jamesie could then have turned his attention to developing business interests in the area. Fish, lumber, coal and land were all possibilities but Jamesie was not interested and Donald employed a manager instead. He acquired a neighbouring stone house which he let, and invested in the Nova Scotia coal industry without his stepson.

In February 1885, Jamesie was in Minnesota where he had decided to farm. A loan from Donald was promised but Hill, who was to be the means through which the loan was handed over, noted that the livestock and farming implements offered as collateral were worth less than half the value Jamesie had put on them. Hill assumed interest would be charged and Donald, who was busy with both the Canadian sub-committee and the latest CPR financial crisis, was slow in responding to queries about the transaction. As Hill had surmised, Donald confirmed that there were "personal reasons" for the loan which could not be recommended on business grounds, but by April, Jamesie had changed his mind and decided not to buy the farm. In October, having returned to Montreal, he seems to have made a nuisance of himself, perhaps by being jealous of his mother who was wintering in England. At any rate, he was "packed off suddenly to England" with his family, but he was no happier in the wet and foggy suburban London winter.[26]

Jamesie eventually became a partner in John MacLean and Company, a Montreal wholesale firm dealing in millinery and fancy goods. It proved no more of a success and in the summer of 1891, when its debts exceeded $250,000, the receivers were brought in. Nearly half the debt was owed to the Merchants' Bank, while Donald was the largest individual creditor with $25,596.52 outstanding. In 1897, another effort was made to encourage Jamesie to take up

Norway House, but again without success. That year he moved to Philadelphia with Donald's financial assistance and later he settled in Boston. Donald gave a regular allowance to Jamesie's oldest son, Donald Alexander, and continued to provide financial support to the family, often in the guise of presents to the children.[27]

In addition to helping immediate and more distant family members, as long as he had a professional base in Manitoba, Donald regularly made small charitable donations to churches and educational establishments in or near Winnipeg and to the Manitoba Rifle Association. Nothing indicates that he gave to causes outside the Northwest before 1880, though he probably did contribute in a small way to charitable institutions in Montreal. In November 1880, however, he made a substantial donation towards improvements at Anderson's Institution in Forres and, the following year, gave a small sum to the Mechanics' Institute which, in common with similar organizations in other Scottish towns, provided lectures for workers who had not had a chance to continue their education. In Forres, the Institute also served as a community centre and housed church bazaars and occasional public celebrations.[28]

Education was a topic in which it was always easy to interest Donald. Until his later years, he read voraciously and throughout his life surprised people by the range of subjects on which he could discourse with more than a superficial understanding. But he was aware that the specialist knowledge on which modern life increasingly depended had to be acquired at universities and in research laboratories. Equally, he knew that women were denied academic training in many places because there were no facilities for their further education and he felt an obligation to do something to rectify this situation. In the 1870s, he had helped finance the creation of a boarding school for young women in Winnipeg and in Montreal in 1883, James Barclay, the new minister of St. Paul's Presbyterian Church, persuaded Donald, who was one of his parishioners, to donate $30,000 for the Trafalgar Institute, a boarding school for Protestant girls.

The admission of women to McGill University in Montreal had been debated for some time and was aired again early in September 1884 when the British Association for the Advancement of Science held its annual meeting in the city. The university itself had taken no clear stand, not least because, while many of the professors were in favour of fully integrated teaching, the very powerful principal, Sir John Dawson, had his doubts about women's education in any form and was firmly against co-education. Though a fine administrator, Dawson's views were retrogressive in many respects: he believed the Bible was a literal account of man's early history and scorned those who predicted air travel. Guided by Dawson, the board of governors had been content to let the arguments in favour of women's education swell up and die down again of their own accord, so they were taken aback when, entirely on his own initiative, Donald sent a cheque for $50,000 to establish an endowment to provide for the education of women at McGill. It was the largest gift the university had ever received and the governors promptly invited Donald to join the board.

Though the cheque had not been anticipated, the university was able to arrange for classes to begin immediately, the income from the endowment being used to meet the costs of repeating for women-only lectures in classics, mathematics, French, German, English and chemistry. The money was sufficient to support the first two years of a bachelor of arts degree and, that autumn, the faculty drew up proposals for the remaining two years. Required courses, which would be sufficient for a degree, would be single sex; honours classes, would be mixed, as would elective classes should the young ladies choose to attend them. The proposal generated a vigorous public debate, with some people, especially faculty members, arguing that Donald's money should be used to improve facilities to which both women and men could have access.

In making provision for the education of girls and women, Donald was identifying himself with an idea which was just beginning to take hold elsewhere and, in assuming women would take degrees, he and McGill were somewhat in the van. The first women's colleges had been established at Cambridge only a decade earlier and in 1878, the University of London was the first academic body in the UK to admit women for degrees on the same terms as men. Oxford University did not grant women degrees until after World War I. As McGill was setting up its first classes for women, Queen Margaret College at the University of Glasgow was opening its doors as Scotland's first college for women. American universities, where the college system had never taken hold, had begun to admit women but had mixed views on co-education.

In 1886, Dawson approached Donald for a further endowment which would finance the faculty's proposals for the third and fourth years of the women's degree course and, in October, received $70,000 with a further $1,600 "being Interest at the rate of 5 percent per annum, on seventy thousand dollars from the 1st of May last, to meet the current expense of the Special Classes for Women until further revenue is derived from the principal sum." Dawson offered to draw up a deed covering both this donation and the original one and Donald agreed. Into it, the principal incorporated his own views on separate education. There was to be a "distinct separate class in the Faculty of Arts" and on no account was any money to be "applied directly or indirectly to sustain mixed classes of the two sexes." It also contained reference to the establishment "as soon as possible" of a separate college. As far as Dawson was concerned, all the classes would be taught there whereas Donald, if pressed, would almost certainly have said he saw no harm in mixed classes, though he clearly favoured a women's college which would provide young ladies with a secure environment in which their intellects could flourish. It is, however, extremely unlikely that any debate about the merits of separate education ever took place between the two men. Donald did not interfere with the running of Anderson's Institution or the Trafalgar Institute just as he did not expect to find Dawson making suggestions as to how to run the Bank of Montreal of which Donald had become president in 1887. Having given the money to the university, he left it to the principal to arrange the details in the manner he thought most appropriate.[29]

In 1889, the university's chancellor, who was also the chair of the board of governors, died. It was expected that his successor would be the brewer, John H.R. Molson, the most senior governor, but he declined. William McDonald (Macdonald after his knighthood), the tobacco magnate and another great McGill benefactor, was asked to survey his fellow governors and reported that Donald was their unanimous choice as the next chancellor.

That October, as Peter Redpath, who had made his fortune in sugar, led Donald, in his black gown and red hood, to the chancellor's chair, the students cheered and sang "For he's a jolly good fellow." Donald was beginning to develop a formula for his public speeches, starting with a graceful compliment to his colleagues or hosts — in this case he noted that the other governors were more qualified to fill the post to which they had elected him — and continuing, when appropriate, with a summation of some of the previous speakers' relevant remarks which led him into the observations he wished to make himself. In his inaugural address, Donald came quickly to the point that the university required increased financial support for the arts, applied science and law. It also needed a new gymnasium, convocation hall and dining room and endowments for more of the professorships. He then observed that "something is required to be done for the Donalda department for women. Some of us had hoped that by this time there would have been such a college in existence, but from certain causes it has not been brought about. However, I think that we may feel assured that before the lady undergraduates who join us this year are ready to leave the college, they will have a habitat of their own."[30]

The college as a concept was inaugurated that year, with permission from the queen for it to be called the Royal Victoria College. The students, however, chose to honour their founder by calling themselves Donaldas and their debating society was Delta Sigma, standing for Donald Smith. In 1897, when complaints were made that the women's programme was costing the university money, Donald made a further grant of $4,000.

The college added music to its curriculum and developed plans to link the courses to the examinations of the Associated Board of the Royal Academy of Music and the Royal College of Music in London. This scheme was so popular that in 1890, Donald bought the former home of a wealthy Montrealer and university benefactor, Thomas Workman, and presented it for the use of music students. He brought Clara Lichtenstein, a pianist and former pupil of Liszt, from Edinburgh to be director of music and when, in 1904, the college's music programme was taken over by the university as the Montreal Conservatory, Lichtenstein became its deputy director. At the turn of the century, the music department's most outstanding pupil was Pauline Lighthouse, a soprano. Lichtenstein felt Lighthouse needed further training after her graduation from McGill and arranged for Donald to give her $50 a month to study in Europe. She eventually settled in London, taking the stage name Pauline Donalda as a compliment to her benefactor.

The "certain causes" which delayed Donald's desire to provide the women with "a habitat of their own" had their roots in the university's divided opinion about co-education and little progress was made until Dawson died in 1893. In 1885, Donald had paid for furnishing three classrooms, a lobby and a waiting room in the arts building and in 1889, more space seems to have been made available. It was only in 1893, however, when Donald purchased land on Sherbrooke Street, next to the McGill campus, that construction of a separate college building could begin. Architects who had designed stations and other buildings for the CPR were brought in to draw up plans and supervise the work and the final bill for the elegant college came close to $400,000. Carpets were specially woven in Scotland, the linen was made in Ireland and each piece of crockery and silverware was stamped with the college crest. There was an assembly hall and various meeting rooms and Donald donated an overdecorated piano. Unfortunately, the architects' experience of creating public spaces did not transfer easily to the requirements of college buildings and they made provision for only thirty-seven bedrooms, as opposed to the hundred which had been requested. Donald dealt with this problem in 1909 by buying the neighbouring house into which the college could expand.[31]

Donald appointed the first principal, Hilda Oakeley. She was only thirty-four and a somewhat surprising choice, given that she supported the suffragettes and had been working as an assistant to Beatrice Webb, one of the founders of the Fabian Society. But Oakeley was an intelligent, well-spoken woman with an unwavering commitment to education and an understanding of the milieu which Donald wanted to provide for the young women. He wrote her to say that he had "every confidence that your supervision of it will be of the most beneficial character — not alone in teaching its pupils to become clever or even learned women, but also in instilling into their minds those principles and sentiments without which they cannot be true gentlewomen." As Donald admitted in a letter to his brother, he had been influenced by memories of their sister Margaret and her scholarly ambitions when he founded the college, but the concept of the gentlewoman, learned from his mother, also underpinned his thinking. Miss Oakeley's successor, Ethel Hurlbatt, whom Donald also engaged, was told the story of old Mrs. Smith asking if the grand ladies he had met were gentlewomen and quickly grasped that the college was to be "more than a residence, something more than a social and recreational centre." Donald "had a liking for English ideals in the field of women's education," his first principal recalled, and trusted that under her guidance the college "would naturally develop in ways that he would approve. His great hope was that it would help Canadian girls to realise the ideal of womanhood, and he believed that there were colleges in England which might serve as a pattern to follow."[32]

The college building was not quite finished when Oakeley took up her post in September 1899, but classes began the day after she arrived. What the staff and students lacked, the CPR was instructed to provide.

What, Oakeley naively asked, was the CPR? "In Canada," her interlocutor replied, "first comes Royalty and then comes the C.P.R."[33]

As for royalty and the Royal Victoria College, Donald commissioned Princess Louise, wife of the former governor general, the Marquess of Lorne, to sculpt a statue of her mother, the queen, to stand in front of the college. It was *in situ* long before it was possible to arrange the official unveiling, which also marked the formal opening of the college. In high spirits, the male students regularly removed the cover — once to celebrate the relief of Ladysmith in the South African war. On that occasion, the old queen was stuck all over with Union Jacks.

Donald was unable to see his creation until October 10, 1900 when he paid a private visit and met all the students. Two weeks later, on the first of November 1900, Lady Minto, wife of the governor general, finally performed the unveiling ceremony. It was preceded by a grand dinner at Dorchester Street where the Mintos mingled with McGill staff, with Donald's railway friends, Van Horne, Angus and Shaughnessy, and with Sir Edward Clouston, president of the Bank of Montreal. The personal and financial strains shared by these men during the construction of the CPR had created an indissoluble bond which, to a lesser extent, also linked their wives and children. They could be certain of invitations to special occasions such as this dinner and regularly shared more private social gatherings too.

Over a thousand of "the most notable figures in the business, professional and educational circles of the city" were invited to the college for what the *Gazette* described as "one of the most brilliant social occasions that has taken place in Montreal of late years." The building was strung with lights in the McGill colours of red and white and, in the fashion of the time, a huge transparency showing the McGill coat of arms, a shield with an open book and three red birds, was erected above the doorway. As Lady Minto removed the statue's cover for the last time, the letters VR flashed on in lights above her head and the huge crowd, watching from the street despite the showers, joined the choir and dignitaries singing "God Save the Queen." For Donald, it was a perfect occasion, offering a dramatic gesture which could be enjoyed by the public at large as well as by his invited guests, but simultaneously allowed him to remain in the background while the focus was on the vice regal party and the college itself.[34]

Some two years earlier, when the university governors were discussing McGill's financial needs, Sir William Macdonald had pointed out that the Royal Victoria College would be expensive to run. At least $10,000 a year would be required, he estimated. Then, to tease Donald, he said that he would give a million dollars to the arts faculty if Donald would give the women a matching sum. It was not a challenge Donald could refuse since he had already begun the practice of making some of his charitable donations dependent on a further sum being raised from other quarters. Rather than hand the money over directly, he put aside a million dollars worth of railway shares and annually transferred to the college the interest which they had earned. It was never less than $42,000 and between 1898 and 1922, he and his heirs paid about $800,000 in interest to the college. In 1924, after the royal charter which Donald had been trying to achieve, had finally been granted and the college was at last incorporated, the shares which formed the principal, together with the interest for the two previous years, were given to the RVC. Insurance, maintenance and other costs had also been met by Donald from time to time.

Donald's commitment to music education and performance was not confined to the Royal Victoria College. He had scarcely returned from Richard Hardisty's funeral before he helped to establish the Montreal Philharmonic Society which undertook to present a series of orchestral concerts in the city. In 1883, the Royal College of Music was incorporated in London with enthusiastic support from several members of the royal family. Among those who were keen to see it succeed was Princess Louise who suggested to Donald and George Stephen that they might endow a scholarship to enable Canadians to study at the college. They agreed, and later that year the princess forwarded Donald's cheque for £1,500. His cousin's matching sum followed later.

The Montreal Scholarship was open to natives of the city and environs and to people who had lived there for a minimum of five years. Though the principle was established in 1883, nothing was done to implement the plans for a scholarship until late in 1884 when Donald and George Stephen asked that the Governor General, by then Lord Lansdowne, undertake the responsibility. The college president, the Duke of Edinburgh, approved this procedure and, in January 1885, the wheels finally creaked into motion.

It was a somewhat cack-handed affair, for Lansdowne found himself obliged to sort out eligibility, receive and process the applications, find the examiners and the examination room and award the prizes. His correspondence suggests he did not object to the imposition but the necessity of making all the arrangements at the last minute meant that some of the best music students did not apply and those who did had insufficient time to prepare. As a consequence, the examiners felt unable to make an award in the first year. They faced the opposite problem a year later when two candidates were deemed to be of equal merit. They finally settled on Mina Louise Walker but Donald, hearing of the difficulty, "defrayed the cost of the musical education and maintenance" of the second candidate, Ada Moylan, for three years. By 1889, he was serving as a member of the corporation, the body from which the governing council of the Royal College was elected, but took no active part in the management of the college and probably confined his involvement in the corporation to a three year term. The scholarship, however, endured.[35]

Donald's support for McGill was not restricted to the women's college. He endowed the chairs of hygiene and pathology, supported a retirement fund for the staff and contributed to an increase in their salaries. In 1913, he gave $100,000 towards a divinity school and $79,000 towards the college armoury. He took his duties as chancellor seriously and when, in 1895, the university needed to find a new principal, he personally led the search, which finally settled on William Peterson of Dundee University. His greatest interest, however, was in medicine, and when the medical building burned in 1907, he purchased land for a new building and gave $450,000 towards the construction. This was half the cost, the remainder being met by the insurance.

Medicine is a career which Donald might well have pursued had his family had the money to enable him to further his education. It was also a field of knowledge which was beginning to expand rapidly at the end of the nineteenth century when the discovery of bacteria and their capacity to cause disease provoked medical researchers to find ways in which infection could be prevented by techniques such as sterilization and inoculation. The diseases which had killed Margaret and Marianne Smith, the typhoid which regularly swept through overcrowded tenements, the recurrent attacks of malaria which plagued Donald's brother, the tuberculosis which had ruined Thomas Hardisty's last years, and the pulmonary infections from which Donald, Bella and Maggie suffered each winter could all be brought under control by application of the knowledge which was being gained in the medical laboratories. Donald believed that both the prevention of disease and the relief of suffering were deserving of his support.

Robert Palmer Howard, a genial and very popular man, was Donald's doctor and had served on the McGill medical faculty since 1854. In 1882, he became dean of medicine and immediately made known the need for development funds. In 1883, Donald gave $50,000, the Leanchoil Memorial, for this purpose, on condition that it be matched by the same amount, to be called the George Campbell Memorial, honouring the late dean of medicine. One contribution, from George Stephen, matched Donald's gift. Few knew that Leanchoil was the name of the farm on which Donald's mother had spent her happy childhood and he never drew attention to the fact. He used the name as his distinctive, personal cable address in both London and Montreal and, when he bought land in Forres and paid for the building of a hospital on it in 1889, he honoured his mother by naming that hospital after the Stuart farm. In the same year, he also established an endowment for the hospital, though his money was not paid over until 1892 when the people of Forres had completed the hospital and raised their own contribution to the endowment.

Robert Jared Bliss Howard, the dean's son by his first marriage, also studied medicine at McGill, graduating with the faculty's gold medal for overall excellence in 1882. He then studied in Europe, and qualified as a surgeon before returning to Montreal where he became a demonstrator in anatomy and surgery at McGill, as well as being a pathologist and assistant surgeon at Montreal General Hospital, and a surgeon at the Montreal Dispensary. It was doubtless through his father that he met Donald and his family, and in March 1888, he married Maggie. The wedding was to have taken place at Christ Church Cathedral, Bella having retained her Anglican faith after her marriage and brought the children up in the Church of England. Maggie, however, had been very ill that winter and there was some worry that she would not recover in time for the service. She did, but it was held at home on the afternoon of Thursday, March 8. Lunch for the few guests who had been invited to the ceremony was followed by a small reception before the couple left for the southern United States where it was hoped that Maggie would recoup her health. Later in the year, they moved to London where Howard practised as a physician and surgeon.

On the evening before the wedding, Donald arranged for Maggie to sign a legal document declaring her to be separate as to property. It was a perfectly normal procedure for a woman who was wealthy or who was likely to inherit a large sum, whether she was marrying a rich man or, as in Maggie's case, a man who was obliged to make his way by his own energies and skill.

On the surface, it ought to have been a match which pleased Donald and Bella: Howard was a doctor, his family was held in high esteem in Montreal and nothing suggested that he was more interested in Donald's money than his daughter. Maggie had just passed her thirty-fourth birthday and, though elegant and with a good figure, was five years older than her husband and about ten years older than most brides of her generation. It might have been expected that the Smiths were glad that she had found a partner; in fact, they seemed discomfited. Richard Hardisty, who was in Montreal and Ottawa with his daughter Clara that winter, sensed an undercurrent of unease at the wedding. "It seems a relief to Sir Donald that Maggie has gone," Richard wrote to his wife, adding that "it must have given a great deal of thought and trouble till the affair was all over. Riches don't always bring true happiness and if we could see into the dark corners in that well filled house, we would, no doubt, see more to pity than to admire."[36]

Like any other well-to-do family, the Smiths were the topic of many idle tongues and it was rumoured that Bella disapproved of Maggie's marriage. Other stories said that she had broken up an earlier match. It seems likely that she did not want to part with Maggie's companionship, and it is also probably true that no man could be possessed of all the qualities which Donald and Bella would have hoped to find in the one who was to take away their only child. Howard was intelligent, well-mannered and diligent, and his profession was one for which the Smiths had great respect, but nothing suggests he had the breadth of interests, the tolerance or even the energy which Donald himself had and which he found in men such as Sandford Fleming and William Van Horne whose company he enjoyed.

The difficulty Donald and Bella found in accepting Howard as a son-in-law persisted and their dislike of him increased. In 1903, Joseph Pope, who had been Sir John Macdonald's private secretary, observed that Donald did not feel "amiably disposed towards his son-in-law," but did not hazard a guess as to the reason. Suggestions from his descendants that Howard was rather too fond of a drink may well be true but they are not corroborated in the correspondence and diaries of his contemporaries. For his part, Howard doubtless resented the time and attention he and his wife were obliged to devote to the Smiths in their increasingly public role, but there is also evidence that he was arrogant and inclined to be intolerant. These are not qualities which Donald would have found acceptable in anyone and would certainly have found very distressing in the husband of his only child.[37]

Richard's suggestion that there was "more to pity than to admire" in the "dark corners" of the house on Dorchester Street partly reflects Donald and Bella's dissatisfaction at Maggie's marriage but it also suggests that Richard, seeing more of the public persona of his sister and her husband and less of their private lives, was unaware that in one of those dark corners there flourished a powerful love which bound the two together with indissoluble ties.

The strength of that bond, never publicly demonstrated, enabled them to disregard the continuing gossip about their relationship. In August 1888, Sir Henry Tyler of the Grand Trunk was in Montreal where Donald entertained him to dinner. Bella was absent, probably in Carlsbad where she generally went in the summer for her health. "His wife is said to have another husband," Tyler wrote to his wife, "& his daughter, lately married against her mother's wishes, not to be his own — & his family relationships are strange & complicated & not precisely understood. His only son, also, is a trouble."[38]

Maggie's new father-in-law, McGill's dean of medicine, was convinced that Montreal was inadequately provided with hospitals, especially for those who were unable to meet the costs of their medical treatment. He had made an unsuccessful attempt to establish another hospital in 1870 but was defeated by a lack of resources, exacerbated by the economic depression of the early 1880s. There can be little doubt that he discussed his concerns with the cousins and in 1886 they wrote the city council offering a million dollars to pay for the construction of a hospital and provide an endowment for its running. The city was to provide the land which, they pointed out, could be had on Mount Royal, behind the reservoir. The hospital was to be named after the queen and its construction was to mark her golden jubilee, due to be celebrated the following year. A further condition was that Donald and his cousin appoint the directors and closely supervise the management of the project. The purpose of the hospital was "the reception and treatment of sick and injured persons of all races and creeds, without distinction."[39]

The city investigated the land proposal and found it acceptable, noting that there were already streets in the area, some of which "afforded a convenient and unobtrusive route to the cemetery." Having obtained royal consent for the name, the city was then obliged to seek the approval of the provincial legislature for the lease of the land in perpetuity and returned to the legislature in 1887 to have the incorporation authorized. The charter was drawn up by the ubiquitous J.J.C.

Abbott and, because the Montreal General had had difficulties with its directors earlier in the year, was exceptionally detailed, especially when it came to defining who these people were to be. The charter called for the mayor of Montreal and the president of the city's Board of Trade as well as the presidents of the Bank of Montreal and the CPR to be on the hospital's board of directors. The principal of McGill, the dean of the faculty of medicine and, interestingly, the senior resident officer of the Grand Trunk were also to serve. A further eight were to be elected by the exofficio governors who would choose from among a group of associates, each of whom was obliged to donate a minimum of $1,000 plus $20 a year or make a single donation of $5,000.[40]

Before the act of incorporation had passed through the provincial legislature, Donald was obliged to go to England for the Hudson's Bay Company's General Court. To enable the joint gift to be handed over in his absence, the cousins deposited the money in the Bank of Montreal in the name of the governor general, asking him to transfer it to the hospital board when it was incorporated. Like most people in Canada and Britain, Lord Lansdowne appreciated the generosity which the two men had shown. Stephen, himself, however, was becoming increasingly sour. He took personally any attack on the CPR and thought Manitoba's campaign to build railways south of the CPR poor thanks for the risks he and Donald had run to construct the national line. The formal letter explaining the arrangement about the money was dictated by Donald on the eve of his departure but Stephen accompanied it with a private letter in which he gave vent to his feelings. "This donation on the part of Sir Donald & myself cancels fully any obligation either of us are under to Canada the amt *exceeds* anything we ever made in the country & we feel that we have treated Canada very differently to what it seems disposed to treat us." While Donald was undoubtedly exasperated by the difficulties in Manitoba, he would never have expressed himself as Stephen had done nor sanctioned such remarks being made in his name.[41]

As early as the second board meeting, on October 11, 1887, the hospital ran into difficulties. The Montreal General, already overcrowded, had begun a crusade against the new hospital. George Stephen had been a generous benefactor of the General Hospital and it is not improbable that its directors feared losing his contributions. What they wanted was a further extension of their own premises and they mounted a press campaign, commenting adversely on the light and air at the chosen site and its distance from the centre of Montreal. The same points were raised when the directors of the two hospitals conferred later in October, but at that meeting, the Montreal General raised the more valid objection that the hospital's effluent could well pollute the city's water supply. It prompted Donald and his cousin to purchase nearby land which was below the level of the reservoir. The land which the city had made over to the hospital was to be reserved as a park.

Negotiations with the Montreal General did not peter out until 1889 but the governors of the Royal Victoria proceeded with their plans regardless. Donald and Stephen were determined to employ Henry Saxon Snell, an English architect who specialized in hospitals and had designed several large infirmaries in London as well as ones in Hull and Aberdeen. A co-author of a volume on hospital construction and management with a particular interest in the provision of facilities for the poor, Snell nevertheless prepared a large and costly design. Immediately, there was an altercation. The intention had been that one-third of the money would pay for construction and two-thirds would supply the endowment, earnings on which would cover the running of the hospital. Snell's designs, however, reversed that proportion. He was unwilling to reduce the size and the governors were unprepared to pay the extra costs. They also objected to Snell's proposals to heat the building with sixty fireplaces, rather than installing central heating; they thought English building and finishing materials were not essential and that expensive woods such as mahogany in the bathrooms were not needed. Snell did nothing to help his reputation at the end of the project when he tried to charge his five percent fee on the more expensive design rather than on the one which was ultimately built.

Odd compromises were enforced as the governors strove to keep down costs and Snell pressed for the completion of his original plan. The separate entrance and other facilities for medical students were done away with, with the result that for the next sixty years the students had to do without a cloakroom. None of the fireplaces was built, but the chimneys were retained to satisfy Snell's demand for rooftop symmetry. For his part, George Stephen continued to stand by Snell, pointing out that he had considerable experience in his field. At last, at an informal board meeting in August 1890, he grew tired of the sniping and announced that he and Donald would meet any unforeseen expenses. To the original medical, surgical and administration blocks, a children's ward and laundry were added in 1893 and a pathology building with an autopsy theatre and laboratory were added the year after. Total construction costs came to $650,000, in addition to the $77,000 which had been paid for the land.

Neither Donald nor his cousin favoured the formal opening which was performed by the governor general, then Lord Aberdeen, on the afternoon of December 2, 1893. Both men thought the hospital should simply have opened its doors and admitted those in need of treatment. Stephen expressed his disapproval by staying in England and Donald was assumed to have absented himself despite pressure from Aberdeen to attend. He did not join the other governors on the platform and was eventually discovered in a corner, talking to the superintendent who was worried whether the floor would withstand all the visitors who had crowded in after the invited guests.

Robert Craik, chairman of the Royal Victoria's medical board, warned in his opening speech that public funds would be required to run the hospital. In 1894, the founders provided $40,000 to cover the deficit and the following year, they gave $20,000 more. At the beginning of 1896, they gave a further $20,000 to wipe the slate clean. It was only a temporary respite, however, and in 1897 the two set up a permanent endowment fund of $1 million in the form of railway shares. These carried with them the option to purchase further stocks, an arrangement which enabled the hospital to add half a million dollars to the endowment fund in 1898.

The Royal Victoria Hospital was not Donald's only contribution to the queen's golden jubilee. In 1886, he had served as one of the Canadian commissioners to the massive Colonial and Indian Exhibition which displayed the products and resources of the British Empire. The Prince of Wales conceived that an institute, devoted to cultural and technical displays about the colonies would be a satisfying, permanent memorial to the queen's long reign and colonial governments and wealthy individuals contributed to its establishment. Canada gave £20,000 to the Imperial Institute, now the Commonwealth Institute, and Donald gave £5,000, offering at the same time, a further £5,000 from George Stephen.[42]

As with many other wealthy men at the end of the nineteenth century, Donald had accepted that his money carried with it an obligation to help others who were less fortunate. The belief was that, after the industrial revolution, much poverty had been created by the rush of people to the cities where they worked in factories and were unable to provide for their basic sustenance as they had done in rural areas, where they had small garden plots and access to common land for animals. The CPR's engines, for example, were made in urban Montreal; Peter Redpath's sugar refineries and the Molson family breweries were in the city as well, replicating a pattern which was seen in all the major European and North American centres. By the last quarter of the nineteenth century, men who made their fortunes directly or indirectly from such industries understood that they had an obligation to alleviate the poverty of urban, industrial centres. Shaw took up the theme in *Major Barbara*, when the arms manufacturer, Andrew Undershaft, says of London's poor, "They poison us morally and physically; they kill the happiness of society."[43]

By 1890, the main thrust of Donald's charitable giving was established and, with few exceptions, it addressed urban needs, especially those of medicine and education; these two were frequently combined, as in the Royal Victoria Hospital which, besides being open to anyone, was also McGill's teaching hospital. By comparison, what the Northwest needed, Donald believed, was population, and he campaigned vigorously to encourage immigration. This, however, he could not do for Labrador. Instead, he agreed to assist Dr. Wilfred Grenfell's sea-going mission along the Labrador coast, bringing medical treatment and providing hospitals for people who had never had anything more than the amateur doctoring of the Hudson's Bay Company factors. He chaired the Montreal fund raising committee for Grenfell's mission which committed itself to providing $1,000 annually. In fact, this was Donald's personal gift. In 1894, he bought the mission a steam yacht which was converted to a hospital ship and re-christened, without his approval, the *Sir Donald*. In due course, two more vessels, both bearing his name, would succeed the *Sir Donald* on the Labrador coast.

CHAPTER FIFTEEN

THE GREAT NORTHERN 1885–1901

In the ordinary sense of the word he was not considered a good "business" man, altho' he did well for himself.

William Armit, referring to Donald Smith [1]

Driving the last spike at Craigellachie did not mean that Sir Donald Smith and Sir George Stephen could now concentrate on clipping the coupons on their CPR bonds. The company still owed the government just over $29 million and there were other debts to be paid off as well. In March 1886, the company agreed to return 6,793,014 acres of land, valued at $1.50 an acre and wiped out the debt completely with a payment of just under $10 million in May and another of just over $9 million in July that year, the money coming from the sale of mortgage bonds retrieved from the government. Though Barings was initially reluctant to handle the sale, primarily because it misunderstood the circumstances, the firm ultimately took the majority, the remainder going to the Bank of Montreal and the Merchants' Bank.

At least as important as settling the government debt was the need to improve the line substantially. When Donald and Fleming had gone west in November 1885, they had travelled over unballasted track and crossed wooden trestles which were a perpetual fire hazard as sparks flew from the steam engines. Forest fires, often caused by careless construction workers, had denuded mountain sides down which avalanches of snow could now easily slide, so snow sheds had to be built to protect the tracks. In the summer of 1886, when Prime Minister Macdonald made his first journey west, the train averaged 20.86 miles an hour, a big improvement over travel on the Dawson Road, but hardly the speed to which the railway aspired. "The trains creep along at a miserable pace, a sort of steam funeral, and they are always being blocked by luggage trains," wrote a young immigrant named Ernest Humphrys. "In one place we came to a hill and found a goods train with one engine on which could not get up the hill, so they had to take off our engine and shove behind to get it out of the way."[2]

Freight took priority because it was from carrying grain and merchandise, and by providing the country's first express parcel service, that the company expected to make its profits. Nevertheless, money needed to be spent on more engines, more passenger and freight cars, and more sidings to enable trains to pass. It was essential to develop branch lines in Ontario in order to increase traffic and keep the aggressive Grand Trunk at bay, and the company was also obliged to develop connections with eastern Quebec and the maritime provinces. Though the CPR was now fully operational, it was not earning enough to meet its capital expenditure and the banks were still not satisfied with the collateral it could offer. In June 1887, Donald and Stephen personally guaranteed a $2 million loan from the Bank of Montreal, even though it was backed with land grant bonds.[3]

In October that year, Stephen assessed the next year's capital requirements in a letter to Macdonald. Running costs, rolling stock and money for steamers, workshops, terminals and the like would require $15 million. This also meant, he revealed the following month, that he and Donald would once more have to put up the money for the bond interest, payable in January. With the loan, the company would then owe them each $2 million. This financing would only work, however, if the government was prepared to assist in the sale of the remaining land grant bonds by offering a guarantee of four percent. In exchange, the company was prepared to agree to drop the monopoly clause.[4]

The government dithered, wanting to keep its financial obligations to $15 million which would mean a lower guarantee on the bonds. Though Donald retained his usual composure in discussions with the government, he was, as Stephen admitted in a letter to the prime minister, "very excited. He warned me if I consented to anything under 4% interest he would oppose it as a director on the ground that anything less will not produce the amount of money absolutely necessary. He is much dissatisfied and points to the fact that the direct loss on the stock alone caused by the agitation [against the monopoly clause] is today over twelve millions cash." The company was eventually forced to accept a compromise at three and a half percent, and Barings took the whole issue in May. Donald was right, however, for it brought in just over $13.5 million, $1.5 million short of the target.[5]

As for the removal of the monopoly clause, the people of Manitoba soon found that the new line, constructed by the Northern Pacific, did little to alter the freight rates. Charles Brydges, in his enthusiasm for providing land for a Winnipeg terminus, failed to perceive that the American line was not interested in bringing prices down but in forcing the CPR to increase its rates on freight originating on the west coast. The American Interstate Commerce Act of 1887 obliged the NP to apply its lowest rate across the entire network and competition from the CPR, which collected freight on the American coast, carried it north to Vancouver in steamers and then loaded it onto trains, was forcing the American line to charge rates which denied the company the chance of staving off yet another bankruptcy.

In 1889, the CPR for the first time earned enough to meet both its fixed costs and the dividend. By the summer of 1888, Stephen could see this stability coming; he was tired from his exertions on the railway's behalf and angered by Manitoba's campaign against the monopoly clause; as far as he was concerned, there was no need for him to continue to carry the burden, and at the annual general meeting in August 1888, he resigned as president. His place was taken by Van

Horne. Donald missed the AGM, having been in London for the HBC's General Court. In 1914, Stephen, who grew more curmudgeonly as he grew older, claimed that Donald had expected the presidency and was surprised to discover that Stephen had made other arrangements. Since Van Horne was vice-president and Donald was accustomed, in both the HBC and the Bank of Montreal, to a pattern in which the deputy generally succeeded to the senior position, Stephen's allegation seems improbable. He made the remark in a letter to Van Horne which contains several errors, suggesting that Stephen's memory, at the age of eighty-five, may not have been entirely reliable.[6]

In addition to consolidating the line, Van Horne devoted a large amount of his very considerable energies to ensuring that railway cars and stations met his high standards of physical, and especially gustatory, comfort. In Vancouver, Van Horne used some of the profits from land sales to build both an opera house and the Hotel Vancouver. He recognized that passengers waiting for an east bound train or a sea connection to Vancouver Island, Seattle or the far east, would need somewhere to stay and, in a town just emerging from the thick forests of the Pacific coast, a traveller had little choice if he fancied clean sheets. In order to ensure that CPR station yards and approaches served to raise standards in the new city, Van Horne also made building regulations which he expected land purchasers to adhere to. In 1892, when the Hudson's Bay Company was erecting its new store on Granville and Georgia Streets, close to the Hotel Vancouver, it also wanted to put up a corrugated iron warehouse near the waterfront. Regulations, however, required an expenditure of between $25,000 and $30,000, much more than the company was willing to spend. To keep the company from having to rent, Donald took over the plot which the HBC wanted and constructed a three storey warehouse for $25,000, giving the company an option to purchase it at cost after it was finished. "I may add," he wrote to Armit, "that I have no wish to be the owner of House property at Vancouver, and have entered on this undertaking merely because it appeared in no other way could the Company get sufficient accommodation for depot purposes." Donald's only other property in Vancouver was a residential block on the corner of Georgia and Granville Streets, opposite the Hudson's Bay Company store. It was badly built and, when the city was more established, his agents found it difficult to attract tenants.[7]

With the profit on the sale of Vancouver town lots the CPR was able to build its first resort hotel at Banff, christened by Donald in honour of the Scottish county where George Stephen was raised. Early CPR hotels in the mountains were intended to provide meals for travellers and so enable the train to leave behind the heavy dining car before pulling the passenger cars up the steep Rocky Mountain passes but, from the beginning, the Banff Springs Hotel was intended for use by holiday makers and those seeking cures at the spa.

The railway's other outstanding hotel venture was the creation of the Château Frontenac on the citadel at Quebec. The design was the apogee of CPR baronial and the hotel, on the commanding site once occupied by the governors of New France, soon became the talk of North America. The construction was part of a deal with the Quebec government which cancelled liabilities on the North Shore Line which the CPR had taken over in 1885. Initially, the railway lacked the resources to build the hotel, so Donald joined forces with Van Horne, Sandford Fleming, R.B. Angus and other CPR directors to create a private company to undertake the project, the railway putting in $50,000 through a trustee. Van Horne predicted that the hotel would "pay more than 10 per cent the first year that it is opened and will quickly reach twenty per cent" and as soon as it began business in 1893, Donald started to see handsome returns on his $25,000 investment; within a few years, he and the other shareholders sold out to the CPR.[8]

Though Van Horne was now president of the railway, he continued to consult George Stephen as though the relationship were still that of general manager and president. Stephen's feelings about Canadian ingratitude did not stand in his way when it came to protecting the CPR from predators and they did not prevent Donald, a much more loyal Canadian, from working closely with him to this end. The company consolidated its lines in Ontario and Quebec and, through prolonged negotiations, cobbled together bits and pieces of other railroads, building between them where necessary, to create what was called the Short Line to Saint John, New Brunswick. It was intended to carry on to Halifax. The creation of the Short Line involved securing running rights over the New Brunswick Railway in which Donald and Stephen had invested in 1880 and led ultimately to their sale of this line to the CPR. Sir John Macdonald insisted on the Short Line both because it enabled the Maritimes to be included in the CPR's unifying embrace and because it completed a trans-Canada route which would allow British troops to be landed at an Atlantic port during winter and moved to any part of Canada, a particularly important consideration if belligerent Russian talk turned to action. The Short Line made little business sense, however, since the Maritimes had neither the wealth nor the population to support yet another railway company.[9]

What might have made the Short Line a workable arrangement for the CPR was the fast mail service which was meant to cross the Atlantic, landing at Halifax in the winter and Quebec in the summer. The CPR was constructing steamers to develop the Pacific route to Japan, possibly extending to Australia, and the combination of ship and rail was intended to create a fast, British, mail and passenger route from England to the far east. At a time when imperialism was beginning to take hold as a concept which would unite Britain and her dominions (especially the self-governing ones) in the face of real or imagined opponents, the fast Atlantic service was an important consideration. To support it, Donald and Stephen each promised to invest £50,000 in Anderson and Anderson, the British company which secured the transatlantic mail contract. Negotiations over the Atlantic service carried on till the end of 1890 when the Andersons pulled out, blaming Donald and Stephen, as anticipated. Thomas Skinner, who was acting as their London agent for this transaction, had refused to commit them when he discovered the Andersons were planning to skim the cream off everything and were even planning to charge a commission on the government subsidy. They had, Skinner noted in a letter to Van Horne, "a reputation for using up their partners while thriving themselves."[10]

Of much greater importance were two American railway lines of which Donald and Stephen felt obliged to gain control in order to safeguard the CPR. The first of these was the Minneapolis, Saint Paul and Sault Ste. Marie Railway, known as the Soo Line, which had been initiated in 1883 by a group of Minneapolis businessmen, including prominent millers such as William Washburn and Charles Pillsbury. They wanted a railway which would be independent of J.J. Hill and Saint Paul and which would go from the wheat fields of Dakota Territory, via the flour mills of Minneapolis, to the markets in the east. When they failed to induce the Northern Pacific to construct the line, the men undertook it themselves. Four separate companies were set up to build different sections and inevitably, since they were run by millers rather than railway men, they encountered difficulties with both construction costs and operating expenses. Failing to find support in Boston and New York, Washburn approached the Bank of Montreal which, in 1886, agreed to a $750,000 loan.

Jim Hill was dismayed. He had been expecting the Soo Line to collapse of its own accord, but he had not dreamed that it would be supported by his allies, by men who held a large number of shares in his own line. He promptly wrote Stephen, explaining that the Soo Line, especially its western arm, then under construction, was in direct competition with the Manitoba road and that its aim was to capture the freight traffic which would otherwise use the Manitoba road. "I do not question the right of the Bank of Montreal to lend its money wherever it choses [sic], but I think it goes without saying that the Bank of Montreal or any other bank, would not lend money on the security of the enterprise alone, even with personal security, without there was some other motive or reason for it." Hill assumed the CPR wanted control of the line, or at least easy access to it.[11]

As the CPR was building to Sault Ste. Marie with the intention of linking with an American route — precisely in the way Hill and the Northern Pacific had wanted the CPR to do from the beginning — Hill had grounds for his fears. In response to Hill's first letter, Stephen blithely assured him that the policy of the Soo Line was to stop at Minneapolis. Donald was in Nova Scotia, he said, but would see Hill's letter on his return. "I am certain he will agree with me that the value of the Sault line as a feeder to us would be greatly diminished if anything were allowed to happen to alienate from it the support & friendship of the Manitoba Company."[12]

In the face of Hill's particulars in a second letter, Stephen wrote a long and somewhat repetitive defense. "The C.P.R. Co has not and does not mean to have any interest direct or indirect pecuniary or otherwise in the line," he affirmed. "As to Smith and myself we neither of us have or mean to have any personal interest in the Sault line, direct or indirect." Stephen's lengthy protestations were not altogether true, for when the millers were short of cash two years later, they approached Donald and Stephen directly. The two men insisted that the four lines be amalgamated and bought a controlling interest in the new company.

This was not just another business opportunity of which they were happy to take advantage. Donald and Stephen knew that the Grand Trunk had been assiduously building towards Sault Ste. Marie and seeking an American connection which would take traffic south of the Great Lakes. If that American connection also took freight west to the Pacific coast or east to the Atlantic, it would be a double threat to the CPR. The cousins were particularly worried by news of William Vanderbilt's interest in the flour merchants' railway, fearing that his Michigan Central would gain control of the Soo Line and take all the traffic "east to the seabord over the Vanderbilt lines without a pound of it getting onto the Canadian lines at the 'Soo'."[13]

In April 1888, when the cousins' control was confirmed — though the line was not reformed until June — Stephen wrote again because he thought, with some justification, that the takeover had prejudiced Hill against the CPR. "What

Smith and I have done is simply, at our own *cost*, and individual *risk*, to secure such a control over the Sault route as to prevent it *ever* being used against the C.P.R. & the Canadian route to the seabord. The C.P.R. have not one dollar in the thing, directly or indirectly & yet it would appear that for this perhaps our *last* service to the CPR & to Canada, we are to be blamed for aiming 'at owning the whole earth'." The CPR could not afford to take it off their hands until 1890.[14]

The other American line which worried Donald and Stephen was the Duluth, South Shore and Atlantic Railway which linked Sault Ste. Marie and Duluth. The threat here was that the Grand Trunk would use the South Shore line to get to Duluth where it would either construct its own line into Manitoba or link up with the Northern Pacific which, in 1888, was building in Manitoba under its agreement with the provincial government. The Northern Pacific already had lines stretching from Duluth in the direction of the Canadian border, as well as a connection to the Pacific coast, and, in its parlous financial state, would have been glad of income from a deal with the Grand Trunk. On July 6, Donald and Stephen secured control of the South Shore shares and immediately cabled Hill to let him know what they had done. A week later, Stephen wrote a long and friendly letter, aimed at accounting for their actions and at rebuilding the bridges which had come down as Hill and Van Horne had fought in the best interests of their respective lines.

"Our object in this move as also in our deal with the 'Soo' Coy was entirely the protection of the Canadian business of the C.P.R.," Stephen explained, "& not in the least with the object of adding to the extent of one cent to our means." They were only interested in protecting the CPR's Manitoba business, Stephen stressed. "Both Smith and myself would like nothing better than to work with you in every possible way for the mutual benefit of all our interests, and while on the subject, let me say what I dare say you are not aware of, that is that we each of us have a greater pecuniary interest, in one way & another, in the St. P. M & M than we have in the C.P.R. but if it were otherwise & we had no money in your road, we should still take the greatest pleasure in doing anything we could to secure and increase its prosperity."

He added that Donald had been seriously ill in London, a personal note which he knew would evoke Hill's sympathy. "He is very strong & would live to an old age if he could be made to take some rest & otherwise take care of himself. When he leaves us he will not leave us many friends like him & this I am sure you must feel as strongly as I do."[15]

Ten days later, Stephen wrote again, by way of a personal postscript to his previous letter. His subject was the Montana Central Railway, an investment in which Hill had at one time suggested Donald and Stephen might like to join him, "but somehow the matter never took definite shape."[16]

In 1886, Hill had talked to Donald and Stephen about building a line of rail from the Manitoba road to Helena, Montana where he had discovered that there was a good supply of lignite. The cousins immediately offered to build a link from the CPR to the border if that would prove useful; they also indicated that they would be happy to invest in this new venture. At that point, however, Hill was not confident that he could trust the two Canadians who were absorbed by the needs of the CPR and seemed disinclined to take him into their confidence. When he parcelled out the shares in the Montana Central Railway, the Great Falls Water

Power and Light Company, and the Red Mountain Coal Mining Company, the Montreal associates were not included.

In 1888, however, several things happened to renew the old, close relationship. Norman Kittson died in May, provoking affectionate memories of the circumstances which had brought them all together ten years earlier. In the spring of 1888, they were forced to think very carefully about those early years for, to the great satisfaction of the Saint Paul gossips, Jesse Farley's prolonged suit, claiming an interest in the Manitoba road, finally came out into the open in a long and detailed court case. Then, John Kennedy decided that his health did not warrant a continued, active interest in Hill's railway concerns and he withdrew. To retain control of both the Manitoba road and the Montana Central, Hill called on Donald and Stephen to help buy up some of the banker's shares. They were both delighted to be involved in the Montana line, "not as you can easily understand that the mere pecuniary advantage can be of any great consequence to either of us but it would be a pleasure to feel that we were not objects of distrust & dislike to all of our old friends," Stephen wrote, adding that he did not "mind being excluded from the Montana business half as much as Smith who seemed to grieve over the exclusion & once or twice remarked on the fact of associates being taken in who could do no good & had no kind of claim to be considered in any way but that feeling has all passed away & whatever you may do now or whatever you do nothing will not make [sic] any difference in our feeling towards you personally or towards the old road."[17]

The incorporation of the Montana Central into the Saint Paul, Minneapolis and Manitoba Railway, the extension of the Manitoba road east to Lake Superior and the construction of huge grain carriers to operate the Great Lakes trade from Duluth to Buffalo meant that the associates' road was undoubtedly a force to be reckoned with. It was also obvious to anyone with an eye for the railroad business that it was only a matter of time before the Manitoba road headed for the Pacific. To Henry Villard, president of Oregon Transcontinental, the holding company which controlled the Northern Pacific and the Oregon Railway and Navigation Company, it meant that it was time to stop the Manitoba road. It was, however, a short lived ambition, for as soon as Hill heard that Villard was snooping around both Kennedy's unsold stock and the shares which were loose on the market, he called on Donald and George Stephen again. They rejoined the board, took up 1,200 shares which might have fallen into Villard's hands and agreed to support Hill in acquiring any other shares which might be needed to secure the Manitoba line. Together with Hill, they also acquired 15,000 shares in Oregon Transcontinental. The Union Pacific, which connected with the Oregon Railway, owned a large amount of Oregon Transcontinental stock but the shares acquired by Donald, Stephen and Hill, together with a similar number owned by a sympathetic Oregon railway man named Elijah Smith, gave the Manitoba road an opportunity to divide and conquer.

Having corralled Villard, Donald, Stephen and Hill began to consider whether they would be better off constructing their own line to the Pacific or taking over an existing one. A takeover would be economically more sound as it was unlikely that there would be sufficient traffic to warrant two lines running in parallel to Washington or Oregon, but the fight to acquire the Northern Pacific with its Seattle terminus would be expensive and exhausting; it might also be a failure.

Building a new line would not be cheap, but it would be entirely under the control of the Manitoba road and so offered a more reliable way forward. This was the option they chose.

A line to the west coast could not, however, be constructed by a company capitalized, as the Saint Paul, Minneapolis and Manitoba Railway was, at only \$15 million. Separate companies had already had to be formed for the Great Lakes shipping business and for the Montana Central and the same would have to be done again. It would, however, be necessary to raise a good deal more money than these ventures had required and the managing company would require considerable powers. The Minneapolis and Saint Cloud Railroad, chartered in 1856 when legislatures saw no reason to curtail the activities of railway companies, had been acquired to build the connection to Lake Superior and Hill now proposed renaming that company the Great Northern Railway and using it both to consolidate the existing operations and to raise money for the westward construction.

In the spring of 1889, as Donald and Stephen tried to sort out the difficulties with the Short Line and the fast Atlantic contract, they were buoyed up by the exciting opportunities the new American venture offered. Thomas Skinner was in Montreal on fast Atlantic service business and was caught up in the enthusiasm, agreeing to broker new shares in London. "It would be an inexpressible satisfaction to me," Stephen wrote after the three of them had been to Saint Paul to see Hill, "to hear of Villard & his friends waking up some fine morning & find themselves owned & controlled by the new Coy. By the way about the name of the new coy. dont you think it would be a blunder to omit the word "Manitoba" from the title? How would 'Manitoba & Great Northern Railway Co' do?"[18]

It would not do, as far as Hill was concerned, and the cousins lost their Canadian reference. In September 1889, both Donald and Stephen joined the board of the new company.

The Great Northern was capitalized at \$40 million, half of which was issued in preferred stock, paying dividends of six percent a year, tax-free. Manitoba road stockholders were entitled to one share of the preferred stock for every share they held in the old company but were only required to pay half the par value of \$100. The remaining amount was made up by transferring the shares in subordinate lines to the new company. The rails, rolling stock and so forth were leased by the Manitoba road to the Great Northern which guaranteed to pay six percent dividends on the entire capital stock for the ninety-nine year term of the lease.

Montana, Idaho and Washington each permitted railways heading west to build without being incorporated in those states, but there was some question as to whether the Great Northern could actually build in Montana since it did not own any lines there. The Montana Central, however, was incorporated in the state. Therefore, the Great Northern "invited" the Manitoba road, which controlled the Montana Central, to build the line to the coast, though raising the funds for it remained the responsibility of the Great Northern.

There was little comparison between the westward construction of the Great Northern and the building of the CPR a few years earlier. Physically, the American task was easier, despite the fact that another pass had to be found through the mountains, while, financially, it was a sellers' market: bankers courted Jim Hill, eager to handle the bond issue. To be sure of success, the men created a pool to keep up the value of shares in the Manitoba road, thus making the new bond issue more attractive when it finally came out. In 1890, the bond sale was handed over to Baring Brothers, but in November that year, the bank collapsed. It had over-extended itself in an unwise investment in the Buenos Aires Water Supply and Drainage Company and then found itself unable to repay the British loans it had secured in order to remain afloat. The Bank of England, with guarantees from other British banks, stepped in to protect Barings' clients, and the bank itself reformed as a public limited company. Donald and Stephen agreed to help out and each invested £50,000 in the new firm which promised to repay at one hundred and twenty as soon as the family could afford to re-purchase its bank. The rapidity with which a million pounds was found to restore the bank demonstrates the breadth of friendships it had cultivated since its inception — friendships which ensured that its business flourished and that it had no difficulty in disposing of the Great Northern bonds.[19]

The last spike of the Great Northern was driven, high in the Cascade Mountains, on January 16, 1893. It was cold, none of the company's directors was present and, were it not for the demands of a photographer, there would have been no ceremony at all. In June, however, shortly before the first through train was run from Saint Paul to the coast, the Minnesota city decided it had something to celebrate. Triumphal arches were erected, parades moved brassily through them and Saint Paul journals devoted acres of newsprint to the Great Northern's achievement. On the evening of June 9, a grand banquet was held at the Aberdeen Hotel. Hill's American colleagues and the politicians whom he had wisely courted over the years were present and recognized by the great crowd. Stephen was in London where he had settled; the lawyers and bankers of New York did not stir themselves to support Hill in front of the flag waving crowds, though many of them sent messages of congratulations. Of his old associates, only Donald made the effort to show his admiration and respect for Hill by attending. For him, it was inconvenient, a quick dash to Saint Paul before setting out for London and the HBC's General Court, but inconvenience was no reason to absent himself on such an occasion.

Among the plump and lusty mid-westerners, Donald was a thin and reticent mystery. "Who is the white-haired gentleman in the old fashioned clothes?" they asked. Beneath his massive, tangled eyebrows, his spectacles glinted in the gas light as he listened attentively to the conversation of his fellow guests. When it was time for toasts and speeches, Hill realized that most of the diners had not solved the riddle. He introduced Sir Donald Smith. Here was the transport pioneer whose name was familiar to everyone in the room. Only yesterday, the *Pioneer Press* had published his comments on the early days of the Saint Paul, Minneapolis and Manitoba and his graceful compliment to James Hill as " a capable, able man — a man able to grasp all the facts of the situation and to pluck the flower of success from the nettle of difficulty." Donald Smith, they knew, was an essential component in the forces which had brought prosperity to their city. Their approving cheers soared upwards.[20]

The cheers that June evening had about them an air of hope — hope that the prosperity symbolized by the Great Northern was not a chimera. In the previous month, the stock market had crashed in New York, initiating a depression which would last, especially in the United States, until the turn of the century. Railways which were under-capitalized or poorly managed went to the wall. The Great Northern, on the other hand, was superbly managed, not least because Hill was the first to see that, by reducing freight rates but increasing volume, he could not merely maintain but actually increase the line's earnings. To cope with longer and heavier trains, gradients and curves had to be reduced to a minimum, the tracks had to be top quality, the engines had to be powerful and the box cars sturdy. But the investment in the line was amply repaid.

Villard, who controlled the Northern Pacific was, by contrast, very good at arranging financial packages but a poor manager of railroads. "It has not been run as a railway for years, but as a device for creating bonds to be sold," Hill sneered. Knowing this, he was not averse to a rate war which helped to push the Northern Pacific into receivership in the summer of 1893. It took two years to reach an agreement with the German banks which held the majority of the Northern Pacific bonds and with the American re-organization committee. On the May 10, 1895, Stephen and Hill, with Thomas Skinner acting for the German bankers, put their names to the London agreement, so called because it was signed in the library of George Stephen's London house. The men agreed to pay the Northern Pacific's interest charges of just over $6 million a year in exchange for which the Great Northern received the majority of the Northern Pacific stock. In New York, J.P. Morgan and Company agreed to head a syndicate to underwrite the securities of the re-organized company.[21]

The ink was scarcely dry on the agreement before it began to come apart. Minnesota had passed a law forbidding any railway from buying the securities or otherwise gaining control of a parallel line. Hill's lawyers declared that the decree could not be applied retrospectively and that therefore the Great Northern, chartered in 1856 as the Minneapolis and Saint Cloud, would not be affected by the legislation. They were wrong.

In April 1896, Hill was back in Stephen's London library, this time with J.P. Morgan who had taken over the re-organization of the Northern Pacific. The new London memorandum called for Donald, Stephen and Hill to purchase a large number of shares which would be exchanged for securities in the new company when Morgan re-organized it. The memorandum said explicitly that the signatories were creating an alliance to protect the common interests of the Northern Pacific and the Great Northern, and said that the lines would not build in each other's territory and would share business where they were in competition. It was a *de facto* amalgamation of the two companies, but carefully constructed to keep the agreement on the right side of the law. It was also an agreement which gave Donald Smith a substantial holding in the Northern Pacific.

The London memorandum allowed Morgan to create a voting trust which effectively gave him control of the management of the Northern Pacific and he did his best to keep Hill at arm's length while profiting from his advice. It was not until November 1900 that Morgan finally gave up the trust and managerial control passed to Hill. A few months later, Hill used some of the Great Northern's surplus earnings which Minnesota law forbade him to distribute as profits to shareholders, to acquire ninety-seven percent of the Chicago, Burlington and Quincy shares. The purchase gave both the Great Northern and the Northern Pacific a Chicago outlet and was expected to produce a net income of $25 million by the end of 1906. Yet again, it added to Donald's rapidly accumulating wealth.

The growing power, and sometimes the aggression, of the Great Northern proved an increasing worry to Van Horne who disliked having to rely on connections with the American company to carry traffic from the Soo and South Shore lines into Canadian territory. In 1892, when a small and incomplete railway called the Duluth and Winnipeg was in financial difficulties, it approached Van Horne for help. Investigation revealed that the Duluth and Winnipeg, when completed, could join with the South Shore line and take traffic from Sault Ste. Marie through to Winnipeg without having to rely on Hill's goodwill. Furthermore, the Duluth and Winnipeg owned nearly eighteen and a half thousand acres of valuable iron-bearing land in the Mesabi and Vermilion ranges and leased as much again. Railway companies had clear, but unwritten, understandings of what was "their" territory and any invasion was seen as an act of aggression. The Duluth and Winnipeg, when complete, would undoubtedly be in Hill's territory and the CPR's acquisition of the line would unquestionably be perceived as belligerent.

Van Horne was not one to shirk from a fight, but neither he nor his directors seemed to be aware that one of the causes of the Duluth and Winnipeg's financial trouble was its inability to repay a loan from J.J. Hill. The upshot was that in July, Donald and Stephen agreed to lend money for the purchase on the security of Duluth and Winnipeg bonds. They then changed their minds about the security, thinking that it would be better that neither of them "should appear to be concerned in the matter in any way" and agreed to take other bonds instead. Donald was growing a little tired of the Soo line and its entanglements — the cousins had lent money the previous year to try to help it out of difficulties and had been forced to sell shares at a loss in order to do so. He was more annoyed by what Stephen expressed as "the '*matter of course*' way he & I have been exhorted to come to the assistance of the CPR Co when help was needed, and without reference to the sacrifice of our personal interests which giving the requested assistance involved, and the apparently general idea of the Board that it is all good business for us, & the obligation if any is & ought to be on our side."[22]

Despite the feeling that their support was taken for granted, Donald and Stephen provided the cash for the CPR's loan to the South Shore line which in turn paid off Hill's loan. As a result, the Duluth and Winnipeg became part of the CPR stable. Hill was extremely angry.

The CPR struggled to build an extension to the border but the depression meant the company had great difficulties in exploiting this or any of its other American lines to their full potential. In 1894, Stephen was writing to Van Horne that he had felt for some time that they were not as closely supervised as they should be "considering the enormous stake we have in them." Their acquisition, he thought, had been a mistake.[23]

Hill maintained a persistent pressure on the CPR, constantly provoking arguments with Van Horne about rates and other details of their working agreements. He was especially uncooperative when it came to the Duluth and Winnipeg. Both men professed admiration for each other, and rightly so since they were among the foremost railway men on the continent. Nevertheless, they worked for what they perceived to be opposing lines and that brought them into conflict. In 1894, Hill was biding his time, unwilling to come to an agreement about the Duluth and Winnipeg, and spent an entire meeting avoiding the subject. "Then he said he would think it over, and if I would try to think out some scheme, we could discuss it at St. Paul on my way back from the Pacific Coast. I promised to do so; and then, taking me affectionately by the arm, he said: 'Van, it is a very nice thing that although we may disagree about business matters, our personal relations are so pleasant. We would do anything for each other.' (The skunk.)"[24]

Donald, having a foot in each camp, was called upon to be a peacemaker but the best he could come up with was an unworkable deal which the men accepted out of courtesy to him. The depression and the CPR's dwindling dividends finally persuaded Stephen to sell all his shares in the trans-Canada line, but by then he and Donald had agreed that the Duluth and Winnipeg was a millstone round the Canadian railway's neck and pressed Van Horne to sell it to Hill. The transaction took place in 1896.

Donald and Stephen were right in seeing the line as an unnecessary drain on the CPR's purse and Van Horne seems never to have grasped that its real value lay in the iron ore lines which it controlled. Hill and his sons bought even more ore land and decided to play a waiting game, convinced that the price of iron ore would increase as Andrew Carnegie's US Steel Corporation developed. They set up a trust which purchased the land the Hills had bought, paying no more than the $4 million they had given for the land. In 1906, the trust finally signed a lease with the US Steel Corporation; Hill estimated that the royalties which he had negotiated would come to about $425 million, all of which would go to the trust's beneficiaries, the stockholders of the Great Northern Railway. Once again, a vast sum would be pouring into Donald's bank account.

When asked why he had shared the vast wealth of the iron ore lands when he could easily have kept all the money for himself, Hill replied that he did it because he wanted to. He did not need the money and neither did Donald, Kennedy and Stephen. It was, however, a way of saying thank you to them for standing by him and his ideas, especially through the troubled days which followed the takeover of the Chicago, Burlington and Quincy.

One of the benefits of that acquisition was thought to be that it would keep Edward Harriman at bay. In 1895, the Oregon Railway and Navigation Company had gone into receivership, taking with it the Union Pacific. For Hill and his associates, this would have been yet another inconsequential railway failure, but for the fact that the Great Northern was dependent on the Union Pacific for access to the Pacific Ocean port of Portland. Reorganization of the Union Pacific was in the hands of Jacob Schiff, a senior partner in the merchant bankers, Kuhn, Loeb and Company and son-in-law of Solomon Loeb, one of its founders, but the dominant force was Harriman, a broker who had hitherto confined himself to railways which were no threat to the Great Northern.

Harriman was both angry and worried by Hill's acquisition of the Burlington line for it gave the Great Northern and Northern Pacific access to the northern Pacific coast of the United States without having to rely on the Union Pacific. Late in April 1901, Harriman decided to corner the Northern Pacific's common stock and oblige Hill and Morgan to include him in the management of the Burlington line. With Schiff's help, Harriman acquired $60 million worth of shares and Hill began to suspect that it was not so much a raid on the Northern Pacific as an attack on J. Pierpont Morgan; Harriman, he suspected, was backed by John D. and William Rockefeller, both of whom would have been glad to have Morgan out of the way.

Hill immediately sought confirmation that Donald, Stephen, Gaspard Farrer at Barings, and Morgan, who was in Switzerland, would back his own retaliatory buying spree. He had discovered that Harriman was buying a mixture of common and preferred stock but would soon realize that he had to seize the common stock if he was to control the company. Hill had to buy it first. By the afternoon of Saturday, May 4, he had agreements that his colleagues would back him in the acquisition of $15 million or $16 million worth of common stock. He got their backing barely in time for Harriman had just grasped the importance of the common stock. He, however, was sick in bed with appendicitis, and was obliged to telephone his instructions to Kuhn, Loeb. They, however, could do nothing, for Schiff, whose authority was required, was in the synagogue and would not work on the sabbath. On Monday morning, Hill easily got the shares he needed.

Harriman's frantic buying had created a bear market. Prices rose to insane heights as brokers sold shares they did not have, confident that in a day or two prices would fall and they would make a handsome profit out of the difference between the buying and the selling price. On Tuesday, May 7, the deadline for delivery of the stocks which had been bought in the previous weeks, the brokers found they had no Northern Pacific shares and were unable to obtain any. It was within Hill's power to bankrupt nearly every stockbroker and bank in New York by insisting that the shares he, Donald, Stephen and their friends had purchased be handed over, but he agreed to a compromise put forward by a worried Jacob Schiff. If Hill would allow the brokers to purchase from the Northern Pacific enough shares to meet their obligations, he would ensure that Harriman came to the conference table prepared to work peacefully with Hill and to allow him to retain control of the management of the Burlington and Quincy.

To protect the Great Northern and its allied lines from a similar raid in future, Hill determined to create a holding company, to be called Northern Securities. He could not, however, establish the company without the full cooperation of Donald, George Stephen and John Kennedy who had retained his shares, though ill-health kept him from taking an active part in the management of the Great Northern. "Briefly we put into a security company which will have a capitalization of two hundred million dollars, our Gt Northern shares and a majority of the shares of Nor. Pacific common," Hill wrote to Donald by way of explanation in August 1901. "This gives us control of both companies and as they own practically all of the C.B & Q shares, we absolutely control all three lines with a mileage of about 20,000 miles." All the lines were well equipped and well supplied with terminals, he explained, and the Great Northern and Northern Pacific could expect to make a profit of about $10 million that year.[25]

> Allowing for an increase for the next five or six years equal to one third of the ratio of the past five years, the net income of the three roads which will practically come to the Nor. Pac. and Gt. Northern will give us an amount for dividends equal to four times our present dividend on the Nor. Pac. In any event we should add some $350,000,000 to $400,000,000 to the balance of our investment and at the same time make our position as a property much more secure. In other words we should make fully four times as much in the coming six years as we have ever made since the beginning of our railway work.[26]

Donald did not want more investments; he neither wanted nor needed more money, but he could hardly refuse to comply with a request which could lead to the stabilization of the American railway situation and make the life of his friend Jim Hill a little easier. Northern Securities was incorporated in New Jersey, where the law made such things easier, with a capital of $400 million, twice Hill's estimate. When the men handed over their Great Northern shares, Hill was found to have just over 80,000, Kennedy had 75,000, Donald had 54,000 and Stephen had nearly 50,000. Together with a handful of other large shareholders, they owned nearly thirty percent of the company.

Their collaboration in this new venture immediately gave it great prestige and people clamoured for stock, but the scheme also aroused widespread negative comment. It was a trust intended to prevent competition and raise freight rates, opponents argued. Hill was adamant that this was not the case. "The Northern Securities Company is organized to deal in high-class securities; to hold the same for the benefit of its shareholders, and to advance the interests of the corporations whose securities it owns," he insisted to the Saint Paul *Globe*, in December. "Its powers do not include the operations of railways, banking, or mining, nor the buying and selling of securities or properties of others on commission; it is purely an investment company."[27]

Such a holding company had never before been applied to railways and the critics were vociferous. President Theodore Roosevelt, previously thought to be one of Hill's friends, authorized a suit against Northern Securities in February 1902 on the basis that it contravened the Sherman Anti-Trust Law of 1890. It was March 1904 before the courts reached a final decision which went against Northern Securities. Hill then set about converting the company's shares back into railway shares, giving each man a proportion in relation to the Northern Securities stock he held. Harriman, however, insisted on receiving the precise shares he had contributed, an arrangement which would have put him in control of the Northern Pacific again. Another year passed before the courts decided against him.

As Donald and George Stephen developed their programme of charitable donations, it was Great Northern and, later, Northern Securities stock which formed the basis of their endowments. Their million dollar endowment of the Royal Victoria Hospital in 1897, for example, took the form of eight thousand preferred shares in the Great Northern. When a rights issue took place the following year, as the donors knew it would, the trustees acquired and then sold their new shares, adding half a million dollars to the hospital's funds.

In 1901, the Prince of Wales, later King George V, spoke to Donald about the financial difficulties of London hospitals which were supported from a central reserve which was desperately low. George Stephen had been trying to establish an endowment fund but had found it difficult to interest other philanthropists in the idea. The result of the prince's overture was the launch of King Edward's Hospital Fund for London, named after Queen Victoria's eldest son and the prince's father. It was set up with a donation of £200,000 each from Donald and his cousin, the gift taking the form of shares in Northern Securities. It tickled Gaspard Farrer of Baring Brothers. "Thus at one stroke have they lightened themselves of their superfluous burden of property, have contributed to the sick & poor & last but not least helped on the cause of NS." The donation prohibited the sale of the shares for five years without their consent. "Every one is asking what security [it] is that is likely to increase so much in value," Farrer noted approvingly.[28]

CHAPTER SIXTEEN

PARLIAMENT AND MANITOBA SCHOOLS 1886–1896

Life would be a poor thing at best if it were made up only of material success and material achievements.
Sir Donald Smith [1]

In the decade which followed the completion of the Canadian Pacific Railway from Montreal to the Pacific Ocean, Sir Donald Smith was extraordinarily busy. After his sixty-sixth birthday in August 1886, a point at which he might have considered retiring, he became deputy governor and subsequently governor of the Hudson's Bay Company; he led the company's Canadian sub-committee in sorting out the difficult problems which arose as a consequence of the land boom in Manitoba; he assumed the presidency of the Bank of Montreal; he was occupied with a variety of railway issues, ranging from Jesse Farley's case against the associates who created the Saint Paul, Minneapolis and Manitoba Railway to the financing of the Canadian Pacific Railway, the Great Northern and the Soo lines. These business interests on both sides of the Atlantic and across the North American continent commanded his intellectual energies as well as demanding a remarkable amount of travel, but he still found time to serve as McGill University's chancellor and to attend to the details of many charitable benefactions, the largest of them being the hospital and women's college in Montreal.

The work and the incessant journeys by train and ship would have tired a younger man, but Donald added to his burdens by re-entering Canadian political life and once again serving as a member of parliament. The pressure to bring him into an alliance with the Conservative Party began late in 1885 when the Tories were casting around for a candidate to stand for Winnipeg in the general election due to take place in the near future — though Macdonald had yet to determine the date. The depression had bred a good deal of dissatisfaction, especially in Nova Scotia, Quebec and Manitoba and in all three provinces, the

Liberal Party was reaping the benefits. Manitoba had not had a strong representative of any political persuasion in the federal parliament since Donald's defeat in 1880 and it badly needed a man who could make peace between the province, with its clamouring against the CPR's monopoly, and Ottawa, with its continual disallowance of provincial railway legislation. Despite his association with the CPR, Donald was both popular and a mediator, willing to speak up for the best interests of Manitoba without caring about the party line. He had always got on well with the Métis community, who needed reassurance following the execution of Louis Riel, and he could be counted on to watch out for their interests once more. To the Conservatives of Manitoba, he seemed an ideal choice.

At the same time, Donald, like many members of the Scots Presbyterian business community in Montreal, was increasingly dismayed by Edward Blake's behaviour. At a time when mature political leaders should have been seeking to heal the wounds which had been created by the fighting in Saskatchewan and Riel's execution, Edward Blake, the leader of the Liberal Party, was picking off the scabs and scratching at the tender flesh beneath.

Early in March 1886, Donald told the prime minister how dismayed he was by Blake's speech the previous week when he had resuscitated both the Pacific Scandal and the quarrel on the floor of the House in 1878. "When a year or so back, I saw him so deeply, so feelingly, as it seemed, interested in the pirouetting and fine points of some Ballet Girls," Donald wrote with a touch of sarcasm, "I had hoped that there was still left in him some of the milk of human tenderness and kindness, but it is evident that in his heart and thoughts so much space is required for self worship as to leave no room for those finer feelings, those instincts of charity and goodwill towards others, the absence of which stamps a man as unworthy to be considered a Christian man or a gentleman." It made Donald think that he would like to be back in the Commons again so that he could have an opportunity of chastising Blake.[2]

His antipathy towards the Liberal leader had not subsided in May when Stephen wrote Macdonald, observing that Donald "feels if possible more angry with Blak[e] than I do myself & that is saying a good deal & will be ready I have no doubt to do all he can to prevent such a malignant pessimist ever having any say in the Govt of Canada." Prevention could take the form of offering financial assistance to the Conservatives but equally it could mean that he would stand in opposition to Blake and the Liberals.[3]

The business community's dislike of Blake increased when it realized that he had no clear economic policy; while he seemed to support the continuation of Macdonald's protective tariff, he did nothing to damp down the growing popular demand for commercial union with the United States, a notion which horrified most Canadian financiers and industrialists on both economic and patriotic grounds.

In reality, Donald could not stand for election because no CPR shareholder was allowed to sit in the House of Commons. "Should Mr. Smith become eligible I should be glad to see him an MP," Macdonald wrote to William Scarth in February. Scarth, who was ostensibly the head of the North West Land Company but in fact much more interested in developing a political career, was one of Macdonald's strongest supporters in Manitoba and a regular conduit of informa-

Donald Smith, 1895

Sandford Fleming

Charles Brydges, 1870

Lord Strathcona

Lord Strathcona with Sir Wilfrid Laurier and Canadian officers during Queen Victoria's golden jubilee, 1897.

Glencoe House

Glencoe House (detail)

Glencoe House (detail)

Colonsay House

Strathcona's Horse at Buckingham Palace, February 15, 1901.

Lord Strathcona, September 1908

Lord Strathcona with his granddaughter, Frances Howard, at the Quebec tercentenary celebrations, July 1908.

Lord Strathcona unveiling a plaque at Fort Garry, Winnipeg, August 25, 1909.

Lord Strathcona by the hollow tree in Stanley Park with Clarence Chipman, Canadian head of the HBC, and C.S. Douglas, the mayor of Vancouver, August 31, 1909.

Lord Strathcona with Father Lacombe, Government House, Edmonton, September 7, 1909.

Lord Strathcona, 1907

Lord Strathcona leaving St. Mark's Church after his wife's funeral, November 19, 1913; his daughter Maggie is on his arm, his grandsons are behind them; the bearded man in the back is his son-in-law, Dr. Howard.

Lord Strathcona with Prime Minister Robert Borden, London, 1912.

tion on the Conservative cause in the province. In May, Scarth reported rumours that Donald would be taken into the cabinet as a minister without portfolio to serve as the voice of the Northwest in the upper echelons of Canadian government. "I am sure this would be a great card so far as this Province & the Northwest is concerned," Scarth wrote. "His ability, wealth, & influence if on our side would help Conservatism very much," he observed, adding that the UK directors of the land company did not appear to object to his taking a more active role in politics himself, though Donald was opposed to his being a candidate. Under Van Horne, the CPR was becoming more overtly a Tory supporter but Donald continued to believe that the railway and its employees, including those who worked for the land company, should remain neutral.[4]

In the spring of 1886, parliament rescinded the legislation prohibiting CPR shareholders from sitting in the House and throughout the summer Scarth continued to press Macdonald to obtain Donald's assent to stand in his old constituency. For his part, Donald explained that he "was not eager to return to political life" and asked for time for reflection. By October, he had told Scarth that he would only stand as an independent and that he would not campaign. Scarth was convinced that he could swing the Tory vote behind Donald but as autumn turned to winter it became increasingly clear that Scarth, as usual, was unduly optimistic. Candidates from both parties were honing their rhetoric while voices less in tune with Scarth's views began to complain that Donald was not resident and could therefore not properly represent the people of Winnipeg; neither could he be counted on to express the almost universal Manitoba opinion that the CPR monopoly was bad for the province.[5]

By January, Macdonald's son, Hugh John, who shared a legal practice in Winnipeg with Stewart Tupper, was warning that Donald stood no chance if he insisted on standing as an independent. "The fact that you are anxious to have him in the House as Minister for Winnipeg ties our hands," he added, because they had neither Donald's agreement to stand nor the freedom to select another candidate.[6]

Donald had sailed for England in the middle of December and was there throughout January, attending to HBC matters when he was not sick in bed. Communication between Winnipeg, Ottawa and London was slow, but by the middle of January, Donald had made it clear that he could not uphold opposition to the federal government's policy of disallowing provincial legislation which infringed the CPR monopoly. With this message, he effectively disqualified himself and Scarth was nominated instead. To Macdonald, Donald cabled on January 21 that his Winnipeg friends had indicated his own chances of election were not good. Furthermore, he was ill and unable to canvas.

Before sailing for England, Donald had discussed his uncertainty about standing for Winnipeg with George Stephen's brother-in-law, James Cantlie. A woollen merchant, he was a director of both the Cobourg and Almonte woollen companies in which Donald and George Stephen were interested, was one of Montreal's most influential businessmen, and frequently saw Donald on both professional and social occasions. He pointed out that if Donald were really interested in resuming a political career, he could assure his nomination for Montreal West. Cantlie took the idea to the local Conservative Association which corresponded with Donald while he was in England but, in Ottawa, Macdonald had the wisdom to ask George Stephen to sound out his cousin. "Smith consents," was Stephen's bald cable on January 27. Donald was a little more expansive in his telegram to the Montreal party, saying that he accepted the nomination "if electors are satisfied with my assurance that as an independent member, uninfluenced by any other considerations than those having in view the best interests of our common country, I will if elected, use every effort to further the material progress of the Dominion, and to promote the prosperity of the City of Montreal."[7]

Donald returned to Montreal on February 15 and went straight to a nomination meeting. "I am disposed to judge of measures more than of men," he told his supporters.

> At the same time, if a Government may have made some blunders, I am not disposed to oppose them because of this. We know that success depends not on absolute perfection, but that with individuals as with governments, to make fewest mistakes is the criterion of success. I will not be disposed to denounce the whole policy of a Government because of this measure or of that measure, provided it be not one of principle and one calculated to be injurious to the community at large. I come forward as an independent candidate, prepared to give my support to what I believe is in the interests of my constituents and of vital interest to the Dominion.[8]

To Macdonald, he explained that his health was "not at all what I could wish and the Doctors would not approve of my going into the excitement of an election contest," adding that since it was so late in the day, he did not feel that "merely personal consideration" should compel the Montreal Conservatives to search for someone else to stand against the Liberals' economic policies.[9]

To both Liberals and Conservatives among Canadian businessmen and industrialists, Donald's value lay in his opposition to commercial union and his support of Macdonald's protective tariff. "We know, and we are not ashamed to own, that we are a smaller and poorer people at this very moment than those on the other side of the line," Donald said at his adoption meeting. "While they maintain high protective tariffs, if we allowed everything to come in here just as they should like, we all know what would very soon become of Canada. We must judge facts by the circumstances of the moment, and of the place; while free trade may be very good for England and while I might support it there with certain modifications, I should be very sorry to see it introduced in this country and would oppose its adoption." The effect of Macdonald's National Policy, he argued, had been "materially to increase the demand for labour and raise the wages of the workman, without adding to the costs of the necessaries of life. If you have not your industries 'in full blast,' you can have no prosperity."[10]

The tariff encouraged the production of Canadian goods for the Canadian market. "If we had not the National Policy," he argued, "Canada would have been swamped by the importation of goods from the United States and elsewhere, and we would neither have manufacturers in the country nor employment for our people." What he added to Macdonald's policy was a conviction that the country should provide technical education for those who were going to work in industry.

"It is the workman of today who is being fitted to become the employer of the future," he declared.[11]

On February 22, he achieved an easy victory at the polls. The people of Montreal, he said in his victory speech, had declared that there "should be no retrograding, no going back to an era of depression and soup kitchens." He would have preferred "to have a little leisure, but there are times when for the public good a man must not study his own convenience."[12]

During the first parliamentary session, Donald stayed at the Russell House when he was in Ottawa and detested its smoky, men's club atmosphere every bit as much as he had seventeen years earlier when he first entered parliament. The following year, Sandford Fleming and his daughter found him rooms on Metcalf Street, within walking distance of the House. By this time, Donald employed a manservant who took care of his clothes, saw to his meals and generally looked after him, usually travelling with him whenever he went to Ottawa, to England or on his various journeys through Canada and the United States. Though he was "a dependable little lad" and not hard to please, it was a relief to both of them when Bank Cottage came available in the spring of 1889 and they were able to move to more satisfactory quarters.[13]

Donald was regularly appointed to the standing committees on Railways, Canals and Telegraphs, the one on Standing Orders and the committee on Banking and Commerce, but he appears to have spent little time in Ottawa and spoke infrequently. Having contributed to the re-election of the Conservatives and the continuation of the National Policy, he seemed to feel he had done his duty and took scant interest in parliamentary proceedings. Home Rule for Ireland was a topic on everyone's lips and he sensibly suggested it was not a matter for the Canadian parliament, but added that he was in favour of "some measure of local government ... which will enable them to conduct their local affairs." Not surprisingly, he also spoke on the disallowance of a Manitoba Railway Bill, adding that "while the idea appears to prevail in this House, as it does throughout the country, that the gentlemen who undertook the contract for building the Canadian Pacific Railway have been dipping their hands very freely into the public Treasury, and have made vast profits by their connection with it, the actual facts are quite otherwise; and that as regards two of the individuals most actively engaged in it, their income today is at least $100,000 less annually than it was at the time they undertook the work, and that they would be so much richer today had they not pledged every sixpence they possessed, with a view of carrying on the enterprise to a completion." Had parliamentarians and the general public been aware of the vast profits George Stephen and Donald Smith were making from their American railway investments, they would have been much less inclined to assume that it was Canadian cash in their bank accounts.[14]

Donald said virtually nothing in the House in 1888, though he had dealings with the government when he sorted out problems with the CPR's land grant bonds. There were also difficulties with Scarth whose preference for a political career in Ottawa meant he was not attending to his work for the Canada North West Land Company. Though Donald had always had misgivings about Scarth's political involvement, he and Stephen had been the only ones to speak in favour of allowing him to stand for election. Now, however, because land sales were picking up following the depression of the 1880s, they put increasing pressure on him to resign his parliamentary seat and devote all his time to his work. Macdonald, on the other hand, felt obliged to protect him in his dual role since he was one of Manitoba's strongest and most committed Tories.

The importation of intoxicating liquors into the Northwest prompted Donald to speak in 1889 while, in 1890, his voice was roused by a new banking act to which he and many other bankers objected. On the whole, however, he regretted that he had agreed to become an MP again; in March 1889 he observed to William Armit with relief that parliament was to be prorogued in two or three weeks "and I will be heartily glad to be freed of the bother of going to Ottawa which I by no means relish."[15]

Where he did play a political role, albeit a covert one, was in trying to help Macdonald achieve press coverage which was sympathetic to the National Policy and, prior to the abolition of the CPR's monopoly clause, to the Conservatives' disallowance of Manitoba railway legislation. Macdonald hoped that the CPR itself would buy into *La Minerve*, a Conservative Montreal paper which needed financial support, but Stephen rejected the proposal, pointing out that anything he and Donald had done in that way in the past had not worked well. "The paper once the investment is made controls the investor, for instance Smith's interest in the Globe and our interest in the [Montreal] Herald not to mention others."[16]

Stephen also rejected a request that the CPR help finance a Tory newspaper in Winnipeg but, in September 1888, Donald made a five year loan of $26,000 to the *Manitoba Free Press*, receiving as collateral seven hundred and ninety-six shares with a par value of $100 each. They were held in trust by William Alloway who, in the loan agreement, promised to vote at board meetings in accordance with Donald's instructions. In February the following year, Van Horne bought a weak Conservative paper, *The Call*, for $33,500 and promptly handed it over to the *Free Press* which increased its share capital from $100,000 to $133,500, giving the three hundred and thirty-five new shares to Van Horne. About 1890, the *Free Press* acquired *The Sun*, paying $40,000 which Van Horne helped the newspaper to secure, probably by guaranteeing a bank overdraft.[17]

William Luxton, who thus lost all control of the newspaper he had founded, nevertheless failed to perceive that his new proprietors were calling a different tune. They had transferred their shares in trust to John Mather, a Winnipeg businessman, but neither he nor Van Horne could oblige Luxton to comply with their wishes. "I fear I might as well try to control the wind," Van Horne expostulated. Luxton was against Macdonald's protective tariff and against the CPR monopoly, the two points on which, above all others, Donald and Van Horne expected the support of the *Free Press*. The paper was broadly Liberal and was expected to maintain good relations with the Liberal provincial government while leading both the politicians and the voters towards a greater acceptance of the CPR and its policies. But Luxton thought of himself as a free agent, able to support those causes which he believed to be good for the west and to attack those which he thought harmful. He overlooked the fact that he had sold his independence when he borrowed money he could not repay.[18]

Shortly after Donald's loan fell due, he and Van Horne discovered that Luxton had not merely launched an attack on Thomas Greenway, the Liberal premier of Manitoba: he had then excused himself to two provincial Liberals who also wanted to bring Luxton into line, by explaining that he was merely following the orders of his proprietors. Luxton was summarily dismissed and replaced by Molyneux St. John, a CPR publicist but a Liberal. This, Donald and Van Horne hoped, would enable him to write copy in favour of the railway while retaining the goodwill of the provincial politicians. Unfortunately, a good press officer is not necessarily a good newspaper editor and the *Free Press* readership dwindled. "I am a good deal concerned about the situation of the *Free Press*, and I know that others who are largely interested are equally concerned," Van Horne wrote in the summer of 1894, adding that the paper was "milk-and-waterish."[19]

A year later, he was more explicit, saying that the "principal man in the F.P." was dissatisfied with the editorial management and believed that the paper was "gradually losing influence." Gently, and with great courtesy, Van Horne dismissed St. John. "The long and short of it is that the people who have money at stake in the concern think that some new deal is necessary to save the property." The new editor was D.L. Beaton who pursued an unthinking pro-Conservative editorial line. By 1897, this so annoyed the Liberal politician, Clifford Sifton, that he began negotiating for the paper. Donald and Van Horne were so glad to be rid of it that they did not mind selling it at a loss.[20]

His experience as the MP for Montreal West had convinced Donald that his resumption of a parliamentary career was serving no useful purpose and giving him no satisfaction. He had no zest for legislative argument and was not passionately engaged by any of the topics of debate. Manitoba was not a fledgling now and did not need his protection; Montreal never had. The only issue which did arouse his interest was the protective tariff.

The Conservatives, however, saw matters rather differently. On February 4, 1891, a group in Montreal wrote Macdonald, asking him to ask Donald to stand for re-election later that spring. He was on his way back from England and they wanted the letter to be waiting for him on his return. Though he had been ill, worried and overworked, the prime minister was in good humour when he wrote Donald, touching just the right nerve to bring the desired response. "It is of great importance to Canada's interests in fact I think to its existence as a portion of the British Empire that we should succeed in the coming contest. The Grits are going to fight with desperation as this is their last chance." Once the country was "safe," Donald could resign after the first session on health or business grounds.[21]

The note was waiting for him when the *Teutonic* docked at New York. He had scarcely opened the front door at Dorchester Street before Charles Tupper, who had been his travelling companion on the voyage from Liverpool, was shown in and began pressing him to allow his name to go forward. It seemed likely that he would be elected by acclamation. Senator George Drummond, vice president of the Bank of Montreal, called with the same message and so did several others. Donald capitulated. Though Blake had resigned as the leader of the Liberals, being replaced by Wilfrid Laurier, the campaign to bring down the trade barriers had not abated. Its supporters, Donald felt, were trying to place Canada "in respect of her Commercial relations if not also politically, at the feet of the United States" and this must be withstood "but I had hoped that some other person than myself would have been found to take the necessary stand in this way in Montreal West," he told the prime minister. He would, of course, be an independent.[22]

Winnipeg, in the meantime, was in exactly the same quandary it had been in at the last general election. The Canada North West Land Company directors had insisted that Scarth choose between parliament and the company and he sensibly opted to retain his job. His best replacement, he argued, would be Donald Smith. Hugh John Macdonald and Stewart Tupper agreed and, according to Scarth, they all thought he would be elected by acclamation. Their worry was that a Liberal would go in by acclamation and they wanted to preclude this by making an early announcement of a strong and popular candidate.

Both Donald and the prime minister told Scarth and his friends that Donald had consented to run for Montreal West, but that did not diminish the pressure. Van Horne joined the battle on February 11 with a letter to Macdonald in which he said that "if he alone can carry Winnipeg you have only to say the word. In fact he told me that I might say to you something to this effect."[23]

To this, Macdonald replied with an extraordinary cable. "Sir Donald must run for West Montreal. I will get nomination for Winnipeg too without his assent."[24]

The intention seems to have been to have Donald nominated for Winnipeg without his consent and to keep him in the field until the last minute when the doubling up of nominations would be "discovered." The Conservatives hoped that Donald's candidature would so intimidate the Liberals that they would decide that it was not worth while opposing him. At the last minute, the Tories would merely switch candidates while the Liberals would be compelled to find someone to nominate and initiate a campaign which they would stand little chance of winning.

None of this was committed to paper and certainly not to the untrustworthy wires of the telegraph company, even if they were owned by the CPR. Donald could see what the prime minister was playing at but the Winnipeg Tories were oblivious to the machinations. As a result, they sent Donald a barrage of telegrams, wanting to know when he would formally assent to his nomination, when he would appoint an agent and when he would arrive in Winnipeg. He found it immensely distressing for he could neither tell Scarth, Tupper and Hugh John Macdonald what they wanted to hear nor, if he were to help secure a Conservative victory in Winnipeg, could he tell them the truth. "Sir Donald is so polite that the telegrams asking his intentions put him in a nervous state because he can't answer them," Van Horne, who knew all sides of the story, explained to the prime minister, adding that he had persuaded Donald to leave the management of the matter to Macdonald and had told Scarth and his colleagues to deal with Ottawa and not with their intended candidate. "He feels much embarrassment," Van Horne, cabled a week later, warning that if the situation was not cleared up, the Conservatives risked losing in Winnipeg.[25]

Two days later, on February 22, Hugh John Macdonald was nominated and on the fifth of March, he won Donald's old seat of Selkirk while Donald himself was victorious in Montreal. At least some of Hugh John's achievement was due to Van Horne who campaigned vigorously among the CPR workers, explaining to them why a Conservative government was good for the country, good for the CPR and therefore good for their jobs. "The CPR vote will be practically unanimous

— not one in one hundred even doubtful," he crowed to Macdonald a week before the election.[26]

Initially, Donald's parliamentary concerns reflected his business interests. He wrote the governor general in March on behalf of the Hudson's Bay Company and eleven other Canadian businesses objecting to an act of the Manitoba legislature which was prejudicial to companies not incorporated in the province. In April, he wrote John Thompson, the minister of justice, on behalf of all the Montreal banks. They wanted judges' salaries to be increased because those who lived in cities, which is to say most judges, could not manage on what they were being paid. In May, he raised on the floor of the House both payments to judges and the salary of the Canadian high commissioner in London. He agreed with the opposition that the high commissioner's salary of $10,000 a year and his expenses of $2,000 should not be distinguished but he also thought the combined figure should be $20,000. "The position of High Commissioner of Canada ... should be made such as to enable him to entertain, to some extent, out of the proceeds of his salary, as is done by almost all other representatives," he told the House.[27]

The greatest concern in the early days of the new parliament, however, was the state of Sir John Macdonald's health. He was seventy-six, just five years older than Donald, but he was exhausted, not merely from the strains of the election campaign but from the rigours of a long political career, guiding Canada towards Confederation and leading the country through the first years of nationhood. Early on the morning of May 28, he suffered a mild stroke. His doctor called Dr. George Ross and Donald's own doctor, James Stewart, up from Montreal and they confirmed his diagnosis. While marvelling at the rapidity with which the prime minister appeared to be recovering, they agreed with the prescription: complete rest and no political or parliamentary activities for several weeks. The news flew around Ottawa and quickly spread throughout the country. There was no obvious successor; the Conservatives were fearful and the Liberals were cheerful ghouls in waiting.

On the afternoon of May 29, Macdonald suffered a second, massive stroke. Again his doctor called in colleagues, including Sir James Grant who had tended to Richard Hardisty after his fatal accident. "Entire loss of speech. Haemorrhage on the brain. Condition hopeless," he cabled to Macdonald's Quebec lieutenant, Sir Hector Langevin.[28]

The following day, the news was on the front page of every Canadian paper. Close to the prime ministerial residence, the CPR pitched a tent and installed a telegraph operator to cable the latest news to the waiting world. On the second of June, all members of parliament were summoned and the next day, Donald went up to the capital. Sir John seemed to rally briefly on June 4, but two days later, on a fine summer evening, the CPR operator tapped out the news the whole country had been waiting for and dreading. The prime minister had died at a quarter past ten.

Donald sent a wreath from himself and Bella and another from the Hudson's Bay Company to the state funeral on June 9. Following the service in Ottawa, a CPR train, draped in mourning, took the body to Kingston, the Ontario town where Macdonald had begun his life in Canada. Every station along the route was shrouded in black. Donald was keenly aware that the country had lost a great leader, as he wrote to the Marquess of Lorne, the former governor general, on the day of the funeral.

> The death of Sir John Macdonald not only removes the greatest man in Canada but for whom the confederation of these Provinces might never have been achieved, but it takes away the source of patriotic inspiration of our best men. I was late in entering political life, but I at once, as if I had been a much younger man, enrolled myself under his banner and regret nothing so much as the temporary estrangement which circumstances unhappily brought about. Notwithstanding this, I never once ceased to hold him in regard and was truly rejoiced when it became possible for me to return openly to my allegiance.[29]

At that emotional moment, Donald may have thought of himself as "enrolled under Macdonald's banner" but in truth he always kept his independence and his freedom to disagree on matters of principle. His allegiance only held good as long as he believed Macdonald was right.

One of the reasons Macdonald had served so long as leader of the Conservative Party was that there was no obvious successor. No other man had his charisma and his capacity to reconcile the different factions within the party, to keep a balance between the needs and demands of the various provinces and to win the confidence of both English and French speaking voters. On his death, the situation was exacerbated for the party by impending charges of corruption against Macdonald's old colleague, Hector Langevin. After a fruitless search for documents in which Macdonald was thought to have named his successor, the governor general asked J.J.C. Abbott, the CPR solicitor and leader of the party in the senate, to form the new government. Sir John Thompson, who had declined the prime ministership partly because he did not want the post and partly because he knew that his conversion to Roman Catholicism meant he would be unpopular in parts of Ontario, was leader in the Commons. The appointment of Abbott was a stop-gap measure until the Conservatives could find themselves a new leader, a search they were driven to the following year when Abbott resigned to go overseas for medical treatment. Charles Tupper flatly refused to take on the leadership himself, claiming that he did not want to stand in the way of Sir John Thompson, who assumed leadership of the party and the office of prime minister in December 1892.

Though he was appointed to the usual committees, Donald rarely appeared in the House and, under Thompson, was less interested in politics than he had been under Macdonald. In March 1893, he spoke about coal mines in Nova Scotia when some parliamentarians expressed fears that a new company, with American capital, would put the country's natural resources and its commitment to the British Empire at risk. Some MPs wanted to disallow Nova Scotia legislation affecting the mine.

The company had been formed by various businessmen, including Van Horne, and Donald, who owned a mine in Cape Breton. Dominion Coal, as the new firm was called, brought together several independent mines in the province with a view to saving expenses by coordinating the management and upgrading the equipment used to extract the coal. Dividends at Donald's mine had been ten percent, substantially above the returns made by many other shares at the time, and he and his colleagues determined to increase the operating capital in the new company in order to invest in new machinery without diminishing the dividends. Their new partners had come from Boston. As the mines were under contract to the British navy, the Canadian MPs wanted to ensure that part American ownership would not put the defense of the realm at risk. It was a business transaction, not a barter in Canadian sovereignty, Donald told the House. The idea that the Americans might shut the mines or sell to the enemy in the event of a war between Britain and Russia was ridiculous since the mines operated under Canadian law. With that outburst, he fell silent again.

In December 1894, while Sir John Thompson was staying at Windsor Castle as a guest of Queen Victoria, he collapsed at lunch and died. He was replaced by Mackenzie Bowell, another competent Conservative without the skills and talents of a natural leader. Across the floor, the Liberals recognized that, in Wilfrid Laurier, they had at their head a man capable of leading both his party and the country and they watched and waited for their opportunity.

Throughout the years after Macdonald's death, a problem had been festering in Manitoba. Abbott and Thompson had been aware of it but their attempts to deal with it had merely made it worse. Under Bowell's government, it came to a head.

The delegates sent from Fort Garry to Ottawa to negotiate the terms of Manitoba's entry into Confederation in 1870 carried a list of terms which had been altered by both Louis Riel and Archbishop Taché. At the prelate's request, a demand for denominational schools was included in the list. With one or two minor hiccups, this dual system had worked satisfactorily and the English and French communities in the province had lived peacefully; the settlements remained apart but they were good neighbours. The Anglophone population was much larger than its Francophone counterpart and the number of English speakers was growing rapidly as immigrants were absorbed. Even in the early days of Manitoba, there were two or three Protestant sects represented among the English and Scots, and the influx of newcomers increased the range of non-conformist churches to be found in the province. An inevitable consequence of such variety was that English schools were Protestant in name but non-denominational in practice; religious education was deemed a matter for parents and the church of their choice. By contrast, the Métis, a more cohesive but less powerful group, accepted church schools as the norm.

In 1888, the Quebec government determined to settle an old problem. When the British defeated the French in Canada in 1759, they seized the substantial landed estates which had been given to the Jesuit missionaries. Control was assumed by the British crown and subsequently by the government of Quebec. In 1888, the land was sold, the proceeds going to the Society of Jesus which was required to use them to support education in Quebec. Some minor points were referred to the Pope for arbitration. The very notion of papal consultation inflamed Irish Protestants, none more than D'Alton McCarthy, an Ontario Conservative who was convinced that the Jesuit Estates Act was driving Quebec into the arms of the Liberals.

An imperialist, McCarthy believed that tolerance of Canada's cultural mosaic would lead to the break-up of the country. As far as he was concerned, bilingualism and biculturalism had no place outside Quebec. In Manitoba, his fiery speeches in favour of a homogeneous nation roused the sympathies of those who had inherited John Schultz's political mantle, and before 1889 was out, they had proposed the abolition of separate schools and of French as one of the province's official languages. On purely economic grounds, the abolition of the dual school system made sense and probably would have carried in saner times, but coupled with anti-French, anti-Catholic hysteria, the proposal was offensive to the Métis and to all tolerant men. A further objection appeared when the Protestant clergy grasped that the new, unified school system was to be non-denominational, or "Godless" as they preferred to call it.

In February 1890, the Liberal premier, Thomas Greenway, introduced an act providing for a secular school system, and when it passed with a large majority, the lieutenant governor, then John Schultz, gave his assent. Archbishop Taché had hoped he would reserve his decision or pass it to the federal government, but since it accorded with Schultz's own views about Catholics and Métis, he had no wish to impede its progress. The prelate was persuaded to hold his objections until the 1891 election had passed, and it was only late in the year that a court case was finally brought to test its validity. A Catholic, and subsequently an Anglican, tax payer challenged the city of Winnipeg's right to make them pay taxes for non-denominational schools. The Manitoba courts went against them, the Supreme Court of Canada upheld their position and the Judicial Committee of the Privy Council came down on the side of the Manitoba courts.

Manitoba's French Catholics then determined to make an appeal under the British North America Act which had established Canadian Confederation. While the act clearly stated that education was a provincial, not a federal matter, it gave a minority, deprived of the educational system it had enjoyed at the time of joining Confederation, the right to appeal to the governor general in council. Should the appeal go against the provincial government, the federal powers could introduce remedial legislation to enforce the decision of the governor general in council. An appeal and the risk of remedial legislation was the last thing Mackenzie Bowell wanted to face. The Conservative Party was weak and would be torn apart as MPs from Quebec supported their brethren in Manitoba while those from Ontario would be vociferous in their support for non-denominational schools. Bowell could almost hear Laurier rehearsing his first prime ministerial speech.

Early in 1895, the governor general decided to intervene.

Stanley had resigned in September 1893 when he had inherited his father's estates and become the Earl of Derby. His replacement was John Campbell Gordon, the Earl of Aberdeen and the first Marquess of Aberdeen and Temair. Ishbel Aberdeen, his wife, had pronounced views on many matters, including the importance of breaking down artificial social barriers, whether on her husband's estate in Scotland or at the governor general's residence in Ottawa. She was keenly interested in social work and it never crossed her mind to hold back or seek advice before enthusiastically taking up some new worthy cause. What she saw as good works, others often saw as meddling.

The tendency not to look before she leapt, coupled with a fine disregard for how things could be paid for, had enabled her to bring her husband close to bankruptcy, the shock of which caused her to suffer a nervous breakdown. The doctors recommended travel and, in the summer of 1890, the Aberdeens set out for Canada. Donald had met them previously and as soon as he knew they were in Montreal, lent them a carriage and entertained them to dinner. Bella had not returned from the spa in Carlsbad, but he asked Shaughnessy, Dr. Barclay from St. Paul's Church, and various other bank and railway colleagues. To Lady Aberdeen's delight, Father Lacombe was visiting and she was able to quiz him on his work among the Indians on the prairies. Donald was his usual attentive self, offering the Aberdeens the use of Silver Heights and putting a private car on the CPR at their disposal.

"It must be confessed that Manitoba is extremely flat as seen about here," Lady Aberdeen reported to her journal, "but this is a dear little snug house, enlarged from an original farm & I can conceive of no more Good Samaritan like action than to place this haven of rest at the disposal of globe-trotters like ourselves who are not yet wholly hardened to 3 days & nights in the train, even tho' it be in a private car."[30]

In September the following year, Donald again hosted a dinner for the Aberdeens, calling on his usual array of relatives, HBC, Bank of Montreal and CPR colleagues to make up the numbers. It reminded the Aberdeens "v much of last year's party, but minus Father Lacombe alas!" Lady Aberdeen was seated between Donald and Shaughnessy and was treated to a full flow of reminiscences about the creation of the Saint Paul, Minneapolis and Manitoba Railway. "The first year the railway did not pay 1 per cent in two and a half years it was paying 80 p. cent, & on one occasion the dividend was 173 per cent," she noted enthusiastically in her journal.[31]

Donald had clearly captivated Ishbel Aberdeen and he became one of her enthusiasms. For his part, while he was happy to have an appreciative audience when he recalled the old days, he was fully aware that Canadians would find her a handful as the wife of the governor general. Even Lord Aberdeen, with his pronounced Liberal bias was a worry. "As to Lord Aberdeen's appointment," he wrote to Sir William Butler who had reported on conditions west of Fort Garry in 1870, "we can only hope for the best. We have so far been especially favoured by Providence in the matter of Governors-General. In this case the fact of Lord Aberdeen's being a great favourite with Mr. Gladstone will not predispose many in his favour; but I believe he is earnest and industrious and a Scotsman of rank and lineage, which in itself signifies a great deal. Then, as I need hardly remind you, there is her ladyship!" Butler, an Irish Catholic, would have understood that Donald was teasing him by assuming the importance of being a Scot; both men had obviously seen enough of Lady Aberdeen to know that Canadians would not be allowed to sit idly by if the governor general's wife thought they should be engaged in improving activities.[32]

Early in 1895, the Conservative cabinet was divided over the Manitoba schools question: some argued that they should go to the country and deal with the Manitoba issue when they were sure of their strength; others believed that they should hear the appeal to the governor general in council first. For his part, Donald did not "believe the Government as at present constituted with B as leader" stood any chance if it went to the people, as Sir Charles Tupper reported from London to his son, Charles Hibbert Tupper.[33]

Throughout 1895, it became increasingly apparent that Bowell could lead neither his party nor the country and on January 4, 1896, seven cabinet ministers resigned, attempting to force Bowell to resign himself. What the ministers had not foreseen was that the Aberdeens so disliked Sir Charles, the only obvious alternative leader, that they refused to accept Bowell's resignation. It took nearly two weeks to persuade them to agree to Bowell's compromise which called for Tupper to return as secretary of state and leader of the party in the House of Commons until April when parliament would be dissolved. This was sufficient to bring six of the ministers back on January 15, but Aberdeen had to summon Donald and Senator Drummond to dinner in Ottawa on the twenty-ninth of March to help him persuade Charles Hibbert Tupper, who had been minister of justice, to rescind his resignation.

Lord Aberdeen acknowledged that Sir Charles Tupper had no choice but to introduce remedial legislation, but privately, with his wife's enthusiastic support, he set about trying to find a compromise. The aim was to "give a loophole for the Dominion Govt to drop the remedial legislation to which it is now pledged & which if carried through & imposed on Manitoba against its will, will produce such a lamentable religious war," Ishbel Aberdeen melodramatically explained in her journal. Had the Aberdeens' covert plan been successful, the unconstitutionality of their actions might well have been disregarded. As it was, they made trouble for themselves and Charles Tupper and for Donald Smith, the agent of their good intentions.[34]

Late in January, Donald chaired the quinquennial McGill dinner at which both the Aberdeens and Tupper were guests. Aberdeen took the opportunity to have a private conversation with Donald who, Lady Aberdeen reported, was "very anxious for some compromise about the school question." In subsequent talks, Donald agreed to go to Manitoba to see what he could do to make peace. "He is the only man left who might possibly persuade the Manitoba Legislature to listen to reason & to take the task of remedying the grievance of the minority into their own hands, & at the same time have influence with the Archbishop to make him willing to accept the offer," Lady Aberdeen noted. "H.E. entreated him to try & finally Sir Donald offered to go off to Winnipeg himself."[35]

The immediate difficulty was that Donald was seriously ill. He had fallen and broken his right arm in the summer and had not allowed time for the bones and the damaged tendons to mend properly. In London in the autumn, he had caught a severe chill but refused to take care of himself, and a rough transatlantic voyage at the end of October knocked his plastered arm about and caused it to become inflamed. He was delirious when Van Horne met him at the station in Montreal on November 2, and the doctors were not certain he would recover. A relapse in December meant he should still have been confined to bed in January and February, but he insisted on travelling to Ottawa, hosting the McGill dinner, and attending CPR meetings. The effort exhausted him and he was subject to fits of uncontrollable shaking, probably signs of a fever. Dr. Stewart refused to allow him to go west until the middle of February, and when Donald finally did set out, the doctor became his travelling companion because both men feared a relapse.[36]

In the meantime, Tupper was also consulting Donald in January and February of 1896, seeking his views on the political situation generally and on ways of dealing with the disarray in the Conservative Party. He also discussed the Manitoba schools problem and, following a lunch in Montreal on February 8, Donald was able to tell Aberdeen that Tupper shared the governor general's views that some discreet, unofficial negotiations might pave the way for a reconciliation between the two Manitoba factions. The rest of the cabinet knew nothing of these intentions — so much so that half an hour before the train was due to depart for Winnipeg, Bowell invited Donald to join him for lunch.[37]

In Winnipeg, Donald stayed at the Manitoba Hotel, Silver Heights having burned to the ground in November 1892. "I am sorry to lose it with its associations of twenty and more years," he had written to Clarence Chipman, "but its loss is of less consequence to my friends now that there are not only decent but, I am told very comfortable hotels in Winnipeg."[38]

In the Manitoba capital, Donald soon discovered that neither Premier Greenway, whose Liberals had won a resounding victory in the provincial elections in January, nor Monsignor Langevin, who had succeeded Taché as Archbishop of St. Boniface, was inclined to compromise. The provincial leader had just had his views vindicated by his electorate while the church leader could see that it was only a matter of time before the federal government's remedial legislation would enforce the desired result. If neither a compromise nor remedial legislation were achieved before the imminent general election, then it was apparent that Roman Catholics would not support the Conservatives and both the provincial Liberals and Manitoba's Catholics would be rewarded with a Liberal federal government which would be able to effect a compromise because it had greater sympathy with both parties in the dispute.

Donald did succeed in wearing down some of Greenway's obduracy and both he and the archbishop agreed that they would go to Ottawa for a conference with the government. Back in Ottawa on February 25, Donald briefed the governor general and Charles Tupper. Not long after, Bowell was also informed of the results of the visit. Neither the Liberals nor the press were long in deducing that something was afoot and on the second of March, D'Alton McCarthy demanded to know what was going on. In response, Tupper was vague, saying that communications between Donald and Bowell were private.

Greenway then played his next card, which was to cable Donald and explain that representatives of the provincial government could "only proceed to Ottawa for the purpose of holding a conference upon the official invitation of the Dominion Government. As you are aware we are not to blame for the situation. I fully appreciate your very kind office in this matter." In short, as Donald was not an official emissary, Greenway and his colleagues could not give an official response to the invitation to go to Ottawa.[39]

On the fourth of March, the cabinet debated what its reply should be and on the ninth, Tupper read Greenway's cable to the House, omitting the line in which the premier pointed out that the Manitoba government was "not to blame for the situation." Tupper made no effort to get Greenway's permission to publicize what purported to be a private telegram and failed to obtain Donald's agreement because he and Bella had slipped away to New York for a day or two. The Conservatives dug a deeper and deeper hole for themselves as they revealed that some of them, at least, had been fully aware of what Donald had been trying to achieve in Winnipeg. Greenway exacerbated the situation with a statement in the Manitoba legislature objecting to the omission of the sentence about blame.

On the nineteenth of March, Donald attempted to clarify the situation, beginning in his customary way, with a résumé of his associations with the Northwest and pointing out that separate schools had existed in Manitoba before the province joined Confederation and that those involved with the negotiations in 1870 had expected this situation to continue. Of his February visit, he stated

> I wish to say very distinctly that I did not go at the instance of the Government. It is true that I had the privilege of communicating with His Excellency the Governor General, not so much as Her Majesty's representative here, but as one who, as we all know, has taken a very warm and deep interest in everything that is for the benefit of Canada. Having incidentally had an opportunity of speaking of this very important matter of the Manitoba school question, His Excellency was good enough to express to me his very great desire that it should be satisfactorily settled in one way or the other so as to be agreeable not only to the people of that province, but also to the people of the Dominion as a whole, desiring it should be disposed of outside altogether of party politics, for we know that the Governor General never allows himself to become a partisan.... I myself was greatly impressed with the view that were it possible to dispose of this matter outside of Parliament, it would be for the general good; and I consequently determined to go to Manitoba with the view of seeing Mr. Greenway and some of his colleagues, and of endeavouring to ascertain if there could not be found a satisfactory way out of the difficulty.[40]

Donald wanted to see the second reading of the remedial bill passed by acclamation and for this to be followed by a federal-provincial conference which would resolve the question and preclude the necessity for the final reading of the bill.

Ishbel Aberdeen was in the House to listen to Donald's speech and sent a complimentary note to him afterwards, scarcely guessing that she had just heard him provide the fodder the Liberals had been waiting for. The following day, Richard Cartwright pointed out that Donald had gone to Winnipeg at the behest of the governor general but that Charles Tupper had told the House that Donald had had no authority to negotiate.

> I draw no distinction between what His Excellency may do, in his capacity of Governor General, and in his private capacity. He must be assumed to have been advised by his Ministers in all the steps he took, or else responsible government in Canada becomes a farce. Under those circumstances, I call upon the leader of the House to explain how it came to pass that His

> Excellency communicated, with the consent of his advisers, no doubt, with the hon. member for Montreal West, and how, that being done, the leader of the House deemed it within his right to tell the hon. member for Simcoe (Mr. McCarthy), that Sir Donald Smith was not authorized on behalf of the Government to negotiate with the Premier or administration of Manitoba with reference to, or on the subject of, the school law of the province.[41]

Prevaricating, Tupper responded by saying that neither he nor any other member of the government had been aware of any communication between Donald and the governor general, but Cartwright and other Liberals pressed home the principle of ministerial responsibility. Trying to protect the Aberdeens, Donald interjected that he had not gone west at the instance of the governor general. Had he gone privately.

Under government instructions or at the request of the governor general, the Liberals demanded. How he had gone to Winnipeg?

"By train; by the Canadian Pacific Railway!" the House shouted.[42]

The opposition hammered at the question of the governor general's authority and his constitutional duty to act on the advice of his ministers until Tupper finally caved in and agreed that the government would take the responsibility. At tea time, during a break in the wrangling, Donald slipped away to Rideau Hall to brief the Aberdeens on the latest developments.

The upshot of all the arguing was that the government sent an official delegation to try to effect the settlement Donald had been working on. Donald did his best to persuade Tupper that it should be a bi-partisan commission including Laurier or his nominees but Tupper was reluctant and Bowell flatly refused. Consequently, Donald, together with Arthur Dickey, the minister of justice, and Senator Alphonse Desjardins, the minister of militia, returned to Winnipeg for a fruitless conversation with Clifford Sifton and the provincial secretary, Douglas Cameron. Neither of the Winnipeg men had any intention of cooperating, while Premier Greenway held himself aloof with a diplomatic illness. The mission failed.

By this time, it was too late to introduce the remedial legislation. Parliament's time had expired and a general election had to be called. The Conservatives were going to the country with several strikes against them and without a strong captain who could take the party and the country with him. For some, there was an alternative to Charles Tupper as head of the party and a campaign to make Donald the new leader began to gather momentum. It had support both inside and outside parliament and Donald had "hundreds of letters from all over the country, urging him that he ought to come forward as Premier," Lady Aberdeen confided to her journal. "But this he felt he could not do, although Sir Mackenzie told him yesterday that if he was asked for advice by H.E. when resigning as to whom was to be his successor that he would advise Sir Donald & that moreover he would serve under him."[43]

Donald had no intention of allowing himself to be made prime minister of Canada. He knew he was not cut out for the hustings or for the incessant negotiating and compromises which would be necessary to keep English and French

Canada in equilibrium. He had never even been a cabinet minister. He had already agreed to be one of the Canadian representatives on the Pacific Cable Commission in London but now accepted Tupper's invitation to be Canada's third high commissioner to the United Kingdom.

For Donald, there were several advantages to the move to London, among them his obligations to the Hudson's Bay Company. He had been devoting a good deal of time to HBC affairs, primarily because the company needed to be restructured to adapt to the demands of the twentieth century. It could no longer consider itself as a fur trading operation first and foremost and had to accept that the wintering partners were part of its history. The company's future lay in its land grant, most of it as yet unsold, and in developing its stores to serve the cities and towns which were growing up throughout Canada. Bringing the company into the modern world was not an easy job for, as Van Horne burst out one day, it was "one of the most hidebound concerns in existence. The London board is a collection of persnickety and narrow-minded men who don't know enough about business to manage a peanut stand.... There are two or three good fellows among them, but they don't know any *business*, and the H.B. Co. is going to pot in consequence.... Sir Donald is the only one in the lot who wears a hat a man's size." Obviously Donald would find it easier to wear this hat if he were in London.[44]

For both Donald and Bella, residence in the English capital held the additional attraction of allowing them to be close to Maggie and her children. The first grandchild, Frances Margaret, had been born in 1889 and she was followed by Donald Sterling in 1891, Robert Henry in 1893, Edith Mary in 1895, and Arthur Jared who was to appear at the end of May, a few days after his paternal grandparents disembarked at Liverpool. The arrival in London was tinged with sadness, however, for Annie Kane, George Stephen's wife to whom Bella had been very close, had died in April that year.

Donald had other, much more private reasons for finding the London posting useful. In 1894, he had acquired extensive property at Glencoe in the Scottish highlands and was in the process of building a grand house there. Though Glencoe is resonant with Scottish history, it is Macdonald territory and on the opposite side of the country from the Grants and Stuarts from whom Donald was descended. The estate was bought at auction through Donald's Scottish solicitors, Skene Edwards and Garson, and there is nothing to suggest that either Donald or Bella saw it before the purchase was completed. For them, the important point was to acquire Scottish property.

Donald's first surviving will was made in 1888, no doubt prompted by Maggie's marriage and the thoughts about his own mortality which such an occasion would arouse. In addition to various benefactions, the testament made provision for Bella, Maggie, Jamesie and other relatives. It was drawn up by John Sterling, regarded as the most discreet man in New York. He was lawyer to many of North America's wealthiest men and knew their most intimate secrets, none of which he ever revealed. A somewhat eccentric bachelor, Sterling was so careful of public opinion that he compelled his housemaid to enter by the back door lest people get the wrong idea. He was not sure the will was "watertight," as he phrased it, but was doing his best to reduce the risk of quarrels among the legatees.[45]

Donald's real worry was that Bella's and Maggie's right to inherit might be challenged in court and the more money he made, the greater the risk seemed to be. For public consumption, Donald and Bella dated their "marriage" to March 9, 1853. It was then that they had been left alone together at the Chief Factor's house in North West River and it was ten months before Maggie's birth. At that point, however, they had not gone through any ceremony, valid or otherwise, and there was no doubt that their daughter was illegitimate. Sir George Simpson was correct when he assured Donald that Bella's marriage to James Grant was not valid because her father had no authority to marry them, a fact which made Jamesie (to say nothing of most other children born in Labrador) illegitimate too and precluded the need for a divorce when his parents wished to marry others. Donald had acquired the right to marry people in Labrador when the Anglican bishop of Newfoundland made him a lay preacher and the governor, Sir Alexander Bannerman, made him a justice of the peace, but that hardly gave him power to conduct a marriage to which he himself was a party. Neither is there any evidence that this marriage or any of the others he conducted was registered at the Colonial Office as required. In the eyes of the law, therefore, Bella was, at best, Donald's common law wife.

It is hard to imagine who might have challenged the will, but the possibility, however remote, of acquiring a large amount of money without working for it makes men do silly things. Gossip about the Smiths' marital arrangements persisted; Andrew Kenyon had tried to get Sir John Macdonald to use it against Donald in the 1878 election campaign; Sir Henry Tyler had reported to his wife the stories, largely incorrect, which he had picked up in Montreal in 1888; and Jamesie's brother-in-law was to attempt to use the information to blackmail Maggie after Donald's death. Most compelling of all, however, was the memory of Barbara Smith's attempt to overturn John Stuart's will in favour of his country wife, Mary Taylor.

One possible way around the problem was for Donald to argue that Scottish rather than English or Canadian law applied to him. In Scotland, it was sufficient for a couple to declare that they lived together as man and wife for their marriage to be considered valid by the courts, and children born before that declaration were considered to be as legitimate as those born after, providing there was no impediment to the marriage at the time of their birth. To comply with Scottish law, Donald would need to prove that he was domiciled in Scotland, or at least to demonstrate that he intended to return to the country of his birth. Acquiring a residence would be the way of doing so. To purchase hundreds of acres at Glencoe was a rather grandiose way of achieving a Scottish home but to the unenquiring mind it made more sense than a wealthy man buying a simple cottage. Because Glencoe was not served by rail and all but inaccessible by road, he bought a yacht, the *Morag*, to take him from the railhead at Oban around to Ballachulish on Loch Leven. It was on the yacht in the summer of 1895 that he had fallen and broken his arm.

It soon became apparent, however, that a Scottish domicile was not sufficient. Since 1847, Scots had been required to register their marriages, regardless of whether they had been performed by clergy or were marriages by consent. In a quandary about how to validate the marriage and confer legitimacy on Maggie, Donald confessed his problem to John Sterling who then arranged for the couple to go through a private marriage ceremony. On Monday, March 9, 1896, their forty-third "wedding" anniversary, when Donald was seventy-five years old and Bella was two months short of her seventy-first birthday, they were married in a civil ceremony at the Windsor Hotel, New York, in the presence of John Sterling and his law partner, Arthur Shearman. We "do again take each other for husband and wife," they swore. "I know this was the greatest possible relief to his mind," Sterling recalled in 1914. In Ottawa, meanwhile, Charles Tupper was desperately trying to find Donald to get his permission to read out Premier Greenway's cable about the proposed delegation to the capital. He could hardly have guessed why the member for Montreal West was absent.[46]

CHAPTER SEVENTEEN

HIGH COMMISSIONER 1896–1899

Lord Strathcona presides most afternoons and every evening at some meeting or another, and speechifies with great aplomb on art, music, medicine, science, university extension, French Employment, and every other interest that is glad to enlist the dear old gentleman's presence — and purse.
Gaspard Farrer [1]

The House of Commons was prorogued on April 23, 1896 and parliament was dissolved the following day. Before the cabinet rushed into the election campaign, Donald was sworn in as a privy councillor in preparation for his new duties as Canada's representative in the United Kingdom.

The post of high commissioner had been created in 1880 by Sir John A. Macdonald who felt that a self-governing colony such as Canada could not have its interests adequately represented by the governor general who, however sympathetic he might be to Canadian concerns, was obliged to give precedence to Britain's wishes in any disagreement. Increasingly, there were matters on which the two nations differed, trade and foreign affairs being the most prominent. Britain was still responsible for Canada's external affairs, and it was important to have a voice in London to represent the Canadian point of view and ensure that it was not overlooked by British ministers, government officials and diplomats. Canada needed someone in London with a thorough knowledge of her agricultural and manufacturing communities to speak on her behalf and she needed an enthusiast who would encourage people to take up land in the Northwest.

An immigration office had been established in London in 1868 and the following year Sir John Rose had become an informal representative with responsibility for managing Canada's foreign debt which was largely in British hands. The first high commissioner was Sir Alexander Galt who was instructed to take orders on immigration questions from the Ministry of Agriculture, which was then responsible for these matters, and on the handling of the national debt from the finance minister. Galt found that a salary of $10,000 and a one-off payment of $4,000 to cover expenses was not enough to keep him, his wife and his vast brood of children. Charles Tupper replaced him in 1883 and for most of the time did not take a salary as he retained his cabinet office.[2]

In 1891, Donald had argued in the House of Commons that the high commissioner's salary should be higher, not because he had any idea that he might be in line for the post but because he felt that "it would be only showing a proper regard to the dignity and the position of Canada to make a worthy allowance for the High Commissioner." For his part, when he accepted the position, he had no intention of living within the confines of his salary and allowance, nor had he any need to do so. The allowances were passed on to the secretary to cover expenses for which there was otherwise no allocation, while all Donald's travel, entertainment and increased domestic expenditure consequent on his representational role were met from his own funds.[3]

Tupper had been living in a house on Cromwell Road, near the cluster of museums which had grown up on the site of the Great Exhibition of 1851. Donald considered this official residence to be below the standards appropriate for the high commissioner and, while improvements were made, he and Bella moved into Brown's Hotel in Piccadilly, long their habitual London address. In the end, however, they decided against living in Cromwell Road, whatever improvements were made, and early in the new year they moved into 53 Cadogan Square. The house was new by London standards, having been completed by the developer, R.G. Trollope, about 1889. In all likelihood, Trollope's ninety-nine year lease on the house and stables was by way of payment for his work in developing the Cadogan estate. The square was much more fashionable than Cromwell Road, attracting army officers and titled gentlemen and their ladies. Lord Balfour of Burleigh, a resourceful Scottish businessman and representative peer who had married the Aberdeens' youngest daughter, lived at number 47. The Smiths' house, which was taken furnished, was probably acquired on a five year lease and when the term was up, they moved to 28 Grosvenor Square.

This square, on land owned for generations by the Dukes of Westminster, was unquestionably higher up the social ladder, with the Marquess of Bath, the Dukes of Portland and Somerset and Lord William Cecil all living there. It was, however, further away from the High Commission offices in Victoria Street and much less convenient for St. Columba's, the Scots Presbyterian church which Donald attended. While Grosvenor Square had the advantage of being closer to Maggie and the children in Queen Anne Street, its principal attraction was its size. It spread over four floors, with servants' rooms in the attic and, in 1902, had just been completely redesigned inside, though that cannot necessarily be judged to have been in its favour since, in 1916, a tenant's agent described it as "the worst planned house in Mayfair."[4]

The Smiths had not yet arrived in London when Donald's promotion from Knight Commander to Knight Grand Cross of the Order of St. Michael and St. George was announced. At the end of 1895, Tupper had been working away behind the scenes with a view to securing him a peerage, pointing out to the colonial secretary, Joseph Chamberlain, that Donald deserved it as much as George Stephen, created Lord Mount Stephen in 1891, had deserved his. For the same purpose, Tupper saw Aberdeen who gladly endorsed the idea, but Tupper's efforts were rejected and he only succeeded in ameliorating Donald's position in the ranks of knighthood. Even that caused Donald to observe that "the bestowal of it has been *very* awkward for me owing to circumstances you fully understand, and more for the sake of my friends than from any feeling on the subject on my own part, I cannot help regretting exceedingly it was not withheld." The awkwardness, which almost certainly also lay behind the refusal of the peerage, was the ambiguity surrounding the Smiths' marriage.[5]

Victorian England was both prudish and two-faced when it came to questions of marriage and legitimacy. The queen's own happy marriage set a standard by which she judged other people's marital circumstances and it therefore became a model for the behaviour of her subjects, but during her reign parliament also felt a need to clarify the regulations governing these matters and to provide for the registration of marriages and births. In part, the nineteenth century legislation reflected men's ancient concern that their titles and property be inherited by their own bloodline and not by children their wives may have conceived by other men and passed off as their spouse's progeny. In part, more articulate laws and stricter social canons were a response to the watering down of tightly knit communities brought about by increased travel and the penetration into the upper classes of newly rich industrialists and wealthy Americans who sought to marry their money to aristocratic titles.

Because divorce could only be achieved by the very expensive and very public process of a court case, it was accepted, especially amongst the wealthy and those with long pedigrees, that unhappy marriages would continue while the partners lived separate lives, though presenting a united front on important public or private social occasions. Infidelity was less scandalous than divorce. The Prince of Wales was a notorious philanderer and his long-standing affair with Mrs. Keppel (to whom he was also unfaithful) was well known, but on public occasions and many semi-private ones, it was always Princess Alexandra who was at his side. The arbiters of social mores found it much easier to deal with the prince's duplicity than to deal with an enduring, stable, loving but irregular marriage such as Donald Smith's.

When Donald was first made a knight, the obligation to attend at court for the ceremony was dispensed with, as was customary when recipients of such honours lived overseas. He had since been presented to Queen Victoria and had been entertained to lunch at Windsor Castle, together with Bella and Maggie and a great many others, when he was a Canadian representative to the Colonial and Indian Exhibition mounted to celebrate Victoria's golden jubilee. The possibility of a peerage and the actuality of a promotion to Knight Grand Cross, however, meant that he could not hide in a crowd and the queen could not overlook the gossip which always attended Donald's introduction to new individuals and circumstances; the fact that the promotion was in the offing was doubtless one of the reasons, though not the only one, for the New York marriage ceremony. As a very private man, reluctant even to reveal the train of thought leading to business decisions, Donald was intensely embarrassed by questions about his marriage,

Maggie's legitimacy and his relationship to Jamesie. While he enjoyed the recognition which his honours conferred, he hated the attendant prying into his private life. Tupper, a self-seeking busybody, took the credit for Donald's promotion in the ranks of knighthood without perceiving the extent to which it would discomfit his so-called friend.

In the summer of 1896, Donald had a good deal more on his mind than the July investiture at Windsor Castle. For a start, Bella was not well. She had not been able to shake the cold which had taken hold in the spring and her usual journey to the spa at Carlsbad did not bring any significant improvement. In September, Donald observed in a letter to Ishbel Aberdeen that Bella had been "an invalid ever since we left Canada" and in the same month, Agnes Macdonald, Sir John's widow, noted that she looked "dreadfully ill." It was spring 1897 before Bella regained her health.[6]

In August 1896, John Smith fell seriously ill and Donald rushed north to be with his brother in what he feared would be his final days. John rallied, but it became clear to Donald on this trip that he needed to provide for the security of his brother's children, a gesture which would also ease his brother's worries and contribute to his physical health. Donald purchased what came to be known as Stuart Lodge, a three bedroom house, with room for two servants, in Polwarth Terrace, Edinburgh. Though he remained the owner, the house was held in trust for his nieces and subsequently for Eliza's heirs. It proved a wise move, for John died on March 1, 1899 and Eliza was widowed early. The house and the regular allowance he provided his nieces did much to make their later years more comfortable.[7]

Donald spent part of the summer of 1896 dealing with Hudson's Bay Company business in the run up to the July General Court, and he went to Glasgow, in his capacity as chancellor of McGill, to attend celebrations honouring Lord Kelvin, the physicist whose experiments in thermodynamics had led to the discovery of the principles of refrigeration and whose work on the transatlantic cable had helped link Britain and Canada. It was also Lord Kelvin, as Donald reminded the listeners to his address, who, with William Siemens, had suggested that Niagara Falls could be a source of hydroelectric power.

Recognition of colonial lawyers in British courts occupied some of Donald's time that summer, as did a Board of Trade conference which tried to find a satisfactory solution to tariff inconsistencies throughout the empire.

On the afternoon of the first of July, Donald and Bella hosted the first of their famous and extravagant Dominion Day parties. It took place in the elaborate foyers of the Imperial Institute to which Donald and Lord Mount Stephen had contributed ten years earlier and, with it, the Smiths launched the custom of engaging Canadian music students studying in London to entertain the guests. By comparison with some of their later ventures, this was a small affair with only five or six hundred guests, but it was, nonetheless, the largest gathering of Canadians London had ever seen. It was also an opportunity for Donald to meet a wide range of businessmen and politicians whose influence could be used to benefit Canadian interests. Few outside the London financial community had ever heard of Donald when his appointment was announced and, to judge by the impression he made on Beckles Willson, the *Daily Mail* reporter who became his first biographer, most people did not rate him very highly on a first meeting. "He is not an imposing figure," Willson noted in his journal, "nor, in spite of his great age, and white beard, patriarchal. My impression is of a shrewd, quiet, rather 'pawky' Scotch business man. Talks with great deliberation and almost with humility. Odd contrast to Tupper, with his aggressiveness, his loud voice, and physical vigour." Because he was not an imposing figure and not a good public speaker, though he no longer flinched at the task, and because he was quiet, Donald slipped almost unnoticed into London's political and social world.[8]

As far as Canada and Canadians were concerned, the biggest news of the summer was the defeat of Charles Tupper and the Conservatives at the June general election. Donald had not expected this turnabout and immediately proposed setting out for Ottawa. Though he expressed his request for permission to return in very general terms, he wanted to discover for himself what the future was likely to bring and whether he would be retained as high commissioner. Tupper, clinging to power for as long as he possibly could, would have none of it. Donald was to stay in London to deal with the contract for the fast Atlantic service and the Pacific cable conference. Tupper, who turned petulant when Aberdeen would not accept his nominations to fill gaps in the senate and on the bench, finally resigned on July 8 and ten days later Donald was on the *Laconia* out of Liverpool. In Ottawa, the new prime minister, Wilfrid Laurier, quickly assured Donald that he wanted him to remain as high commissioner.

Laurier, a lawyer by training, was given a British name and, in his youth, acquired a firm grounding in English language and literature. It was, he believed, the only way in which he could defend French Canada from her Anglophone compatriots, though he read so deeply that one suspects duty had turned to pleasure long before he arrived at the House of Commons. The new prime minister was twenty-one years younger than the high commissioner and a determined Liberal. Though not conventionally handsome, he was elegant, with a thick shock of curly chestnut hair, just beginning to be tinged with white. Tall and graceful, Laurier was judged to be the best dressed public man in Canada and observers joked that aspiring young Liberals hoped that, in learning to remove their overcoats as he did, they might also acquire his political skills. Both Donald and Laurier firmly believed that their private lives were no one's business but their own and always refused journalists' requests for interviews which touched on their domestic affairs. Both were the subject of considerable gossip, Donald because of his relationship with Bella and her children and Laurier because of his close friendship with Emilie Lavergne, the wife of his law partner.

What drew the two men together, however, was a commitment to Canada and to the forging of a Canadian identity in an international context. With complementary and contrasting views, they supported and corrected each other and together worked towards a consensus which would define Canada within the empire. In the process, they forged a firm friendship based on mutual admiration and respect.

There was much talk of imperialism at the end of the nineteenth century. Britain felt impelled to expand not only because it needed new sources of raw materials and new markets but also because it needed to demonstrate its superiority over newly united countries such as Italy, Germany and the United States. British prestige was enhanced by increasing the number of countries school children could colour red. Cyprus, South Africa, Kenya, Rhodesia, British New Guinea, North Borneo and parts of Burma all came under British control in the last two decades of the century. At home, poets, novelists and newspaper writers generated an aura of excitement, sometimes bordering on the jingoistic, as they fed their readers stories of the strange people and exciting adventures British soldiers and explorers encountered on the empire's frontiers. The compulsion to inform the British public about its overseas empire lay behind the Colonial and Indian Exhibition of 1886 and behind its transformation into the permanent displays and research facilities of the Imperial Institute.

One of the Canadian high commissioner's jobs was to contribute to this education process by lectures and exhibitions which attempted to strip away the layers of ignorance about Canada, its history, its population and its wealth of natural resources. At the Royal Colonial Institute in April 1898, Donald produced a succinct account of the history of British Columbia before 1859 and of Manitoba and the North West Territories up to 1869. It was, of course, the familiar story of the North West Company and the HBC, but he delivered it objectively and without reference to his and his family's involvement in the development of these areas. He then gave a brief account of circumstances in Ontario and Quebec, following it with a clear statement of his views on emigration and trade, outlining a position which he was to repeat over and over again in the coming years.

> We must not forget that the future of the outlying portions of the Empire is largely bound up in the emigration question. In my opinion it is to the interest, if it is not the duty, of all the Fellows of the Royal Colonial Institute to do what they can to direct emigration so that it may be retained within the British Empire. It is by emigration in the past that the colonies have made the wonderful progress witnessed during the 60 years reign of our Sovereign. It is the emigration to the Colonies that is making the United Kingdom less dependent year by year upon foreign countries for her food supplies, and it is emigration to the Colonies that has provided such large markets for British products — markets that are astonishing when compared with the trade between the United Kingdom and foreign countries with ten times the population of the self-governing colonies. It is by encouraging emigration to the British colonies that you will ensure the expansion of these markets which afford greater possibilities for the British trade than those in any other parts of the world. And last but not least it is by thus adding to the population of the Colonies that we shall increase their wealth and strength, and be enabled to maintain with their help the position of being the greatest Empire the world has ever seen. What we want in Canada are more people and more capital.[9]

Donald's office produced school packs and exhibitions which toured the country and maintained sets of lantern slides to accompany lectures to businessmen on the nature of the Canadian economy. "Peaches are cheaper in Canada in the autumn than apples are in London," Donald declared in a lecture to the Imperial Institute, adding that "tons upon tons of superb Canadian turkeys are annually imported for the Christmas markets" and that "Canada exports more cheese to Great Britain than all the rest of the world put together, and is rapidly taking up the same position with regard to butter and bacon."[10]

When he addressed the Birmingham Chamber of Commerce in 1900, it was because he was asked to explain why the manufacturing interests of the West Midlands seemed to be making little headway in the Canadian market. By that point, he knew that he had to start with a brief sketch of the country, its transportation systems and its resources and he repeated the need for emigration to develop future markets. Since direct taxation was impractical in a sparsely populated country, he explained, the Canadian government raised revenue by taxing imports and Britain was favoured with a twenty-five percent reduction. Despite this bias, the United States was still Canada's foremost trading partner, even when British goods were better. The reasons were lower American prices occasioned by lower production costs and the Americans' geographical advantage. British goods, he warned, were not always adapted to the Canadian market and little research was done before attempting to sell them there. In short, the assumptions of empire, the belief that the colonies must want British goods, were preventing British manufacturers from reaching their intended market.[11]

Partly because it was in their interests to do so, Canadians argued that communications should play an important role in uniting the empire and ensuring its security in the face of potential threats from Russia, Germany and Italy. The fast Atlantic service, linking Britain with Hong Kong via the CPR's trains and Pacific steamers, was advocated as a tie which would bind the empire together and this All Red Route was one which Donald continued to support, even though the British government showed no interest in subsidizing the north Atlantic crossing. As late as 1908, he was warning that Britain needed to have control over the means by which she imported her foodstuffs and raw materials. Furthermore, a link such as the All Red Route, by then taking in Australasia as well, would facilitate improved commercial relations and encourage capital investment and emigration. Trade with China and Japan was sure to develop, he told his audience, "and the nation which first secures control of it will mainly reap the advantage of the situation."[12]

Canada had better luck with the Pacific Cable. It had first been advocated in 1879 when Sandford Fleming pointed out that Britain would enjoy more secure communications with her eastern colonies if a line went via Canada and a cable on the floor of the Pacific. At one point, he established a company, with Donald as one of the directors, which would be responsible for laying the cable and managing the line. The project made little headway because two related commercial companies, the Eastern Telegraph and the Eastern Extension Telegraph, were already providing a service across Europe to Asia and Australia and Fleming's proposals were seen by some as self-serving. In fact, Fleming did not care about the cable as a business venture: he was promoting it in the interests of the empire. As the imperial idea, and with it the fear of a threat to the empire, took hold, he saw that it made more sense for the cable to be owned and controlled by the governments in whose interest it was to be established. By 1893, the Canadian government supported this view and sent Fleming with Mackenzie Bowell to Australia to sound out the state governments there. This led to Canada hosting a conference in Ottawa in 1894 at which she and the Australian colonies demanded action on the Pacific cable. A year later, when Lord Salisbury's government came to power in London and Joseph Chamberlain, Britain's most ardent imperialist, took office as colonial secretary, progress at last began to be made.

Donald was appointed one of the Canadian delegates to the Pacific Cable Conference which met first in July 1896, just before he went to Ottawa to meet Laurier. For the next four years, the Pacific cable was a thread running through his diplomatic duties as the colonies negotiated with the mother government about rates of subsidy, surveying the route and security of the line. The Eastern Extension Company tried to scupper progress at every turn and it was not until the last day of December 1900 that a contract was finally awarded for the laying of the cable. Donald was then appointed to the joint government commission responsible for managing the company. To his embarrassment, it soon transpired that the greatest number of errors and the greatest delays in transmitting messages were occurring in Canada, frequently on CPR cables. Errors were often caused by breaks in the lines but telegraph operators were careless too. In 1909, the chairman of the Pacific Cable Board, Henry Primrose, was obliged to point out that for every thousand errors made in Canada, only one hundred and seventy-six occurred in Australia. The average time of transmission from Bamfield, on the east coast of Vancouver Island, to Montreal was 317 minutes on one day in January 1909 while it was 443, or nearly seven and a half hours, on another. This was hardly the service which was expected and Donald swiftly took up the matter with Thomas Shaughnessy, by then CPR president.[13]

Uniform postage rates for mail between Britain and various parts of her empire also attracted the attention of imperial enthusiasts and Canada forced the issue at the end of 1897 by charging the equivalent of a British penny for letters to the UK. Donald attended the imperial postage conference the following summer and at Christmas 1898, penny postage came into force throughout the empire.

Late nineteenth century British imperialism was always coloured by the changing relationship between Britain and her self-governing colonies. Canada, South Africa, Australia and New Zealand were governed, for the most part, by men who had been born in the UK or who accepted the Westminster parliamentary model without question. They understood the principles of democratic government and increasingly demanded to be treated as independent entities, much in the way grown children who have set up homes for themselves expect to be allowed to make their own decisions. The countries of black Africa which had recently fallen under British influence had none of this experience and were disregarded in the clamour for a greater say in foreign policy. India, too, was not thought to be eligible for inclusion in fora where such issues were decided.

On matters of foreign policy and defense, Prime Minister Laurier and his high commissioner were much less enthusiastic about imperialism. Laurier particularly favoured a greater independence for Canada, or at least a greater say in imperial foreign policy where Canadian interests were concerned. Both men felt that the demands of the empire should not be allowed to diminish the importance of more strictly Canadian needs or restrict the growth of Canadian nationalism. Britain's lacklustre support for Canada when Americans transgressed Canadian rights in the Klondike during the gold rush of 1897 reinforced both men's view that Canada needed its own independent voice, albeit one which could be heard within an imperial context. In Washington in 1871 Donald had advised Macdonald that it was important to ensure that Canada retained rights to navigation on the Yukon River, of which the Klondike was a tributary, and proof of his conviction was now at hand. Britain, ostensibly Canada's voice in international affairs, had been prepared to throw away Canada's rights in the Yukon in 1871 because she was oblivious to their importance and little had changed by 1899 when Britain's representatives on the Alaska Boundary Commission felt they could agree to a compromise which was unacceptable to Canada.[14]

Initially, the self-governing colonies toyed with the idea of electing representatives to parliament in London but this was not a course of action Donald approved of. "As at present constituted, Parliament is occupied largely with local affairs, of little or no Imperial significance, important though they may be in themselves," he told an audience at the University of Aberdeen in 1900; "and in these circumstances it is not clear to me where the usefulness of Colonial members in either House would be apparent." He had no doubt that the time was fast approaching when "all parts of the Empire," by which he presumably meant India and the African countries as well, "will want to have a voice in Imperial foreign policy, and in other subjects affecting the well-being of the community in general." He was reluctant, especially in a public context, to say how this might be brought about, but suggested that an "Imperial Council" meeting regularly to discuss these matters could be a way forward, "even if the Council were only consultative at the commencement." In the end, each colony achieved its independence in its own way, but the seeds of an imperial council were established in the colonial conferences which, at Canada's insistence, were held regularly every four years. Eventually, these gatherings became the biennial Commonwealth Heads of Government Meetings.[15]

While Donald's thoughts about imperialism were primarily occupied with Canada controlling her own destiny, he also had one or two ideas about the outward manifestations of her independence. A case in point was the Canadian flag. In a letter to the Aberdeens written at the beginning of May 1897, he suggested that the queen's diamond jubilee year would offer a good occasion for Canada to stop using the red ensign and the Union Jack and adopt a flag of her own. He recommended a maple leaf, an idea which did not find favour until Canada's centennial year.[16]

When the Smiths moved to London, they retained their house in Montreal and occupied it once or twice a year when they visited Canada. Donald still owned Norway House and still hoped Jamesie might occupy it. The Hardisty house in Lachine was in Bella's name and, with still more additions, was let to tenants who ran it as a hotel. In Scotland, the Glencoe estate included Invercoe, a house in the village of Ballachulish on the shores of Loch Leven, as well as a seven bedroom shooting lodge and various houses for farm workers, estate managers and crofters. The Smiths were at Invercoe in September 1895 when Donald made a foolish mistake which suggested that his years in Canada had obliterated his appreciation of the sensitivities of Scottish clans.

Lord Archibald Campbell, the second son of the Duke of Argyll and brother of the Marquess of Lorne, was a cheerful and adventurous man who had visited Canada on several occasions and had almost certainly met Donald there. He was an enthusiastic supporter of the Celtic revival and had founded a festival of Scottish arts and culture at Oban, the west coast port where the trains terminated and from which the Smiths sailed to reach Glencoe. Campbell had formed a pipe band on the Argyll estate at Inverary, about thirty miles south of Ballachulish, and wanted to take it to the Oban mod that September. He had never been to Glencoe and also wanted to thank the choirs of Ballachulish and Glencoe for their help in setting up the mod and maintaining its high standards, so he decided to take his band to Oban by an indirect route through the Coe glen. Both Donald and the minister, Dr. Alex Stewart, whose writings in Gaelic contributed to the renaissance of Celtic culture, agreed to Campbell's proposal and Donald offered to entertain the band at Invercoe before taking them in the *Morag* to Oban. Both men, like Campbell, were oblivious to the insult the visit would cause to some of Donald's tenants.

In February 1692, the Macdonalds had been slow to accept William and Mary as the new monarchs of a united kingdom. When the undersecretary of state did receive the formal acknowledgement in Edinburgh, he suppressed the papers and ordered the Glenlyon Campbells to kill every Macdonald in the Coe valley. At the time the orders were received, the Campbells had been the guests of the Macdonalds, under a false pretext, for two weeks, so the vicious slaughter of men, women and children early in the morning of February 13 was a transgression of traditional highland hospitality, to say nothing of being a bloody end to a monstrous deceit. It is one of the most infamous stories in Scottish history which every Scottish child learns and Donald would have had his memory refreshed when he purchased Glencoe since the property included the island of St. Munda, the traditional burial place of the chiefs of the Macdonalds of Glencoe. But he, like Campbell and the Rev. Dr. Stewart, had focussed on the artistic and traditional values represented by the pipe band and assumed that time had dulled the emotions roused by the massacre.

At Glencoe, some Macdonalds were incensed when they learned that Lord Archibald Campbell had had the effrontery to plan a march through their glen, however peaceable his intentions and despite the fact that there was not a single Campbell in his pipe band. The *Glasgow Herald* wrote a tongue in cheek editorial, suggesting that the pipers would play laments in atonement for past crimes as they walked through the glen and that, in turn, provoked a spate of letters decrying Lord Archibald's "stupendous impudence."[17]

Bolting the barn door after their insensitivity had let the horse out, Donald and the Celtic revivalists did their best to pacify the irate Macdonalds and assure them that no slight was intended. It was Scottish traditions and Scottish culture which should be celebrated and not the country's divisive past. In the event, the "march" proved something of a storm in a whisky glass.

By the time they reached the upper entry to the glen, on the afternoon of September 9, the men were three hours behind schedule and the light was fading. Instead of walking, the seven pipers and three drummers found themselves "rattling smartly down the glen" in a coach and four, while Campbell and his daughter, Elspeth, travelled in a landau in which a bicycle was prominent. Before it got too dark, Miss Campbell set her bicycle on the rough drovers' road with a view to pedalling her way to Ballachulish. "The nature of the path, however, soon made this mode of locomotion somewhat toilsome," the *Herald* explained to its readers, "and the young lady resumed her seat in the carriage." The Macdonalds stayed in their crofts and only the winking of their lights behind twitching curtains suggested they were watching this curious procession.[18]

At the Clachaig Inn, where the wild mountain pass broadens into lush greenery, the band was greeted by Dr. Stewart and an inquisitive crowd. By then, it was too dark to see that the inn, which Donald owned, bore the sign: "No Hawkers. No Circulars. No Campbells." Plans to walk the remaining six miles were abandoned and the pipers, accompanied by those who had come up to greet them, rode down to Ballachulish. Villagers with torches lit the way to Invercoe House where the band played and two local choirs sang their welcome.

No doubt those Macdonalds who had fulminated against this quaint excursion soon saw that they had been egged on by the press and one or two malcontents, but they were also canny enough to perceive that life at Glencoe was about to change and that they were to be among the beneficiaries. The estate, which had been sold by the previous owner's widower, had been on the market for some time and the reserve price had been lowered to £13,330 shortly before it was auctioned in Edinburgh in 1894. Though Donald and Bella would rarely spend more than one month in twelve at Glencoe, they would add substantially to the income of the area by offering both temporary and permanent employment and they unquestionably had more prestige than the widower who seems to have depended on the village post office for his livelihood.[19]

In 1895, Donald commissioned Rowand Atkinson to design a new house for him at Glencoe. Though he had houses scattered across Canada and would acquire more homes before his life was out, Donald only once had an opportunity to say exactly what he wanted. The site he chose was on a hill above the village of Ballachulish with a view to Loch Leven and the burial grounds on St. Munda. Terraces were cut in the hillside to make a garden while behind it, the Pap of Glencoe rose in the mists. Atkinson was Scotland's most famous architect, known for his baronial style, and his instructions seem to have been to create a family seat which would commemorate Donald's marriage to Bella and to provide a Scottish base for future generations. Because of the sloping site, the house ranged between two and three storeys with an attic containing servants' quarters. In addition to bedrooms in the main body of the house, wings to either side provided nearly two dozen bedrooms for the many guests whom the Smiths were to entertain.

On the main floor of the centre block, there was a lounge with a grand piano, a drawing room with a spinet, a morning room, a library and a dining room, as well as two bedrooms, cloakrooms and the like. The multi-coloured ceilings were elaborately plastered with thistles, fleurs-de-lis, roses, maple leaves and oak leaves, all reminiscent of the English, Scottish and Canadian blood which mingled in the veins of Maggie's children. Pretty tiles surrounded the fireplaces and the grates were decorated with beautiful brasswork. The principal staircase, floored with white marble, was not as grand as the one in Dorchester Street, but nonetheless made a striking impression. Upstairs, the master bedroom had both a bathroom and a dressing room *en suite*. Pantries and other facilities to make the servants' lives easier were dotted about.

Throughout, the house was lined with blue asbestos, now known to be a dangerous carcinogenic but then valued as an efficient fire retardant. Thick doors were stuffed with asbestos between the hardwood panels and the interconnecting rooms on the ground floor all had air locks. These ensured privacy, as servants would close one door before opening the next, but they would also slow the spread of fire. Fifty years had passed since Donald had damaged his eyes at Mingan and since Bella had been forced to flee when her uncle Corcoran's house had burned at Albany, but neither of them had forgotten the horror of those experiences. They insisted that Glencoe House have the highest standards of fireproofing.

Outside, the house was faced with local grey granite and trimmed with polished red sandstone. Carved into the stone above some of the windows was Donald's crest, a beaver gnawing at the base of a maple tree, sometimes with *Perseverance* on a scroll, sometimes surmounted by a thistle and sometimes by a fleur-de-lis. The beaver, the tree and the motto, all taken directly from the North West Company's coat of arms, demonstrated again how Donald traced his lineage through his uncles and cousins who had explored Canada's prairie provinces, discovered British Columbia's northern lakes, and traced the Fraser River to its mouth. The beaver also linked Donald with the Canadian Pacific Railway for Van Horne, in designing the company's corporate symbol, had paid Donald a subtle compliment in selecting his beaver, gnawing some maple leaves, as the railway's identifying image.

Above other windows at Glencoe House were carved *DAS* and *ISS*, the latter sometimes in the Latin style as *JSS*. In spelling out in its decorative motifs the experiences and nationalities which had come together in their marriage, the house was a grand love letter from Donald to Bella in celebration of their life together. The initials, hers separate to indicate that she was an individual in her own right and not merely his adjunct, were the baronial equivalent of the school boy's DAS + ISS TRUE.

When a man devotes his thoughts and his energies to devising a gift which is not merely a present but a love token, his beloved, if she returns his affection, is wisest if she acknowledges her lover's motivating passion rather than its outward manifestation. Bella kept her thoughts to herself, but she hated Glencoe. More often than not, the mountains behind the house, all rounded outpourings of ancient volcanoes, were shrouded in cloud and the mist poured down through the valley to envelop the house and embrace the fog rolling in off Loch Leven. The grouse moors were so dank that in the first year the Smiths were in Glencoe, before the new house was built, the paper covered cartridges disintegrated.

Bella enjoyed having her grandchildren around her at Glencoe House and liked to listen to their lively stories about competing with seals for the salmon in the loch, but she had done her fishing a long time ago. The month or six weeks they spent at Glencoe each year was punctuated by visits, often by Canadian or American businessmen and politicians who clearly appreciated the hospitality. But Donald would nip off to London for two or three days, leaving Bella and Maggie to deal with gentlemen, often without their wives, with whom they had very little in common. Bella was always glad to see old friends such as Sandford Fleming and his daughters, but she did feel trapped and not a little bored at Glencoe. She was seldom without her knitting: there were few young mothers in London, Montreal or Glencoe who did not receive a shawl or jacket or boots for their newborn children, but busy hands were no substitute for companionship. And Donald's cables of affection were no substitute for the man.

By the spring of 1897, perhaps because Whitehall and Windsor had had an opportunity to judge Donald at first hand, it was finally decided to raise him to the peerage. The celebrations to mark the diamond jubilee of Queen Victoria's accession to the throne were also a factor, for the occasion was to be used to honour many men, both at home and in the colonies. Once again, it raised the question of Donald's marriage and when he was in New York at the end of April, on his way back from Canada where he had gone on government and Great Northern business, he arranged for John Sterling to provide a notarized statement confirming the Labrador marriage.

Back in London, when Donald met Chamberlain on other matters, he was told that a peerage would be offered. In response, he expressed his desire "that it should descend to my daughter and only child Mrs. Howard, but he seemed to think this course so very unusual as to be all but impossible if not wholly so." Donald was in two minds about whether to accept the peerage and sought Sterling's advice. "My own feeling would be to decline the offer," he confessed, "but the matter has been in the minds of many of my friends for so long and their insistence that I should not again — for in a sence [sic] it was known this had been proposed before — refuse the proffered distinction has been so strong that I almost feel myself precluded from saying so."

Donald was also worried that Jamesie might misunderstand and think that he, and his son after him, would inherit the title. As Donald was back in London and could not conceive of dealing with such a matter except face to face, he asked Sterling to either invite Jamesie to New York or go to Montreal "though not ostensibly for that purpose" and explain to him "that as my wife's sone [sic] by a former marriage, but not mine, he has legally no standing as respects myself and consequently in a legal view [is] entitled to no consideration or privilege on account of his being my stepson and adopted son. His son should also be made to know this as otherwise much that would be awkward might arise from his being ignorant of the facts." In the strictest sense of the word, Jamesie was not even his adopted son; no legal steps had ever been taken to formalize the arrangement though Jamesie also referred to himself as being Donald's adopted son.[20]

Jamesie had been a worry over the years but his response on this occasion was all that Donald could have wished — except that it was sent to Maggie.

> I know mother would have written me on the subject if she had been able. I believe that her hope to live long enough to see Sir

> Donald raised to the Peerage has kept her alive through her most severe illness this winter. She need have no misgiving, that I would attempt to claim any succession to the new title. I am as well aware as anyone can be that you are the only child of Sir Donald and my mother. Many people here, who do not know the circumstances, think that I am your full brother, just because I have been brought up by Sir Donald as a son. He certainly has been like a real father to me from the time my own father deserted my mother and left Labrador. I feel so much gratitude and love for him for all that he has done for me and mine that I could never be guilty of the meanness of making any claim adverse to the interest of one whom I know to be his only child.[21]

Bella's health was still enough of a worry that Jamesie did not write her directly but asked Maggie to pass on the contents of his letter if she thought their mother well enough to read it.

In the same post, Jamesie's son, Donald Alexander, known to the family as Aleck, also wrote his aunt Maggie to say, "My father is really just as much rejoiced as if he were his real son."[22]

The diamond jubilee honours were officially announced on the evening of June 21. Though he had had time to consider by what title he would like to be known, Donald had reached no conclusion, nor would he for some time to come. Many assumed he would be Lord Glencoe and some people even addressed him by that title. Mount Stephen was not consulted on Donald's title and, at the end of August, incorrectly assumed that no decision had yet been reached. "What a strange creature he is, so Indian like in his love of mystery & secretiveness," he wrote to J.J. Hill. Mount Stephen was not the one to talk. His letter to Hill had for its main purpose the expression of thanks for a portrait of his late wife which Hill had arranged to be made from a photograph. It was not, perhaps the most appropriate moment at which to reveal that in November he was going to marry Gian Tufnell, a lady-in-waiting to Princess Mary, the mother of the future Queen Mary.[23]

Some time before his cousin wrote J.J. Hill, Donald had settled on Lord Strathcona and Mount Royal of Glencoe, in the County of Argyll, and of Mount Royal, in the Province of Quebec and Dominion of Canada. Though "Strathcona" sounds like a Scottish word, reminiscent of Strathmore, Strathclyde and even Strathconan, it was created by the new baron. "Strath" is Gaelic for "broad valley" and "cona," a reference to the River Coe, flowing through the glen to Loch Leven. Mount Royal, of course, is the mountain after which Montreal is named and both McGill University and the Royal Victoria Hospital are at its base.

In choosing Strathcona, Donald placed an emphasis on the Scottish seat through which he was demonstrating the legitimacy of his heirs, but Leanchoil must have been tempting, with its links to his mother's family. The word was still resonant with meaning for him and he still used it as his personal cable address in the UK; it was also the code by which he was referred to in confidential cables between J.J. Hill, Van Horne and Lord Mount Stephen. It was, however, a word which was bound to be mispronounced in England and Canada and that was sufficient argument against it. He might have incorporated a reference to St. Lawrence, alluding both to the Canadian river and to the parish kirk at Forres. In 1894, he had a seal with the beaver, a lion, a thistle and the gridiron on which St. Lawrence was martyred, but Strathcona and St. Lawrence had an inappropriate religious overtone and a less satisfying sonority than Strathcona and Mount Royal.

As a baron, Donald was also expected to have a coat of arms and crest and he registered his in Scotland on the twenty-second of August. The crest was easily determined: he chose the beaver gnawing at the maple tree with *Perseverance* as his motto above it. The escutcheon which formed the centre of the coat of arms was divided into three bands. On top was what the heralds referred to as a demi-lion rampant; in the middle was "a hammer surmounted by a nail in saltire of the last," meaning that the hammer and the nail, of the sort which had been pounded into thousands of railway sleepers, including the CPR's last spike, were crossed diagonally in the manner of the cross of St. Andrew, Scotland's patron saint. In the bottom band was "a canoe with four men paddling," and flowing out from the front of the boat was a flag with NW inscribed on it. The image is taken directly from the North West Company's own crest in which a canoe is being paddled by eight Indians while a bearded man in European dress, including a beaver hat, sits in the middle. The company flag flies from the stern.[24]

London was *en fête* for the old queen's diamond jubilee. Representatives from India and the self-governing colonies gathered for the celebrations and for the colonial conference which was also scheduled for June. Many besides Donald received honours that summer, among them Sandford Fleming who was knighted. Lord Aberdeen and Donald arranged for Wilfrid Laurier to be knighted during the celebrations, but kept it a secret from the prime minister until the last minute to prevent him from turning it down. Laurier was one of the stars of the festivities; he turned the ladies' heads wherever he went and easily carried the lead at the colonial conference. Donald was delighted to be able to introduce such a man as his country's leader and the two men cemented a friendship that summer that was to last the rest of their lives. Frederick Borden, Laurier's militia minister, commented on it after a visit to Glencoe in September 1900. "There is no doubt I think of the friendship of Lord Strathcona both, & *especially*, to yourself personally & to the Government as a whole. Equally is there no doubt of his personal dislike of Tupper & contempt for many of those who surround him."[25]

As the actual date of Queen Victoria's accession, June 20, fell on a Sunday in 1897, celebrations began the following day with a state dinner at Buckingham Palace and a reception to follow. While the dinner was a relatively small "family" affair for the queen and her numerous royal relatives, the reception was a grand and formal occasion, organized, so it was alleged, by courtiers who wanted to take the wind out of Alfred Harmsworth's sails.

Two years earlier, Harmsworth, later to become Lord Northcliffe, had founded the *Daily Mail* and in the jubilee year, Beckles Willson, a Canadian, had written a long series of articles about Canada under the banner "Our Western Empire." These accounts heralded the colonial conference and when Willson and Harmsworth, in the full flush of their imperial enthusiasm, discovered that the visiting premiers, being unknown, were unwelcome in the best London drawing rooms, they set about providing a countervailing force. The newspaper was filled with profiles of the men and their countries and Willson, in Harmsworth's name, organized a grand reception at the proprietor's Berkeley Square home. Nellie Melba, the great Australian soprano, her compatriot, the contralto Ada Crossley, and Jan Paderewski, the famous Polish pianist, were all engaged to entertain the guests. The premiers were invited and so too was the cream of London society, starting with the Prince of Wales. After fifteen hundred invitations had gone out for June 21, the palace announced its reception, accusing Harmsworth of "pushful Imperialism." "I am afraid I also am laying myself open to the charge of pushful Imperialism," Donald acknowledged, for the reception was precisely the sort of occasion he wanted in order to bring Canada to the fore.[26]

It was a glittering evening, especially when the colonial premiers and their countries' UK representatives arrived, resplendent in their Windsor uniforms, with knee breeches, cocked hats and swords, after the Buckingham Palace party. At midnight, the announcement of the new honours added to the excitement of the evening.

On the following day, a massive parade wound its way through London to St. Paul's Cathedral. Canada contributed an official militia contingent of two hundred men, enlarged by a further twelve "officers" who were so eager to be in London for the celebrations that they wheedled their way into the militia as temporary officers. The queen decreed that she was too lame to mount the grand flight of steps at the cathedral, so the service of thanksgiving for her long reign took place outdoors and she followed it from her carriage. On Thursday, June 24, Donald was present as the colonial conference got under way and that evening he and Bella joined government and diplomatic officials for another reception at Buckingham Palace. On June 29, he hosted a Dominion Day dinner for three hundred gentlemen.[27]

It fell to Rudyard Kipling to remind the British not to mistake the pomp and glory of the jubilee celebrations for anything other than surface polish. Published in *The Times* on July 17, "Recessional" warned of the dangers of "frantic boast and foolish word" and reminded its readers that "all our pomp of yesterday/Is one with Nineveh and Tyre!" The poem's message that God expected "an humble and a contrite heart" was exactly attuned to Donald's own thinking; it chimed with the eleventh paraphrase which exhorted him to choose celestial wisdom over material glory and reminded him that his houses, his money, his new title, his grand hospitality, were worthless if his spiritual core was hollow. He cut out the poem and kept it on his desk until he had committed it to memory.[28]

On July 6, Donald paused in the busy round of jubilee activities to chair the Hudson's Bay Company's General Court at the City Terminus Hotel. The HBC occupied at least a day a week when Donald was in London and meetings were more frequent in the weeks immediately before and after the General Court. Though it interfered to some extent with his duties as high commissioner, he felt no compunction about accepting the nomination for re-election as governor that summer. After acknowledging the congratulations on his peerage, he drew the shareholders' attention to the many men they did not know who were the bedrock of the company.

> It is a long life — looking back almost 60 years — in a country much of which is also outside what is usually known as civilization, but such has been the life of many of those who were connected with your service. They have been many of them more self-sacrificing than I have been, and I feel that they deserve your

> best opinion and your best wishes in every respect. Isolated as they are, thousands of miles from the common haunts of civilised men, it is often no easy matter for a man to reconcile himself to the duties he has before him; and to my knowledge there are those in the country who have sacrificed themselves — not only their pleasure and their convenience, — but their very lives in doing their duty to the Hudson's Bay Company. I think it is only fitting that I should say for these gentlemen, that I believe no corporation and no body of men have ever been before more honestly, more honourably and more efficiently served than you and those who preceded you for so many years back.[29]

The more the HBC grew away from its fur trading past and turned itself into a chain of stores, the more the investors appreciated stories from a man who had once been a fur trader himself. Donald increasingly enjoyed reminiscing, but he was also aware that the Deed Poll of 1893, guaranteeing the rights of the old wintering partners, would need defending in the coming years. All newcomers were now on salary and the Deed Poll would only survive on the sufferance of the board and the shareholders. As Archibald McDonald at Qu'Appelle had remarked when he returned his signed agreement for the 1893 Deed Poll, "Undoubtedly there was a feeling of uneasiness, as to what the result of the Guarantee would be in the event of my friend Sir Donald Smith leaving the Board."[30]

The summer of 1897 was a busy one, partly as a consequence of the jubilee, and several weeks passed before Donald was able to find time to correct the transcript of his speech and prepare it for publication. It was trying for William Ware, who had replaced Armit as the company's secretary; so too was Donald's absent mindedness when it came to cashing the cheque for his fee as governor. On several occasions over the coming years, the staff would be obliged to remind him to deposit the money so that they could settle the company's accounts and, on one occasion, they had to provide him with a new cheque since the original was out of date. This reflected a carelessness about his own welfare —he was more interested in his work — but it also related to the fact that he did not believe in accepting money for directorships until he had served the complete term to which the fee referred. In the case of the Third National Bank of New York, which paid him in advance and was probably seeking his influence as much as his advice, the cheque went into the vault and stayed there, much to the annoyance of Joseph Hardisty who liked things to be tidy. He equally declined to cash his CPR director's cheques while he was high commissioner, worrying lest his railway and his government interests conflict. On his death, his solicitors presented them all for payment.[31]

At the end of the summer, Lord and Lady Strathcona were in Montreal for the annual meeting of the British Medical Association where, Donald said, he hoped that the doctors would have learned the "climactic advantages of [Canada's] position as a health resort, and as a new field of travel in the case of those requiring both rest and change — without the necessity of giving the change to the waiters and the rest to the keepers of the hotels." Bella's visits to Carlsbad and Nice had obviously made an impression![32]

In October, he addressed the medical students at Middlesex Hospital. The invitation came from his own doctor, William Pasteur, and he had assumed that he would merely be handing out prizes and mouthing a few generalities, until it was made clear to him that something a little more substantial was expected. What he offered his listeners (after a brief advertisement for Canada's health giving properties) was a concise catalogue of the physical attributes and health, the diseases and the treatments among the natives of Labrador. Children often died of lung diseases; rheumatism was rare, fevers were common; baldness and loss of hair colour were unusual. "So long as the natives keep to their own food and habits — they live largely on meat and fish, always cooked, and upon wild berries and fruits — they generally retain their teeth, in fact I have seen teeth worn almost to the gums without showing signs of decay. But in the case of the natives of the Interior, who soon adopted the food of the white men, they soon lost their teeth; and from indigestion, and it may be from other causes incident to the change of living, their lives were often shortened." He also told them about steam baths and the use of juniper as an antiseptic and observed that a positive attitude did much to further recovery. The speech was tailored for his audience, presenting his observations and stating what he perceived to be cause and effect with regard to health and life expectancy. Unlike some of his speeches to less cohesive groups, this one was devoid of generalities and revealed that he had lost none of his interest in medicine. The following year, the British Medical Association elected him an honourary member.[33]

When he was in Canada in the summer, Donald had been to Ottawa for discussions with Clifford Sifton, the minister of the interior and now the man responsible for immigration. Both he and the high commissioner were keen to develop an immigration policy which would bring to the country men who would occupy the lands of the Northwest. This involved Donald speaking at every possible opportunity in order to increase people's awareness of the country; it also meant that he made numerous efforts to get Canadian events covered by the British press. As none of the UK papers had Canadian correspondents, this was not easy. The only newspaper which regularly carried any Canadian news was *The Times* which, as Donald pointed out to Laurier, "has a comparatively limited circulation, and does not reach the middle class. Consequently very little information relating to the commercial or industrial progress of the country reaches the larger public, and a valuable medium for educating the people of the United Kingdom about the resources and capabilities of Canada is lacking." He thought that if Laurier could feed him with news, he could pass it on to the press. Unfortunately, he could not make the papers print it any more than he could make the general public read the *Canada Gazette* which George Stephen had founded in 1882 in a bid to inform people about the Northwest and encourage investment in the CPR.[34]

Throughout Britain, a network of immigration agents maintained contacts with communities which might want to seek a new future in Canada. Donald was meant to supervise these agents but Sifton's office corresponded directly and the agents bypassed London to file their reports and accounts to Ottawa. Donald repeatedly complained that the arrangement was unsatisfactory, pointing out that "if any supervision is to be exercised over the Agents and their work, it can only be effectively carried out if they receive their instructions and make their reports through this office. If this is not done no supervision can be effectual." Sifton, however, was not willing to give up direct management of his agents, the more so since Donald had a host of other problems calling for his attention and his secretary, Joseph Colmer, who carried much responsibility in the office, was known to be unsympathetic to the Liberal Party.[35]

The flow of emigrants from Britain tended to reflect agricultural conditions in the UK and the attractiveness of the publicity material produced to entice men and their families to the Northwest. In France, Germany and the Scandinavian countries, however, Donald's job was significantly more difficult because it was illegal to advocate emigration. In 1898, Donald visited Germany and Austria to discover for himself what the restrictions were and how Canada might deal with them. Agents for the various steamship companies received capitation fees for each emigrant who passed through their hands and one of his tasks was to encourage the agents, though he and Sifton also hoped that he would be able to negotiate changes to the bonus system which would reduce Canada's expenses. As well, Donald wanted to use the trip to learn more about the kaiser's new law, designed to tighten up restrictions against promoting emigration. He had only a limited grasp of how his behaviour would be perceived by less liberal eyes. "The arrogance of the Canadian, Lord Strathcona," fulminated the *Hamburger Nachrichten*, "and the utter disrespect shown by him for the laws of the Empire in publicly conducting his emigration propaganda on German soil and in the very teeth of the authorities, demand that vigorous representations should be made at once to the British Government which is, we presume, still responsible for this Colony. While apart from the weakening of the Fatherland which the success of such propaganda entails, the attempt to lure our fellow-countrymen to this desolate, sub-arctic region is, upon humane grounds alone, to be denounced as criminal."[36]

The objections were not confined to the public prints. Count Hatzfeldt, the German ambassador, complained to Lord Salisbury who was both prime minister and foreign secretary. In turn, Chamberlain sent his private secretary, Lord Ampthill, to the high commissioner's office. The fact that Donald was not summoned to the Colonial Office indicates that Chamberlain was not inclined to take the complaint seriously but it still made Donald uncomfortable. In response, he wrote Chamberlain to say that his German visit related to emigration by people from Galicia, then part of the Austro-Hungarian empire, who were obliged to use the ports of Bremen and Hamburg and who travelled in German ships. That was true, but it certainly was not the whole truth. He had had lengthy discussions with the shipping companies and the agents about the German law prohibiting emigration propaganda and about the secret bonus system which was meant to induce the agents to encourage emigrants to go to Canada rather than the United States or South America. On his return to London in March, he had written three reports to Sifton outlining in detail what he had done, who he had seen and what suggestions had been made by the shipping agents. "I have not the slightest idea what gave rise to the action of the German Government in the matter," he wrote to Sifton following Count Hatzfeldt's complaint, but he worried that his reports might have been leaked and reached the ears of the German consul in Ottawa. Loose tongues in Hamburg or Berlin, were also a possibility, he acknowledged, a more likely explanation in view of the fact that the German minister for the interior complained to the British ambassador in Berlin.[37]

Donald was very uncomfortable with an emigration system which required him to breach German law, less because of the illegality than because it was impossible to work confidentially when such a large number of people were involved. Ostensibly, dealings were through the North Atlantic Trading Company, a loose coalition of continental shipping agents, but it still involved Canadian officials breaking the law. Since it was also apparent that demands on his own time were increasing almost daily, he suggested that the post of inspector for immigration agencies be created on his staff. The idea was a good one and the Canadian High Commission in London has had an immigration officer ever since. Unfortunately, in the first instance, Sifton and Laurier decided to appoint W.T.R. Preston who had been the Ontario organizer for the Liberal Party and was owed a favour. He was arrogant and argumentative, two-faced, and fond of pursuing petty arguments, enunciating them in long-winded and repetitive detail in letters to Laurier. His disruptive behaviour in the emigration office led ultimately to a hearing before the public accounts committee and his removal from responsibilities in London.

In 1899, Preston reformed the North Atlantic Trading Company, using his son-in-law and his relatives to set up the new arrangement. Donald objected, arguing that it contravened the laws in Germany and other European countries which prohibited emigration propaganda. He said it was wrong for the Canadian government to be party to such an arrangement and advised that if it had to go ahead, it should be on the basis of letters of agreement rather than a formal contract. He would object more strongly, he said, had it not been clear that the Department of the Interior favoured the agreement. Preston's creation of a Canadian Labour Bureau to sell steamship tickets to emigrants further angered many people. It was a private company giving every appearance of being a branch of the Canadian government, even to the extent of allowing the emigration office to pay surreptitiously for its heat and telephones.

Disputes over expense claims, printers' bills and the opening of confidential mail ran on for years. Donald tried to bring people into line but, as he had warned Sifton, because he exercised no direct responsibility, he found it impossible to bring Preston to heel or to ensure that he managed his staff properly. Acres of paper, most of it directed to Laurier or Sifton, was wasted in Preston's incessantly regurgitated arguments and his ire was further roused when Joseph Colmer resigned in exasperation and was replaced by William Griffith with whom Preston had quarrelled when Griffith was in the emigration office.

Preston's behaviour finally wore down even Laurier's patience.

> Allow me to call to your attention the tone in which you speak of the High Commissioner. You say that you should not be allowed to be made the victim of Lord Strathcona's spleen. I am much surprised at the tone of this remark as in the many conversations I had the pleasure of having with you during your stay in Ottawa, you not only always spoke with consideration of Lord Strathcona, but you always expressed yourself as gratified at his uniform kindness and courtesy. I certainly shared then and still share now this opinion. I told you before and I beg to repeat that Lord Strathcona spoke in the most

> complimentary terms of yourself and the manner in which you discharge your work. The only fault he ever found with you was that you were unduly aggressive in your relations with the different agents and employees of the Government on the other side.[38]

In 1907, Preston was sent to the far east and courtesy and good manners returned to the emigration office.

The one interesting point to emerge from all the squabbling was that Preston overspent his budget and found himself early in 1905 unable to pay the rent or taxes on the emigration office in Trafalgar Square. He mentioned this to Donald who borrowed enough money from the bank to cover the overdue payments. It happened again at the end of April 1905, but on this occasion Donald personally borrowed the money to enable the emigration department to meet its obligations.[39]

As the century wound to a close, Donald became increasingly better known to British men and women beyond the financial circles in which he had moved in the past. His huge Dominion Day dinners for influential gentlemen and the receptions which he and Bella hosted for mixed company at the end of the day came to be events for which invitations were eagerly sought. Donald accepted virtually every request to speak about Canada and became adept at turning any public speech around to emigration, trade and Canadian loyalty to the crown.

On February 15, 1898, Donald was introduced to the House of Lords by Lord Balfour of Burleigh and Lord Bagot and took his oath of allegiance on bended knee. On July 8 that year, he made his maiden speech, introducing the second reading of the Deceased Wife's Sister Bill. It was an extraordinary topic with which to make his debut, even though he happened to believe the principle which it embodied. In Britain, the law accepted that a married couple were as one and that therefore a man's sister-in-law was to be treated as though she were his own sister. Similarly, a woman's brother-in-law was to be treated as her own brother. From this it followed that marriage to the sister of one's deceased wife or to the brother of one's deceased husband was incestuous. The restriction contradicted the injunction in *Deuteronomy* calling upon a man to marry his brother's widow if she had not borne him any children, but it was nonetheless strictly adhered to. One of Henry VIII's reasons for divorcing Catherine of Aragon was that he had offended the Almighty by marrying her, since she was his brother's widow. When Canada wanted to appoint Sir Alexander Galt as high commissioner, it had first been necessary to obtain Queen Victoria's dispensation because he had married his deceased wife's sister. The queen decided that since such a marriage was legal in the United States where it had taken place and because Lady Galt had been received in Canadian society, the couple could be allowed to occupy a position in British society as well.[40]

The bill, which had been thrown out on previous occasions and was to be defeated many more times, was not about moral issues but about the inheritance of real property in Britain by children considered illegitimate under British law. It was not designed to make marrying one's deceased wife's sister legal in Britain but merely to permit recognition of such marriages where they had been legally contracted and thus to accept succession to real property in the UK.

"Why should the children of such marriages, when they come home to the Mother Country, bear the mark of illegitimacy?" Donald demanded of his fellow peers.[41]

The Marriage Law Reform Association which had asked Donald to introduce the bill saw it as a first step towards making marriage with a deceased wife's sister legal in Britain but were prepared to approach the subject gradually since earlier efforts to bring in wider reforms had failed. Donald pointed out that the law sanctioning such marriages in the colonies had been signed by the queen and should therefore be recognized in the UK but he accepted that in committee the proposed legislation would be altered to forbid recognition of marriages which had taken place abroad solely for the purpose of circumventing British law on this point.

As a representative of the largest self-governing colony in which such marriages were legal, Donald was a logical person to speak in the interests of the bill but the fact that he agreed to do so in the light of the continuing gossip about his own marriage suggests both an insensitivity on the part of those who asked him to introduce the second reading and a remarkable self-confidence on his own part. "His Labrador lordship," Queen Victoria is said to have sniffed, "should be the last to meddle in these matters." She is also said to have observed that Bella had obviously not been consulted on the subject. As the legitimacy of both Jamesie and Maggie was questionable, the queen had a point, but she was well wide of the mark if she thought that Bella had no influence over her husband or if she thought that Donald did not take her feelings into account. Donald certainly had obtained Laurier's official approval before agreeing to speak and the presence of both the Prince of Wales and his son, the Duke of York, in the House of Lords that July afternoon suggests that the royal family was also prepared to support the idea. Though it passed through the Lords, the Commons defeated the bill as it did its successor, which Donald introduced two years later. It fell to a later generation to change the law.[42]

Throughout 1898, Donald's social life grew increasingly busy. Privately, he and Bella saw Sandford Fleming whenever he was in London or they were in Canada and they frequently had Agnes Macdonald, the prime minister's widow, for a Sunday quiet lunch in London. Canadian businessmen and politicians with whom they had more than just a professional link also came to the house for dinner and Bella was "at home" one day a week. In the summer, J.J. Hill sent Adolf Müller-Ury, a young German artist who had emigrated to the United States and whom he wanted to encourage, to paint portraits of George Mount Stephen and Lord Strathcona as gifts for these friends. After starting on Donald's picture, Müller-Ury came down with a cold and was obliged to interrupt his work for a week, as he explained in a letter to his patron, adding, "Lord Strathcona is one of the most charming & magnetic man I ever seen & I am sure that his portrait will be even more successful than the one of Lord Mount Stephen. Lord Strathcona showed much kindness when I was ill — in coming twice to see me. His wife was quite sick again — & if better I would have an order to paint her."[43]

Most of these private activities were unrecorded but there is enough evidence to suggest that the Strathconas were busier than many couples half their age. Donald's professional social life, however, was even fuller and was beginning to be conducted on a very grand scale. In July 1898, the fourth Earl of Minto was appointed governor general and Donald gave a dinner for him at the Athenaeum Club, inviting senior members of the British cabinet and Canadian ministers who were in London for the imperial postage conference. In Montreal in December, he again hosted the Mintos. "Last week we had very hard work at Montreal," Minto groaned in a letter to his brother. "Old Strathcona is a dear old man but his hospitality was simply overpowering. Huge luncheons and dinners every day & receptions in the evening — the receptions consisting of formal presentations — and as one night there were around 1,000 present, we were quite exhausted." Minto grumbled and was rude, but the governor general's budget was so restricted that without Donald's hospitality, he could not afford to be in Montreal. Nor was entertaining on such a scale peculiar to Donald and Bella, though people did comment on how lavish they were. In 1903, for example, when the Alaska Boundary Commission was meeting in London, Lady Lansdowne, wife of the foreign secretary, gave a reception for 2,000.[44]

It was partly with a view to improving their opportunities for official entertaining that the Strathconas leased Knebworth House in 1899. Many of the English capital's residents perceive their homes there as temporary because their hearts are in the countryside. Amongst the established families, those hearts are ensconced in large, sometimes palatial mansions previously occupied by their forefathers, but less wealthy people also own houses and cottages in rural villages to which they retreat at weekends and at holiday times. This was especially so at the turn of the century when London was foggy and dirty. Families either lived in the country, to be joined by the *paterfamilias* at weekends, or they all migrated on Friday evenings, returning to London on Sunday evening or Monday morning. Oscar Wilde's *The Importance of Being Earnest* hinges on this custom. "The season," when daughters were launched in London society, involved staying in London throughout July at a time when coal fires were not lit and the air was comparatively smog free. In such an environment, both social and atmospheric, it was inevitable that Donald and Bella should seek a country house which would be close enough to London for weekend use, unlike Glencoe which required a night and a day to reach.

Knebworth, had been built around a courtyard in the early sixteenth century. In 1811, however, three sides were pulled down and the fourth received an extensive Victorian gothic overlay. Eight towers were added and battlements were constructed on the roof; later, gargoyles and a miscellany of heraldic devices were attached. For Donald and Bella, and even more for some of their Canadian visitors, however, there was much in the house to delight them. The banqueting hall with its musicians' gallery, though somewhat altered in the seventeenth century and later painted, was essentially as it was originally made and so too was the state drawing room where Queen Elizabeth had been received in 1588. An inscription over a fireplace recorded her visit. When the Strathconas occupied the house, it was believed that the queen had spent the night there and the bed she was thought to have occupied was pointed out to visitors. "I at once lay down on the bed to say I had slept in the same bed as the great Queen," the usually staid Joseph Pope noted in his diary when he was a house guest in 1903.[45]

A further attraction was the fact that the house had been inherited in 1843 by Edward Bulwer who had added Lytton to his surname in recognition of the fact that the Lyttons had owned the property in the fifteenth century. Inheritance of the house had often been indirect, through cousins or through women whose names had changed with marriage and it was a well-established tradition to assume the Lytton name on inheritance. The library where Bulwer Lytton had written such popular historical novels as *The Last Days of Pompeii* and *Rienzi* had been preserved for the edification of visitors. His son, Robert, the first earl of Lytton, had inherited his father's talent for facile verse which he published as Owen Meredith. As the first viceroy of India, he had gathered a collection of souvenirs which, during Donald's occupancy of the house, were displayed in a room off the state drawing room.

"The present owner, Lord Lytton," Pope confided to his diary, "grandson of the novelist[,] is too poor to keep it up. He rents it to Lord Strathcona for £2,000 a year." The gardens were used for large outdoor parties on summer afternoons and the 156 acres of deer park surrounding the house gave overnight visitors plenty of scope for walks in the fresh air; on Sundays, house guests were expected to join Knebworth villagers in the parish church of St. Mary and St. Thomas of Canterbury, built 800 years before in the grounds of the house.

Knewbworth was used for summer garden parties, replete with military bands and vast numbers of guests. Eight thousand were invited on one occasion and five thousand turned up. Among those who regularly received invitations was Joseph Chamberlain, of whom the politician Henry Labouchere remarked in 1896, "he is clever but a gentleman he will never be." Some found the colonial secretary's forthright style abrasive and there is no indication that Donald and Chamberlain ever became personal friends, perhaps for that reason. Politically and diplomatically, however, they saw eye to eye on many issues, differing primarily when Donald put Canadian issues before what Chamberlain saw as greater imperial demands.[46]

Chamberlain's political base was in Birmingham, the heavily industrialized Midlands city, where he had been mayor from 1873 to 1876. He had scant time for privilege, believing that each man should be given the opportunity to make the best of his life. It was a view with which Donald could easily sympathize and he was therefore receptive to Chamberlain's suggestion, in 1899, that he help in the creation of the University of Birmingham. Specifically, Chamberlain wanted Donald to support a faculty of commerce, a field of study which had been established in North America but was rare in England. No university in the UK offered commerce as a subject in which young men could take their first degree.

When Donald returned from his brother's funeral in Edinburgh, he wrote Chamberlain, agreeing to give £25,000 to the university's endowment fund as soon as it raised the remainder of its goal of £300,000. Chamberlain then sent a letter to Andrew Carnegie who promptly responded that he would "like to class myself with that anonymous fellow-countryman of whom you speak, and promise you £25,000 as he has, upon the same conditions." Carnegie's money was to be used to help "the gifted sons of the poor" whose education would be "not only a matter of benefit to themselves, but probably to the community."[47]

Donald's correspondence with Chamberlain was exceedingly formal, even by his own strict standards, and suggests that he felt uncomfortable dealing with the colonial secretary on non-government business. "I am very sensible of the kind way in which you refer to my own little efforts to forward the good work you have undertaken of providing Birmingham with a university which while affording scientific teaching will not overlook what is of not less importance that of giving to its young men a sound and efficient commercial education and training," he wrote with all the old fashioned circumlocutions of his youthful Hudson's Bay Company letters. The principle of summarizing the letter to which the writer is replying is here, as in so many of his formal letters, so thoroughly adhered to that there is no need to see Chamberlain's letter to know what he said.[48]

It appears that the men met after this letter was sent and Chamberlain, perhaps pointing out that Carnegie had given £25,000 to be used as a scholarship fund, persuaded Donald to commit himself to a further £25,000. Perceiving his commitment to the commerce faculty, Chamberlain suggested that this second sum should be invested separately, the income to be used specifically for that department. The fund could, suggested Chamberlain, be called the Strathcona Trust. While approving the use to which the money would be put, Donald insisted on anonymity. "On all occasions where it was possible I have declined permitting my name to be associated with any little contribution it may have been my good fortune to be able to make," he explained. The Birmingham donation was so secret that when the university decided to express its gratitude to its major benefactors by awarding them honourary doctorates in 1909, Chamberlain was obliged to intervene to ensure that Donald was among the recipients.[49]

While his gifts to McGill University were very public, virtually no one knew that in 1888, he had given £2,000 to St. John's College, Cambridge, a condition of the donation being that his name should "in no wise be used or mentioned in connection with it." The university had awarded him an honourary doctorate in 1887, years before any other academic body thought to do so. In all likelihood, the degree was prompted by Donald MacAlister, a Scottish divine and medical doctor who had met Donald in Montreal during the British Association for the Advancement of Science meeting there in 1884. MacAlister had invested all his spare money in the CPR because, according to his wife, he believed in it and in Donald Smith. Following the degree ceremony in 1887, MacAlister and two friends returned to Montreal and Donald, Stephen and Van Horne took the visitors with them on a journey to Vancouver on the completed line. It was probably in the course of quizzing the men about British university life that Donald expressed a wish to become a fellow of St. John's College; he made his gift when this was granted the following year. In 1894, he gave the college a further £10,000, again refusing any public acknowledgement.[50]

His link with the University of Aberdeen, by contrast, began in public and continued in that vein. In July 1899, the university awarded him an honourary doctorate and in the autumn a group of students nominated him for the post of rector. His opponent was Sir Edward Grey, the Liberal politician who was to become foreign secretary when his party returned to power in 1905. Donald, however, refused to conduct a political campaign, a decision which anyone familiar with his later Canadian political career would have recognized as characteristic but a wise move as well, given his continuing role as Canada's high commissioner. Sir Edward, perceiving that a wealthy Conservative could do more for the university than a Liberal of more ordinary means, withdrew from the contest and

Donald was elected by acclamation. In his rectorial address in December the following year, Donald apologized for spoiling the students' campaigning fun and remarked that he understood they had managed to enjoy themselves anyway. He carefully remained silent on the fact that this had led them into conflict with the police who injured several students with their truncheons. Despite this unpleasant incident, the rectorial election was the beginning of a happy association with the university which lasted until Donald's death.

CHAPTER EIGHTEEN

THE BOER WAR 1900

I have been reading your doings in South Africa with great surprise. Little did I think in the old days that you would ever make a soldier. Peace, I thought, was more in your line.
Former Hudson's Bay Company employee in a letter to Lord Strathcona [1]

During his term as high commissioner, Lord Strathcona helped to enunciate many aspects of Canada's relationship with Great Britain and thus contributed to the definition of British imperialism as it flourished at the end of the nineteenth century. Communications, trade, tariffs, emigration, and foreign policy were all reassessed as Canada grew towards nationhood within the context of the empire and, in each of these spheres, Donald helped to determine the extent of Canada's independence. His views in turn were modified by Laurier's Canadian patriotism on the one hand and by Chamberlain's grand imperial schemes on the other. No topic, however, contributed more to the creation of both a Canadian and an imperial identity than that of defense.

In the abstract, agreement on the role of the colonies in defending themselves and defending the empire could be reached quickly or could be postponed indefinitely. In the face of a real threat, the strengths and weaknesses of policies and principles assumed a clarity they lacked when they were largely theoretical and, in application, policies were coloured and sometimes distorted by the personalities who implemented them.

In 1895, when the Duke of Cambridge, at the age of seventy-six, was finally forced to resign as commander-in-chief, his replacement, Garnet Wolseley, by then Lord Wolseley, began to reorganise imperial defenses which had suffered from having the same rather ineffectual leader for thirty-nine years. Canada was asked to prepare a plan which would show how she would contribute to her own defense in the event of invasion. The cabinet found it easiest to postpone dealing with the request, especially since the government was in turmoil following the death of Macdonald. Early in 1898, one of Donald's callers at the High Commission offices was Lieutenant General

Sir Henry Wilkinson who was hoping for a more specific statement concerning Canada's contribution to imperial defense than the evasions and platitudes he had received hitherto. Donald tended to point out that Canada had not developed a military force, nor seen a need for one, but had created an infrastructure through building the CPR and its associated telegraph system to enable imperial troops to move across Canada quickly and efficiently should the need arise. This was not what the War Office had in mind.

A year earlier, Donald had been sympathetic to the idea of an imperial defense force to which the colonies would contribute men and equipment. Sam Hughes, the eccentric MP for the Ontario riding of Victoria North and opposition defense critic, was a militia officer and a voluble advocate of imperial unity and an integrated force. In 1897, Donald paid for him to visit Australasia where he lectured enthusiastically on the need for colonial military contributions to imperial defense. By the time Hughes returned in 1898, however, Donald had begun to appreciate Laurier's argument that Canada should decide each case on its merits and not be obliged by a blanket agreement to fight for a cause or a part of the world in which she had no interest and for which she had no sympathy.

The appointment of the Earl of Minto as governor general in July 1898, together with the assignment of Edward Hutton as commander of the Canadian militia earlier in the same year, ensured that imperial defense was thrust to the forefront of Canadian policy considerations, whatever the desires of Laurier's cabinet, and the war in South Africa a year later threw those considerations into sharp relief.

Gilbert John Murray Kynynmond Elliot, the fourth Earl of Minto, was not the Colonial Office's first choice as governor general of Canada nor even its second but he lobbied hard for the post, calling in favours and reminding men in influential positions of the duties of friendship. In the circumstances, it is ironic that one of Minto's ambitions as governor general was to stamp out patronage and political interference, especially in the militia. Minto's military experience was negligible, consisting largely of ceremonial duties at Buckingham Palace during his brief stint with the Scots Fusiliers, acting as aide-de-camp or secretary to various military commanders, and serving as Lansdowne's military secretary when he was governor general of Canada. In this latter capacity, the Canadian government had asked him to prepare various defense plans which it then never tabled in parliament and, in 1885, on his own initiative, Minto drew up schemes to raise Canadian forces to serve in the various skirmishes in which the imperial army was then involved. The War Office took this as an offer of troops and Prime Minister Macdonald was obliged to point out to Minto that the militia was restricted by law to the defense of Canada and that the raising of troops for any other purpose would require an act of parliament.

When he returned to Canada as governor general, Minto was much impressed with his own authority and blind to the fact that in the intervening thirteen years Canada had achieved a greater measure of self-government and would not be dictated to by the viceroy. As a firm believer in the unity of the empire, Minto was reluctant to accept that self-governing colonies such as Canada intended to determine their futures within the empire without reference to London and might, on occasion, prefer a course of action which was not in line with England's views. Moreover, he took at face value his honourary title as commander in chief of the Canadian militia and determined to use his position to enforce a thorough overhaul.

The Colonial Office was fully aware of the doctrine of ministerial responsibility, by then well established in Canada, and generally managed to collaborate with Laurier to keep Minto in line when he exceeded his ill-defined authority. But Joseph Chamberlain and his colleagues had been appalled when the War Office announced that it would be sending Major General Edward Hutton to command the Canadian militia. Keeping him under control would be a much more difficult job and they urged Lansdowne to think again, but their pleas were disregarded.

Hutton was arrogant and had quarrelled with people wherever he went. He did not know the meaning of the word tact and was oblivious to the fact that, as head of the militia, he was under the control of the Canadian civil authority. Minto's appointment delighted him because he perceived it as confirmation of his determination to reform the militia and purge it of what he saw as political interference. He was right to think that the Liberal and Conservative Parties both saw the militia as an easy way to dispense patronage but wrong to believe that he was free to act against it without reference to his political masters. Though Minto was occasionally a little perturbed by some of Hutton's excesses, he believed that enthusiasm for the empire and a commitment to its defense held sway in the hearts of the average Canadian; if necessary, Laurier's apparent caution in the face of Hutton's ambitions could be overruled by an appeal to the populace at large. The struggle between the cabinet and the head of the militia erupted publicly when the Boer War brought Hutton and Laurier out of their corners and into the ring.

For much of the century, Britain had been jostling with the Boers for control of South Africa. The UK had already established colonies in Cape Province and in the area to the north east in what was to become Rhodesia. Transvaal had been annexed in 1877 but the Dutch farmers, or Boers, who had settled there determined to regain their independence, which they did following a successful battle in 1881. Ostensibly, the Transvaal still acknowledged British suzerainty but this was not enough for Cecil Rhodes' British South Africa Company which sought a confederation under the British crown of all the South African colonies, not least as a protection against Germany's plans to establish a similar band of control through the middle of the continent. In 1895, in a bid to overthrow Paul Kruger, president of the Transvaal, Leander Jameson of the British South Africa Company launched a foolish raid during which he was soundly trounced by the Boers.

Political control meant little to the British adventurers who rushed to the province when gold was discovered. The Boers objected to these Uitlanders and refused to grant them the citizenship which would have enabled them to exploit the gold fields. The Boers' intransigence and British expansionist ambitions inevitably led to an escalation of the disagreement in the Transvaal. On October 10, 1899, the Boers delivered an ultimatum: differences were to be settled by arbitration, British troops were to be withdrawn and those soldiers on their way to Cape Town were not to be landed. Britain refused to accept that a little agrarian republic could stand in its way and war against the Transvaal and the Orange Free State was declared the following day.

The South African war was a conflict for which Britain was totally unprepared. There were not enough uniforms to kit out the army in peace time let alone in war and those there were blue and red, entirely unsuited to the veld on which the battles were to be fought. In domestic life, pills had replaced liquid medicines but the army was still equipped with cumbersome pharmaceutical boxes filled with glass bottles. Medical orderlies were ignorant of even basic hygiene and the army doctors were hopelessly out of touch with contemporary medical practice. It was said that Britain did not want to encourage war by preparing for it, but there were no stockpiles of weapons, apart from some rifles with faulty bores, and the arms manufacturers had great difficulties in meeting the sudden surge in the demand for ordnance. Simple things like maps were unavailable and the system for replenishing supplies of horses was so scandalously inadequate that an enquiry into their procurement was set up as early as 1900.

Worst of all was the fact that the senior command of the army was overstaffed and disorganized and, despite all the talk, nothing had been done to devise a way of bringing colonial troops to the aid of the empire or to train those who volunteered. When the war was over, Donald sat on a commission of inquiry which concluded

> if the war teaches us anything it is this, that throughout the Empire, in the United Kingdom, its colonies and dependencies, there is a reserve of military strength which, for many reasons, we cannot and do not wish to convert into a vast standing army, but to which we may be glad to turn again in our hour of need, as we did in 1899. In that year there was no preparation whatever for utilising these great resources. Nothing had been thought out either as to pay or organisation, as to conditions of service, or even as to arms. The new force was not to be discouraged, but it was allowed to equip itself, and it was denied anything beyond the barest complement of trained officers.[2]

In an additional comment on the scarcity of adequately trained men, Sir George Taubman-Goldie observed that "it produced the most perilous international situation in which the Empire has found itself since the days of Napoleon. Only an extraordinary combination of fortunate circumstances, external and internal, saved the Empire during the early months of 1900, and there is no reason to expect a repetition of such fortune if, as appears probable, the next national emergency finds us still discussing our preparations." This lack of preparation was rich soil into which a man like Hutton could seed his own plans for creating a Canadian army out of the militia and contributing troops to an imperial armed force.[3]

In July 1899, J. Davis Allan, the secretary of the Cape Town and London South African Association, was in Ottawa where he met Minto, Laurier and Tupper. As a result of that conversation, he cabled Chamberlain to say that

Laurier had agreed to introduce a resolution affirming Canada's support for imperial supremacy throughout South Africa, but would only do so if Chamberlain wished it. "If Sir Wilfrid Laurier is correctly reported," the colonial secretary wrote to Donald on the fourteenth, "I hasten to say that such a resolution of sympathy and support as he suggests would be most cordially welcomed by Her Majesty's Government."[4]

Donald promptly conveyed the message but it caught Laurier by surprise because Davis Allan had misrepresented his views. He was not prepared to commit Canadian men to fight in South Africa and could be sure that Quebec would flatly refuse to endorse what it saw as an irrelevant English war. On the other hand, Tupper had been present at that conversation and would surely make political capital out of it if Laurier offered no expression of support. The newspapers of Anglophone Canada were already braying excitedly in favour of sending soldiers to the looming war.

In the meantime, negotiations between Chamberlain and Kruger were becoming increasingly hostile. The colonial secretary saw Donald on the twenty-sixth and urged him to encourage Laurier to make a statement. He followed up his plea with a letter on the following day. "The opinion of a great self-governing Dominion, such as yours, whose leader is not of British origin, could hardly fail to impress powerfully the gentlemen of the Volksraad and persuade them to adopt a more reasonable view of their position and ours. It might have the further useful effect of checking some of that sympathy and encouragement which the Boers are receiving from many in the United States, who are, I gather, wretchedly informed as to the merits of the present dispute."[5]

Laurier cabled Donald to say that the matter required "careful handling" but on the thirty-first, he introduced a motion which made no reference to sending military aid but did support the political liberty of the Outlanders. "I consider that the action of the Dominion marks a distinct stage in the history of Imperial relations," Chamberlain responded thankfully in a note to the high commissioner. Unfortunately, it had no impact on the Boers whatsoever.[6]

What Chamberlain did not tell Donald, nor was it his business to do so, was that he was also communicating with the governor general. Would Canada make a military contribution in the event of war, he had asked, and if so, what form would it be likely to take? Minto's duty was to seek an answer to this inquiry from his responsible ministers, either Laurier or Frederick Borden who headed the Militia Department. Instead, he went directly to Hutton and asked him to prepare a contingency plan. The general immediately drew up a scheme to send 1,200 men and identified the officers to lead them. He, of course, was to be at the fore. It was cabled to Wolseley and the following day, July 4, Minto mentioned Chamberlain's query to Laurier. He did not, however, acknowledge that Hutton had already devised a plan and forwarded it to London. Since Laurier indicated that Canada would not wish to contribute to one of Britain's foreign wars, Minto may well have decided that his silence was justified.

In the meantime, Sam Hughes, with visions of himself bravely leading a valorous Canadian contingent, drew up his own scheme. He sent a copy to Hutton, who suppressed it, and a copy to Borden who, despite Hutton's objections, passed it to the cabinet which, in turn, asked Minto to forward it to London. The governor general declined to do so on the grounds that Hughes, not being a trained army officer, was incapable of leading the Canadian volunteers. Whether prompted by vanity or political nous, Hughes also sent a copy of his plan directly to Chamberlain.

The colonial secretary may not have been a gentleman but he was prompt with his bread and butter letters and immediately wrote a note to Hughes, thanking him for his patriotism. In accordance with form, it was sent via Minto who was annoyed to find that an upstart volunteer had succeeded, despite efforts to suppress him. Minto asked Hutton to take him down a peg or two. Hutton's arrogance was easily matched by Hughes' own and he responded to the reprimand with a vicious attack on Hutton, Minto and the British army. Hutton responded in kind. "You might as well try to fly to the moon as to take the field alongside of British regulars," he spat.[7]

Hughes retaliated by starting to recruit volunteers and Hutton responded by accusing him of violating the Army Act which defines who may gather forces for the regular army. Laurier's cabinet was exasperated by this very public slanging match but also perceived that Hughes had come up with a solution to its dilemma. The militia was, by definition, a domestic force and could not be sent overseas without a change in the law. The cabinet was divided over sending a large official contingent at Canada's expense, which was what the War Office wanted, sending smaller units which Britain would pay for and which would be attached to the British army, which was what Chamberlain was seeking, or refusing to get involved at all. Volunteers, however, could do as they wished and the government need not stand in their way.

This opportunity of doing something while doing nothing disappeared at the beginning of October when the War Office asked the Colonial Office to send a circular cable to the colonial governments which had offered help. As it applied to Canada, the War Office was referring to Hutton's scheme to send 1,200 men, a contingency plan the existence of which was still denied by Minto and Hutton. Instead of thanking the people of Canada in a general way for offers of help, as the War Office intended, the Colonial Office carelessly referred to "offers to serve in South Africa." Canada had made no such offer but someone, probably in the Militia Department, made sure the press knew that unauthorized offers had been made. At the same time, the correspondence between Hughes and Hutton became public. The Anglophone press was wild with excitement, insisting that Canada send troops, and the cabinet finally bowed to pressure and, soon after war was declared, offered a contingent.

"I fully appreciate the difficulties you had to meet in determining to send a contingent to South Africa," Donald wrote to the prime minister. "Happily, the people here were so favourably impressed with the unmistakable and enthusiastic loyalty of the people of the Dominion as a whole that the strictures of one or two Quebec newspapers were hardly noticed."[8]

In announcing that a contingent would be sent, Laurier warned that it was not to be considered a precedent, but at a dinner in honour of the officers immediately prior to their departure, Hutton contradicted the premier by predicting that Canada would send up to 100,000 men to save the empire. The following night, Minto seemed to side with Hutton when he declared him to be the best general in Canada since Confederation. It was Borden and his ministry which recruited the men, not Hutton, who nevertheless quarrelled with all the senior officials in the Militia Department. Under pressure, Borden began to drink and, as on previous occasions, was belligerent as a consequence. As a short term measure, Laurier wrote Minto, complaining that Hutton's speech transgressed onto political grounds and implying that Minto, too, was not maintaining an apolitical stance.

In South Africa, the British troops and their colonial reinforcements easily outnumbered the Boers, but Kruger's men outmanoeuvred their foes with no difficulty. England's soldiers marched in order, dismounted to fire their guns and followed the regulations issued by their out-of-date and inflexible officers. The Boers knew their territory intimately and had no need of maps. They were capable of controlling their horses with their knees while they hunted on the veld or, in this case, shot British soldiers; unencumbered by a rule book, they fought to win and inflicted one defeat after another on the British army.

By December, the War Office was grateful for Canada's offer of a second contingent. London asked for mounted men who could shoot from the saddle but Hutton, as usual convinced that he knew best, decided to recruit from the mounted militia: he would send urban gentlemen of whom he could be proud. Even Minto, who urged Hutton to recruit from the Northwest, was disgusted. Hutton, still refusing to believe he was under the thumb of the civil authority, quarrelled again with Borden over the purchase of horses for the contingent.

Laurier, Minto, Lansdowne at the War Office, and Chamberlain at the Colonial Office all knew aspects of the seething hatred which was building up against Hutton in Ottawa and it was clear to Laurier and his colleagues that Minto was conducting a vindictive campaign against Sam Hughes. Though Donald must have got wind of some of the problems, he was generally kept in the dark. At Laurier's request, he urged Lansdowne to ensure the second Canadian contingent was commanded by a Canadian but was probably unaware that both Hutton and Minto did not believe any Canadian was capable of doing so.

Well before he discovered that Hutton had disregarded the War Office's request and Minto's advice in recruiting the second Canadian contingent, Donald understood that the British army was taking a beating in South Africa because its men could not match the Boers' skills in the saddle in unmarked territory. He also perceived that the mounted police force which he had helped to establish in the unmapped Northwest would be more than capable of tackling the Boers on their own terms. He decided to intervene in the provision of Canadian forces for the war in South Africa. Beckles Willson, the author of the 1915 biography of Lord Strathcona, claims to have been one of the first to know of Donald's intention and suggests that he was mulling over the idea as early as November 1899.[9]

He turned the notion over in his mind through much of December and on New Year's Eve sent Laurier a telegram outlining his proposal.

> Very confidential. Should like to provide and send to South Africa my personal fund squadron mounted men and officers say four hundred men and horses from North West, single men if possible. Force will be Canadian but distinct from Government contingent. Men must be expert marksmen, at home in saddle, and efficient as rough riders and rangers. I propose pay cost shipment similar that of Canadian contingent and transport if you approve proposal. Would like use of Government organization for recruiting force, if that is practicable.[10]

Laurier's acceptance arrived on the third of January, coupled with a note that the Militia Department would need three or four days to complete arrangements for the second contingent and would then be available to raise the new squadron. Donald was in bed with his familiar winter cold when Laurier's reply reached him and it was not until the ninth that he was able to sound out Chamberlain. The astonished colonial secretary asked to have the offer in writing so he could present it to his cabinet colleagues.

Donald's letter repeated his cable to Laurier, except that someone seems to have told him that four hundred men would be the equivalent of two squadrons. He reiterated that he would pay the cost of the equipment and the transport to South Africa where the force would be taken over by the imperial government. He confirmed that the dominion government would assist in raising the troops but wanted assurances that "the force proposed to be raised would be of substantial benefit in South Africa." He had already discussed the broad principles with Lansdowne who was probably responsible for directing Donald to Chamberlain and may even have planted the idea in Donald's mind in the first place, if Beckles Willson is correct in claiming that the notion of providing the rough riders was suggested to Donald by someone else. Donald concluded his letter by pointing out that "for the moment, at any rate, I do not wish my name to be publicly mentioned in connection with it."[11]

The request for anonymity, which had been passed to Laurier on January 6, was fruitless, perhaps not surprisingly in view of the antagonisms and leaks to the press which characterized the quarrel between Hutton and the Militia Department. By the twelfth, the story was in the Canadian press. The following day, Donald drafted a cable for Laurier, beginning with a complaint about the premature publicity and outlining his intentions in greater detail. On the fourteenth, he read it to Lansdowne before sending it to Ottawa. The horses were to be purchased in consultation with General Hutton; medical tests for the officers and men were to be arranged in consultation with Donald's Montreal doctor, James Stewart, again in conjunction with Hutton. When the engagement was completed, the men were to retain their clothes and necessaries but their horses, arms and equipment were to be the property of the imperial government. Selection of the men was to be "entirely non-political; only qualification being thorough fitness and suitability of officers and men for services required." He reiterated his desire to have the "benefit of experience of Gen. Hutton in the selection of men and purchase of horses, arms and equipment; officers to be nominated by him and names & particulars submitted my approval." Payment would, of course, be made through the Bank of Montreal and Donald had already earmarked £150,000 for that purpose in Canada. He assumed that further expenditure would be required in London and the British press put the final figure at £200,000. They probably underestimated it.[12]

The cable left a bitter taste in Laurier's mouth. The offer was more than generous and it would certainly help his government to be able to lay both the cost and the political responsibility for this force at Donald's door, but the references to Hutton were unwelcome. The last thing the Militia Department needed was a further opportunity for the general to interfere and perhaps even to defy Donald's clear instructions and put his gift in jeopardy. Laurier discussed it with the cabinet and then cabled. "Before replying more fully to your last telegram Gov. think you should be informed that Hutton's relations with them so unsatisfactory that his cooperation with the Ministry of Militia cannot be relied on." The following day, Laurier wrote in greater detail and the day after, the cabinet decided to press for Hutton's recall.[13]

Donald was startled to discover that his reference to disregarding political factors in the recruitment of his force was seen in Ottawa as reflecting the views of the War Office which would, in turn, have got them from Hutton and Minto and their long standing campaign to wipe out what they saw as political interference in the militia. As Lansdowne had approved the draft offer letter, he would have sanctioned the reference to "non-political" selection but he is unlikely to have recommended it in the first place. The phrase is entirely in keeping with Donald's views expressed in election campaigns as early as 1871 when he declared himself to be in favour of whatever was good for the people of the Northwest "without distinction of race, party or creed." His concern now was that the mounted troop should be "thoroughly efficient in every way, that the men and the officers should be the most suitable that can be obtained for the services for which they are likely to be required. And further, that the equipment and armament should be as perfect as possible."[14]

Though Donald would have been aware of the newspaper coverage of the Hutton-Hughes row and would have known that the general had attracted a good deal of controversy, he had to point out to Laurier that he was "quite unaware" of the government's problems with Hutton when he suggested the general might represent him in making arrangements with the Department of Militia.[15]

In place of Hutton, the Canadian government invited Sam Steele to raise Donald's force of rough riders, and was immediately reprimanded for doing so without consulting their benefactor. While the troublesome Sam Hughes was desperate for a post and Donald was not averse to helping him, it was immediately apparent that Steele was an inspired choice. He had served with the North West Mounted Police since its inception and was widely known and respected by the men who had worked with him. He had dispensed rough justice along the CPR tracks as the railway was being built and, when the labourers struck in March 1885 because they had not been paid since winter began, he had faced an armed mob and cowed them into submission.

Steele had subsequently used a mixture of intelligence, bravado and common sense to keep the peace in the Yukon gold fields and was immensely popular with the young officers who had seen him in action or knew of his accomplishments. His campaign against corruption in Dawson proved to be a campaign against Clifford Sifton, the minister of the interior, and, in the autumn of 1899, Steele found himself still in the Mounties but without a job. He had volunteered to go to South Africa with the second contingent when Borden offered him the opportunity to recruit, and then lead, what was beginning to be called Strathcona's Horse.

Steele had the pick of the best riders and marksmen in the Northwest. Most of the men he chose were on leave from the North West Mounted Police, though some had resigned their commissions to farm in the area and a few were good enough to be Mounties but had never joined the service. Americans flooded across the border, begging to sign up with the new squadrons, but this was to be a purely Canadian force and they were politely sent home again. It took Steele a mere two weeks to raise five hundred and ninety-six men, including twenty-nine officers. While Steele was recruiting and equipping his men, Donald kept up a stream of encouraging letters, urging him to spare no expense to ensure the men's comfort and efficiency.[16]

Strathcona's Horse assembled in Ottawa, where they sent many a lady's heart aflutter when they paraded through the streets or joined the young women at balls and skating parties, but the flirtations were short lived for the men were only in the capital for two weeks before setting out for Halifax where they embarked for Pretoria on March 17. Donald had hoped to be there to see them off but at the beginning of February there were still traces of pleurisy in his lungs and his doctors insisted he remain in London. The fact that he was not in South Africa escaped some of his Canadian correspondents who wrote "General Strathcona" to comment enthusiastically on his military exploits! One letter was so full of praise for his "well known bravery and skill on the battlefield of which the newspapers are now full," that he sent it to Sam Steele, noting that it was "wrongly addressed."[17]

The moment Steele was appointed to raise Strathcona's Horse, the cabinet turned its attention to getting rid of Hutton. On the nineteenth of January, Laurier asked Minto to arrange for the general to be recalled. Minto refused, saying that the problem lay with Borden who drank to excess and should be dismissed. Laurier pointed out that no one else would take on the Militia Department while Hutton was there and suggested there were two ways of handling the situation. One was to arrange for the War Office to place him on active service in South Africa while the other was for the Canadian government to dismiss him. The former was to be preferred. Minto, however, continued to defend the general. He asked Laurier for a written memo on his objections while he himself prepared a paper on Canadian military administration. In it, he laid bare his ignorance of Canadian constitutional arrangements and especially the relationship between the general officer commanding and the minister of militia. His catalogue of corruption in the cabinet and Borden's department merely served to reinforce the ministers' view that Hutton had to go.

By now, Laurier was keeping Donald fully briefed because it was inevitable that he was going to be needed as a channel of communication with the War Office and the Colonial Office since Minto was either unwilling to forward documents or accompanied them with his own biased arguments. At the beginning of February, Laurier told Donald that the preference was for London to repost Hutton. "While desirous of having him recalled, we think you should be informed confidentially [that] he is meddlesome, ignores [the] authority of his minister [and] constantly acts as one who holds himself independent [of the] civil authority," Laurier damningly wrote. He asked Donald to sound out Chamberlain and possibly Lansdowne as well.[18]

The colonial secretary was not surprised to learn that Hutton had been behaving true to form and on February 3, Donald was able to cable that Chamberlain had agreed to speak to Lansdowne and arrange for Hutton to be posted to South Africa. The War Office, in turn, told Minto that it was trying to find a suitable position for Hutton, but the governor general said nothing about this to the prime minister. Indeed, he urged the War Office to delay. While Laurier and his cabinet waited for news from London, Borden discovered that Hutton had marked down for courses at the Royal Military College in Kingston two officers whose retirement was imminent. Hutton complied with his request to give the places to younger men, but then told one of those whose name was removed from the list that he had been ousted because of his political activities on behalf of the opposition. For the cabinet, this was the last straw and Laurier told Minto that Hutton must be removed.

Minto insisted that this be a formal order in council. He did not want to deal with the controversy quietly but sought an official, public argument in which he was convinced the Canadian public would back Hutton. He urged the general to refuse to accept his dismissal and to demand a royal commission. Hutton promptly set to work preparing his list of grievances and girding his loins for an all out battle with the Canadian government.

As soon as the dismissal document reached the Colonial Office, a shrewd civil servant named John Anderson deduced that Minto had not told Laurier that the War Office was looking for a South African post for Hutton. Chamberlain was horrified by the embarrassment which would be caused when it became publicly known that Hutton had been dismissed by a colonial government and asked the War Office to arrange his immediate recall. He then asked Donald to cable Laurier to say he was trying to arrange matters discreetly, pointing out that an *official* request must necessarily have an *official* reply. To this Donald added, "Would it not be better, matter now being arranged as you desire, to withdraw official despatch?"[19]

Laurier agreed that it should be held in abeyance, noting that, all along, he would have preferred confidential, unofficial communication on the subject. Though Donald had a bit of a struggle to get the Colonial Office to grasp the idea that the request could be placed in limbo, he finally succeeded in getting his idea across.

News that Hutton had been recalled for "special service" reached Ottawa on February 10 and Hutton resigned immediately. On February 13, the opposition, sensing that all was not as it appeared to be, questioned Laurier about Hutton's recall and the prime minister responded with platitudes. That night, however, Hutton's friends gave him a farewell dinner at which he spoke intemperately of political interference in the militia. To ensure that his remarks, made at a private dinner, did not remain private, he handed the text of his speech to the *Ottawa Citizen* which printed it *verbatim*.

The cabinet was livid and when the opposition raised the question of Hutton's return to the UK again on February 19, Laurier admitted that the general had been dismissed. Under the circumstances, he explained to Chamberlain, he could not rescind the order in council and would be obliged to publish the relevant correspondence which had passed between London and Ottawa. The Canadian public, in the meantime, proved Minto's assessment of their enthusiasm for Hutton to be entirely wrong. The ladies missed the teas and dances he and his wife had arranged at Earnscliffe, Macdonald's old home, but no one thought twice about his ambitions for the Canadian militia.

Once in London, Hutton called on Donald and reported the high commissioner to be "extremely indignant at the Canadian Government for having taken the organisation of his Corp[s] out of my hands, & at their having made much party political capital out of it all." As Laurier went out of his way to avoid turning the dismissal of Hutton into a political issue, Hutton seems, once again, to have put his own idiosyncratic interpretation on the words of others.[20]

It took the dismissal of another militia commander, Lord Dundonald, and the replacement of Lord Wolseley at the head of the British army before British military commanders finally grasped that when they were heading the Canadian militia, the civilian government, whether corrupt or otherwise, was their employer and, in the last analysis, had to be obeyed. The Hutton incident brought Donald and Laurier closer together because they saw eye to eye on how it should be handled, even though Donald was privately sympathetic to complaints of political interference in the Militia Department. "I'm afraid it will take years or some great national danger to put our military service on a plane above party interests," he remarked to Beckles Willson when Dundonald was dismissed.[21]

In South Africa, Strathcona's Horse comported themselves well, though the British military leaders were taken aback by how much the colonial troops drank and Steele was, and would continue to be, too drunk too often. He had a reputation as a bully but his men held him in the greatest esteem; it may be that the rough language, which was effective in the Northwest, was misunderstood in the drawing rooms of Ottawa and among the gentlemen officers in South Africa.

Steele's men had signed up for a minimum of six months and a maximum of a year and when they were pressed by British officers to extend their engagement, refused to do so. Those who were still in the NWMP had not been released indefinitely and those who had families and farms could not rely on friends to plant and harvest yet again. On January 21, 1901, the day before Queen Victoria died, the regiment set sail from Cape Town, resplendent in new uniforms and hats sent out by their patron. They reached London on St. Valentine's Day and were immediately engulfed in hospitality. On February 15, they paraded at Buckingham Palace where they were presented with the first of the Boer War medals and the king pinned the medal of the Royal Victorian Order, fourth class, on Steele's tunic.

Donald gave two luncheons, one at the Metropole Hotel to honour all the officers and men, the other at the Savoy for the officers alone. In both cases, as with the dinners hosted by British officials, military, church and political leaders were also among the guests. At the Metropole, where Donald was loudly cheered as he entered the room, it was assumed that a Church of England prelate would say grace. Instead, Donald invited the only man in the room who was not in full military uniform or formal morning dress to do the honours. He was John McDougall whose sister, Eliza, had married Bella's brother, Richard Hardisty. He had been born on the prairies before the North West Mounted Police had even been thought of and it was he who had been ordained at the first missionary conference in Winnipeg in 1872. His strong Canadian accent pronouncing a simple blessing made it clear to the assembled British dignitaries that this was not an imperial or even a Canadian occasion: it belonged to the Northwest.

The lunch at the Savoy was equally grand, with Chamberlain, Wolseley and Lord Roberts among the guests. Unfortunately, Steele was drunk when he arrived and kept drinking. Donald had to prevent him from making an unscheduled speech in the middle of the meal but there was little he could do about much of his unsavoury behaviour. Sir Frederick Williams-Taylor, Inspector-General of the Bank of Montreal, subsequently said that Donald had had a cheque for $10,000 in his pocket and had intended to make Steele a present of it but his behaviour, coupled with insults aimed at Lord Roberts, made him change his mind.[22]

Donald saw his corps off at Euston Station on February 23 and, when they reached Halifax, they were met by Williams-Taylor who gave each man the difference between his British army pay and the NWMP salary which they had foregone in South Africa. This doubled the men's pay and, for good measure, each received a bonus as well.

Sir Charles Tupper had played no part in the raising of Strathcona's Horse nor had he been able to comply with Donald's request that he see them off at Halifax the year before. The day after they embarked, however, he decided to ingratiate himself with Donald. He wrote a letter to Chamberlain in which he said that "all Canadians will rejoice if his great services to the Crown at an important crisis are recognized by arranging that his Peerage shall descend to his only child, the Hon. Mrs. Howard. She is the wife of Dr. Howard of 31 Queen Anne Street who is the first Canadian who took the Fellowship of the Royal College of Surgeons. His father was the most eminent physician in Montreal, and a professor in the McGill University. Mrs. Howard would grace any position, and her family of sons and daughters are bright and interesting. You can imagine what it would be for Lord Strathcona, like myself so near the close of life, to feel that his grandson, Donald Howard, would one day wear his title."[23]

At the same time, Tupper wrote Donald, saying that he hoped Donald would replace Minto as governor general and also that he was sure the crown would recognize his contribution to the war effort by ensuring that the peerage descended to his daughter. He added that a general election was shortly due in Canada and he expected to be returned to power. "I will say no more than to beg you on no condition to vacate the High Commissionership before a general election takes place."[24]

In a letter the following month, Tupper sent Donald a copy of his letter to Chamberlain, together with the colonial secretary's reply in which he pointed out that the question of Maggie inheriting the peerage had been discussed in 1897 and turned down. "It is possible that these difficulties may be ultimately surmounted and you may count on my seizing any opportunity of securing the desired result," Chamberlain had said.[25]

The colonial secretary was as good as his word. He raised the subject with Lord Salisbury, the prime minister, and he in turn broached the subject with the queen. In view of the fact that Britain was at war and there were many other topics to discuss at a royal audience, the decision was reached remarkably quickly. A confidential letter from Chamberlain arrived on Donald's desk on May 19.

"The intimation conveyed in it came as a great surprise," Donald wrote, mindful of what Tupper had said, but also remembering that inheritance of titles by women was generally frowned on, especially for a peerage as new as his. "My daughter, Mrs. Howard, I am happy to say is a woman of culture with all the instincts of a gentlewoman and devotes herself to educating and bringing up her children so that they may be no discredit to any position she may occupy. For her sake then and for theirs and for the gratification it will afford our friends, I greatly appreciate the step the Queen has been graciously pleased to authorize." Old Mrs. Smith's insistence that position counted for nothing if ladies were not "gentlewomen" still rang true in Donald's ears.[26]

Donald did not change his title with the new peerage but he was obliged to alter his coat of arms. He added two supporters —the figures on either side of the escutcheon. One was "a navvy standing on a railway sleeper, chaired and railed." The rail is gripped by the chair and the man, bearded and in rough working clothes, is about to swing a hammer down to nail the chair to the sleeper. The other supporter was a trooper of Strathcona's Horse. Like the beaver, the supporters were "all proper," that is, in their natural colours. As a Scottish peer, he was entitled to two mottos so below the escutcheon he added a new motto, *Agmina Ducens*. Donald's choice, as he expressed it in English, was "in the van," though the Latin is now sometimes translated as "a leader of men." To his contemporaries, it seemed a curious decision because, as the principal of McGill, William Peterson, who gave Donald the Latin translation, commented, "for all his eagerness to be 'in the van,' one can never think of him as anything but essentially modest and unassertive. You all know what his bearing was on the various occasions on which he was seen in our midst, — inwardly glad, no doubt, to receive the homage of our love and praise, but genuinely anxious at the same time that no one should be put to any inconvenience because of him."[27]

Not only was he not "in the van" socially, his ideas were not new; he was not an inventive man or a strong leader in any sense. What he did perceive was how to put into effect the ideas of other men. He saw how the Saint Paul, Minneapolis and Manitoba Railway could improve the Hudson's Bay Company's travel arrangements, but he did not think of building the railway in the first place. He gave university education for women to Montreal and, with his cousin, gave that city a great teaching hospital, but he did not conceive of the need for these institutions. His choice of a second motto, however, suggests that he did perceive himself to be at the forefront, and perhaps he was in the sense that, as soon as he was convinced of the worth of a new idea, he acted on it. When telephones were still new fangled inventions, he had one installed; as soon as the transatlantic cable was laid, he used it regularly for HBC business; as soon as the need for a college in Manitoba was explained to him, he contributed to its establishment.

With the creation of the second peerage, Donald began to occupy a position as the grand old man of the empire. There was a genuine outpouring of affection for him, and when he visited Montreal in the autumn for the official opening of Royal Victoria College, McGill students met his train, unhitched the horses from his carriage and pulled it through the streets to the house on Dorchester Street, despite the pouring rain.

On the fifteenth of November, he was invited to a meeting where reference was made to his role in the construction of the CPR, the establishing of the Pacific cable and his contributions to settling the dispute with Louis Riel in 1869-1870. Other speakers commented on his care for the sick and his provision of education in Montreal and on the raising of Strathcona's Horse. The citizens of Montreal determined to erect a statue in his honour.

In response to the flattering speeches, Donald asserted that his greatest contribution, despite all he had done since, was the service he had accomplished in the Northwest. "I do not wish to seem to forget that I have been very fortunate in the country which now for over sixty years has been the country of my adoption. Looking back now, I do not see where greater opportunities of usefulness could have offered themselves than in connection with a young and growing country such as this." He knew that it was likely to be a rather emotional meeting. "It is said that out of the fulness of the heart the mouth speaketh; but sometimes, as you all know, the heart is too full for words." He had taken the precaution of writing down his final sentences. "This expression of your good-will for me is very precious to me. I find in it strength and comfort, and support and it will always continue in the years that may lie before me among my most pleasant recollections."[28]

CHAPTER NINETEEN

A MARVEL OF A MAN 1900–1907

Lord Strathcona is indeed a wonder. Though he bears the burden of eighty-six years, he is as erect as ever, as keen, as alert, as eager as the youngest.

Sir William Robertson Nicoll [1]

Though Lord Strathcona's reputation had expanded well beyond Britain's financial community by the time Britain declared war on South Africa, it was the contribution of Donald's mounted regiment and the second peerage which brought him to the attention of the wider public. In April 1900, he replied to the toast to colonial forces at the Press Club annual dinner and in the same month, at a banquet honouring the men who were negotiating the creation of the Australian Commonwealth, he was asked to respond to the toast to home and colonial legislatures. At the installation of the new sheriffs of London in September, he replied to a similar toast. The pattern was to continue for the next decade and a half.

The people of Forres had better reason than many to know their most famous living son and in September they bestowed on him the freedom of the royal burgh. It was something of a family occasion: Donald was accompanied by Bella and Maggie and her husband, and John's married daughter, by now widowed, also attended. The streets were decorated with bunting and two local volunteer companies lined the streets. The town's largest building, the Mechanics' Institute, had been given over to a fund raising bazaar in aid of Forres Free Church, so the ceremony took place in the United Presbyterian Church. Inevitably, it began with the second paraphrase, "O God of Bethel," by which the Scots confirmed their identity with their forefathers and with generations of Scots to come.

It was a joyful occasion at which Donald allowed the city fathers to reveal that he had been the source of the anonymous donation to Anderson's Institution in November 1880. Donald, himself, was in bubbling good spirits, jesting that schoolboys do not always appreciate their school days. "There may be some reasons, and I daresay one is sometimes connected with the might and strength of the right arm of our master — for we know that this plays a very important part in the pursuit of learning in early days." He spoke fondly of his youth, playing on Cluny

Hill and the banks of the Findhorn and, to the delight of his listeners, joked about his being "very modest, as all Scotsmen are." In the same vein, he observed that "it appears to be an ordinance and provision of Providence that Scotsmen should scatter themselves about through every portion of the Empire, and I think they will be found all over the world, that they may do good and teach other races."[2]

Donald seemed to be much more at ease among his fellow Scots and his little jokes were always well received by them. The following year, when he was made a freeman of Aberdeen, an honour which, a few weeks earlier, had been bestowed on his cousin, George Stephen, he referred to himself as "the Baby freeman of your city," adding, "When one arrives at my age, it is an intense satisfaction to know that one is still young in any capacity, and I appreciate especially that I am a younger citizen of the granite city than Lord Mount Stephen."[3]

When in Forres to receive the freedom of the burgh, he took advantage of his age and experience to suggest that the Free Church, whose bazaar he opened in the afternoon, and the United Presbyterians, both of which had split from the Church of Scotland, should consider re-uniting as had happened in Canada.

This happy day in his native town was made the more remarkable by the fact that two days earlier, on September 9, Donald had travelled from Glencoe to London, taking the overnight train. He had done a day's work in the capital, then boarded the night train, arriving in Forres on the morning of September 11. At the end of the afternoon, he was on the overnight train again and a week later was on it once more, heading for Glencoe where Frederick Borden, the militia minister, was his guest. At the beginning of October, he was on his way to Montreal for the opening of Royal Victoria College. Bella described his arrangements for the Canadian trip as "very hurried." By most people's standards, all his travel plans were fixed in a rush at the last minute but on this occasion he must have given very short notice for it was one of the rare occasions when she did not accompany him.[4]

Donald had celebrated his eightieth birthday that August and might well have been expected to have begun to reduce his responsibilities. When he was in Montreal in October, he cut back to the extent of forming the Royal Trust Company and handing over to it all the Private Cash Accounts which he had managed for so many years. The company was an extension of the Bank of Montreal and all its directors were directors of the new operation, including Donald, who was president. He ended his letter in which he told his clients of the new arrangements by pointing out that he would still be happy to be of use in any way that he could. There was no question of retirement.

It was probably as well that the accounts, share certificates and other documents were transferred when they were for, on the twenty-third of January 1901, a fire in the Board of Trade building in Montreal destroyed the bulk of Donald's business records and some personal material as well. Letters, ledgers and account books all vanished, along with papers such a treatise on the Naskapi which he had written long years before. In a few hours, the tangible evidence of so much that he had worked on, so much that he had achieved, was reduced to ashes. "The loss to him of these papers meant more than the value of his whole estate," his lawyer, John Sterling, observed to J.J. Hill.[5]

He had little time to ponder his loss, however, for the night before the fire, the life of the old queen, whose health had been failing for much of the previous year, finally drew to a close. Queen Victoria had been little more than a year older than Donald; he had met her many times since that spring day in 1838 when he had hoped to catch a glimpse of her in her carriage and, though they had never been close, her death marked the passing of an era of which he too had been part and reminded him of his own mortality.

On the second of February, Donald and Bella travelled to the royal mausoleum at Frogmore for the interment. Suffering from her winter cold, Bella was far from well and Donald was especially grateful when Sir Thomas Barlow, who was their doctor as well as the queen's principal physician, insisted she return to London on an early train and saw her "safely and comfortably into the railway carriage." Her condition deteriorated and she was still confined to bed near the end of March though she was, by that time, recovering. Donald himself had pleurisy in both lungs but ignored it, "attending deputations to his majesty and other functions, going out in the bitter east winds though the doctors have forbidden him to leave the house and have warned him that he does so at the peril of his life."[6]

The queen had been reluctant to allow her children to stray very far from home and generally refused to countenance any transatlantic journey for either them or her grandchildren. Her death, however, removed this impediment to North American travel and Donald quickly took advantage of it, suggesting that the Duke and Duchess of Cornwall and York, the future King George V and Queen Mary, visit Canada.

The acceptance of the Canadian invitation caused an immediate flurry of excitement, not least in Montreal where there was no vice-regal residence beyond Donald's house on Dorchester Street which Lord Minto used when he visited the city. The impending royal visit more than doubled the problem, since beds needed to be found for both Minto and the English guests. For the Strathconas, the matter was further exacerbated by the fact that Lucinda Crawford, their housekeeper for many years, died in September shortly before the royal party arrived in Montreal.

As soon as the trip was confirmed, Donald had offered his house to the Duke and Duchess who agreed to take up his invitation. Then Montagu Allan, son of Sir Hugh who had been at the centre of the Pacific Scandal in 1873, offered his own palatial home, Ravenscrag, implying that he would vacate it for the duration of the royal visit. Not knowing where to turn, Minto wrote to Sir Edward Clouston, general manager of the Bank of Montreal, for advice. "You know how small his house is," he moaned of the Dorchester Street building, not bothering to add that he disapproved of railways and the men who built them across the Canadian prairies, just as he disapproved of new wealth and new fashions in ladies' clothes. By July, Minto knew that the visitors would include the Duke and Duchess, Prince Alexander of Teck, nineteen staff, including three ladies, and a further twenty-eight servants, among them three maids for the duchess and two valets for the duke. Where to put them all?[7]

Clouston and Donald were ahead of Minto. They commissioned an architect to draw the rooms in order to help the royal party determine who was to have which one and he created a conservatory to link Donald's house with its neighbour which he had bought from Duncan McIntyre. The architect also designed a temporary reception room which could accommodate two thousand guests. The remainder of the royal party were provided for at Royal Victoria College and the

Mintos were guests of R.B. Angus. Donald bought new suites of Canadian bird's eye maple furniture for the bedrooms of the duke and duchess, much to the Minto's disgust. Modern furniture was no more to his taste than Canadian design.

More successful in his eyes were the seven special cars the CPR built for the transnational journey. *Cornwall* and *York* were the royal coaches, complete with crests on the exterior and "elaborate and artistic" interiors equipped with telephones and electric lights. *Sandringham*, the royal estate in Norfolk, gave its name to the dining car while *India*, *South Africa*, *Australasia* and *Canada* christened the kitchen and baggage cars. To Minto's satisfaction, proof of their suitability was given when the royal couple reported themselves delighted with the luxury provided.[8]

The efficiency of the arrangements, however, did nothing to satisfy Minto, who disliked going to Montreal at the best of times, and especially on this occasion, "with French & English hating each other like cat & dog — two reception committees, one English, the other French, a corrupt mayor and general quarrelling and poor old Strathcona attempting to lead society[,] the ways of which he is ignorant of, with a squaw wife who is absolutely hopeless what could he expect."[9]

More disconcerting than the governor general's prejudices was the fact that organization of the Montreal reception had fallen into "bad hands," as Minto reported to Chamberlain in the Colonial Office. "We were aware of suspicious characters being in Montreal whose presence caused anxiety — the officer com^ding the District and the Commissioner of the Police were thoroughly dissatisfied as to the actual safety of the Duke's attendance, Lord Strathcona and Senator Drummond (Chairman of the general reception committee) were equally so, and the former told me that from a conversation he had had with the Mayor he believed he would be thankful for a hint from me not to hold it — it had got into such bad hands, that respectable people were refusing to take their wives to it, and there seemed actual risk in the Duke's attendance."[10]

Salvation came from an unexpected quarter. US President William McKinley was shot on September 6 while he visited the Pan-American Fair in Buffalo. He appeared to be recovering, but suffered a relapse and died on September 14. As a "mark of respect," the civic reception, scheduled for September 18, was cancelled and Donald and Bella called off the second of their dinner parties planned for the following day when McKinley was buried.

Montrealers had no intention of allowing the American misfortune to interfere with their pleasure, however, and thousands thronged the streets to see the elaborate decorations and illuminations put up in honour of the royal visitors. A huge crown with coloured lights had been placed on the Bank of Montreal; George Stephen's house was outlined in lights and there were coloured lanterns in the garden; Shaughnessy's house was a blaze of light, beside which Donald's home, with a crest in electric light over the door, seemed decidedly, if typically, modest.

The royal visitors were met at the train station by the governor general, the prime minister, other dignitaries, and Donald and Bella. While the official party made its way across Montreal, accompanied by the Royal Scots, complete with pipe band, the Strathconas nipped around the back way and were at their front door to greet the duke and duchess when they stepped out of their carriage into the autumn drizzle. The rain did nothing to dampen the enthusiasm of three thousand young men and women from the snow shoe club, the fire brigade, McGill University and other similar organizations. They mounted a torchlight parade along Dorchester Street to Donald's house and there played the national anthem and shouted and cheered with pleasure. Fireworks from the top of Mount Royal rounded off the day. Donald's guests at dinner, tucked inside and secure from the jollity, included Maggie and Dr. Howard, Minto, Laurier, Van Horne, Angus, Shaughnessy and Clouston as well as other political and business leaders and a sprinkling of respectable young ladies to partner the royal aides. Van Horne's invitation was in fact for September 19, but it seems likely that space was found for him and perhaps for some others who would be forced to forgo the cancelled dinner the following night.[11]

The next day, Donald was decked out in his gold embroidered robe as chancellor of McGill to welcome the royal guests again. They both received honourary doctorates at Royal Victoria College —hers being the first ever given to a woman at McGill — before carrying on to open a new medical building at the university and visit the Royal Victoria Hospital. When they left the following morning, they might have been forgiven for wondering if there was any part of Montreal for which Donald had not been responsible.

Donald and Bella remained in Canada till the duke and duchess returned to Montreal early in November when there was another, much less public dinner at Dorchester Street before the royal couple returned to England. The menu was the same as it had been in September: oysters, consommé, and an enormous selection of fowl, meat and game, ranging from chicken and pheasant to venison and lamb, followed by a pudding and biscuits.

In the intervening eight weeks, Donald travelled to Ottawa to deal with immigration questions and the increasingly vexatious matter of the provincial agents general. Long before the federation of the Canadian provinces, colonies such as Nova Scotia had had representatives in London and, as the post-Confederation provinces developed more sophisticated industries and more complex trade demands, they too sent representatives to London, rightly arguing that they knew more about the details of provincial matters than even the most assiduous high commissioner could be expected to know. The agents general, however, felt that they should be entitled to the same privileges and the same access to the colonial authorities that Donald enjoyed. The British government thought otherwise.

The cabinet's initial reluctance to allow a colony to have a permanent representative at all had given way to an appreciation of the greater efficiency brought about by direct communication with the high commissioner. Direct communication with the agents general of the provinces, however, would lead to confusion. As Donald was forced to explain on more than one occasion, the British North America Act was very explicit in saying that it was the federal government which conducted relations with the British government and not the governments of the individual provinces. The agent general for British Columbia proved particularly recalcitrant, pointing out that the Australian states were accredited to the British government. Donald was driven to constitutional lessons and to observing that the new country of Australia was facing difficulties precisely because it had not taken full cognizance of the question of foreign representation when it drew up its constitutional document; it was now trying to find a way of, in effect, demoting its constituent states. It would be foolish for Canada to take a retrograde step and put itself in Australia's position. The BC agent general, John Turner, who had previously been the province's premier, nevertheless felt he could go behind Donald's back and convince his successor, Richard McBride, to request accreditation to the colonial office, saying that Donald would approve. The fib soon made its way to Laurier's desk and Turner discovered that the prime minister entirely shared the high commissioner's views.[12]

Donald developed a cold when he was in Canada in the autumn of 1901 and his health deteriorated in London's smoggy air. It was Christmas before he could shake it, but he did himself no favours by working late in the High Commission offices and attending HBC board meetings anyway. As Bella said, "he was done up with work & travelling & fidgetting [sic] to get to his office." Part of his trouble was that his cold and influenza had brought with them an ear infection which exacerbated the deafness from which he was beginning to suffer.[13]

When he and Bella had got back to London in November, they found the city buzzing with excitement over the forthcoming coronation. Innumerable celebrations were planned; the colonial prime ministers were due and there would be a colonial conference; colonial troops were required for the coronation parade and decorations would fill the city. Bella was the "ostensible chief" of a Canadian stand at a huge coronation fair designed to raise money for the children's hospital in Great Ormond Street and both Maggie and Agnes Macdonald were her lieutenants. Donald ordered $250 worth of Indian handiwork for sale at the stall and seems to have paid for a good deal else besides. "I need not say that all the old Lord is allowed to pay for & do, he pays for, & *does* like a prince," Lady Macdonald reported.[14]

The subject which provoked the greatest amount of bother and the greatest amount of cable traffic between London and Ottawa, however, was the coronation arch. It seems to have been Preston's notion and smacks of his handiwork in the sense that it was a good idea but not properly thought through.

The idea was to build an arch across Whitehall, the road which connects Trafalgar Square with the Houses of Parliament and Westminster Abbey, passing the main government offices on the way. It would form part of the coronation parade route and any decoration mounted in Whitehall would also be seen by the thousands of visitors flocking to London for the celebrations. The plan was to use the arch as a means of promoting Canada and encouraging emigration. The role model was an arch, built entirely of wheat, which had been erected in Winnipeg.

In April, Donald decreed that the arch was to span the entire street and not sit in the centre, forcing traffic to go around it. He said it must incorporate "design features" and not just be made of wheat, and that it should be capable of being illuminated. He also noted that it would be essential to employ an architect in the UK. In April, he stressed that it "must be done in such a way so as to cause no reflection upon the taste and good judgment of the Government, and at the same time give to Canada the character of advertisement which we all so much desire."[15]

Squabbles over Canada's insistence on designing the arch in Ottawa, and the consequent need to re-design it in London, arguments over costs, the electricity company's profiteering as London dressed itself up for the coronation, and difficulties in finding sheaves of wheat long after the harvest had been brought in nearly finished the project. In the end, Ottawa authorized the spending of $10,000 and Donald committed himself to paying the difference between that and what it would take to do it properly. Had Ottawa even half guessed at the impact the arch would make, it would not have begrudged the money.

The arch was sixty feet wide, fifty feet high and had a central opening of twenty-five feet, enough for a London double decker bus to pass through. About twenty tons of wheat, grasses and other grains were fastened to the frame and, at a level where pedestrians could clearly see them and admire their size, grains of wheat filled narrow glass panels. Maple leaves, apples and cobs of corn were included in the decorative structure, while illuminations — pictures on glass which were lit from behind at night — showed Canadian scenes to passers by. The whole arch was outlined with four thousand lights. On each side of the arch, a dove, emblematic of the peace which had just been achieved in South Africa, perched over the British coat of arms. A huge sign on one side read "Canada, Britain's Granary" and on the other, less subtly, was the message "Free Homes for Millions."

Unfortunately, the king developed appendicitis and instead of proceeding down the aisle at Westminster Abbey, found himself comatose in a hospital operating theatre. As soon as it was certain that he would recover, London gave itself over to partying. The longer the coronation was delayed, the longer the good times would last. Crowds flocked to see the Canadian arch, choking Whitehall at every opportunity. On July 1, Canadian troops idling their time away while they waited for the coronation, celebrated Canada's national holiday by parading down Whitehall to be reviewed by Donald's erstwhile house guest, now more generally referred to as the Prince of Wales. Photographs of the soldiers passing through the arch appeared in all the magazines and newspapers and were flashed up on screens in music halls which treated their audiences to scenes of preparations for the coronation. On July 7, the *Daily Express* reported that people on the buses which travelled along Whitehall and under the arch were failing to alight at their destination. Instead, they remained on the bus so they could travel under the arch again.

When General Kitchener returned from South Africa, the somewhat drooping arch was, as *The Times* reported, "literally spruced up for the occasion with fresh wreaths of fir. It had also a picture of Lord Kitchener, with the inscription 'Hero in Peace and War'." "Welcome to our Heroes" gave the other soldiers their due and crimson drapery completed the effect. It was not common to turn on the lights of such decorations every night and Canada was one of the few to illuminate on the night of the Kitchener celebrations, to the delight of the "black stream of people which ebbed and flowed beneath, rendering vehicular traffic practically impossible." The crowds and the traffic jams began to tell on the temper of the police who finally demanded the arch be removed as a traffic hazard. A gift of £50 from Canada to the Metropolitan and City Police Orphanage convinced the bobbies that it was not quite the danger they thought.[16]

At Laurier's insistence, the arch was refreshed again for the coronation. Having authorized the expenditure of $10,000, Canada actually spent $33,000, including the cost of collecting and shipping the grain. Another $11,075 went on various electrical fittings to adapt the arch for Kitchener's celebrations and to revitalize it for the coronation. The impact, however, was so great that parliament willingly passed a special vote to cover the extra costs. Even the most curmudgeonly of MPs recognized that no amount of conventional publicity could equal the effect of the coronation arch.

Coronation lunches, dinners, banquets and receptions surrounded the colonial conference which began on July 18. On the 26th, the Strathconas gave a huge garden party at Knebworth and on August 11, they hosted a dinner party in honour of the colonial premiers — "64 guests 8 at each table & 8 tables. House decorated with flowers & palms[.] Electric light in ceiling. Each table covered with rich silver & delicate glass a large silver basket of red roses ferns & leaves on each." Princess Louise and her husband, now the Duke of Argyll, headed the guest list which also included the "Aberdeen's," as Agnes Macdonald reported with her usual flair for the misplaced or unnecessary apostrophe.[17]

King Edward VII and Queen Alexandra were finally crowned on August 9 and the Hudson's Bay Company celebrated by giving to everyone who had been in the company's service for more than twelve months ten percent of their salaries. The emigration campaign conducted by the Canadian government, in the person of Donald and his staff, and by the CPR agents, had resulted in a steady surge in land sales and the HBC dividends reflected this. From 2.5 percent in 1891 and 1892, payouts had risen to 8.65 percent in 1902 and were about to skyrocket to the astonishing figure of 50 percent in the years immediately prior to the first world war. It was nevertheless a period of general economic instability with inflation steadily eroding the value of wages. In April 1903, Donald made a personal cash gift to everyone who had been in the company's employ for the previous twelve months to encourage them to stay with the HBC. Shortly after, the company finally introduced a pension scheme for its staff.

By the middle of August, London social life and the coronation celebrations finally came to a halt. Donald dashed up to Forres to lay the foundation stone of the new United Free Church on August 13 and, shortly afterwards, Bella set out for the baths at Carlsbad. Late in the month, they finally escaped to Glencoe where they remained till early October. Towards the start of that month Donald's propensity for sprained and broken limbs reasserted itself and one of his legs was in plaster till the middle of December. Early the following summer, he sprained his ankle.

The commission of inquiry into the South African war first sat on October 8, 1902 and, though Donald missed this session because he was in Liverpool as a guest of the city's Provision Trades Association for the opening of the new Exchange, he attended virtually all the others. As the commission met almost daily, it occupied a huge amount of his time until the middle of March 1903.

The spring of 1903 brought Canadian delegates to the meetings of the Alaska boundary commission and the dinners and entertaining which invariably attended such negotiations. It also brought the news that Lord Lytton had married and could soon be expected to want the use of Knebworth. Quietly, Donald began to keep an eye out for country houses near London and in July, he instructed his agents to purchase Debden Hall.

The house was set in a grand park in Essex and the core of the building seems to have been erected some time in the seventeenth century. In 1795, Richard Chiswell, "an eminent Turkey merchant," decided to rebuild it and commissioned Henry Holland to design the changes. He created new façades for three of the four sides while, for the west side, he devised an Ionic portico. When Donald bought the house, the entrance was through a much admired avenue of lime and chestnuts approaching from the south to meet another carriage drive coming from the north. Oak floors, doors and wainscotting, and marble and oak mantlepieces featured on the ground floor which also had "enriched plaster" ceilings. An oak staircase with mahogany rails led to the first floor which had six principal bed and dressing rooms. Twelve bedrooms occupied the second floor and there were five bedrooms for servants in the attic.[18]

The estate had vegetable gardens, 130 acres of timbered park, a lake stocked with fish and nearly five thousand acres of land for shooting pheasants, partridges, hares and other small animals and birds. There were forty-two farms, two of which had five bedroom houses, as well as thirty-five cottages. The ancient church of Debden, on the property, came with an eleven bedroom rectory. The estate had its own spring and several wells and Debden Hall had central heating, an almost unheard of luxury in an English country house at that time. Two oil fired generators produced electricity for the house and the owner of the estate was entitled to call himself Lord of the Manor of Debden.

While he owned Debden, Donald increased the estate by 753 acres, making judicious purchases of neighbouring farms, and bringing the total purchase price to £138,527. In 1903, the annual income was just over £4,229, farm rents having been reduced to enable the tenants to make a living. The increase of thirteen and a half percent in the amount of land, coupled with a general increase in economic prosperity, led to a growth of nearly forty-seven percent in the estate's annual income during Donald's ownership. He substantially improved the drainage, especially for domestic waste, and provided running water for the houses and cottages which had previously been without.

For all that the manor house was modern and well appointed by the standards of the time, it was not as Donald wanted it to be and he made substantial alterations before moving in. He moved the drawing room so that it, rather than the billiard room, had the casement windows opening onto a terrace and the west lawn. He built a second, servants' staircase, and substantially improved the facilities for the domestic staff, including providing separate accommodation for six of the men and two of the women. When he bought it, the house had two interconnecting bedrooms with a dressing room off one of them, a suite of rooms clearly intended for use by the master and mistress of the house. Donald and Bella had these completely re-done, creating one bedroom with a dressing room and a bathroom, replete with modern fittings. The Strathconas' worries about fire had not abated and they had the house fitted throughout with "fire hydrants with hose & complete attachments." They also put in a telephone. The improvements to the house and the estate were estimated to have cost about £12,000. All the changes meant that it was the summer of 1908 before they finally gave up Knebworth and moved to Debden Hall.[19]

As well as incessantly entertaining and being entertained, Donald also faced a regular stream of visitors to his office in Victoria Street. "Poor old Lord Strathcona must be worried to death with callers from every quarter," John McConnell wrote to his fiancée in July 1904 after he had spent more than an hour in the queue to see the high commissioner. "They are hanging around waiting to see him all day long and they tell me at the office here that the old gentleman rarely leaves his office before seven or eight o'clock at night and he is in his 85th year."[20]

Some were at Donald's office by appointment on government or Hudson's Bay Company business, others were messengers from banks or commercial interests and others, by far the greatest number, were men and women seeking favours. Up to seventy people a day passed through the office, and a mixed bag they were. John McConnell, for example, was selling shares in the Canadian company, Standard Chemicals, but more important than persuading Lord Strathcona to buy some was the host of introductions he could, and did, provide.

At the other end of the social and economic scale were men who were little more than beggars, hoping that they could come up with a sad story to loosen his lordship's purse strings. More often than not, they were successful and emerged from Donald's office with a smile and £5 or £10 tucked securely in their pockets.

Others were a cut above these people on the social scale but no more committed to repaying their loans, despite their promissory notes. "There is nothing further yet from Mr. H.N. Moody respecting his debt of £500 and accrued interest," Joseph Colmer wrote at the beginning of October 1904, "but I suppose we must allow this to stand over, in view of his father's letter to you." Colmer had resigned as secretary to the high commissioner, but continued to work as Donald's private secretary, a post which took on added importance after Joseph Hardisty's death in Montreal in 1906. He was constantly engaged in an effort to keep track of the loans and in the thankless task of trying to arrange repayment. "I suppose we shall never get the $600 from Fabre. It was lent to him in October 1897 — seven years ago, and he neither writes nor pays." The Canadian MP, Henry Nathan, owed £300 which was due in August 1903 "but you told me not to do anything in the matter, and I do not know whether he has written you on the subject." As a rule, when letters demanding repayment were answered, they contained an affirmation that the money was a gift, despite the fact that notes promising repayment had been signed.[21]

It was the secretaries, the bookkeepers and the lawyers who suffered from this failure to distinguish between a loan and a gift, none more so than the very proper William Garson, Donald's Scottish solicitor.

> I was running over the stubs of a cheque-book with Lord Strathcona, checking up the various items, when I came across the record of a cheque for one hundred pounds made out to a man who I knew to be unworthy. Calling Lord Strathcona's attention to it, I expressed my surprise, but, as he made no comment, I said nothing more, and continued running through the stubs of the cheque-book.
>
> To my amazement, I shortly came across another cheque for the same amount, made out to the same individual. This time I ventured to suggest to Lord Strathcona that the man's reputation did not justify confidence in him and that if he desired an investigation, I believed the reputation would be amply borne out by specific evidence. I waited for a reply, but he still kept silence, and I went on looking over the stubs.

> Finally, I came across a third cheque for the same amount to the order of the same individual. When I called his attention to it, he said, in his quiet way: "Well, Garson, if one in twenty is worthy —"[22]

Joseph Hardisty, Colmer, and various others kept records of the loans from 1880 onwards. By 1913, the only years in which all loans had been repaid were 1885, 1886 and 1894. The total still owing for 1887 was $23,830, a sum far in excess of the outstanding debts for any other year.

Others in the queue outside Donald's door were not after loans but outright gifts for worthy causes. While some people sought charitable donations in writing and others, especially the well connected ladies, made their requests through Bella or Maggie, many people decided to chance their luck in person or made an appearance at Victoria Street because someone had arranged an introduction. Like most people, Donald found it difficult to turn down a supplicant in person; if he did refuse a man to his face, he did not expect an argument and was more than a little taken aback when he found the Rev. John Antle challenging his decision.

Antle, a Newfoundlander whose circle in Brighouse would have included Nathan Norman's family, was operating a mission boat along the coast of British Columbia, working with fishermen and loggers and trying to keep the Indian women from prostitution. He had come to England partly to publicize the work he was doing in Canada and partly in the hope of raising money from wealthy individuals in the UK. Friends had secured an appointment at the high commission, a procedure which, in itself, took eleven days in 1908.

Donald immediately told Antle that he would not support the mission work, a bluntness which so startled the missionary that he sat down when he had pointedly not been invited to do so. Thinking he had nothing to lose, he tried to explain the work the mission was doing, but Donald became "very impatient and rather aggressive. First of all, he said, he did not approve of persons coming from Canada to collect the pence of the poor for building their institutions."

> By this time, I had got over my diffidence and was on my feet facing him again. My reply to this attack was not one penny of what I had collected by my missionary talks had been given to the Columbia Coast Mission but to the charities in England. "In coming to you, Lord Strathcona, I am not coming to the poor of England but to the rich of Canada."
>
> He returned to the attack and declared he objected very strongly to missionaries coming to England from Canada and giving the people [the impression] there were no schools, no churches, no hospitals, "while we," he said, "spend thousands of pounds advertising Canada and assuring the people they will not lack schools or churches when they go to Canada."
>
> I said, "you should not do it."
>
> "Why not?" he asked.
>
> "Because it is not [t]rue," I replied. "Where you settle these people — where the thousands that your transportation compa-

> nies bring to Canada to settle, in those areas, there are no schools or churches, and if it were not for beggars — as you call us missionaries — there would be none of the services which are considered necessary to civilization."
>
> I was angry and[,] advancing as I spoke, had backed Lord Strathcona to the fireplace. He reached to a side table and pulled out a letter file. Opening it he showed me a pile of letters and said, "These are all begging letters from institutions equally as important as your own."
>
> I remarked that it was only natural that a man of his position and wealth should receive these appeals, but I said, "Is it a fair question to ask you how many you have replied to favorably?"
>
> He appeared amazed at my temerity in thus questioning him. There was a long pause and I fully expected to be shown the door, then he blurted out, "Give you five hundred pounds!"
>
> It was my turn to be astonished and I hastily sought the support of the chair I had pushed aside in my anger.[23]

Having been beaten, Donald capitulated with good grace. He met the Rev. Antle on subsequent occasions and quizzed him in a friendly manner about the work which was being done on the west coast. And when Antle boarded the *Empress of Britain* to return to Canada, he found a cordial note wishing him Godspeed.

Another person who waited her turn in the High Commission queue was Agnes Macdonald. The prime minister had left what little money he had to three trustees: his son Hugh John, his long time secretary Joseph Pope, and Fred White, the comptroller of the NWMP. They were to invest it on his widow's behalf. The bulk of the work, however, fell on a man named Ferguson and, on his death, on a man named Sinclair. They were slow with accounts and, for many years, Sinclair did not keep any at all. He secretly borrowed from the estate for his own uses, though he repaid with interest in due course. Poor Lady Macdonald was at her wits', end, not only because she had a very limited income but also because she rarely knew what it was. Moreover, the transfer of her allowance from Canada to England was frequently late and she could never be sure whether it would come at all. At one point she consulted Lord Mount Stephen who was so disenchanted with Canada and all things Canadian that he advised her to sell her Canadian Pacific Railway shares as he himself had done. To her later regret, the baroness complied with this advice.

In despair, she finally turned to Lord Strathcona. She saw Donald and Bella socially but did not feel free to discuss her business matters on such occasions and so joined the crowds in Victoria Street. "Lord Strathcona is *most* kind, ever ready to suggest & talk to me, but he is never at home, always to be seen at his office, & to say truth Mr. Colmer's manner is so unpleasant to me when I go there that I *never* go when it can by any possibility be avoided," she wrote to Pope at the end of 1900, adding "I d'ont in the least think Colmer means to be rude but he is priggish & rather vulgar."[24]

As soon as he realized what her difficulties were, Donald recommended transferring responsibility for her investments to the Royal Trust. He promised that the management charges would not exceed those she was currently paying and was confident the interest would equal what she was getting. Unfortunately, because her investments were so inefficiently handled, it took years for her trustees to agree to the transfer and then effect it. For her, these were years of incessant worry and she became increasingly dependent on the advice and consideration which Donald was able to offer her. "Indeed, his interest and kindness are very touching, seeing he was not even a party man & saw so little of either of us," she remarked to Pope in 1902.[25]

Donald soon removed her from the High Commission queue and he and Bella treated her as a personal friend: she was invited to quiet family meals on Sundays and received invitations to formal dinners for visiting Canadian dignitaries. Both Donald and Bella showed more than a superficial concern for the Macdonalds' disabled daughter, Mary, and visited her without waiting for an invitation. When Mary grew deaf, Donald arranged for Dr. Barlow to examine her and then to remove the polyps which had caused the loss of hearing. The bill was a fraction of Barlow's normal charge, either because he had been persuaded by Donald to be considerate of the baroness's restricted means or because Donald made up the difference.

"He indeed is more than good in taking an interest in my small affairs," she wrote to Pope in 1906. "I am touched to observe his friendliness & interest & that he is never too busy or pre-occupied to omit asking about my trifling amusements.

"How strangely the wheel of life goes round!

"That the day is here in which Donald Smith is such a friend to me!"[26]

Two years earlier, he had solved another problem for her. "Unasked, out of his wonderful kindness & sagacity that wonderful old Lord Strathcona saw my unspoken & unsleeping perplexity —saw — or rather divined it, & suggested Andrew [sic] Lang, Manager of Bank of Montreal as guardian for my poor Mary *in case of my death*."[27]

Donald also arranged for her to visit his lawyers in London and make a codicil to her will by which her goddaughters, who were her brother's children, would inherit the money which their father had left to her. "He is literally & remorselessly *besieged* when got at. People have no mercy, I c'ant join in, when I *do* his kindness consideration and interest is beyond belief — then me thinks how little I or mine deserve it from him," she wrote to Pope on another occasion.[28]

Though Lady Macdonald was always fairly frank in her correspondence with Pope, and increasingly gushing about the help she was receiving from Donald and about the kindness both he and Bella showed to Mary, it was very late in the day when she finally confessed that Donald had also been paying her winter rent and fuel bills. She and Mary moved to Italy towards the end of each year because life was much cheaper there, and Donald had taken to presenting her with a cheque to keep a roof over their heads and coal in their grates. While she was undoubtedly grateful for it, and it helps to explain her innumerable references to "dear kind Lord S," it was equally a source of worry to her. "This cheque is always given at the last minute before we leave England and I cannot possibly *count* on it for a moment," she explained to Pope in 1913. "He is an old man, and might forget it, or intend to discontinue it, or alas! pass away from us, who so love & revere the splendid old man; and would miss him in every possible way." It was the last option which finally stopped the cheques, but not before the transfer to the Royal Trust had at last been completed and the baroness's accounts put on a steady footing.[29]

In addition to making gifts and unsecured loans which he only half expected to see repaid, Donald continued his Canadian business of lending money on reliable security, though his British transactions never equalled the Canadian in either the amounts lent or the number of people he dealt with. One of his long standing British debtors was Major General Sir John Carstairs McNeill, the nephew of George Stephen's old school fellow, Field Marshal Donald Stewart and consequently one of Donald's very distant relatives.

As a young man, McNeill had been military secretary to Governor General Sir John Young (later Lord Lisgar). The tour of duty lasted from 1868 to 1872, an exciting time for the young soldier who travelled to the North West with General Wolseley in the summer of 1870. A distinguished military career, coupled with good breeding and a long Scottish lineage, brought him a position as ADC to George, Duke of Cambridge, Commander-in-Chief of the British Army, and, when he left the army in 1890, as an equerry to the Duke's cousin, Queen Victoria. No doubt it was his love of sport, rather than his army experience or Scottish background, which fostered his friendship with the Prince of Wales and ensured his knighthood when Edward acceded to the throne.

McNeill owned the islands of Colonsay and Oronsay which lie off the west coast of Scotland, just north of Islay and west of Jura. In total, they are only nine miles long with Oronsay accessible from Colonsay by foot across the sands at low tide. They have been inhabited at least since the Middle Stone Age but their names derive from Saint Columba, the Irish missionary who brought Christianity to Scotland, and his assistant, Saint Oran. John Macdonald of Islay, the first Lord of the Isles, founded an Augustinian priory on Oronsay in the second quarter of the fourteenth century and the ruins of the church and monastic buildings, with their elaborate Celtic stonework, gargoyles, carvings of priests in vestments and funerary depictions of knights in armour are rich with reminders of both the secular and the religious life of the time.

The Campbells and the Macdonalds squabbled over Colonsay and Oronsay until 1701 when Malcolm McNeill acquired the estate from the Duke of Argyll, a Campbell. It passed by purchase among collateral branches of the McNeill family until 1870 when Lord Colonsay sold the islands for £40,000 to his brother, John McNeill. Seven years later, John McNeill sold the islands to his nephew, John Carstairs McNeill, for the grossly exaggerated sum of £80,072. McNeill compounded his folly in paying such an excessive price for the islands by a failure to manage either his finances or his investments prudently; neither was his friendship with the Prince of Wales designed to keep his personal spending under control.

In April 1886, he wrote "Dear Uncle Donald" from Osborne, Queen Victoria's residence on the Isle of Wight, saying he had spoken to Lord Mount Stephen who thought his cousin might help. A farm on Colonsay was about to become vacant and McNeill wanted to borrow money in order to purchase stock for it. In May, Donald provided £2,500 at four percent, to be repaid on demand or on the sale of Colonsay and Oronsay. The following May, McNeill had £5,000 on the same terms.[30]

The mortgages which Donald and others had on the property hung over McNeill's head for the rest of his life. He talked about selling the islands to rid himself of the debts but had not got round to doing so when he died suddenly in May 1904. McNeill had never married and neither his heirs nor any of his other relatives wanted the islands. In June 1904, Donald sent to his Scottish solicitors for the papers relating to his loans to McNeill and before the year was out, he had purchased the islands for £44,000, a sum which covered the money owing to him and paid off the other debts. For an additional £3,000, he bought the superiority from the Duke of Argyll. Astonishingly, the McNeills had never acquired this important right which allowed the owner to collect rents while enabling the tenants to bequeath the property they occupied to subsequent generations.

Donald immediately set about making improvements on Colonsay, by far the larger of the two islands. In 1722, at the little hamlet of Kiloran, Colonsay House had been erected, almost certainly on the site of a monastic ruin. Later generations of McNeills extended the house but it was Donald who undertook the first series of major alterations, adding a second storey and attic to some of the earlier additions and substantially upgrading the service courtyard. Between the purchase and the spring of 1909, he spent nearly £14,000 on improvements on the island, nearly half of that amount going on the house. A road was built and the pier improved. General repairs required another £1,000. Set against these expenses was an annual income from rents of £1,500. The potential rental income from property occupied or managed in Donald's own name added a further £500 to the annual value of the property he had acquired.

No sooner had he purchased the islands than numerous petitions concerning leases and tenancies began to arrive. The McNeills wrote concerning which moveable possessions were theirs and not included in the sale. They also wanted to erect a memorial to the general and Donald agreed to contribute £50, half the cost. Miss Jamieson wanted to purchase the buckboard. (She was given it, but denied permission to use it on the island.) The question of servants had to be settled. The housekeeper engaged a cook, an under housemaid and a laundry maid and had instructions to find two table maids, a kitchen maid and an additional laundry maid.

Towards the end of July 1905, the solicitors were in London explaining to Lord Strathcona that there was only one horse at Colonsay which could run in carriage and there was a heavy mare for carting luggage. At least one more horse was needed. As for carriages, the only ones at the house were a four wheeled dog cart and a luggage cart which was "practically useless". A landau, a two wheeled dog cart, a light wagonette and a luggage cart would be useful, the lawyers reported. His Lordship might also want to consider a pony cart for the children, for it was clear from the beginning that Colonsay was going to be a family house in a way that Glencoe never managed to be.

The solicitors presented even the most minute questions to Donald and he made all but the most insignificant decisions about the islands, the farms, the buildings and the staff. Points in which he had no interest, such as guns, fishing rods, tennis, croquet and bowls sets were left for the Howards to determine. The fact that Maggie was never encouraged to concern herself with the management of investments and property which would one day be hers reflects Donald's view, common among his generation, that women did not belong in the board room, even though he thought they should be well educated. The fact that Dr. Howard was never given the opportunity to contribute reflects the fact that Donald had not grown to like him any more than he had when Maggie married him. Howard, with his wife and children, spent the obligatory holidays in Glencoe and, later, Colonsay, and weekends at Knebworth and Debden; he attended many of the official dinners which the Strathconas hosted in London and Montreal, but no camaraderie, no bond of affection, ever grew up between Donald and his son-in-law. Howard may have sacrificed something of his medical career in the interests of his wife's family but a large measure of Donald's disappointment derived from the fact that Maggie's husband never distinguished himself. During the Boer War, he worked at the Guards' Hospital in London and he also practised as a laryngologist, working from his home in Queen Anne Street, but medical biographies for the first part of this century imply that he did very little at all; his promise of brilliance was never fulfilled.

In the midst of the house purchases, the routine High Commission business, the problems with Preston and the North Atlantic Trading Company, worries about Northern Securities and the inevitable dinners and speeches, Donald continued as governor of the Hudson's Bay Company, playing an active role in its day to day management and leading the semi-annual General Courts. More often than not, he was too busy to check the proofs of his speeches and Ware struggled to get him to do it so he could publish the Court proceedings. The Governor and Committee continued to interest themselves in the minutiae of Canadian business, from the sale of individual plots of land to the supply of crockery for the shops. In 1906, the Canada North West Land Company decided to sell off its land as quickly as it could since prices were rapidly rising. Seeing that the future would demand increasing quantities of electric power, it converted itself into Canada North West Energy.

In the summer of 1904, Donald made what was to prove to be his last trip to Forres, laying the foundation stone for the new parish church of St. Laurence and visiting Leanchoil Hospital. A gift of £1,500 wiped out the deficit in the church building fund or, as the reporters at the time preferred it, paid for the steeple of the new church.

Laurier won the federal election in November that year and Borden hoped that it would provide an opportunity for him to succeed Donald as high commissioner. The prime minister, however, saw no reason to change an arrangement with which he was more than happy, and Donald remained in post.[31]

He continued to take an interest in the House of Lords, though he rarely spoke in order to avoid a conflict of interest with his duties as Canada's representative in the UK. He had no difficulty, however, in introducing the second reading of an amendment to the 1886 Medical Act to allow reciprocal recognition of medical qualifications where these had been issued by Canadian provincial, rather than federal authorities. And a year later, in 1906, he once more supported a Colonial Marriages Bill.

Bella was seriously ill again in the late autumn of 1905 and Donald delayed his Canadian trip until Christmas as a consequence. It was a rough crossing which even Donald, by now the world record holder for transatlantic voyages, found unpleasant. In Montreal, he arranged for the adjoining house which had been used by the Duke and Duchess in 1901 to be furnished so the new governor general, Earl Grey, could use it whenever he wished.

In the spring of 1906, Robert Baden-Powell, having returned to England following the organization of South Africa's police force, finally settled down to drafting his proposal for a new society which would teach English boys the rudiments of self-reliance which he had witnessed among young South Africans. *Scouting for Boys* as he called the book which grew out of this proposal, fitted in with thinking then current that boys should be prepared to defend the empire. The South African war and the commission of inquiry which followed it had made it abundantly clear that not only was Britain unprepared, she was unable to make herself ready in short order, not least because most young men were neither physically nor mentally able to make a quick transition from civilian to military life. Boys needed regular training which could be turned to advantage in a national emergency. Strength of character was required but this needed to be reinforced by skills such as the capacity to observe and remember details, the ability to swim and judge distances, and the knowledge of how to use a compass, cook and give first aid. A number of eminent men were sent copies of the original paper, including both Donald and Earl Grey. Donald thought it "one of the finest plans for the betterment of the race that has been evolved in our time," and in 1913 he promised $25,000 to enable the Scout movement to be established in Canada.[32]

While Baden-Powell was drawing up his proposals for Boy Scouts, Sir Frederick Borden was thinking along similar lines. Most Canadian schools had neither the staff nor the resources to teach any form of physical education though the contribution exercise made to general health was beginning to be generally understood. At the time, it was also believed that regular and disciplined exercise such as calisthenics or military drill fostered greater discipline in all other aspects of school activity, and organisations such as the Young Men's Christian Association believed controlled exercise could help young men lead a more upright life. Borden perceived that such exercise, taught in school, would assist "not only the bodily development of all classes and both sexes" but, married to military drill for the boys, would create a group of men who could "take part in the defence of their homes and country."[33]

In 1907, the Militia Department began to train physical education teachers, both at normal schools and in special after-school classes. Early in 1909, or possibly late in 1908, when he was in London, Borden discussed his aims with Donald, who immediately offered to help. In response to a paper outlining the plan, Donald wrote that he had "long entertained the opinion that such training as that you are striving for is of the highest value in developing the moral, physical and intellectual qualities of children, as well as that valuable quality known as patriotism." He gave $250,000, the intention being that it would be invested to provide a return of $10,000 a year. When it became clear a few weeks later that $12,000 a year would be required, he added $50,000 to his original donation. A year later, in October 1910, he felt more money was needed and sent a further $200,000.[34]

As usual, Donald requested anonymity but in this case, he wasted his breath. Not only was his initial gift announced, it became the topic of an enthusiastic parliamentary debate. Contradicting Donald's instructions that his name was not to be associated with the enterprise, Borden set up the Strathcona Trust which devised a set of guidelines with which schools were to comply in order to obtain financial support for the programme. Not all approved of the military element of the trust's aims but most were prepared to go along with it in order to finance physical education courses.

The older Donald grew, the more he seemed to feel obliged to disperse his great wealth. Maggie and her children were more than adequately provided for; Jamesie and his children received a regular allowance and smaller sums were employed to look after various female relatives. Donald knew that he and Bella could not have much longer to enjoy the fruits of his investments and felt increasingly free to dispose of his surplus. When fire swept through San Francisco following an earthquake in the spring of 1906, he immediately sent off a cheque for $10,000. In 1907, he gave $5,000 to the YMCA in Ottawa. This was the first of a long series of gifts to Canadian branches of the YMCA, the total finally coming to $196,300. Earlier, he had given £25,000 towards a new building for Marischal College at the University of Aberdeen.

The university celebrated its four hundredth anniversary in 1907 and the occasion provided Donald with an opportunity to indulge in the most elaborate entertainment he ever devised or, at any rate, that he ever paid for. When his term as rector expired in 1902, he had been elected chancellor of the university for life and it was in this capacity that the principal consulted him during a weekend visit to Knebworth in June 1907. Donald confirmed that he wanted to be involved in the celebrations and added that his contribution would be a dinner "at which he desired not only all the Delegates and invited Guests but all Graduates and other members of the University taking part in the Celebrations should be invited to be present. His Lordship had further indicated his desire that no apparent difficulties, financial or otherwise, should be allowed to stand in the way of carrying out his plan in the best possible manner."[35]

The main impediment to carrying out Donald's wishes was that there was no place in Aberdeen large enough to seat 2,500 for a banquet, but since "no apparent difficulties" were to stand in the way, the university set about creating a temporary building, inevitably called Strathcona Hall. Its construction also resolved the university's dilemma of where to hold a reception to which nearly five thousand were to be invited. Conveniently, the city had just cleared a tenement facing the gate to Marischal College and the land provided the ideal site for the hall which was built of timber and decorated with garlands of flowers and greenery. The hall cost £3,400 and £4,500 was spent on feeding the guests.

All of Aberdeen celebrated the anniversary; important guests were housed with townspeople; citizens decorated their houses in festive style; students processed by torchlight through the streets and held a sports day to which all were welcome. The lord provost, the magistrates and the town council entertained the university and were the scholars' guests in turn. Through three days of celebrations there was music: pipers from the Gordon Highlanders played Scottish airs, the Aberdeen Male Voice Choir serenaded diners, the Artillery Volunteers played "Land of Hope and Glory" and selections from *Yeoman of the Guard*, while young men ran races and showed their skill at hammer throwing; Herr Stanislaus Wurm's White Viennese Orchestra played the *William Tell* overture and "Ave Maria" and selections from *Spring Chicken* at the art gallery reception and when the king and queen arrived on the last day, it was the band of the Scots Greys with works by Wagner, Elgar and Grieg. To ensure that everyone in Aberdeen had a chance to celebrate, Donald gave £1,000 to provide entertainment for the poor of the city.

A host of people from all over the world received honourary degrees at Donald's hands on the morning of September 26, the second day of the celebrations. "Genius makes its own rules," wrote Leslie MacKenzie in the flowery prose with which he recorded the ceremony in the university's account of its party.

> Mr. Carnegie, answering to his name, rose promptly and mounted the platform. But the emotion of the moment was for once his master. He looked up at the face of old Strathcona; their eyes met, and we knew that, for the instant the whole world was lost to them. Mr. Carnegie instantly held out his hand and the Chancellor took it; but in doing so, he laid down the Mystic Cap and thus it happened that Mr. Carnegie was never created a Doctor! ... We accepted the omen. Mr. Carnegie is a maker of Universities; he cannot be made by them.[36]

Despite the jollity pervading the celebrations — Lord Balfour of Burleigh suggested an honourary doctorate to the Meteorological Society for fixing the perfect autumn weather — Donald's speech at the degree ceremony was neither especially cheerful nor self-congratulatory. Scottish universities needed to look to their laurels, he said, because they were in danger of failing to adapt to modern life. North American universities "enjoy a considerable advantage in the ease and readiness with which, unhampered as they are by any venerable traditions, they can adapt themselves to the practical needs of the various constituencies which they seek to serve." He suggested it was time for changes to the 1889 Scottish Universities Act which restricted the opportunities for change. North American universities "have never accepted the view that Universities must necessarily be institutions cloistered and apart from the main current of public life and service. On the contrary, they make a training for citizenship, and for public usefulness the basis and foundation of much of their educational activity."[37]

On the morning of the twenty-seventh, the king and queen arrived in Aberdeen and the cheers of the welcoming students drowned out the playing of the national anthem, much to the disgust of *The Times* whose correspondent thought the enthusiasm showed a lack of dignity and respect. Perhaps he overlooked the fact that many in the crowd believed the monarch had only come because "uncle Donald" had asked him to.

Donald's dinner that night was cooked in London by Lyons, the mass caterers who had restaurants throughout the English capital. It was shipped north by special train, together with the thousands of glasses, plates, knives and forks needed for the occasion. Another special took the waiters and their equipment back. Strathcona Hall was far too large for diners to hear the speakers and the toasts, a problem which Andrew Carnegie dealt with by giving his speech to the press and advising those who could hear him to read it in the morning. "The Chancellor wished to dine a few friends," he began, pointing out that the crowd at the banquet were only a few of Donald's many friends.

> But to understand his triumphs you must know the power behind the throne, Lady Strathcona — the special counsel, not the silent partner. Is it not positively amazing what the Scot can grow to imagine, undertake, and accomplish if caught young enough and transplanted to the stimulating climate and conditions of Canada, the home of many of our English speaking race? The North American continent appears the most fruitful developing ground in the world for the human plant provided it is started right — that means among the heather. Whether it be a railroad across the continent to the Pacific, or a monster hall in Aberdeen, it's all the same to the transplanted Lord Chancellor, who inherits the virtues of both lands and the foibles of neither.[38]

The heather and the stimulating Canadian climate had made an amazing man and so too had Bella, not because she was out of sight, directing affairs, but because she was always there for him, in spirit if not in person. Her steadfast friendship, to say nothing of her love, was not dependent on his position or his possessions but on the man himself.

CHAPTER TWENTY

THE GRAND OLD MAN 1908–1914

Rising at 8 o'clock, Lord Strathcona went as usual to the Canadian offices at Victoria Street where he remained attending to business matters until 8 o'clock at night.
The Times, *describing how Lord Strathcona spent his ninetieth birthday.* [1]

The Canadian High Commission offices in Victoria Street were known to some as "The Lighthouse" because when most businesses were closed for the day, the lights still burning in Lord Strathcona's office guided travellers on their way. In fact, though Donald may have risen at eight o'clock, he tended to spend the mornings at home looking after his own affairs, in the City seeing to Bank of Montreal or Hudson's Bay Company business, or down the road from the High Commission offices at meetings with the colonial secretary or other government ministers. "I have breakfast at 9 A.M. and dinner at 9 P.M. and that gives me eleven hours daily for work," he would explain to those who wondered how he managed to achieve so much.[2]

"I was very much struck by the simplicity of his life," Edward Greenshields noted in his diary after dinner at the Strathconas' house in Montreal in January 1907. "He ate vary sparingly and drank a good deal of milk."[3]

Donald thought that a simple diet also helped him keep up his energies. "I am able to do more work, more alert work, on two meals than I could possibly do on three; and I eat sparingly. I believe that the secret of health and long life is to live regularly and sparingly as respects food. Above all, cultivate a contented mind."[4]

It was the contented mind, one which felt no need to reveal itself or seek the approbation of others, which disconcerted many who would have been more at ease with a man who did not keep his own counsel. A dietician, on the other hand, or even a Boy Scout, would have been tempted to say something about the diet. Donald had been doing without lunch since his Labrador days but it was only late in life that he decided he would manage just as well by confining himself to what he liked best. Vilhjalmur Stefansson, the Arctic explorer, described the dinners he attended at Grosvenor Square in 1912. "As course after course was served to the rest of us, he would converse, drinking a sip or two of each wine as it was poured. Sometime during the middle of the dinner, his tray was brought: several medium-soft boiled eggs broken into a large bowl with plenty of butter and with extra butter in a side dish, and, I believe, a quart of whole milk, or perhaps half and half. My impression is that they also brought him toast, but that he barely nibbled it, using it a bit as if it were a napkin." Donald would not have forgotten the scurvy he helped to eradicate in Labrador and it seems more than likely that meals in private, and especially at Debden where there was a good kitchen garden, would have contributed to a more balanced diet than Stefansson saw. Also, he ate at public luncheons and dinners so often that he would have found himself consuming a more balanced diet despite his fondness for eggs and dairy products.

Vigorous though Donald still was in the early years of the century, he made several attempts to resign as president of the Bank of Montreal but each of them was rebuffed until 1904 when the bank finally gave way. The resignation took effect in 1905, but Donald remained as honourary president for the rest of his life. His withdrawal was not prompted by a desire to cut down on his work but by the belief that he could not serve the bank sufficiently well if he were in London most of the time. In fact, after his resignation from the bank, he took on more work, both in relation to establishing the fast Atlantic service and in agreeing, in 1908, to be president of the National Hospital for the Paralysed and Epileptic which was about to launch a fundraising campaign. The British Home and Hospital for Incurables also gained his active support when it initiated an appeal to enable it to build a new wing.

Donald's time was also taken up by a new business venture. It started as an oil exploration company, then joined forces with Burmah Oil and finally developed into Anglo-Persian Oil which, in due course, became British Petroleum.

William Knox D'Arcy was one of Donald's neighbours in Grosvenor Square. Married to the actress Nina Boucicault, he gave grand parties with actors and famous singers among the guests. He had made his fortune in the gold fields of Australia but was not inclined to settle for a life of theatres and bonhomie when he returned to England and, in May 1901, he acquired a sixty year concession to search for oil in Persia. By the autumn of 1903, when oil had still not been struck, he was forced to admit that he could not continue much longer to pay out for fees and exploration costs. Nor could he find anyone who was willing to invest when there was no evidence that oil would ever be discovered.

The British navy had converted to oil, a controversial decision in view of the fact that the country had no secure source of that fuel whereas it still had huge reserves of coal. The navy's need for oil was, however, sufficient to warrant D'Arcy's approaching the Admiralty's Fuel Oil Committee with a request for a loan of £120,000 in exchange for an undertaking to supply the navy in due course. The Admiralty was prepared to cooperate but Austen Chamberlain, recently appointed as chancellor of the exchequer, rejected the proposal on the grounds that a loan would never find approval in the House of Commons.

The Foreign and India Offices were also willing to cooperate. Russia was seeking a warm water port and Whitehall saw D'Arcy's presence in southern Iran as a bulwark against tsarist intervention. Foreign Secretary Lord Lansdowne had publicly declared that spring that any fortified port or naval base in the Persian Gulf would be perceived as a threat to Britain because it endangered her communication with India.

With the navy, the India Office and the Foreign Office in accord, the problem defined itself as a need to find a non-governmental source of financial support for D'Arcy's concessionary rights. A prominent and wealthy man who was committed to the British empire was needed, less for his money than to lead by example and bring others in after him. "I rather smiled at being asked to take it up in the first instance," Donald acknowledged. By and large, he had not undertaken any new investments since his appointment as high commissioner, believing that he should fight shy of any conflict of interest, and would have declined the Persian oilfields proposal had Lord Selbourne, the first lord of the admiralty, not been so insistent. As it was, he had only two questions. Was it in the interest of the Royal Navy and, if so, would £50,000 do?[5]

Donald's agreement gave D'Arcy the support he needed to approach Burmah Oil, a Glasgow based company which had been selling the products of its Burmese wells to India as kerosine. It was the only British oil company of any significance and already had a contract to supply the navy. The arrangement with Burmah called for that company to put up £95,000 and for Donald to supply £5,000 for what everyone hoped would be an interim exploration company. Assuming oil was found, a new exploitation company would be established and the shares would be transferred accordingly.

Oil in economically viable quantities was finally discovered in 1908 and the Anglo-Persian Oil Company was formed in 1909. While the real business would be handled by the Burmah executives, it was essential that the new company have a chairman whose name would inspire confidence in investment circles and Charles Wallace, who had long been associated with Burmah Oil and was a director of the new company, recommended Lord Strathcona who had, as he pointed out, stuck by the company from the moment he agreed to be involved. Only when the new Liberal government confirmed to Donald that it concurred with its Conservative predecessor's policy on naval fuel and supported the view that a reliable source of oil should be in British hands, did Donald accept the chairmanship.

The company's tribulations were not yet over, however, for the oil which had been discovered was in such a remote part of Persia that both pipelines and a refinery had to be constructed before it could be sold and before Donald, D'Arcy or Burmah Oil could start to recoup their investments. By 1911, Burmah was distinctly uneasy. So too was the new first lord of the admiralty, Winston Churchill. Germany was rearming and making increasingly belligerent noises. The British navy had reverted to Welsh coal but Churchill was certain that the only way naval superiority could be achieved was through a flotilla of light weight, oil powered vessels. A committee of inquiry was set up to determine whether a secure supply could actually be achieved and whether the navy's construction programme should be altered as a result. While the committee was deliberating, Royal Dutch Shell began to realize that the prize of the Persian oilfields might be within its grasp.

As the Admiralty and the Foreign Office argued about whether collaboration with the Dutch would solve the problem and whether the Dutch would supply the Germans if they gained control, Anglo-Persian Oil moved closer to bankruptcy. In November 1912, Burmah Oil capitulated to Anglo-Persian's pleas and arranged a further loan of £100,000 while Donald and D'Arcy found an additional £50,000 between them. Churchill then insisted that the navy would have to buy forward, that is, it would have to agree a price for oil to be delivered at a future date. Furthermore, these purchases would have to be made from a reliable company in British hands, so an agreement was made with Anglo-Persian.

In July 1913, secret negotiations between a cabinet committee and Anglo-Persian centred on the oil company's need for £2 million to enable it to fulfill its Admiralty contract. Churchill argued that it should be viewed purely as a business investment but others recalled Donald's evidence before the Oil Fuel Committee while Churchill's predecessor as first lord of the admiralty, Reginald McKenna, "explained to other members of the Committee that he remembered well Lord Strathcona's interviews with him on the subject, and that he was satisfied that Lord Strathcona had only interested himself in the Company for purely patriotic reasons and at the urgent insistence of the Government and therefore that the Government were under obligations to the Company other than those of an ordinary business nature." This view carried the day and the purchase of debentures was arranged through the Bank of England. Nothing was said in public to avoid alerting foreign powers to the fact that Britain now had an extensive, publicly owned, and secure source of oil for her navy and a monopoly on the Iranian oilfields.[6]

At the end of July 1908, Donald paid a short visit to Canada to attend some of the celebrations marking the tercentenary of the founding of Quebec by Samuel de Champlain. He had been reluctant to go since he was tied up in the middle of the month with the HBC General Court and was due back in Canada in September, but a cable from Laurier in the early part of July persuaded him to change his mind and he took his eldest granddaughter, Frances, with him. His autumn visit was meant to couple business in Ottawa with a trip out west where he had agreed to be president of the celebrations marking the centenary of the exploration of the Fraser River by Simon Fraser and John Stuart. That journey had to be postponed when, early in September, a Royal Navy salute was fired too close to his eardrum and rendered him deaf. Dr. Barlow ordered immediate rest in hopes that the ear would heal itself but Donald never properly recovered his hearing. "Dear kind old Lord Strathcona is very deaf," Agnes Macdonald recorded in 1910, but added that he "thinks his hearing much worse than it really is." From the time of the accident, his hearing slowly deteriorated and colds inevitably exacerbated his ability to pick up conversations, especially in a crowded room.[7]

The postponed journey to western Canada was revived in the summer of 1909 but instead of being a quiet visit to some of his former haunts, punctuated by reminiscences with those of his old cronies who still survived, the trip transposed itself into an exercise that was little short of a royal progress. Bella chose not to go with him, her desire to see the Rocky Mountains being easily overcome by her greater desire to avoid being travel sick from sea to sea, to say nothing of being travel sick from Liverpool to New York and back again. Donald did, however, take Frances with him again. Then a charming young lady of twenty, she was joined by her eldest brother, Donald, who was just eighteen and shortly to begin his last year at Eton. The apparent focal point of their visit was the meeting of the British Association for the Advancement of Science in Winnipeg but as soon as people in western Canada learned that Donald would be visiting, they clamoured for speeches and presentations and dinners and any number of other public gatherings.

By the end of July, Clarence Chipman, head of the HBC operations in Canada, realized that if some control were not exercised over the impending trip it could turn into a chaotic fiasco. He wrote Edward Clouston at the Bank of Montreal and suggested they sort out a programme, assuming they could discover when Donald was due to arrive. "On receipt of your letter I obtained by cable some information in regard to Lord Strathcona's movements," Clouston replied, "the gist of which I telegraphed you to-day. The cable adds that he has engaged passage on the "Empress" sailing on the 13th of this month, but with him that does not amount to much. If, however, he should come out I will try and arrange the programme you suggest."[8]

Clouston was right to be sceptical. Donald and the children left Euston on August 14 and sailed on the *Mauretania*. They scarcely had time to catch their breath in Montreal before they were off to Winnipeg. Thomas Shaughnessy, the CPR president, arranged a special to pick up Donald and his group at Fort William on the morning of August 24 and Donald asked Chipman to join him there so the two of them could settle down to some HBC work.

Sandford Fleming had retired from the company's board of directors in 1907 and had been replaced by Leonard Cunliffe whose financial activities included a substantial investment in Harrod's, the London department store which had recently established itself as *the* emporium for wealthy Londoners. Donald and Fleming had long remained the only HBC directors who regularly spent time in both England and Canada and Cunliffe recognized that if he were to do more than collect his dividends, he would have to learn about Canada and the company's business there.

Donald's policy of not putting the company's land on the market until there was a substantial demand for it was paying off and the HBC was making huge profits from land sales. The stores, on the other hand, were doing a mediocre business and Cunliffe wanted to look more closely at this side of the operation. He took with him Richard Burbidge, Harrod's general manager, and their wives, combining a holiday with their work. Burbidge had been briefed by Donald in London in August and he and Cunliffe had met Chipman in Fort William the day before.

Cunliffe and Burbidge were appalled by what they discovered on their journey. Such stores as there were were badly managed, badly stocked and had little concept of marketing themselves or their goods. The solution proposed by Cunliffe and Burbidge was to raise more money to build more stores and improve or replace those which already existed, and to follow the familiar HBC rut of splitting the business into three departments: land, fur and sales shops. They also revived the Canadian Committee. Unfortunately, they made three serious errors, though it would be some years before they became apparent. The first was to allow nepotism to take such control over the sales shops that Burbidge's lazy son was put in charge and any pretext of efficient management went out the window. The second was to assume that Canadians needed and wanted stores stocked with British goods and that British merchandising styles would transplant, unchanged, to Toronto, Vancouver and the prairie cities. The stores ran huge press advertisements, but they were of little use if customers did not want the goods on offer. In January 1874, Donald had failed to persuade the Governor and Committee that the company needed "a person perfectly conversant with the quality and description of goods required for the Trade," and nothing had changed.[9]

Burbidge and Cunliffe's third mistake was not to learn the lesson which history had repeatedly taught the HBC and which the company had repeatedly failed to comprehend. It needed a George Simpson figure, dynamic, energetic and with a grasp of all aspects of the business. Such a person needed to be based in Canada and to tie together the three separate strands of land, fur and sales shops. This man ought to be a personification of the company, complex though it was. Simpson was such a figure; Donald might have been had he been willing or able to be so single minded and not allowed railways, politics, diplomacy and a myriad other interests to take his eye off the HBC ball.

Donald and his companions arrived at Winnipeg at half past eight that evening, to be met at the station by members of Strathcona's Horse and school cadets. Much to Donald's delight, the school band was in kilts. The travellers emerged from the station to find the streets strung with red, white and blue lights and crowded with people. The city hall was outlined in lights and emblazoned in red and white lettering across the front was "Welcome Lord Strathcona, Craigellachie." The lieutenant governor's residence, where they stayed, had flags and bunting on the verandahs while the Royal Alexandra Hotel, where most of Donald's meetings took place, was festooned with flags and glittering lights.

The next morning, Donald received the press on the verandah at Government House, reminiscing about old friends and asking after those who were still alive. He admitted that he was amazed at the speed with which Winnipeg had grown and at the size of the buildings which now dotted its skyline. He also confessed to greatly regretting the destruction by fire of his house at Silver Heights. Though he did not reveal this to the press or his host, he always preferred to stay in his own accommodation rather than being someone's guest.

At noon, he moved to the city hall where three huge chairs had been brought out from the council chamber and placed at the top of the steps. There, Donald was soon joined by council officials and his old friend J.J. Hill. In response to the civic speech of welcome, with its familiar references to the Hudson's Bay Company and the CPR, Donald was equally courteous but, at the same time, showed how far he and the country had moved from the cantankerous days of fighting off railway competition. "I am glad to have been one of those who undertook a work then considered by many as premature, but which has helped to consolidate the Dominion from ocean to ocean, and which with the assistance of the other Railways now being constructed will open up many more millions of acres of land for settlement."[10]

The news that Donald was planning a western visit had prompted many other Manitoba organisations to honour him or to seek his advice. Foremost among these was the Canadian Club which wanted to ensure that the gate to Fort

Garry, virtually all that was left of the historic Hudson's Bay Company building, was singled out for posterity with a commemorative brass plaque. Donald, who was the honourary president of the Association of Canadian Clubs, unveiled it, pulling aside the Union Jack which had been raised in the fort the day Louis Riel's Franco-Irish flag was lowered for the last time. The British flag had been saved by Colin Inkster, an industrious English half-breed whom Donald had known since 1870 and who, as sheriff of Winnipeg, had packed off the disputed ballots after the 1878 recount. At the Canadian Club luncheon which followed, when Donald rose to reply to the mayor's introduction, the entire crowd stood and cheered him, waving their handkerchiefs in the air. It almost rendered superfluous Hill's proposal of a vote of thanks to Donald for all he had done for the Northwest.

Lunch was followed promptly by a Board of Trade reception and the time between five and seven in the evening, which Chipman had set aside for Donald to put his feet up, was promptly filled with press interviews. That evening, the British Association launched its conference.

Before he set off for another British Association meeting the following morning, Donald cabled Shaughnessy to say how much he had enjoyed the train journey and how impressed he was by "the great work all but accomplished in double tracking, the improvement of gradients and generally everything done for facilitating traffic and resulting in large economies in working. Have seen all this with the greatest interest and much appreciate the opportunity."[11]

Strathcona's Horse had disbanded immediately following its return from South Africa but the regiment had reformed and was based at Winnipeg. Its official name had just changed from the Royal Canadian Mounted Rifles to Strathcona's Horse and Donald was delighted to accept the regiment's invitation to a luncheon which celebrated its new identity. He was likewise pleased to have Sam Steele and his officers as his companions on the train journey to Lower Fort Garry, the old Hudson's Bay Company fort about ten miles downriver from Winnipeg, where a reception had been arranged for the delegates to the British Association conference. Back in Winnipeg, Donald was the guest of honour at a Government House dinner. The next night, he gave a dinner which was followed by a garden party at Government House and on Saturday, he hosted his own party in the gardens at Silver Heights where he still maintened a farm and the buffalo run. On his instructions, invitations were issued in the names of Lord and Lady Strathcona, a gesture which demonstrated to the men and women of Winnipeg that Bella still shared his life and his thoughts, even though she had not come with him. Two thousand attended the party.

In between the public celebrations, he was called on by people and societies who wished to pay their respects, generally by presenting formal addresses, elaborately inscribed and decorated, on parchment or expensive paper. With some, he was politely formal while with others, such as the St. Andrew's Society which he had helped to found nearly forty years earlier, he was much more ebullient and, by his standards, nearly garrulous in his response. He also received groups who sought his advice or his intervention. A band of Sioux and another of Cree arrived to see him, more from curiosity than need, while a group of Chippewa from Portage la Prairie, including Yellow Quill and Short Bear, sought his help over what they considered to be an unfair treaty.

A rather more delicate meeting took place on August 27 when the committee of the Selkirk Centennial Exhibition called. Chipman had written to warn Donald that the committee hoped he would become its president and wanted to tender him a banquet which they believed would encourage a positive response. He also warned that the exhibition, designed to celebrate the hundredth anniversary of the arrival of the Selkirk settlers in 1812, "is being boomed here but is by no means an assured accomplishment." He advised Donald to accept the courtesies in order to avoid causing offense but to be cautious about committing himself. Two days later, on August 18, he wrote again to explain that the Selkirk committee, having found there was no time for yet another banquet, was trying to impose itself on the Canadian Club luncheon. Chipman advised keeping them separate.[12]

The exhibition committee was not trying to mount a sophisticated version of the annual fall fair; it was trying to stage an international exhibition of the calibre of the American centennial exposition at Philadelphia in 1876 or the big celebrations which had marked Queen Victoria's golden and diamond jubilees. The men admitted that they were short of time for such an ambitious programme and also recognized that Donald could not give their project any serious consideration when there were so many other demands on his time while he was in Winnipeg. They also accepted that they could not ask him to be honourary president until they had secured the finance for their project. What they really wanted was advice. In a letter written after the meeting, they explained that they calculated they would need $2,500,000 over three years from the federal government, in addition to support from provincial governments and other sources. Laurier, they said, had indicated privately that he was in favour of their project; what they wanted from Donald was help in turning this into a public commitment and a willingness to see the necessary legislation through the House. In addition, they sought approval for their scheme from the imperial government and wanted to know if he could help and whether he recommended sending a commissioner to the UK. These were sensible questions, though the fact that they had to be asked suggests that neither Hugh Sutherland, the chair, nor his committee members, were sufficiently sophisticated and worldly wise to be able to achieve their ends, either financial or organizational.

On September 8, while still on his travels, Donald replied, agreeing to do what he could to help but getting straight to the point about where the responsibilities lay.

> You and your colleagues will, however, I know, recognize that it must rest mainly with yourselves to put the subject you have so much at heart so clearly and intelligently before the Prime Minister, and strengthen it with such local influence as you can command, to convince him, and the members of the Government, that the result accruing from your Centennial Celebration will be of such paramount importance, not to Winnipeg, or Manitoba alone, but to the whole Dominion, that he and they may feel themselves justified in contributing the large sum —for, of course, it is a very large sum — for the purpose.[13]

He added that he would do what he could to help in the UK but pointed out that he could only act on instructions from the Canadian government.

A year later, Sutherland wrote to say they had trimmed their budget to $5 million. They had commitments of $1.75 million but were still trying to persuade the federal government to back the project. This never happened; the men had overstretched themselves and Ottawa was unwilling to throw money into a scheme which was doomed to failure because it was so far behind schedule and because the committee had allowed its ambitions to exceed its grasp. The grandiose plans collapsed in 1911 and the centennial was marked with a modest display of Red River artifacts, coupled with an exhibition about local manufacturing and agriculture.

As soon as the Winnipeg press began writing about Donald's visit and had its copy picked up by papers across Canada, invitations from other cities and other organisations began to arrive. Almost every settlement between Winnipeg and the Pacific wanted to offer a banquet or present an illuminated scroll or guide Donald around towns and small cities which had been dusty settlements on the prairies when he last visited. All were turned down for the outward journey but where they could be fitted in on the return, acceptances were cabled.

After the garden party at Silver Heights, Donald and the grandchildren boarded the *Earnscliffe*, the private railway car which had been provided for their use throughout the journey, while Chipman and Clouston took their places in the *Pacific*. They did not leave, however, before sending cables to the Howards at Glencoe with a separate one sending "much love" to Bella. Messages also went to William Garson, Donald's Scottish solicitor, and Joseph Colmer, his secretary in London, and continued to do so at intervals throughout the time they were in Canada. Less frequently, Griffith also received messages at the high commission. Each of the businessmen in turn kept Donald abreast of events which concerned him; he was never more than a few hours away from work. Chipman was also assiduous with his cable communications but in his case he was trying to ensure that everyone knew what the plans were, where they were going and when they expected to be there. By nature a cheerful man, he was clearly enjoying himself and was buoyed up by the fact that Donald was too. "His lordship is in rare good form," he cabled William Whyte, vice president of the CPR. "When returning may spend Sunday in the mountains."[14]

They went straight through to Vancouver which they reached on the morning of August 31. A pipe band played "Cock o' the North" as the train steamed into the station and the band of the Sixth Regiment topped it with "See the Conquering Hero Comes." A group of school cadets formed a guard of honour. "No special pomp and circumstance marked the return to Vancouver of the veteran statesman," *The Daily News-Advertiser* assured its readers, as if guards of honour and bands greeted the arrival of every CPR train.

> It is a pleasant thing to see the venerable statesman carrying his years so lightly, for he is now in his 89th year. The burden of an Imperial statesmanship and of a strenuous life have left him slightly stooped, a grand and noble age has silvered his hair, but he still treads firmly and gives the impression of a man who ... may yet be spared ... for many years to come, and though his

> years show in his voice his diction is clear, crisp and faultless, and the grey eyes behind his glasses still mirror the intrepid spirit, whilst his face is kind and gentle, and, as yet, scarcely seamed by the passage of nearly a century of toil.[15]

A Board of Trade reception was followed by a visit to the Hudson's Bay Company store and a Canadian Club luncheon. Deputations then came to see him at the Hotel Vancouver, seeking his support for a highland regiment and a music society. It was a day of bright sunshine and light breezes and in keeping with the still-undiminished Vancouver tradition of hospitality for out-of-town guests, Donald was taken for a drive in Stanley Park which had once been reserved for military use but was now a public amenity of virgin forest, rich with massive Douglas firs. Following local custom, they paused to have their photograph taken beside the hollow tree.

Donald was then whisked up to the roof of Spencer's, a department store which had been established by a former member of Strathcona's Horse. Though it was closer to the waterfront than the HBC store, it was high enough to give a panoramic view of the city and to show Donald what had become of Van Horne's designs for the huge land grant the CPR had received in order to induce it to build from Port Moody to the eastern edge of Burrard Inlet. Next on the list was Vancouver General Hospital where the mayor's wife and the ladies' auxiliary waited with tea. One suspects the reception was a trifle dull because Donald and his hosts were able to get away in time to make a surprise call on the Strathcona Sailors' Institute which also functioned as a loggers' home. Around the world, port cities were notorious for fleecing sailors and the British and Foreign Sailors' Society tried to provide lodgings where men could obtain a clean bed and meals without falling into the arms of lodging house keepers who were always sober enough to rob drunken seamen or claim a commission for handing them over to agents who sought replacements for sailors who had jumped ship.

Donald was tired by the end of the day and the cold which he had managed to keep under control in the previous week had turned nasty. It also affected his hearing. He nevertheless showed up to the banquet at the Hotel Vancouver in full evening dress with all the honours and insignia such an occasion demanded. His speech contained the usual references to the All Red Route, closer imperial ties and the wonderful future which lay ahead of Canada. He also suggested that there should be one or two cruisers on the Pacific coast to protect the fisheries, a comment which reflects the fact that the Liberals were trying to avoid making a cash contribution to the British navy by planning to develop Canada's own sea defenses at some unspecified future date. In fact, Ottawa thought his remarks could have been stronger, as Griffith cabled from London two weeks later. "Minister Marine feels that you might well aid him by making stronger public utterance on navy question. I gather he would [like] you to take the line that this country expected Canada to take substantial steps creation navy and would be much disappointed unless this done. He feels unless stronger general support[,] matter will resolve itself into cash contribution," which was what the Conservatives preferred.[16]

At ten to eight the following morning, Donald and the grandchildren, together with Chipman and Clouston, boarded Lieutenant Governor Dunsmuir's steam yacht, the *Dolaura*, and a few minutes later set out for Victoria. The Canadian Club was hosting a lunch in honour of Lord Grey, the governor general, and it had been expanded to include Donald as well. Lunch was in progress when they arrived at the Empress Hotel, a fact which implies either that accepting the offer of a ride in Dunsmuir's yacht had been a miscalculation or that the men had consciously chosen to be late in order not to detract from an occasion which was meant to focus on the governor general.

After lunch, the official engagements were over for the day but Donald had agreed to have tea with Dallas Helmcken, the son of Dr. John Helmcken, a retired chief factor and BC politician who had negotiated the province's entry into Confederation and had subsequently been involved in discussions over the CPR's route. The visit would offer a chance to reminisce with Dr. Helmcken and to discover from his son news of the Royal Jubilee Hospital where Donald had endowed the Strathcona Wing. The following day, after a visit from a delegation wishing to establish an experimental farm on HBC land, he visited the hospital and also called on St. Joseph's Hospital. The next stop was the University School where Chipman had two boys studying and where a third, who had been travelling with him, was about to be enrolled. Donald addressed the cadet corps, advising the boys that "no kind of labor is in itself demeaning. Let all work honestly at whatever they would find to do and in time their efforts would be rewarded by the respect and honour of their fellow men." He then shook hands with each lad, the youngest of whom was only seven, and persuaded their teacher to let them have a half day's holiday.[17]

At two in the afternoon, they set out for Vancouver and thence to New Westminster where the *Earnscliffe* and the *Pacific* awaited them. The pipers outside the train the next morning roused them for yet more formalities. A drive through the streets of New Westminster and a visit to the city's market where he was cheered, preceded a hospital tour and a visit to the Simon Fraser monument which he had been unable to unveil a year earlier. Fifteen hundred school children sang "The Maple Leaf Forever" while a little boy in a kilt presented Frances with a bouquet. Donald must have been flattered by the *News-Advertiser*'s description of her as his niece! At lunch, he pleased his listeners by telling them that it had been John Stuart's description of their province which had caused him to throw away his Indian job offer and take his chances in Canada and concluded, "It is not meet that I should say 'Good bye' to you but rather 'Au revoir'." At the age of eighty-nine, it seemed that he was thinking of his next journey to the Pacific.[18]

On Saturday, the train halted at Kamloops for speeches and the presentation of a book about the Thompson River country and then carried on to Vernon, at the head of Lake Okanagan, where the train stopped for a purely private visit. When Lord Aberdeen was governor general, he and his wife had bought Coldstream Ranch, a fruit farm a little to the south east of Vernon. They had consistently failed to make it pay its way and Donald had several times been pressed to help; in 1897 he had tried without success to form a syndicate to take it off the Aberdeens' hands.

The train was met by W.M. Megaw, a prominent local merchant and former mayor of Vernon, who drove Donald and Chipman over the bluffs to the ranch. About three miles out of town, the horses started to become unmanageable because the whippletree was striking their hindquarters. They bolted as they descended a steep hill at the bottom of which the road curved sharply and ran parallel to the shores of Lake Kalamalka. As the horses careened forward, Megaw, acknowledged as "one of the best whips in the country," realized that the animals would probably miss the curve and plunge over the cliff into the lake. With great force, he wheeled the horses, forcing them to crash into the barbed wire fence. The carriage overturned and the men were thrown out. Chipman was unhurt but the muscles in Donald's right arm and hand were badly torn and Megaw's leg was broken below the knee. "It is a miracle that we escaped with our lives," Donald said, giving the credit for their survival to Megaw's skill. Chipman agreed, and in sending good wishes for their driver's speedy recovery, noted that "the rest of the party thanks to Mr. Megaw's presence of mind in the face of great danger escaped what might have been something we did not want to think about."[19]

Battered and bruised, the travellers returned to the train by automobile and a doctor from Revelstoke joined them at Golden on the eastern bank of the Columbia River. There was little he could do for Donald beyond urging him to rest and providing a sling to help him keep his arm and hand immobile. The travellers spent Sunday morning enjoying the scenery at Lake Louise and reached Banff in the afternoon.

On Monday, they were at Calgary where young Donald Howard sensibly sent his parents at Glencoe a cable. "We had carriage accident at Vernon driver seriously injured. Grandfather's arm slightly but getting on nicely. Mention this in case exaggerated reports might reach you. Expect arrive Montreal eleventh. All quite well much love to Grandmother and all." On the same day, Donald sent his own message to Bella, also at Glencoe. "Hope all quite well. On our way back to Montreal where arrive eleventh and expect to be with you soon. All well and send love." He made no mention of the accident but his silence did not stop the news spreading and the High Commission was finally forced to issue what Griffith described as a "judicious" statement to the press.[20]

Though they were only in Calgary for a few hours, it allowed Donald an opportunity to introduce his grandchildren to some of their Hardisty relatives. In this family reunion, the lead was taken by William's daughter, Isabella, who had been brought up by Richard Hardisty after her father's death and had later married James Lougheed who was to become one of the wealthiest men in Alberta.[21]

From Calgary, the party travelled north to Edmonton, stopping at Strathcona, then a municipality on the capital's southern outskirts though soon to be incorporated in the city. Here, while a huge bonfire blazed a welcome on the hills beyond, Donald reviewed the men of the 101st Fusiliers. "Clad in a Prince Albert, with a cape thrown across his shoulders to protect him from the evening chill, and leaning slightly on the arm of Lieut.-Governor Bulyea, Lord Strathcona advanced along the line of soldiery," the *Edmonton Evening Journal* reported, providing a rare observation on Donald's clothes, but one which demonstrated that he was hardly a follower of fashion. Most men had years ago given up Prince Alberts, the double breasted, knee length coats favoured by Queen Victoria's husband.[22]

Donald had hoped to spend the night in Strathcona as he was feeling the effects of interrupted sleep caused by trying to avoid lying on his injured arm.

Edmonton, however, had arranged an illuminated procession to Government House where it was assumed he would stay and Donald consented to adhere to the programme but he declined the offer of hospitality, returning instead to the Canadian Northern Railway station to which the private cars had been moved. The decision was a disappointment for Richard Hardisty, Bella's nephew and the son of her favourite brother, who was now one of Edmonton's leading citizens. He and his wife had offered accommodation to the grandchildren, for whom there was not sufficient room at Government House, though the Hardistys, too, seem to have been under the impression that Frances and Donald were a niece and nephew.

The morning of the following day, Tuesday, September 7, was given over to business discussions with Chipman and a group of men who were hoping to acquire HBC land on which to build a new hospital and Donald also talked to an *Edmonton Journal* reporter who described him as "taking as much enthusiastic delight in his trip as a boy."[23]

A drive around Edmonton brought Donald to Government House for a garden party. There, one of the first people he encountered was Father Lacombe, then eighty-two years old and still ministering to the Indians and the mixed-blood people of the prairies. Katherine Hughes, Lacombe's biographer and one of the guests, watched as their faces lit up when they met. The priest caught sight of the sling and

> put out a quick hand of sympathy, suddenly mindful of the other's age and the fatigues of his journey.
>
> He spoke of his fears: but Strathcona brushed them aside laughingly as he would have done on their trip to St. Paul forty years earlier: and the old priest murmured his admiration:
>
> "Ha, that is like you, always — you never would complain!"[24]

The afternoon was exceptionally hot but the two men found seats in the shade beneath the trees where they caught up with each other's news, and reminded themselves of the old days, the days when the Métis, driven further and further west by the scarcity of buffalo, had begun to trade at Edmonton; the days when the CPR was an unfulfilled promise; the day when Father Lacombe was president of that same august line of steel for an hour. Now, the Métis who had moved west were old too and many had neither the wherewithal to feed themselves nor shelter for their last years. Father Lacombe was building a home for them, a refuge which would also teach young Métis practical skills such as farming so they could avoid the fate of their grandparents. Perhaps the great man could send "a little souvenir," a reminder of the days when these hunters were masters of the prairies and purveyors of the pemmican which kept the Nor'Westers alive in their long journeys from Montreal to the mountains. Donald nodded, and the two silver haired, black coated men continued to recall friends long gone and adventures which could never be understood by even the best disposed bankers and aristocrats in London. When he returned to Montreal, Donald posted his "souvenir." It was a cheque for $10,000.

The CNR tracks took the travellers through Battleford to Saskatoon where they spent an hour and a half. At Regina, Donald met dignitaries at city hall and attended a reception, but the party was back on the train and heading for Winnipeg within three hours. The train pulled into the station in the Manitoba capital just after seven and at 7.45 Sam Steele appeared as Donald had asked him to. Steele sent Donald numerous long and self-aggrandizing letters, the essence of which showed him to be floundering around without work and in need of financial support. He could not re-join the police and the army in peace time had little use for him. In 1909, he was responsible for a military district which spread from Winnipeg to the Rockies and was involved in a number of charitable activities, including the Strathcona Trust for Physical and Military Training in Schools which Donald had founded that spring. It was not enough to occupy him fully or to pay him adequately and at Donald's death, Steele owed him $6,000 which his solicitors judged they would not be able to recoup. Certainly Colmer had no luck in his attempts to have the money repaid.

Steele's audience was short. Donald had cancelled a review of the cadets because his arm was painful and he wanted to get straight back to Montreal. The train left Winnipeg at eight o'clock and the next morning arrived at Fort William. The journey only took about twelve hours and the train probably pulled into a siding to allow Donald to sleep without knocking his arm about. The following morning, he and Chipman met Whyte, R.B. Angus, and Shaughnessy from the CPR. Shaughnessy and Whyte were heading west on their annual tour of inspection and Whyte had instigated the meeting because he wanted to discuss a block of land south of Medicine Hat in Alberta. Opinions about this portion of the fertile belt had varied widely over the years, some thinking that it was arid and infertile and others believing that there was sufficient rain to enable the soil to grow abundant crops. Meteorological records finally revealed that both opinions were correct: years of drought were followed by years of rain. Fleming had advocated that the CPR be built through the more northerly Yellowhead Pass because his surveys had been done in drought years; the syndicate had decided on Kicking Horse Pass in one of the wet years. The company had refused to take any of its land grant in the area during dry years and Van Horne had contravened this decision when the rains were doing their job.

The HBC had also accepted just over 102,000 acres in the area and the CPR purchased it from the company in order to have an uninterrupted block which, in an arid season, it set about irrigating. The land had been unsaleable and no individual settler could afford to bring water down from the Bow River. The CPR, on the other hand, believed it could bring in water and still sell the land at a profit. This proved to be an expensive and not altogether rewarding exercise since the rains returned when the irrigation system was nearly completed.

Back in Montreal on Sunday, Donald was met with a sharp cable from Maggie. "Cubatus caduceum all well love." The Latin may have come from the CPR code book which Donald and his family used or it may have formed part of their own family code: *cubatus* is probably a typographical error for *cubitus*, Latin for elbow with the implication of returning, while *caduceum* is a reference to, if not a typographical error for *caduceus*, the winged staff of Mercury, entwined with serpents and the symbol of the medical profession. The translation, possibly appended by Chipman since it appears in his letter book, is "Have been expecting to hear from you. Are you well? What date do you leave?" As Glencoe had had no messages since the report of the carriage accident, it is hardly surprising that Bella and Maggie were waiting for news.

A proposed return date was probably cabled before Donald and the grandchildren set out for Ottawa where they were the guests of the Lauriers. The visit to the prime minister and his wife appeared to give substance to the rumours then current in Canadian political circles that Donald's retirement was imminent. The *Daily Mail* correspondent was sufficiently convinced of their truth that he cabled a story to London, reporting that Donald had confirmed in an interview that his successor would soon be appointed. To Griffith's inquiry about the veracity of the paragraph, Donald responded that it was not true, but neither was it worth bothering to contradict it.

Donald was in Hamilton for a dinner of the Canadian Manufacturers Association on September 16 when he received a cable from his grandson saying that his mother expected him back in time to return to Eton on September 25. "Would have liked all of us go together but no doubt your mother has good reasons for urging your being Eton 25th instant," Donald responded, agreeing that his namesake could try to book a passage from New York in two days time. The cable traffic does not reveal whether a passage was unavailable or whether Donald's wishes held sway. In any event, when Donald returned to England, he was accompanied by both grandchildren.

For the moment, however, he had business to attend to. On the 17th, the day he returned from Hamilton, he hosted a dinner at the Canada Club for the delegates to the convention of Canadian Clubs, repaying some of the hospitality he had enjoyed in the west. While he was in Montreal on this trip he also saw the Archbishop of Montreal, Paul Bruchési, who was making plans for the Eucharistic Conference, due to take place in Montreal in a year's time. Donald gave £1,000 to support it and also put his house at the disposal of the Catholic church to accommodate the visiting bishops.

Canada's maritime provinces were not to be outdone by their western compatriots and invitations had come from Fredericton, which Donald declined, and Halifax, which he accepted. The special left Montreal on Sunday and stopped at Pictou at seven o'clock the following morning. E.M. McDonald, his Nova Scotia solicitor who looked after the property, was asked to meet the train with any papers which might be relevant, and warned that they would have precisely one hour in which to conduct their business. Halifax fared little better. Donald seems to have accepted the invitation to the city because D.C. Fraser, the lieutenant governor, had captained the Canadian curling team which had visited Scotland the year before and the two men were friendly as a result. The train pulled in just before eleven; there were no bands or crowds of people and none of the festive atmosphere of the visit to the west. After a drive through the suburbs, they arrived at Government House where Donald was interviewed by a journalist from the *Morning Chronicle* who was not quite sure what the point of the meeting was. He told his readers that Donald wore steel-rimmed bi-focals and that "his face is full and his skin as smooth and well colored as that of a healthy girl." For his part, Donald remembered staying at the Waverley Hotel — "a very cosy, comfortable place" — when he was sick in 1864 and remarked that Nova Scotia had a good school system. After lunch with the lieutenant governor, Donald and his grandchildren were back on the train and were in Montreal in time for dinner.[25]

Two days later, Donald sent his car to the station to collect Lord Balfour of Burleigh who was then chair of the Royal Commission on Closer Trade Relations between Canada and the West Indies. They had breakfast together at Dorchester Street after which they took a special to Ottawa for what Donald described as "a very satisfactory interview" with Laurier. He was back in Ottawa for a few hours the following day, starting with a hastily arranged lunch with Laurier from which he went to Bank Cottage to see Auguste Lemieux, the postmaster general. The main topic of conversation at these meetings was the cable conference, proposed for London the following year, and meant to encourage the development of more cable connections throughout the empire. At least as important were the discussions centring on the need to improve the notoriously weak Canadian links in the cable system.

At Bank Cottage, he also saw Henry Morgan, founder of a successful chain of department stores in Quebec, a part of Canada which the HBC had yet to touch. In May and June the previous year, he had rented from Morgan bedroom furniture, including sixteen beds, as well as bedding, tables and chairs and a sideboard. Governor General Grey had been using the Strathconas' Montreal house and its neighbour which Donald still owned and it seems likely that the meeting with Morgan was designed to come to a more permanent arrangement about the furniture. As Lord Minto had found some years earlier, the house was invaluable in providing the means by which the governor general could have a presence in French Canada and among the influential Scots-Canadian business community in Montreal. In 1911, when Grey was about to be replaced by the Duke of Connaught, one of Queen Victoria's younger sons, Donald spent $50,000 on alterations to the house, money which Grey thought wasted. He nonetheless advised the duke to broach the subject of the house with Donald. "Think it important that your R.H. should know nothing of this —but perhaps you might say how very useful the loan of his comfortable house has been to me etc. Your R.H. would not be going too far in saying that I attribute a great part of the influence I have been able to make felt in Montreal to the right I have enjoyed of using his house etc. etc."[26]

Another caller at Bank Cottage was Andrew Miller of the Ottawa *Free Press* who negotiated a loan of $3,000 to enable him to buy a newspaper in the Northwest. He also undertook a history of Strathcona's Horse for which Donald provided documents, though he declined to endorse it when sent the manuscript in 1914.[27]

That evening in Montreal, Donald hosted a dinner for forty-five men, including Richard Cartwright, Sandford Fleming and young Donald Howard. The next morning, Donald and the grandchildren were on the train for New York where they boarded the *Empress of Ireland* and sailed for Liverpool.

Back in London, Bella's fretting and Dr. Barlow's advice sent Donald packing off to Glencoe to allow some time for his right arm to recuperate. He had found before that sleeping on a sprained or broken arm at sea was a very painful experience and his hand and arm were undoubtedly worse when the ship docked than they were when it had set sail. It must have seemed more than a little unfair when, on December 21, his left arm was injured when he was knocked over in the street outside the High Commission offices as a consequence of a collision between a car and a bus.

He was still very deaf and, though he did not like to admit it, his hearing problems, his difficulties writing because of the repeated damage to his hand and arm, and the regular colds and pleurisy were beginning to wear him down. His short term memory was not quite as good as it used to be and he kept mislaying his HBC governor's cheques. Bella's health was also a worry. Like Donald, she was subject to regular chest infections and she also had difficulties with rheumatism in the damp winters. More dismaying, however, was the fact that her mind was beginning to wander and she was showing the first signs of dementia. By 1912, she was "quite batty," according to Joseph Pope and in August 1913 the sister of the Lord Chancellor observed in her diary, "Lady S ... is not I think quite *compos mentis*." Her condition seems to have been variable and people such as Agnes Macdonald who saw her privately and might have remarked on her behaviour or conversation appear to have made no comment. Bella continued to preside at official dinners at Grosvenor Square and to attend formal functions at court and elsewhere but Maggie was generally around to keep an eye on her and she increasingly served as her father's official companion and hostess.[28]

For several years, Sir Thomas Barlow had been recommending retirement and at last Donald decided to follow his advice. Stories about his impending departure from the high commissioner's office had circulated almost from the day of his appointment but they were all without foundation. On March 5, however, he wrote Laurier, asking to be relieved on the first of July.

The prime minister was not at all pleased to receive the letter and chose to interpret it as being subject to confirmation. "I keep this letter to myself and will not communicate it to anybody until I hear again from you that it is your absolute and settled determination," he wrote. "In the mean time let me express the hope that you will reconsider the question. I make due allowance for the fact that you may desire at your time of life to be disconnected with the duties of the office. Permit me to observe, however, that your resignation will be the cause in Canada of universal regret, and I still hope that you may defer this determination." Prime Ministers always have political debts to pay and the high commissionership was a ripe plum with which Laurier might have rewarded support for controversial legislation or contributions to the party coffers. The fact that Laurier preferred to keep Donald in office, even on the eve of his ninetieth birthday, shows not only the esteem in which he was held but also the value of the service he continued to provide.[29]

Donald was flattered by Laurier's response but answered that he did not want the date of his resignation to remain indefinite, the more so since, at the beginning of April, his right arm was still painful and his left continued to bother him after the accident in London. "It is, however, needless for me to say that I am truly grateful for your consideration and kindness to me now as on all occasions, and in deference to your wish that I will reconsider the question, I would suggest that instead of the 1st of July, my resignation should take effect at the end of the fiscal year, 31st March, 1911, or with the close of the present calendar year 31st December, as may be most convenient for you in appointing my successor." In response, Laurier expressed his regrets and asked Donald to delay until after the imperial conference, scheduled for the summer of 1911. To this, Donald acceded.[30]

From Canada's point of view, it was fortuitous that he did, for King Edward died in May that year. "Dear old Uncle Donald," as the king had called him, echoing John Carstairs McNeill, was perfectly aware of the monarch's gambling, his numerous extra-marital affairs and his various other indiscretions, but these did not stand in the way of his respect for the crown as an institution or of his admiration for the way in which the king had executed his official duties. His bond with Queen Alexandra, however, was one of mutual affection, coloured, on his part, with demonstrations of old fashioned chivalry. The new king, George V, and Queen Mary, who, as the Duke and Duchess of Cornwall and York, had been Donald's house guests in Montreal in 1901, were not due to be crowned until the summer of 1911. At this point of transition, Canada needed to have in London a man who was familiar with the protocol and procedures demanded by a coronation. As well, since Donald had an easy entrée into royal circles, it would be desirable for him to remain in post to smooth the way.

Board meetings of the HBC and Anglo-Persian Oil were interspersed in a familiar round of official openings, formal luncheons and dinners and High Commission business throughout 1910. He chaired meetings of the British and Foreign Sailors' Society; he gave £10,000 to endow a chair of agriculture at the University of Aberdeen; he hosted the usual Dominion Day reception, this year at the Queen's Hall; and he turned the first sod for the erection of the Canadian building at the Festival of the Empire, due to be held in 1911.

On his ninetieth birthday, on August 6, he went to work as usual but congratulatory messages streamed in all day. The king, the queen, Queen Alexandra, the Duke of Connaught, Princess Louise and the Duke of Argyll all sent cables. So too did the governor general, Laurier and a great many Canadian friends, both personal and official. The British and Foreign Sailors' Society published *Canada's Coeur de Lion*, a volume of encomiums, to mark the occasion. Though grateful for the kindness, Donald found it all very embarrassing and was glad when his birthday was over and the thank you notes written.

In January 1911, Maggie escorted her father to Kent where he unveiled a statue of General Wolfe in the village of Westerham and had tea in Quebec House where Wolfe had lived and which was then occupied by Beckles Willson, who had written a biography of Donald published in 1902 and was to write another, published in 1915. Much of the first half of 1911, however, was given over to preparations for the coronation and the imperial conference. The coronation itself was on June 22 but in advance were levées at the palaces, dinner parties and receptions for visiting dignitaries and the huge Festival of the Empire exhibition at Crystal Palace. Canada was now so much better known that no need was felt for a public manifestation such as the coronation arch of 1902. Britain generally was less excited about this celebration: imperial enthusiasms were waning, there was no recent military victory to contribute to the party spirit and there was a growing unease about what appeared to be Germany's aggressive intentions.

On June 16, Donald unveiled a plaque at the Westminster Palace Hotel to commemorate the 1866 conference, held there, which led to the creation of the Dominion of Canada. Laurier was in London for the coronation and Donald insisted that he make a public announcement of his resignation as high commissioner at the Dominion Day dinner on June 30. Even then, when the tables were swollen with visiting dignitaries, the prime minister fudged the issue, saying only that Donald would be leaving "at an early date." Donald had already told the Dominion Day organizing committee that this would be his last dinner, but Laurier was doing his best to keep the date as vague as possible for as long as possible. Once again, fate was to take a hand in ensuring that Donald did not have his way.[31]

Laurier returned to Canada to fight a general election. Though he had retained power in the 1908 election, he put it at risk by developing a policy of reciprocity with the United States. Loyalty to Britain was still a dominant factor in the Canadian political makeup, even if imperialism was no longer as powerful as it had been, and the signing of a treaty with the US early in 1911 seemed to disregard the strong emotional and economic ties linking Britain and Canada. Across Canada, the English press agreed with the *Montreal Star* which described the policy as "anti-Canadian, anti-British and anti-Empire." The treaty also gave some unthinking American politicians the opportunity to boast that the stars and stripes would one day fly over the entire continent. Laurier, who was striving to increase Canada's independence, would never have accepted the American embrace but the treaty gave his political opponents the opportunity to tax him with it anyway, while those contending for the Francophone vote condemned him for his naval bill which, it said, marked him as a British imperialist, prepared to commit Canada to fight some future British war.[32]

Donald disliked the reciprocity treaty because he felt it diminished the strength of Canada's ties with the UK and, in common with the rest of the Canadian business community, believed it would damage trade rather than succour it. In the line of duty, he did his best to defend the policy, but he was not happy doing so. The Canadian electorate felt no such compunction and, in September, turned Laurier and the Liberals out of office.

The new prime minister, Robert Borden, was a fifty-seven year old Maritimer who had led the Conservatives since 1901. The cousin of Frederick Borden, the former militia minister, he had none of Laurier's charisma and none of his charm. His party was disunited and his policies on important issues such as the navy were poorly thought out. His electoral victory said more about Laurier's reciprocity treaty than it did about what the Tories had to offer Canada.

The election took place on September 21. On September 23, Donald was on the *Mauretania*, sailing from Liverpool to New York. He reached Montreal on September 29 and the next day spent a few hours in Ottawa having lunch with Borden and visiting Laurier. On Tuesday, October 3, he paid a quick visit to McGill, had a brief meeting with the governor general, Lord Grey, and boarded the train for New York. On Wednesday, he was back on the *Mauretania* and bound for Liverpool. Even by Donald's standards, this was a speedy journey and the fact that the *Mauretania* had made such a rapid round trip provoked admiring comment in the press.

The moment the outcome of the election was known, people began to speculate on who the next high commissioner would be. Stories were circulating in Ottawa that the post would be offered to Sir Edmund Osler, a Tory stalwart who, with Donald, had been a townsite trustee for the Canada North West Land

Company. Osler himself had no interest in the post, but this did not stop tongues wagging. Van Horne was advocating Laurier, the appointment to be made after a decent interval so it would not appear as though he were deserting his party. "Lord Strathcona could be induced to hang on as long as necessary," he observed, "although he wishes to retire." William Peterson, McGill's principal, wrote Borden the day Donald called on him to say that he thought the high commissioner "would quite like to be *urged* to stay, — at least in the meantime."[33]

The man who *really was* after the high commissionership was Lord Grey, the governor general. Sir Charles Fitzpatrick, chief justice of the supreme court, asked Joseph Pope to call by a few days after the election and about two weeks before the Greys were due to depart. He pointed out that Grey "was not well off, had no employment in sight, and that Sir CF had reason to believe he would be glad of the job." He asked Pope to broach the matter with Borden. Pope was taken aback and pointed out that he did not know Borden well enough to make such a suggestion. He did, however, agree to raise it with Laurier who "received the whole project with disfavour." Like most people with political experience, he assumed that Borden had already decided who would be rewarded with the job and, in any event, he felt that Grey was too impulsive to be a good high commissioner.[34]

In fact, the man Borden was thinking of was Lord Strathcona, if only because it had not crossed his mind to offer the post to anyone else. Donald "gladly consented to discharge the duties" until Borden could appoint a successor and assumed he had only a few months to go.[35]

Back in London, he resumed his old habits. On October 17, he was the guest speaker at the 288th Cutlers' Feast in Sheffield where he told the assembled diners that his association with the city went back to his boyhood when he had a penknife of Sheffield steel; on October 21 he was with a deputation from the British and Foreign Sailors' Society which presented a painting to Nelson's ship, the *Victory*, preserved as a museum in Portsmouth. Donald had paid for the painting, even if it was the society's gift. On October 26, he was gazetted an honourary colonel of Strathcona's Horse, and so it continued. In February 1912, however, Donald fell seriously ill. He had battled with colds and pleurisy throughout his life but on this occasion it was influenza coupled with pleurisy. He had not recovered his strength from the Canadian trip and the virus took a firm hold.

"High Commissioner down with influenza," Griffith cabled Borden on February 19. "Barlow reassuring I feel uneasy." Griffith reported on the twentieth that Donald was slightly better and Borden sent a cable wishing a speedy recovery. To this, Donald insisted on making his own response: "am holding my own and somewhat easier," and the following day he sent off a telegram relating to the impending bankruptcy of the Hudson Bay and Pacific Railway.[36]

Anxiety was nevertheless widespread and the king sent a messenger to inquire after the high commissioner's health, as did Princess Louise and her husband, the Duke of Argyll. *The Times* carried a daily bulletin on his health from February 20 till March 12. It was not until March 29 that the paper was able to report that, although still confined to his room, Lord Strathcona expected to "be about again next week."

On February 24, when it was apparent that Donald was likely to survive, Griffith wrote Borden again. "One fact I think I should mention to you and it is that Lord Strathcona is losing courage with respect to his health. Until a few months ago all his arrangements were entered into as if he were a man of fifty, now he frequently turns to me and asks, 'I wonder if it is realised that I am ninety years old?' To me, I fear, this is significant."[37]

He was weak throughout the spring and could hardly hold a pen to attend to his correspondence but gradually his strength returned and he began to deal with some of the High Commission's more pressing problems. Foremost among these was the need to find new premises. The offices in Victoria Street were convenient for the government buildings in Whitehall but they were rather gloomy and very crowded. In December, Borden had said that the High Commission should find new offices or build its own.

Australia was in the process of constructing a building for itself in the Strand, which leads east from Trafalgar Square towards London's financial district, and South Africa was thinking about new premises as well. In 1905, London began the construction of the Kingsway, a north-south street to link the Strand with Holborn about a third of a mile to the north. At the same time, one of the London Underground lines was being extended. It was a huge and lengthy building project which included the demolition of twenty-eight acres of slums. In 1912, many of the gaps had not been filled, and Lord Grey, having failed to become high commissioner, had accepted the chairmanship of Dominion Site, a company which had taken an option on a large portion of the unoccupied land at the Strand end of the Kingsway where it intended to construct accommodation for the self-governing colonies. Grey was enthusiastic about this grandiose scheme and refused to believe that Canada would not want offices in the new building. Donald, on the other hand, thought the site unsuitable and the price too high, and was not prepared to be pushed by Grey into a proposition which he thought would not satisfy Canada's needs.

In June 1912, George Foster, the minister of trade and commerce, and Sir Edmund Osler arrived in London to help Donald examine possible sites and assist in the negotiations. They narrowed their choice to two; one was a hotel on the east side of Trafalgar Square, while the other was the site of Westminster Hospital on the south side of the Thames, immediately across from the Houses of Parliament. The latter was Donald's preference and, even when he was ill in bed, he had had discussions about it. It was a cumbersome procedure because he was negotiating with a committee, and one of the members had persuaded the others that the land should be sold leasehold rather than freehold. Negotiations dragged on for months and Grey continued to press for his Dominion Site. Eventually, Foster and Osler left without having concluded a deal.

The men were distracted from their investigations by the arrival of Prime Minister Borden, paying his first official visit to Britain in his capacity as Canada's leader. Innumerable invitations to private and public functions were sent to him through the High Commission and it fell to Donald to advise on which to accept and which to decline. To Donald's annoyance, Borden arrived two days after the Dominion Day dinner and reception. The Strathconas had a small dinner for sixteen on the Sunday after Borden reached London; the king and queen had lunch for fifty a week later and there were garden parties and a court ball as well as banquets and dinners given by the Chamber of Commerce, the Admiralty, and the Canada Club. On July 25, Donald entertained seventy-nine guests, all male, to dinner at Grosvenor Square and offered a reception, which included ladies, to follow.

The wining and dining were tiring in themselves, but Donald also had strict ideas about protocol during prime ministerial visits. While Borden appreciated the courtesy and consideration which he was shown, he was much more casual about such matters than the high commissioner.

> During my visit as Prime Minister in 1912 he was in evidence on every occasion. He met us at the station upon our arrival in London; he regularly called upon us at our hotel; when I left London to visit Paris, I found him (to my great astonishment) waiting for me at the hotel door early in the morning in order to accompany me to the train. On that occasion he reproached me for not having given him formal notice of my departure; and he seemed to feel that his failure to attend would have been almost a disgrace. He was so earnest on the subject that when I returned from Paris, I gave him by telegraph the formal notice which he desired, and of course I found him again at the station to meet us.[38]

When Donald was younger, he would not have met Borden at Euston Station; he would have gone to Liverpool. A few years earlier, it had taken some effort to persuade him that the journey to the port to meet Laurier was not necessary and he subsequently formulated a compromise: Griffith went to Liverpool and Donald restricted himself to the train station in London.

As soon as the official party had departed, Donald and Bella set out for Glencoe where they spent most of August, all of September and the first few days of October. As a consequence, he was rested and more vigorous when he returned to London. His first official duty was to lay a wreath in St. Paul's Cathedral to commemorate the centenary of the death of Sir Isaac Brock in the Battle of Queenston Heights during the War of 1812. A few days later, Bella accompanied him to the British Home and Hospital for Incurables where he laid the foundation stone for the Queen Alexandra wing. In the middle of November, he received the Royal Society of Arts' Albert Medal honouring his services to railways and resources, commerce and industry in Canada.

In November, however, he was in bed with a very bad cold and Bella was also unwell. The cold was followed by "a rather severe accident (at Christmas) to my right leg, which upset me a good deal, as Sir Thomas Barlow ... was somewhat apprehensive of the possible result."[39]

In the summer, Donald had reiterated his wish to retire, and the accident, together with his most recent cold, reinforced this desire. Borden's letter of December 19, therefore, did not get the reception the prime minister intended. He offered $5,000 to engage an assistant secretary to help with "the increased work in connection with the exceedingly responsible and important office which you fill." Borden had been impressed with what he had seen in the summer and by the acuity and experience which Donald brought to the question of finding new offices for the high commission. "You do not need to be assured my dear Lord Strathcona of the very great appreciation which all the members of our Government place upon the continuance of your services as High Commissioner. It would be most unfortunate if you should persevere in the suggestion of retiring which you mentioned to me when I was in London." In a separate cable, he proposed increasing Griffith's allowance by $1,000, a fair gesture in view of the fact that he was carrying more and more responsibility for the day to day operation of the high commission.[40]

Donald immediately cabled acceptance of the offer to increase Griffith's allowance but it was February 2 before he felt up to responding to Borden's offer of an assistant secretary. He said that Canada was far better known than it had been when he became high commissioner in 1896 "and is now so thoroughly in the minds of the people that although the volume of the work has largely increased the duties are much less exacting than they then were and the staff which has been considerably increased is as it at present exists quite capable of coping with the requirements." In short, what was needed was not more staff but a new high commissioner. "I shall therefore be greatly indebted if you will kindly relieve me from the duties of the office in May next when I shall have served seventeen years." He carried on to thank both Borden and Laurier and their staff for their support "throughout my long service, a service in the interests of Canada which to me has been one of love."[41]

Borden had undoubtedly got the measure of his high commissioner and responded in terms which were highly complimentary but also largely true.

> I need not assure you that we are greatly disturbed at your suggestion of retirement in May next. Your wonderful capacity to deal wisely with the interests of the country committed to your hands, your most earnest and untiring devotion to duty, the great position which you hold outside of all official responsibility and the prestige of your name throughout the Empire have combined to render most regrettable any early termination of your public service. While agreeing that the considerations affecting your health are of the first importance and must first be regarded may I venture to express the most earnest hope that you will reconsider your decision to retire from the High Commissionership in May next. At least I hope you will not retire until I have the opportunity of a personal interview at which the subject may be more fully and effectively discussed than it is possible to do by correspondence.[42]

The flattery worked and Donald responded to the prime minister's "far too indulgent message" by agreeing to delay his retirement until he and Borden could talk.[43]

Meetings with British and Canadian officials and the speeches and public duties which still fell on Donald required more and more effort and he found that it took longer and longer to recuperate from that effort. The man people saw in private was no longer the energetic figure with which they had been familiar before his bout with influenza in the winter and spring of 1912. "I feel I am bound to give you my personal impression about the state of Lord Strathcona's health, as of late I regret greatly to say he appears to be failing fast," Griffith wrote to Borden in March. "Yesterday afternoon he seemed to me to be quite dazed while here and it is only too evident that he is in a precarious state, his margin of health is narrow, although of course it is quite possible he may go on for a year or two longer."[44]

The message roused no sympathy in Borden and nothing changed in the Victoria Street offices.

Canadian fiscal policies and British investment in Canada occupied Donald's attention at the beginning of the year, as did an anonymous letter to *The Economist* which suggested that land was going out of cultivation in Canada. In fact, a severe winter had killed off some of the wheat crop and Donald argued that clarifying the situation with an official letter would do more harm than good because it would precipitate a controversy which would be picked up by newspapers with a much wider circulation. It was a view which Borden and his cabinet colleagues shared.

In April, Donald was busy with the Canadian Arctic Expedition. It was an initiative of Vilhjalmur Stefansson who, though born in the Icelandic community in Manitoba, had emigrated to the United States and become an American citizen. His plan was to conduct a scientific exploration of the Arctic which had yet to be accurately mapped because no one was sure where the land stopped and the ice started. He had secured for his expedition an American crew and financial support which would have allowed him to claim for the United States any discoveries he might make, but because he did not have as much money as he felt he needed, he had approached Borden for additional Canadian backing for his projected journey. Clarifying the location of its northern extremities has been a concern for Canada throughout this century and the prime minister quickly persuaded the cabinet that Canada should take over the Arctic expedition in its entirety.

Borden recommended that Stefansson discuss his project with Donald; his Labrador experience and the HBC's long involvement in the Arctic could be useful. So too would be his contacts among the scientific communities in British universities. Stefansson spoke at the Royal Geological Society in London and Donald paid his way to attend the International Geological Congress in Rome.

Stefansson planned to take pemmican as the basic ration and was dismayed to discover that some of his scientists wanted to test it to discover its makeup. "Strathcona agreed that, while it was never too late to question the quality of any particular lot of pemmican, it was at least a century too late to question pemmican as a travel ration." Quite what this ration really was is hard to guess since it was ordered from Bovril in England! The arguments and the delays meant that the pemmican was late leaving the UK, late into Halifax and risked arriving at Esquimalt after the navy, which was supporting the expedition, had departed for the north. It only took a few moments for Donald to ensure that the CPR provided an express service across the country. "For this extraordinary service the expedition was charged ordinary freight rates only. Strathcona was a[s] pleased with himself as a boy who has just shot his first rabbit," Stefansson recalled.[45]

Donald also sorted out travel arrangements for scientists and other British crew members. On the eighteenth of April, Stefansson went to the High Commission to say good-bye and express his thanks for Donald's support. "The old man handed me his personal check for a thousand pounds, saying that it would be a good thing for me to have a little money for which I did not have to account to anyone. I protested, not too firmly, that the naval service had been very generous and would undoubtedly be considerate at all times. Strathcona said that I could not know much about auditors. They never felt, he said, that they were earning their salaries unless they were able to find some item to disallow. I laughed and said that I would report to him about that when I got back. He smiled and said, 'I shall not be here'."[46]

The journey had an unhappy ending; Stefansson's ship was crushed in the ice and he left it, saying that he was going to hunt caribou and would be back in ten days. In fact, he spent five years exploring the Arctic without contacting the lead ship. The men, most of whom had no previous Arctic experience, were rescued in September 1914, but eleven of them had died.

The Canada Club, the Hudson's Bay Company, the British and Foreign Sailors' Society, the Hospital and Home for Incurables and many other charities occupied Donald's attention in the spring and summer. The only concession to his failing strength was the decision to separate the men's dinner for Dominion Day and the mixed reception, holding one on the first of July and the other a day later.

On August 3, *The Times* announced that it was Lord Strathcona's birthday and congratulatory telegrams once again inundated Grosvenor Square and the high commission. The fact that the paper got the day wrong was glossed over. The British and foreign press all wanted more than *The Times*' formal announcement and journalists pestered the high commissioner for interviews. "The best way to live to an old age," he told the reporters, "is by not thinking about age at all, but just going on doing your work."[47]

The American Bar Association held its annual conference at the Royal Victoria College in Montreal in September 1913 and invited Viscount Haldane, Britain's Lord Chancellor, to be one of the guest speakers. Donald wanted to see Sterling in New York in order to make some changes to his will to bring the Scottish and American versions of the codicils into line. As well, he wanted to change two of his trustees, replacing George Stephen with Maggie and Alexander Lang, the Bank of Montreal manager, with his Scottish solicitor, William Garson. The matter could have been dealt with by post, but that was not his way. It consequently made sense to him that he should combine his trip with Haldane's. Bella, having been unhappy about letting him travel to Canada alone in 1911, determined to go with him.

The formality which Donald showed towards Canadian prime ministers visiting England applied equally to the Lord Chancellor as far as Donald was concerned, and he made it clear that he would escort him and his sister to Euston Station where they would catch the boat train for Liverpool. Donald and Bella were late arriving at the Haldane residence — probably because Bella was confused, it being on this morning that Haldane's sister observed that she was not quite *compos mentis*. At any event, they reached the station on time and Donald ensured that the Haldanes were settled while Maggie, who was travelling with them, looked after her mother. Donald then left the platform, possibly for a last minute briefing with Griffith or a chat with station staff to whom he always showed consideration. The train was due to depart at 1150 and Donald had not reappeared when it started to pull out. "He arrived as the train was on the move, and with surprising agility — he is 93 years of age —" *The Times* reminded its readers, "managed to board the rear portion, and reached his reserve saloon by means of the connecting corridor." "The old gentleman is wonderfully on the spot," enthused Miss Haldane.[48]

The visit was scarcely less hurried than the one he had made in 1911 and, as usual, he had decided to travel at the last minute. He spent Friday and part of Saturday with Sterling in New York before heading north. He admitted to the *Montreal Gazette* that it was unlikely that he would be able to make many more visits to Canada, "but I would be loath to believe that this one must necessarily be my last." He reminisced about the early days of transatlantic travel and the changes he had seen but his mind was by no means confined to the past. "At some future day means of traffic may again be revolutionized, and the people of that time will look upon us of today as having been the victims of very grave discomfort. I imagine it may not be long before people may be crossing the Atlantic in the air, but I think it will be very long before such a method of passage can be made as comfortable, especially for an old man, as that of our great ocean greyhounds of today."[49]

Donald had two busy days in Montreal, with Bar Association dinners on both the Sunday and the Monday. At Monday's dinner, he refused to eat the partridge, explaining to US Chief Justice White that it was "either killed out of season or had been in ice for a year and was unfit to eat."[50]

That day, in his capacity as chancellor of McGill, he had conferred degrees and on either Sunday or Monday he also saw both Borden and Van Horne. Conversation with the prime minister would have centred on his retirement and the difficulty in finding suitable office accommodation in London. The discussion with Van Horne, while friendly, was fundamentally unsatisfactory.

Sometime in 1890 or early 1891, Van Horne had purchased two hundred acres on Minister's Island, just off the New Brunswick holiday resort of St. Andrew's and close to the US border. His enthusiasm for his new acquisition was infectious and Donald observed that he would like to have some land there too. Van Horne offered to split his purchase on condition that Donald build a summer home on his half as Van Horne intended to do. The men agreed and Donald sent a cheque. Van Horne returned it since, in his mind, the deal was only valid if a house was built. Donald posted the cheque again and it went back and forth several more times before Van Horne agreed to keep it on the understanding that he would return it if the house was not built.

Van Horne made several efforts to get Donald to go to Minister's Island with him so the two could agree on where they would build but Donald was always occupied with something else.

> Finally he told me to go ahead and make my own selection and he would be quite content, whereupon I proceeded with the building of my house leaving him with what I thought the most favorable site but I could not afterwards get him to make any move towards building — he was too busy and after seven or eight years I brought up the matter with him in the presence of Sir Thomas Shaughnessy and Mr. R.B. Angus

> pointing out to him the embarrassment of my position with half the property remaining unimproved and in an unsightly condition and without roads or fences whereupon he asked me to treat the property as my own and go on with any improvements upon it that I thought best, the cost of which he should make good if he should build and in the event of his not building immediately he would absolve me from any claim in the matter.[51]

In the fall of 1911, Garson was trying to make sure all loose ends were tied up while Lord Strathcona was still around to explain any unclear points. He discovered that there were no title deeds and no other documentary evidence to prove ownership of the land on Minister's Island and wrote the Royal Trust to see if it could clear up the matter. At the end of October, Donald discovered what had happened and wrote the Royal Trust himself to say that "he regrets very much that Mr. Garson had taken it upon himself to give any instruction in this connection." The matter was a personal one between him and Van Horne.[52]

For his part, Van Horne was glad to have the interference because he too wanted the matter cleared up. At the beginning of November, he wrote to say that he had made improvements on Donald's land, building roads and fences and planting trees. He was not concerned about the expenditure but he did not like the fact that he felt constrained in his plans for the island and wanted to settle with Donald. "I should at least wish to return the money you advanced with compound interest (for nothing less would be just to you) and to make good any advance that may have occurred in the value of land on the Island."[53]

Donald did not reply but his obligation to Van Horne did nag his conscience and he raised the subject when he was in Montreal in 1913. He was under the impression that Van Horne had never cashed his cheque and wanted to know if he should sign a discharge. If the cheque had been cashed, he did not want his money back. Given the inconvenience he had caused his old friend, it was the least he could say. Unfortunately, while the matter was thus settled between the two men, there was no documentation of their agreement.

On the second of September, Donald and Bella were again on the train bound for New York where Donald had another meeting with Sterling about his will. The *Lusitania*, the ship on which they had crossed, sailed for Liverpool the following day and they were on it. Lord Haldane and his sister were also on board and she reported to her diary that one day she "had an interesting talk with old Lord Strathcona" who told her about the circumstances which had prompted him to go to Canada so many years ago. At the end of their chat, he "was most anxious to escort me back to my cabin. Not bad at 93!"[54]

On their return, Donald and Bella went immediately to Glencoe for a month's respite. They were back in London in time for the October 15 wedding of Queen Victoria's grandson, Prince Arthur of Connaught, whose father was governor general of Canada.

At the beginning of November, Bella had another cold but was not confined to bed. On fine days, she liked to walk her Yorkshire terrier in Grosvenor Square and, on Friday, November 7, she was doing just that when she collapsed. She showed signs of influenza and these soon turned to pneumonia. Barlow was optimistic so Donald, though concerned, assumed she would recover. About noon on November 12, however, she took a sudden turn for the worse and Barlow was compelled to tell Lord Strathcona she might not survive.

Donald was shocked. Barlow's earlier confidence, the fact that she was nearly five years younger than he was and her success in shaking off so many chest infections in the past had led him to believe that she would outlive him. Now, his Bellefeuille was trembling as she never had before. He held her hand and his soft Scottish burr caressed her ears with sweet encouragement. This tiny figure, dwarfed by the huge white pillows, was the only person in the world who could always speak without dissembling to the chairman, the high commissioner, the governor, the president. She had loved him when he was a Labrador trader smelling of salt fish and she had never lost sight of the man she loved. She had seduced him and made him love her and he had never stopped doing so. They had shared their lives for more than sixty years and Donald could not conceive of life without her. About half past seven that evening she slipped into unconsciousness and an hour later her heart gave up the battle.

On November 17, he sat down to acknowledge Charles Tupper's letter of condolence and revealed his feelings in a way he rarely did. Her death, he said, was "the greatest sorrow I have ever experienced. She was my stay and comforter throughout a long life, and I can hardly yet realize that she has passed away from me. You, my dear Sir Charles, have been through the same trial, and only those who have done so can fully realize what it means, after so many years of dear companionship."[55]

The funeral took place on November 19 at St. Mark's, North Audley Street, just a few yards from Grosvenor Square, where Bella had worshipped. Queen Alexandra sent a wreath as did the Duchess of Albany, one of Victoria's widowed daughters-in-law. Members of the royal family never attend funerals other than those of their own relatives but both Queen Alexandra and the Duke of Connaught sent representatives. The service was taken jointly by the vicar, Herbert Cronshaw, and Dr. Archibald Fleming, the minister from St. Columba's where Donald worshipped. The burial was at Highgate Cemetery. "A large & representative Funeral it was on a bleak black day," Agnes Macdonald observed to Pope.[56]

Donald did his best to pull himself together and concentrate on his work. To some extent, he had no choice for when Leonard Cunliffe and Richard Burbidge had worked their way onto the board of the HBC, they were determined to force more shares to be issued in order to raise capital to expand the stores. As the company paid dividends of fifty percent in 1913, it might have been assumed that it already had sufficient resources to pay for the expansion. Nevertheless, five days after Bella's funeral, Donald presided over an extraordinary General Court to consider increasing the capital of the company. He was too deaf to contribute actively to either this meeting or the General Court the previous June but he nevertheless felt it his duty to be present and to prepare speeches for others to read on his behalf.

Before the extraordinary General Court, he met Wilfred Grenfell for lunch at the HBC offices. The two had kept in touch over the years because Donald had remained an active supporter of the hospital ship and other mission work in which Grenfell and his colleagues were engaged on the Labrador coast. Their visits also gave him an opportunity to catch up on news of those he had known so many years ago and, if he heard any of them were in difficulty, to send off parcels of food and clothing, gifts which were worth a good deal more than money in a land without shops.

When they met in 1913, Donald asked after the *Strathcona*. It, and a previous *Strathcona,* had replaced the *Sir Donald* in Grenfell's medical work on the coast. "He was dismayed to hear that her boilers had blown out, and that she was laid up owing to the lack of the necessary funds to replace them. It seems almost superfluous to say that he at once ordered them to be replaced at his expense so as to make the ship as efficient as possible, and the day after I received a letter to confirm his wishes."

Grenfell had not seen Donald for two years and the last time they had met,

> so far as his keen interest in life was concerned, his natural force seemed in no way abated. He still found his greatest pleasure in a full day's work, and when the day itself had gone, the same sufficient satisfaction in the company of the long-time partner of his life — and of their family.
>
> This time, however, a blind man could realize a vast difference in his attitude toward the world. The same interest, the same courage, but no longer the same man. He seemed to me like one of the great solitary rocks of our barren coast, which, from time immemorial, far out in the wide ocean, during the season of open water, has raised its head above the gigantic rollers of the Atlantic, and in winter, towered over the resistless grinding of the Atlantic field ice.
>
> Alone left of his generation, Lord Strathcona seemed now to me to loom up as just such another wonder. The discussion on the business which had brought us together had come to an end. We were thinking of saying good-bye, when suddenly he leaned over toward me and said, "You will let me know about the boilers for the hospital ship? See that they are done as well as they can be and come and see me before you go back to Labrador." The word seemed involuntarily to have carried his thought back to the long-ago scenes of that country where first he had met the wife whom he had loved so truly. It seemed to me that his white head bent a little lower, as he added, "Doctor, a terrible blow has come to me since you were here last, —terrible! terrible!" he repeated.[57]

Donald did his best to get into the High Commission offices after Bella's death and early in January he forced the promoters of the Central Railway of Canada, whose line was never built, to publicly correct their claims that the Canadian government had promised them a subsidy.

Jamesie wrote early in the month and the contents of his letter "greatly excited" Donald who "directed that Mr. Smith and a friend of his should be cabled to come over here and that they should be treated 'liberally'." Griffith, who reported Donald's distress to Borden, assumed that it related to the fact that Bella had stated in her will that Maggie was her only child by Lord Strathcona but it seems more likely that Jamesie had got himself into financial difficulties again. In any event, he did not go to England. He did, however, sell his share of the old Hardisty house in Lachine to Maggie. Bella had left it to them both, exactly replicating the unsatisfactory arrangement her father had made for her and her brother William so many years before.

On January 8, 1914, *The Times* reported that Donald, who had been confined to his room with a cold was much better and expected to resume work that day. He did not. His condition deteriorated and Barlow, who had been worried about heart disease for some time, feared the worst. It would be an exaggeration to say that his patient had lost the will to live, but with Bella gone there seemed little reason to carry on.

On January 17, William Garson was summoned from Edinburgh. He chartered a train and set a record for the journey to London, stopping only at Carlisle and Crewe to change engines and crews. While he waited for his lawyer, Donald insisted on attending to High Commission business. Laurier had condemned Lord Grey as impetuous but he was also presumptuous and Donald was very angry. On the fifth of January, two days before he was to set sail on a voyage round the world to drum up enthusiasm for the Dominion Site, Grey had written Donald, asking him to forward a letter to Borden. He pointed out that an article in the Montreal *Herald* suggested that "there is a difference of opinion between you and me. I am deleting this passage and all other press references that have been sent to me suggesting that you are in favour of the Westminster Hospital site." Grey was sure that when Donald heard all the arguments, he would favour the Dominion Site.[58]

Donald was sure he would not and wanted to make certain that Borden received a succinct statement of the case while he had breath left to make it. Borden and his cabinet colleagues had already come to the conclusion that the time was not right for spending such a sum as Grey had in mind and Donald wanted to reinforce this opinion.

> An enormously expensive edifice near the Strand on the plan put before me by Earl Grey, with an elevation overtopping not only the Commonwealth [of Australia] and other buildings in the immediate vicinity, but the dome of the great Cathedral, St. Paul's, I could not possibly regard as other than an unpardonable expenditure, and in my mind such a vast building with a dominating pinnacle erected as a striking advertisement would provoke ridicule rather than bring advantage to our great country and its people. I am more convinced every day that it is not in the grand architectural effect of the offices of the Dominion in London that the requirements of the situation are to be found, but in the work that is actually done within them in the interests of the Canadian people.[59]

Donald advised trying to extend the lease on Victoria Chambers.

On Sunday, while churches across Canada prayed for Lord Strathcona's recovery and the king and queen requested that they be kept informed of his condition, Donald began to issue his final instructions to his lawyers. The bulk of his American investments had been taken care of by the establishment of fourteen different trusts. His own personal account had investments worth $11.99 million while a trust in Bella's name had investments worth close to $1.5 million. The income from both of these had gone to Donald. As well, he and Bella had a joint trust with investments worth just over $1.2 million.

Donald and Maggie had a joint trust which was probably set up at the same time as the joint trust with Bella since the investments were worth exactly the same. The first $4,000 earned by this trust was payable to Maggie and the remainder to her father but on his death, she was to receive all the income and to have the power to distribute the capital among her children, the implication being that it would be invested on their behalf. Maggie had her own trust, with investments worth $7.8 million and each of her five children had trusts with 2,000 Great Northern and 2,200 Northern Pacific shares valued in total at a little over £2 million. Another quarter of a million dollars had been invested for Frances and Donald had settled an additional 2,500 Northern Pacific shares on her when she married Captain James Kitson of the Royal Navy in May 1913. Except for this marriage trust and the joint trust with Maggie, the income from all these investments was paid to Donald during his lifetime. The trust for Jamesie had investments worth just over $167,000 and the income was paid to him. By 1914, he had borrowed nearly $4,000 against the income and shares had to be sold as a consequence. These US trusts accounted for just over $26.5 million in total.

On Sunday, Garson and Wilson, his young clerk, settled into chairs by Donald's bed where he was propped up by pillows with his deed box in his lap. Now that he knew where he was going to die, there was no need to worry about making the Scottish and American legacies dovetail. He revoked his January 1896 will and the codicils added in May that year, in January 1899 and the two he had sorted out with Sterling on his rushed trip to Canada the previous autumn.

Colonsay and Oronsay, he said, were no longer to go to into a trust but were to be inherited by Maggie and her male heirs. The same was to happen with the various parcels of land which made up the Glencoe estate but £500,000, presumably to be acquired through selling some of the land, was to be invested in what became known as the Peerage Trust. "I am desirous of making provision for the suitable maintenance of the dignity of the said peerage," he had stated when the original trust was established in 1903. He had seen the difficulties Agnes Macdonald had faced when, having accepted a peerage as a posthumous honour for her husband, she found herself unable to afford the coronation robes or any of the social obligations which British society assumed a peeress would undertake, and wanted do his best to ensure that his grandson, and his heirs in turn would not find themselves in a similar situation. The income from the Peerage Trust was to be paid to the baroness and the capital was to be made over to Maggie's male heir, "but I strongly recommend that such heir shall thereupon create a new trust in terms similar to the trust created by these presents so as to ensure the continuance of due provision for maintaining the honour and dignity of the Peerage in the persons of himself and his successors."[60]

All that remained was to be inherited by Maggie after other bequests and legacies had been provided for and any beneficiaries who contested the will were to forfeit their legacies.

Norway House at Pictou and the associated land and buildings were given to Jamesie. The executors, to whom everything was left in trust while the legacies were sorted out, were to invest £25,000 for Jamesie; he was to have the income and his children were to inherit the capital. Another £5,000 in trust was added, probably on the following day.

By default, as it were, Maggie thus inherited Silver Heights, the house on Dorchester Street in Montreal and Debden Hall as well as all the investment properties. Unfortunately, Donald forgot to mention Minister's Island and Garson wasted little time in ensuring that Van Horne repaid the estate for the one hundred acres in which Donald had shown so little interest.

Donald then instructed his executors, who were Maggie, John Sterling, William Garson and his brother James, to set aside £20,000 and invest it on behalf of Margaret Smith, his brother John's unmarried daughter, and to do the same for her sister, Eliza. The capital from both investments passed to Eliza's children on her death. Stuart Lodge, where Margaret lived, was already held for them in trust.

Next, Donald said, he wanted to dispose of £100,000 in charitable gifts. St. John's College, Cambridge was to receive £10,000, an intention which had figured in his earliest will and was repeated again in 1896. The trustees were to reclaim the $120,000 which had been given to the Donalda Endowment at the Royal Victoria College in Montreal and were to add to it enough money to total a million dollars which was to form a new endowment for the college. Donald still owned the land on which the college was built but it was to be given to the college when it was finally incorporated, a process which was taking an exceedingly long time because, to the dismay of the Canadians, Skene Edwards and Garson had failed to consult McGill on the wording of the royal charter, the first draft of which was unacceptable to the university.

Donald was very conscious of the fact that most of his fabulous wealth had been earned through his American investments and felt an obligation to give something back to the country. Apart from contributing to disaster appeals in the United States, he had given nothing by way of support for schools, churches or hospitals. Now, he offered £100,000 to Yale University "for the promotion of the modern sciences and for instructions in the practical questions arising from the application of scientific knowledge to the Industrial, Social and Economical problems of the time, it being my special desire to have the said sum expended so far as in the opinion of my Trustees may be deemed advisable for instruction in civil and mechanical engineering, with special reference to the construction, equipment and operation of transportation of passengers and freight whether by land or water and the financial and legislative questions involved." This had been corrected to read "with special reference to the problems connected with the economical and efficient transportation of passengers and freight" etc. but the lawyers failed to incorporate the change when the papers were presented for signature and so the reference to "construction, equipment and operation" remained. Donald said that his wishes might be carried out by the erection of a building or the endowment of a chair but he also hoped there would be one or more scholarships, preferably for railway employees or their children.[61]

Next, he gave £100,000 towards the endowment of a maintenance fund for the Royal Victoria Hospital in Montreal. A similar sum was to be given by George Stephen.

At this point, he had given away not £100,000 but nearly £400,000 and Donald was not through yet. Garson had never had any real picture of his client's wealth because nearly all of it derived from investments in North America and was handled by Sterling. Now, he was aghast at the way money seemed to be flowing out of the Strathcona coffers. Perhaps his lordship should stop. Nonsense, Donald declared, there was plenty more. And so there was.[62]

He gave £5,000 to make up the full endowment for the Chair of Agriculture at Aberdeen University and £10,000 to the maintenance fund of Leanchoil Hospital, the latter to be in Bella's name. Other hospitals and academic institutions also benefitted.

He then cancelled three debts. The first was a substantial one owed by the estate of Richard Cartwright, who had been Laurier's finance minister and whose loan had been covered by shares which had subsequently lost their value; his son was negotiating with Sterling to try to find some means of settling the debt, neither man suspecting that Donald was going to resolve their problem for them. The second debt was the remainder of a mortgage which William White, deputy postmaster general of Canada under the Liberals, had been paying off, and which his estate had continued to repay after his death; and the third was a moderate sum, backed by mining shares, which was owed by George Foster, the Conservative minister of trade and commerce, who had borrowed the money in 1898. Maggie later cancelled two more debts owed to her father.

Donald also put his mind to annuities for those to whom he had been providing support for many years. These included the daughters of his cousin, Hugh Lindsay Stuart; other female Stuart relatives; Margaret McLennan who had been Bella's maid for many years; and several old Hudson's Bay Company factors, including Dr. Helmcken whom Donald had visited in Victoria in 1909, Colin Rankin with whom he had maintained a warm friendship for most of his life, and Roderick MacFarlane, who still pestered all and sundry about the inequities of the company's arrangements for its retired chief factors.

Other bequests included £1,000 for William Garson and his brother James, the same for Joseph Colmer and William Griffith and a thousand guineas to Dr. Barlow and his colleague, Dr. Pasteur. Donald later thought again about the doctors and doubled their legacies.

Garson and Wilson left their client in order to type up his new will and give some shape to his requests, but when they returned the following day, they discovered that he had more to add. Jamesie's son, Donald Alexander, was to continue to receive an allowance of $50 a month and the allowance to Mr. MacInnes at Glencoe was to be maintained. A thousand pounds was to go to St. Columba's Church where he had worshipped in London and the same was to go to St. Mark's which Bella had attended. The ministers of both churches were also to receive £1,000 each. Abraham May, who assisted Joseph Colmer in his duties as private secretary, was to be dealt with generously; the Grey Nuns in Montreal were to receive $2,000 and May would identify those who were to receive a further $3,000. Both Borden and Lady Laurier were to be given £1,000. Towards the end of this list, he remembered his son-in-law and instructed that he should have five hundred HBC shares, the same number also being transferred to Maggie's eldest son.

As well, there was a record, prepared by Colmer, of all those organizations in Britain and Canada which had been promised money on condition that other sums be raised first. These came close to $45,000 and nearly all were eventually paid. In addition, Donald pointed out that he had just committed up to $3,000 for a new boiler for Grenfell's hospital ship and had given a guarantee of up to £5,000 for the Crystal Palace exhibition, scheduled for 1915.

When he finally reached the end of his long list, "Lord Strathcona expressed a desire to be buried by the side of his wife in Highgate Cemetery, and suggested that any mausoleum to be erected should be simple, but not foolishly simple." It was a wish which, in many ways, summed up the man. His love for his wife far exceeded his desire for any honours which the country might bestow and he intended that this should be demonstrated in death as much as in life. As for the mausoleum, any canny Scot would know that excessive simplicity would be as laughable as excessive grandeur. What was required was a design which led the eye and the mind to the spiritual purpose of the grave marker.

Donald's will stated clearly that he was a resident Scot and he now urged Garson and Wilson to record the statement he was about to make. He then carefully recounted the circumstances of Bella's marriage to James Grant, noting that her father had "no authority to perform the marriage ceremony outside the territory of the Hudson's Bay Company." He explained that Bella and Grant had separated shortly after Jamesie's birth, that the Anglican bishop had subsequently appointed him a lay preacher, and that the governor of Newfoundland had given him the authority to perform marriages and christenings. He then revealed the circumstances of his marriage to Bella with one crucial error. The ceremony, he said, took place in 1852. In fact, Jamesie was born in June 1852 and his parents separated later that year. Muddling dates is easily done and Donald may well have meant 1853, the year in which his relationship with Bella was consummated, since March 9, 1853 is the date he gave out for publications such as the peerage guides. His deathbed statement says, "I myself performed the ceremony in the presence of a number of witnesses including several Orcadians. I considered that if in the circumstances stated the marriage should be deemed irregular, still as I was then a domiciled Scotsman, which I still am, the marriage would be regularized and validated and any children of the union would be duly legitimized by going through a formal marriage ceremony with my wife at any time thereafter." This he did in New York, as Maggie discovered that day for the first time. In fact, of course, the marriage ceremony in Labrador did not take place until 1859 but rearranging the dates gave Maggie a legitimacy which might otherwise have been questioned. A summary of the statement, conveniently omitting the dates, was prepared and signed by Barlow and Pasteur as a true statement of the deathbed declaration. It concludes, "Lord Strathcona then took Mrs. Howard's hand and said she was the only child by his marriage and the only child he ever had."[63]

The gossip about his marriage had carried on behind Donald's back for sixty years. He had ignored it but the irregularity of his arrangements weighed on his conscience, not for his sake or Bella's, but for Maggie's. He may have feared that Jamesie would try to make a claim on the estate after his death but nothing in Jamesie's behaviour suggested he would behave in this way. The truth would seem to be that, having brought his daughter from the backwoods of Labrador to the Court of St. James, he did not want to see his achievements torn away by small minded courtiers or lawyers.

Joseph Colmer was summoned on January 20. "I think I was the only friend, outside the family circle and the Doctors, who saw Lord Strathcona a few hours before he passed away. I shall never forget it. Propped up in his bed he looked like a grand old patriarch. His eye was as keen as ever, his voice as clear as a Bell. He was quite calm and collected, although he knew very well that he might pass away at any moment, and he told me what he wanted to say to me without a falter and without hesitating for a single word."[64]

Dr. Archibald Fleming, the minister at St. Columba's, entered the room as Colmer left. They prayed together and Donald repeated the second paraphrase as he so often had before. He had recited it at his mother's knee and repeated it when he suffered the excruciating pain of frostbite in Newfoundland in 1864; it was sung when he was made a freeman of Forres; it was a thread which had wound its way through his life, tying the Scots lad to the fur trader, to the Canadian man of business to the high commissioner. "O God of Bethel!" he began and, without stumbling, recited each verse.

O God of Bethel! by whose hand
thy people still are fed;
Who through this weary pilgrimage
hast all our fathers led:
Our vows, our pray'rs, we now present
before thy throne of grace:
God of our fathers! be the God
of their succeeding race.
Through each perplexing path of life
our wand'ring footsteps guide;
Give us each day our daily bread,
and raiment fit provide.
O spread thy cov'ring wings around,
till all our wand'rings cease,
And at our Father's loved abode
our souls arrive in peace.
Such blessings from thy gracious hand
our humble pray'rs implore;
And thou shalt be our chosen God,
and portion evermore.

Not long after he had recited these words, he drifted off to sleep and at ten minutes to two on the morning of January 21, 1914, with his daughter, her husband and Dr. Barlow by his side, Donald Alexander Smith, Baron Strathcona of Glencoe and Mount Royal, drew his last breath.

"Old standing heart disease (mitral)," Barlow wrote in the space on the death certificate reserved for cause, adding that the patient had had the condition for many years. As well as gout, he suffered from "Bronchial Catarrh & Heart Failure."

Messages of sympathy were sent by the king, the Duke of Argyll, the Lord Mayor of London and countless friends and relatives as well as by business and political leaders. Canadian Pacific shares dropped on the London market and other Canadian shares followed suit.

The Duke of Connaught, governor general of Canada, sent a telegram, praising Donald's "lofty ideals, his splendid patriotism, as well as his distinguished services as High Commissioner." In Canada, flags on the Bank of Montreal and CPR buildings flew at half mast. In the House of Commons, Borden moved an adjournment as a mark of respect, observing in his speech, "I have known many men in my own lifetime who have been inspired by a high sense of duty, but I do not know of any man in my acquaintance and knowledge who has been inspired by a higher conception of duty than was Lord Strathcona."[65]

In seconding the motion, Laurier's affection for the man and his understanding of the breadth of his interests was expressed with the gracefulness Donald had so much appreciated. "Since Sir John Macdonald, I do not think there has been any Canadian whose loss has occasioned so deep and so universal sorrow. He is mourned by His Majesty, by the authorities of commerce and finance in London whose equal he showed himself to be, by the poor of London for his generosity, by the people of Scotland with whom he remained in close relations to the end, and by Canadians, high and low, rich and poor, of whatever race or creed."[66]

The Dean and Chapter offered burial at Westminster Abbey, but Maggie explained that it had been one of her father's last wishes to lie beside his wife at Highgate Cemetery. An attempt was made to provide a combined funeral at St. Columba's and the Abbey but the logistics proved impossible so Dr. Fleming joined the Dean at the Abbey on Monday, January 26.

The previous day, Fleming had made Donald's life the focal point of his sermon, describing him as "a humble Christian and a deeply religious man." He then recounted some of the death bed conversation he had had on Tuesday, not by way of breaching a confidence but because, "speaking as one who was delivering a testimony, he bade me report it to others." He said

> that in his long life he had learned a great toleration, and had come to realize that God reveals Himself to His faithful people by the lips of all the Churches; for it had been his experience that he could receive benefit from them all; so that to him denominational distinctions, and even the distinction between Protestant and Roman, almost ceased to exist in view of the great elemental truths which all, according to their ability, strove to represent: the "Good and Great Creator" could and would reveal Himself somehow to us through them all. Such was the wide sweep of this great man's spiritual vision, and such the large charity of this great heart. Yet it was ever to the simple worship of his boyhood ... that his thoughts returned; and never shall those who were around him forget the emotion with which they heard him repeat, not many hours before he died, without error, pause or confusion, the whole of the Second Paraphrase, so dear to Scottish hearts.[67]

Monday dawned grey and damp. At Grosvenor Square, Fleming conducted a private service for Maggie, Dr. Howard and their children, for John Smith's daughters and Eliza's children, and for close friends. Shortly before eleven, the "glass framed motor-hearse" pulled out of Grosvenor Square, followed by a dozen cars bearing the chief mourners. Slowly, the cortege moved down Park Lane, past Apsley House, once the home of the Duke of Wellington in whose victory at Waterloo Donald's father-in-law had played a tiny part. The cars moved to Victoria Street, where the High Commission was shut and the Union Jack flew at half mast. All along the route, crowds gathered, heads bowed, and many houses had drawn their blinds as a mark of respect.[68]

When the doors of Westminster Abbey opened, the fog surged up the aisle, shrouding the mourners with a physical manifestation of the gloom they felt in their hearts. The pall bearers shouldered the coffin. How light he was, this man who had loomed so large in the lives of so many. They adjusted the weight: Lord Lansdowne, once governor general, head of the War Office when Strathcona's Horse was created; Lord Aberdeen, governor general when the Manitoba schools question threatened Canadian Confederation; the Reverend George Adam Smith, principal of the University of Aberdeen; Sir William Osler, Regius Professor of Medicine at Oxford, once McGill's star medical student, and the professorial guide for Donald's son-in-law; Sir Lewis Harcourt, the colonial secretary; Sir Thomas Skinner, deputy governor of the Hudson's Bay Company; William Griffith, secretary at the high commission; the Duke of Argyll, another governor general and a great believer in the future of Canada; Lord Lichfield, once a deputy governor of the Hudson's Bay Company; Sir Vansittart Bowater, Lord Mayor of London. The last two were substitutes, standing in for Sir Charles Tupper and Lord Minto, both too ill themselves to attend the funeral. The procession of clergy and choristers started up the aisle with their sombre burden and the choir began to sing. "O God of Bethel by whose hand thy people still are fed."

On the purple pall lay the family's wreath of lily of the valley; Queen Alexandra's cross-shaped tribute of lilies and heliotrope orchids followed with her inscription: "In sorrowful memory of one of the Empire's kindest of men and the greatest of benefactors." The king, Queen Alexandra, Princess Louise and the prime minister all sent representatives; ambassadors, high commissioners, university leaders, company directors, railway men, hospital governors, the Salvation Army, bankers, all came to pay their respects. Here and there among the black coats and hats were flashes of colour. Gold braid glinted on military uniforms and the Liverpool Scottish, of which Donald had been honourary colonel, sent five officers in uniform.

It was a simple service: the congregation sang Psalm 90 with its reference to living for threescore years and ten, and the choir sang the fourth paraphrase, "How still and peaceful is the grave." There was music, short readings from the Bible and the Lord's Prayer but no sermon, no evocation of the long life whose conclusion they were mourning. To the "Dead March" from *Saul*, the coffin was carried out of the church and placed again in the hearse.

The cortege proceeded along Whitehall, past the Houses of Parliament, a fire-charred ruin when Donald had first seen them in 1838 and now a collage of

Victorian Gothic pinnacles, already black with coal dust from London's foggy air. Rounding Trafalgar Square, they passed St. Martin-in-the-Fields where Bella's father had been christened one hundred and twenty years before. Slowly, they headed north, reaching Highgate Cemetery about one o'clock. A carpet of floral tributes marked the grave. Here, Dr. Fleming read the committal service, combining Church of England and Church of Scotland rites. Then Donald returned to Bella for the last time.

POSTSCRIPT

God of our fathers! be the God
of their succeeding race.
Second Paraphrase

Before the end of January 1914, a committee, organized by Joseph Colmer and including many Canadians and men with long-standing Canadian interests, met to consider "arranging for some memorial" of Lord Strathcona's life and work in London. Westminster Abbey approved the idea of a window which was placed in the north aisle, near the west door. Lord Strathcona's coat of arms is surrounded by the collar of St. Michael and St. George, the order of knighthood to which he belonged. The shields of Canada, the Hudson's Bay Company, Manitoba and Quebec are included, along with the regimental badges of the Liverpool Scottish and Strathcona's Horse. An inscription describes Lord Strathcona as "a great Canadian imperialist and philanthropist." Contributions to the fund to erect the memorial were restricted to five guineas per person to allow men and women from all walks of life to contribute equally. Though the money was quickly raised, it was thought inappropriate to celebrate Lord Strathcona's life while war raged through Europe and the window was not dedicated until Dominion Day 1919.[1]

The bequest to Yale University caused some consternation because there was no clear idea of how Lord Strathcona intended the money to be spent. In the end, the university opted for the construction of Strathcona Hall which visitors to New Haven can still see.

When the University of Birmingham erected a new commerce building in 1964, it decided that the time for secrecy was long past and publicly acknowledged earlier generosity by calling it the Strathcona Building. It too may be seen on the campus.

The house by the Mosset Burn in Forres was torn down to make way for a widening of the bridge but a plaque has been erected on the bridge to mark the site. Anderson's Institution where Donald Smith went to school still faces the High Street and Sueno's Stone and the witches stones may still be seen as can Nelson's Tower on Cluny Hill. Leanchoil Hospital still serves the community. The family memorial, erected in 1875 by Donald Smith and his brother, was removed when the people of Forres decided that a graveyard jutting into the High Street was unsightly. At the Falconer Museum in Tolbooth Street, may be seen souvenirs of Donald Smith's career, including the engraved powder horn and the silver pocket watch given to him when he left for Canada.

The Hudson's Bay Company's headquarters at Lachine were sold to the Sisters of St. Anne who replaced the old house with a convent building which they still use. Opposite it, on the other side of the canal, is the only surviving fur trade building, a warehouse which now serves as a museum of the fur trade. Across the St. Lawrence River, the Kahnawake Reserve continues to be a Mohawk settlement but the men are now famed not for their canoeing skills but for their apparent lack of fear when working at heights as they do when employed to erect the steel frames of skyscrapers.

Dorchester Street in Montreal became Dorchester Boulevard and now is called René Levesque Boulevard. Lord Strathcona's house there became a home for old ladies and the site is now occupied by the Canadian Centre for Architecture. Royal Victoria College on Sherbrooke Street is easily recognized by the statue of the old queen at the bottom of its steps. The building now houses McGill University's music department and a large portrait of Lord Strathcona hangs in the entrance hall. Also on Sherbrooke Street is Strathcona Hall, built by the YMCA.

The Montreal Scholarship for students at the Royal College of Music in London still exists but is now worth very little and is used to support students who need help with expenses.

The Royal Victoria Hospital, with various modern additions, continues to care for the men, women and children of Montreal. The sharp eyed can just make out the intertwined initials of Donald Smith and George Stephen in two roundels high on the hospital facade.

The house at Silver Heights was burned to the ground in Lord Strathcona's lifetime. He retained the garden and the farm but all the land was sold after his death and the houses built on it are part of the Winnipeg suburb of Silver Heights. The buffalo herd formed the nucleus of a herd established at Banff earlier in this century and that herd has, more recently, been used to reintroduce buffalo onto the American plains. The gate and part of the old wall of Fort Garry are still standing, concealed behind a Petro Canada service station. Fort Garry Court, the Winnipeg apartment block which was built in 1902, incorporating stone from the walls of Fort Garry, was destroyed by fire in February 1976. Lower Fort Garry, the stone fort, still exists and is open to visitors.

James Hardisty Smith never occupied Norway House in Pictou, Nova Scotia and it was sold soon after he inherited it. It has since been converted to a geriatric hospital for Rebeccas, the wives of Shriners, the charitable organisation linked to the Masons in North America.

The house at Matapedia was abandoned and, in 1913, when it was burgled, it was not thought to be worth repairing. The basement had caved in and the roof was leaking.

Lord Strathcona's first London home, at 53 Cadogan Square, still exists as a private home and is still part of the Cadogan estate. His home in Grosvenor Square, together with all the other buildings at the west end of the square, was torn down to make way for the United States Embassy, erected in 1957-1958. Brown's Hotel, where he regularly stayed on visits to London, still caters for the discreet and wealthy. Knebworth, the Strathconas' first country house, has had some modern features added by Sir Edward Lutyens, a son-in-law of the first Earl of Lytton, but is otherwise not much changed. Debden Hall was sold within weeks of Lord Strathcona's death and was demolished in 1936.

The house at Glencoe was occupied for some time by Frances Kitson, Lord Strathcona's favourite granddaughter, and her family. During the first world war it was used as a convalescent home for wounded servicemen. Both wings have been destroyed, one by dry rot and one by fire, but the main body of the house has survived and is now a listed building. It is used by the local health service as a geriatric hospital and the stable block now houses the ambulance service.

Though the little island of Oronsay has been sold, Colonsay is still owned by Lord Strathcona's descendants and forms the principal residence of the present Lord Strathcona and his son who is gradually taking over from his father the management of the estate.

The mausoleum at Highgate Cemetery, London, where both Lord and Lady Strathcona are buried, was restored in 1987 and is now used by the Friends of Highgate Cemetery as a little office from which they can inform visitors about the many interesting graves and monuments in the cemetery.

The plaque commemorating the 1866 Confederation conference which Lord Strathcona unveiled in 1911 was moved to Canada when the Westminster Palace Hotel was torn down and the plaque can now be seen outside the parliamentary library in Ottawa.

Many of Lord Strathcona's pictures were given at his death to the Montreal Museum of Fine Art and in 1927, his grandson gave the museum Tissot's *October*. A smaller copy of the picture, made by Tissot in 1878, the year after he painted the original, recently sold at Sotheby's New York for nearly two million pounds. Turner's *Mercury and Argus* was sold to the National Gallery, Ottawa, in 1951; *The Communicants* is in a private collection, but on loan to the Art Gallery and Museum of Perth, in Scotland. The majority of Lord Strathcona's papers have been destroyed, but most of those which have survived, together with the diamond encrusted last spike, have been donated to Canadian institutions in recent years. It is, says Euan Howard, the present Lord Strathcona, where they belong.

APPENDIX I DONATIONS AND BEQUESTS

This list of charitable donations made by Lord Strathcona in the course of his life or carried out by his executors after his death is far from complete. He attempted to keep at least some of his charitable contributions secret and it is quite possible that not all have yet surfaced. More important, however, is the fact that accounts have only survived in any detail for the last few years of his life when his solicitors and accountants on both sides of the Atlantic were trying to ensure that they understood all the aspects of his financial dealings. It seems likely that the multitude of small donations which occur in his last years are a reflection of a policy of charitable contribution which began many years earlier. It also seems likely that many of the gifts shown here were made annually. Where a possible date for a first contribution is available, the contributions are entered annually; in other cases, the sole reference to annual subscriptions or donations is recorded.

In many cases, gifts to individuals are to relieve hardship but some cheques have clearly been made out to individuals (usually women) who are collecting for a particular charitable cause. Efforts have been made to eliminate those gifts which were probably not charitable in intent, with the exception of a few oral bequests.

The list does not include regular gifts to people such as Rosa Pitts, Lady Strathcona's nurse in her last years, nor does it include gratuities to doctors, the wives of his secretaries at the High Commission, or most of his gifts to Sir John A. Macdonald's widow. Neither does it show the regular allowances to family members such as his brother's daughters or the granddaughters of his mother's brother, Peter Stuart. Emily Nelson, a Mortimer descendant in Nova Scotia, also received financial support.

Occasionally, a secretary or solicitor was unable to resist a comment on the gift and these have been included in quotation marks. In a few instances, the amount is not known but reference to the donation has been included to show the breadth or type of contributions he made. All figures in guineas have been rounded down.

	$	£
date unknown		
Standard Building, Sherbrooke, land used for new city hall		
gold medal for best pupil of year at Roslyn Ladies' College, Montreal		
church in Schreiber, Ontario	1,000	
insurance on Royal Victoria College		
purchase of Bell homestead; monument in Brantford Ontario	500	
Miss Lavinia Herd, New Orleans (annual from ?; increased to $150 in 1913)	100	
construction of Little Britain Presbyterian Church	1,000	
silver cups to the Forres and Northern Fat Cattle Club		
Poplar Institute (building fund; possibly sailors' mission)		1,500
House for Incurables (Roman Catholic), Montreal	10,000	
Catholic High School in St. Patrick's Parish, Montreal	5,000	
portrait of James McGill for Redpath Library, McGill University		
Lord Strathcona Cup for Montreal Bankers' Hockey League		
1871		
orphans of the Convent of St. Boniface		2
Ladies' Higher Boarding and Day School, Winnipeg	250	
Winnipeg collection for sufferers of Chicago fire	50	
c 1872		
to help establish Manitoba College	250	
1873		
Ladies' School, Winnipeg	100	
Ladies' School, Winnipeg	50	
1874		
Roman Catholic Church, Winnipeg	25	
Manitoba Rifle Association cup and plate	60	
to complete St. Boniface Cathedral	100	
Rev. George Young, missionary in Northwest	50	
1876		
to send Manitoba farm products to CNE if matched by $75	25	
1877		
prize for competition in drill of Winnipeg Field Battery	25	
1878		
prize for competition in drill of Winnipeg Field Battery	25	
Winnipeg Presbyterian Church	50	
1879		
towards Knox Church building fund, Winnipeg	750	
towards restoration of St. James' Church, Winnipeg	200	
1880		
for sufferers of fire in Hull	400	
towards prize money for Manitoba Rifle Association competition	50	

	$	£
Fund for the benefit of the families of HBC officers connected with the Home Service		250
Anderson's Institution, Forres		
1881		
share of salary of chair of Science and Literature, Manitoba College	500	
Manitoba Rifle Association cup (engraved "Presented by a Patron") Mechanics' Institute, Forres		150
1882		
botanical garden, Winnipeg	500	
McGill University	1,000	
Presbyterian College, Montreal	100	
share of salary of chair of Science and Literature Manitoba College	500	
1883		
Trafalgar Institute (Protestant girls boarding school, Montreal)	30,000	
McGill University	1,000	
Presbyterian College, Montreal	100	
endowment of Medical Faculty, McGill University (Leanchoil Memorial) on condition that it be matched by the people of Montreal (Campbell Memorial)	50,000	
share of salary, chair of Science and Literature, Manitoba College	500	
charity for indigent Scots in London		800
endowment of Montreal Scholarship at Royal College of Music, London; similar sum contributed by George Stephen		1,500
1884		
McGill University	1,000	
Presbyterian College, Montreal	100	
Donalda Endowment for the Higher Education of Women	50,000	
1885		
McGill University	1,000	
Presbyterian College, Montreal	100	
1886		
tuition and expenses for Ada Moylan to attend Royal College of Music, London (est.)		150
McGill University	1,000	
Chair of evangelical theology, Presbyterian College, Montreal	100	
Royal Victoria Hospital construction and endowment	500,000	
additional land for Royal Victoria Hospital	38,500	
Imperial Institute (now Commonwealth Institute)		5,000
Donalda Endowment for the Higher Education of Women	70,000	
interest on the above for preceding year	1,600	
Victoria Rifles Association, Montreal	500	
1887		
tuition and expenses for Ada Moylan to attend Royal College of Music, London (est)		150

	$	£
Chair of evangelical theology, Presbyterian College, Montreal	100	
1888		
Manitoba Rifle Association challenge cup		
tuition and expenses for Ada Moylan to attend Royal College of Music, London (est)		150
Chair of evangelical theology, Presbyterian College, Montreal	100	
St. John's College, Cambridge		2,000
1889		
land for Leanchoil Hospital, Forres		238
building Leanchoil Hospital		5,000
Chair of evangelical theology, Presbyterian College, Montreal	100	
1890		
Mrs. James Green Stuart (widow of HBC man)	25	
purchase of Workman house for Royal Victoria College	47,500	
Forres Golf club		20
gift to tide over Isaac Cowie till HBC can decide on his request for financial support		100
1891		
Forres St. Laurence Cricket Club		10
1892		
endowment for Leanchoil Hospital		3,000
blankets and linen for Leanchoil Hospital		
Mansion House Fund for victims of fire in St. John's		1,500
addition to Manitoba College	5,000	
Dallas Supplementary Endowment Fund, for a benefice in Forres		150
1893		
McGill Medical Faculty, endowment for Chair of Hygiene	50,000	
McGill Medical Faculty, endowment for Chair of Pathology	50,000	
Cromdale Church (plus American organ)		50
1894		
Grenfell Mission	1,000	
curling pond and tennis green, Forres		50
steam yacht for Grenfell Mission		
St. John's College, Cambridge		10,000
sufferers of fire in Hinckley, Minnesota	5,000	
sufferers of Hinckley fire, from Lady Smith	1,000	
deficit in first year's running costs of Royal Victoria Hospital	20,000	
contribution to McGill pension fund	50,000	
purchase of land for Royal Victoria Hospital	5,888	
1895		
Grenfell Mission	1,000	
to complete building fund for Manitoba College	5,000	

	$	£
1896		
Grenfell Mission	1,000	
to pay off accumulated deficits of Royal Victoria Hospital	10,000	
1897		
permanent endowment of Royal Victoria Hospital (preferred shares in Great Northern Railway)	500,000	
Grenfell Mission	1,000	
Victorian Order of Nurses	5,000	
McGill University to cover deficit said to have been caused by Donalda programme	4,000	
1898		
Grenfell Mission	1,000	
Calgary General Hospital funds	100	
shares in Great Northern to Royal Victoria Hospital in trust; income to be used (value of shares shown)	4,000	
annual contributions by Lord Strathcona or his trustees to Royal Victoria College from 1898 to 1922 of not less than $42,000 per year, the payments representing interest on the sum required to make up the original endowment of $120,000 to $1m, the interest totalling more than	800,000	
development of new curriculum at Royal Victoria College	4,000	
new stock in Great Northern Railway sold under terms of endowment and added to capital, Royal Victoria Hospital	504,000	
1899		
University of Birmingham		50,000
Grenfell Mission	1,000	
1900		
Grenfell Mission	1,000	
Victorian Order of Nurses	5,000	
Hamilton Normal School of Domestic Science and Art		
gift to Forres United Free Church bazaar to raise money for new church		
Strathcona's Horse		200,000
"handsome gift" to Victoria Church, Montreal, renovation fund		
1901		
Grenfell Mission	1,000	
Castlehill United Free Church, Forres		100
Castlehill United Free Church, Forres (from Lady Strathcona)		50
Provincial Royal Jubilee Hospital, Victoria, for construction of Strathcona Wing	5,000	
1902		
Keith North United Free Church Hall		10
Coronation Gift (for King Edward Hospital for Officers)		200
Grenfell Mission	1,000	
make up separation allowance for Sara Gillies (husband with Strathcona's Horse) plus gift ($10)	110	
plus other, regular, gifts of between $30 and $100 (see below)		

	$	£
Forres United Free High Church		1,600
King Edward's Hospital Fund for London		200,000
purchase of land for Royal Victoria Hospital	6,126	
1903		
Grenfell Mission	1,000	
Catholic Sailors' Club, Montreal	1,000	
1904		
Strathcona School (Protestant, Outremont) to be used for an endowment fund for scholarships	1,000	
Women's Art Association, Montreal	500	
Amateur Athletic Association, Montreal	500	
Grenfell Mission	1,000	
church at Bonnie Doon		150
University of Manchester	20,000	
Parish church of St. Laurence, Forres		1,500
University of Manitoba, Faculty of Science	5,000	
1905		
McVicar Memorial Church, Montreal	1,000	
Grenfell Mission	1,000	
Mrs. Stewart, Edmonton	25	
Miss Francis [sic] Scott, Ottawa	20	
W.A. Fife, Edmonton	50	
Rev. Sister St. Vincent de Paul, Levis, Quebec	125	
Mary G. Gould, Montreal	150	
Edward C. Russell, Ottawa	60	
concert hall, Catholic Sailors' Club, Montreal	1,000	
University of Manitoba, Faculty of Science	5,000	
1906		
Grenfell Mission	1,000	
Academy, Rawdon, Quebec	1,000	
San Francisco earthquake sufferers	10,000	
Calgary General Hospital to erect a surgical wing	1,000	
Essex Bishopric fund		1,000
Amateur Athletic Association, Montreal	1,000	
gift to destitute family of deceased HBC employee		100
contribution to new building at Marischal College, Aberdeen		25,000
hospitality, Aberdeen University quartercentenary		3,400
entertainment for the poor of Aberdeen on the occasion of the University's quartercentenary		1,000
Forres Lawn Tennis Club		100
University of Manitoba, Science Faculty	5,000	
Pictou Cottage Hospital	1,000	
1907		
Grenfell Mission	1,000	
Manitoba Rifle Association	200	
CPR Association Football Club	100	

	$	£
Provincial Exhibition, Quebec	200	
YMCA Ottawa	5,000	
Fresh Air Fund (Montreal)	100	
St. John's Church, Morrisburg	5	
Hospice, St. Joseph de la Déliverance	100	
Ladies' Benevolent Society	25	
Printers and Newspaper Writers Association	100	
Charlotte Eaton	100	
Dominion Assembly, Knights of Labour	100	
Grey Lacrosse Club, Winnipeg	50	
Montreal Trades and Labour Council	100	
Union 145 Typographique Jacques Cartier	100	
Hervey Institute	200	
Sons of Scotland Camp, Erin	50	
Conseil Central Nationale des Metiers et du Travail de Montreal	50	
The Montreal Dispensary	50	
John Horn, Longeuil (Canadian amateur historian)	100	
L'Assistance Publique	100	
Rev. Sister Aloysia	150	
family of late John Balsillie, but Lord Strathcona had the proceeds of his life policy	2,000	
Winnipeg Industrial Exhibition	100	
Rev. George Bryce (probably for University of Manitoba)	5,000	
Presbyterian College, Montreal	2,750	
McGill College Book Club	10	
University of Manitoba, Science Faculty	5,000	
Montreal Sailors' Institute	100	
Montreal Diet Dispensary	50	
Lachine Snowshoe Club	50	
Industrial Rooms, Montreal	25	
Rev. Sisters St. Vincent de Paul	50	
Aberdeen Assembly No. 91	50	
St. Paul's Church, Montreal (probably contributed regularly before this)	200	
1908		
Montreal Holly Snow Shoe Club	50	
Montreal Horse Show Association	100	
Grand Bazaar, Gananoque	25	
Quebec Rifle Association	100	
British Army and Navy Veterans Association	120	
Montreal Canine Association	100	
Manitoba Provincial Rifle Association	200	
Grenfell Mission	1,000	
Verdun Methodist Church	50	
CPR Football Club, Montreal	100	
Society of the Friends of the Poor	25	
Montreal Cricket Club	100	
Quebec Tercentenary	1,000	
Forest and Stream Club	50	
Winnipeg Lawn Tennis Club	100	
Municipal Reform Association, Montreal	50	

	$	£
Alexandra Hospital	1,000	
Provincial Exhibition, Quebec	350	
National Trades and Labour Council	100	
Methodist Church, Lachine	1,000	
John Horn	100	
Miss R. Desjardins, for her studies in Paris	100	
Fernie, BC Relief Fund	5,000	
support for boat for Rev. John Antle's mission to BC coastal loggers		500
Quebec Tercentenary Celebrations	1,000	
Victoria Rifles of Canada	2,000	
Montreal Diet Dispensary	50	
Lachine Snowshoe Club	50	
Dominion Assembly, Order of Knights of Labour, Montreal	100	
University College Hospital, London		1,000
St. Paul's Church, Montreal	200	
Montreal Sailors' Institute	100	
1909		
Grenfell Mission	1,000	
Strathcona Trust for Physical and Military Training in Schools	250,000	
history of Quebec Battlefields	1,000	
King Edward's Hospital for Officers, London		100
Strathcona Trust for Physical and Military Training in Schools	50,000	
rebuild chapel & convent, Church of the Blessed Sacrament, Point aux Trembles, Montreal; burnt down; inadequately insured	200	
Rendell Manse, Scotland	100	
McGill Medical Buildings (plus site for their construction)	450,000	
augmenting McGill University salaries	50,000	
Father Lacombe's home for poor Métis, Alberta	10,000	
Knox Church, Peterborough, Ontario	1,000	
biology laboratory, Cambridge (not paid till after his death)	1,000	
purchase of Learmont house for Royal Victoria College, to be used for Conservatory of Music	18,000	
repairs to Learmont house	700	
Montreal Horse Show Association	100	
Manitoba Provincial Rifles Association	200	
Holly Snow Shoe Club, Montreal	50	
Quebec Rifle Association	100	
Municipal Reform Association, Montreal	50	
1910		
emergency typhoid hospital in Montreal	25,000	
support for International Eucharistic Conference, Montreal		
Grenfell Mission	1,000	
King Edward's Hospital for Officers, London		100
Salvation Army		10
Toynbee Hall		5
Hospital of St. John of Jerusalem		31
Tabernacle Baptist Church, Montreal	1,000	
Barnes Wesleyan Methodist Church, London		50

	$	£
International Interchange of Students		100
Chair of Agriculture, University of Aberdeen		10,000
Archbishop's Western Canada Fund		1,100
Strathcona Trust for physical and military training in schools (plus promise of $20,000 per year)	200,000	
Montreal Horse Show Association	100	
Manitoba Provincial Rifles Association	200	
Holly Snow Shoe Club, Montreal	50	
Montreal Sailors' Institute	100	
Quebec Rifle Association	100	
Municipal Reform Association	50	
1911		
Montreal Flower Mission	1,000	
for a portrait of Prince Francis of Teck for Middlesex Hospital		26
Prince Francis of Teck Memorial Fund in aid of Middlesex Hospital		26
Rev. John Kerr towards book on curling		100
London Chamber of Commerce Education Fund		52
University College Hospital for Lucas portrait		5
Saffron Walden Town Band		3
Saffron Walden Ancient Maye Fund		2
Lorne Horticultural Society, Oban		6
Widdington Band		2
Boys' Naval Brigade		5
Wesleyan Church, Boston, Lancashire		5
Galt Church, Ontario	500	
ten percent of guarantee to London musical congress		50
Miss Juliette Gauthier, Paris, for her musical education		200
Grenfell Mission	1,000	
YMCA Canada		100
painting for HMS Victory		50
St. Columba's Church, London, endowment fund		1,000
King Edward's Hospital for Officers, London		100
band instruments for Mansfield House Settlement, London		15
Victoria Rifles, Montreal	1,000	
Trades and Labour Council	100	
yearly contribution to Liverpool Scottish Regiment		250
church window, St. Andrew's, London		250
Forres Coronation celebrations		100
Faversham Church		10
Gustav Lanctot, to assist with college studies, London		200
Mrs. Garrison re her son's studies		35
Miss R. Desjardins to continue studies		300
Montreal Horse Show Association	100	
Reid Taylor for concert expenses		25
Mrs. Baird, Andover, NB, gift for son	500	
Asiatic Exploration Fund		525
Royal Albert Orphan Asylum		100
Western Infirmary, Glasgow		2
Debden Church		30
annual donation, South African National Union		1

	$	£
Bishop's Stortford Cricket club		3
McGill University Cricket Club	100	
Hygiene Exhibition, London		500
Homes for Little Boys		100
hospital in Liverpool		100
Rev. Gavin Lang		100
M.A. Gillies, husband of Sara Gillies (see 1902)	100	
Women's Hospital, Soho Square, London		100
Mrs. Leslie Wood on leaving for Canada		100
Seaman's Mission Society, Saint John	1,000	
Wilhelm Garry concert		8
Debden Cricket Club		2
Sir Frederick Young Fund		50
Mrs. Baird, Andover	100	
Australian Antarctic Expedition		1,000
West London Hospital		25
Colonial Troops Entertainment Committee		250
British Empire League's entertainment of Colonial Visitors		52
ten percent (final instalment) of guarantee for musical congress, London		50
Elchies Church, Scotland		250
Wimbush Coronation festivities		10
gift to members of 79th Cameron Highlanders of Canada visiting England		2,010
Post Office Orphan Homes		1
Guy Maingy of London to continue studies		25
Mr. Maskelyne of Somerset to continue studies		3
John Grant of Glenlivet to continue studies		5
Mrs. Ballam of London to continue studies		3
St. Giles Parish Church, London		5
Bon Accord Military Band, Aberdeen		10
Shaw Memorial Church, Montreal	100	
Franco-British Guild, Paris		1,000
Coronation festivities for patients at British Home and Hospital for Incurables		20
Presbyterian College, Saint John for Gov. Fraser memorial	2,000	
Fresh Air Fund, Montreal	100	
Calvin Presbyterian Church, Montreal	1,000	
Lochaber Agricultural Society, Fort William, Scotland		2
YMCA		
Vancouver	25,000	
Winnipeg	25,000	
Winnipeg (from Lady S and Mrs. Howard)	10,000	
Guelph	5,000	
Halifax	10,000	
Brantford	10,000	
Galt	5,000	
Nelson	5,000	
Victoria	5,000	
Brandon	5,000	
Fort William	10,000	
South Molton, Devon, to buy books		10
Lords and Commons Committee for Entertaining Colonial Visitors		250
Viscountess Horncastle		25

	$	£
Mrs. Janet Bell	200	
Navy League, Vancouver, to purchase launch	3,000	
Rev. R.G. MacBeth, Paris, Ontario	2,500	
John Horn	100	
J.P. Morgan, Hamilton	100	
Debden Football Club		2
Church Hall, Carnoustie Church, Scotland		20
Children's holiday fund		3
Portsmouth Bible class to visit London		3
Miss M. Thompson, Edmonton	300	
John MacLeod, Nova Scotia for anti-tuberculosis publications	500	
Mrs. Walker to go to Canada		5
Debden Coronation festivities		65
King Edward VII Rest Home, Malta		100
Prince of Wales memorial at Holyhead		500
Prince of Wales memorial at Milford Haven		500
testimonial for Archdeacon Sinclair		10
Mrs. Calder, Milngavie		5
Mrs. N.M. McLeod of Glasgow to apprentice son as dentist		20
memorial hall, St.Andrew's University, New Brunswick		500
Children's Hospital, Winnipeg	5,000	
motor boat for mission work in Stromness		10
Mrs. Nora Turner, 3rd payment to keep son at school		10
Rev. Alexander Robertson for mission work in Venice		50
Mrs. W. Thomson, Glasgow		2
Manitoba Provincial Rifle Association	250	
Salvation Army, Regent Street, London		20
Provincial Exhibition, New Westminster	250	
annual donation to Caledonian Horticultural Society		2
annual donation to Aberdeen University Union		5
Forres Hockey Club		2
Romford Village Institute		10
King Edward Memorial, Montreal	2,500	
for purchase of picture for Guildhall, London		105
for Carlyle memorial		25
gift to E.H.W. Crossley		10
National Association of Old Scholars Clubs		10
Church hall, Baptist Church, New Barnet, London		10
Edinburgh hospital and dispensary		5
Evening News Children's Fund		2
annual donation to Atlantic Union		1
Orphan Working School		10
bazaar funds, Naval Volunteer Reserve, Glasgow		10
Governesses Benevolent Society of Scotland		10
French Benevolent Society of London		10
Royal General Dispensary		10
Mrs. Morrison of Glasgow		3
Rev. Dr. Morgan, Wales		3
Reynold's Newspaper for Sandwichmen's Christmas dinner		3
Canadian Public Health Association, Montreal	2,500	
Aberdeen University Celtic Society		2

	$	£
Queen Alexandra Wing, British Home and Hospital for Incurables		2,000
Presbyterian College, Montreal	2,750	
St. Paul's Church, Montreal	200	
Ottawa Boys' Home (annual donation)	500	
Danish Gathering, Ottawa	50	
Knebworth Congregational Sunday School		5
Browning Settlement, London		25
United Free Church of Grantown		5
Imperial Sunday Alliance		10
manse of Durness Church, Scotland		50
Imperial Arts League, London, annual subscription		10
Mrs. A.M. (Sara) Gillies, Toronto	100	
National Society for the Prevention of Cruelty to Children, London		5
Queensferry Sailors' Home		25
Holy Trinity Church, Bardesley		10
London Gaelic Society		10
Royal Hospital for Sick Children, Glasgow		5
Mrs. Alice Thomson		1
League of Mercy, Hitchin		21
British Antarctic Society		200
Natural History Society, Montreal annual subscription	4	
Holly Snow Shoe Club, Montreal	100	
Ninga Church, Ninga (annual donation)	200	
St. Paul's United Free Church, Perth, Scotland		10
Bishop's Stortford Hospital		10
Forsyth Memorial, Quebec	1,000	
Watrous Presbyterian Church, Saskatchewan	1,000	
Dickens Fund		100
Mrs. Baird, Andover	4,000	
Lady Macdonald		200
Lundy Memorial, Portage la Prairie	100	
C.E.D. Black of London		5
Mrs. Christie Murray, London		3
Christmas entertainment, British Home and Hospital for Incurables		5
Strathcona's Horse helmets	3,000	
Forres Soldiers' Club		100
Rev. A.L. Macinnes, Glencoe		50
gift to Rev. A.L. Macinnes, Glencoe for the poor of Glencoe		10
Mrs. Otillie Wright, Montreal	2,000	
J.C. Taylor, assistant secretary, High Commissioner's Office for son's education at Cambridge		50
Mount Royal Club (servants' Christmas Box)	4	
Montreal Sailors' Institute	100	
Quebec Rifle Association	100	
Municipal Reform Association, Montreal	50	
1912		
church manse fund, Fork River	100	
John Miller, Toronto	500	
Montreal Sailors' Institute	100	
Montreal Sailors' Institute (special donation)	1,000	

	$	£
Mrs. R. Gerrish		10
for widow of parliamentary messenger		10
Rev. Kenneth Ross		10
Good Templars, Glasgow		10
King Edward's Hospital for Officers, London, fourth of five promised donations		100
Rev. Canon Perkins		100
Railway Guards Universal Friendly Society		5
Church Army winter work		10
Mrs. Holmes, Canada, re expenses of bishop's illness		100
YMCA		
Montreal	200	
Montreal, building fund	2,000	
Belville	5,000	
Cobalt	2,000	
Berlin, Ontario (now Kitchener)	4,820	
New Westminster	5,000	
Collingwood	1,000	
Sault Ste. Marie	5,000	
Ottawa	3,000	
Owen Sound	1,000	
Woodstock, Ontario	3,000	
Ballachulish and Glencoe Ambulance Class Concert		1
Quebec Rifle Association	150	
Mrs. M. Shepherd, London, for her daughter		3
Crown Court Church, London (Church of Scotland)		500
Miss Desjardins, Paris, to continue her studies		350
Juliette Gauthier, Venice, to continue her studies		300
Grenfell Mission	1,000	
Victoria Rifles, Montreal	1,000	
Queen Mary Coronation Hostel, B.C.	100,000	
Prof. Sir W. Ramsey, Aberdeen, for Asiatic exploration		500
H. Russell Stephenson, Montreal		100
Lady Grey		100
Crown Princess of Sweden		250
Imperial Institute		50,000
Mansion House Titanic Fund		1,000
North American Fund for survivors of the Titanic	5,000	
London Gaelic Services		10
Liverpool Scottish Regiment		200
building for National Naval Cadets, London		50
Imperial Cadet Association		100
Municipal Reform Association, Montreal	150	
Mrs. Garrison (for her son's studies)		150
Lord Plymouth re guarantee for Festival of Empire (Festival of All Red Route)		1,898
Lockyer (Lochaber?) presentation		10
Piobaireachd Society subscription and gift		9
Montreal Association for the Blind	10,000	
Mendelssohn Choir, Toronto	200	
Trades and Labour Council, Montreal	150	
McGill University Medical Faculty to reequip building after 1907 fire	450,000	

	$	£
Queen Mary Coronation Hostel (via Lady Minto)		1,027
Mrs. Janet Annand, Newton		50
Lochaber Agricultural Society, Fort William		2
Mrs. Hamilton, London		3
Boys Club		10
Sara Gillies, Canada		25
Mrs. Christie Murray, London		3
Cartier Centenary, Montreal	2,500	
Judge Prowse, Newfoundland		200
Lady Strong, Ottawa	100	
St. John's Ambulance, Windsor Review Funds		100
Natural History Society, Montreal (annual subscription)	4	
Marischal Memorial, Aberdeen		100
London School of Tropical Medicine		1,000
Dalhousie University, Halifax	15,000	
Sir Frederick Young Fund (annual donation plus £50 gift)		100
to clerk of parliament for police outing		1
Forres Soldiers' Association		100
Fresh Air Fund, Montreal	100	
Mrs. O. McDonnell, Montreal	100	
Mrs. N. Turner, Seaford, to keep her boy at school (fourth of five gifts)		10
Lachine General Hospital	1,000	
National Central Trades and Labour Council	100	
Boy Scouts' Memorial		10
Mrs. Campbell Mackenzie, wife of director of Royal Academy of Music		20
Miss G. Sandham, London		50
Ramsgate, Las Palmas and New Zealand Sailors' Rest Home		300
Knox College, Toronto, building fund	25,000	
seventy percent guarantee, London Chamber of Commerce Entertainment Fund		35
McLeod Memorial, St. Columba's Church, London		25
Gustav Lanctot, to continue his studies		25
passage to Canada for Creighton family		5
Robert Garrison, for his studies		50
Manitoba Provincial Rifle Association	250	
A. Jensen, Montreal, gift to continue studies (which he did not do)	200	
St. Bees Church, Westville	1,500	
Caledonian Horticultural Society, Edinburgh		2
Argyll and Southern Highlanders, Ballachulish		3
Ballachulish and Glencoe Shinty Club		10
Mrs. C. Geary, Liverpool		100
Appin Manse Fund		10
Highland Society, Fort William, to take choir to Inverness		10
Montreal Kennel Club (for cup)	100	
Mrs. A. Daubnere, London		4
Victoria University, Manchester, towards Morley's portrait		10
to pay off debt of Forres Mechanics Football Club		30
towards repairs of United Free Church, Ballachulish		100
Miss MacKelvie, Calgary, to return to London to resume studies		100
trophies for Fleet		150
Bishop's Stortford Cricket Club		3

	$	£
Lister Memorial		10
annual donation, Aberdeen University Union		5
Rev. John Kerr		100
Seaman's Institute, Victoria	1,000	
Manse Fund, Gairloch Free Presbyterian Church		50
Mrs. Hugh MacIntosh, Kinlochleven		50
Rev. A.S. MacInnes, Glencoe		100
St. Thomas Roman Catholic Church, Keith		100
Captain John Campbell, Rothesay		104
Lord Farquhar, "no details (political propaganda)"		200
Miss Connor, Glencoe		5
Ed. Gascoigne (out of pocket £4/4, rest as gift)		20
manse repairs, established church, Ballachulish		70
Huntington Flood Funds		100
Montenegrin Refugees Fund		50
memorial to Archbishop Machray in Sidney Sussex College Chapel, Cambridge		200
Mme Donalda		100
Scottish Agricultural Organisation		20
International Interchange of Students		250
St. Giles Presbyterian Church, Montreal	1,000	
British Science Guild, London		100
Commercial Travellers' Schools		10
British Home and Hospital for Incurables (as from Lady Strathcona)		250
Schreiber Church, Ontario	1,000	
HRH Duchess of Connaught (for nurses assoc)	50,000	
Aberdeen Chrysanthemum Society		2
Church Nursing Brigade		3
London Gaelic Society		2
United Methodist Church, Cardiff		5
Blind Braille Library, London		10
Rev. R.G. MacBeth, Paris, Ontario	100	
Rev. T.B. Paynter for church funds		15
Holly Snow Shoe Club, Montreal	100	
League of Mercy, Hitchin (includes £10 from Lady Strathcona)		31
Baroness Macdonald		200
Miss M. Crosse to continue studies in Vienna		40
Manitoba Curling Club, Winnipeg	100	
Aberdeen University Medical Unit		120
Balkan War Fund (refugees)		5
Tronbridge Testimonial, London		55
Mrs. McIntosh, Kinlochleven		60
patients' entertainments, British Home and Hospital for Incurables		5
Presbyterian College, Montreal	2,750	
St. Paul's Church, Montreal	200	
Calgary University	25,000	
Strathcona Hospital, Edmonton	25,000	
National Council of Public Morals		5
Church Hall, Keith, Scotland		100
Mrs. Dawson, Aberdeen		3
Reynold's Newspaper Sandwichmen's Christmas dinner		3

	$	£
Danish Gathering, Ottawa	20	
Knights of Labour, Montreal	100	
National Exhibition, Toronto (for cup)	100	
Hospice St. Joseph de la Deliverance, Levis	300	
Mrs. A.M. (Sara) Gillies, Toronto	100	
Montreal Horse Show Association	100	
Lorne Horticultural Society, Oban		3
1913		
Ottawa Choral Society	200	
Mrs. J. Miller, Toronto	125	
Sir W. Ramsey, Aberdeen, Asiatic exploration		500
Miss Johnson, Cheltenham		50
Mrs. Paul Stewart, Scotland		25
Mrs. Campbell MacKenzie, London		10
James O'Regan, Ottawa, further gift towards son's education	150	
A. Hodkinson, Manchester "so-called temperance work"		80
Mrs. Hamilton		5
Nelson's portrait fund		3
Charity Organisation Society, Montreal	150	
Mrs. Macaulay, Montreal	150	
Austro-Hungarian White Cross Society		5
Stockbridge Day Nursery		25
Henniker Heaton Welcome Fund		31
testimonial, Brook, Station Master, Euston		100
General Booth Memorial, Salvation Army,Toronto	5,000	
University College Hospital, London		10
King Edward's Hospital for Officers, London, final grant		100
Sir George White memorial		25
St. Boniface Orphanage		10
Paddington Children's Hospital		2
Knox Presbyterian Church, Strathcona, Alberta	2,000	
Mrs. E. Sharpe, Vancouver	100	
Mr. W. Lane	100	
Hospital for Sick Children, Glasgow		3
Railway Guards Universal Friendly Society		5
Rev. James Olphert, Barnes, re colleague's illness		5
St. Luke's Church, Souris, Quebec	1,000	
Portage la Prairie Hospital, Manitoba	1,500	
St. Andrew's College, Toronto	20,000	
Presbyterian Church, Point à Brillant	100	
Bible Society, Winnipeg	3,000	
Piobaireachd Society, Scotland		1
Brotherhood of Saint Andrew		100
British Antarctic Fund		1,000
Grenfell Mission	1,000	
Victoria Rifles, Montreal	1,000	
Montreal Boys' Home	5,000	
Mrs. Godfrey Evans		10
Essex Regimental Presentation		5
Quebec Rifle Association	150	

	$	£
Montreal Horse Show Association	100	
final contribution to Cavendish Club		300
Mrs McIntosh, Kinlochleven		25
First Highland Cadet Battalion, Boy Scouts		50
Lister Memorial		100
Mrs. and Miss Henry, towards passage to Canada		20
St. Patrick's Anglican Mission, Kelwood	150	
Queen's University, Kingston (women's residence)	2,000	
Presbyterian Church (via Earl Grey)	300	
Edinburgh Play Centre		10
Mrs. June C. Cooper, Ireland		10
St. John's Club, East Dulwich		2
Robert Garrison, for his studies		125
National Hospital for Paralysed and Epileptic		1,000
Canadian Arctic Expedition		1,000
American Ohio Flood Fund	5,000	
St. Anne's Home, London		3
Trades and Labour Council, Montreal	100	
Liverpool Scottish Regiment		200
Richards Memorial, London		20
Municipal Reform Association	150	
Citadel Cricket Club, Inverness		3
Argonaut Rowing Club, Toronto (towards crew's expenses to Henley)	1,000	
Winnipeg Industrial Exhibition	1,000	
Rev. D. Henderson (blind clergyman)	500	
Union Mission for Men, Toronto	1,500	
Juliette Gauthier, Florence, to continue her studies		100
Judge Prowse, Newfoundland		100
for portrait of the king for United Services Club		100
Aviation Cup Competition		10
Rev. John Kerr, Kirleton		150
Society for Protecting Women and Children, Montreal	100	
Congregation de Notre Dame, Ste. Anne de Bellevue	1,000	
YMCA		
New Glasgow	1,000	
Port Arthur	3,500	
Orillia	5,000	
St. Thomas	5,000	
Sherbrooke	2,000	
Oban	20	
Calgary	10,000	
Toronto	15,000	
Cobalt	1,000	
Revelstoke	2,000	
Oshawa	1,000	
Lethbridge	2,500	
Hamilton		5,000
Miss M. White, Staines		10
A. Rosenstranch for Jewish Mission		10
Miss M. Armstrong	100	

	$	£
McGill University, dining hall etc.	100,000	
Regina Disaster Fund	10,000	
Hospice L'Assomption, Quebec	1,500	
Civil Service Sports		100
Miss Shurmer		10
McGill University, armoury, etc.	100,000	
Pincher Creek Hospital, Alberta	1,000	
Ontario Tercentenary Celebrations	1,000	
Clerk of Parliament for Doorkeepers' Outing		1
Thaxted Church repairs		21
Mrs. N. Turner, final amount promised		10
Australian Club, London		10
Sir Frederick Young Fund		50
John Horn	100	
London Tuberculosis Sanatorium	15,000	
Caledonian Christian Club		50
Church Lads Brigade		3
Miss M. Thompson, Edmonton	1,000	
Father Lacombe, towards work in Canada	2,000	
Mr. H.J. Osborne		2
H. Bussell		3
Crystal Palace Acquisition Fund		10,000
Thomas Hillman		10
United Methodist Church, Okehampton		25
guarantee, 1915 Crystal Palace Exhibition		5,000
Miss Desjardins, to continue her studies		150
Manitoba Provincial Rifle Association	250	
Mrs. E.J. Ferguson, London (but returned)	1,000	
Fresh Air Fund, Montreal	100	
King Edward National Sanatorium Association of Canada	125,000	
Lyttleton Memorial		5
Lochaber Gathering, Fort William		2
Mr. Somerset, Winchester		8
Robert Garrison, re his studies		250
National Central Trades Council	100	
Aberdeen University Union		5
Argyll and Sutherland Highlanders, Ballachulish		3
Imperial Cadet Corps, London	50	
International Association of Medical Museums	5,000	
Miss E. Chapman, Quebec	100	
Ballachulish and Glencoe Shinty Club		10
National Reserves, Ballachulish		3
St. Andrew's Church bazaar, London		5
London Lock Hospital		50
Boy Scouts of Canada	5,000	
plus, for next two years	10,000	
bazaar fund, British and Foreign Sailors Society, Portsmouth		105
Miss Lambert		5
Edinburgh University Settlement Association		100
Caledonian Horticultural Society		2

	$	£
Central City Mission, Vancouver	5,000	
St. Mary's College, Halifax	2,000	
British Empire Shakespeare Society		10
Women's Christian Temperance Union, Toronto	1,500	
Sweated Industries League		100
Miss Sullivan		100
Hitchin District League of Mercy (includes £10 from Lady Strathcona)		31
Mrs. A.S. Rutter		5
Bishop's Stortford Cricket Club		3
new boiler for Hospital Ship Strathcona, Grenfell Mission (up to); paid after his death	3,000	
Jennifer Goode		6
Danish Gathering, Ottawa	50	
Holy Trinity church School, Tewkesbury		20
Reynold's Newspaper Sandwichmen's Christmas dinner		3
Toynbee Hall		5
Camberwell Dispensary		10
Scottish Memorial to General Booth		20
Knebworth Church		100
Miss Pigott		10
Maurice Peterson		150
Rev. Herbert Cronshaw, vicar, St. Mark's North Audley Street, London		100
Mme Lessore		50
Mrs. M.R. Hamilton		1
Rev. A.S. Macinnes, Glencoe		100
Rev. A.S. Macinnes for the poor of Glencoe		25
Rev. D.J. Learoyd for church expenses and the poor of Debden		50
Miss L. Johnson		25
Geike Presentation fund		3
Hospice des Soeurs de la Charité, Rimouski	150	
New York American Christmas Fund (Christmas dinner for the poor)	1,000	
Presbyterian Church, Florence	250	
1914		
Lorne Horticultural Society, Oban		3
Saffron Walden Hospital		10
Aberdeen Chrysanthemum Society		2
Mrs. Campbell MacKenzie		5
Manitoba Provincial Rifle Association	250	
Holly Snow Shoe Club, Montreal	100	
Miss M. Gard, musical studies		100
Miss G. Sandham, London		10
1914 (in will)		
Royal Victoria Hospital	5,000	
King Edward's Hospital Fund		200,000
Leanchoil Hospital		10,000
Yale University	500,000	
St. John's College, Cambridge		10,000
Royal Victoria College	380,000	
Royal Victoria College Maintenance Fund		100,000

	$	£
Chair of Agriculture, Aberdeen University		5,000
Rt. Hon. John Burns for maintenance of about 50 lepers in the UK		5,000
maintenance of Leanchoil Hospital		10,000
Queen Alexandra Extension, Home and Hospital for Incurables, Streatham		2,000
National Hospital for Paralysed and Epileptic		2,000
Middlesex Hospital, London		2,000
University College Hospital, London		2,000
Church of Scotland Fund for Aged and Infirm Ministers		10,000
Extension Fund, Queen's University, Kingston Ontario		20,000
endowment of professorship, Presbyterian College, Montreal		12,000
January 19, 1914 (oral bequests)		
St. Columba's Church, London		1,000
Dr. Fleming of St. Columba's		1,000
St. Mark's Church		1,000
Rev. Mr. Cronshaw of St. Mark's		1,000
Grey Nuns and some others	3,000	
Sir Robert Borden		1,000
Lady Laurier		1,000
Miss Fraser Tytler (for her homes)		1,000
retired Chief Factors, HBC, annual allowance (approx)		1,000
1924		
from the trustees of Lord Strathcona's will, the principal of the endowment to Royal Victoria College with interest for years since 1922	1,202,500	
TOTAL	$7,520,601	£1,026,381

APPENDIX II SHARES AND INVESTMENTS

Most of Lord Strathcona's business papers were destroyed by fire and this list has therefore been compiled from secondary sources; it should not be assumed that it is complete. The value of the different shares fluctuated according to market conditions; some non-business shares, such as the Restigouche Salmon Club, were worth a good deal more than one might assume and markedly increased in value, while others, such as The Knowledge Publishing Company, were virtually worthless. Those shares which were intended as a charitable contribution, for example the Duchess of Sutherland's Cripples Guild, have been omitted.

Transport and Communication
Albany and Susquehanna Rail Road
Alberta Railway and Irrigation Company
Atchison Topeka and Santa Fe Railway
The Baltimore and Ohio Railway
Bell Telephone Company of Canada (some stock was part of Royal Victoria College legacy)
Black Diamond Steam Ship Company
Canadian Pacific Railway Company
Chicago, Burlington and Quincy Rail Road
Chicago and Eastern Illinois Rail Road
Chicago and Erie Rail Road
Chicago Milwaukee and Saint Paul Railway Company
Chicago and Northwestern Railway
Colorado and Southern Railway
Chicago Union Station
Commercial Cable Company
Cunard Steamship Company
Dorval Turnpike Trust
East Tennessee Valley Railway
Grand Rapids Rail Road
Great Northern Railway (now Burlington and Northern)
Havana Central Railroads Company (Van Horne company); purchased in 1906
Hocking Valley Railway
Illinois Central Rail Road Company
Kanawha and Michigan Railway

Kansas City Railway Terminal
Lake Champlain and St. Lawrence Junction Railway
Lake Shore and Michigan Southern Railway
Louisville and Nashville Rail Road
Manhattan Railway Company
Manitoba Cartage and Warehousing Company
Manitoba South Western Colonization Railway Company
Minneapolis, Saint Paul and Sault Ste. Marie Railway Company (the Soo Line)
Minneapolis, Sault Ste. Marie and Atlantic Railway
Minneapolis Street Railway Company (amalgamated with Saint Paul City Railway Company to become Twin Cities Rapid Transit Company)
Minneapolis Union Railway Company
Mitchell Line of Steamships
Mobile and Ohio Rail Road
Montana Central Railway (part of the holdings of Montana Securities)
Montreal Park and Island Railway
Morris and Essex Rail Road
National Transit Company
New Brunswick Railway; bought with George Stephen in 1880; increased holding in 1881; added $50,000 in 1887; ultimately amalgamated with CPR
New York Elevated Rail Road
New York Transit Company
New York Westchester and Boston Railway
Norfolk and Western Railway
Northern Pacific Railway; later amalgamated with the Great Northern Railway
Ontario and Quebec Railway Company
Oregon and Washington Rail Road and Navigation Company
Oregon Rail Road and Navigation Company
Oregon Short Line
Pacific Coast Railway Company
Pacific Telegraph Company
Paducah and Illinois Railway Company
Pennsylvania Railway Company
Peoria and Eastern Railway
Pittsburg, Cincinnati, Chicago and St. Louis Railway
Pittsburg, Shenango and Lake Erie Rail Road
Pullman Palace Car Company
Red River and Assiniboine Bridge Company
Saint Louis and San Francisco Railway Company
Saint Paul City Railway Company
Saint Paul, Minneapolis and Manitoba Railway Company; formally acquired in 1879; later incorporated in the Great Northern)
Saint Paul and Sioux City Rail Road
Saskatchewan and Western Railway Company
Sault Ste. Marie Bridge Company
The South and North Alabama Rail Road
Southern Railway
Southern Pacific Rail Road
Toledo and Ohio Central Railway
Union Forwarding and Railway Company
Union Pacific Rail Road
Victoria Rolling Stock Company
West India Railway Company, Kingston, Jamaica
Winnipeg and Assiniboine Bridge Company
Winnipeg and Western Transportation Company
Wisconsin Central Railway

Insurance and Financial Institutions
Accident Insurance Company of North America
American Steam Boiler Insurance Company
Bank of Commerce
Bank of Toronto
Bank of Montreal
Baring Brothers
Citizens Insurance and Investment Company of Canada
Civic Investment Company
Commercial Bank of Scotland
Glyn Mills and Company
Hand in Hand Mutual Fire Insurance Company
Huron and Bruce Loan and Investment Company (see Standard Loan below)
Imperial Colonial Finance Company
London and Canadian Loan and Agency Company
London and Lancashire Life Association
Mackay Companies
Merchants' Bank of Canada
Montreal Investment Association; had invested $7,000 some years before 1869; a vehicle for Private Cash investments
Montreal City and District Savings Bank
Montreal Investment Trust
Montreal Loan and Mortgage Company
Montreal Safe Deposit Company
Montreal Trust and Deposit Company
Northern Life Assurance Company
Northern Securities
Ontario Bank
Port Arthur and Fort William Mortgage Company
Royal Trust Company
Scottish Union and National Insurance Company
Security Loan and Savings Company of St. Catherines, Ontario
Standard Loan Company (took over Huron and Bruce Loan and Savings Company in 1905)
Standard Reliance Mortgage Corporation

Hotels
Algonquin Hotel Company
Canada Pacific Hotel, Winnipeg
Canadian Pacific Hotels
Château Frontenac
Hertfordshire Public House Trust Company Limited
Iroquois House Hotel
Muskoka Lakes Navigation and Hotel Company
Ritz Carlton Hotel, Montreal; shares worth $50,000 plus bonds acquired in 1910
St. Louis Hotel, Lachine, created from Richard and Margaret Hardisty's retirement home; also called Strathcona Hotel
Windsor Hotel, Montreal

Manufacturing and Power
British Empire Steel Company
Canada Paper Company
Canada Rolling Stock Company
Cedar Rapids (Quebec) Manufacturing and Power Company
Citizens Light and Power Company; shares sold in 1903
Cold Brook Rolling Mills Company
Cornwall Manufacturing Company
Dominion Iron and Steel; previously British Empire Steel; later Dominion Steel
Great Falls Water Power and Land Company (part of the holdings of Montana Securities)

Economy Engine and Machine Company
Imperial Writing Machine
Lachine Rapids Hydraulic and Land Company; shares sold in 1903
Lake of the Woods Milling Company
Manitoba Electric and Gas Light Company
Minneapolis Mill Company (with St. Anthony Falls Water Power Company, controlled all the water power on the Mississippi)
Montreal Light, Heat, and Power Company
Nova Scotia Steel and Coal Company
Patent Elbow Company Limited
Pease Foundry (hot water boilers, heaters etc.)
Royal Electric Company
St. Anthony Falls Water Power Company
Standard Light and Power Company; shares sold in 1903
United States Steel Corporation
Victoria Rolling Stock Company
West Indian Electric Company, Kingston, Jamaica

Newspapers, Presses, Publications
Annual Review Publishing Company, Toronto; bought fourteen shares in March 1907; in 1912 agreed to buy $1,000 worth of shares if owners could find a further $4,000 to clear their debt; they did; shares not issued before Lord Strathcona died; confusion resulted
Dominion Illustrated Publishing Company
Globe Printing Company
The Interior Publishing Company
The Knowledge Publishing Company
Kootenay Mail Publishing Company
London Advertiser Newspaper Printing and Publishing Company
Mail Printing and Publishing Company (Toronto)
Manitoba Free Press, shares taken in 1888 as security for a loan which was not repaid; controlling interest with Van Horne acquired in 1893 and sold in 1898 to Clifford Sifton
Montreal Gazette
Montreal Herald
Moon Publishing Company
Ontario Publishing Company
Standard Newspaper (Winnipeg)
Westminster Review Company

Natural Resources (including land, ranches and houses)
Abbey Effervescent Salt Company
Abbott-Mitchell Iron and Steel Company of Ontario
Acadia Pulp and Paper; sold to liquidator in 1914; became Macleod Pulp Company
Adams Tobacco Company
Alberta Railway and Coal Company
Amalgamated Asbestos Corporation
Anglo-American Oil
Anglo-Persian Oil Company
Atlantic Refining Company
Baynes Land Colliery Company
BC Cooperage and Jute Company
BC Sugar Refinery
British South Africa Company
Brompton Lake Asbestos Company; acquired in 1900
Buckeye Pipeline Company
Calgary and Medicine Hat Land Company
Canada North West Land Company
Canadian Peat Fuel Company
Civic Investment and Industrial Company

Climax Coal Company
Colonsay and Oronsay; besides family house, land included farms, hotel, cottages, fishing rights
Columbia American Mining Company
Concessions Syndicate (re Anglo-Persian Oil)
Consolidated Banner Gold and Silver Mining Company
Corogitz Anthracite Coal Mining Company, Queen Charlotte Islands, BC
Crescent Goldmining Company of Marmora
Crescent Pipe Line Company
Debden; besides the house and private estate, the property included farms and houses which were let to tenants
Dominion Coal
Eureka Pipe Line Company
Five Sisters Building, Victoria
Forsyth Granite and Marble Company
Fort Garry Court; apartment block in Winnipeg, built on site of Canada Pacific Hotel
Galena Signal Oil Company
Glencoe; besides the house and shooting rights which were not let, the estate included shops, cottages, inns, the Loch Leven Power Company and land let to British Aluminium
Globe Cattle Company
Great Falls City Land Company
Great Northern Iron Ore Properties
Highland Mining Company
High River Horse Ranche
houses on Buckley Road, Kilburn, London
house at 279 University Street, Montreal
Indiana Pipe Line Company
Inter-Colonial Coal Mining Company, Nova Scotia
International Coal Company
land with buildings on Sanguinet Street, Montreal; bought from William Chennell in July 1877
land at Mansfield, Pontiac County, Quebec, previously owned by Thomas Taylor (George Simpson's manservant and brother of John Stuart's country wife); acquired in February 1874 and sold for $5,000 to Henry Connolly (HBC officer from Esquimaux Bay) in August 1876
twenty lots in Lachine, purchased from James Bissett (HBC officer and later Smith's private secretary and attorney) in 1879
land at Pointe aux Trembles, eastern outskirts of Montreal, with stone house, barn, stables etc. and their contents, bought for $10,000 from William Stephen (one of George Stephen's relatives, possibly Donald Smith's uncle) in October 1880, sold in June 1883
land in Manitoba sold by Henry Nathan (MP from Victoria) in April 1881
land with eight brick and stone dwellings, houses and out-buildings on St. Martin Street, Montreal, acquired at a sheriff sale in August 1881
fifty acres and a house at Matapedia, near the railway station, purchased from George Stephen in August 1881; this was part of the fishing camp established by Stephen on land acquired from the Intercolonial Railway
three hundred and twenty acres of land, probably in Manitoba, sold by the HBC in December 1882 to Smith, R.B. Angus, William Bain Scarth and Edward Boyd Osler
land along the lower St. Lawrence; iron ore exploration by John Carson of Montreal; $20,000 invested in April 1907; also wanted to buy other property with molybdenite; land not to be purchased in Lord Strathcona's name
land associated with St. Anthony Falls Water Power and Minneapolis Mill; held by the Minneapolis Trust till sold to the Great Northern Railway in 1904
land bought jointly with George Stephen in 1880, location unknown
Laurentide Paper Company
Laurentide Pulp Company
McGill Armoury; land provided by Lord Strathcona in 1913; drill hall built by government
Manitoba Brick and Pottery Company
Minneapolis Stock Yard and Packing Company
Mond Nickel Company

Montreal residence and associated buildings: nine houses on Baile and Fort Streets; stone house and outbuildings on Dorchester Street, acquired from the widow Auger in November 1876; Ferme des Prêtres at Fort and Baile Streets, bought from Seminaire de St. Sulpice in April 1881
New Walrond Ranche Company (cattle ranch near Fort McLeod, Alberta)
Northwest Coal and Navigation Company
Northwestern Mining Development Company
Ohio Oil Company
Playa d'Oro Mining Company, Kentucky
Prairie Oil and Gas Company
Puget's Sound Agricultural Company
Queen Charlotte Island Coal Mine Exploration Company
Red Mountain Consolidated Mining Company (part of the holdings of Montana Securities; the claims were never really worked)
St. Andrews Land Company (owned hotels and land in New Brunswick; three Canadian, eleven American shareholders)
Silver Heights, house and land six miles west of Winnipeg
Southern Pipe Line Company
Standard Chemical Company (formerly Standard Chemical Iron and Lumber Company; principal business was marketing acetone in Europe)
Standard Oil of California
Standard Oil of Indiana
Standard Oil of New Jersey
Standard Oil of New York
Strathcona Building; office and residential block on the corner of Georgia and Granville Streets, Vancouver
Strathcona Coal Company, River Herbert, Cumberland County, Nova Scotia; four square miles of coal areas, seven seams of coal, one hundred and fifty acres real estate, timberland, twenty-six miners' houses, school etc.
Thunder Bay Silver Mining Company; acquired in 1882
Twin City Stockyards Company
United States Water Purification Association
Union Tank Line Company
Vacuum Oil Company
Winnipeg Waterworks Company

Retail Outlets
Army and Navy Co-operative Society
Hudson's Bay Company

Textiles
Almonte Knitting Company
Canada Cotton Manufacturing Company
The Coalicook Cotton Company
Dominion Textile Company
Dominion Cotton Mills
Globe Woollen Mills
Merchants Cotton Company
Paton Manufacturing Company
Rosamond Woollen Company of Almonte

Government Bonds
City of New York
City of Ottawa
City of Toronto
Corporation of Montreal
Government of Canada
Province of New Brunswick
United Kingdom government

Miscellaneous

Argyll's Motor Company
Clifton Park (Blackpool) Racecourse Syndicate
Forest and Stream Club
Manitoba Club
Montreal Board of Trade
Montreal Exposition Company
Mount Royal Golf Club
Pageants Limited, a company set up to tour British theatre productions in Canada and so avoid American dominance of Canadian theatres; it owned Imperial Theatres of Canada and Dominion Productions
Restigouche Salmon Club
Royal Montreal Golf Club
Scottish Home Industries Association

Mortgages

John Bain (Winnipeg lawyer) on property at Shoal Lake, Manitoba
A.G.B. Bannatyne on land in the parish of St. Clement's, Manitoba
Walter Beckett on land with houses and other buildings in Sherbrooke, Quebec
Horace Bélanger's house and land, Lachine; arranged through Hopkins in 1861
Judge Louis Bétournay, $4,000, supplied in 1874
Brewster's property, City of Montreal
Augustin Cantin's land in St. Ann's Ward, Montreal; a subrogation from the Hon. James Hamilton
Communauté des Soeurs des Saints Noms de Jésus et Marie de Hochelaga for convent and other buildings at the foot of St. Mary Street in Montreal; initially a subrogation from John Redpath in 1874; then mortgages in 1876 and 1877
E.G. Conklin on thirty-nine lots and some other property in Winnipeg
John Stoughton Dennis (Dominion Surveyor) and his wife on property in Cooper Street, Ottawa, acquired in January 1876
John Stoughton Dennis and his wife on land in Hull, Quebec, acquired in January 1876
John Stoughton Dennis and his wife on land in St. Boniface, Manitoba, acquired in 1879
Pierre Dorion land at the corner of St. Lawrence Main and Ontario Street in Montreal; a subrogation acquired from Paschal Dagenais
John Grant on property at St. Vital, Manitoba, acquired in 1878; subsequently entangled in election bribery charges against Smith
Thomas Hardisty's land, Main Road, Upper Lachine; on his death in 1877 at least some of this land was sold to James Bissett
William Lucas Hardisty's house in Lachine (probably purchased from James Bissett)
M.W. Howard on property in Winnipeg
Lucius Seth Huntington (the man who revealed the Pacific Scandal in the Canadian parliament in 1873) and his wife, E.C. Huntington, John Earl Brown: $10,000 re mining claim in Nevada, California; deed to 30.91 acres received as collateral
Hubert Ives on property in St. Ann's Ward, Montreal, including a two storey brick building occupied by Miller Brothers and Mitchell as a machinist's shop
John and Peter Jackson on farm land in Côte St. Paul and Côte St. Pierre, Montreal
John Kenny and others (including William Fisher Luxton) of the Standard Printing Company on a house, other buildings, fixtures and fittings on the east side of Main Street, Winnipeg; this is *Free Press* building
Lt. Col. Charles King on property in Sherbrooke, Quebec
Emelie Labelle, a small mortgage on unspecified land
Jean Olivier Lautier debt (possibly not a mortgage); a subrogation from the late George Simpson
D. McArthur (employed in HBC office, Montreal), place unspecified, but presumably Montreal
James McKay's land in St. James and St. Boniface, Manitoba
Joseph McPherson's house and land, Pictou, Nova Scotia
New Auburn Woollen Mill, Peterborough, Ontario; mortgage bought from George Stephen in April 1871
William Frederick Powell, Ottawa: $1,000 for townsite land in Manitoba, granted in 1876

John Renshaw on two plots of land with buildings etc. in St. Ann's Ward, Montreal; initially given in November 1879, renewed for an increased sum in February 1882

William Roberts on land on Sherbrooke Street, Montreal

Rosamond Woollen Mill, St. Anthony Falls, Minnesota; $25,000 provided in October 1880 and renewed in 1885

estate of James Ross at McGill and St. Paul Streets, Montreal, to be paid off with half the rents from the McGill Street properties

William Shaw on property in Montreal

Helen Smith on land at Algoma, Ontario

Rev. F.A. Toupin on land and property in the west and centre wards of Montreal

Lt. Col. William White (former deputy postmaster general); $6,900 at 5.5 percent negotiated with Joseph Hardisty in 1894 on property in Wurtemburg Street in Ottawa; a further $1,000 was agreed in 1897; some of the money was repaid before his death and his estate repaid $100; $6,731.70 was owing in January 1914 when Lord Strathcona cancelled the debt

Loans

Donald Smith lent large and small sums to many people from all walks of life. As a rule, collateral took the form of life insurance policies, shares or property. Rarely were loans unsecured. The interest rate ranged from four and a half percent to eight percent but generally hovered between five and seven percent, depending on the market rates at the time. Many small borrowers were Hudson's Bay Company officers and there is no evidence to suggest Smith habitually lent to people he had not met in a political, professional or social context, though loans to people he did not know were arranged through his agents. Capacity to repay and the likelihood of doing so, together with the viability of the collateral, seem to have been the factors which determined whether most loan requests were granted. The following list indicates some of the more interesting loans for which evidence has survived.

Viscount Anson: £8,500; Lord Strathcona's daughter cancelled the debt after her father's death

James Bissett (Hudson's Bay Company officer and subsequently Smith's private secretary and attorney) and his brother: $20,000 for an "improved nail cutting machine," the patent taken as collateral

Sedley Blanchard (HBC lawyer in Winnipeg): $12,000 with an interest in Manitoba Cartage and Warehousing Company as security

Richard Cartwright (finance minister under Laurier): $8,000, followed in 1899 by a loan for $20,000; $5,000 was repaid; with interest to January 21, 1914 the sum owing was $45,613.39; the loans were amply covered by securities which lost their value; after Cartwright's death in 1912, his son was negotiating repayment terms on behalf of the estate with Lord Strathcona's New York lawyer when Strathcona himself died; when his will was published, the Cartwright estate discovered that the debt had been cancelled

Robert Cunningham and William Coldwell, Manitoba Queen's Printers: $2,800

Simon James Dawson (MP and engineer of the Dawson Route, the corduroy road between Lake Superior and Lake of the Woods): $700

Arthur Doughty, first dominion archivist: $500, twice

George Foster (former Conservative finance minister): $10,000 borrowed on April 15, 1898 with mining shares offered as collateral; by January 1914, interest had nearly doubled the amount owed; debt cancelled in Strathcona's will

Sir George Kirkpatrick (Lieutenant Governor of Ontario when loan contracted in 1897): sum unknown; had not been repaid when Strathcona died in 1914

Major General John Carstairs McNeill: £2,500 in May 1886 and £5,000 in May 1887, the Scottish islands of Colonsay and Oronsay given as collateral

Manitoba Colonization Society: $1,000 in 1879

Andrew Miller: $3,000 in 1909 to purchase a newspaper in the Northwest; $1,100 was still owing when Strathcona died and the debt was cancelled by his daughter

New Brunswick Railway Company: $32,850.16

Saint Paul, Minneapolis and Manitoba Railway: $500,000; "temporary loan" April-July 1881

Sam Steele: £150 to his wife to enable her to join him in South Africa when he was helping to set up the police force there; two other loans totalling £6,000

Richard White, Montreal Gazette Printing Company: $10,000; overdue in December 1902

APPENDIX III EQUIVALENCE: THE VALUE OF THE POUND AND THE DOLLAR IN THE NINETEENTH CENTURY

Comparability:

Several currencies existed alongside each other in mid-nineteenth century Canada and most businessmen moved fluently between them. Decimal currency such as is now used in Canada was introduced on January 1, 1858 at which time there were a hundred mills in one cent as well as one hundred cents in a dollar. The British pound sterling co-existed with decimal currency until 1871 when it was officially withdrawn from circulation. Most Canadians converted quickly to decimal currency but sterling continued to be a factor in Canadian economic life because British merchant banks and the London stock exchange were important in financing the country's economic development.

Sterling remained a familiar but unofficial unit of measure in the Northwest and other areas dominated by the Hudson's Bay Company after 1858 because, although accounts were computed in decimal currency, outfits were initially valued in sterling and the prices furs made at auction in London were reported in sterling. In addition, the officers were paid in sterling and the dividends earned by the wintering partners were in sterling. As soon as Esquimaux Bay began to report directly to London, its accounts reverted from decimal currency to sterling.

Halifax currency, in which the HBC had also kept accounts, continued to be a unit of measure in parallel with the pound sterling and the Canadian dollar. This was especially true in the Maritime provinces. Donald Smith's loan to Joseph McPherson in 1869, for example, was in Halifax currency.

In the Northwest, the Hudson's Bay Company also used its own currency. Printed in London or, more often, stamped into copper or brass, the currency represented a portion of a made beaver. These tokens facilitated trade in the HBC posts and remained in circulation until the middle of the present century. Their value reflected the price pelts fetched at auction in Montreal or London with the result that the currency depreciated in value as the market for beaver dried up.

American decimal currency also appeared in Canada from time to time and figured frequently in conversations and correspondence of men like Donald Smith and George Stephen whose business involved sales and purchases on the American market.

As a general rule the relationship between the currencies in the nineteenth century was as follows:

Sterling	Canadian Dollar	US Dollar	Halifax Currency
£1.00	$5.00	$5.00	$3.89[1]

Donald Smith and his friends virtually never distinguished between the American and Canadian dollar in terms of its value. Minor fluctuations affected the relationship between the dollar and the pound, but the dollar rarely slipped below $4.90 to the pound and rarely went above $5.10. The rule of thumb throughout the period with which this book is concerned, and indeed for much longer, was $5 to the pound. In July 1996, the ratio was $ Cdn 2.11 to the pound and $ US 1.55 to the pound.

Value:

While the ratios between the currencies remained fairly constant, the values of the currencies themselves fluctuated according to economic condition. As a rule, prices in Canada fell between 1874 and 1896 because internal transportation and communication improved, freight rates and the cost of insurance diminished, and technological improvements allowed more goods to be produced more cheaply. The following table shows the average prices for selected years between 1868 and 1913, where 1913 is 100. The final column indicates the value of the Canadian dollar today in relation to those prices. It means that in 1944, approximately $14.55 would be required to purchase what one dollar could buy in 1913. Consequently, we can say that Lord Strathcona's bequest of $380,000 to the Royal Victoria College was worth $5,529,000 by today's standards.

1868	92.9	1882	93.2	1905	82.1
1873	100.4	1886	75.3	1910	91.7
1874	100.8	1890	80.0	1913	100.0
1878	79.8	1896	64.3	1994	1454.7[2]
1879	81.3	1900	77.4		

This means that his donation of two hundred dollars towards the restoration of St. James Church, Winnipeg in 1878 would be worth $3645.86 dollars today ([100/79.8] x $200 x [1994 figure/100]).

The cost of living in Britain was relatively stable prior to the First World War because Britain was still on the gold standard. Figures for the UK, where January 1974 is 100, show the following:

1914	11.1	1974	100.0	1994	568.5[3]

1 Mitchell, *Statistical Contributions*, vol. 2, p. 56.
2 Mitchell, *Statistical Contributions*, vol. 2, p. 56 and *Statistics Canada.*
3 UK Central Statistical Office.

APPENDIX IV GENEALOGICAL CHARTS

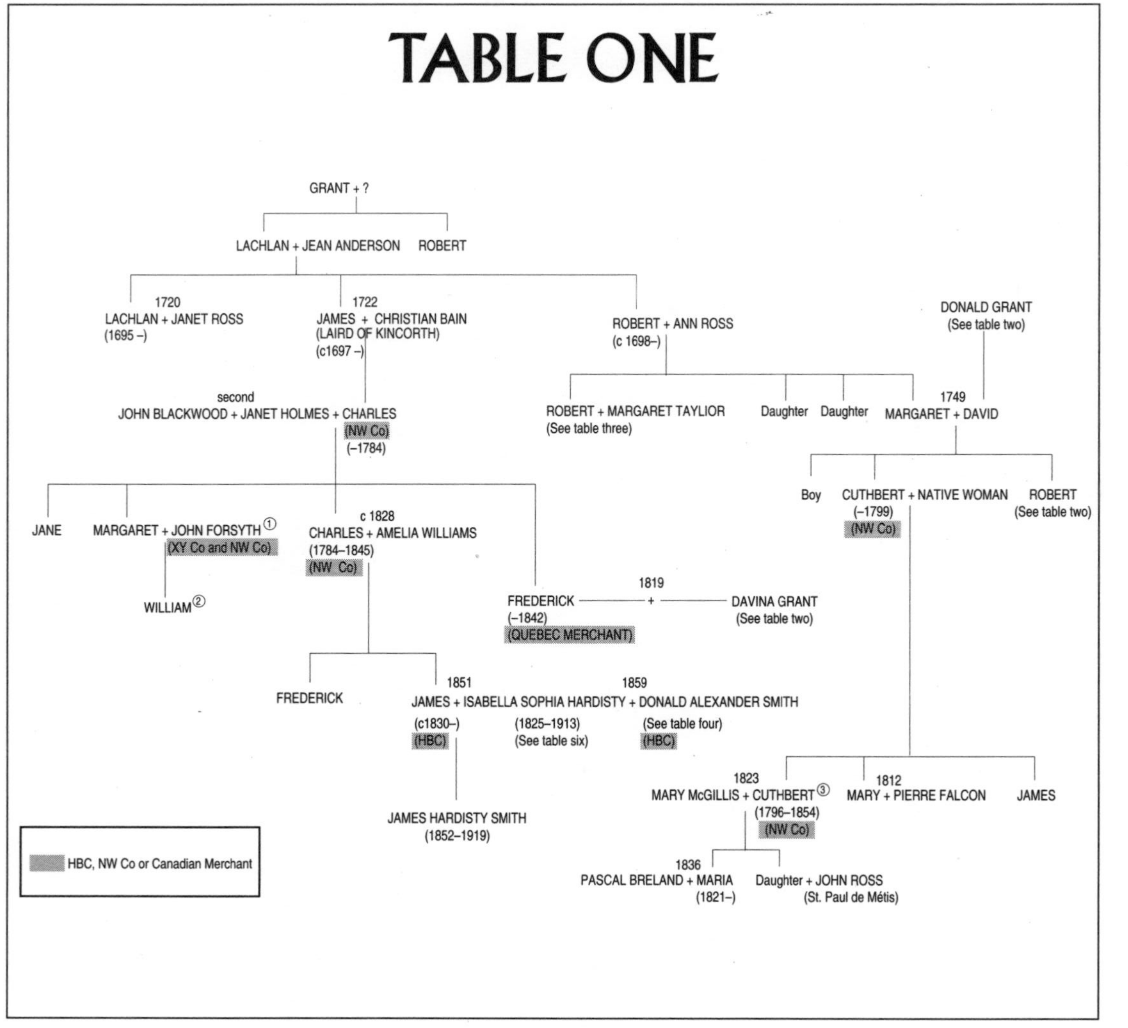

TABLE ONE
GRANT + ?
LACHLAN + JEAN ANDERSON
ROBERT
1720
LACHLAN + JANET ROSS
(1695 –)
1722
JAMES + CHRISTIAN BAIN
(LAIRD OF KINCORTH)
(c1697 –)
ROBERT + ANN ROSS
(c 1698–)
DONALD GRANT
(See table two)
second
JOHN BLACKWOOD + JANET HOLMES + CHARLES
(NW Co)
(–1784)
ROBERT + MARGARET TAYLIOR
(See table three)
Daughter
Daughter
1749
MARGARET + DAVID
JANE
MARGARET + JOHN FORSYTH ①
(XY Co and NW Co)
c 1828
CHARLES + AMELIA WILLIAMS
(1784–1845)
(NW Co)
Boy
CUTHBERT + NATIVE WOMAN
(–1799)
(NW Co)
ROBERT
(See table two)
WILLIAM ②
1819
FREDERICK
+
DAVINA GRANT
(–1842)
(QUEBEC MERCHANT)
(See table two)
FREDERICK
1851
1859
JAMES + ISABELLA SOPHIA HARDISTY + DONALD ALEXANDER SMITH
(c1830–)
(HBC)
(1825–1913)
(See table six)
(See table four)
(HBC)
JAMES HARDISTY SMITH
(1852–1919)
1823
MARY McGILLIS + CUTHBERT ③
(1796–1854)
(NW Co)
1812
MARY + PIERRE FALCON
JAMES
1836
PASCAL BRELAND + MARIA
(1821–)
Daughter + JOHN ROSS
(St. Paul de Métis)
HBC, NW Co or Canadian Merchant

TABLE TWO

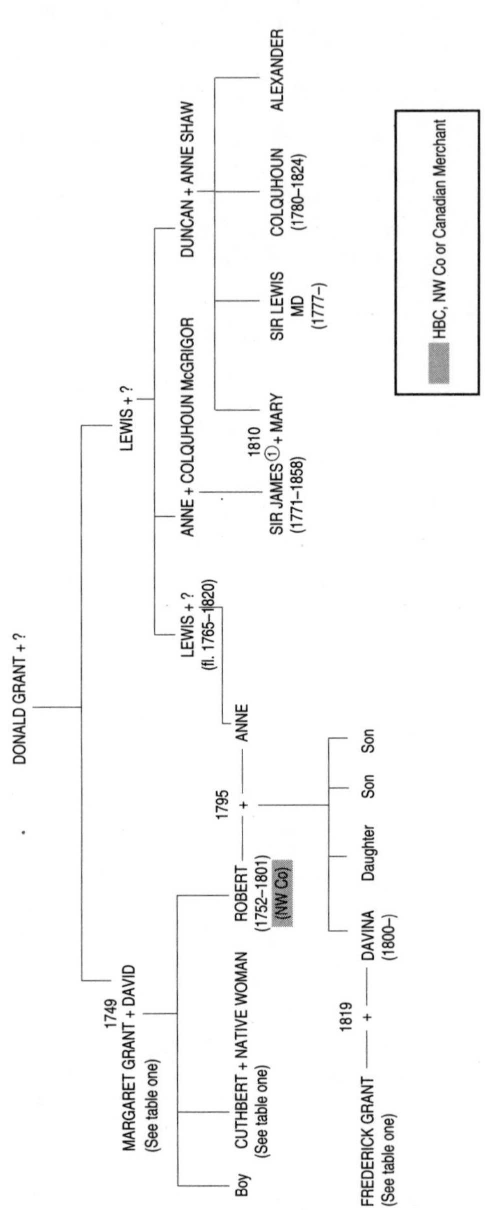
DONALD GRANT + ?
1749
MARGARET GRANT + DAVID
(See table one)
LEWIS + ?
(fl. 1765–1820)
LEWIS + ?
ANNE + COLQUHOUN McGRIGOR
DUNCAN + ANNE SHAW
Boy
CUTHBERT + NATIVE WOMAN
(See table one)
ROBERT
(1752–1801)
(NW Co)
1795
ANNE
1810
SIR JAMES ① + MARY
(1771–1858)
SIR LEWIS
MD
(1777–)
COLQUHOUN
(1780–1824)
ALEXANDER
1819
FREDERICK GRANT
(See table one)
DAVINA
(1800–)
Daughter
Son
Son
HBC, NW Co or Canadian Merchant

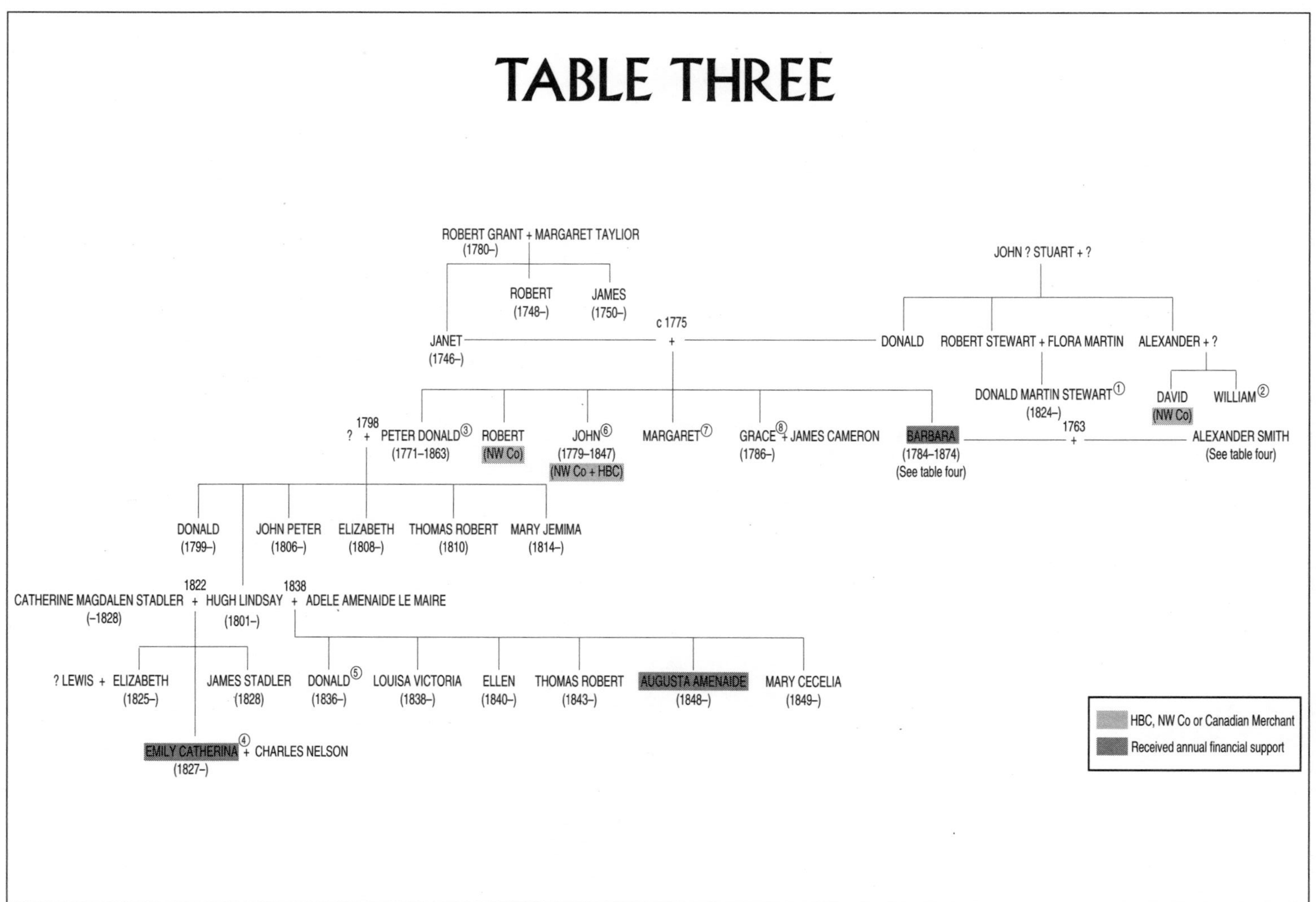
TABLE THREE
ROBERT GRANT + MARGARET TAYLIOR (1780–)
ROBERT (1748–)
JAMES (1750–)
JOHN ? STUART + ?
JANET (1746–)
c 1775 +
DONALD
ROBERT STEWART + FLORA MARTIN
ALEXANDER + ?
DONALD MARTIN STEWART ① (1824–)
DAVID (NW Co)
WILLIAM ②
1798 ? + PETER DONALD ③ (1771–1863)
ROBERT (NW Co)
JOHN ⑥ (1779–1847) (NW Co + HBC)
MARGARET ⑦
GRACE ⑧ + JAMES CAMERON (1786–)
BARBARA (1784–1874) (See table four)
1763 +
ALEXANDER SMITH (See table four)
DONALD (1799–)
JOHN PETER (1806–)
ELIZABETH (1808–)
THOMAS ROBERT (1810)
MARY JEMIMA (1814–)
CATHERINE MAGDALEN STADLER (–1828)
1822 + HUGH LINDSAY (1801–)
1838 + ADELE AMENAIDE LE MAIRE
? LEWIS + ELIZABETH (1825–)
JAMES STADLER (1828)
DONALD ⑤ (1836–)
LOUISA VICTORIA (1838–)
ELLEN (1840–)
THOMAS ROBERT (1843–)
AUGUSTA AMENAIDE (1848–)
MARY CECELIA (1849–)
EMILY CATHERINA ④ + CHARLES NELSON (1827–)
HBC, NW Co or Canadian Merchant
Received annual financial support

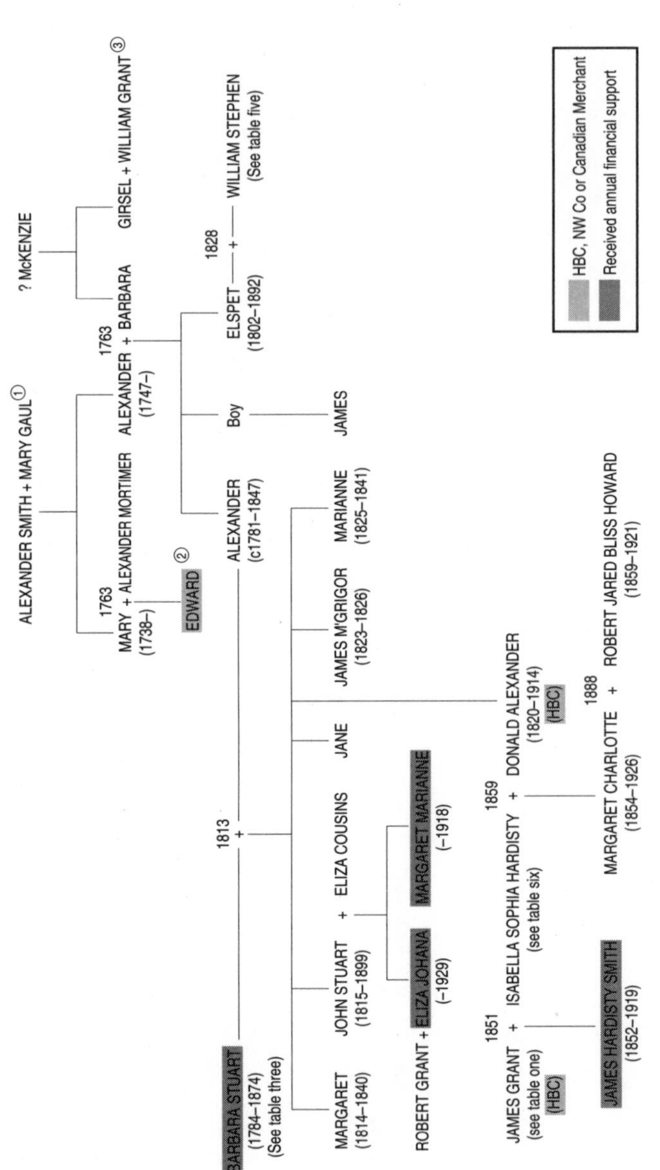
TABLE FOUR
ALEXANDER SMITH + MARY GAUL ①
? McKENZIE
1763
MARY + ALEXANDER MORTIMER
(1738–)
EDWARD ②
1763
ALEXANDER + BARBARA
(1747–)
GIRSEL + WILLIAM GRANT ③
ALEXANDER
(c1781–1847)
Boy
JAMES
1828
ELSPET + WILLIAM STEPHEN
(1802–1892)
(See table five)
BARBARA STUART
(1784–1874)
(See table three)
1813
MARGARET
(1814–1840)
JOHN STUART + ELIZA COUSINS
(1815–1899)
JANE
JAMES M'GRIGOR
(1823–1826)
MARIANNE
(1825–1841)
ROBERT GRANT + ELIZA JOHANA
(–1929)
MARGARET MARIANNE
(–1918)
DONALD ALEXANDER
(1820–1914)
(HBC)
1851
JAMES GRANT + ISABELLA SOPHIA HARDISTY + DONALD ALEXANDER
(see table one)
(HBC)
(see table six)
1859
JAMES HARDISTY SMITH
(1852–1919)
1888
MARGARET CHARLOTTE + ROBERT JARED BLISS HOWARD
(1854–1926)
(1859–1921)
HBC, NW Co or Canadian Merchant
Received annual financial support

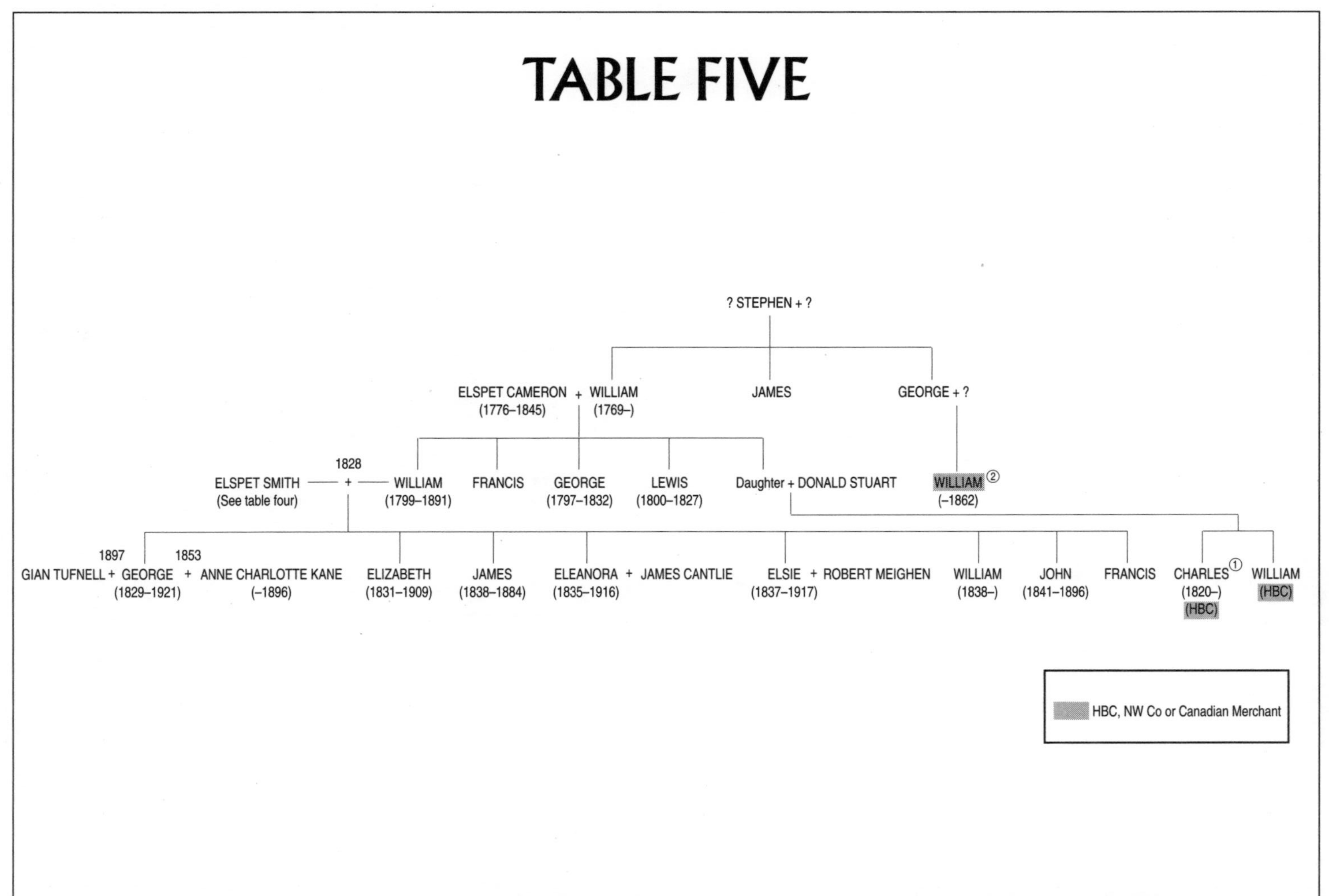
TABLE FIVE
? STEPHEN + ?
ELSPET CAMERON + WILLIAM
(1776–1845) (1769–)
JAMES
GEORGE + ?
1828
ELSPET SMITH + WILLIAM
(See table four) (1799–1891)
FRANCIS
GEORGE
(1797–1832)
LEWIS
(1800–1827)
Daughter + DONALD STUART
WILLIAM ②
(–1862)
1897
GIAN TUFNELL + GEORGE
(1829–1921)
1853
+ ANNE CHARLOTTE KANE
(–1896)
ELIZABETH
(1831–1909)
JAMES
(1838–1884)
ELEANORA + JAMES CANTLIE
(1835–1916)
ELSIE + ROBERT MEIGHEN
(1837–1917)
WILLIAM
(1838–)
JOHN
(1841–1896)
FRANCIS
CHARLES ①
(1820–)
(HBC)
WILLIAM
(HBC)
HBC, NW Co or Canadian Merchant

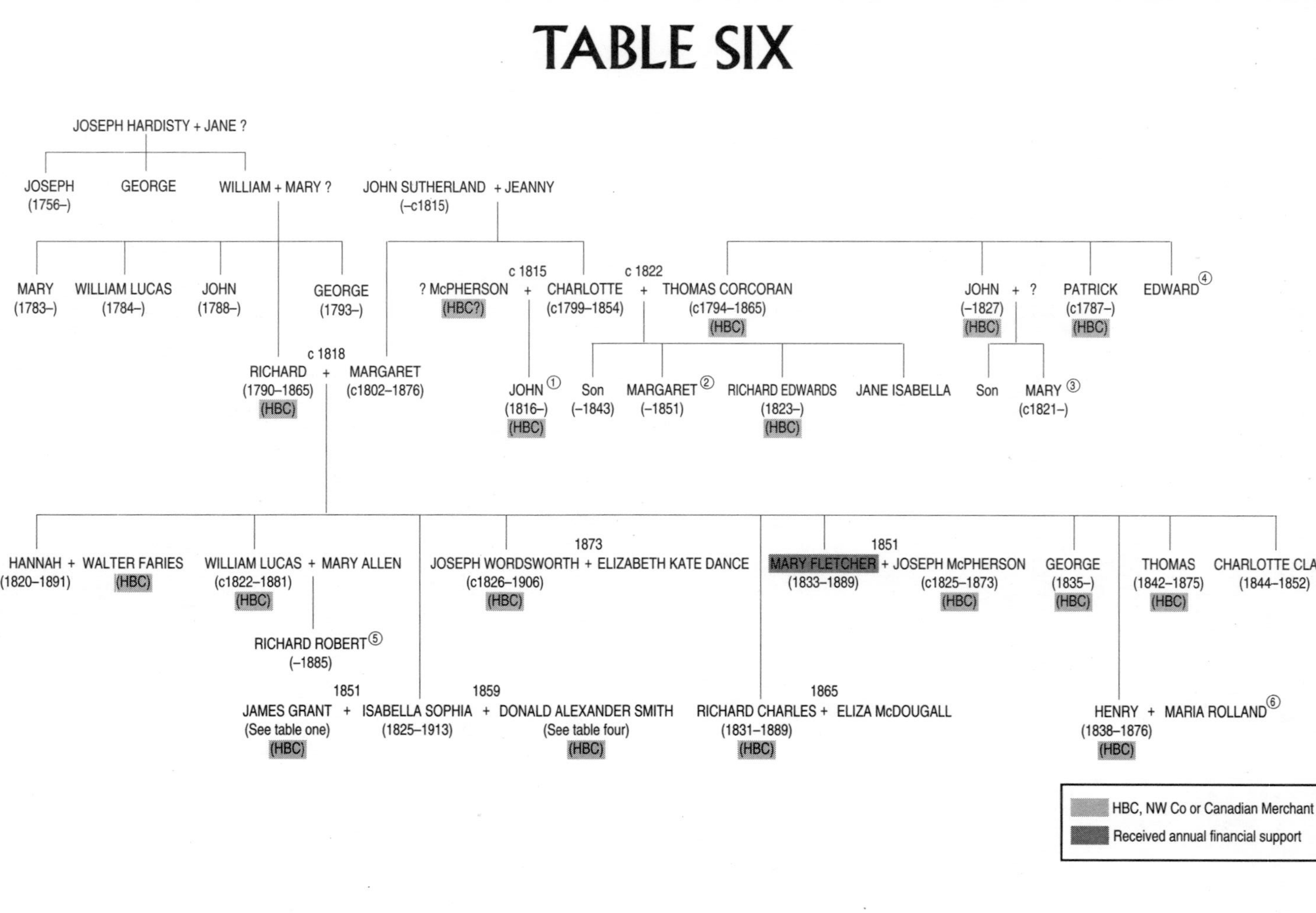
TABLE SIX
JOSEPH HARDISTY + JANE ?
JOSEPH (1756–)
GEORGE
WILLIAM + MARY ?
JOHN SUTHERLAND (–c1815) + JEANNY
MARY (1783–)
WILLIAM LUCAS (1784–)
JOHN (1788–)
GEORGE (1793–)
c 1815
? McPHERSON (HBC?) + CHARLOTTE (c1799–1854)
c 1822
+ THOMAS CORCORAN (c1794–1865) (HBC)
JOHN (–1827) (HBC) + ?
PATRICK (c1787–) (HBC)
EDWARD (4)
c 1818
RICHARD (1790–1865) (HBC) + MARGARET (c1802–1876)
JOHN (1) (1816–) (HBC)
Son (–1843)
MARGARET (2) (–1851)
RICHARD EDWARDS (1823–) (HBC)
JANE ISABELLA
Son
MARY (3) (c1821–)
HANNAH (1820–1891) + WALTER FARIES (HBC)
WILLIAM LUCAS (c1822–1881) (HBC) + MARY ALLEN
1873
JOSEPH WORDSWORTH (c1826–1906) (HBC) + ELIZABETH KATE DANCE
1851
MARY FLETCHER (1833–1889) + JOSEPH McPHERSON (c1825–1873) (HBC)
GEORGE (1835–) (HBC)
THOMAS (1842–1875) (HBC)
CHARLOTTE CLARA (1844–1852)
RICHARD ROBERT (5) (–1885)
1851
JAMES GRANT (See table one) (HBC) + ISABELLA SOPHIA (1825–1913)
1859
+ DONALD ALEXANDER SMITH (See table four) (HBC)
1865
RICHARD CHARLES (1831–1889) (HBC) + ELIZA McDOUGALL
HENRY (1838–1876) (HBC) + MARIA ROLLAND (6)
HBC, NW Co or Canadian Merchant
Received annual financial support

NOTES

Chapter One: **The Early Years 1820-1838**

1 *The New Statistical Account*, 1845, vol. xiii and *The Third Statistical Account*, *passim.*
2 Willson, vol. 1, p. 5; *Forres Gazette*, April 29, 1874.
3 Willson, vol. 1, p. 10.
4 Willson, vol. 1, p. 12.
5 Speech by Lord Strathcona at first annual dinner of Forres Academy Club, August 17, 1904, *Elgin Courant*, August 19, 1904.
6 Cited in Willson, vol. 1, p. 13n.
7 *Forres Gazette*, April 29 and May 6, 1874.
8 *Forres Gazette*, April 29, 1874.
9 *Forres Gazette*, April 15, 1874.
10 *Forres Gazette*, April 1, 1874.
11 *Forres Gazette*, May 27, 1874.
12 Lauder, p. 149.
13 Lauder, p. 156.
14 Willson, vol. 1, p. 13, quoting an unidentified source, presumably a correspondent from Forres.
15 Willson, vol. 1, p. 193, quoting a letter from Ethel Hurlbatt, then Warden of Royal Victoria College, Montreal.
16 Alexander Kerr to James Alves, December 1, 1833, NAC, MG 24, I 26.
17 See Appendix IV for details of the Grants and other relatives in the North West Company.
18 Willson, vol. 1, p. 17, citing a letter from John Stuart to William McGillivray, a North West Company director.
19 George Simpson, *Part of a Dispatch from George Simpson*, E.E. Rich, ed., London, Hudson's Bay Record Society, 1947, pp. 25-26.
20 Cited in Willson, vol. 1, p. 34.
21 Donald Smith to Barbara Smith, April 30, 1838, Willson, vol. 1, pp. 37-38.
22 *Ibid.*
23 Simpson to James Keith, April 20, 1838, HBC Archives, B. 134/c/38.
24 Simpson to Keith, April 25, 1838, HBC Archives, B. 134/c/38.
25 Willson, vol. 1, p. 39.
26 Donald Smith to Barbara Smith, May 9, 1838, Willson, vol. 1, p. 40.
27 *Ibid.*

Chapter Two: **The Little Emperor and the King's Posts 1838–1847**

1 Two metrical paraphrases in particular weave like leitmotifs through Donald Smith's life. The eleventh, based on *Proverbs* iii, 13-17, was one of them.

O happy is the man who hears instruction's warning voice,
And who celestial wisdom makes his early only choice.
For she has treasures greater far than east or west unfold,
And her rewards more precious are than all their stores of gold.

In her right hand she holds to view a length of happy days;
Riches, with splendid honors joined are what her left displays.
She guides the young with innocence in pleasure's path to tread;
A crown of glory she bestows upon the hoary head.
According as her labours rise, so other rewards increase;
Her ways are ways of pleasantness and all her paths are peace.

2 McKenzie to Keith, June 18, 1838, HBC Archives, B. 134/c/38. Willson, vol. 1, pp. 52-54, is quite explicit in saying that the *Royal William*, stopped at Fraserville on June 27 and docked at Quebec on June 30, and that Smith arrived in Montreal on July 2, but McKenzie's letter is clearly dated June 18 and a file note on it indicates it was received on June 21, a Monday. In 1908, when Lord Strathcona addressed the Savage Club on June 20, he observed that it was "seventy years to a day" since he first landed in Canada. He may have meant Montreal, rather than Canada, or may actually have said so and been misreported in *The Times* of June 22, 1908. Willson's information may have come from *Lloyds List* which does give June 30 for the arrival at Quebec but the paper is frequently inaccurate because it reports the dates when vessels registered their arrival, not when they actually arrived. As the *Royal William* carried no cargo, there would have been no pressure on Captain Agar to make a prompt official report.

3 Willson, vol. 1, p. 57; Carlyle, *Reminiscences*, p. 136n.

4 Stuart to Stewart, May 10, 1838, Willson, vol. 1, p. 43.

5 Simpson to Keith, April 20, 1838, HBC Archives, D. 4/17.

6 Hudson's Bay Company Royal Charter, *Charters, Statutes, etc.* p. 11.

7 Lord Strathcona, speech to a meeting of the Royal Colonial Institute, April 13, 1897, NAC, MG 29, A 5; *Charters Statues etc.* p. 11.

8 Stuart to Smith, October 2, 1838, Willson, vol. 1, p. 70-71.

9 Margaret and Mary were the daughters of George Taylor, a Hudson's Bay Company sloopmaster, and a native woman. Their brother, Thomas, was Simpson's personal servant. Simpson had fathered two illegitimate children in Scotland and at least five by four different women in Canada before establishing his relationship with Margaret Taylor.

10 Willson, vol. 1, p. 66.

11 Ellice to Keith, [July 14, 1838], HBC Archives, B. 134/c/39; Willson, vol. 1, p. 68.

12 Connolly to Keith, July 7, 1838, HBC Archives, B. 134/c/39.

13 Donald Smith to Barbara Smith, November 8, 1838, Willson, vol. 1, pp. 69-70.

14 Abstracts of Servants Accounts, HBC Archives, B. 134/g/13.

15 Cited in Willson, vol. 1, pp. 85-88.

16 Donald Smith to Margaret Smith, [nd], Willson, vol. 1, p. 85.

17 Enclosure in Connolly to Keith, November 29, 1839, HBC Archives, B. 134/c/44.

18 Willson, vol. 1, p. 86.

19 Williams, ed., "The 'Character Book' of Governor George Simpson," *Miscellany*, pp. 220-221. The value of experience in James Keith's office was also recognized by McPherson who, four months after John Stuart's request, wrote Keith seeking a place for his son Joseph who would be joining the company in the near future. Simpson to McPherson, October 14 and October 28, 1843, HBC Archives, D. 4/63.

20 Stuart to Simpson, August 24, 1841, HBC Archives, D. 5/6.

21 Stuart to Keith, January 24, 1842 and April 2, 1843, HBC Archives, B. 134/c/51 and B. 134/c/55.

22 James McKenzie to John McKenzie (deputising for James Keith who was on leave of absence), November 18, 1843, HBC Archives, B. 134/c/56.

23 Littlejohn and Drew, *The Gulf of St. Lawrence*, p. 159; Willson, p. 89.

24 Simpson to McPherson, March 1, 1844, HBC Archives, D. 4/64; Simpson to Barnston, March 29, 1844, HBC Archives, B. 214/c/1.

25 Letter written in 1844, in Willson, vol. 1, p. 88.

26 Cited in Willson, vol. 1, p. 90.

27 Smith to Barnston, January 21, 1845, HBC Archives, B. 214/c/1. The first copy of this letter in the file is dated January 21, 1844 and another copy appears later, dated July 21, 1845. As Barnston wrote Duncan Finlayson at Montreal on March 22, 1845

(B. 134/c/58) saying he was forwarding Donald Smith's remarks, it seems certain that the second copy contains a slip of the pen. Smith was in the habit of writing different letters to the same person on the same day, the distinction being the subject dealt with and whether they were official, personal or private. A letter on the management of the business at Mingan is also dated January 21, 1845 and one on personal finances was written the following day, suggesting that he was taking advantage of a passing vessel to communicate with Tadoussac.

28 Barnston to Finlayson, December 27, 1844, HBC Archives, B. 134/c/58.
29 Smith to Barnston, January 21, 1845, HBC Archives, B. 214/c/1.
30 Barnston to Smith, March 18, 1845, HBC Archives, B. 214/c/1.
31 Smith to Barnston, August 17 and August 24, 1844 and January 21, 1845; Simpson to Barnston, September 4, 1844, HBC Archives, B. 214/c/1.
32 Smith to Barnston, January 21, 1845, HBC Archives, B. 214/c/1.
33 *Ibid.*
34 Barnston to Smith, August 12, 1846, HBC Archives, B. 132/c/1.
35 Smith to Barnston, October 10, 1845, HBC Archives, B. 214/c/1.
36 Smith to Finlayson, August 3, 1847, HBC Archives, B. 134/c/64.
37 Smith to Barnston, March 2, 1846, HBC Archives, B. 214/c/1.
38 Simpson to Smith, September 4, 1845, HBC Archives, D. 4/67.
39 Smith to Simpson, October 15, 1845, HBC Archives, D. 5/15.
40 On his memory for facts and figures, see, for example, Joseph Colmer, cited in Willson, vol. 2, p. 495.
41 Smith to Barnston, October 10, 1845, HBC Archives, B. 214/c/1.
42 Smith to McKenzie, September 1, 1846, HBC Archives B. 170/c/1.
43 Smith to Finlayson, November 10, 1846 and July 21, 1847, HBC Archives, B. 134/c/62 and B. 134/c/64.
44 Smith to Finlayson, November 10, 1846 and July 21, 1847, HBC Archives, B. 134/c/62 and B. 134/c/64; Smith to Barnston, October 12, 1846 and March 19, 1847, HBC Archives B. 214/c/1.
45 Simpson to Barnston, December 20, 1846, January 1, 1847, and January 22, 1847, HBC Archives, B. 214/c/1; Williams, ed., "The 'Character Book' of Governor George Simpson," *Miscellany,* p. 195.
46 Smith to Barnston, March 19, 1847, HBC Archives, B. 214/c/1.
47 *Ibid.*
48 *Ibid.*
49 Williams, ed., "The 'Character Book' of Governor George Simpson," p. 231 and Barnston to Finlayson, May 29, 1847, HBC Archives, B. 134/c/63.
50 Barnston to Simpson, December 3, 1847, HBC Archives, D. 5/20.
51 "Notes and Stray Recollections," NAC, MG 29, A 5.
52 Barnston to Finlayson, July 13, 1847, HBC Archives B. 134/c/1; Finlayson to Barnston, July 21, 1847 and August 20, 1847, B. 214/c/1; Barnston to Simpson, November 5, 1847 and November 27, 1847, D. 5/20.
53 Barnston to Simpson, November 5, 1847, HBC Archives, D. 5/20.
54 Simpson to Barnston, November 13, 1847, HBC Archives, D. 4/69.
55 Barnston to Simpson, December 3, 1847, HBC Archives, D. 5/20.
56 McKenzie to Simpson, December 13, 1847 and December 18, 1847, HBC Archives, D. 4/67.
57 "Notes and Stray Recollections," NAC, MG 29, A 5; Simpson to Smith, January 19, 1848, HBC Archives, D. 4/69.

Chapter Three: **Esquimaux Bay 1847–1852**

1 Cited in Willson, vol. 1, p. 94.
2 Hardisty to Simpson, September 16, 1847, HBC Archives D. 5/20; Simpson to Barnston, May 11, 1847, HBC Archives, D. 4/68; November 13, 1847 and January 18, 1848, HBC Archives, B. 214/c/1; Simpson to Governor and Committee, December 11, 1847, HBC Archives, D. 4/69.

3 Simpson to Nourse, January 18, 1848, HBC Archives, D. 4/37; Simpson to Barnston, January 18, 1848 and March 6, 1848, HBC Archives, B. 214/c/1.
4 "Notes and Stray Recollections," NAC, MG 29, A 5.; Jane Smith to HBC secretary George Smith, July 21, 1848, HBC Archives A. 10/25; Smith to Simpson, January 20, 1848, HBC Archives, D. 5/22. The silver watch which Donald was given before his departure from Forres must have been deemed to be of sentimental value and not worthy of repair since it never appears on the watch repair list; alternatively, it was rarely, if ever, used because of its sentimental value or its unreliability.
5 McKenzie to Simpson, January 24, 1848; Smith to Simpson, January 24, 1848 and January 26, 1848, HBC Archives, D. 5/21.
6 Simpson to Barnston, January 18, 1848, HBC Archives, B. 214/c/1; Barnston circular letter to posts below Tadoussac, January 31, 1848 and Smith to Simpson, February 2, 1848, HBC Archives, D. 5/21. A letter dated February 10 says they left Tadoussac on February 2, but this appears to be a slip of the pen.
7 Smith to Simpson, February 10 and 17, 1848, HBC Archives, D. 5/21. The sick Mohawk, whose name was written Sagayenhas by George Barnston, was still ill in the summer. On July 3 he had reached Tadoussac and was sent from there back to Lachine.
8 Smith to Simpson, March 4, 1848, HBC Archives, D. 5/21.
9 Smith to Simpson, April 7, 1848, HBC Archives, D.5/22.
10 Smith to Simpson, June 10, 1848, HBC Archives, D. 5/22.
11 Smith to Simpson, July 14, 1848, HBC Archives, D. 5/22 and Smith to Hopkins, October 16, 1864, B. 134/c/96.
12 Donald Smith to Barbara Smith, [nd], Willson, vol. 1, pp. 116-117.
13 Field Marshal Sir Donald Stewart to his wife, November 30, 1878, in Elmslie, *Field Marshal Sir Donald Stewart*, p. 226-7; Jane Smith to Hudson's Bay House, June 21, 1848 [misdated July 21], HBC Archives, A. 10/25. The draft response is at the bottom of the page.
14 Smith to Simpson, July 14, 1848, HBC Archives, D. 5/22.
15 Hallock, p. 755.
16 Hallock, pp. 758-759.
17 Smith to Barnston, January 21, 1845, HBC Archives, B. 214/c/1.
18 Hallock, p. 755.
19 Joseph Beioley, Rupert House Report, 1823-1824, HBC Archives, B. 186/e/6.
20 M.H. Pentony to Joseph Hardisty, February 20, 1852, HBC Archives, E. 69/2.
21 Officers and Servants in the Hudson's Bay Company Employ, HBC Archives, A. 30/3.
22 Diary of John Macdonell in Gates, *Five Fur Traders*, pp. 133-4 and Harmon, *Journal*, pp. 65-66. The fact that Jeanny could both read and write English suggests that her father may have been a Hudson's Bay Company officer who took care over her education. Indians were, however, occasionally admitted to the schools and the traders' surprise seems to come from finding such abilities in a native woman, rather than one of mixed-blood.
23 George Budge, George Grot and Samuel Harvey to John Hodgson at Albany, October 8, 1809, HBC Archives, A. 1/50; Albany Journal, March 30, 1812, HBC Archives, B. 3/a/115.
24 Isabella Hardisty at Matawagamingue to her brother Richard, January 16, 1845, Glenbow, M5908, Box 8.
25 Richard Hardisty to George Simpson, September 16, 1847, HBC Archives, D. 5/20; Richard Hardisty to his son Richard, April 15, 1865; Margaret Hardisty to her son Richard, September 3, 1867 and April 8, 1872, Glenbow, M5908, Box 8.
26 Register of Baptisms and Burials at Eastmain, HBC Archives, B. 59/z/1 and *Prince of Wales* log, HBC Archives, C. 1/834.
27 Richard Hardisty to George Simpson, January 23, 1843 and January 30, 1844, HBC Archives, D. 5/8 and D. 5/10.
28 Isabella Hardisty to her brother Richard, January 16, 1845, Glenbow, M5908, Box 8.
29 Richard Hardisty to his son Richard, January 15, 1845, Glenbow, M5908, Box 8.
30 No photographs of George, Henry or Charlotte appear to have survived.

31 Hardisty to Archibald Barclay, July 14, 1849 and July 16, 1850, HBC Archives, A. 11/58; Hardisty to Simpson, September 25, 1849, HBC Archives, D. 5/26; Simpson to Hardisty, March 28, 1850, HBC Archives, D. 4/71.
32 Cited in Willson, vol. 1, p. 117.
33 Smith to Simpson, September 21, 1850, HBC Archives, D. 5/28.
34 Hardisty to Simpson, September 25, 1849, HBC Archives, D. 5/26.
35 *Ibid.*
36 Barbara Smith to Simpson, January 1, 1850, HBC Archives, D. 5/27; Simpson to Barbara Smith, January 30, 1850, HBC Archives, D. 4/70.
37 Brown, *Strangers in Blood*, p. 136; Barbara Smith to James Keith, July 15, 1851, NAC, MG 19, A 41; W.G. Smith to Simpson, October 25, 1850, January 17, 1851 and September 16, 1851, HBC Archives, D. 5/29, D. 5/30 and D. 5/31; Scottish Record Office, CS 17/Minute Book, vol. 70, pp. 646-647.
38 Hardisty to Simpson, September 23 and October 21, 1850, HBC Archives, D. 5/28 and D. 5/29.
39 Hardisty to Simpson, [nd, probably about July 20, 1850], HBC Archives, B. 153/a/12.
40 The son of one of the senior North West Company directors, Simon McGillivray had been assigned to Hamilton Inlet in 1821 and remained there till ill health forced his retirement in 1839. Simpson seems to have left him in Labrador to keep him from making trouble elsewhere, but seized the opportunity of his resignation to try to force some improvements on the district.
41 Smith to Simpson, September 21, 1850, HBC Archives, D. 5/28.
42 Simpson to Hardisty, March 20, 1851, HBC Archives, D. 4/72.
43 Hardisty to Simpson, October 21, 1850, HBC Archives, D. 5/29.
44 Smith to Simpson, October 26, 1850, HBC Archives, D. 5/29.
45 North West River Journal, January 28, 1851, notes that Smith and Lyne [sic] arrived late that evening and that Cameron had drowned on December 15. The information is repeated in a fairer hand in February, but the cooper is now called Lyall and the drowning is said to have happened on December 18. As the diarist would have had a better opportunity to learn the facts while the men were at North West River, it seems likely that the latter entry is more reliable; HBC Archives B. 153/a/12; Hardisty to Simpson, July 16, 1851, HBC Archives D. 5/31.
46 Simpson to Hardisty, July 29, 1851, HBC Archives, D. 4/43.
47 Hardisty to Simpson, September 21, 1851, HBC Archives, D. 5/31.
48 Cited in Willson, vol. 1, p. 227.
49 Smith to Simpson, July 17, 1851, HBC Archives, D. 5/31.
50 Isabella Hardisty to her brother Richard, July 18, 1851, Glenbow, M5908, Box 8.
51 Richard Hardisty to his son Richard, August 11, 1852, Glenbow, M5908, Box 8.
52 Smith to Simpson, September 20, 1851, HBC Archives, D. 5/31.
53 Smith to Simpson, July 17, 1851, HBC Archives, D. 5/31.
54 Hardisty to Simpson, July 16, 1851, HBC Archives, D. 5/31.
55 Richard Hardisty to his son Richard, August 11, 1852, Glenbow, M475.
56 Simpson to Hardisty and Simpson to Smith, March 26, 1852, HBC Archives, D. 4/44.
57 Hallock, p. 755.
58 Smith to Simpson, October 7, 1851, HBC Archives, D. 5/32.
59 Smith to Simpson, September 22, 1852, HBC Archives, D. 5/34.
60 Smith to Simpson, September 23, 1852, HBC Archives, D. 5/34.
61 Smith to Simpson, October 14, 1852, HBC Archives, D. 5/32.
62 *Ibid.*
63 *Ibid.*
64 *Ibid.*

Chapter Four: **Chief Trader 1852–1861**

1 Willson, vol. 1, p. 122.
2 Mary McPherson to Joseph Hardisty, August 30, 1856, HBC Archives, E. 69/2; Isabella Grant to Richard Hardisty, October 12, 1853, Glenbow, M5908, Box 8.

3 Isabella Grant to Richard Hardisty, October 12, 1853, Glenbow, M5908, Box 8; Smith to Simpson, October 13, 1853, HBC Archives, D. 5/38.
4 Mary McPherson to Joseph Hardisty, August 30, 1856, HBC Archives, E. 69/2; Isabella Grant to Richard Hardisty, October 12, 1853, Glenbow, M5908, Box 8.
5 Smith to Simpson, October 13, 1853, HBC Archives, D. 5/38.
6 Isabella Grant to Richard Hardisty, October 12, 1853, Glenbow, M5908, Box 8.
7 Isabella Grant to Richard Hardisty, October 14, 1855, Glenbow, M5908, Box 8.
8 Smith to Simpson, October 12, 1853, HBC Archives, D. 5/38.
9 Simpson to Smith, April 1, 1853, HBC Archives, D. 4/59.
10 Baikie, *Labrador Memories*, pp. 9-10.
11 *Periodical Accounts*, vol. 21, p. 215 and vol. 22, p. 441.
12 Simpson to Smith, [nd] March 1854, HBC Archives, D. 4/81.
13 Smith to Barclay, September 28, 1854, HBC Archives, A. 11/58.
14 Barclay's reprimand is quoted in Smith's response.
15 Simpson to Hardisty, April 19, 1855, HBC Archives, D. 4/50.
16 Simpson to Smith, March 29, 1855, HBC Archives, D. 4/50.
17 Smith to Simpson, September 26, 1855 and October 20, 1855, HBC Archives, D. 5/40; Simpson to Grant, January 24, 1856, HBC Archives, D. 4/51.
18 Simpson to Smith, March 15, 1856, HBC Archives, D. 4/83; Isabella Grant to Richard Hardisty, October 14, 1855, Glenbow, M5908, Box 8.
19 Isabella Grant to Mary McPherson, April 6, 1856, Glenbow, M941, Box 1.
20 Mary McPherson to Joseph Hardisty, August 30, 1856, HBC Archives, E. 69/2.
21 Bell to James Watt at Montreal, September 25, 1855, HBC Archives, B. 134/c/72; Simpson to Smith, March 15, 1856, HBC Archives, D. 4/51.
22 Donald Smith to W.G. Smith, June 27, 1856, HBC Archives, B. 134/c/73.
23 Smith to Simpson, October 20, 1856, HBC Archives, D. 5/42.
24 *Labrador Memories*, p. 11-12. Words in parentheses were missing in the original manuscript and supplied by the editors.
25 *Labrador Memories*, pp. 12-13.
26 *Labrador Memories*, p. 14.
27 *Labrador Memories*, p. 13.
28 *Periodical Accounts*, vol. 22, p. 442.
29 *Periodical Accounts*, vol. 22, p. 445.
30 *Periodical Accounts*, vol. 22, p. 446.
31 *Ibid.*
32 "Notes and Stray Recollections," NAC, MG 29, A 5.
33 *Periodical Accounts*, vol. 22, p. 448.
34 Elsner to Smith, September 7, 1858, HBC Archives, B. 134/c/77.
35 Simpson to Smith, March 26, 1858, D. 4/54.
36 Simpson, *Narrative of a Journey*, pp. 45-46.
37 *Report from the Select Committee*, p. 48; Simpson, *Narrative of a Journey*, pp. 55-56.
38 *Report from the Select Committee*, p. 330.
39 Smith to Simpson, September 10, 1857, HBC Archives, D. 5/45.
40 Smith to Kernaghan, January 18, 1857, Willson, vol. 1, pp. 146-147.
41 Rigolet Journal, HBC Archives, B. 183/a/13 and Simpson to Smith, March 26, 1858, HBC Archives, D. 4/54.
42 Smith to Simpson, September 10, 1857, HBC Archives, D. 5/45.
43 Simpson to Smith, March 26, 1858, HBC Archives, D. 4/54.
44 Simpson to Smith, March 23, 1859, HBC Archives, D. 4/84.
45 *Ibid.*
46 Donald Smith to W.G. Smith, September 20, 1858, HBC Archives, D. 5/47.
47 Smith to Simpson, October 19, 1859, HBC Archives, D. 5/50.
48 Simpson to Smith, March 15, 1856, HBC Archives, D. 4/83.
49 Smith to Fraser, August 10, 1859, HBC Archives, A. 11/58.
50 Willson, vol. 1, p. 124.
51 North West River Journal, August 19, 1855, HBC Archives, B. 153/a/15.

52 *Periodical Accounts*, vol. 22, p. 446.
53 Fleming, Notes, probably for an article or speech, NAC, MG 29, B 1, vol. 96.
54 Hallock, p. 759.
55 Willson, vol. 1, pp. 158 - 160.
56 Baikie, *Labrador Memories*, p. 16.
57 James Fraser, cited in Willson, vol. 1, p. 228.
58 Willson, vol. 1, p. 229.
59 Willson, vol. 1, pp.159-160 and Smith to Simpson, October 6, 1860, HBC Archives, B. 134/c/80.

Chapter Five: **Chief Factor 1862–1869**

1 Willson, vol. 1, p. 227.
2 Fraser to Hopkins, February 4, 1862, March 26, 1862 and May 15, 1862, HBC Archives, B. 134/c/85.
3 Fraser to Smith, May 9, 1862, HBC Archives, A.6/37.
4 Smith to Hopkins, August 16, 1862, HBC Archives, B. 134/c/87.
5 Smith to Hopkins, August 16, 1862; August 21, 1863; March 21, 1864, HBC Archives, B. 134/c/87; B. 134/c/91; B. 134/c/93.
6 Fraser to Smith, May 12, 1863, HBC Archives, A. 6/38.
7 *Ibid.*
8 Smith to Fraser, July 22, 1863, Willson, vol. 1, p. 166.
9 Smith to Hopkins, [nd], Willson, vol. 1, pp. 180-181.
10 Watkin, *Canada and the States*, p. 124-125.
11 Head to Smith et al, July 22, 1863, Willson, vol. 1, p. 184.
12 Smith to Fraser, July 22, 1863, HBC Archives, A. 11/58.
13 Hopkins and his brothers, though forced to make their way in the world from an early age, nonetheless developed a strong interest in the arts. His elder brother's first born was the poet, Gerard Manley Hopkins.
14 Connolly to Hopkins, October 4, 1862, HBC Archives, B. 134/c/88.
15 Smith to Hopkins, September 19, 1864, HBC Archives, B. 134/c/95.
16 Willson, vol. 1, p. 115 and statement by Kenyon enclosed in Peter Ryan to Sir John A. Macdonald, December 31, 1878, NAC MG 26, A, vol. 306. In the 1878 letter, the ungrateful Kenyon discusses the Smiths' domestic relations and claims the offer to educate his child was a trap. By this time, he had been dismissed by the HBC, was unemployed and was trying to sell this so-called information to the Conservative Party.
17 Smith to Hopkins, October 16, 1864, HBC Archives, B. 134/c/96.
18 Smith to Hopkins, November 24 and 26, 1864, HBC Archives, B. 134/c/96 and Willson, vol. 1, pp. 11, 190-192 and 217. Smith left his bedding behind at Nathan Norman's home and it was returned the following year; the Scotch plaid which his mother had given him when he left home was accidentally omitted, however, and remained with Norman's descendants as a souvenir at least until the early years of this century.
19 Willson, vol. 1, p. 207. Willson's unnamed source places this incident in 1866 but he must have misremembered. Smith was not in Montreal before June 1, 1866 but in March that year he was writing to Hopkins about his cousin in a way which makes it clear they had already met. As well, a letter from Stephen to Smith, in HBC Archives B. 132/c/1, is dated February 1, 1865.
20 Stephen to Smith, February 1, 1865, HBC Archives, B. 132/c/1 and Smith to Hopkins, December 28, 1866, HBC Archives, B. 134/c/104.
21 Smith to Fraser, March 28, 1865, HBC Archives, A. 10/61.
22 Thomas, *Forgotten Railways: Scotland*, pp. 184-198 and Willson, vol. 1, p. 194.
23 Smith to Fraser, March 13, 1865, HBC Archives, A. 10/61 and Smith to Fraser, [nd], cited in Willson, vol. 1, p. 195.
24 Colvile to Lampson, [nd], Willson, vol. 1, pp. 194-195.
25 Smith to Barnston, [nd], Willson, vol. 1, p. 199.
26 *Report of the Governor and Committee*, July 5, 1866, p. 28, HBC Archives.

27 Smith to Fraser, March 13, 16, 20, 25, 28, 1865, HBC Archives, A. 10/61 and Fraser to Smith, June 9, 1865, HBC Archives, A. 6/39.
28 Willson, vol. 1, p. 200; William Armit to Beckles Willson, July 8, 1915, NAC, MG 29, A 11. The Armit letter is among the Roderick MacFarlane Papers, though it clearly belongs to the Beckles Willson Papers, MG 30, D 5, among the correspondence he accumulated in preparation for his 1915 biography of Lord Strathcona.
29 Willson, vol. 1, p. 201; W.G. Smith to John Stuart Smith, June 16, 1865, HBC Archives, A. 5/30; Davis to W.G. Smith, June 15, 1865, HBC Archives, A.10/61; Smith to Fraser, October 15, 1865, HBC Archives, A. 11/58.
30 Smith to Hopkins, October 15, 1865, HBC Archives, B. 134/c/100.
31 Hopkins to Smith, November 1, 1865, HBC Archives, B. 134/b/23; Smith to Hopkins, November 24, 1865, HBC Archives, B. 134/c/100; Hopkins to William Hardisty, May 6, 1867, HBC Archives, B. 134/b/27 and Smith to Richard Hardisty, November 19, 1865, Glenbow, M5908, Box 8.
32 Smith to Hopkins, November 24, 1865, HBC Archives, B. 134/c/100.
33 Fraser to Hopkins, November 30, 1865, HBC Archives, B. 134/c/100 and December 14, 1865, HBC Archives, A. 6/40.
34 Smith to Hopkins, January 25, 1866, HBC Archives, B. 134/c/101.
35 Fraser to Moravian Brethren, December 13, 1865, Moravian Church Archives.
36 Smith to Hopkins, January 25, 1866, HBC Archives, B. 134/c/101.
37 Smith to Hopkins, March 3 and March 17, 1866, HBC Archives, B. 134/c/101; Smith to Hopkins, May 1, 1866, HBC Archives, B. 134/c/102 and Smith to Hopkins, May 23, 1867, HBC Archives, B. 134/c/106.
38 Smith to Hopkins, June 8, 1866, HBC Archives, A. 11/31.
39 Smith to Hopkins, March 3, 1866, HBC Archives, B. 134/c/101 and Smith to Hopkins, June 19, 1866, HBC Archives, B. 134/c/102.
40 Smith to Hopkins, March 3, 1866, HBC Archives, B. 134/c/102 and Willson, vol. 1, p. 213.
41 Cited in Willson, vol. 1, p. 209-213.
42 Smith to Fraser, August 4, 1866, HBC Archives, A. 11/51.
43 Smith to Hopkins, August 11, 1866, HBC Archives, B. 134/c/103.
44 Smith to Fraser, August 23, 1866, HBC Archives, A. 11/58.
45 Smith to Hopkins, December 28, 1866, HBC Archives, B. 134/c/104 and Maggie Smith to her uncle, Richard Hardisty, April 16, 1867, Glenbow, M5908, Box 8.
46 *Annales de la Propagation de la Foi*, 1868, cited in Willson, vol. 1, pp. 223-224; North West River Journal, July 21, 1867, HBC Archives, B. 153/a/18; Church to Smith, September 6, 1869, HBC Archives, B. 134/c/115. Church's letter is largely given over to complaints about his standard of living, obviously provoked by instructions to reduce his costs. "If I have to send a requisition to Montreal for ever dozen of Eggs or pound of fresh meat I beg for house use I would have to ask at least 6 weeks before the time and then phraps not get an answer I have lived since I came to Bersimis has cheaply as possable and never had to Live on as poor fare in my life before if you where to look at the amounts paid per annum for fresh meat & before I came you would find they amount nearly to as mutch as my House Expences alltogether."
47 Donald Smith to W.G. Smith, October 18, 1867, HBC Archives, A. 11/58.
48 Charles Linder, "Report of the Year 1867-1868," in *Periodical Accounts*, vol. 20.
49 Smith to W.G. Smith, October 18, 1867, HBC Archives, A. 11/58.
50 Murdoch McPherson to Joseph McPherson, March 2, 1859, Glenbow, M941.
51 Lampson to Northcote, November 26, 1868, cited in Willson, vol. 1, pp. 224-225.
52 W.G. Smith to Donald Smith, April 21, 1869, HBC Archives, A. 6/43.
53 Donald Smith to W.G. Smith, October 1, 1869, HBC Archives, B. 134/b/29; W.G. Smith to Donald Smith, October 21, 1869, HBC Archives, A. 6/45 and Simpson circular letter to Private Cash customers, March 1855, B. 134/b/11.
54 William Lucas Hardisty to Smith, May 13, 1869, HBC Archives, B. 134/c/114 and Alexander Christie to Smith, July 28, 1869, HBC Archives, B. 134/c/115.
55 McPherson to Smith, June 8, 1869 and July 28, 1869, HBC Archives, B. 134/c/114 and B. 134/c/115.

56 Correspondence and newspaper clippings concerning Joseph McPherson and his family, Glenbow, M941; Patterson, *History of the County of Pictou*, passim; mortgage and other documents concerning Norway House, HBC Archives, E. 33/1.

Chapter Six: **Louis Riel and the Northwest 1869–1870**

1 Butler, *The Great Lone Land*, p. 42.
2 Accounts of the disturbances at Red River are found in Morton, *Manitoba: A History*, Stanley, *Riel*, Morton, ed., *Begg's Red River Journal*, Donald Smith's unpublished report on his mission in PRO, CO42/685, the published report in Canada Sessional Papers, 1870, vol. 5, no. 12 and Canada, *House of Commons Debates*, April 2 and 3, 1875.
3 *New York Times*, May 5, 1869; Smith to Hopkins, October 12, 1864, NAC, MG 30, D 5.
4 Fleming, *Memorial*, pp. 7 and 22.
5 Mactavish to W.G. Smith, August 10, 1869, HBC Archives, A. 11/99.
6 Mactavish to W.G. Smith, October 13, 1869, HBC Archives, A. 12/45.
7 Bowles, "Manitoba's Government House," p. 4.
8 Howe to McDougall, October 31, 1869, cited in Willson, vol. 1, p. 264.
9 Cited in Morton, *Manitoba: A History*, p. 130.
10 Smith to Howe, November 24, 1869, Sessional Paper, no. 12.
11 Howe to McDougall, December 7, 1869, Sessional Paper, no. 12.
12 Thomas Hardisty to Joseph Hargrave, October 19, 1869, HBC Archives, B. 235/c/1.
13 Donald Smith to W.G. Smith, November 26, 1869, HBC Archives, A. 11/33.
14 Smith to Kittson, November 25, 1869, HBC Archives, B. 134/b/29.
15 Stephen to Macdonald, November 27, 1869, NAC, MG 26, A, vol. 102.
16 Macdonald to Stephen, November 29, 1869 and December 1, 1869, NAC, MG 26, A, vol. 516.
17 Donald Smith to W.G. Smith, December 3, 1869, HBC Archives, A. 11/33.
18 *Ibid.*
19 W.G. Smith to Donald Smith, December 2, 1869, HBC Archives, A. 6/45.
20 Rose to Macdonald, December 9, 1869, NAC, MG 26, A, vol. 101.
21 Macdonald to Smith, December 12, 1869, NAC, MG 26, A, vol. 516.
22 Donald Smith to W.G. Smith, December 15, 1869, HBC Archives, A. 11/33 and Macdonald to Stephen, December 9, 1869, NAC, MG 26, A, vol. 516.
23 Smith to Macdonald, December 20, 1869, NAC, MG 26, A, vol. 102.
24 Mactavish to W.G. Smith, December 28, 1869, HBC Archives, D. 1/11; Willson, vol. 1, p. 311.
25 HBC Accounts for 1869 and 1870, HBC Archives D. 26/25; Tupper, *Recollections*, p. 106.
26 Macdonald to Rose, January 21, 1870, NAC, MG 26, A, vol. 516.
27 Tupper, *Recollections*, 107-118.
28 Morton, ed., *Begg's Red River Journal*, p. 252.
29 Healy, *Women of Red River*, p. 47 and Willson, vol. 1, pp. 326-327.
30 Morton, ed., *Begg's Red River Journal*, p. 200.

Aujourd'hui sa couronne
Est un songe passé
Et le trône qu'on lui donne
Est un trône percé
Main il dit qu'à présent
Il est bien suffisant.

31 Smith to Macdonald, January 8, 1870, NAC, MG 26 A, vol. 102.
32 Begg, *Creation*, pp. 219-220.
33 Morton, ed., *Begg's Red River Journal*, p. 264.
34 *The New Nation*, January 21, 1870, cited in Morton, ed., *Begg's Red River Journal*, p. 265.
35 PRO, CO42/685; Thibault to Howe, January 22, 1870, cited in Wilson, vol. 1, p. 328; *Statement of Claims Made upon the Dominion Government*, 1871. Donald Smith was not paid a fee for his work on behalf of the government in the winter of 1869-1870, nor did he seek one.

36 Papers on Red River Disturbance, PRO, CO42/685.
37 *Ibid.*
38 *The New Nation*, January 21, 1870, cited in Morton, ed., *Begg's Red River Journal*, p. 273. By describing his wife as a native of Rupert's Land, Donald Smith conveyed to his listeners the fact that she was of mixed blood.
39 Mactavish to W.G. Smith, January 22, 1870, HBC Archives, D. 11/1.
40 Smith to an unknown correspondent, [nd], cited in Willson, vol. 1, p. 242.
41 Papers on Red River Disturbance, PRO, CO42/685.
42 *The New Nation*, February 11, 1870, cited in Stanley, *Riel*, p. 94.
43 Smith, "Report as Canadian Commissioner to Red River," *Sessional Paper*, no. 12. This printed version of the report is inconsistent in its spellings which have here been corrected.
44 *The New Nation*, February 11, 1870, cited in Stanley, *Riel*, p. 96.
45 Morton, ed., *Begg's Red River Journal*, p. 303.
46 *The New Nation*, February 18, 1870, cited in Stanley, *Riel*, p. 107.
47 Papers on Red River Disturbance, PRO, CO42/685.
48 *Ibid.*
49 *Ibid.*
50 Martin, *James J. Hill*, pp. 74-75.
51 Smith to Northcote, May 9, 1870, cited in Willson, vol. 1, pp. 379-380.
52 Northcote diary, April 21, 1870, BL, Add. 50,063A.
53 Northcote diary, April 24, 1870, BL, Add. 50,063A.
54 Northcote to Lampson, April 24, 1870, BL, Add. 50,056.
55 John McTavish to W.G. Smith, August 3, 1870, HBC Archives, A. 11/99; Donald Smith to W.G. Smith, August 1, 1870, HBC Archives, D. 11/1.
56 Smith to Lampson and Committee, August 1, 1870, HBC Archives, A. 11/51.
57 Donald Smith to W.G. Smith, August 1, 1870, HBC Archives, D. 11/1.
58 Donald Smith to W.G. Smith, August 21, 1870, HBC Archives, A. 11/7.
59 *Ibid.*
60 Wolseley to Louisa Wolseley, August 21, 1870, Hove, W/P.1.
61 Lower Fort Garry Journal, August 23, 1870, HBC Archives, B. 303/a/1.
62 Wolseley to Louisa Wolseley, August 24, 1870, Hove, W/P.1.
63 Young, *Manitoba Memories*, p. 188.
64 Wemyss Simpson to Smith, enclosed in Smith to Dugald Mactavish, April 13, 1871, HBC Archives, B. 134/c/120.
65 Young, *Manitoba Memories*, pp. 189-190.
66 Butler, *Great Lone Land*, pp. 192-193.
67 Donald Smith to W.G. Smith, August 27, 1870, HBC Archives, A. 11/99.

Chapter Seven: **A Representative Man 1870–1871**

1 Smith, Election address, *Manitoban*, December 3, 1870.
2 *The Manitoba News-Letter*, September 13, 1870.
3 Begg and Nursey, *Ten Years in Winnipeg*, passim; Hill, *From Home to Home*, p. 61; Healy, *Winnipeg's Early Days*, p. 22 and passim.
4 John McTavish to W.G. Smith, June 25, 1870 and July 12, 1870, HBC Archives, A. 11/99; Smith to Armit, February 19, 1871, HBC Archives, A. 11/100.
5 Donald Smith to W.G. Smith, September 17, 1870, HBC Archives, A. 11/99.
6 Donald Smith to W.G. Smith, October 10, 1870 and October 19, 1870, HBC Archives, D. 11/1.
7 Donald Smith to W.G. Smith, October 19, 1870 and January 22, 1871, HBC Archives, A. 11/99 and A. 11/100; Edward Trail to Adams Archibald, [nd], PAM, G12/A1.
8 Butler, *Great Lone Land*, pp. 299-300. The animal to which he refers is the cabrit, a name for the pronghorn or American antelope.
9 Richard Hardisty to Christie, December 28, 1870, copied and sent to Smith with a note that it was "a plain statement of facts," HBC Archives, D. 12/2. The worry about miners refers to a belief that a gold rush was imminent.

10 Lieutenant Butler's Report, March 10, 1871, in *Great Lone Land*, p.381.
11 Donald Smith to W.G. Smith, September 24, 1870, HBC Archives, A. 11/99; Smith to George Stephen, February 5, 1871, HBC Archives, D. 11/2; Red River Rebellion, Miscellaneous Papers, HBC Archives, E. 9/1.
12 Donald Smith to W.G. Smith, October 10, 1870, HBC Archives, D. 11/1.
13 Johnson to Simpson, April 9, 1857, extract in Skene, Edwards and Garson, Box A40.
14 Smith to McDonald, September 20, 1870, PABC, A/D/20/G19.
15 Jean d'Artigue, *Six Years in the Canadian North-West*, p. 45.
16 Donald Smith to W.G. Smith, September 17, 1870, HBC Archives, A. 11/99.
17 Northcote to Smith, January 6, 1871, HBC Archives, A. 7/4.
18 Graham to Northcote, January 21, 1871, HBC Archives, A. 11/100.
19 Graham to Northcote, a second letter dated January 21, 1871, HBC Archives, A. 11/100.
20 *Ibid.*
21 Smith to Lampson, February 19, 1871, HBC Archives, A. 11/100.
22 Smith to Stephen, February 5, 1871, HBC Archives, D. 11/2.
23 *Manitoban*, December 31, 1870; the newspaper report sent to London is undated and unsourced but probably appeared in Saint Paul's *Pioneer Press*, in which case it would have been forwarded to Montreal by Norman Kittson and sent from there to London by Dugald Mactavish; it is in HBC Archives, A. 11/99.
24 Willson, vol. 1, p. 402.
25 *Manitoban*, March 18, 1871.
26 *Manitoban*, May 2, 1874.
27 Smith Deed Register, Hudson's Bay Company Archives, E. 33/1.
28 Edgar Andrew Collard, "All Our Yesterdays", *Montreal Gazette*, April 9, 1955.
29 *Manitoban*, December 3, 1870.
30 *Manitoban*, December 17, 1870.
31 *Manitoban*, February 25, 1871.
32 *Manitoban*, March 25, 1871.
33 Armit to Mactavish, February 21, 1871 and March 10, 1871, HBC Archives, A. 11/34; Lampson to Smith, January 6, 1871, HBC Archives, A. 7/4.
34 "Memorandum," addressed to Mr. Cunningham, cited in Willson, vol. 1, p. 413.
35 *Journal of High Commission*, written by Donald Smith and addressed to Curtis Lampson, cited in Willson, vol. 1, pp. 414-415.
36 Macdonald to Tupper, April 27, 1871, cited in Willson, vol. 1, p. 417.
37 *Verbatim Transcript of Proceedings*, General Court, November 22, 1870, pp. 11-12, HBC Archives, A. 2/17; "Opinion of Sir Roundell Palmer and Montague Bere," February 21, 1871, HBC Archives, A. 39/8.
38 Northcote diary, April 21, 1870, BL, Add. 50,063A.
39 Campbell to MacFarlane, January 31, 1871 and June 2, 1871, NAC, MG 29, A 11.
40 Fortescue to unnamed correspondent, [nd], cited in Willson, vol. 1, p. 426.
41 Cited in Willson, vol. 1, p. 427.
42 "Opinions of the Attorney-General [R.P. Collier] and Mr. Jessel, QC," June 29, 1870, James McDougall Papers, cited in Oleson, "The Commissioned Officers of the Hudson's Bay Company," p. 24.
43 Smith to Armit, June 28, 1871, HBC Archives, A. 10/83.
44 Smith to MacFarlane, October 16, 1871, NAC, MG 29, A 11, and Smith to Armit, April 8, 1872, HBC Archives, A. 10/85.
45 Lockhart to MacFarlane, December 28, 1871, NAC, MG 29, A 11 and Hamilton to unnamed correspondent, probably MacFarlane, [nd], cited in Willson, vol. 1, p. 429.
46 Lockhart to MacFarlane, December 28, 1871, NAC, MG 29, A 11; Smith to Anderson, [nd], cited in Willson, vol. 1, p. 430.

Chapter Eight: **Chief Commissioner 1871–1873**

1 From a letter by Donald Smith, February 11, 1873, cited in Willson, vol. 1, p. 520-521.
2 Graham to Northcote, January 21, 1871, HBC Archives, A. 11/100.
3 Graham to Northcote, January 31, 1871, HBC Archives, A. 11/100.

4 Graham to Lampson, April 4, 1871, HBC Archives, A. 10/83 and Minute Book, August 1, 1871, HBC Archives, A. 1/149; Armit to Smith, April 17, 1872, HBC Archives, A. 6/47.
5 Bank of Montreal Resolve Book, NAC, MG 28, II 2.
6 Smith, Deed Register, HBC Archives, E. 33/1; NAC, MG 29, A 5, vol. 14; Skene Edwards and Garson, Box A32.
7 Grant, *Ocean to Ocean,* pp. 84-85.
8 Casault to her friend Mrs. Bowles, December 12, 1870, NAC, MG 29, C 119.
9 Skene Edwards and Garson, Box A40. Prior to 1869, the Hudson's Bay Company sold none of its land but leased plots for 999 years, a system which allowed it to retain its monopoly. The Rupert's Land Act of 1868 stipulated that titles to land conferred by the HBC should be confirmed by the crown. This involved applying for a patent which converted leases to full ownership. Silver Heights was the subject of a court case in 1908 when a claim, based on a misunderstanding of the leasehold principle, was brought by one of the Rowand descendants. Smith had successfully applied for patents to all the Silver Heights land and as soon as the facts became known, the Rowand solicitors withdrew, saying they would offer no evidence and could see that they could not win the case.
10 Skene Edwards and Garson, A40.
11 Proclamation, October 3, 1871, cited in Stanley, *Riel*; Smith to Armit, October 8, 1871, HBC Archives, A. 12/14.
12 Stanley, *Riel*, pp. 169-171; Hamilton to an unnamed correspondent, November 2, 1871, cited in Willson, vol. 1, p. 448; Bryce, *Manitoba Memories*, p. 216. O'Donoghue's name is now generally spelled with a "g", though the letter was often omitted during his lifetime.
13 Elliott, *Winnipeg As It Is*, p. 1.
14 Major Mulvey in *Manitoba Liberal*, cited in Young, *Manitoba Memories*, p. 219-220.
15 Young, *Manitoba Memories*, p. 226.
16 Stanley, *Riel*, pp. 173-175.
17 Smith to Armit, October 11, 1871, HBC Archives, A. 12/14.
18 *Report of the Select Committee*, 1874.
19 *Ibid.*
20 Smith to Armit, February 11 and November 28, 1873, HBC Archives, A. 12/14; January 10, 1874, HBC Archives, A. 12/15.
21 Smith to Armit, January 23, 1872, HBC Archives, A. 12/14.
22 Smith to Armit, December 2, 1872, HBC Archives, A. 12/14.
23 Smith to Armit, December 2, 1872, January 24, 1873, and April 11, 1873, HBC Archives, A. 12/14.
24 Smith to Armit, May 15, 1874, HBC Archives, A. 12/15.
25 Smith to Archibald, October 24, 1871, HBC Archives, D. 11/1; *Manitoban*, March 4, 1872; *Debates of the House of Commons*, March 11, 1878.
26 Smith to Armit, August 26, 1872 and November 24, 1872, HBC Archives, A. 12/14.
27 Bissett to Armit, October 17, 1873, HBC Archives, A. 11/34 and Thomas Hardisty to Richard Hardisty, January 30, 1874, Glenbow, M5908, Box 8.
28 *Manitoban*, February 26, 1872 and Willson, vol. 1, p. 488-492.
29 McDougall, *In the Days of the Red River Rebellion*, pp. 237-238.
30 *Manitoba Weekly Free Press*, [nd], in HBC Archives, A. 12/14 and Schultz to John Gunn, September 23, 1872, PAM, MG14/B29.
31 Hamilton to MacFarlane, December 21, 1872, NAC, MG 29, A 11, vol. 1.

Chapter Nine: **The Pacific Scandal 1873**

1 Henry Hardisty to MacFarlane, January 18, 1874, NAC, MG 29 A 11, vol. 1.
2 Report of a Committee of the Canadian Privy Council, April 19, 1871 in HBC Archives, A. 13/18.
3 Canada, *Sessional Papers,* vol. 5, no. 44, *Statement of Claims; Commons Debates*, March 23, 1876.

4 Smith to Armit, January 12, 1872, April 11, 1872, November 15, 1872, January 31, 1873, April 4, 1873, October 24, 1873, HBC Archives, A. 12/14 and June 5, 1873, HBC Archives, D. 11/5.
5 Testimony of Donald Smith, *Report of the Select Committee*.
6 Cited in Willson, vol. 1, p. 465.
7 *Report of the Royal Commissioners*.
8 *Ibid*.
9 *Ibid*.
10 *Ibid*.
11 *Report of the Royal Commissioners*; Armit to Smith, June 6, 1872, HBC Archives, A. 6/47.
12 Smith to Armit, November 8, 1872, HBC Archives, A. 12/14.
13 Healy, *Winnipeg's Early Days*, p. 25.
14 *Report of the Royal Commissioners*.
15 Smith to Northcote, October 1873, cited in Willson, vol. 1, p. 465.
16 Rose to Macdonald, May 1, 1873, NAC, MG 26, A, vol. 258.
17 Campbell to Alexander Morris, November 29, 1873, PAM, MG12/B2.
18 Smith to Armit, October 24, 1873, HBC Archives, A. 12/14; Smith to Macdonald, two cables in September 1873, dates unclear, NAC, MG 26, A, vol. 126. In 1878, Tupper accused Smith of having promised in these cables to support the government but in fact they make no commitment beyond the date at which he hoped to arrive in Ottawa.
19 Morris to Macdonald, September 20, 1873, PAM, MG12/B1.
20 Smith to Armit, October 24, 1873, HBC Archives, A. 12/14; Clarke to Richard Hardisty, October 13, 1873, Glenbow, M477, Box 2.
21 Memoirs of Angus McKay, cited in MacGregor, *Senator Hardisty's Prairies,* p. 108; Cowie, *Company of Adventurers*, p. 460; Henry Hardisty to Roderick MacFarlane, January 18, 1874, NAC, MG 29, A 11.
22 *Report of the Select Committee*, Ottawa, 1874; Smith to Armit, October 24, 1873, HBC Archives, A. 12/14.
23 Campbell to Morris, November 29, 1873, PAM, MG12/B2.
24 "Memorandum for Mr. Buckingham," quoted in Willson, vol. 1, p. 478.
25 *Debates of the House of Commons*, May 10, 1878.
26 *Ibid*.
27 Campbell to Morris, November 29, 1873, PAM, MG12/B2.
28 *Toronto Mail*, November 6, 1873.
29 Young, *Public Men and Public Life*, vol. 2, p. 153.
30 Burt, "Peter Mitchell on John A. Macdonald," p. 217 and *Report of the Select Committee*.
31 *Debates of the House of Commons*, May 10, 1878.
32 *Globe*, November 7, 1873.

Chapter Ten: **Land Commissioner 1874–1879**

1 Butler, *Great Lone Land*, p. 331. He is describing the confluence of the North and South Saskatchewan Rivers.
2 *Manitoban*, November 21, 1874.
3 Armit to Smith, July 9, 1872, HBC Archives, A. 6/47.
4 Armit to Smith, December 9, 1872 and July 22, 1873, HBC Archives, A. 6/47 and A. 6/48.
5 Northcote to Smith, December 3, 1872, HBC Archives, A. 7/4.
6 Northcote to Smith, December 27, 1873, HBC Archives, A. 7/4.
7 Colvile to Smith, February 11, 1873, HBC Archives, A. 7/4.
8 Minutes, July 8, 1873, HBC Archives, A. 1/149.
9 Armit to Smith, December 24, 1872, HBC Archives, A. 6/47.
10 Minutes, July 15, 1873, HBC Archives, A. 1/149.
11 Armit to Smith, May 5, 1874, HBC Archives, A. 6/48.
12 Colvile to Grahame, June 5, 1874, HBC Archives, A. 7/4.

13 Grahame to Smith, March 25, 1874, HBC Archives, D. 16/1.
14 Grahame to Bissett, August 17, 1874 and Grahame to Smith, November 19, 1874, HBC Archives, D. 14/1 and Smith to Grahame, January 15, 1875, HBC Archives, D. 20/2.
15 Grahame to Smith, February 18, 1875, HBC Archives, D. 12/1.
16 Smith to Grahame, May [3], 1875, HBC Archives, D. 20/2; Grahame to Smith, June 16, 1875, HBC Archives, D. 14/2.
17 Smith to Grahame, July 29 and July 31, 1876, HBC Archives, D. 20/5; Armit to Smith, October 11, 1876, HBC Archives, A. 6/50; Smith to Armit, June 8 and June 15, 1877, HBC Archives, A. 12/15.
18 The Deed of Surrender is printed in full in Appendix A of Bowsfield, ed., *The Letters of Charles John Brydges, 1879-1882*.
19 Smith to Armit, December 22, 1871, HBC Archives, A. 12/14.
20 Smith to Armit, May 17, June 21 and December 20, 1872, HBC Archives, A. 12/14.
21 Smith to Armit, January 25, January 31, March 13, May 17, June 7, July 19, September 7 and September 29, 1878, HBC Archives, A. 12/15.
22 Smith to Armit, February 25, 1876, HBC Archives, A. 12/15.
23 Smith to Armit, November 21, 1872, HBC Archives, D. 11/3; March 9, 1874, July 17, July 21, July 28, August 10, 1876, October 11, 1878, HBC Archives, A. 12/15.
24 Smith to Armit, August 25, 1876, HBC Archives, A. 12/15.
25 Mills to Smith, June 29, 1877, HBC Archives, D. 12/1.
26 Northcote to Lampson, April 20, 1870, BL, Add. 50,056; Smith to Armit, October 21, November 11, December 25, 1874; January 4, 1875, HBC Archives, A. 12/15.
27 Smith to Armit, May 14, September 24, 1875, HBC Archives, A. 12/14. See also Galbraith, "Land Policies."
28 Goschen to Smith, February 4, 1875, HBC Archives, A. 7/4; *Report of the Governor and Committee and Proceedings of the General Court*, June 29, November 10, 1875; June 27, November 9, 1876; June 29, 1979; July 4, 1910; Goschen to Mackenzie, July 27, 1875 and Mackenzie to Goschen, August 18, 1875, NAC, MG 26, B.
29 Smith to Rankin, May 10, June 19, June 24, July 29, 1875, NAC, MG 29, A 12; Isabella Smith to Rankin, July 13, 1875, NAC, MG 29, A 11.
30 Smith to Fleming, November 19, 1875, NAC, MG 29, B 1, vol.48; Share Ledger, August 13, 1875, HBC Archives, A. 40/15, Dividend Payments, HBC Archives, A. 42/15. The initial entry in the share ledger makes the mistake of recording two hundred shares for Donald Smith but this is immediately corrected, giving him one hundred and same number to Fleming.
31 Smith to Armit, June 22, 1877, HBC Archives, A. 12/15.
32 *Manitoban*, December 3, 1870; Smith to Armit, October 11, 1878, HBC Archives, A. 12/15.
33 Smith to Secretary of State, November 16, 1872, HBC Archives, D. 11/3.
34 Armit to Smith, April 12, 1872, HBC Archives, A. 6/47.
35 Smith to Armit, May 24, 1872, HBC Archives, A. 12/14; May 19, 1876, HBC Archives, A. 12/15.
36 Smith to Armit, August 14, 1872, HBC Archives, A. 12/14.
37 Smith to Armit, May 19, 1876 and August 17, 1877, HBC Archives, A. 12/15.
38 *Manitoba Free Press*, August 31 and September 24, 1878; Skene Edwards and Garson, Box A32; Smith to Armit, July 4, 1879, HBC Archives, A. 12/15.
39 Smith to Armit, July 4, 1879, HBC Archives, A. 12/15; Brydges to Armit, September 6, 1889, HBC Archives, A. 12/19 and April 28, June 1, September 5, 1881, HBC Archives, A. 12/20; Brydges to Smith, May 30, 1881, HBC Archives, E. 33/3; Skene Edwards and Garson, A32.
40 Smith Deed Register, HBC Archives, E. 33/1.
41 Skene Edwards and Garson, A32.
42 Langevin to Morris, June 2, 1875 and Smith to Morris, December 17, 1875, PAM, MG12/B1.
43 *Journals of the House of Commons*, April 1, 1874.

44 Canada, *Report of the Select Committee*, in *Journals of the House of Commons*, 1874; Taché to Monseigneur LaFlèche, Bishop of Three Rivers, in Robert Rumilly, *Histoire de la Province de Québec*, vol. 1, 1941, p. 301, cited in Stanley, *Riel*, p. 206. Taché said that Macdonald had lied "comme ferait un voyou."
45 Beckles Willson, who may have seen the memorial, says it records Margaret's death as having taken place in 1841 but her obituary appears in the *Forres Gazette* for February 6, 1840. Since it is unlikely that she was born in 1813, the year of her parents' marriage, she was probably twenty-six when she died in January, rather than twenty-seven as Willson records.
46 Thomas Hardisty to Richard Hardisty, January 30, 1874, Glenbow, M5908/Box 8.
47 Smith to Rankin, May 23, 1876, NAC, MG 29, A 12.
48 Smith to Mary McPherson, November 6, 1878, HBC Archives, D. 11/7.
49 William Lucas Hardisty to Grahame, March 28, 1877, HBC Archives, D. 20/6; Richard Hardisty to Donald Smith, draft of a letter dated July 17, 1877, Glenbow, M5908, Box 8. Papers in the Skene Edwards and Garson collection, especially in A32, reveal some of the many wills of family, friends and Hudson's Bay Company employees which involved Smith as an executor, a tutor or as a person with power of attorney to act on behalf of heirs, creditors or debtors.
50 James Bissett to John McIntyre, October 31, 1874, NAC, MG 29, A 21.
51 *Montreal Herald*, [nd], in HBC Archives, D. 20/4.
52 Goschen to Grahame, November 17, 1877, HBC Archives, D. 19/4.
53 John McTavish to McDougall, June 19, 1878, McDougall Papers, cited in Oleson, "Fur Trade Party," p. 133; Hargrave and Christie to McDougall, June 19, 1878, HBC Archives, E. 21/3.
54 John McTavish to Richard Hardisty, October 7, 1878, McDougall Papers, cited in Oleson, "Fur Trade Party," p. 159.
55 Grahame to Armit, July 19, 1878, HBC Archives, A. 33/6.
56 Hargrave, Circular to members of The Fur Trade Party, October 7, 1878, McDougall Papers, cited in Oleson, "Fur Trade Party," p. 158.
57 Smith to Armit, October 18, 1878, HBC Archives, D. 11/7.
58 Smith to John McTavish, October 22, 1878 and Smith to Armit, October 25, 1878, HBC Archives, D. 11/7.
59 Armit to Smith, November 5, 1878, HBC Archives, A.6/51; Grahame to Armit, November 22, 1878, D. 16/1.
60 Armit to Smith, November 5, 1878, HBC Archives, A. 6/51.
61 Smith to Armit, November 28, 1878 and Smith to McTavish, November 30, 1878, HBC Archives, D. 11/7.
62 Smith to Armit, December 3, 1878, HBC Archives, D. 11/7.
63 Smith to Grahame, December 6, 1878, HBC Archives, D. 20/11 and Grahame to Armit, November 22, 1878, D. 16/1.
64 Grahame to John McTavish, November 20, 1878, HBC Archives, D. 16/1.
65 John McTavish to Grahame, November 30, 1878, HBC Archives, D. 20/11 and minutes of a Fur Trade Party meeting, December 2, 1878, McDougall Papers, cited in Oleson, "Fur Trade Party," p. 188.
66 Fur Trade Party to Grahame, December 14, 1878, McDougall Papers, cited in Oleson, "Fur Trade Party," p. 194.
67 Armit to Grahame, November 19, 1878, HBC Archives, A. 6/51.
68 Minutes, February 21-26, 1879, HBC Archives, A. 1/151.
69 Smith to Armit, February 27, 1879, HBC Archives, A. 12/15.
70 Fur Trade Party Minutes, March 18, 1879, Glenbow, M5908, Box 8; Bissett diary, March 18-15, 1879, NAC, MG 19, A 49. Smith frequently sent cables as soon as a transatlantic liner was close enough to a port — particularly New York — to enable him to do so. It implies that he used the voyage to think through the implications of the work he had just done in Europe and that he put in motion whatever course of events should follow as soon as he was able to communicate with his colleagues in North America.

71 John McTavish to Fur Trade Party Members, April 9, 1879, Glenbow, M5908, Box 8.
72 Oleson, "Fur Trade Party," pp. 241-243.
73 Armit to Smith, June 19, 1878, HBC Archives, A. 6/51.
74 Smith to Sweeny, May 28, 1878 and Smith to McTavish, May 28, 1878, HBC Archives, D. 11/7.
75 Smith to Armit, October 25, 1878, HBC Archives, D. 11/7 and *Debates of the House of Commons*, April 5, 1880.
76 Smith to Armit, February 25, 1879, HBC Archives, A. 12/15.

Chapter Eleven: **The Saint Paul, Minneapolis and Manitoba Railway 1870–1880**

1 *Manitoba Free Press*, December 5, 1879, reporting the inaugural journey of the Saint Paul, Minneapolis and Manitoba Railway.
2 Casault to Mrs. Bowles, November 9, 1870, NAC, MG 29, C 119.
3 Smith to John McTavish, December 2, 1871, HBC Archives, D. 11/3; Smith to Armit, January 23, 1872, HBC Archives, A. 12/14.
4 Casault to Mrs. Bowles, November 25, 1870, NAC, MG 29, C 119.
5 Graham to Lampson, April 4, 1871, HBC Archives, A. 10/83; *Farley vs Kittson*, Smith Deposition.
6 Hill to Hester Pollock, May 15, 1915, Hill Papers, contains an outline of the history of the Minnesota and Pacific from 1854 to 1862 when it was restructured and renamed.
7 Donald Smith to W.G. Smith, October 3, 1870, HBC Archives, A. 11/99.
8 Kittson to Armit, March 9, 1871 and May 1, 1871, HBC Archives, A. 10/83.
9 Smith to Armit, November 6, 1871, HBC Archives, A. 12/14; *Canada Gazette*, December 16, 1871.
10 Cooke to Armit, January 17, 1872, HBC Archives, A. 10/85.
11 Hill to his grandmother, Mary Riggs Hill, August 1, 1856, cited in Martin, *James J. Hill*, p. 27.
12 Paton to Morris, September 5, 1873, PAM, MG12/B1.
13 *Farley vs Kittson*, Smith Deposition; Hill to Bryce, May 5, 1915, PAM, MG14/C15.
14 Barnes to Morris, September 25, 1873, PAM, MG 12/B1.
15 *Ibid.*
16 Hill to Bryce, May 5, 1915, PAM, MG14/C15.
17 *Farley vs Kittson*, Smith Deposition.
18 Smith to Armit, April 2, 1874, HBC Archives, A. 12/15 and *Farley vs Kittson*, Hill Deposition.
19 Kittson to Smith, March 26, 1874, HBC Archives, A. 12/15.
20 Smith to Armit, April 2, 1874, HBC Archives, A. 12/15.
21 *Farley vs Kittson*, Smith and Stephen Depositions.
22 *Farley vs Kittson*, Hill and Farley Depositions.
23 March 20, 1874, Bank of Montreal Resolve Book, NAC, MG 28, II 2.
24 Barnes to Farley, February 6, 1877, *Farley vs Kittson*, Farley Deposition.
25 The figures are in Kittson to Stephen, September 17, 1877, and enclosure, Hill Papers.
26 Barnes to Farley, June 27, 1877, *Farley vs Kittson*, Farley Deposition.
27 Hill to Kittson, July 31, 1877, Hill Papers, P-1.
28 Modern historians have suggested that the captain of the *International* would willingly have endangered his passengers, and his cargo in order to comply with instructions to ram the *Manitoba*. There is no evidence of such an order having been given by any of the people to whom it has been attributed and all the contemporary accounts describe the collision as an accident.
29 Hill to Smith, August 4, 1877, Hill Papers, P-1.
30 Dufferin, *Journal*, p. 320.
31 Dufferin to Mackenzie, August 10, 1877, NAC, MG 26, B.
32 *Manitoba Free Press*, August 15, 1877.

33 Correspondence between Hill and Stephen in the Hill papers indicates that Stephen planned this trip and negotiated the dates; the story that a toss of a coin determined whether he and Angus would go to Saint Paul or Saint Louis is charming but untrue.
34 *Manitoba Free Press*, August 20, 1878.
35 *Manitoba Free Press*, October 9, 1877.
36 Angus to Walter Watson, October 31, 1877, NAC, MG 29, A 28.
37 Smith to Kittson, October 31, 1877, Hill Papers.
38 Smith to Kittson, January 8, 1878, Hill Papers.
39 Hill to Stephen, January 16, 1878, Hill Papers, P-1.
40 Stephen to Kennedy, January 14, 1878 and January 29, 1878, Minnesota Historical Society, Saint Paul and Pacific Railway Papers, 22.c.3.8F.
41 Associates' draft agreement, "Defendant's Exhibit No. 14," *Farley vs Kittson*.
42 Gilbert, "The Unaccountable Fifth," revealed the fact that Kennedy had received the shares. Only knowledge of the fifth explains Angus' letter to Sterling in which he discusses supporting the railway's stock in the American market. "I presume Mr. Tod will take 1/5 for Mr. Kennedy. Stephen, Hill and Smith take 1/5 each and Mr. McIntyre joins me in taking the remaining fifth." By 1883, Angus and McIntyre had acquired enough of the shares to make them co-partners with the associates. Angus to Sterling, July 25, 1883, NAC, MG 29, A 28.
43 Stephen and Smith to Kennedy, January 29, 1878, Minnesota Historical Society, Saint Paul and Pacific Papers, 22.c.3.8F; Hill to Kittson, February 18, 1878, Hill Papers, P-1.
44 *Daily Globe*, April 1, 1878, cited in Martin, p. 154.
45 *Debates of the House of Commons*, March 28, 1878.
46 *Debates of the House of Commons*, April 4, 1878.
47 *Ibid.*
48 *Ibid.*
49 Stephen to Hill, April 8, 1878, Hill Papers.
50 *Debates of the House of Commons*, May 8 and 9, 1878.
51 *Debates of the House of Commons*, May 10, 1878.
52 Preston, *Life and Times*, p. 112. On a great many points, Preston's biography is an unreliable mixture of his own bias and factual error but his comment on Donald Smith's excitement derives from a personal conversation and is therefore probably correct.
53 Stephen to Kennedy, July 18, 1878, Minnesota Historical Society, 22.c.3.9B; Smith to Stephen, June 8, 1878, HBC Archives, D. 11/7.
54 Smith to Hill, November 5, 1878, HBC Archives, D. 11/7.
55 Hill to Stephen, January 10, 1879, Hill Papers, P-3.
56 *Manitoba Daily Free Press*, December 5, 1878.
57 Ham, *Reminiscences*, p. 45.
58 Stephen to Hill, February 20, 1879, Hill Papers.
59 Stephen to Hill, March 19, 1879, Hill Papers.
60 Stephen to Hill, March 20, 1879, Hill Papers.
61 Stephen to Kennedy, November 28, 1878, Minnesota Historical Society, 22.c.3.9B.
62 Kennedy to Farley, January 30, 1879 in *Farley vs Kittson*, Stephen Deposition.
63 Stephen to Hill, January 17, 1879, Hill Papers.
64 Angus to Goldwyn Smith, August 16, 1879, NAC, MG 29, A 28.
65 Grahame to Armit, October 21, 1879, HBC Archives, D. 13/4.
66 Grahame to Armit, December 1, 1879, HBC Archives, D. 13/4.
67 Angus to Kennedy Tod, July 28, 1880, Hill Papers, R-26.

Chapter Twelve: **The Canadian Pacific Railway 1880–1885**

1 Stephen to Macdonald, February 9, 1885, NAC, MG 26, A, vol. 268.
2 *Manitoba Daily Free Press*, September 24, 1878.
3 *Manitoba Daily Free Press*, September 25, 1878.
4 *Manitoba Daily Free Press*, September 27, 1878 (and earlier for ballot instructions).
5 *Manitoba Daily Free Press*, November 6, 1878; Davin to Macdonald, February 22, 1879, NAC, MG 26, A, vol. 355.

6 *Debates of the House of Commons*, May 7, 1879.
7 Morris to Macdonald, November 22, 1879, NAC, MG 26, A, vol. 252A.
8 *Manitoba Daily Free Press*, September 3, 1880.
9 It has been claimed that Donald Smith spent $30,000 on this election campaign, but there cannot be a scrap of truth in such an allegation. His officially recorded expenditure in 1878 had been $1,647.30 compared to Morris' $1,410.83 (*Manitoba Daily Free Press*, December 7, 1878). Even if his actual expenditure had been double or treble this amount, it nowhere approximated the sum which it is claimed he spent for a much shorter campaign in 1880. In today's terms, $30,000 is the equivalent of nearly $8 million, or just over a million dollars per Selkirk voter.
10 *Manitoba Daily Free Press*, September 3, 1880.
11 Memorandum, June 15, 1880, NAC, MG 26, F, vol. 5.
12 McIntyre to Macdonald, July 5, 1880, NAC, MG 26, A, vol. 127.
13 Stephen to Macdonald, July 9, 1880, NAC, MG 26, A, vol. 267.
14 Angus to Stephen, September 11 and 15 and December 31, 1880, Hill Papers.
15 Bank of Montreal Resolve Book, September 28, 1880 and January 7, 1881, NAC, MG 28, II, 2.
16 Hill to Angus, October 19, 1880, Hill Papers, P-5.
17 Stephen to Rose, December 16, 1880, and Stephen to Macdonald, December 16, 1880, NAC, MG 26, A, vol. 268 and 267.
18 Smith to Stephen, January 9, 1881, cited in Willson, vol. 2, p. 98.
19 Stephen to Macdonald, January 23, 1881, NAC, MG 26, A, vol. 268.
20 *Debates of the House of Commons*, December 14, 1880.
21 *Debates of the House of Commons*, January 8, 1881.
22 *Debates of the House of Commons*, December 17, 1880.
23 Hill to Kennedy, February 1, 1882 [misdated 1881], Hill Papers, P-5; Angus to Smith, March 7, 1882, Angus to Stephen, March 16, 1882, Angus to Kennedy, June 4, 1882, NAC, MG 29, A 28.
24 C.W. Allen to Macdonald, November 24, 1879, NAC, MG 26, A, vol. 311; Hill to Angus, March 6, 1883 and Hill to Kennedy, July 26, 1883, Hill Papers, P-7.
25 Colvile to Brydges, January 6, 1881, HBC Archives, A. 6/78.
26 Smith to MacFarlane, January 10, 1884, NAC, MG 29, A 11, vol. 1.
27 Smith Deed Register, HBC Archives, E. 33/1 and Levine, *Scrum Wars*, p. 16.
28 Macdonald to Stephen, November 20, 1883, NAC, MG 29, A 30.
29 Stephen to Macdonald, January 3, 1884, NAC, MG 26, A, vol. 269; Preston, pp. 170-173; Levine, *Scrum Wars*, p. 41. Preston and Levine, following him, err in saying Smith acquired a large stake in the *Globe* at the time of Brown's death. Seventy-six shares were temporarily assigned to him as collateral in September 1880 but his first purchase was not made until 1886 when he bought ninety shares at $500 each. In 1904, he still held only these shares; he had 810 with a face value of $100 each in 1913 at which time they were worth only seventy-five percent of par. By 1918, the value had slipped to $48,600 or sixty percent of par. Smith Deed Register, HBC Archives, E. 33/1 and Skene Edwards and Garson, A/42.
30 Angus to Hill, September 20, 1882, Hill Papers.
31 Winnipeg *Sun*, September 30, 1882.
32 Kennedy to Hill, November 4, 1882, Hill Papers.
33 *Ibid.*
34 Stephen to Macdonald, March 22, 1883, NAC, MG 26, A, vol. 267.
35 Hill to Kennedy, May 28, 1883, Hill Papers, P-7.
36 Enclosure in Angus to Van Horne, March 21, 1882, NAC, MG 29, A 28.
37 T.E. Wilson, "The Last of the Pathfinders, as related to W.E. Round," pp. 57-58, cited in Berton who fills in the blanks which Wilson (or Round) inserted following Rogers' frequent use of "Blue," vol. 2, p. 166.
38 Hughes, *Black-Robe Voyageur*, p. 234.
39 Skene Edwards and Garson, Box A32.
40 Skelton, *Life and Letters of Laurier*, vol. 1, p. 273.

41 Bank of Montreal Resolve Book, January 2, 1884, NAC, MG 28, II, 2.
42 *Globe*, February 1, 1884, cited in Berton, vol. 2, p. 261.
43 Stephen to Macdonald, January 25, 1884, NAC, MG 26, A, vol. 269.
44 Stephen to Macdonald, February 10, 1884, NAC, MG 26, A, vol. 268.
45 Lansdowne to Lord Claude Hamilton, February 24, 1884, NAC, MG 27, I, B 6.
46 Kennedy to Hill, March 1, 1884; Stephen to Hill, March 22, 1884, Hill Papers.
47 Bank of Montreal Resolve Book, April 4, 1884, NAC, MG 28, II, 2.
48 Stephen to Macdonald, November 7, 1885, NAC, MG 26, A, vol. 269.
49 Stephen to Macdonald, December 10, 1884, NAC, MG 26, A, vol. 268.
50 Stephen to Macdonald, February 9, 1885, NAC, MG 26, A, vol. 269.
51 Beckles Willson's 1915 biography recounts the story in vol. 2, p. 116. His text was read by Van Horne who edited several sections and re-wrote others. A variant occurs on pp. 115-116 of Vaughan's biography of Van Horne but it is almost certainly drawn from Willson. Pierre Berton's history of the CPR, vol. 2, p. 352, attributes the remark to Stephen, citing James Bonar's pamphlet, *The Inauguration of Trans Canada Transportation*. In turn, Bonar quotes Randolph Bruce, a former lieutenant governor of British Columbia, who heard the story from Van Horne.
52 Stephen to Macdonald, January 14, 1885, NAC, MG 26, A, vol. 269. The letter is mistakenly dated December 14, 1885 and is misfiled as a consequence.
53 Wrigley to Smith, April 5, 1885, HBC Archives, D. 17/1.
54 *Manitoba Daily Free Press*, May 25, 1885.
55 Macdonald to Stephen, May 26, 1885, NAC, MG 29, A 30.
56 Fragment of a memo by Van Horne, probably written in 1914 or early 1915 to help Willson prepare his biography of Donald Smith, NAC, MG 30, D 5.
57 Stephen to Macdonald, October 3, 1885, NAC, MG 26, A, vol. 269.
58 Fleming diary, October 31, 1885, NAC, MG 29, B 1, vol. 81; letter from an unidentified correspondent to Richard Hardisty, November 12, 1885, Glenbow, M5908, Box 8.
59 Vaughan, p. 131.
60 Fleming, "Memories of the Mountains," pp. 32-33.
61 *Ibid.*
62 *Daily British Colonist*, November 19, 1885; Stewart, *Steele*, p. 156.
63 Willson, vol. 2, pp. 124-125.

Chapter Thirteen: **The Canadian Sub-committee 1880–1889**

1 George Ham, *Reminiscences of a Raconteur*, p. 51.
2 Verbatim Transcript, General Court, June 24, 1879, HBC Archives, A. 2/36.
3 Minutes of a meeting to consider a report on the management of the company's business at Winnipeg, March 13, 1883, HBC Archives, A. 67/59.
4 Armit to Smith, October 13, 1880, HBC Archives, A. 6/52.
5 Rea, Introduction to Bowsfield, ed., *Letters 1883-1889*, p. xxvii.
6 Armit to Brydges, July 9, 1879, HBC Archives, A. 6/51.
7 Average prices are quoted in Bowsfield, ed., *Letters 1883-1889*, p. xxvii. Pierre Berton in *The Last Spike* offers a detailed account of the boom and land speculation in Chapter Two.
8 Armit to Grahame, February 8, 1882, HBC Archives, D. 19/9.
9 Fleming, draft of a pamphlet presented to the Governor and Committee, October 31, 1882, NAC, MG 29, B 1, vol. 112. The text is printed as an appendix in Bowsfield, ed., *Letters 1879-1882*; Grahame to Armit, January 20, 1882, HBC Archives, D. 13/5.
10 Fleming diary, 1882, NAC, MG 29, B 1, vol. 81.
11 Colvile to Brydges, May 10 and 11, 1882, HBC Archives, A. 7/5.
12 Colvile to Smith, June 20, 1882, HBC Archives, A. 7/5.
13 Share Ledger S-Z, 1879-1890, HBC Archives, A. 40/19.
14 Fleming diary, August 12, 1882, NAC, MG 29, B 1, vol. 81; Rose to Macdonald, January 4, 1883, NAC, MG 26, A, vol. 259.
15 James Coyne to George Bryce, September 9, 1915, PAM, MG14/C15.

16 Minutes of October 17, 1882, HBC Archives, A. 1/152; Armit to Grahame, March 6, 1883, HBC Archives, D. 20/25; Grahame to Colvile, August 5, 1884, Robert Hamilton to Smith, August 23, 1884, and Armit to Grahame, September 9, 1884, HBC Archives, D. 46/8.
17 Fleming pamphlet draft, October 31, 1882, NAC, MG 29, B 1, vol. 112; Armit to Rose, November 17 and 27, 1882, HBC Archives, A. 6/45.
18 Smith to Fleming, January 6, 1883, NAC, MG 29, B 1, vol. 48.
19 Armit to Brydges, December 12, 1882, HBC Archives, A. 6/54.
20 Colvile to Brydges, May 29, 1883, HBC Archives, A. 7/5.
21 Armit's report to the Governor and Committee, [nd], NAC, MG 29, B 1, vol. 112.
22 Share Ledger, S-Z, 1879-1890, HBC Archives, A. 40/19.
23 Verbatim Report, General Court, December 4, 1888, HBC Archives, A. 2/45.
24 Verbatim Report, General Court, November 22, 1883, HBC Archives, A. 2/45.
25 List of men elected, November 24, 1883, as distributed by William Armit the day after the General Court, HBC Archives, D. 19/10.
26 Stephen to Macdonald, December 3, 1883, NAC, MG 26, A, vol. 267.
27 Rose to Macdonald, December 1, 1883, NAC, MG 26, A, vol. 259.
28 Rose to Macdonald, December 29, 1883, enclosing his letter of December 17 to the Governor and Committee, NAC, MG 26, A, vol. 259.
29 Rose to Macdonald, September 11, 1884, NAC, MG 26, A, vol. 259.
30 Copy of a resolution passed by the Governor and Committee, January 22, 1884 and copy of a resolution passed on January 29, 1884, NAC, MG 29, B 1, vol. 96.
31 Fleming to Colvile, April 16, 1884, NAC, MG 29, B 1, vol.11. The draft of this document is in vol. 96.
32 Minutes of the meeting of the Governor and Committee, May 1, 1884, in Canadian Sub-committee Papers, HBC Archives, D. 45/1.
33 See, for example, Brydges to Armit, August 6, 1884, September 24, 1884, HBC Archives, D. 46/6; October 1, 1884, HBC Archives, D. 46/7; Smith to Brydges, March 19, 1885, HBC Archives, D. 44/1.
34 Minutes of July 8, 1884 meeting of Governor and Committee, HBC Archives, D. 46/3; Smith Deed Register, HBC Archives, E. 33/1.
35 Brydges to Smith, January 26, 1885, HBC Archives, D. 46/6.
36 Minutes of the Canadian Sub-committee, February 7, 1885, HBC Archives, D. 44/2.
37 Minutes of the Governor and Committee, April 14, 1885, HBC Archives, D. 46/19.
38 Smith to Armit, April 21, 1885, HBC Archives, D. 44/1.
39 Cable, Armit to Smith, [nd, probably June 2, 1885], HBC Archives, A. 12/53.
40 Memorandum from the Canadian Sub-committee to the Governor and Committee, July 3, 1885, HBC Archives, D. 44/1. Another copy may be found in A. 12/53.
41 Smith to Fleming, July 25, 1885, NAC, MG 29, B 1, vol. 48; Armit to Brydges, July 28, 1885, HBC Archives, D. 46/22.
42 Verbatim Report, General Court, December 15, 1885, HBC Archives, D. 46/26.
43 Armit to Brydges, January 6, January 27, July 7 and July 14, 1886, HBC Archives, A. 6/56.
44 Smith to Fleming, June 27, 1887, NAC, MG 29, B 1, vol. 48; Armit to Brydges, January 26, 1888, HBC Archives, A. 6/57; Brydges to Armit, May 2, 1888, HBC Archives, A. 12/26.
45 Armit to Brydges, June 6, 1888 and July 1, 1888, HBC Archives, A. 6/58; Armit to Brydges, August 2, 1888, not traced in HBC Archives but cited in Armit to Brydges, October 25, 1888, HBC Archives A. 6/58; Rose to Brydges, August 7, 1888, not found in HBC Archives but cited in Brydges to Armit, October 25, 1888, HBC Archives, A. 12/26; Brydges to J.W. Kendrick, August 27, 1888, A. 72/9; McNaught to Brydges, October 18, 1888, HBC Archives, A. 27/9.
46 Brydges to Armit, September 21, 1888, HBC Archives, A. 12/26; Armit to Brydges, [nd, probably October 10 or 11, 1888], HBC Archives, A. 10/82a; Brydges to Armit, October 12, 1888, HBC Archives, A. 12/26; Armit to Brydges, October 17 and 18, 1888, HBC Archives, A. 6/58.

47 Memo on proposed compromise on Northern Pacific sale, October 2, 1889, HBC Archives, A. 72/9; memo on history of Northern Pacific negotiations, February 12, 1897, HBC Archives, A. 12/L 67/1.
48 Armit to Smith, December 18, 1888, HBC Archives, A. 7/5; Armit to Brydges, January 17, 1889, HBC Archives, A. 6/58.
49 Smith to Armit, March 14, 1889, HBC Archives, A. 12/53.
50 Smith to Fleming, June 20, 1887, NAC, MG 29, B 1, vol. 48.
51 Fleming diaries, September 6, 28 and 29, 1887, November 11, 1889, NAC, MG 29, B 1, vol. 81; Smith to Fleming, December 22, 1888 and January 29, 1889, NAC, MG 29, B 1, vol. 48.

Chapter Fourteen: **A Man of Substance 1886–1896**

1 Carnegie speech, September 27, 1906, in Anderson, ed., *Record of the Celebration*, p. 207.
2 Smith to Bell, October 26, 1876 and April 9, 1877, NAC, MG 29, B 15, vol. 33.
3 Deed of sale from Widow Auger to Smith, November 6, 1876, deeds of sale from Sulpicians to Smith, April 30, 1881 and February 16, 1889, Skene Edwards and Garson, A32.
4 *Montreal Street Directory*, 1877-1878; MacKay, *Square Mile*, p. 103; deed of sale, McIntyre to Smith, June 8, 1888, Smith to Drinkwater, 1887, Skene Edwards and Garson, A32.
5 Agreements, December 1884, with Plante and Dubuc, masons, Hutchison and Steele, architects, John McLean, plasterer, J.H. Hutchison, mason, Messrs C. Garth and Company, plumbers, Walter Scott, painter and John Allan, carpenter and joiner; statement of Montreal rental property; Craddock Simpson to Smith, June 16, 1881, Skene Edwards and Garson, A32; MacKay, *Square Mile*, p. 113.
6 Draft insurance contract [nd], builders' etc. agreements, December 1884, Skene Edwards and Garson, A32; MacKay, *Square Mile*, pp. 112-113; *Montreal Star*, March 9, 1888; *Montreal Gazette*, September 14, 1888 and *Montreal Gazette*, April 16, 1955; photographs, McCord Museum, Montreal; Lord Grey to Lord Strathcona, December 11, 1907, NAC, MG 27, II, B 2, vol. 6.
7 Angus to Laurie, May 2, 1887, NAC, MG 29, A 28; Butlin and Joll, *Turner*, vol. 1, pp. 217-281 and vol. 2, plate 372.
8 *Montreal Gazette*, September 14, 1888.
9 Richmond, *Lord Strathcona*, p. 243.
10 *Montreal Gazette*, September 14, 1888; Sir Henry Tyler to his wife, August 26, 1888, NAC, MG 29, A 31; valuation of contents of Dorchester Street house, Craddock Simpson, [nd], NAC, MG 29, A 5, vol. 1.
11 Angus to Thomas Laurie and Son, April 25, 1885, NAC, MG 29, A 28.
12 Elphinstone to Lansdowne, November 17 and November 24, 1885, NAC, MG 27, I, B 6.
13 Lansdowne to Macdonald, November 29, 1885, NAC, MG 27, I, B 6.
14 Stephen to Macdonald, December 17, 1885, NAC, MG 27. I, B 6.
15 Smith to Macdonald, January 28, 1886, NAC, MG 26, A, vol. 265.
16 Smith to Lansdowne, February 1, 1886, NAC, MG 27, I, B 6.
17 Smith to Macdonald, February 23, 1886, NAC, MG 26, A, vol. 265.
18 Eleventh paraphrase; see Chapter Two, 1n.
19 Roderick McKenzie to Roderick MacFarlane, December 14, 1879; Richard Hardisty to MacFarlane, February 28, 1880 and January 10, 1881, NAC, MG 29, A 11, vol. 1; Grahame to Armit, January 20, 1881, HBC Archives, D. 13/5.
20 Smith to Richard Hardisty, November 11, 1881, Glenbow, M5908, Box 8; Hardisty to Smith, August 8, 1880, Glenbow, M477, Box 7; Smith to Grahame, June 8, 1882, HBC Archives, D. 20/69.
21 Smith to Richard Hardisty, October 7, 1885, Glenbow, M5908, Box 8.
22 Smith to Hill, February 2, 1884, Hill Papers.
23 Joseph Hardisty to Hill, February 15, 1884, Hill Papers; Joseph Hardisty to Richard Hardisty, September 12, 1884, Glenbow, M5908, Box 8.

24 Richard Hardisty to Smith, October 24, 1884, HBC Archives, D. 18/5; Smith to Richard Hardisty, October 7, 1885, Glenbow, M5908, Box 8; Joseph Hardisty to Richard Hardisty, December 17, 1885, Glenbow, M477, Box 7.
25 Richard Hardisty to Eliza Hardisty, November 9, 1887, Glenbow, M477, Box 7.
26 Norway House papers, Skene Edwards and Garson, A32; Hill to Smith, February 20, 1885, Hill Papers, P-2, vol. 11 and April 6, 1885, vol. 12; Joseph Hardisty to Richard Hardisty, December 17, 1885, Glenbow, M477, Box 7. Emma Davis was the sister of Horace Davis who worked in the advertising department of the *Montreal Standard*; following Lord Strathcona's death, he attempted to blackmail Maggie by threatening to reveal the circumstances of the Labrador marriage.
27 Court papers for John MacLean and Company insolvency hearing, Skene Edwards and Garson, A32; *Montreal Gazette*, July 24, 1891; Sterling to Smith, October 22 and 28, 1897, private collection.
28 *Forres, Elgin and Nairn Gazette*, November 24, 1880 and October 5, 1881.
29 Smith to McGill governors, October 6, 1886, cited in Roscoe, *The Royal Victoria College*, p. 25; notarial deed of donation, October 16, 1886, cited in Gillett, *We Walked Very Warily*, p. 89.
30 *Montreal Gazette*, November 1, 1889.
31 Deed of sale, November 13, 1893, Skene Edwards and Garson, A32.
32 Smith to Oakeley, September 4, 1899, cited in Gillett, *We Walked Very Warily*, pp. 166-167; Willson, vol. 1, p. 15; Hurlbatt manuscript, cited in Roscoe, *The Royal Victoria College*, p. 33; Oakeley, *My Adventures*, p. 81.
33 Oakeley, *My Adventures*, p. 81.
34 *Montreal Gazette*, November 2, 1900.
35 Minutes of the meetings of the Executive and Finance Committees of the Royal College of Music, December 13, 1883, January 29, 1885, May 21, 1885; Royal College of Music Annual Reports, 1884, 1886 and 1891; Lansdowne correspondence, January and February 1885, NAC, MG 27, I, B 6; *Montreal Gazette*, October 28, 1889.
36 Richard Hardisty to Eliza Hardisty, March 11, 1888, Glenbow, M5908, Box 8.
37 Pope diary, May 10, 1903, NAC, Mg 30, E 86, vol. 43; for an example of Howard's intolerance, see his belligerent letter to Skene Edwards and Garson, September 29, 1914, NAC, MG 29, A 5, vol. 6, in which he is scornful of the Roman Catholic church and dismisses a request for the donation of land for a public park in Lachine as "an audacious attempt at begging with no possible excuse."
38 Tyler to his wife Margaret, August 28, 1888 (continued the following day), NAC, MG 29, A 31.
39 Royal Victoria Hospital Charter, cited in Lewis, *Royal Victoria Hospital*, p. 311.
40 Report of city of Montreal commission to investigate the proposed hospital site, cited in Lewis, *Royal Victoria Hospital*, p. 7.
41 Stephen to Lansdowne, June 10, 1887, NAC, MG 27, I, B 6.
42 Smith to Tupper, July 17, 1886, NAC, MG 26, F, vol. 6.
43 *Major Barbara*, Act II.

Chapter Fifteen: **The Great Northern 1885–1901**

1 Armit to Willson, July 8, 1915, NAC, MG 29, A 11, vol. 1.
2 Humphrys, "The Shiny House," p. 51.
3 Bank of Montreal Resolve Book, June 17, 1887, NAC, MG 28, II, 2.
4 Stephen to Macdonald, October 19, 1887 and November 11, 1887, NAC, MG 26 A, vol. 270.
5 Stephen to Macdonald, March 17, 1888, NAC, MG 26, A, vol. 271.
6 Mount Stephen to Van Horne, November 17, 1914, NAC, MG 29, A 60.
7 Smith to Armit, April 5, 1892, HBC Archives, A. 12/53.
8 Van Horne to Stephen, December 14, 1891, copy enclosed in a letter to Fleming, December 15, 1891, NAC, MG 29 B1, vol. 51.
9 Details of the acquisition and subsequent sale of the New Brunswick Railway are in Skene Edwards and Garson, A32. The Short Line was a total of 481.7 miles, of which

211.3 were constructed by the CPR, the remainder having been built by other companies. See Lamb, *History of the Canadian Pacific Railway*, p. 170 for details.

10 Stephen to Macdonald, October 21, 1889; Stephen to Van Horne, October 14, 1889; Skinner to Van Horne, November 1, 1889, NAC, MG 26, A, vol. 288.
11 Hill to Stephen, May 18, 1886, Hill Papers, P-14.
12 Stephen to Hill, May 23, 1886, Hill Papers.
13 Stephen to Macdonald, January 29, 1888, NAC, MG 256, A, vol. 271.
14 Stephen to Macdonald, April 22, 1888, NAC, MG 26, A, vol. 271.
15 Stephen to Hill, July 16, 1888, Hill Papers.
16 Stephen to Hill, July 25, 1888, Hill Papers.
17 *Ibid.*
18 Stephen to Hill, May 31, 1889, Hill Papers.
19 When the renewed Baring Brothers collapsed in 1995, again because it had over-extended itself, a similar rescue package was proposed and the Bank of England sought guarantees from English banks to enable it to support the enfeebled company. In this case, however, Barings was unable to state the precise extent of its liability and the other banks were unwilling to expose themselves to a risk of unknown limits. As a result, the directors had little option but to agree to a takeover.
20 *The Saint Paul Pioneer Press*, June 8, 1893.
21 Hill to Stephen, October 20, 1894, Hill Papers, P-15.
22 Stephen to Van Horne, July 24, 1892 and January 19, 1892, PAC, MG 29, A 60.
23 Stephen to Van Horne, February 24, 1894, PAC, MG 29, A 60.
24 Van Horne to Mount Stephen, June 20, 1894, cited in Lamb, *History of the Canadian Pacific*, p. 203.
25 Hill to Strathcona, August 13, 1901, Hill Papers, P-17.
26 *Ibid.*
27 Saint Paul *Globe*, December 22, 1901.
28 September 3, 1902, Farrer to Hill, Hill Papers.

Chapter Sixteen: **Parliament and Manitoba Schools 1886–1896**

1 Donald Smith, *Montreal Gazette*, November 16, 1900.
2 Smith to Macdonald, March 2, 1886, NAC, MG 26, A, vol. 265.
3 Stephen to Macdonald, May 27, 1886, NAC, MG 26, A, vol. 270.
4 Macdonald to Scarth, February 9, 1886, NAC, MG 27, I, E 19; Scarth to Macdonald, May 5, 1886, NAC, MG 26, A, vol. 261.
5 Willson, vol. 2, p. 135.
6 Hugh John Macdonald to J.A. Macdonald, January 7, 1887, NAC, MG 26, A, vol. 537.
7 Stephen to Macdonald, January 27, 1887, NAC, MG 26, A, vol. 270; Willson, vol. 2, p. 136.
8 Cited in Willson, vol. 2, p. 137.
9 Smith to Macdonald, February 16, 1887, NAC, MG 26, A, vol. 265.
10 Cited in Willson, vol. 2, pp. 138-139.
11 Cited in Willson, vol. 2, p. 143 and p. 142.
12 Cited in Willson, vol. 2, p. 145.
13 Smith to Fleming, December 22, 1888 and January 29, 1889, NAC, MG 29, B 1, vol. 48. The passenger register for a voyage of the *Teutonic* leaving New York for Liverpool on November 18, 1891, (PRO BT 26/14) names Robert Adams, an unmarried Englishman of twenty-six, as Sir Donald Smith's manservant. The same man may have been working for him in 1888. The register is unreliable, giving Smith's age as forty-eight when in fact he was seventy-one!
14 *Debates of the House of Commons*, April 25, May 26, 1887.
15 Smith to Armit, March 26, 1889, HBC Archives, D. 44/1.
16 Stephen to Macdonald, August 12, 1888, NAC, MG 26, A, vol. 271.
17 Loan agreement, September 6, 1888, NAC, MG 29, A 5, vol. 12; Van Horne to St. John, August 14, 1894 and Van Horne to William Luxton, September 17, 1895, NAC, MG 29, A 60, vol. 52.

18 Van Horne to Macdonald, February 3, 1891, NAC, MG 26, A, vol. 288.
19 Van Horne to St. John, July 31, 1894, NAC, MG 29, A 60, vol. 52.
20 Van Horne to St. John, July 6, 1895, NAC, MG 29, A 60, vol. 52.
21 Macdonald to Smith, February 5, 1891, NAC, MG 26, A, vol. 533.
22 Smith to Macdonald, February 6, 1891, NAC, MG 26, A, vol. 265.
23 Van Horne to Macdonald, February 11, 1891, NAC, MG 26, A, vol. 288.
24 Macdonald to Van Horne, February 12, 1891, NAC, MG 26, A, vol. 288.
25 Van Horne to Macdonald, February 14 and 20, 1891, NAC, MG 26, A, vol. 288.
26 Van Horne to Macdonald, February 28, 1891, NAC, MG 26, A, vol. 288.
27 *Debates of the House of Commons*, May 26, 1891.
28 Grant to Langevin, May 29, 1891, *Ottawa Free Press*, May 30, 1891.
29 Smith to Lorne, June 9, 1891, cited in Willson, vol. 2, p. 152.
30 Aberdeen Journal, October 1, 1890, NAC, MG 27, I, B5.
31 Aberdeen Journal, September 15, 1891, NAC, MG 27, I, B 5.
32 Smith to Butler, [nd, approx. August 1893], cited in Willson, vol. 2, p. 153.
33 Charles Tupper to his son Charles Hibbert Tupper, February 9, 1895, NAC, G 26, F, vol. 9.
34 Aberdeen Journal, January 30, 1896, NAC, MG 27, I B5.
35 Aberdeen Journal, January 24 and February 25, 1896, NAC, MG 27, I B5.
36 Ware to Chipman, October 26, 1895, HBC Archives, A. 6/121; Smith to Ware, November 8 and 19, 1895, HBC Archives, A. 12/53; Smith to Tupper, December 18, 1895, NAC, MG 26, F, vol. 10; Van Horne to Willson, [nd, probably 1915], MG 30, D 5; Aberdeen Journal, February 25, 1896, NAC, MG 27, I B5.
37 *Commons Debates*, March 20, 1896.
38 Smith to Chipman, December 3, 1892, HBC Archives, D. 26/5.
39 Greenway to Smith, March 2, 1896, MG 26, E 1 (A), vol. 15.
40 *Commons Debates*, March 19, 1896.
41 *Commons Debates*, March 20, 1896.
42 *Ibid*.
43 Aberdeen Journal, April 24, 1896, NAC, MG 27, I B5.
44 Van Horne to William Whyte, c. 1891, cited in Vaughan, *Van Horne*, p. 196.
45 Sterling to Smith, June 12, 1888, private collection.
46 Marriage certificate, March 9, 1896; Sterling to James Garson, March 6, 1914, private collection.
"Whenever the father is a domiciled Scotchman, it is of no consequence in what country his natural children have been born, or his marriage with the mother of those children celebrated; neither does it matter what the law of that country may have been in regard to the legitimation *per subsequens matrimoniem* — but that in such a case it is the law of Scotland alone which must give the rule in the question of legitimation, and that within Scotland at least, and to all proper Scotch effects the legitimation of the child is unquestionably worked out by the mere fact of the subsequent marriage." Shelford, *A Practical Treatise*, pp. 788-789.

Chapter Seventeen: **High Commissioner 1896–1899**

1 Farrer to Hill, August 4, 1899, Baring Brothers Archives, cited in Gilbert, *The End of the Road*, pp. 163-4.
2 Secretary of State to Galt, May 20, 1880, NAC, MG 30, D 5.
3 *Debates of the House of Commons*, May 26, 1891; bank pass book for 1912 and 1913, Skene Edwards and Garson, A32; Griffith to Borden, February 14, 1914, NAC, MG 26, H, vol. 154. The frequently repeated stories that Lord Strathcona did not accept the high commissioner's salary are inaccurate as his pass book shows.
4 Grosvenor building agreements, cited in *Survey of London*, p. 145.
5 Tupper Journal, December 17, 1895, NAC, MG 26, F, vol. 24; Tupper, *Recollections*, p. 313; Smith to Tupper, June 25, 1896, NAC, MG 26, F, vol. 11. Tupper's journal entry and his published memoirs are not entirely in accord. In the journal he says he went to see Lord Aberdeen because Chamberlain had agreed his case would be

strengthened if the governor general backed it, whereas in his book he says that when he went to see Aberdeen he discovered the peerage had already been approved; "some kind friend, however, put a spoke in the wheel." In fact, as Tupper should have known, honours for people in the colonies had to be initiated there, not in London, and it is extremely unlikely that official approval was given and then revoked. The "kind friend" doubtless asked about the legitimacy of the Smith's marriage.

6 Smith to Lady Aberdeen, September 17, 1896, NAC, MG 27, I B 5; Agnes Macdonald to Joseph Pope, September 3, 1896, NAC, MG 30, E 86.
7 Stuart Lodge papers, and Deed of Directions, private collection.
8 Willson, *From Quebec to Piccadilly*, p. 49.
9 Lecture to the Royal Colonial Institute, April 13, 1898, NAC, MG 29, A 5. This text, which appears to be a later copy, is erroneously dated April 13, 1897.
10 Lecture to the Imperial Institute, [nd, probably early 1901], NAC, MG 29, A 5.
11 "The Commercial Relations of Canada and Great Britain," [nd, probably spring 1900], NAC, MG 29, A 5.
12 "The All Red Route," a paper read to the Royal Colonial Institute (now the Royal Commonwealth Society) on April 7, 1908, NAC, MG 29 A 5.
13 Primrose to Laurier, February 18, 1909, NAC, MG 26, G.
14 Laurier to Smith, May 26, 1899, NAC, MG 26, G.
15 "Imperialism and the Unity of the Empire," December 18, 1900, NAC, MG 29, A 5.
16 Smith to Aberdeen, May 1, 1897, NAC, MG 27, I B 5.
17 Letter to the editor from "A Glencoe MacDonald," *Glasgow Herald*, September 2, 1895.
18 *Glasgow Herald*, September 10, 1895.
19 *Scotsman*, September 1, 1894.
20 Copy of letter, Smith to Sterling, May 1897 [date incomplete], private collection.
21 James Hardisty Smith to Margaret Howard, May 25, 1897, private collection.
22 Alexander Smith to Margaret Howard, May 25, 1897, private collection.
23 Mount Stephen to Hill, August 23, 1897; Hill Papers.
24 Notes on Strathcona New York Trust, Skene Edwards and Garson; *Burke's Peerage*, 1900, p.1431. The arms were modified following Lord Strathcona's death and now show four men *rowing* a wooden canoe.
25 Borden to Laurier, September 21, 1900, NAC, MG 26, G.
26 Willson, vol. 2, p. 263.
27 Haycock, *Sam Hughes*, p. 63; St. Aubyn, *Queen Victoria*, p. 547.
28 *Times*, July 17, 1897; Willson, vol. 2, p. 278.
29 Minutes of the General Court, July 6, 1897, HBC Archives, A. 2/45.
30 McDonald to Chipman, February 10, 1893, HBC Archives, D. 26/5.
31 Cheque, September 4, 1889, on Third National Bank of New York and notes about cashing it, Skene Edwards and Garson, A32; Shaughnessy to Willson, July 23, 1915, NAC, MG 30, D 5.
32 Speech to Middlesex Hospital School students, [October 7, 1897], NAC, MG 29, A 5.
33 *Ibid.*
34 Strathcona to Laurier, August 20, 1896, cited in Willson, vol. 2, p. 257.
35 Smith to Sifton, July 16, 1897, NAC, MG 27, II D 15, vol. 33. Canada has never resolved the question of responsibility for immigration or for trade and commerce in its foreign missions. The officers responsible for these areas are usually, but not always, housed within the high commission or embassy building as a matter of administrative and economic convenience but have not necessarily been part of the same chain of command. Frequently, immigration and trade officers have been posted abroad by their respective ministries and have followed a career structure which bears no relation to that followed by staff in the department responsible for Canada's foreign affairs.
36 Cited in Willson, vol. 2, p. 294.
37 Strathcona to Chamberlain, May 17, 1898 and Strathcona to Sifton, May 18, 1989, MG 27, II D 15, vol. 33. The reports of the visit to the continent are dated March 23,

1898 and can be found in NAC, RG 25, A 1, vol. 97. Substantial extracts from these reports are in Willson, vol. 2, pp. 295-304.
38 Laurier to Preston, February 6, 1906, NAC, MG 26, G.
39 Preston to Rodolfe Boudreau, Laurier's private secretary, May 6, 1905, NAC, MG 26, G.
40 *Deuteronomy* 25:5; Lorne Papers, NAC, MG 27, I B4.
41 *Parliamentary Debates*, July 8, 1898.
42 Willson, vol. 2, p. 316.
43 Müller-Ury to Hill, June 13, 1898, Hill Papers.
44 Minto to his brother, Peter Elliot, December 25, 1898, NAC, MG 27, II B I, vol. 35. Minto has dated the letter 1899 and it is filed accordingly. Diary of Joseph Pope, May 1, 1903, NAC, MG 30, E 86, vol. 43.
45 Pope, diary entry for May 9, 1903, NAC, MG 30, E 86, vol. 43.
46 Labouchere to George Curzon, April 6, 1896, India Office Library, Curzon Papers.
47 Carnegie to Chamberlain, March 30, 1899, University of Birmingham, JC12.
48 Strathcona to Chamberlain, May 16, 1899, University of Birmingham, JC12.
49 Strathcona to Chamberlain, May 24, 1899, University of Birmingham, JC12.
50 Smith to Charles Taylor, Master of St. John's College and Vice-Chancellor of Cambridge University, July 16, 1888, St. John's College, Smith Papers.

Chapter Eighteen: **The Boer War 1900**

1 Cited in Willson, vol. 2, p. 361.
2 *Report of His Majesty's Commissioners*, vol. 1, p. 83.
3 *Report of His Majesty's Commissioners*, vol. 1, p. 149.
4 Chamberlain to Strathcona, July 14, 1899, cited in Willson, vol. 2, pp. 331-332.
5 Chamberlain to Strathcona, July 27, 1899, cited in Willson, vol. 2, p. 332.
6 Strathcona to Chamberlain, July 30, 1899, University of Birmingham, JC11; Chamberlain to Strathcona, [August 1, 1899], cited in Willson, vol. 2, p. 333.
7 *Globe*, October 4, 1899.
8 Strathcona to Laurier, [nd], cited in Willson, vol. 2, p. 335.
9 Willson, vol. 2, p. 336.
10 Strathcona to Laurier, December 31, 1899, NAC, MG 26, G.
11 Strathcona to Chamberlain, January 10, 1900, University of Birmingham, JC11; Willson, *From Quebec to Piccadilly*, p. 106.
12 Strathcona to Laurier, January 13, 1900, NAC, MG 26, G.
13 Laurier to Strathcona, January 15, 1900, NAC, MG 26, G.
14 *Manitoban*, November 17, 1871; Strathcona to Laurier, January 19, 1900, cited in Willson, vol. 2, p. 343.
15 Strathcona to Laurier, January 17, 1900, NAC, MG 26, G.
16 Sources vary when citing the number of officers and men in Strathcona's Horse. The figures here are taken from the report of the British commission of enquiry into the war on which Lord Strathcona sat. It records a final total of twenty-nine officers and five hundred and sixty-eight other ranks. Twelve men were killed or died of wounds, fourteen died of disease, twenty-four were wounded and forty-eight were invalided.
17 Cited in Willson, vol. 2, p. 361.
18 Laurier to Strathcona, February 1, 1900, NAC, MG 26 G.
19 Strathcona to Laurier, February 13, 1900, NAC, MG 27, II BI, vol. 5.
20 Hutton to Minto, March 2, 1900, NAC, MG 27, II B 1, vol. 15.
21 Cited in Willson, vol. 2, p. 350.
22 According to a letter by Agar Adamson, Steele lost his way while looking for the toilets and urinated on a kitchen stove. Later he was sick on the carpet. Adamson to his wife, [nd], cited in Gwyn, *Private Capital*, pp. 363-364.
23 Tupper to Chamberlain, March 18, 1900, NAC, MG 26, F, vol. 12.
24 Tupper to Strathcona, March 18, 1900, NAC, MG 26, F, vol. 12.
25 Chamberlain to Tupper, March 31, 1900, University of Birmingham, JC15.
26 Lord Strathcona to Chamberlain, May 19, 1900, University of Birmingham, JC11.

27 Cited in Willson, vol. 2, p. 471.
28 *Montreal Gazette*, November 16, 1900.

Chapter Nineteen: **A Marvel of a Man 1900–1907**

1 Cited in Willson, vol. 2, p. 409.
2 *Elgin Courant and Courier*, September 14, 1900.
3 Strathcona, Speech on being presented with the freedom of the city of Aberdeen, [nd], NAC, MG 29, A 5.
4 Lady Strathcona to Van Horne, October 6, 1900, MG 29, A 60, vol. 54.
5 Sterling to Hill, August 20, 1914, Hill Papers.
6 Strathcona to Barlow, February 7, 1901, Welcome Foundation, Barlow Papers; Farrer to Sterling, March 23, 1901, cited in Gilbert, *End of the Road*, p. 164.
7 Minto to Clouston, May 27, 1901, NAC, RG 7, G 23, vol. 3.
8 *Montreal Gazette*, September 3, 1901; Minto to Chamberlain, October 23, 1901, University of Birmingham, JC14.
9 Minto to his brother, Peter Elliot, November 30, 1901, NAC, MG 27, II BI, vol 35.
10 Minto to Chamberlain, October 23, 1901, University of Birmingham, JC14.
11 *Montreal Gazette*, September 19, 1901; invitation in Van Horne Papers, NAC, MG 29 A 60, vol. 89.
12 Willson, vol. 2, pp. 414-416.
13 Agnes Macdonald to Pope, quoting Lady Strathcona, December 4, 1901, and January 26, 1902, NAC, MG 30, E 86, Macdonald estate papers.
14 Agnes Macdonald to Pope, July 9, 1902, NAC, MG 30, E 86, Macdonald estate papers. The total value of the Indian goods actually sent was $104.60; NAC, MG 29, A 5, vol. 25 for the initial request and vol. 9 for the payment.
15 Preston to James Smart, deputy minister of the interior, April 12, 1902, NAC, RG 76, B 1, vol. 225.
16 *Times*, July 14, 1902.
17 Agnes Macdonald to Pope, August 12, 1902, NAC, MG 30, E 86, Macdonald estate papers.
18 Neale, *Views of the Seats*; sale catalogue, 1903, Essex Record Office, B2787.
19 Sale catalogue, 1914, Essex Record Office, A1012; Skene Edwards and Garson, A42.
20 John McConnell to Lily Griffith, July 5, 1904, private collection.
21 Notes and accounts re loans, 1880-1913, and letter, October 1, 1904 from Colmer, private collection. The Colmer letter is unsigned but is written on personal letter paper bearing his London address.
22 Cited in Willson, vol. 2, pp. 499-500.
23 Ms autobiography of the Rev. John Antle, Glenbow, M 321.
24 Agnes Macdonald to Pope, December 20, 1900, NAC, MG 30, E 86, Macdonald estate papers.
25 Agnes Macdonald to Pope, January 26, 1902.
26 Agnes Macdonald to Pope, April 22, 1906.
27 Agnes Macdonald to Pope, October 31, 1904. Lang's first name was Alexander.
28 Agnes Macdonald to Pope, October 12, 1909.
29 Agnes Macdonald to Pope, March 3, 1913.
30 McNeill to Smith, April 11, [1886]; promissory notes, May 20, 1886 and May 4, 1887, Skene Edwards and Garson, A32.
31 Borden to Laurier, January 10, 1905, NAC, MG 26, G.
32 Cited in Willson, vol. 2, p. 421.
33 Borden to Walter Scott, Premier of Saskatchewan, January 29, 1909, cited in Sutherland, *Children in English-Canadian Society*, p. 191.
34 Strathcona to Borden, March 18, 1909, NAC, MG 29, A 5, vol. 24.
35 Anderson, ed., *Record of the Celebration*, p. 47.
36 Anderson, ed., *Record of the Celebration*, pp. 137-138.
37 Anderson, ed., *Record of the Celebration*, p. 152.
38 Anderson, ed., *Record of the Celebration*, p. 207.

Chapter Twenty: **The Grand Old Man 1908–1914**

1 *Times*, August 8, 1910.
2 Cited in Willson, vol. 2, p. 440.
3 Greenshields diary, January 23, 1907, cited in MacKay, *The Square Mile*, p. 170.
4 Collard, "All Our Yesterdays," *Montreal Gazette*, April 9, 1955.
5 Great Britain, *Minutes of Evidence Taken Before the Departmental Committee on Oil Fuel at the Admiralty*, December 29, 1911, p. 97.
6 Memorandum of a meeting on July 10, 1913 with the Cabinet Committee to consider the question of the Admiralty Contract for Oil Fuel, private collection.
7 Agnes Macdonald to Pope, January 5, 1910, NAC, MG 30, E 86, Macdonald estate papers.
8 Clouston to Chipman, August 6, 1909, HBC Archives, D. 26/38.
9 Smith to Armit, January 10, 1874, HBC Archives, A. 12/15.
10 Response to welcoming speech, HBC Archives, D. 26/38.
11 Strathcona to Shaughnessy, August 26, 1909, HBC Archives, D. 26/38.
12 Chipman to Strathcona, August 16 and 18, 1909, HBC Archives, D. 26/38.
13 Strathcona to Hugh Sutherland, September 8, 1909, HBC Archives, D. 26/38.
14 Chipman to Whyte, August 30, 1909, HBC Archives, D. 26/38.
15 *Daily News-Advertiser*, September 1, 1909.
16 Griffith to Strathcona, September 16, 1909, HBC Archives, D. 26/38.
17 *The Colonist*, September 3, 1909.
18 *Daily News-Advertiser*, September 3, 1909.
19 Strathcona interview, *Edmonton Evening Journal*, September 7, 1909; Chipman to C.D. Sims, HBC officer at Vernon, September 6, 1909, HBC Archives, D. 26/38.
20 Donald Howard to his parents and Lord Strathcona to Lady Strathcona, September 6, 1909, HBC Archives, D. 26/38.
21 A senator, James Lougheed was the grandfather of Peter Lougheed who became premier of Alberta in 1971.
22 *Edmonton Evening Journal*, September 7, 1909.
23 *Ibid*.
24 Hughes, *Black Robe*, p. 453.
25 *Halifax Morning Chronicle*, September 21, 1909.
26 Grey to Duke of Connaught, September 14, 1911, NAC, MG 27, II B2, vol. 29.
27 Correspondence, 1909-1914, Private Collection.
28 Pope, diary, July 7, 1912, NAC, MG 30, E 86, vol. 43; Miss Haldane, diary, August 23, 1913, National Library of Scotland, MS20054.
29 Laurier to Strathcona, March 15, 1910, Willson, vol. 2, pp. 425-426.
30 Strathcona to Laurier, April 8, 1910, Willson, vol. 2, p. 426; Laurier to Strathcona, April 26, 1910, NAC, MG 29, A 5, vol. 25.
31 *Times*, June 30, 1911.
32 Levine, *Scrum Wars*, pp. 76-77;
33 Van Horne to Graham, September 27, 1911, NAC, MG 29, A 60; Peterson to Borden, October 3, 1911, MG 26, H, vol. 252.
34 Pope diary, September 25, 1911, NAC, MG 30, E 86, vol. 43.
35 Strathcona to Borden, February 2, 1913, NAC, MG 26, H, vol. 173.
36 Griffith to Borden, February 19,1912; Borden to Strathcona, February 21, 1912; Strathcona to Borden, February 22 and 23, 1912; NAC, MG 26, H, vol. 132.
37 Griffith to Borden, February 24, 1912, NAC, MG 26, H, vol. 132.
38 Willson, vol. 2, p. 433.
39 Strathcona to Borden, February 8, 1913, NAC, MG 26, H, vol. 73.
40 Borden to Strathcona, December 19, 1912, NAC, MG 26, H, vols. 132 and 154.
41 Strathcona to Borden, February 2, 1913, NAC, MG 26, H, vol. 173.
42 Borden to Strathcona, February 28, 1913, NAC, MG 26, H. vol. 173.
43 Strathcona to Borden, March 6, 1913, NAC, MG 26, H, vol. 173.
44 Griffith to Borden, March 24, 1913, NAC, MG 26, H, vol. 154.
45 Stefansson, *Discovery*, p. 151.

46 Stefansson, *Discovery*, p. 152.
47 *Boston Post*, January 21, 1914.
48 *Times*, August 25, 1913; Haldane diary, August 23, 1913, National Library of Scotland, MS20054.
49 *Montreal Gazette*, September 1, 1913.
50 Haldane diary, August 23, 1913, National Library of Scotland MS20054. The reference is to the dinner on September 1; some portions of the diary have been written retrospectively.
51 Van Horne to Skene Edwards and Garson, March 26, 1915, NAC, MG29, A 60, vol. 86.
52 H. Robertson, Royal Trust, to Van Horne, October 28, 1911, NAC, MG 29, A 60, vol. 86.
53 Van Horne to Strathcona, November 1, 1911, NAC, MG 29, A 60, vol. 86.
54 Haldane diary, [nd], National Library of Scotland, MS20054.
55 Strathcona to Tupper, November 17, 1913, cited in Willson, vol. 2, pp. 450-451.
56 Agnes Macdonald to Pope, November 29, 1913, NAC, MG 30, E 86, Macdonald estate papers.
57 Wilfred Grenfell, cited in Willson, vol. 2, pp. 480-481.
58 Grey to Strathcona, January 5, 1914, NAC, MG 26, H, vol. 43.
59 Strathcona to Borden, January 17, 1914, NAC, MG 26, H, vol. 173.
60 Codicil, June 15, 1903, Skene Edwards and Garson, A42.
61 Skene Edwards and Garson, A42.
62 The present Lord Strathcona and his siblings were told this story by Wilson whom they, as children, dubbed "Changeable Weather" since that was the first thing he said to them each time he greeted the family, umbrella at the ready, at the train station in Edinburgh.
63 Statement, Skene Edwards and Garson, A42; private collection.
64 Colmer to Borden, January 30, 1914, NAC, MG 26, H, vol. 26.
65 Cited in Willson, vol. 2, pp. 454-455.
66 Cited in Willson, vol. 2, p. 456.
67 *Times,* January 26, 1914.
68 *Times,* January 27, 1914.

Postscript

1 Colmer to Borden, January 30, 1914, NAC, MG 26, H, vol. 26.

Appendix IV: **Genealogical Charts**

Table One

1 Inherited Scottish estate and changed name to Forsyth Grant. He was executor of Charles Grant, husband of Amelia Williams and father of James Grant.
2 Inherited the estate of Frederick Grant, Quebec merchant.
3 Cuthbert Grant had several other partners besides Mary McGillis.

Table Two

1 Head of Wellington's medical services after 1812 in the Peninsular War; head of the Army Medical Department, 1815-1851.

Table Three

1 Field Marshal; a school friend of George Stephen's and, in adult life, a fishing companion in both Canada and Scotland.
2 Woollen merchant. Initially based at Cateaton Street (now Gresham Street) in London; acted as banker for John Stuart and, until he moved to the west country, for Donald Smith.
3 Served in the army for most of his life; held the honourary position of Fort Major of Belfast from retirement until his death. His son, Hugh, described himself as having

been born "in the army." Hugh was a doctor, another member of the family to have benefitted from the influence of Sir James M'Grigor.

4 Lived in Saint John, New Brunswick.

5 A daughter, Sydney R.A., born in 1857 so presumably Donald's child, received a regular allowance from Lord Strathcona.

6 John Stuart had at least four country wives. He appears not to have had children by Françoise Laurain; by another woman, he had a daughter, Isabel; by Catherine Lavallé he had two sons, William and Donald; there is no evidence that he had children by Mary Taylor whom he refused to marry after bringing her to Scotland shortly after he retired.

7 The youngest daughter of Janet and Donald Stuart, she drowned en route to Orkney on a visit to family there.

8 Grace died before 1851. Her children by James Cameron were William, Donald, Helen, Grace, Charles Stuart, Isabella and Christian. The last married James Stuart.

Table Four

1 Variously spelled Gaul, Gall, Gawl, Gallaway, Gauld and Gald.

2 Built Norway House, Pictou, Nova Scotia.

3 The children of Girsel McKenzie and William Grant were the models for the Cheeryble brothers in Dickens' *Nicholas Nickelby.*

Table Five

1 Resigned from the HBC in 1872 because of ill health.

2 This William Stephen was a wholesale dry goods merchant in Montreal. His cousin William (1799-1891) joined him in business there in 1847.

Table Six

1 John had entered the HBC service by 1833. He was posted to the Columbia River district in 1840 and retired from the service in 1845, presumably to pursue another career in the west. The family lost track of him. John's father either died or abandoned his mother not long after John was born and he was raised as Thomas Corcoran's son, though no formal adoption ever took place.

2 Margaret was a nun in a convent on the outskirts of Montreal.

3 Mary's brother seems not to have survived childhood. Her mother may also have died. Her father returned to the UK in 1826 and Mary was raised by Thomas and Charlotte Corcoran.

4 The Corcoran brothers, from County Mayo, Ireland, appear to have used the HBC as a means of obtaining passage to Canada and setting themselves up on a farm at Rawdon, Quebec. Patrick left the HBC early to farm there and Thomas joined them after his wife's death. Richard Edwards Corcoran also left the HBC to farm at Rawdon.

5 Killed at Batoche. He had six siblings, including a sister, Isabella, who was raised by Richard and Eliza Hardisty following her father's death.

6 Two of their children were raised by Richard and Eliza Hardisty following Henry's death.

ILLUSTRATION CREDITS

Frontispiece: Private collection; photograph supplied by the National Portrait Gallery, London.

First Group:

Page One:
1. Private collection
2. Hudson's Bay Company Archives / Provincial Archives of Manitoba 1987/363-E-700-S/275
3. Private collection

Page Two:
1. Private colletction
2. Notman Photographic Archives 78,494-BI
3. Private collection

Page Three:
1. National Archives of Canada C33690
2. Notman Photographic Archives 66962-BI
3. Hudson's Bay Company Archives / Provincial Archives of Manitoba 1987/363-E-700-H/42 (N7386)
4. National Archives of Canada C06688D

Page Four:
1. National Archives of Canada PA 25569
2. Hudson's Bay Company Archives 1987/363-F-131/25 (N 13336)
3. James J. Hill Papers, James J. Hill Reference Library, St. Paul, Minnesota.
4. James J. Hill Papers, James J. Hill Reference Library, St. Paul, Minnesota.

Page Five:
1. Glenbow Museum and Archives NA 292-2
2. Hudson's Bay Company Archives / Provincial Archives of Manitoba 1979/53-84 (N13334)
3. Hudson's Bay Company Archives / Provincial Archives of Manitoba 1979/53-54 (N6278)
4. Hudson's Bay Company Archives / Provincial Archives of Manitoba 1987/363-E-700-H/41 (N13335)

Page Six:
1. Notman Photographic Archives MP004 87

2. Notman Photographic Archives 81628-BII
3. Notman Photographic Archives 63,346-I
4. Notman Photographic Archives 11918-BII

Page Seven:
1. Glenbow Museum and Archives NA-4967-1
2. Glenbow Museum and Archives NA-4967-112
3. Glenbow Museum and Archives NA-1494-6

Page Eight:
1. Notman Photographic Archives 49247-BII
2. Provincial Archives of Manitoba Smith 1
3. Notman Photographic Archives 4267-view

Second Group:

Page One:
1. Notman Photographic Archives 110,266-II

Page Two:
1. Notman Photographic Archives 46,192-BI
2. Notman Photographic Archives MP 101/80
3. Hudson's Bay Company Archives / Provincial Archives of Manitoba 1987/363-S-58/2

Page Three:
1. National Archives of Canada C15291

Page Four:
1. Robert McDonald
2. Robert McDonald
3. Robert McDonald

Page Five:
1. McDonald/Robert McDonald
2. Glenbow Museum and Archives NA2235-9

Page Six:
1. National Archives of Canada PA29365

Page Seven:
1. National Archives of Canada PA24777
2. Provincial Archives of Manitoba, Events 14-3 (N7615)
3. Hudson's Bay Company Archives / Provincial Archives of Manitoba 1987/363-S-58/7 (N13338)
4. Glenbow Museum and Archives NA-1328-61371

Page Eight:
1. Notman Photographic Archives 166,275-II
2. National Archives of Canada C49723
3. *Daily Sketch*, January 22, 1914. Used by permission of The British Library.

BIBLIOGRAPHY

UNPUBLISHED SOURCES

British Library
Add. 50,056 Iddesleigh Papers. Correspondence of Sir Stafford Northcote. 1870.
Add. 50,063A Iddesleigh Papers. Diary of Sir Stafford Northcote. 1870.

Essex Record Office
B2787 Auction Catalogue, Debden Hall. 1903.
A1012 Auction Catalogue, Debden Hall. 1914.

Glenbow Museum and Archives
M321 Antle and Dibney Family Papers.
M477 Richard Hardisty Papers.
M941 Patrick McPherson Papers.
M5908 Richard Hardisty Papers.

Hove Public Library
W/P.1 Garnet Wolseley Papers.

Hudson's Bay Company Archives
The Hudson's Bay Company, the National Archives in Ottawa and the Public Record Office in London all use different classification systems. Since both the National Archives and the PRO indicate the number of the HBC original, only the HBC references have been used. In 1994, the archives were officially donated by the company to the Provincial Archives of Manitoba.

James Jerome Hill Reference Library
J.J. Hill Papers. (The letterpress books, 1866-1916, are also available on microfilm at the National Archives of Canada.) Citations from the incoming correspondence all refer to the General Correspondence series. Citations from the letterpress volumes referring to the Saint Paul, Minneapolis and Manitoba Railway are all in the P series while the Canadian Pacific Railway references are all from the R series.

Minnesota Historical Society
St. Paul and Pacific Railway Papers.
J.W. Taylor Papers.

Moravian Church
Correspondence with Hudson's Bay Company.

National Archives of Canada
MG 17, B 2 Papers of the Church Missionary Society (microfilm copy of papers now at the University of Birmingham).

MG 19, A 41 James Keith Papers.
MG 24, B 29 Joseph Howe Papers.
MG 24, D 21 Baring Papers.
MG 24, I 26 Alves Papers.
MG 26, A Sir John A. Macdonald Papers.
MG 26, B Sir Alexander Mackenzie Papers.
MG 26, D Sir John Thompson Papers.
MG 26, E Sir Mackenzie Bowell Papers.
MG 26, F Charles Tupper Papers.
MG 26, G Sir Wilfrid Laurier Papers.
MG 26, H Sir Robert Borden Papers.
MG 27, I B 3 Lord Dufferin Papers.
MG 27, I B 4 Marquess of Lorne Papers.
MG 27, I B 5 Lord and Lady Aberdeen Papers.
MG 27, I B 6 Lord Lansdowne Papers.
MG 27, I B 7 Lord Monck Papers.
MG 27, I E 19 William Bain Scarth Papers. These are copies, the originals of which are in the Public Archives of Ontario.
MG 27, II B 1 Lord Minto Papers.
MG 27, II B 2 Earl Grey Papers.
MG 27, II D 15 Clifford Sifton Papers.
MG 28, II 2 Bank of Montreal Papers.
MG 29, A 5 Lord Strathcona Papers.
MG 29, A 11 Roderick MacFarlane Papers.
MG 29, A 12 Colin Rankin Papers.
MG 29, A 21 John McIntyre Papers.
MG 29, A 28 R.B. Angus Papers.
MG 29, A 30 George Stephen Papers.
MG 29, A 31 Sir Henry Tyler Papers.
MG 29, A 49 James Bissett Papers.
MG 29, A 60 Sir William Van Horne Papers. The originals of some of these are in the Canadian Railroad Historical Association Archives, St. Constant, Quebec.
MG 29, A 676 Keith Papers.
MG 29, B 1 Sir Sandford Fleming Papers.
MG 29, B 15 Bell Papers.
MG 29, C 19 Mary Casault Papers.
MG 29, C 26 Edward T. Fletcher Papers.
MG 29, C 73 Robert Sutherland Papers.
MG 29, C 108 Journal of Ethel M. Davis.
MG 30, D 5 Beckles Willson Papers.
MG 30, D 71 Katherine Hughes Papers.
MG 30, E 86 Joseph Pope Papers.
RG 6 Records of the Department of the Secretary of State.
RG 7 Records of the Office of the Governor General.
RG 25 Records of the Department of External Affairs.
RG 76 Records of the Immigration Branch.

National Library of Scotland
MS12556 Lord Minto Papers.
MS20054 Haldane Papers.

Provincial Archives of British Columbia
A/D/20/G19 Archibald McDonald Papers.

Provincial Archives of Manitoba
MG2 C22 John Inkster Papers.
MG12 A1 Adams Archibald Papers.
MG12 B1,2 Alexander Morris Papers.
MG14 B29 John Gunn Papers.
MG14 B30 Colin Inkster Papers.
MG14 C14 Charles Acton Burrows Papers.
MG14 C15 George Bryce Papers.
MG14 C20 Alexander McArthur Papers.
P 981-983 W.L. Morton Papers.

Public Record Office, London
CO 42/684, 685 Colonial Office papers on Red River disturbance, 1869-70.
WO 25 Military careers and marriages of John Stuart Smith, Hugh Lindsay Stuart and Peter Stuart.
WO 76 John Stuart Smith's career.

Royal College of Music Archives
Minute Books of the Executive and Finance Committees 1883-1885.
Annual Reports, 1884, 1885, 1886, 1889, 1891.

Saint John's College, University of Cambridge
Donald Smith, Lord Strathcona Papers.

Scottish Record Office
CS 17/Minute Book, vol. 70.

University of Birmingham
Joseph Chamberlain Papers.

The Welcome Foundation
Thomas Barlow Papers.

Private Collections
Lord Strathcona and Mount Royal. Papers of the first Lord Strathcona.
Skene Edwards and Garson, WS. Papers of Lord Strathcona. (Some of these papers are on deposit at the Scottish Record Office.)

Theses and Dissertations
Belvin, Cleophas. "A Study in Canadian Entrepreneurship and Politics: The Early Career of Donald A. Smith 1838-1876." MA Thesis for Bishop's University, 1992.
Oleson, Robert Valdimar. "The Commissioned Officers of the Hudson's Bay Company and the Deed Poll in the 1870's, with Particular Emphasis on the Fur Trade Party, 1878-1879." MA Dissertation for the University of Manitoba, 1978.

GOVERNMENT DOCUMENTS

Canada
Journals of the House of Commons. Ottawa. 1871-1874.
Debates of the House of Commons. Ottawa. 1871-1881, 1886- 1896.
Sessional Papers. Vol. 5, no. 12. *Correspondence & Papers connected with Recent Occurrences in the North-West Territories*. Ottawa. 1870.
— Vol. 5, no. 44. *Statement of Claims Made on the Dominion Government, Consequent upon the Insurrection in the North-West Territories*. Ottawa. 1871.
Report of the Select Committee on the Causes of the Difficulties in the North-West Territory in

1869-70. Ottawa. 1874.

Report of the Royal Commission. Journals of the House of Commons. Vol. 7, appendix 1. Ottawa. 1873.

Great Britain

Report from the Select Committee on the Hudson's Bay Company; Together with the Proceedings of the Committee, Minutes and Evidence, Appendix and Index. London. Ordered by the House of Commons to be Printed, 31 July and 11 August 1857. Session 2, vol. 11.

Parliamentary Debates, House of Lords. London. 1897-1914.

Journals of the House of Lords. London. 1898-1914.

Report of His Majesty's Commissioners Appointed to Inquire into the Military Preparations and other matters connected with the War in South Africa. London. 1903.

Admiralty Committee on the Use of Oil Fuel in the Navy. Departmental and other Reports and Minutes of Evidence From December 1911 to February 1912 and Interim Report of the Committee Dated January 19th, 1912. London, HMSO.

Manitoba

Silver Heights. Government of Manitoba, Historic Resources Branch. 1985.

United States

United States Circuit Court, District of Minnesota. *Jesse P. Farley vs N.W. Kittson, et al. Transcript of the Record*. Chicago Legal News Company, 1888.

BOOKS AND JOURNALS

Anderson, J.P. ed. *Record of the Celebration of the Quartercentenary of the University of Aberdeen*. Aberdeen. 1907.

Andrew's Directory of London. 1793.

The Army List. 1839-1866.

Artibise, Alan F.J. *Winnipeg, A Social History of Urban Growth, 1874-1914*. Montreal and Kingston. McGill- Queen's University Press, 1975.

d'Artigue, Jean. *Six Years in the Canadian North-West*. L.C. Corbett and S. Smith, trans. Toronto. Hunter Rose and Co., 1882.

Baikie, Margaret. *Labrador Memories, Reflections at Mulligan*. Happy Valley, Labrador. Them Days, [nd].

Begg, Alexander. *The Creation of Manitoba; or, A History of the Red River Troubles*. Toronto. Hunter, Rose and Co., 1871.

— *History of the North West*. Toronto. Hunter, Rose and Co., 1894.

— and Nursey, Walter R. *Ten Years in Winnipeg, A Narration of the Principal Events in the History of the City of Winnipeg from the Year A.D., 1870, to the Year A.D., 1879, Inclusive*. Winnipeg, 1879.

Bernard, Jean-Paul. *Les Rebellions de 1837-1838, Les patriotes du Bas-Canada de la memoire collective et chez les historiens*. Montreal. Boreal Express, 1983.

Berton, Pierre. *The Great Railway*. Vol. 1, *The National Dream, 1871-1881*, Toronto. McClelland and Stewart, 1970. Vol. 2, *The Last Spike, 1881-1885*, Toronto McClelland and Stewart, 1971.

Blackwood, Hariot Georgina, Marchioness of Dufferin and Ava. *My Canadian Journal 1872-1878*. London. John Murray, 1891.

Bolus, Malvina, ed. *People and Pelts: Selected Papers of the Second North American Fur Trade Conference*. Winnipeg. Peguis Publishers, 1972.

Boulton, Major. *Reminiscences of the North-West Rebellion*. Toronto. Grip Printing and Publishing Co., 1886.

Bowles, Frances. "Manitoba's Government House." *Transactions of the Historical and Scientific Society of Manitoba*, series III, no. 25, 1969-70 (Special Supplement).

Bowsfield, Hartwell, ed. *The James Wickes Taylor Correspondence 1859-1870*. Manitoba Record Society Publications, vol. 3, 1968.

— *The Letters of Charles John Brydges, 1879-1882*. Winnipeg. Hudson's Bay Record Society, 1977.

— *The Letters of Charles John Brydges, 1883-1889*. Winnipeg. Hudson's Bay Record Society, 1981.

Boyle's General London Guide. 1794, 1797-8.

Bredin, Thomas F. "The Red River Academy." *The Beaver*, winter 1974, pp. 10-17.

Brotman, Ruth C. *Pauline Donalda: The Life and Career of a Canadian Prima Donna*. Montreal. [Privately published], 1975.

Brown, Jennifer S.H. *Strangers in Blood: Fur Trade Company Families in Indian Country*. Vancouver. University of British Columbia Press, 1980.

— and Jacqueline Peterson, eds. *The New Peoples: Being and Becoming Métis in North America*. Winnipeg. University of Manitoba Press, 1985.

Burke, Bernard. *A Genealogical and Heraldic Dictionary of the Peerage and Baronetage*, 62nd ed. London. Harrison and Sons, 1900.

Burr, Anna Robeson. *The Portrait of a Banker: James Stillman 1850-1918*. New York. Duffield and Co., 1927.

Burt, A.L. "Peter Mitchell on John A Macdonald." *The Canadian Historical Review*, vol. 42., no. 3, pp. 209-227.

Butler, William Francis. *The Great Lone Land*. Tokyo. Charles E. Tuttle Co., 1968.

Butlin, Martin and Evelyn Joll. *The Paintings of J.M.W. Turner*. Yale University Press for Paul Mellon Centre for Studies in British Art and the Tate Gallery, 1984.

Campbell, Lydia, *Sketches of Labrador Life*. Happy Valley, Labrador. Them Days, 1980.

Carlyle, Thomas. *Reminiscences*. C.E. Norton, ed. London. Dent, 1932.

Cartwright, Richard. *Reminiscences*. Toronto. William Briggs, 1912.

Collard, Edgar Andrew. *Montreal: The Days That Are No More*. Toronto. Doubleday, 1976.

Corley, T.A.B. *A History of the Burmah Oil Company 1886-1924*. London. Heinemann, 1983.

Cowie, Isaac. *The Company of Adventurers, A Narrative of Seven Years in the Service of the Hudson's Bay Company during 1867-1874 on the Buffalo Plains with Historical and Biographical Notes and Comments*. Toronto. William Briggs, 1913.

Creighton, Donald Grant. *John A. Macdonald, The Old Chieftain*. Toronto. The Macmillan Company of Canada Limited, 1955.

Cruise, David and Alison Griffiths. *Lords of the Line, The Men Who Built the CPR*. Toronto. Viking, 1988.

Debrett's Peerage, Baronetage, Knightage and Companionage, 1894.

Dennison, Merrill. *Canada's First Bank, A History of the Bank of Montreal*. Toronto. McClelland and Stewart, 1967.

Elliott, George B. *Winnipeg As It Is in 1874 and As It Was in 1860*. Winnipeg. The Daily Free Press Group, [1874].

Elmslie, G.R. *Field-Marshal Sir Donald Stewart, An Account of His Life, Mainly in his own Words*. London. John Murray, 1903.

Engelbourg, Saul and Leonard Bushkoff. *The Man Who Found the Money: John Stewart Kennedy and the Financing of the Western Railroads*. Michigan State University Press. East Lancing, Michigan, 1996.

Ferrier, Ronald. *History of the British Petroleum Company*. Cambridge University Press, 1982.

Fleming, Sandford. *Memorial of the People of Red River to the British and Canadian Governments with remarks on the Colonization of Central British North America and the Establishment of a Great Territorial Road from Canada to British Columbia*. Quebec. Hunter, Rose and Co., for the Legislative Assembly, 1863.

— "Memories of the Mountains." *Canadian Alpine Journal*, vol. 1, no. 1, 1907, pp. 9-33.

Frost, Stanley Brice. *McGill University for the Advancement of Learning*. Montreal and Kingston. McGill-Queen's University Press, 1980.

Galbraith, John S. *The Little Emperor, Governor Simpson of the Hudson's Bay Company*. Toronto. Macmillan, 1976.

— "Land Policies of the Hudson's Bay Company." *Canadian Historical Review*, vol. 32, no. 1, March 1951, pp. 1-21.

Gates, Charles M., ed. *Five Fur Traders of the Northwest*. St. Paul. Minnesota Historical Society, 1965.

Gilbert, Heather. *The Life of Lord Mount Stephen*. Vol. 1, *Awakening Continent, 1829-1891*. University of Aberdeen Press, 1965. Vol. 2, *End of the Road, 1891-1921*. University of Aberdeen Press, 1977.

— "King Edward's Hospital Fund for London: the First 25 Years." *Social and Economic Administration*, vol. 8, no. 1, pp. 43-63.

— "The Unaccountable Fifth." *Minnesota History*, vol. 42, no. 5, spring 1971, pp. 175-177.

— "Mount Stephen: A study in environments." *Northern Scotland*, vol. 1, no. 2, 1973, pp. 177-197.

Gluek, Alvin C. *Minnesota and the Manifest Destiny of the Canadian Northwest*. University of Toronto Press, 1965.

Gordon, Ishbel, Marchioness of Aberdeen and Temair. *The Canadian Journal of Lady Aberdeen 1893-1898*. Ed. John T. Saywell. Toronto. The Champlain Society, 1960.

Grant, George M. *Ocean to Ocean, Sandford Fleming's Expedition Through Canada in 1872*. London. Sampson Low, Marston, Searle, and Rivington, 1877.

Green, Lorne. *Chief Engineer, Life of a Nation Builder — Sandford Fleming*. Toronto. Dundurn Press, 1993.

Greenberg, Dolores. "A Study of Capital Alliances: The St. Paul and Pacific." *Canadian Historical Review*, vol. 57, no. 1, March 1976, pp. 25-39.

Gwyn, Sandra. *The Private Capital: Ambition and Love in the Age of Macdonald and Laurier*. Toronto. McClelland and Stewart, Ltd., 1984.

Hallock, Charles. "Three Months in Labrador." *Harpers New Monthly Magazine*, vol. 22, no. cxxxi, April 1861, pp. 577-599 and May 1861, pp. 743-765.

Halkerston, Peter. *A Digest on the Law of Scotland Relating to Marriage*. Edinburgh, 1831.

Ham, G.H. *Reminiscences of a Raconteur Between the 40s and the 20s*. Toronto. The Musson Book Company, 1921.

Hamilton, Henry, ed. *The Third Statistical Account of Scotland*. Glasgow. Collins, 1965.

Harmon, Daniel Williams. *A Journal of Voyages and Travels in the Interior of North America*. Andover. Flagg and Gould, 1820.

Haycock. Ronald G. *Sam Hughes, The Public Career of a Controversial Canadian 1885-1916*. Wilfrid Laurier University Press in collaboration with the Canadian War Museum, the Canadian Museum of Civilization, National Museums of Canada, 1986.

Healy, W.J. *Women of Red River: Being a Book Written from the Recollections of Women Surviving from the Red River Era*. Winnipeg. Russell Lang and Co., 1923.

— *Winnipeg's Early Days*. Winnipeg. Stovel Company, 1927.

Hedges, James B. *The Federal Railway Land Subsidy Policy of Canada*. Cambridge, Massachusetts. Harvard University Press, 1934.

— *Building the Canadian West: Land and Colonization Policies of the CPR*. New York. Macmillan, 1939.

Hill, J.J. *Highways of Progress*. London. Hodder and Stoughton, 1910.

Hilliker, John. *Canada's Department of External Affairs*. Vol. 1, *The Early Years 1909-1946*. Montreal and Kingston. The Institute of Public Administration of Canada and McGill-Queen's University Press, 1990.

Hind, Henry Youle. *Explorations in the Interior of the Labrador Peninsula*. London. Longman Green, 1863.

Howard, R. Palmer. *The Chief: Doctor William Osler*. Science History Publications U.S.A., 1983.

Hudson's Bay Company. *Charters, Statutes, Orders in Council, etc., relating to the Hudson's Bay Company*. London. Hudson's Bay Company, 1931.

Hughes, Katherine. *Father Lacombe, The Black-Robe Voyageur*. New York. Moffat, Yard and Co., 1911.

Humphrys, Ruth. "The Shiny House and the Man Who Built It." *The Beaver*, spring 1977, pp. 49-52.

Kelly's Handbook to the Titled, Landed and Official Classes for 1894. London.

Kent's Directory of London. 1794-1805. London.

Kerr, J. Lennox. *Wilfred Grenfell, His Life and Work*. Toronto. Ryerson Press, 1959.

Lamb, W. Kaye. *History of the Canadian Pacific Railway*. New York. Macmillan, 1977.

Lang, Andrew. *Life, Letters, and Diaries of Sir Stafford Northcote, First Earl of Iddesleigh*.

Edinburgh. William Blackwood and Sons, 1891.

Lauder, Sir Thomas Dick. *An Account of the Great Floods of August 1829 in the Province of Moray and Adjoining Districts*. Edinburgh. Adam Black, 1830.

Le Bourdais, D.M. "North West River." *The Beaver*, spring 1963, pp. 14-21.

Levine, Alan. *Scrum Wars: The Prime Ministers and the Media*. Toronto. Dundurn Press, 1993.

Lewis, D. Sclater. *Royal Victoria Hospital 1887-1947*. Montreal. McGill University Press, 1969.

Littlejohn, Bruce and Wayland Drew. *A Sea Within: the Gulf of St. Lawrence*. Toronto. McClelland and Stewart, 1984.

Loder, John de Vere. *Colonsay and Oronsay in the Isles of Argyll, Their Flora, Fauna, History and Topography*. Edinburgh. Oliver and Boyd, 1935.

Long, Dorothy E.T. "The Elusive Mr. Ellice." *The Canadian Historical Review*, March 1942, pp. 42-57.

Lownde's Directory of London. 1793-1797. London.

[MacAlister, E.F.K.] *Sir Donald MacAlister of Tarbert*, by his wife. London. Macmillan and Co., 1935.

McDougall, John. *In the Days of the Red River Rebellion*. University of Alberta Press, 1983.

MacGregor, J.G. *Senator Hardisty's Prairies, 1849-1889*. Saskatoon. Western Producer Prairie Books, 1978.

— *John Rowand, Czar of the Prairies*. Western Producer Prairie Books, 1978.

MacKay, Donald. *The Square Mile: Merchant Princes of Montreal*. Vancouver. Douglas and McIntyre, 1987.

MacKay, Douglas. *The Honourable Company, A History of the Hudson's Bay Company*. Indianapolis. The Bobbs-Merrill Company, 1936.

McLeod, Margaret Arnett and W.L. Morton. *Cuthbert Grant of Grantown, Warden of the Plains of Red River*. Toronto. McClelland and Stewart, 1963.

McNaughton, John. *Lord Strathcona*. Oxford University Press, 1926.

Martin, Albro. *James J. Hill and the Opening of the Northwest*. New York. Oxford University Press, 1975. [Reprinted by Minnesota Historical Society, 1991.]

Masters, D.C. "Financing the C.P.R., 1880-5." *The Canadian Historical Review*, vol. 24, no. 4, December 1943, pp. 350-361.

The Medical Directory. 1889-1895. London. J. and A. Churchill.

Miller, Carman. *The Canadian Career of the Fourth Earl of Minto, the Education of a Viceroy*. Waterloo, Ontario. Wilfrid Laurier University Press, 1980.

Miller, J.R. "D'Alton McCarthy, Jr.: A Protestant Irishman Abroad." *Boswell's Children, The Art of the Biographer*. R.B. Fleming, ed. Toronto and Oxford. Dundurn Press, 1992.

Mitchell, Elaine Allan. *Fort Timiskaming and the Fur Trade*. University of Toronto Press, 1977.

Mitchell, H. *Statistical Contributions to Canadian Economic History*. Vol. 2, *Statistics of Prices*. Toronto. Macmillan, 1931.

Montreal Street Directory. 1861-1891.

Morton, Arthur S. *A History of the Canadian West to 1870-71*. Edinburgh. Thomas Nelson and Sons [1939].

— and Chester Martin. *History of Prairie Settlement and "Dominion Lands" Policy*. Toronto. The Macmillan Co. of Canada, 1938.

Morton, W.L., ed. *Alexander Begg's Red River Journal and Other Papers Relative to the Red River Resistance of 1869-1870*. Toronto. Champlain Society, 1956.

— *Manitoba: A History*. University of Toronto Press, 1957.

— "Donald Smith and Governor George Simpson." *The Beaver*, autumn 1978, pp 4-9.

Myers, Gustavus. *History of Canadian Wealth*. Chicago. Charles H. Kerr, 1914.

Neale, J.P. *Views of the Seats of Noblemen and Gentlemen in England, Wales, Scotland, and Ireland*. London. Sherwood, Neely and Jones, 1819.

The New Statistical Account of Scotland, vol xiii. Edinburgh. William Blackwood and Sons, 1845.

Newman, Peter C. *Company of Adventurers*. Toronto. Viking, 1985, 1987, 1991.

New York City Directory. 1856-1890.

Norwak, J.M. *The Parish of Debden and the Church of St. Mary All Saints*. 1965.

Oakeley, Hilda. *My Adventures in Education*. London. Williams and Norgate Ltd., 1913.

O'Dell, A.C. and Walton, K. *The Highlands and Islands of Scotland*. Edinburgh. Thomas Nelson and Sons, 1962.

Page, William, ed. *A History of Hertfordshire. The Victoria History of the Counties of England, vol. 3*. London, Constable, 1912.

Paget, George, Marquess of Anglesey. *A History of the British Cavalry 1816 to 1919*. Vol. iv, 1899 to 1913. London. Leo Cooper with Secker and Warburg, 1973.

Patterson, the Rev. George. *A history of the County of Pictou Nova Scotia*. Montreal. Dawson Brothers, 1877. (Reprinted by Mika Studio, Belleville, Ontario, 1972.)

Pedley, J.W. *Lord Strathcona*. Toronto. Nichols Co. Ltd., 1915.

Peel, Bruce. "First Steamboats on the Saskatchewan." *The Beaver*, autumn 1964, pp. 16-21.

Penlington, Norman. *Canada and Imperialism 1896-1899*. University of Toronto Press, 1965.

Preston, W.T.R. *The Life and Times of Lord Strathcona*. London. Eveleigh Nash, 1914.

Rampkey, Ronald. *Grenfell of Labrador: A Biography*. University of Toronto Press, 1991.

Rea, J.E. "The Hudson's Bay Company and the North-West Rebellion." *The Beaver*, summer 1982, pp. 43-57.

Reynolds, Louise. *Agnes, The Biography of Lady Macdonald*. Toronto. Samuel Stevens, 1979.

Rich, E.E. *The History of the Hudson's Bay Company, 1670-1870*. London. Hudson's Bay Record Society, 1958.

Richmond, W.R. *The Life of Lord Strathcona*. London, Collins, 1914.

Rife, Clarence W. "Norman W. Kittson, a Fur-Trader at Pembina." *Minnesota History*, vol. 6, no. 3, September 1925, pp. 225-52.

Robertson, Erasmus. *The Law of Legitimation by Subsequent Marriage*. London and Edinburgh. 1829.

Ross, George. *Getting into Parliament and After*. Toronto. William Briggs, 1913.

St. Aubyn, Giles. *Queen Victoria, A Portrait*. London. Sceptre, 1991.

Schull, Joseph. *Laurier, The First Canadian*. Toronto. Macmillan, 1965.

– *Rebellion, the Rising in French Canada 1837*. Toronto. Macmillan, 1971.

Shelford, Leonard. *A Practical Treatise of the Law of Marriage and Divorce, and Registration as Altered by the Recent Statutes ... and the Conflict Between the Laws of England and Scotland Respecting Divorce and Legitimacy*. London, S. Sweet, 1841.

Sheppard, F.H.W., ed. *Survey of London*, vol. xl, *The Grosvenor Estate in Mayfair*, part ii, The Buildings. London. The Athlone Press for the Greater London Council, 1980.

Siggins, Maggie. *Riel, A Life of Revolution*. Toronto. Harper Collins, 1994.

Simpson, George. *Narrative of a Journey Round the World, During the Years 1841 and 1842. London. Henry Colburn, 1847.*

– *Part of a Dispatch from George Simpson Esqr Governor of Ruperts Land to the Governor & committee of the Hudson's Bay Company London*. E.E. Rich ed. London. Champlain Society for Hudson's Bay Record Society, 1947.

Skelton, Oscar D. *The Life and Letters of Sir Wilfrid Laurier*. Toronto. Oxford University Press, 1921 and McClelland and Stewart, 1965.

– *The Railway Builders*. Toronto. Glasgow, Brook and Co., 1920.

Skilling, H. Gordon. *Canadian Representation Abroad: From Agency to Embassy*. Toronto. Ryerson Press, 1945.

Society for the Furtherance of the Gospel. *Periodical Accounts Relating to the Missions of the Church of the United Brethren Established Among the Heathen*. London, vols. 20-22.

Solicitor. *Marriage and Marriage Ceremonies According to the Law of Scotland*. 1898.

Stanley, G.F.G. "The Fur Trade Party." *The Beaver*, September 1953, pp. 35-39 and December 1953, pp. 21-25.

– *Louis Riel*. Toronto. Ryerson Press, 1963.

Steele, Samuel Benfield. *Forty Years in Canada*. London. Herbert Jenkins, [1905].

Stewart, Robert. *Sam Steele, Lion of the Frontier*. Toronto. Doubleday, 1979.

Stefansson, Vilhjalmur. *Discovery: The Autobiography of Vilhjalmur Stefansson*. New York. McGraw Hill, 1964.

Stevens, Paul and Saywell, John T. eds. *Lord Minto's Canadian Papers, A Selection of the Public and Private Papers of the Fourth Earl of Minto 1898-1904*. Toronto. The Champlain

Society, 1981.

Stroud, Dorothy. *Henry Holland 1745-1806*. London. Art and Technics, 1950.

— *Henry Holland, His Life and Architecture*. London. Country Life Limited, 1966.

Sutherland, Neil. *Children in English-Canadian Society: Framing the Twentieth-Century Consensus*. University of Toronto Press, 1976.

Terry, Neville. *The Royal Vic*. Montreal. McGill University Press, 1994.

Thomas, John. *Forgotten Railways: Scotland*. Newton Abbott, Devon, David and Charles, 1976.

Thomson, Dale C. *Alexander Mackenzie, Clear Grit*. Toronto. Macmillan, 1960.

Tway, Duane C. "The Wintering Partners and the Hudson's Bay Company 1863-1871." *The Canadian Historical Review*, March 1952, pp. 50-63.

— "The Wintering Partners and the Hudson's Bay Company 1867-1879." *The Canadian Historical Review*, September 1960, pp. 215-223.

Tupper, Charles. *Recollections of Sixty Years*. London. Cassell and Co., 1914.

Universal British Directory. 1793-1794, 1797.

Van Kirk, Sylvia. *Many Tender Ties, Women in Fur Trade Society in Western Canada, 1670-1870*. Winnipeg. Watson and Dwyer Publishing, 1981.

Vaughan, Walter. *The Life and Work of Sir William Van Horne*. New York. The Century Co., 1920.

Victoria. *The Letters of Queen Victoria*, third series, vol. 1. George Buckle, ed. London, John Murray, 1930.

Waite, Peter. *Arduous Destiny: Canada 1874-96*. Toronto. McClelland and Stewart, 1971.

Wakefield's London Directory. 1794.

Walford, Edward. *The Windsor Peerage*. London. Chatto and Windus, 1894.

Wallace, W. Stewart. "Strathspey in the Canadian Fur Trade." *Essays in Canadian History*. Ralph Flenley ed. Toronto. Macmillan, 1939, pp. 278-295.

—, ed. *Documents Relating to the North West Company*. Toronto. The Champlain Society, 1934.

Watkin, Edward W. *Canada and the States, Recollections 1851 to 1886*. London. Ward Lock and Co., [1887].

Williams, Glyndwr, ed. *Hudson's Bay Miscellany, 1670-1870*. Winnipeg. Hudson's Bay Record Society, 1975.

Willson, Beckles. *The Great Company*. Toronto. Copp Clark, 1899.

— *Lord Strathcona, The Story of His Life*. London. Methuen and Co., 1902.

— *The Life of Lord Strathcona and Mount Royal*. Cambridge University Press, 1915.

— *From Quebec to Piccadilly and Other Places: Some Anglo-Canadian Memories*. London. Jonathan Cape, 1929.

Wilson, Keith. *Donald Smith and the Canadian Pacific Railway*. Book Society of Canada Ltd., 1978.

Woods, Shirley E. Jr. *The Molson Saga 1763-1983*. Toronto. Doubleday Canada Ltd., 1983.

Young, George. *Manitoba Memories, Leaves from my Life in the Prairie Provinces, 1868-1884*. Toronto. William Briggs, 1897.

Young, James. *Public Men and Public Life in Canada, The Story of the Canadian Confederacy*, vol. 2. Toronto. William Briggs, 1912.

NEWSPAPERS AND PERIODICALS

Boston Post, 1914

Calgary Herald. November 1913.

The Colonist (Victoria). November 1885, September 1909.

The Daily News-Advertiser (Vancouver). September 1909.

The Edmonton Evening Journal. September 1909.

Elgin Courant. 1847-1916. *Passim*.

Forres, Elgin and Nairn Gazette. 1840-1925. *Passim*.

Glasgow Herald. 1904-1912. *Passim*.

The Globe (Saint Paul). December 1901.

The Globe (Toronto). 1870-1914. *Passim.*
Halifax Morning Chronicle. September 1909.
Inverness Courier. 1838.
The Mail (Toronto). November 1873.
Manitoba Daily Free Press. 1874-1914. *Passim.*
Manitoban. 1870-1874. *Passim.*
The Manitoba News-Letter. 1870.
Montreal Gazette. 1869-1914, 1955. *Passim.*
Montreal Star. 1888.
New York Times. 1869-1914. *Passim.*
Regina Leader. October 1889.
The Saint Paul Pioneer Press. May and June 1893.
The Times. 1885-1914. *Passim.*
Vancouver Daily World. August and September 1909.
Vancouver Province. August 1909.
Winnipeg Sun. September 1882.

INDEX

N